Yearbook of International Sports Arbitration 2015

Antoine Duval · Antonio Rigozzi
Editors

Yearbook of International Sports Arbitration 2015

ASSER PRESS

Springer

Editors
Antoine Duval
ASSER International Sports Law Centre
T.M.C. Asser Instituut
The Hague
The Netherlands

Antonio Rigozzi
Faculté de droit
Université de Neuchâtel
Neuchâtel
Switzerland

Assistant Editor
Erika Hasler
Levy Kaufmann-Kohler
Geneva
Switzerland

ISBN 978-94-6265-128-9 ISBN 978-94-6265-129-6 (eBook)
DOI 10.1007/978-94-6265-129-6

Library of Congress Control Number: 2016945765

Published by T.M.C. ASSER PRESS, The Hague, The Netherlands www.asserpress.nl
Produced and distributed for T.M.C. ASSER PRESS by Springer-Verlag Berlin Heidelberg

Printed on acid-free paper

This Springer imprint is published by Springer Nature
The registered company is Springer-Verlag GmbH Berlin Heidelberg

Preface[1]

The publication of this inaugural issue of the Yearbook of International Sports Arbitration could not be more timely. 2015 has been a momentous year for the Court of Arbitration for Sport and international sports (law) in general, and 2016 promises to be just as eventful.

On a systemic level, just as the curtains were drawn on 2014 with the *SV Wilhelmshaven* case taking the stage,[2] 2015 was off to an explosive start with the Munich *Oberlandesgericht*'s decision in Claudia Pechstein's dispute against the International Skating Union.[3] Pechstein's challenge to the CAS system, which led to the German regional court's decision refusing to enforce a CAS award that had previously been upheld by the Swiss Federal Tribunal, has been seen as a dramatic setback for the world court of sports. The questions raised in and around the *Wilhelmshaven* and *Pechstein* cases deserve the international sports community's utmost attention and cannot be left unanswered: a point starkly illustrated, among others, by the CAS's unprecedented initiative, in March 2015, of issuing a press release stating its position in the aftermath of the OLG München's decision in the *Pechstein* case. That said, as recognized by the German court itself, the value of having a single body adjudicating international sports disputes by fast, flexible and relatively inexpensive arbitration cannot reasonably be questioned.

In light of the foregoing, it is only fitting for the YISA 2015 to open with Jan Paulsson's firm reminder of the indispensable function the CAS was set up to fulfil in the international sports arena. The CAS's usefulness and legitimacy arise from and must be assessed in the light of that very function. Professor Paulsson rightly points out that, without the CAS, the international sports community would return to the chaos that reigned before that institution's establishment. In view of this, those who call for the CAS's dismantlement bear the responsibility of putting

[1]The editors would like to thank Erika Hasler for her outstanding editorial assistance and Marine Montejo for her support in reviewing the proofs.

[2]See Duval's commentary at pp. 315–334.

[3]See Maisonneuve's commentary at pp. 335–347.

forward a valid and viable alternative. Returning to the *status quo ante* is an untenable proposition.

The fairness and usefulness of the CAS system must also be assessed in light of the (quality of) the awards rendered by its panels in the ever-growing number of cases that are adjudicated every year.[4] While commentators and the courts were busy discussing the virtues and flaws of the CAS system, CAS panels continued to play their fundamental role in interpreting sports regulations and deciding disputes. In this respect too, 2015 has witnessed many important developments. The *Juventus* case showed the importance of the interpretive approach and techniques adopted in dealing with complex regulations and confirmed that CAS is far from being a kind of rubberstamp body confirming the sports-governing authorities' decisions.[5] In this case the arbitrators showed that they were fully prepared to test the validity of sports regulations against the relevant national law as well as the broader EU law context, and to disapply any regulation or interpretation that would not meet such legality test.

Reverting to Prof. Paulsson's appraisal, more than three decades after its creation, the CAS remains above all "a fascinating example of transnational institution-building". This is apparent, inter alia, in the influence of different legal traditions upon its practice and procedures.[6] The increasing sophistication of the system was equally visible, in the past year's case law, in the panels' approach to procedural issues such as standing to appeal[7] and the impact of the amended Article R57 of the CAS Code on the admissibility of evidence,[8] but also in their jurisdictional rulings.[9]

The CAS's case law in 2015 was further marked by the sensitive questions arising from violent nationalist incidents and the attendant issues of liability.[10] More generally, football law—from transfers and so-called sell-on clauses[11] to domestic rules on the promotion and relegation of clubs[12]—has continued to generate interesting decisions.

While football disputes take up a great share of the CAS's docket, another source of complex legal questions as well as high-profile disputes is anti-doping. 2015 has seen the entry into force of the third edition of the WADA Code, and the decisions applying the WADC's new provisions have begun to emerge.

---

[4]2015 was also a record-breaking year with regard to the number of new cases registered, almost 500 (see Reeb M. (2015) Message from the Secretary General. CAS Bulletin (Issue 2) 4).

[5]See Duval's commentary at pp. 155–168.

[6]See Ioannidis' article at pp. 17–38.

[7]See Zagklis' commentary at pp. 219–234 and Anderson's commentary at pp. 203–218.

[8]See Levy's commentary at pp. 169–186.

[9]See Crespo and Torchetti's commentary at pp. 275–297.

[10]See Zagklis' commentary.

[11]See Lambrecht's commentary at pp. 187–202 and Colantuoni and Devlies' article at pp. 73–91.

[12]See Haindlova's commentary at pp. 299–312.

The regulations may have changed, but the challenging questions arising from the constantly evolving doping techniques and the difficulty of integrating scientifically sound detection and analytical methods, as well as appropriate evidentiary rules and practices into a coherent (and fair) legal framework remain unabated. In the *Dutee Chand* case, one of the most sensitive decisions in 2015, science and the law have again shown their respective limits at the crossroads of eligibility rules based on gender.[13] Still in the realm of disciplinary and eligibility disputes, only months after the conclusion of the Council of Europe's Convention on the Manipulation of Sports Competitions (in September 2014), Vanessa Vanakorn's case in the wake of the 2014 Sochi Winter Olympic Games was the object of much media attention. The CAS award in the *Vanakorn* case shows that while sports-governing bodies have a legitimate interest in vigorously fighting any kind of sports fraud or manipulation, be it doping or match-fixing, the athletes' rights and fundamental principles of law cannot be overlooked.[14]

International sports arbitration is not the exclusive remit of the CAS. In addition to the important role played by the courts[15] and national sports arbitration tribunals (which will certainly be the object of future studies in this Yearbook), the Basketball Arbitral Tribunal, soon to celebrate its 10th anniversary, is undoubtedly another very successful experiment in the institutionalized resolution of sports-related disputes. The significance of the BAT can no longer be ignored by sports law practitioners and academics, which is why, after the short introduction included in the present volume,[16] the YISA will devote a specific section to the review of its case law in future issues. Finally, being seated in Switzerland, both the CAS and the BAT are subject to the supervisory jurisdiction of the Swiss Federal Tribunal. Accordingly, every volume of the YISA will include a final section providing an overview of the SFT's most significant decisions with regard to sports arbitration in the relevant year.[17]

The production of this inaugural volume would have been impossible without the dedication of our contributors, who deserve our deepest gratitude. The diversity of their profiles and backgrounds is truly remarkable, and I hope that more sports arbitration practitioners and scholars will be attracted to this new publication in the future, contributing to giving international sports arbitration its *lettres de noblesse*…

Neuchâtel, Switzerland Antonio Rigozzi

[13]See Viret and Wisnosky's article at pp. 39–72 and commentary at pp. 235–273.

[14]See Anderson's commentary.

[15]See Blackshaw and Pachmann's article at pp. 93–110 and Maisonneuve's commentary.

[16]See Hasler's article at pp. 111–152.

[17]See Hasler and Hafner's commentary at pp. 351–388.

Contents

Abbreviations

CAS	Court of Arbitration for Sport
CAS Code	Code of the Court of Arbitration for Sport
CC	Swiss Civil Code
CCP	Swiss Code of Civil Procedure
CHF	Swiss Franc
CJEU	Court of Justice of the European Union
CO	Swiss Code of Obligations
CONI	Comitato Olimpico Nazionale Italiano/Italian Olympic Committee
ECHR	European Convention of Human Rights
ECtHR	European Court of Human Rights
EU	European Union
FIBA	Fédération Internationale de Basketball
FIFA	Fédération Internationale de Football Association
FIFA DC	FIFA Disciplinary Code
FIFA DRC	FIFA Dispute Resolution Chamber
FIFA PSC	FIFA Player Status Committee
FIFA RSTP	FIFA Regulations on the Status and Transfer of Players
FIFA TMS	FIFA Transfer Matching System
IBA Rules	International Bar Association Rules
ICAS	International Council of Arbitration for Sport
IOC	International Olympic Committee
ITC	International Transfer Certificate
NYC	New York Convention on the Recognition and Enforcement of Foreign Arbitral Awards
OJ	Official Journal
PILA	Swiss Private International Law Act
SFT	Swiss Federal Tribunal/Tribunal fédéral suisse
SGB	Sports-Governing Body
TEU	Treaty on European Union
TFEU	Treaty on the Functioning of the European Union
UCI	Union Cycliste Internationale

UEFA	Union of European Football Associations
UEFA FFP	UEFA Financial Fair Play Regulations
WADA	World Anti-Doping Agency
WADA Code	World Anti-Doping Code

Part I
General Articles

Chapter 1
Assessing the Usefulness and Legitimacy of CAS

Jan Paulsson

Abstract Disqualified athletes and their nationalistic supporters tend to be highly critical of the regime of sanctions for violations of the international law of sports, and specifically of the Court of Arbitration for Sport (CAS). The author maintains that CAS promotes public policy and favours fair competition, not the opposite, and that those who condemn CAS tend to be unacquainted with the facts and irresponsible in failing to explain how they would propose to remedy the chaos which would ensue if CAS were suddenly to disappear.

Keywords CAS · Arbitration · International sports law · Fairness · Independence

Contents

This article is an abbreviated version of a keynote speech given by the author on 22 September 2015 in Berlin at a joint DIS/CAS conference. It was first published in the SchiedsVZ—German Arbitration Journal (Issue 6/2015). It is reprinted in this volume with the kind permission of the Verlag C.H. Beck.

J. Paulsson (✉)
University of Miami, Coral Gables, USA
e-mail: jpaulsson@law.miami.edu

J. Paulsson
Three Crowns LLP, Washington, D.C., USA

A. Duval and A. Rigozzi (eds.), *Yearbook of International Sports Arbitration 2015*,
DOI 10.1007/978-94-6265-129-6_1

1.1 Introduction

The Court of Arbitration for Sport (CAS) often deals with sensitive disputes, which arouse powerful passions. It is therefore not surprising that CAS itself becomes a subject of controversy. My own view is that the function that CAS seeks to fulfil in the international community is indispensable. This does not mean that CAS is indispensable. But it does mean that those who raise existential criticisms of CAS have a duty to explain how they consider that this indispensable function would be fulfilled if we listened to them.

I had no part in inventing CAS. I do not have any role in running CAS. It has been ten years since I represented any party as an advocate before CAS. I have sat and continue to serve frequently as a CAS arbitrator, but I could very easily demonstrate that I would be financially better off, if I never did so. I have no role in any sports federation, and I am not even much of a sports fan. I have no favourite teams in any sport. I have never noticed that athletes care about whether I win my law cases and do not see why I should care whether they win their games.

But I have always supported CAS because I thought from the beginning, when the International Olympic Committee (IOC) took the initiative to establish it, that this was a worthwhile experiment. As things have turned out, it has in my view been very successful and continues to be a fascinating example of transnational institution-building. It has replaced the chaos that was there before, and which would have become even worse if CAS had not emerged. That is why I say that those who criticise CAS have a duty to understand what they are talking about before they start tearing things down, and to tell us what they would like to do instead.

I would like to look at our subject from three perspectives. First, the role of federations in enforcing the rules of international sports. Second, the observed behaviour of supporters of the accused. Third, the future: what would happen if we dismantled CAS?

1.2 The Role of International Federations

So let us begin with the international federations (IFs). But why? Isn't the subject CAS, rather than the IFs? That is indeed so. It has been questioned whether CAS is sufficiently independent of the IFs. As a matter of Swiss law, the supreme court of that country in the *Gundel* case (1993)[1] acknowledged CAS's legitimacy in cases, where the IOC itself is not a party to the arbitration. In reaction to *Gundel*, CAS was reformed so that the IOC was no longer involved in its management.

[1]SFT 119 II 271.

And so the Swiss Federal Tribunal is now satisfied that CAS may produce binding arbitral decisions even when the IOC is a party; it so held in the *Lazutina* case (2003).[2] But since courts in other countries might say that "what is good enough for the Swiss Federal Tribunal is not good enough for us", I propose to question whether it is really all that important whether CAS is independent of IFs. My simple point is that IFs are not the true adversaries of athletes suspected of cheating. IFs do not 'win' if suspected athletes are convicted. They do not have a desire to prove that there is cheating. It is bad for the reputation of their sport, and for their own reputation, since they are responsible for the way it is governed. IFs are the representatives of the entire body of competitors, and indirectly of the public. When someone has cheated in the context of the Olympics, his adversaries are the thousands of athletes who competed to get into the Games and the hundreds who actually made it. The same is true of every sport in which competition is organised across borders. Have you ever heard of Oscar Pereiro? I doubt it. He is the Spanish bicycle racer who won the 2006 *Tour de France*, but someone else stood on the highest podium at the finish line and had his name proclaimed throughout the world as the winner. Have you ever heard of Koji Morofushi? He made a magnificent hammer throw in the Athens Olympics on his very last attempt and should have stood on top as the Japanese national anthem was played. Instead Pereiro and Morofushi are names you might look up and see in the record books as answers to questions in a game of *Trivial Pursuit*—who was declared the winner on paper after the man who stole the spotlight was disqualified? They are the victims and the adversaries of those who competed illegitimately, and so are all other competitors. The second-place finisher is obviously not the only victim.

The victims of the cheaters are also the thousands of teenagers who have no realistic prospects of elite status in sports, but do not yet know it, and want to emulate the stars. Teenagers are impressionable, and when cheating is not suppressed they draw the conclusion that to be a champion means to ignore the rules. And so they destroy their health, and some youngsters even lose their lives doing what they think they must to succeed.

This is a matter of public health, and a matter of the gravest concern to all of us. If this is not a matter of public policy, I do not know what is. Can national laws and national law enforcement agencies deal with this problem at the international level? If so, we would not need IFs and we would not need CAS. Can anyone seriously believe that can be a solution?

Is free competition a matter of public policy? I am more than willing to say yes. But then it is a matter of public policy—is it not?—that competition should be fair. So when the IF or the IOC or CAS sanctions the cheater, it is acting in the interest of all competitors, and thus promoting public policy, not the opposite. How else is this supposed to happen? Are the victims supposed to go to the courts of the country of the cheater? Well, who can believe that Pereiro was going to go to ask the American courts to give him back what was taken from him by the American

[2]SFT 129 III 445.

cheater? How many years, how many hundreds of thousands of dollars would that involve? Who can believe that such a step would be taken by a racer who might have finished 20th and received a bonus which matters nothing to anyone else but perhaps determines whether he can continue to earn his living in the sport or not? What a fortunate thing it is that this is not how the system works! Because if it was, different courts might give different decisions, and all would be subject to appeals. And once this process was extended to a multiplicity of national court systems, including countries where the courts are susceptible to political influences and to bribery, all would be lost: total chaos.

Is it really proper and useful to say that IFs are monopolies? After all, that term was conceived to refer to profit-seeking business organisations. Would the world be a better place if each sport had 'competing' IFs? Seriously? Just consider what has happened in the world of boxing, where any number of organisations claim that they designate the world champion. And what would it mean for federations to 'compete', which is the purpose of avoiding monopolies? "Come to us because we have excellent doping controls"? Or, "come to us because we don't have any doping controls at all"? How about: "come to us because we'll give you a license which doesn't contain that nasty CAS clause"? What is the point of treating athletes as consumers who might be free to choose federations in which rules are *not* enforced in a uniform manner? And then what happens? In such chaos, surely the first thing left behind would be public policy.

And if cheaters can mobilise the support of their fans in a rich country to finance law suits that challenge every rule and every action taken by the supervisors of the sport—law suits that are beyond the budgets of most federations not involved in the glamour sports—other cheaters will do the same and simply make it impossible for those federations to play this role. Again, public policy will be defeated.

Let me make a few more observations that have some relation to this basic proposition that federations are not the adversaries of athletes.

1) One international rule of doping controls is remarkably favourable to athletes. There are protocols for the way doping samples must be identified and remain identified throughout the testing process. If any element of that protocol has been disregarded, the athlete must be acquitted. It does not matter if the protocol contains superfluous requirements, such as the use of a seal as well as a lock, and the problem is only that the seal was improperly affixed. The athlete will with absolute certainty be acquitted, even if his competitors might think this is far too indulgent. The federations insist on the discipline of an absolute reliability on the chain of custody.
2) One often-heard argument is that the athlete has been tested a multitude of times but never tested positive before. This often influences his fans a great deal. Who can forget how perhaps the most infamous of all offenders, Lance Armstrong, for so long repeated, again and again, and perfectly truthfully, that no one in his sport had ever been tested as many times as he, with never a single adverse finding. But this of course proves nothing, except perhaps that the science of testing continually follows the science of cheating at some distance.

The inventions of the cheaters come first, and the controllers must struggle to react and to do the reverse engineering. In fact three of the most prominent female runners in history retired several decades ago after having been tested innumerable times but were never ever caught—although there is surely no one left who believes that their grotesque records were obtained without performance-enhancing drugs. They (and those behind them) were simply ahead of the game.

3) Athletes often say that whatever has been found in their body was not performance enhancing. This argument has never fared well. To begin with, the criterion is not just performance-enhancement, but also the health of the athletes, and perhaps more importantly the health of young admirers, who want to copy them in every way. But even if one were only concerned with performance-enhancement, there must be legislation; lines must be drawn; standards must be set. Not everyone agrees with those standards, just as not everyone agrees with speed limits for cars or the danger of 100 ml of shampoo brought aboard an aircraft. Still, those who are subject to regulated activity cannot make up the rules for themselves, each one as it suits him or her.
4) Athletes also argue that they tested positive only because of a highly unusual natural condition which has everything to do with genes and nothing to do with cheating. Perhaps there *is* a one in a thousand chance that the positive finding was the result of a rare biochemical imbalance. If so, of course, 999 positives still do come from cheaters. What do we do—give up all attempts at fair competition because we cannot prove that there can never be a false positive? We do the best we can. Difficult questions never have to do with a single principle, such as avoiding punishment of the innocent, but with the collision of two competing principles when lines must be drawn in the general interest. Whether the cause of disqualification is that the concerned athlete has yielded to unhealthy influences or pressures, or because, just possibly, he or she has a rare genetic makeup, we do not need to make a moral judgment, only an objective legal finding in the interest of those who do manage to compete while satisfying the established standards.
5) What we should never expect is to have evidence of the actual ingestion of the prohibited substance, given how much pressure there is to deny, deny, deny. What we have is science, and science can be debated. Does the fact that one expert questions a detection method mean that the method cannot be used? Again, that would paralyse the entire effort and defeat the public interest in fair competition and public health. And sometimes we do not even have science, but simply compulsory inferences, such as the rule that an athlete who has violated the duty to give information about his or her whereabouts, so as to enable out-of-competition testing, will be deemed to have committed a doping infraction. Need I say it again? Such rules do not indicate a desire on the part of federations to exclude athletes from competition. Their goal is to have more competitors attracted to a sport that promotes instead of undermines health and fair play. And that goal is better achieved by the fair administration of proper rules of competition—which must be uniform.

1.3 The Behaviour of Supporters of the Accused

Now let us turn to the supporters of the accused. Entire nations are jubilant when their representatives win major competitions. So do the leaders of the country, and of course the national sports federations. Who can fail to remember when great Olympic champions mount the victory stand and immediately say that they dedicate their victory to the wonderful dictator of their country who offers great rewards for those who can contribute to his prestige by winning gold medals. Needless to say, such powerful people are more than annoyed when the glory turns into shame, creating enormous incentive to deny wrongdoing. Do not hope for anything from the courts of those countries.

But such effects may also result from *public* pressure. Consider the attitude of the Hungarian press and public when two Hungarian athletes won gold medals in the 2004 Athens Olympics and were promptly disqualified for doping. The two men were friends who trained together but did not compete against each other, because one participated in the hammer throw and the other threw the discus. As it happened, the finals in these two events took place on consecutive nights. On Sunday the 22 August, the hammer thrower led the competition from the very beginning. Then a strange thing happened towards the end; he left the stadium before his last throw and came back with an official some time later. The athlete was entitled to a sixth and final throw, but showed no interest in taking the opportunity to improve his record. He had gone to the doping control tent before the event was over, surprising the staff there, and quickly done a test, which was negative. After his return to the stadium, he engaged in no further competition. So he was done with the controls, and could get on the podium and receive the applause of the packed Olympic stadium. The Hungarian national anthem was played—not the Japanese—and the entire Hungarian nation watched the images in rapture.

On Monday evening, the discus thrower participated in the final of his event and he also won the gold. Dancing broke out on the streets of Budapest. But this time the officials at the control station were ready when he sprinted to the tent to be tested, and insisted on doing it punctiliously, which according to the rules means that a controller must enter the testing room and observe the urine leaving the athlete's body. Rumours had been swirling that the Hungarians were using a contraption concealed between their legs which allowed them to leave a guaranteed clean sample, namely the urine of another person. The discus thrower was very unhappy, and sat in the tent for two hours simply saying he was unable to give a sample. He was offered drinks to help the process, but refused to drink. He finally said that he found the whole business intolerably stressful and insisted on leaving. He was reminded that the refusal to provide a sample would be deemed a positive result and he would thus lose his gold medal. He ignored the warning and left the stadium knowing that he would forfeit his victory.

Since these two athletes were training partners, the doping control officials were now highly suspicious of what had happened the night before and decided to conduct a targeted test of the hammer thrower. They expected that this would be no problem, since they could simply go to find him with the Hungarian team in the Olympic Village Tuesday morning. Indeed, he was scheduled to fly back with the whole Olympic Team one day later. But they found that instead of waiting to return to Hungary as scheduled, to meet the ovations of the public as he walked proudly off the plane, he had decided to drive all the way back to Hungary by car, and had already left at 8 o'clock that morning—just hours after his friend the discus thrower had finally left the control station knowing that he was abandoning his gold medal. It seems that the priority was not to get to Hungary, but to leave Athens.

The control officers naturally concluded that this could not be allowed. The IOC dispatched a small team of inspectors to travel immediately to the suspect's village in Hungary. They presented themselves near midnight on Thursday at the athlete's home, where they found a waiting crowd of journalists and supporters of the athlete, including muscular men straddling loud motorcycles and blocking the way. The controllers were neither trained nor disposed for combat, and retreated to make their report. The IOC then issued an official notification via the Hungarian Olympic Committee requiring the athlete to present himself for testing at a police station at 4 p.m. the following day. He never came. The consequence under the rules was that he was deemed to have committed a doping infraction, and the IOC took away his gold medal as well.

Both of these athletes appealed to CAS, asking that the IOC's decision be overturned.[3] You might think this was astonishing, but perhaps it is understandable in light of the reaction of the Hungarian media and public. Instead of feeling embarrassed by this shameful behaviour, and instead of taking the slightest interest in the true facts of the matter, they 'patriotically' and instinctively defended their athletes—who of course denied all wrongdoing. Seldom have there been as many people, Hungarian journalists and fans having travelled to Lausanne, filling the street outside the venue where the CAS hearings were held. Pushed by this national pride, the athletes told incredible stories. The discus thrower said he was a very shy person whose religious beliefs required him to be modest, and that he had been intimidated and harassed by the officials. Since the official in question was a retired doctor who came to testify and turned out to be an unusually small elderly gentleman, this was hardly convincing in the mouth of a powerful world-class discus thrower who could probably make Arnold Schwarzenegger back down. As for the hammer thrower, he could not even manage to put together a coherent story of just why he absolutely had to drive the long way back to Hungary and why he was so unwilling to be tested properly and thus to defend his gold medal, if indeed he had obtained it fairly.

Another example comes from the United States of America: the case of *Floyd Landis*, the bicycle racer who stole the 2006 *Tour de France*. He had been under the very long shadow of Lance Armstrong, and his results had been relatively modest. Even with Armstrong gone in 2006, things did not look good for Landis in

---

[3]CAS 2004/A/714 & 718, *Fazeckas v. IOC*, Awards of 31 March 2005.

2006 after he almost collapsed in stage 16 of the race and lost ten (10) minutes. But for the next stage he was miraculously restored. He passed every single rider on his own team and thereafter raced onwards solo without support from them in a show of spectacular dominance, climbing away from everyone as though he had a turbo attached to his wheel. And so he became the apparent surprise winner of the *Tour de France*. But the day after the race the bad news came: he had failed his test from stage 17. He swore his innocence. He referred to his strong religious beliefs, and insisted on how he had been brought up always to respect the truth, and the truth was that he had never taken illegal substances. He said that if the result was correct his genes must be to blame, or maybe he was the victim of powerful interests conspiring against another American winner. Ultimately Landis came before CAS, which held a five-day hearing in New York in 2008. He still swore he had never lied. His lawyer harshly attacked the poor staff members of the laboratory which had done the testing and were now subjected to his cross-examination. He suggested that they were guilty of all kinds of dishonesty and professional misconduct. But the Tribunal found against Landis,[4] and he promptly said that he would go to court in America and attack CAS because of its unfairness.

But in May 2010 he suddenly announced that he wished to "clear his conscience" and admit that he had been lying all along. He admitted that he had been using prohibited substances for years. He wrote a book about the pressures of being a professional athlete, and how everyone around him had continuously been guilty of doping.

It is a sad story. Its point for present purposes is simply that a multitude of nationalistic fans believed everything he said, because (one supposes) they wanted to have faith in their champion. Commentators on blogs in America repeated Armstrong's frequent complaint that the French daily newspaper *L'Equipe* was against him because they preferred to report on the success of French racers, and they must somehow have some kind of dark influence with the French laboratories. Landis also had the vocal support of experts who were happy to be in the media and immediately rushed to his side in public comments. For example, a professor of human performance at Rice University in Houston immediately said he found it unlikely that Landis had used illegal substances. He and other experts were happy to support Landis even though they were not aware of the actual off-the-scale test results, nor that there was specific evidence of 'synthetic' testosterone. No matter—Landis started something called the 'Floyd Fairness Fund', and presented his arguments again and again on his blog. American fans responded, completely convinced by his affirmations and ready to condemn everybody in sight: the French, the laboratory technicians, the international cycling federation, and of course CAS for being dishonest and anti-American (even though Landis had appointed an American arbitrator, a prominent private lawyer in New York, who today is the President of the International Bar Association and has never

[4]CAS 2007/A/1394, *Floyd Landis v. USADA*, Award of 30 June 2008.

worked for a sports federation). It is said that Landis collected over one million dollars in public contributions to his legal defence fund, and that is very likely true, because in due course he was sued by some of them and the US authorities, who were threatening him with criminal pursuit on the grounds of fraud, with the possibility of a 20-year prison sentence, in 2012 let him go on the condition that his future earnings be garnished to recompense all contributors who could be traced. Many people had given money without identifying themselves, but the traceable contributions of more than 1700 fans amounted to $ 478,000. One year later, $ 10,000 had been returned. Records for 2014 and 2015 so far show no payments at all.

So to conclude: those who support suspected offenders simply cannot be trusted when they are infused by some form of misplaced patriotic passion. And when we are talking about dictators and other potentates, anxious to protect the champions whose glory they seem anxious to share, they have a lot more than $ 478,000 to spend in the effort.

1.4 Future Directions

And now to end with a series of questions about how the critics of CAS would propose to organise the governance of international sports.

The most excellent institutions should always be conscious of the possibility of improvement and reform. CAS is no exception. All serious people acquainted with its work are likely to have their own suggestions. For example, I have ideas about how to enhance transparency and the appearance of justice. For example, it should be possible to find out easily which arbitrator has been appointed by whom and how many times. Although I have seldom found that fellow CAS arbitrators have been committed to the cause of their appointers, I do not see why full records should not be readily available to the public. Nor have I ever had the feeling that there is a cabal of federations seeking to ensure that whatever any of its members might do in a disciplinary case is upheld by CAS panels. But why should *the federations* nominate a majority of the hundreds of persons who figure on the list of arbitrators qualified to serve in CAS cases? I do not believe that prejudice is caused to the accused in individual cases. I am pretty sure the badminton people do not spend any time trying to figure out how to help the field hockey people and so on. Still, in my view any preponderant formal role of the federations is unnecessary and creates an unfortunate appearance. On the other hand, I would think twice before eliminating the CAS list system, and allowing parties to choose whomever they want as arbitrator. Neither CAS nor the other disputants are capable of performing due diligence on arbitrators from all over the world, to find out anything about unknown nominees from remote countries before their appointment is accepted.

That being said, I do not believe that persons nominated to serve on the list of hundreds of CAS arbitrators should be identified as 'representing' athletes or federations. If you have been listening to me, you will understand that only a foolish 'athlete representative' will think that his duty is to defend the accused athlete, come what may. There are a few such arbitrators, who as incredible as it may seem are incapable of understanding that the huge majority of non-cheating athletes also deserve to be represented, and that in their interest it is imperative to disqualify and suspend those who obtain illicit advantage.

But how should reform come about? Should the individual legal system of every country in the world be entitled to decide that some feature or another of the CAS system is not worthy of respect? Should each legal system be given a chance to say that "what is good enough for the Swiss Federal Tribunal is not good enough for us"?

That would surely be chaos. There would be no end to what judges here or there might include in the concept of public policy. I have heard it said by the lawyers of an accused athlete that CAS is violating human rights because the proceedings are not entirely conducted in Flemish, even though their client-athlete is in the world elite and writes on a blog and conducts interviews in fluent French and English. Will CAS have to conduct its cases in 200 languages? And why should not the fundamental elements of every country's procedural code be held to constitute tests of public policy as far as due process is concerned? Are you familiar with the concept of '*amparo*' known throughout Latin America, that is to say control of the constitutional conformity of any decision affecting any individual's legal rights and obligations? It is of course a matter of public policy. Does this mean that no CAS decision involving a Latin American party could ever be final and binding, because if could be subject to judicial review in this manner?

More chaos.

And what about the special CAS formations which render decisions within 24 h in the context of the Olympic Games, or other similar multi-sport competitions? If CAS is illegitimate, how will decisions be rendered in the framework of such important international events? Just looking at the summer Olympics, does that mean that the next two Games will be subject to the decisions not of CAS arbitrators, but judgments of the courts of Brazil and Japan? How long will those judges take to decide which result should be upheld or nullified? How long before appeals are exhausted? And will the world be convinced by the legitimacy of those decisions? What will happen when they are presented for enforcement in the courts of the losing athletes? And what about cases brought by individuals who finished second or third, or missed the finals, and want their own courts to move them up, or to give damages for loss of earnings because they were deprived of the chance of a better placement in the competition? Let us not even talk about issues of eligibility to compete in the Olympics, because those disputes may arise on the day before the Games and must be decided within hours. Read my lips: *national courts cannot do it.*

More chaos again.

I really do not want to say much about the *Butch Reynolds* case, because it is an old tedious matter which takes long to explain and because I thought it was well behind us. Let me just remind you that this American sprinter, whose world record from 1988 still stands, 27 years later, as the second-fastest time in history, tested positive for anabolic steroids two years later and started a legal process, which included the intervention of the US Supreme Court to lift his suspension, decided by the international federation, and thus allowed him to compete in the US national Olympic trials two years later. The International Association of Athletics Federations (IAAF) did not then belong to the CAS system, so there was no recourse to CAS to uphold or annul the IAAF ban. The US Olympic trials were postponed for four days until Reynolds was allowed to run. Imagine the irritation of other athletes who were ready to compete on the scheduled day. Ultimately Reynolds qualified for the relay, but the Olympics were held in Barcelona and there was no way the US Supreme Court could tell the public authorities in Spain to force the IOC to let Reynolds compete. It was an absolute mess. But it got even worse. Reynolds went back home to Ohio and somehow convinced a US federal court, no less, to award him $ 27.3 million in damages against the IAAF for having damaged his reputation. The IAAF shrugged its shoulders and declared that that judgment had no effect outside Ohio. I guess that meant the IAAF would never again allow the staging of any international events in Ohio, which is a fairly important state including the major cities of Cleveland and Cincinnati—or perhaps even in the United States. Fortunately a federal appellate court overruled the court of first instance on the basis that it had no jurisdiction over the IAAF in Ohio.

Today this could not happen, because the validity of the IAAF ban would have been tested in CAS since by now the IAAF has adopted CAS jurisdiction as the global final dispute resolution mechanism. Is the *Reynolds* scenario the kind of chaos we want to go back to? With the ever-increasing monetisation of international sports, more time would be spent in the courts, I fear, than in the stadium. New 'Reynoldses' would seek the protection of their national courts, which would be more or less effective in light of how powerful their countries might be, and their competitors would go to their own courts to seek to prevent races where they are competing—which might be more or less effective depending on how powerful *their* countries might be. And where would the Olympic Games be held to avoid being embroiled in such disputation? On Mars maybe?

One last example, more up to date. If CAS were neutralised, who would resolve controversies relating to gender? Nature is messy. In most cases, we know who is of what gender. But some women have beards, and some men have none. Beards are not a test of gender, nor is a high-pitched voice. No one has a simple definition, and that includes scientists and laboratories. The issue came up again before CAS this year in relation to a teenage Indian runner named Dutee Chand; you will have seen it everywhere in the international press. She comes from a village in a poor part of India. She began to record impressive results as a junior. A test revealed that she is hyperandrogenetic, which means she has a high level of testosterone when compared to other women. Her serum testosterone reading turned out to be ten (10) nanomoles per litre, whereas not a single woman tested at the IAAF World Championships in 2011 was at that level, and 99 % were below a reading of three (3). On the other hand, a reading of ten (10) is normal for men. And men's measureable athletic performance are on average 10–13 % superior to women's.

Under the IAAF's Hyperandrogenism Regulations, Ms. Chand was suspended on the basis of that test. Such a suspension would end her career before it ever really began. She had little if any understanding of what was happening to her, save that she had always been a girl, raised as a girl, playing with girls, and could not comprehend how it could be denied that she is female. And it was not as if she could suddenly stop something in her body from producing this excess testosterone, so the suspension effectively was exclusion for life. The case came to CAS, where it was recognised as a matter of great importance and delicacy. A panel of three very experienced arbitrators, presided by Justice Annabelle Claire Bennett of the Federal Court of Australia, reviewed numerous expert reports and last March convened a hearing of four days' duration to question the experts and hear legal arguments. In the end, in an exceptionally thorough award, 161 extremely well-written pages, which I think anyone in this room would acknowledge as remarkably serious and sober, dealing exhaustively with difficult issues of procedure and evidential standards as well as the substantive rules and the policies behind them, the CAS Tribunal lifted Ms. Chand's suspension, and declared that the IAAF Regulations *themselves* were suspended for two years to allow for further investigations into their scientific foundations. To put it in a nutshell, the CAS arbitrators found that something was missing: regulations whose purpose is to promote fair competition among women cannot find a satisfactory basis in the simple observation that men have high testosterone levels and men are on the whole stronger and faster. An obvious missing investigation, they noted, must determine whether high levels of testosterone in women really do have the result of enhancing *their* performance. Until that is done, the Regulations are simply inapplicable, as the IAAF has no legally sufficient foundation for them.

Other decision-makers might have devised different solutions. But the CAS award in the Chand case has the double merit of being a fully reasoned and rational decision, and it created a comprehensible and enforceable (provisional) regime for all international athletics competitions. We now have a ruling which is effective worldwide—unless someone interferes with it.

Who could that be? How about one of Ms. Chand's competitors, who might go to the courts of their own home countries, or perhaps some other court where events are held and where her advisors think the courts would be favourable to her, perhaps because none of their own female athletes have so far had the problem of hyperandrogenism. Ms. Chand's presence in the competitions, she might say, is a threat to the plaintiff's economic prospects as a professional athlete; this is a matter of public policy; the CAS decision is not entitled to recognition. And then Ms. Chand's advisors will remember that the Government of India itself has been alerted to the case and has (as is revealed in the CAS award) launched its own inquiry into hyperandrogenism which might reach a different result. Is this a matter for the sovereign determination by 200 States of what they believe to be public policy? Will there be 200 answers, all of them supposedly pro-athlete but some of them in favour of the few (who have abnormal results on some kind of test recognised in some country) and others in favour of the many (who test normally on some other kind of test)?

Once again, this is the road to chaos.

Ladies and gentlemen, I have freely expressed a number of opinions here today, but please note that my conclusions are not in the form of answers, but in questions. I have tried to show that we have a remarkable system in place. It is not perfect: of course it can be improved, of course it should be continuously reevaluated.

Actually, the only question I truly would like to ask is how such improvements should be conceived and implemented. But given the types of challenges that have been raised against CAS, and given that many of them are actually destructive in their nature, I feel impelled to ask many other questions, and to challenge the critics of the system to answer those questions before they run off to tear down the building. These critics are not only nationalistic courts and lawyers who specialise in defending athletes accused of cheating, and whose only objective is to invalidate disciplinary decisions. There are many federations which also find CAS very annoying indeed—an impediment to the old autocratic ways of governing sports. CAS is an institution which provides answers to a wide range of extremely challenging and time-sensitive problems that arise when sports are practiced across borders. Those who do not like the institution are entitled to their opinion, but if they want us to see things their way they have the duty to tell us what they would leave in the wake of whatever it is that they would do with CAS.

Chapter 2
The Influence of Common Law Traditions on the Practice and Procedure Before the Court of Arbitration for Sport (CAS)

Dr. Gregory Ioannidis

Abstract The importance of the Court of Arbitration for Sport in the resolution of sporting disputes has become synonymous with the continuous development of sports law as a separate legal discipline. The unique structure of this supreme Court for sport, along with its composition, have created an unparalleled framework for the practice of sports law and at the same time a need for a better understanding of such practice. The author discusses the particular and unique elements of practice and procedure before the Court of Arbitration for Sport and explains that such practice has several similarities with the traditions of common law systems. He critically assesses specific elements of practice such as the standard of proof, examination of witnesses, the use of presumptions and negative inferences, along with the use by CAS Panels of previous decisions and concludes that although there is no declared system of binding precedent, in practice, CAS Panels, silently, operate a form of such binding precedent. He calls for ICAS to declare a system of binding precedent before the CAS and suggests that such system will restore certainty, predictability, consistency and clarity.

Keywords CAS · Sports Law · Precedent · Procedure · Evidence · Jurisdiction

Contents

Dr. G. Ioannidis (✉)
Department of Law and Criminology, Sheffield Hallam University,
Collegiate Crescent Campus, Sheffield S10 2BQ, UK
e-mail: g.ioannidis@shu.ac.uk

A. Duval and A. Rigozzi (eds.), *Yearbook of International Sports Arbitration 2015*,
DOI 10.1007/978-94-6265-129-6_2

2.1 Introduction

The majority of nations in today's modern world follow one of the two main legal traditions, namely common law or civil law. Civil law is originated in what we call today continental Europe and was developed there. Common law, on the other hand, emerged in England during the Middle Ages and was also applied in British colonies throughout the borders of the British Empire. Its influence on the American legal tradition, as well as on other former and current commonwealth traditions, is evident today.

Common law is generally uncodified and although there is a body of statutory law, it is largely based on judicial precedent. The law, therefore, develops through decided cases with presiding judges deciding upon facts and the law. Although the law is usually interpreted, followed, distinguished or overruled in the two highest courts in England, such as the Supreme Court (formerly known as the House of Lords) and the Court of Appeal, the influence of judicial precedent on lower courts is pre-determined, as they are obliged to follow decisions from the higher courts, because of the binding nature of such decisions. Procedure is largely adversarial, meaning that the facts and the law are presented and argued by the lawyers, with the judge being a moderator.

Civil law, on the other hand, is codified. Nations that follow a civil law legal tradition place emphasis on and follow large codified statutory instruments, which they update regularly. Such codes describe, in a comprehensive manner, substantive law, procedural law and penal law. Although the judge is the supreme arbiter of facts and has powers to investigate, examine and rule on a matter, his/her powers are largely determined by the relevant codes and his/her decision making is confined within the limitations created by such codes. The judge's powers, in a civil law legal tradition, therefore, are less crucial in the 'creation' of the law, than those of parliament with its legislative decision making.

Before we examine the influence of English common law on the practice and procedure before the CAS, it is necessary to evaluate the origins of this unique legal tradition.

2.2 The Origins of Common Law and Its Historical Development

English Common Law finds its origins in the early Middle Ages in the Kings Court (*Curia Regis*). This royal court was based in Westminster, London and was responsible for the administration of justice for most of the country. As it was the case with many courts in those days, the court was more concerned with the application of remedies, rather than the application of any procedural rights. It was after the Norman Conquest in 1066 that, through a system of *writs* (royal orders), such remedies would be afforded to applicants for wrongs suffered. Although the Norman Conquest had a heavy influence on society, it did not bring an immediate end to Anglo-Saxon law.[1] Several elements of Anglo-Saxon law survived and continued to influence the administration of justice.[2]

The Normans attempted to influence the administration of justice through the application of customary law they had in Normandy. They spoke French and they did not have professional lawyers, at least, not in the modern sense of the word. Those who were given the task for the administration of justice were clergymen, who had knowledge of Roman law and canon law. It was that time when Roman law emerged in a form of a justice system; however, its presence had no substantial influence. This was because the early Anglo-Saxon system was very sophisticated and because the system of writs had become highly formalised and very rigid in its application. This remedial system of writs became so important in the administration of justice that at the same time it created inflexibility and rigidity. It was this rigidity that led to requests for remedial applications directly to the King, with the result the creation of a separate court: it was the court of *Equity*, or the Chancery, as it is widely known, named after the King's chancellor.

The court of equity was given the task of applying principles of equity based on different sources, such as Roman law and natural law, with the aim to achieve justice. It was the emergence of these improved remedies in the King's court that allowed the clarification of the rigid and complicated system of writs and further set the stone for the creation of the system of common law, approximately during the late twelfth century.

---

[1]Anglo-Saxon law, the body of legal principles that prevailed in England from the 6th century until the Norman Conquest (1066). In conjunction with Scandinavian law and the so-called barbarian laws (*leges barbarorum*) of continental Europe, it made up the body of law called Germanic law. Anglo-Saxon law was written in the vernacular and was relatively free of the Roman influence found in continental laws that were written in Latin. Roman influence on Anglo-Saxon law was indirect and exerted primarily through the church. There was a definite Scandinavian influence upon Anglo-Saxon law as a result of the Viking invasions of the 8th and 9th centuries. Only with the Norman Conquest did Roman law, as embodied in Frankish law, make its influence felt on the laws of England.

[2]Such elements were the jury, ordeals (trials by physical test or combat), the practice of outlawry (putting a person beyond the protection of the law), and writs (orders requiring a person to appear before a court).

Roman law continued to play an important role in the administration of justice, although one may argue that its true influence is being underestimated. The actions, for example, of trespass and adverse possession were evident in the administration of justice and had analogies with Roman law. Similarly, Chancery and maritime courts applied Roman law, whereas the principle of mistake influenced contract law and the Roman law principle of fault was embedded into the law of negligence. It was clear that common law and Roman law (along with other laws such as canon law) co-existed, albeit in competitive terms. Precedent began to emerge and was to be followed and the first books on equity were published and it was not until the seventeenth century when common law prevailed over other laws.

Common law continued to develop rapidly and its unique influence on legal reason and the general administration of justice was to allow for the creation of important legal customs and institutions. Courts of law and equity appeared to function separately until the nineteenth century when writs were abolished. Despite this, common law continued to emerge as the prevailing legal system and some elements from the old system of writs, such as subpoenas and warrants, continue to exist in the present day with regard to the practice of common law. An example of this important influence on legal reason and practice is the writ of *habeas corpus*, which protects individuals from unlawful detention. The writ of habeas corpus developed during the same period as *Magna Carta,* which is one of the most significant developments with regards to individual liberties. One of the most famous and important liberties relates to the premise that no man could be imprisoned or punished without the judgement of his peers. This premise eventually led to the birth of trial by jury, which is one of the most significant creations of common law, although a form of jury trial could also be identified in Ancient Greece.[3]

2.3 The Modern Influence of Common Law on Legal Thinking and the Principle of *Stare Decisis*

It is submitted that it is natural and, indeed, normal to follow previous decisions in everyday affairs. To do so produces several obvious benefits, particularly in terms of accumulated experience, previous knowledge and consistency. The last element

[3]Ancient Athens had a mechanism, called *dikastaí*, to assure that no one could select jurors for their own trial. The institution of trial by jury was ritually depicted by Aeschylus in the *Eumenides*, the third and final play of his *Oresteia* trilogy. In this play the innovation is brought about by the goddess Athena, who summons twelve citizens to sit as jury. The god Apollo takes part in the trial as the advocate for the defendant Orestes, and the Furies as prosecutors for the slain Clytaemnestra. In the event the jury is split six to six, and Athena dictates that in such a case the verdict should henceforth be for acquittal.

of consistency produces an attractive and much desired proposition for the successful development of things. It is not uncommon for modern business mediums to follow previous decisions and to base their procedures on the benefits of accumulated experience from previous decisions. Although there is always the danger that persistent reliance on the same decision may cause inflexibility and, eventually, a static process, it is submitted that ways of evading a rigid adherence to previous practice, do assist in the friction between consistency and instability.

As there is a constant interaction between legal principles and facts, it is arguable that a system which allows a marriage between consistency and adaptability can produce the required levels of fairness and justice. Although this is not an absolute proposition, in general terms, it is fair to say that the Common law system has achieved, to a great extent, this marriage. The most important achievement of the common law system, however, has been the application of uniformity in the development of the law and, consequently, in the administration of justice. Uniformity is, undoubtedly, the element that characterises the unique nature of common law and which serves as a catalyst towards stability and efficiency.

The importance of the common law towards the application of justice and its influence on modern legal reasoning and thinking cannot be dismissed at face value. Modern legal thinking is largely based on the application of legal reasoning, which stems from the accumulated experience and wealth of case-analysis and expertise that judicial creativity and ingenuity offer through the system of judicial precedent.

For the civil lawyer, however, the doctrine of binding precedent may appear obsolete, inflexible, stale and rigid. Indeed, civil lawyers may conclude that the system of binding precedent is unnecessary as it creates an environment of rigidity and oppression. As B. Cardozo argues: "Uniformity ceases to be a good when it becomes uniformity of oppression. The social interest served by symmetry or certainty must then be balanced against the social interest served by equity and fairness or other elements of social welfares."[4] A civil lawyer labours under enormous difficulty to comprehend the necessity and importance of the difficult predicament of a common lawyer, who has to burden himself with complicated long judgements, in an effort to identify just one sentence of the binding *ratio decidendi* and the judges' unfortunate situation where they are bound and required to follow a precedent, which may be 500 years old. Indeed, it has been argued that a common law judge may be "a slave to the past and a despot for the future, bound by the decisions of his dead predecessors and binding for generations to come the judgements of those who will succeed him."[5]

When a condemning and highly polemical view like this is applied, it is easy to understand the civil lawyer's disapproval of the dynamics of common law. This

[4]Cardozo 1921, p. 113.

[5]Goodhart 1934, p. 61.

perception, with respect, is subjective and it does not reflect the true picture of the doctrine of *stare decisis*. The binding nature of the doctrine underpins the essence of the English legal system and its old-established existence and operation serve to demonstrate its important nature. This, however, is not an anathema, nor is a mechanism which makes the law static. The law develops through the decided cases but the rule of the binding nature of the doctrine is not absolute. The Practice Direction of 1966[6] recognises that the House of Lords (changed now to The Supreme Court) may treat previous decisions as binding, but may also depart from them when it appears right to do so. In the premises, it is submitted that any perceived limitations of the doctrine of binding precedent that may be apparent to the civil lawyer, can be dismissed by the relative freedom of the judiciary, for the determination of the scope and reason of previous decisions and the justification for a departure from a previous decision, when the fresh circumstances of a new case warrant so. This freedom of departure from previous decisions has been reluctantly exercised by the highest court in England over the years.[7] Nevertheless, it remains a freedom, upon which the doctrine operates and exercised for the efficient development of the law.

Similarly, it is submitted that the freedom of the judiciary to apply fairness and justice on a given matter is not limited by the application of the doctrine. As Lord Denning, the former Master of the Rolls, argues: "If lawyers hold to their precedents too closely, forgetful of the fundamental principles of truth and justice which they should serve, they may find the whole edifice comes tumbling down about them. Just as the scientist seeks for truth, so the lawyer should seek for justice. Just as the scientist takes his instances and from the builds up his general propositions, so the lawyer should take his precedents and from them build up his general principles. Just as the propositions of the scientist fail to be modified when shown not to fit all instances, or even discarded when shown in error, so the principles of the lawyer should be modified when found to be unsuited to the times or discarded when found to work injustice."[8]

This justifies the reason behind the creation of the Practice Direction of 1966 and it acknowledges the need of judges to be able to depart from the awkward situation where they have to distinguish previous bad precedents on the facts. The relative freedom of judges to depart from previous decisions is an integral part of the English legal system and goes to the root of the doctrine of *stare decisis*. As

---

[6]*Practice Direction* [1966] 3 All ER 77. See also Duxbury 2008, pp. 125–149.

[7]Some commentators submit the necessity of judicial creativity in stronger terms: "…it is an abdication of judicial responsibility for judges, at least in the law of obligations, to decline to develop the common law on the grounds that legislation is more appropriate. Even if a statutory solution would be better, no one can predict whether legislation will, or will not, be passed. It is therefore preferable for judges to proceed as they think fit, whether the decision be in favour or against a development, knowing that the Legislature is free to impose a statutory solution if the common law position is thought unsatisfactory or incomplete." Burrows 2012, p. 258. Duxbury 2008, p. 11.

[8]Denning 1979, pp. 285–314.

Duxbury argues: "The value of the doctrine of precedent to the common law is not simply that it ensures respect for past decisions but also that it ensures that bad decisions do not have to be repeated."[9]

It is also arguable that this freedom has not stretched the boundaries of judicial creativity. Although one would think that common law remains judge-made law, the critical examination and evaluation of the doctrine of binding precedent suggests that there is a fine balance between case law and statute. Notwithstanding the remarkable elements of stability and certainty the doctrine creates, as practitioners are able to determine, to a great extent, a sound legal advice from the outset, the doctrine walks in tandem with the existence of statute. It is statutory law which forms the genesis of a particular law, but it is case law which interprets such law and explains not only the intention of the legislator, but offers guidance as to its correct and purposeful application. It is submitted, therefore, that judge-made case law is important, as is important the existence of statute.

It is with regret that the author has to submit that the relationship between case law and statute has been remarkably unexplored. It is submitted that such relationship is evident even in civil law systems, where statute plays a primary role in the determination of a legal principle. Although previous decisions do not have a binding effect, on judges, in civil law systems, reference to such previous decisions is exercised and has a strong persuasive effect.

The continuous interaction between case law and statute also confirms the dynamic nature of the doctrine of judicial precedent. The relative freedom of the judiciary to depart from previous decisions and distance itself from Parliament, particularly in the light of bad precedents, is exemplified with numerous statements. According to Lord Steyn: "It would certainly be the easy route for the House to say 'let us leave it to Parliament'. On balance my view is that it would be an abdication of our responsibilities with the unfortunate consequence of plunging both branches of the legal profession in England into a state of uncertainty over a prolonged period."[10]

It is this unexplored relationship that forms the basis for a future international system of judicial decision making, in the sphere of the sports law discipline that the author wishes to promote with the present work. Although the CAS does not have a pre-determined application of a specific legal system, the author advocates the importance of common law, in the determination of legal matters before the CAS and its perceived influence in the creation of sports law principles. The common law, it is submitted, plays an important role before the CAS and the doctrine of binding precedent "…exemplifies the general balance which the common law strikes between certainty and adaptability. This general balance is a child of common law's methods, and it represents a large part of its genius."[11]

---

[9]Duxbury 2008, p. 11. See also Hershovitz 2006.

[10]*Arthur Hall v. Simons [2000] 3 WLR 543* at 683.

[11]Lord Justice Laws (2012) Our Lady of the Common Law. ICLR Lecture, p. 3. http://www.iclr.co.uk/assets/media/iclr-annual-lecture-transcript-2011.pdf. Accessed 16 February 2016.

2.4 The CAS and Its Procedure

2.4.1 Origins and Historical Development

The CAS[12] was created in 1983 by the International Olympic Committee and it became operational in 1984. It is an international *quasi-judicial* body, established to settle sporting disputes. Its seat is in Lausanne, Switzerland and its courts are located in Lausanne, New York and Sydney. The CAS also has *ad hoc* divisions in the host cities for the Olympic Games that take place every four years. Its current list comprises 328 arbitrators from 87 countries and such arbitrators are chosen subject to their specialist knowledge of sports law and international arbitration. The CAS hears nearly 300 matters every year.

The main reason for the creation of the CAS lies in the increasing need for specialist expertise in the handling of complicated and controversial sporting disputes. This expertise included the need to settle any dispute, beforehand, via the method of arbitration and/or mediation. As Matthieu Reeb explains: "The idea of creating an arbitral jurisdiction devoted to resolving disputes directly or indirectly related to sport had been launched. Another reason for setting up such an arbitral institution was the need to create a specialised authority capable of settling international disputes and offering a flexible, quick and inexpensive procedure. The initial outlines for the concept contained provision for the arbitration procedure to include an attempt to reach a settlement beforehand. It was also intended that the IOC should bear all the operating costs of the court."[13]

In the premises, it is submitted that the practice of sports law before the CAS, over the years, also demonstrates one of the most significant developments in this legal discipline of expertise; that is, an attempt to harmonise not only the procedural framework leading to the resolution of disputes arising from different sports, but also to create a framework of judicial decision making, capable of bridging the gap between different decisions from different disciplinary panels around the world. A harmonisation and consistency in the process of sporting dispute resolution, is the most remarkable achievement of the CAS and a testament of the argument that self-regulation cannot function without an independent, specialist and fast-track type of judicial process. The CAS procedure and application of the disciplinary law, on which the relationship between parties to a sporting dispute is based, have helped not only the procedural economy of the court, but they have also created a framework of uniformity in the application of general principles of law, specific principles of sports law and principles of penal law.

This process of harmonisation and consistency in the application of law and justice to sporting disputes did not commence smoothly. In the first ten years of its existence, the CAS operated with one single contentious procedure irrespective of the dispute in question. The claimant would submit a 'request' before the CAS

[12] In French: *Tribunal arbitral du sport*, TAS.

[13] Reeb 2002, pp. 23–25.

and a panel of arbitrators would rule on its admissibility and, subsequently, would be called to rule upon the matter. The parties, therefore, were free to continue with their action elsewhere should they wished to do so and if they were not happy with the decision.

In 1991, the CAS published an arbitration Guide, which included several arbitration clauses. One of such arbitration clauses was created for inclusion in the rules and regulations of different sporting governing bodies. It read: "Any dispute arising from the present Statutes and Regulations of the… Federation which cannot be settled amicably shall be settled finally by a tribunal composed in accordance with the Statute and Regulations of the Court of Arbitration for Sport to the exclusion of any recourse to the ordinary courts. The parties undertake to comply with the said Statute and Regulations, and to accept in good faith the award rendered and in no way hinder its execution."

This specific clause was the beginning of the creation of a series of similar clauses that were to be included in the regulatory framework of different sports. Not only self-regulation and governance were changing dramatically, in terms of the judicial process, but the CAS was paving the way for its judicial supremacy in the world of sporting dispute resolution. Such arbitration clauses became 'compulsory' in the regulatory framework of sporting governing bodies and from 1992 the Appeals Arbitration division of the CAS (as we know it today) was formed. This section was assigned to hear appeals from the decisions of disciplinary panels of sports bodies. In essence, the decisions re-entered by disciplinary panels were deemed to be decisions at first instance that were appealable to the Appeals Arbitration division of the CAS. Sporting judicial process was shaping up!

2.4.2 The Reforms of 1994

The major reform occurred in 1994 and it was as a result of an important appeal submitted to the CAS in February 1992, by a horse rider named Elmar Gundel. The rider submitted the appeal against the decision rendered at first instance by his federation on charges of horse doping. The initial decision included a ban against the rider and a fine. The CAS issued an Award in October 1992 and it found, partly, in favour of the rider.[14] The rider disagreed with the decision of the CAS and appealed further to the Swiss Federal Tribunal, on the grounds that the CAS Award was not valid and the CAS was not a proper court and it lacked impartiality and independence. In March 1993, the Swiss Federal Tribunal delivered its judgement[15] recognising the CAS as a true court of arbitration. The Federal Tribunal, however, made a crucial point with regards to the independence of the

[14]CAS 92/63, *Gundel v. Fédération Equestre Internationale*, Award of 10 September 1992.

[15]Published in the *Recueil Officiel des Arrêts du Tribunal Fédéral* [Official Digest of Federal Tribunal Judgements] at SFT 119 II 271.

CAS. It stated in its judgement that there were several links between the CAS and the IOC, serious enough to call the CAS' independence into question. Such links made reference to the fact that the CAS was financed almost exclusively by the IOC, the IOC President had enormous power to appoint the CAS arbitrators and the IOC, overall, had the power to modify the CAS statutes. All these facts, the Federal Tribunal argued, were serious enough to create questions of independence and impartiality.

The *Gundel* decision led the CAS to restructure itself and create a more efficient and appropriate mechanism, whereby, all sporting disputes submitted to it could be dealt with more appropriately. The ICAS was created and it took over from the IOC the financial management of the CAS and the overall running of the Court. In addition, two different divisions of hearing disputes were created, the Ordinary Arbitration Division for sole (first) instance disputes and the Appeals Arbitration Division, hearing disputes arising out of decisions taken by sports organisations. This transformation was confirmed with the introduction of the CAS Code, which now forms the procedural guide for practising sports law before the Supreme Court for sport.

2.4.3 The Significance of the Code

The Code is perhaps the most significant document of the CAS. It governs the organisation of the Court as well as the procedure, including the pre-trial process. It is a 70-article-document which is divided into the relevant statutes of bodies working for the settlement of sport-related disputes[16] and the Procedural Rules[17] which govern the Procedure before the CAS.

One of the important functions of the CAS, which was established in 1999, is the creation of the mediation process, whereby parties have the choice, via negotiation and the use of a mediator, to settle their dispute, without the need for a full hearing. The relevant mediation rules set the ground for the mediation process and explain that such process is non-binding and informal. It is a process, however, which observes confidentiality, reduces the parties' costs considerably and offers an expedited procedure.

In the premises, it is submitted that the CAS has the following procedures[18]:

- the ordinary arbitration procedure;
- the appeals arbitration procedure;
- the mediation procedure.

---

[16]Articles S1-S26.

[17]Articles R27-R70.

[18]See The History of the CAS at http://www.tas-cas.org/en/general-information/history-of-the-cas.html. Accessed 16 February 2016.

The proceedings before the CAS are usually twofold, as procedure involves, first, the exchange of written statements and then the oral and live hearing. The Appeals Arbitration procedure also offers the parties the use of Provisional and Conservatory Measures, which, in modern legal systems, are the equivalent of a stay of execution, usually against a decision re-rendered by a sport governing body.

In addition and in essence, there are usually two types of disputes submitted before the CAS, those of a commercial nature and disputes of a disciplinary nature. The former types of disputes may include contractual relationships, such as contracts between players and clubs, sponsorship disputes and even television rights. On the field injuries (civil liability) disputes may even come under this category. The latter type of disputes includes appeals on decisions taken by disciplinary panels of sports governing bodies and are heard before the Appeals Arbitration Division of the CAS. Here, anti-doping disputes have a dominant presence.

Finally, it is not uncommon for the CAS to dismiss an application for an Appeal because of lack of jurisdiction, or because the Applicant was 'manifestly' late in submitting the application.

Advisers, therefore, must ensure that the Appeal is filed within the 21-day time limit provided for by the procedural rules of CAS, or according to the time limit the rules of the appropriate sporting body prescribe. Most importantly, they must ensure that CAS has jurisdiction to hear the Appeal. Such jurisdiction usually derives from the regulatory framework of the sporting governing body in question, or when there is a specific and express arbitration agreement between the parties. A specific clause would normally indicate a route to Appeal, although close attention must be paid to the actual wording of the relevant provision. This is an important point that requires further analysis.

Rules of national governing bodies are usually in line with the rules of international governing bodies, or have been drafted in the same spirit. It may be the case that certain provisions require members to recognise the jurisdiction of CAS, regarding disputes of national dimension. However, the purpose of these provisions may not be to compel CAS to admit in all types of disputes that the national governing body has jurisdiction to hear. In this instance, confusion may be created by the provision which specifically 'recognises' the jurisdiction of CAS. Although such provision may 'recognise' the jurisdiction of CAS, this does not mean that the provision also 'grants' such jurisdiction to CAS. In other words, CAS jurisdiction will be operative only when such jurisdiction is specifically granted by the provisions of the national governing body.[19]

[19]This was evident in four football appeals the author was involved in before the CAS. See CAS 2011/A/2483, *Iraklis Thessaloniki FC v. Hellenic Football Federation & Greek Super League.*

2.5 Common Law or Civil Law?

The main function of the CAS is to resolve sporting disputes between parties. Although such disputes are dealt with via arbitration, in practice, a CAS matter takes the form of a full trial, even at the appellate level, as the general applicable rule is that all appeals before the CAS, take the form of a *de novo* hearing.[20]

The practice of sports law before the CAS, over the years, has contributed enormously towards the creation of a remarkable body of case law, as well as statutory law. A unique *lex sportiva* is now in place, which highlights the importance of the CAS in the development of sports law principles and its influence on the practice and procedure of sports law. It is the creation of this remarkable body of case law which forms the basis of the present work.

The nature of the proceedings before the CAS is undoubtedly private and it is usually private international law and Swiss law that govern the proceedings, particularly, in the absence of an express agreement between the parties as to the application of a specific law. What is not specifically stated, however, is the choice, if any, of the actual legal system that governs the process before the CAS. Given that there is a mixture of arbitrators (judges) from, both, common law and civil law jurisdictions, it becomes imperative for the practising lawyer to identify the appropriate medium and, therefore, conduct the proceedings in the appropriate manner.

From the author's experience, it is submitted that proceedings before the CAS (and even during the pre-trial stage) are conducted with the style one meets in a common law jurisdiction. Although the judges, to a certain extent, apply the 'inquisitorial' civil law style of examination, this is limited to questions, during the proceedings, towards the witnesses and sometimes, towards Counsel for either side. Overall, parties are free to submit the evidence of their choice and test it, during the proceedings, in the common law style of 'adversarial' examination, that is, through Counsel for either side. Such examination of the evidence may take the form of written statements, witness testimonies and even applications for pre-trial disclosure. Even during the proceedings before the panel of judges, the process is very much influenced by the common law tradition, whereby, the process involves opening and closing statements, examination in chief and cross-examination and the right to redirect.

---

[20]Pursuant to Articel R 57 CAS Code, which grants CAS Panels the authority to produce a full review of the facts and the law. See also CAS 2009/A/1880 & 1881, *FC Sion & E. v. Fédération Internationale de Football Association (FIFA) & Al-Ahly Sporting Club*, Award of 1 June 2010, where the panel stated as follows: "…the CAS appeals arbitration allows a full de novo hearing of a case, with all due process guarantees, which can cure any procedural defects or violations of the right to be heard occurred during a federation's (or other sports body's) internal procedure. […] it is the duty of a CAS panel in an appeals arbitration procedure to make its independent determination of whether the Appellant's and Respondent's contentions are correct on the merits, not limiting itself to assessing the correctness of the previous procedure and decision" (paras 142, 146).

It is, however, the parties' references to previous decided cases and the continuous use of such decisions by different panels of judges that would allow one to enquire whether there is a system of *stare decisis* before the CAS. One may produce an attempt at dismissing the existence of such system in the proceedings before the CAS and argue that the CAS panels of judges simply take a note of previous cases, for the sake of consistency and clarity. But is it not this contention that forms the basis for the application of a system of judicial precedent?

It is not disputed that there is now a specific system of *lex sportiva* and the sheer volume of decided cases before the CAS serves to demonstrate that different principles of sports law develop through the examination, analysis and, consequently, via the decisions of the CAS. This only can serve as a catalyst towards a persuasive argument that the CAS does have a system of precedent.[21] As the Panel states in the case of CAS 2002/O/373, *Canadian Olympic Committee & Beckie Scott v International Olympic Committee*: "CAS jurisprudence has notably refined and developed a number of principles of sports law, such as the concepts of strict liability (in doping cases) and fairness, which might be deemed part of an emerging *lex sportiva*."[22]

With this in mind, it is worth examining, both, scholarship and practice, so a determination could be achieved as to whether there is a *de facto* system of *stare decisis* before the CAS. Certain commentators have suggested that the existence of the CAS Awards "demonstrate the existence of a true *stare decisis* doctrine within the field of sports arbitration",[23] whereas others have suggested that CAS arbitrators "…are not generally obliged to follow earlier decisions but they usually do so in the interests of legal certainty."[24] The author is inclined to accept and follow such interpretation, given that the CAS Panels make constant use of previous decided cases, particularly when they identify the *ratio decidendi* in their Awards. It is common practice and, indeed, usual reference to previous decisions can be identified in almost every single CAS Award. Such is the importance of precedent in the procedure and practice before the CAS, that it is now common practice for Counsel to submit a Bundle of Authorities before the CAS Panel, in support of his/her submissions. This is also true in situations where the composition of the CAS Panel is mixed, with arbitrators from common law and civil law jurisdictions adjudicating together upon a sporting dispute.

There are, however, instances, in practice, when CAS arbitrators disagree with the above interpretation. In the case of CAS 2008/A/1545[25] the Panel made refer-

---

[21]For further discussion see CAS 2002/O/373, *Canadian Olympic Committee (COC) & Beckie Scott v. International Olympic Committee (IOC)*, Award of 18 December 2003.

[22]Ibid., para 14.

[23]Kaufmann-Kohler 2007, p. 366.

[24]Blackshaw 2009. Similarly, Mitten and Opie 2010, pp. 283–308.

[25]CAS 2008/A/1545, *Andrea Anderson, LaTasha Colander Clark, Jearl Miles-Clark, Torri Edwards, Chryste Gaines, Monique Hennagan, Passion Richardson v. International Olympic Committee (IOC)*, Award of 16 July 2010.

ence to the case of CAS 97/176 with regards to the value of judicial precedent, where it was stated: "…in arbitration there is no stare decisis. Nevertheless, the Panel feels that CAS rulings form a valuable body of case law and can contribute to strengthen legal predictability in international sports law. Therefore, although not binding, previous CAS decisions can, and should, be taken into attentive consideration by subsequent CAS panels, in order to help developing legitimate expectations among sports bodies and athletes".[26] Similarly, the same Panel also made reference to another CAS Award of CAS 2004/A/628 (award of 28 June 2004), where it was stated: "In CAS jurisprudence there is no principle of binding precedent, or *stare decisis*. However, a CAS Panel will obviously try, if the evidence permits, to come to the same conclusion on matters of law as a previous CAS Panel."[27] Having looked at the two aforementioned authorities, the Panel concluded: "Therefore, although a CAS panel in principle might end up deciding differently from a previous panel, it must accord to previous CAS awards a substantial precedential value and it is up to the party advocating a jurisprudential change to submit persuasive arguments and evidence to that effect."[28]

The above analysis suggests that in the CAS procedure there is no *de jure* recognition of the doctrine of binding precedent, at least, not in theory. In practice, however, it is submitted that the constant use of previous decisions and the undisputed reference of different CAS Panels to the elements of consistency, continuity and legal certainty, suggest that the doctrine of binding precedent operates before the CAS, albeit, with some minor exceptions. The author submits that, in practice, the CAS operates in a similar manner with regards to The Supreme Court in the UK (previously known as the House of Lords), where judges are allowed to depart from their own previous decisions. The fact that 'persuasive arguments' and 'evidence to that effect' may lead towards a jurisprudential change, demonstrate the argument that if CAS Panels feel 'right to do so', they may depart or decide not to follow previous decisions. In fact, in such cases, the CAS Panels go at length to explain the reasons of their 'departure' from previous cases and they tend to do so by distinguishing relevant authorities on the facts and on the merits.

2.5.1 Binding or Persuasive Authority?

One issue, which has remained elusive, over the years, is a clear declaration from the ICAS as to the nature of the Awards pronounced by the CAS. Although the *Anderson*[29] Award explicitly recognises that there is no system of binding prece-

[26]CAS 97/176, *UCI v. Jogert & NCF*, Award of 15 January 1998, para 40.

[27]CAS 2004/A/628, *International Association of Athletics Federations (IAAF) v. USA Track & Field (USATF) & Y.*, Award of 28 June 2004, para 73.

[28]CAS 2008/A/1545, *Andrea Anderson & al. v. IOC*, para 55.

[29]Ibid.

dent before the CAS, nevertheless, such Award also recognises the *'substantial value'* of precedent. This situation appears to be self-conflicting and contradictory and to a certain extent, with respect, it does not assist in the procedure and practice before the CAS.

One explanation for the lack of an explicit declaration of the binding (or otherwise) nature of the CAS Awards is possibly the acknowledgement that arbitral awards do not usually contain any form of precedential nature.[30] This may be true, in the sphere of international arbitration; but is the CAS, in practical and pragmatic terms, an arbitral tribunal or is it a Court, with full power to examine the facts and the law, examine the evidence and the witnesses and produce decisions where future disputes may rely upon for guidance? In pragmatic terms, the CAS procedure and practice resemble practice in a civil or criminal court. The process before the CAS is identical to the process of a civil or criminal court, whereby procedural rules determine the actual practice of Counsel and judges alike and offer guidance as to the rights of litigants. The proceedings are formal and the primary duty of Counsel remains the same: the duty to the Court. Rules of evidence play an important role in the final determination of the matter in question, whereas language and court-etiquette are observed at all times and those practising advocacy at the highest level, are familiar with the appropriate pace, tone of the voice, body posture and eye contact with the judges. These are all issues that play an important role in the proceedings before the CAS and the formal process applies, without an exception, in the Ordinary and the Appeals Divisions of the CAS.

Moreover, the CAS Awards, in their majority, do not have a confidential nature and, unless the parties agree otherwise, are published in the CAS website and are available and free to everyone. In addition, the CAS website contains a specific 'Jurisprudence' section, where those interested can access recent Awards or even the archive where older Awards are stored. This, in essence, creates a useful tool of actual law reporting, similar to the one in the UK. In the author's opinion, this process is substantially relevant and identical to the most important ingredients that form the basis of a common law system.

In the premises, reference needs to be made to statutory interpretation employed by the CAS, which over the years, has assumed an important role in the understanding and appreciation of different relationships in sport. The CAS has assumed a primary role in interpreting rules and regulations of sporting governing bodies. Such regulations, along with the statutes of the said sporting bodies, form the basis of real and actual statutory interpretation and it is, without a doubt, a practice that occurs constantly. One would be hard pressed in discovering one single CAS Award that fails, in one way or another, in its attempt to interpret specific rules and statutes. Such is the importance of the CAS statutory and regulatory interpretation, that practitioners are now able to determine, to a great extent, the outcome of the litigation and advise their clients accordingly.

---

[30] Blackaby et al. 2009.

The above analysis suggests that, in theory, the doctrine of binding precedent does not exist before the CAS. In practice, the author submits, the doctrine of binding precedent is very much exercised and it occurs more often than not. In the limited number of CAS Awards where CAS Panels declared the absence of a system of binding precedent, they also took the opportunity to suggest that there must be good reasons as to why a CAS Panel may decide to depart from a previous authority, regardless of the composition of such Panel. In the author's opinion, the CAS is usually reluctant to disregard previous decisions, particularly where facts and *ratio decidendi* of previous and present matters appear to be and, are, as a matter of fact, identical or similar. In essence, although not specifically stated, it is submitted that some form of unique existence of precedent (in the common law understanding) is exercised before the CAS. One may argue that such precedent is not binding, but such is the force of its application on present and future CAS Panels that one would also accept the premise that the persuasive nature and constant reference to such nature of previous decisions, constitutes a de facto practice of judicial decision making that tends to become binding, in a looser interpretation of the meaning of the word.

2.5.2 The CAS Standard of Proof as an Example of a Practising Common Law Tradition

The common law tradition with regards to the rules of evidence has devised two different standards of proof. In civil matters the standard of proof is on the *balance of probabilities* and this is the standard of proof generally required to be met by either party seeking to discharge the burden of proof. On the other hand, the criminal standard of proof is *beyond reasonable doubt*. In the sporting context, sports law jurisprudence has devised a third standard of proof, which is currently identified between the common law civil and criminal standards of proof. Those practising before the CAS recognise and use the *comfortable satisfaction* standard of proof. The CAS jurisprudence suggests that this standard is above the common law civil standard of proof, but below the common law criminal standard of proof.[31] In the case of *IAAF v. RFEA & Josephine Onyia*[32] such standard of proof was defined as being "greater than a mere balance of probability but less than proof beyond reasonable doubt."

Although specific CAS Panels have suggested in the past that they are not obliged to follow rules of evidence,[33] it is the author's respectful submission that

[31]See the case of CAS 2010/A/2229, *WADA v. FIBV & Berrios*, Award of 28 April 2011. This standard was first used in sport in the case of CAS 96/003 & 004, *Korneev and Gouliev v. IOC*, Award of 4 August 1996. Its true origin in the law can be identified in the Australian case of *Briginshaw v. Briginshaw* [1938] 60 CLR 336.

[32]CAS 2009/A/1805 & 1847, *IAAF v. RFEA and Josephine Onyia*, Award of 22 September 2009.

[33]See CAS 2008/A/1574, *D'Arcy v. Australian Olympic Committee*, Award of 7 July 2008.

this is exactly what they do in practice. One would be hard pressed in identifying situations where CAS Panels did not follow the rules of evidence, particularly, during proceedings. As a matter of fact, CAS Panels have consistently used direct and circumstantial evidence and have proceeded with rulings on whether specific pieces of evidence are admissible or not. From the author's experience before the CAS, such instances have been an integral part of the pre-trial stage of a CAS matter and determined the outcome of such matter during the appeal hearing.[34]

It is also worth stating that there is another similarity between the CAS evidential process and the one in the common law tradition. The standard of proof is normally used at the end of the trial, when all the different pieces of evidence have been submitted and examined. It may be also used in the situation where there is a submission of a no case to answer, particularly where one party has failed to adduce evidence.[35]

The common law civil standard of proof, obviously, is determined on the balance of probabilities. In *Miller v Minister of Pensions* [1947][36] Lord Denning explained: "It must carry a reasonable degree of probability, but not so high as is required in a criminal case. If the evidence is such that the tribunal can say: 'we think it more probable than not', the burden of proof is discharged, but if the probabilities are equal it is not." This suggests that the civil standard of proof requires the party with the burden to prove that the defendant's actions were 'more likely than not'. It has been suggested by Lord Hoffman in the case of *Secretary of State for the Home Department v Rehman* [2001][37] that the only higher degree of probability required by the law is the criminal standard. This means that the civil standard cannot be broken down into different categories with the aim of producing immediate standards.[38]

The common law civil standard of proof, however, has some flexibility in its application. Such flexibility may be interpreted according to the seriousness of the allegation and suggests that if such allegation exists, then the degree of probability needs to be raised.[39] Although this position has now been rejected,[40] it is submitted

[34]See CAS 2005/A/887, *IAAF v. SEGAS, Kenteris & Thanou*.

[35]*Miller v. Cawley* [2002] EWCA Civ 1100, The Times (6 September 2002).

[36]*Miller v. Minister of Pensions* [1947] 2 All ER 372 at 374.

[37]*UKHL 47* [2003] 1 AC 153 at 55.

[38]See the leading judgement of Richards LJ in the case of *R (N) v. Mental Health Review Tribunal (Northern Region)* [2005] EWCA Civ 1605, [2006] QB 468 at 60.

[39]See Denning LJ in *Bater v. Bater* [1951] P 35 at 37.

[40]CAS 2008/A/1574, *D'Arcy v. Australian Olympic Committee*. See also Baroness Hale in *Re B (Children) (Care Proceedings): Standard of Proof* [2008] UKHL 35, [2009] 1 AC 11 at 70–72: "Neither the seriousness of the allegation nor the seriousness of the consequences should make any difference to the standard of proof to be applied in determining the facts. The inherent probabilities are simply something to be taken into account, where, relevant, in deciding where the truth lies.".

that it walks in tandem with the current standard of proof before the CAS. This is true in anti-doping litigation as the WADA Code clearly explains that any anti-doping organisation must establish the alleged anti-doping violation 'to the comfortable satisfaction of the hearing body bearing in mind the seriousness of the allegation which is made.' This, in essence, means that the more serious the allegation the higher the degree of satisfaction and, consequently, the standard of proof.

This submission is well enshrined not only in the CAS jurisprudence but in English and wider common law too, making the argument that the CAS procedure and practice resemble common law, even stronger. For example, the origin of the 'comfortable satisfaction' standard is identified in the Australian case of *Briginshaw v Briginshaw* [1938][41] where Justice Rich stated: "In a serious matter like a charge of adultery the satisfaction of a just and prudent mind cannot be produced by slender and exiguous proofs of circumstances pointing with a wavering figure to an affirmative conclusion. The nature of the allegation requires as a matter of common sense and worldly wisdom the careful weighing of testimony, the close examination of facts proved as a basis of inference and a comfortable satisfaction that the tribunal has reached both a correct and just conclusion." In the English case of *Hornal v Neuberger Products Ltd* [1957][42] it was stated: "The standard of proof depends on the nature of the issue. The more serious the allegation the higher the degree of probability that is required; but it need not, in a civil case, reach the very high standard required by the criminal law." Similarly, in the CAS Award of CAS 2004/O/645, *USADA v Montgomery* it was stated: "…the more serious the allegation the less likely it is that the alleged event occurred and, hence, the stronger the evidence required before the occurrence of the event is demonstrated to be more probable than not."

The substantial influence of the common law traditions, with regards to the standard of proof before the CAS, is also evidenced by the use of other considerations, such as the admissibility of evidence, its rebuttal, the use of presumptions and the use of circumstantial evidence. In anti-doping litigation, for example, the use of presumptions is often. There is a presumption that the onus of proof is with the sporting governing body (or the anti-doping organisation) to establish the alleged offence, provided that the anti-doping test has been conducted properly and executed correctly. To this effect, the common law influence on the rebuttal of a presumption in anti-doping litigation is evident, as such rebuttal must be made on the balance of probabilities. In other words, if the prosecuting authority is alleging a positive anti-doping test and the presumption is that such test was conducted properly, then the athlete has to show how the substance entered his/her body and in doing so he/she must rebut such presumption on the balance of probabilities.[43]

---

[41]Supra 31.

[42]*Hornal v. Neuberger Products Ltd* [1957] 1 QB 247.

[43]CAS 2006/A/1067, *IRB v. Keyter*, Award of 13 October 2006. It was stated by the Panel: "… that the occurrence of a specified circumstance is more probable than its non-occurrence." The athlete may also have the opportunity to demonstrate departures from the International Standards for Testing.

Similarly, the CAS is not agnostic or unfamiliar with the use of circumstantial evidence (for example, the blood profile of an athlete), particularly in anti-doping litigation. The use of negative inferences is also used before the CAS and Counsel, more often than not, are prepared to make submissions in favour of the Panel drawing negative inferences, in the situation where one or more of the opponent's witnesses are refusing to give oral testimony before the Panel. Oral testimony, or lack of it, carries considerable weight in the final determination of a CAS Panel. As it was stated in the CAS Award of CAS 2002/A/385, *T v. FIG*,[44] "[t]he Panel was not afforded the opportunity to form its own impression of the athlete. It is difficult for the Panel to identify further mitigating circumstances if an athlete decides not to appear before the Panel for the hearing of his/her case which may have a very substantial impact on his/her future professional career."[45]

The above analysis, with regards to the standard of proof applied by the CAS, suggests that such application is consistent with common law and given the enormous importance CAS Panels place on the analysis and evaluation of evidence, it is submitted that the influence of traditional common law principles and methods characterises the core of the proceedings before the CAS.

2.6 Conclusion

The analysis in the present work suggests two things: first, the CAS does not consider its decisions to be binding and secondly, the CAS is reluctant to depart from its previous decisions, for reasons of consistency and legal certainty. This, in essence, creates some form of precedent, albeit, not binding in the common law meaning. The reader of this work will probably arrive at the same conclusion, which indicates a synthesis between common law and civil law and, at the same time, demonstrates the unique nature of the operation of the CAS. There is a lot to be said from this marriage of common law and civil law traditions and a lot more to be gained.

For reasons of clarity and legal certainty, the author would recommend some form of declaration, on behalf of the ICAS, to the effect that previous decisions would be followed, where appropriate, particularly when facts and the law of present matters, appear to be in harmony with previous ones. In the author's respectful opinion, this is the silent operation of precedent before the CAS. Such declaration may even be incorporated into the CAS Code and become a binding feature of procedure and practice before the CAS.

[44]CAS 2002/A/385, *T v. FIG*, Award of 23 January 2003, para 57. See also CAS 2004/O/645, *USADA v. Montgomery*, Award of 13 December 2005; CAS 2005/A/884, *Hamilton v. USADA & UCI*, Award of 10 February 2006; CAS 2005/A/887, *IAAF v. SEGAS, Kenteris & Thanou*.

[45]This much is also supported by the new version of the WADA Code 2015.

Although there is a minority of CAS Panels having declared that the CAS does not consider its previous decisions binding and that there is no operation of the doctrine of *stare decisis,* the present analysis indicates exactly the opposite. Where the facts warrant so (and this is true in the majority of anti-doping litigation) the CAS Panels are reluctant to depart from previous decisions, for reasons of consistency and legal certainty. In essence, the CAS operates like another UK Supreme Court, where the judges are not bound by their own previous decisions, but they are vehemently discouraged from departing from them, without a compelling justification.

Opponents of the doctrine of binding precedent may argue that this constant reliance on previous decisions and the unparalleled desire for uniformity may lead to oppression and that a bad decision may bind lower courts for years. This may be true in certain situations, but in the author's opinion, such argument cannot dissuade the use of binding precedent, as the CAS is the Supreme Court in sport and, in practice, its decisions are respected and followed worldwide. Its decisions may not be binding over national courts, but they very much form and determine the structure and synthesis of the regulatory framework and overall self-regulation in modern sport.

It is also true that some problems will always arise with the application of the doctrine of binding precedent. As Rodger suggests: "Because, even in the highest courts, judges will change their minds from time to time. This is nothing to be ashamed of: indeed there is divine precedent for it. As Pope Innocent III remarked in 1215, in a decree issued during the Fourth Lateran Council changing the rules on the impediments to marriage by reason of affinity, 'in the new Testament even God himself made some changes to what he had laid down in the Old'".[46]

Despite some of the criticisms of the doctrine of binding precedent, with regards to how oppressive uniformity could be, the author submits that without a system of binding precedent, confusion and uncertainty usually prevail. This is particularly true in anti-doping litigation, where clarity and consistency in the decision making is important and imperative.

It is submitted that the doctrine of binding precedent promotes convenience and predictability. It also promotes consistency and clarity of legal thought. The law moves and develops through judicial decision making and it is evident that judicial precedent is not static, as it promotes flexibility. Above all, it is clear that precedent is a source of law and as such, a compelling justification exists for the CAS to adopt it.

Finally, it has been suggested in this work that there is a fine balance between case law and statute and that this relationship has been unjustifiably unexplored. The time is right for the CAS to adopt a specific method of statutory interpretation, with aids that would stem from the analysis and interpretation of case law. This is true in a situation where statutes and regulations of sporting governing bodies are unclear and confusing. The CAS is not a stranger to rules of sporting

[46]Rodger 2005, p. 79.

governing bodies who cause friction in the relationship between athletes and the governing bodies themselves. It is true that sometimes the rules of sporting governing bodies resemble the architecture of an ancient building.[47] Several parts are missing and several other parts need to be put in the right place, so the operation of the building is workable. The same can be said for many of the statutes and regulations of sporting bodies. The CAS judges, therefore, need a clear framework and aids of statutory interpretation, which will assist them during the examination and analysis of case law.

It is this unexplored relationship between case law and statute that needs to be at the forefront of any judicial development before the CAS. As it was suggested at the beginning of this work, the influence of common law to the procedure and practice before the CAS is great and it cannot be dismissed at face value. The analysis in this work suggests that there is a fine relationship and a workable marriage between common law and civil law traditions, in the administration and application of justice before the CAS. The author respectfully submits that this is a marriage between equal partners. One needs the other to survive and one cannot function without the other.

In conclusion, it is submitted that the CAS is a necessary mechanism for the resolution of sporting disputes and its operation is important for the development of sports law as a dynamic and separate legal discipline. The CAS procedure and practice, however, can be improved, particularly, with an acknowledgement that a system of precedent operates before the CAS and that previous decisions must be binding on sporting governing bodies and their legislative organs. This is true in the case of WADA and the IAAF, where they both tend not only to recognise the judicial superiority of the CAS, but to follow, indiscriminately, its decisions.

In the author's view, therefore, the silent operation of the doctrine of binding precedent confirms to a great extent the remarkable and considerable influence of common law traditions on the procedure and practice before the CAS. Such influence has crawled into the operation of judicial decision making slowly but steadily and has determined, without stretching the boundaries of judicial creativity, the future not only of self-regulation, but also shaped the development of the discipline of sports law, as a unique, autonomous and specialised body of law.

References

Beloff QCM (2001) Drugs, laws and verspapaks. In: O'Leary J (ed) Drugs and doping in sport: Socio-legal perspectives. Cavendish, London, pp 39–56

[47]Michael Beloff QC suggests: "In my experience, rules of domestic or international federations tend to resemble the architecture of an ancient building: a wing added here, a loft there, a buttress elsewhere, without adequate consideration of whether the additional parts affect adversely the symmetry of the whole", see Beloff 2001, p. 42.

Bersagel A (2012) Is there a stare decisis doctrine in the court of arbitration for sport? An analysis of published awards for anti-doping disputes in track and field. Pepperdine Dispute Resolut Law J 12:189–213

Blackaby N, Partasides QCC, Redfern A, Hunter M (2009) Redfern and hunter on international arbitration, 5th edn. OUP, Oxford

Blackshaw I (2009) Sport, mediation and arbitration. T.M.C Asser Press, The Hague

Burrows A (2012) The relationship between common law and statute law in the law of obligations. Law Q Rev 128:232–258

Cardozo B (1921) The nature of the judicial process. Yale University Press, New Haven, USA

Denning A (1979) The discipline of the law. Butterworths, London

Duxbury N (2008) The nature and authority of precedent. Cambridge University Press, Cambridge

Goodhart A (1934) Precedent in english and continental law. Law Q Rev 50:40–65

Hershovitz S (2006) Integrity and stare decisis. In: Hershovitz S (ed) Exploring law's empire, Oxford University Press, pp. 103–118

Kaufmann-Kohler G (2007) Arbitral precedent: Dream, necessity or excuse? ARB Int 23:357–378

Mitten M, Opie H (2010) 'Sports Law': Implications for the development of international, comparative and national law and global dispute resolution. Tulane L Rev 85:269–322

Reeb M (2002) The role and functions of the court of arbitration for sport (CAS). Int Sports Law J (Issue 2):21–25

Rodger A (2005) A time for everything under law: Some reflections on retrospectivity. Law Q Rev 121:57–79

Chapter 3
The Validity of Analytical Science in Anti-doping—A Scientific and Legal Challenge

Marjolaine Viret and Emily Wisnosky

Comments in the light of the human Growth Hormone trilogy before the CAS.

Abstract The solidity of scientific foundations underlying anti-doping programs is a key aspect of the effectiveness of the World Anti-doping Code. Taking as a starting point recent cases involving human Growth Hormone before the Court of Arbitration for Sport, this article provides insight into the growing complexity of anti-doping analytical science and the challenges arising there from for building a coherent legal framework, as well as the manner in which CAS panels deal with expert evidence in doping disputes, including the Athlete's position in this respect.

Keywords Anti-doping · Expert evidence · Endogenous substances · Laboratory analysis · Human growth hormone · Legal aid

Contents

M. Viret (✉) · E. Wisnosky
School of Law, University of Neuchâtel, Avenue du 1er-Mars 26,
2000 Neuchâtel, Switzerland
e-mail: marjolaine.viret@unine.ch

E. Wisnosky
e-mail: emily.wisnosky@unine.ch

A. Duval and A. Rigozzi (eds.), *Yearbook of International Sports Arbitration 2015*,
DOI 10.1007/978-94-6265-129-6_3

3.1 Introduction

The *Lallukka* CAS award, rendered only weeks before the effective date of the revised 2015 WADA Code, represents the latest episode in a series of three cases involving human Growth Hormone (or 'hGH') brought before the CAS between 2013 and 2015. This 'hGH Trilogy' started with a CAS panel in *Veerpalu v. FIS* refusing to uphold an anti-doping rule violation for lack of reliability of the decision limits[1] used in the hGH analytical test.[2] Less than a year later, another CAS panel in *NADA v. Sinkewitz* took a different position and found that a violation could be upheld irrespective of the reliability of these decision limits.[3] The CAS panel in *WADA v. Lallukka* thus faced the difficult mission to reconcile those two apparently diverging precedents.

The hGH Trilogy illustrates the current challenges facing anti-doping science in upholding the effectiveness and validity of its analytical detection tools. Modern doping practices often involve the abuse of substances which, like hGH, can be endogenously (naturally) produced by the human body. This development creates a new landscape for anti-doping scientists and sports regulators, as compared to

[1]All capitalized terms that are not defined in this article are defined terms in either Appendix 1 of the 2015 WADA Code or in one of the 2015 International Standards. Decision Limits is a defined term in the ISL, however, as explained in Sect. 3.3.2, there rests some ambiguity as to whether the 'decision limits' in regards the hGH analytical test are 'Decision Limits' as contemplated by the ISL. Thus, we only capitalize 'Decision Limits' when speaking specifically of the ISL understanding of 'Decision Limits'.

[2]CAS 2011/A/2566, *Andrus Veerpalu v. International Ski Federation*, Award of 25 March 2013.

[3]CAS 2012/A/2857, *Nationale Anti-Doping Agentur Deutschland v. Patrick Sinkewitz*, Award of 24 February 2014.

the past, when doping practices were largely limited to purely exogenous agents. In particular, regulations must adapt alongside new detection methods capable of distinguishing whether the same substance was taken endogenously or exogenously; an adaptation that is not always straightforward in practice.

After presenting the context of the *Lallukka* CAS award and a summary of the CAS panel's legal analysis and findings (1), we will provide insight into the scientific and regulatory background of the hGH Trilogy to allow for a better understanding of the issues the CAS panels faced in these three awards (2). We will then address two key issues that the awards raise: First, the manner in which CAS panels struggle with fitting the scientific complexity of anti-doping analytics into a legally coherent framework (3); and second, the manner in which CAS panels deal with expert evidence in doping disputes including the position of Athletes in this respect (4).

3.2 The *Lallukka* CAS Award: The Latest Instalment in the hGH Trilogy[4]

3.2.1 The Positive Test

In September 2011, the Finnish cross-country skier Juha Lallukka (the 'skier'), a National-Level Athlete affiliated with the Finnish Ski Association, underwent an Out-of-Competition Test. The analysis by the WADA-accredited laboratory in Helsinki returned an Adverse Analytical Finding for recombinant human Growth Hormone, a synthetic form of exogenously administered hGH.[5] Human Growth Hormone is a non-Specified Substance, and is included in class S2 of the WADA Prohibited List.[6] The laboratory applied the so-called 'Isoform Differential Immunoassays' test (the 'Isoform Test') and reported the Sample positive based on the fact that the ratios between the relevant isoforms detected in the Athlete's Sample exceeded the decision limits as set in the relevant WADA Guidelines,[7] i.e. the ratio values above which laboratories are to report an Adverse Analytical Finding. The skier denied having ever used hGH and requested the analysis of his B Sample, the results of which again exceeded the decision limits.

---

[4]The facts and summary of *WADA v. Lallukka* are adapted from our comment on this CAS award, published as part of our anti-doping reports in Rigozzi et al. 2015, pp. 56–61.

[5]In this article, the abbreviation "hGH" is used as a short form to refer to exogenous hGH. More precisely, the Isoform Test discussed in this article targets only synthetic ('recombinant') exogenously administered hGH.

[6]Category S2 includes: "S2. Peptide Hormones, Growth Factors, Related Substances and Mimetics".

[7]WADA Guidelines: hGH isoform differential immunoassays for anti-doping analyses, version 2.1, 15 June 2014, (hereinafter 'hGH Guidelines'), replaced with effect on 1 September 2015 by Technical Document TD2015GH.

3.2.2 National-Level Proceedings

Before the national-level bodies, the skier successfully challenged the reliability of the decision limits in a disciplinary process that took over two years to complete. The extended duration at the first-instance, conducted before the Finnish National Anti-Doping Agency ('FINADA') Supervisory Board, was due to Juha Lallukka's request in January 2012 for a stay of his proceedings in anticipation of the CAS award in the *Veerpalu* matter.[8] In the *Veerpalu* matter, an Estonian skier, Andrus Veerpalu, also challenged the reliability of the decision limits applied in the hGH Isoform Test. In March 2013, the *Veerpalu* CAS award was released; the CAS panel found that the reliability of the decision limits enshrined in the WADA hGH Guidelines was not sufficiently demonstrated and, therefore, that Andrus Veerpalu did not commit an anti-doping rule violation. Thereupon, the FINADA Supervisory Board resumed the proceedings against Juha Lallukka and decided that the decision limits in the hGH Isoform Test were unreliable, in line with the *Veerpalu* CAS award. In addition, the Supervisory Board held that FINADA had not provided sufficient scientific evidence that the revised decision limits—soon to be published based on the studies that WADA had commissioned after the *Veerpalu* matter—would not be set at values higher than the ratios observed in the skier's Sample. The Board consequently found that no anti-doping rule violation had been committed. The decision was appealed by FINADA, but confirmed on appeal by the Finnish Sports Arbitration Board in December 2013.

3.2.3 CAS Proceedings

WADA appealed the Finnish Sports Arbitration Board's decision to the CAS on the main ground that the decision limits had subsequently been verified by two independent studies (McGill University in Montreal and University of Descartes in Paris), the results of which had been merged into the so-called 'Joint Publication Paper'. WADA also submitted that, in any event, the skier's ratios were so high that they "constitute[d] overwhelming evidence of administration of exogenous hGH, irrespective of whether the Decision Limits as set in WADA's Guidelines are reliable or not".[9]

The *Lallukka* panel first addressed the procedural issues. The skier had argued, in particular, that WADA's appeal was inadmissible for belated filing.[10] After affirming the timeliness of WADA's appeal, the CAS panel addressed the admissibility of documents filed by WADA after submission of its appeal brief.

[8]CAS 2011/A/2566, *Veerpalu v. FIS*.

[9]CAS 2014/A/3488, *WADA v. Lallukka*, Award of 20 November 2014, para 46.

[10]Ibid., para 48.

The submission of a party's brief typically represents the last moment in the proceedings for that party to file evidence in CAS appeal proceedings (Article R51 of the CAS Code). In the particular matter, the documents at stake were the revised 2014 WADA hGH Guidelines, as well as the final version of the Joint Publication Paper arising from the studies conducted after the *Veerpalu* award. The panel considered that the documents had only been made available to WADA after the submission of its appeal brief, that these documents addressed essential questions in the proceedings, as well as the fact that the skier had failed to submit additional comments on these documents—in spite of having been invited to do so—and had not objected to their production. Accordingly, the CAS panel found that 'exceptional circumstances' within the meaning of Article R56 of the CAS Code were realized and that the new evidence should be admitted on the record.[11]

On the merits, the skier's main argument was that the decision limits for the hGH Isoform Test are not reliable. In particular, he submitted that the Joint Publication Paper issued as a result of the two independent studies commissioned by WADA after the *Veerpalu* award left some issues raised by the CAS panel in this award unanswered, so that the decision limits remained unreliable. However, the skier declared that he did "not have the financial means to substantiate his allegations in this regard".[12] The skier, named as a sole respondent in the CAS proceedings, was granted legal aid by the International Council of Arbitration for Sport to cover the travel and accommodation costs for the skier and his counsel to a hearing, as well as for "the costs of any experts, witnesses, or interpreters in connection with a hearing, if necessary".[13] A subsequent request for additional legal aid was denied,[14] but the panel agreed with the Athlete's request to forgo an oral hearing and based its decision on the written submissions.[15]

In evaluating the merits, the CAS panel first resolved in the affirmative the issue of whether an anti-doping rule violation had been committed (1), and then decided on the appropriate sanction (2).

3.2.3.1 The Anti-doping Rule Violation

As a preliminary matter, the CAS panel recalled that the burden of proof is on the Anti-Doping Organization to establish an anti-doping rule violation to the comfortable satisfaction of the panel (Article 3.1 of the WADA Code). The panel also emphasized that the skier did not dispute the manner in which the analysis of his

[11] Ibid., paras 66–72.

[12] Ibid., para 48.

[13] Ibid., para 33.

[14] Ibid., para 42.

[15] Ibid., paras 39–43.

Sample was performed; rather, he challenged the reliability of the decision limits determined by WADA, and argued that physiological or scientific explanations for his high ratios could not be excluded.[16]

Since the skier relied primarily on the findings in the *Veerpalu* award, the CAS panel also stressed the significant developments that had taken place since this first award, in particular[17]:

- In a second hGH matter, *NADA v. Sinkewitz* of February 2014, a CAS panel had sanctioned a German cyclist, ruling that the Athlete's values were so high that there was no "borderline situation which might trigger the benefit of uncertainty in favour of the athlete"[18];
- WADA had commissioned new studies with the purpose of addressing the issues raised by the CAS panel in *Veerpalu v. FIS*; and
- The WADA hGH Guidelines had been updated to reflect the latest revised decision limits based on the Joint Publication Paper drawn from these studies.

The CAS panel turned to the Joint Publication Paper, assessing how the publication addressed the "main points of contention" raised in *Veerpalu v. FIS*.[19] As a starting point, the panel recounted the reasoning in the *Veerpalu* award, whereby the Anti-Doping Organization bears the burden of showing that a violation occurred "by means of a test that is scientifically reliable",[20] which includes the decision limits. Reviewing what they considered the three main points of contention (insufficient sample size, inappropriate exclusion of certain sample data, and uncertainties related to the distribution model used), the CAS panel concluded that "the Joint Publication Paper responded adequately to the concerns expressed" in the *Veerpalu* award.[21]

The panel ended its analysis of whether the decision limits are "scientifically reliable" with a few remarks regarding its role in weighing expert opinions. The CAS panel insisted that it is "not its function to step into the shoes of scientific experts", but that its role is nevertheless "to determine whether the experts' evaluations […] are soundly based on the facts, and whether the experts consequent appreciation of the conclusion be derived [sic] from those facts is equally sound".[22] In the particular matter, the panel considered as relevant factors: (i) the fact that the studies and Joint Publication Paper were "the fruit of a collaborative effort by two independent teams of experts", (ii) that the study was based on a "considerable and large dataset, which has been peer-reviewed and accepted for

[16]Ibid., para 80.

[17]Ibid., para 81.

[18]Ibid., para 81, in reference to CAS 2012/A/2857, *NADA v. Sinkewitz*, para 204.

[19]CAS 2014/A/3488, *WADA v. Lallukka*, para 83 et seq.

[20]Ibid., para 83, quoting CAS 2011/A/2566, *Veerpalu v. FIS*, para 202.

[21]CAS 2014/A/3488, *WADA v. Lallukka*, para 96.

[22]Ibid., para 97.

publication", and (iii) that the study "is said to establish decision limits with a 99.99 % specificity".[23] Based on these factors, the panel declared that "it is not immediately apparent to the Panel how it could conclude that the Joint Publication Paper may be said to be unreliable", and therefore found itself comfortably satisfied of the reliability both of the test and of the decision limits.[24]

According to the CAS panel, this meant the burden of proof was on the Athlete to establish "any particular departure or departures that could have led to a false-positive finding".[25] However, the CAS panel found that the Athlete fell short of discharging this burden. It characterized the Athlete's defence as founded on mere speculations without "any substantiation of his allegations or evidence to support them". Thus, according to the CAS panel, the Athlete failed to establish on a balance of probability how any of the points raised in the commissioned study could reasonably have caused a false positive result.[26]

The CAS panel finally turned to the ultimate question at issue: whether Juha Lallukka committed an anti-doping violation, considering the overall evidence submitted by the parties and its own findings regarding the decision limits. The CAS panel noted that the revised decision limits are "quite close" to the decision limits in the previous version of the WADA hGH Guidelines, so that the decision limits "did not vary in a magnitude that brings them anywhere near the ratio values found on the Athlete".[27] In this respect, turning to a different limb of the reasoning, the CAS panel sought support from the *Sinkewitz* award, considering the following findings relevant:

- The Athlete's ratios in the *Sinkewitz* case did not present a "borderline situation", in the sense that his ratios were "far higher" than WADA's decision limits[28];
- Juha Lallukka's ratios were even higher than Patrick Sinkewitz', "and significantly so"[29]; and
- The decision limits are mere recommendations to the WADA-accredited laboratories, not legally binding as such and therefore do not have the "legal force to distinguish between doping […] and non-doping […]".[30] The panel cited the paragraphs in which the *Sinkewitz* panel relied on expert opinions confirming that Patrick Sinkewitz's ratio values were clearly indicative of the presence of hGH according to their experience.[31]

---

[23]Ibid., para 98.

[24]Ibid.

[25]Ibid.

[26]Ibid., para 99.

[27]Ibid., paras 100–101.

[28]Ibid., para 104.

[29]Ibid., para 105.

[30]Ibid., para 106.

[31]Ibid., para 107.

In a final comment, the panel observed that the Athlete had submitted no evidence showing that his ratio values could have been affected by individual circumstances, and, consequently, "the Athlete is not in a position to prove to the comfortable satisfaction of the Panel that external factors may have had an impact on his ratio values, which could have led to a false positive".[32]

The CAS panel finally addressed a further objection of the Athlete, whereby applying the revised decision limits to a Sample analysis conducted in 2011 would amount to an impermissible retroactive application of the law. The CAS panel reiterated its position that the decision limits "are not rules as such", rather they are described in the WADA hGH Guidelines and "merely constitute figures upon which reliance may be placed by means of evidence to determine whether an anti-doping violation has or has not occurred in application of the rules".[33] The evidence adduced by WADA to this effect had been admitted to the CAS proceedings, confirming that the skier's ratio values were "at a level that violate the applicable rules, irrespective of whether one places reliance on [the] level set by the 2010 Guidelines or the higher level that later emerged".[34] Recalling that the prohibition of retroactivity does not apply to evidentiary matters, the CAS panel rejected the objection.[35]

With respect to due process, the CAS panel rejected the skier's claims for compensation against WADA for undue delays in the proceedings, holding that WADA had "dealt with the Athlete's situation without undue delay and conducted itself in a fashion which is beyond reproach and scrupulously, in accordance with the interests of all the parties".[36]

3.2.3.2 The Sanction

Having considered itself comfortably satisfied that the analytical findings revealed the presence of hGH and thus that an anti-doping rule violation occurred, the CAS panel turned to the determination of the appropriate sanction. The CAS panel refused to follow WADA's claims that the facts of the matter, i.e. the detection of hGH or the fact that the skier had chosen to contest the allegations, could per se represent an aggravating circumstance under Article 10.6 of the Finnish Anti-Doping Regulations (equivalent to Article 10.6 of the 2009 WADA Code). Accordingly, the CAS panel imposed a standard two-year Ineligibility period, but

---

[32]Ibid., para 109.

[33]Ibid., para 113.

[34]Ibid., para 114.

[35]Ibid., paras 115–116.

[36]Ibid., para 120.

gave the skier credit of the Provisional Suspension and refused—for fairness reasons—to disqualify results achieved in the period during which the skier had been "cleared" by his two national hearing panels.[37]

3.3 Background of the hGH Trilogy

3.3.1 Challenges for Anti-doping Science

The abuse of human Growth Hormone in sport—especially in its synthetic ('recombinant') form—has been a central topic in anti-doping for a considerable amount of time. While it is known that there is a widespread misuse of the substance in Athlete circles for its anabolic properties, its genuine effectiveness on sports performance is controversial and its detection is far from straightforward.[38] During the 2015 WADA Code implementation process, hGH has been included as a target substance—along with EPO and related substances—in the new Technical Document for Sport Specific Analysis (TD2014SSA)[39] enacted by WADA. This document imposes minimum levels of analysis based on a risk assessment for certain categories of substances in particular sports. The importance attributed to combatting hGH in anti-doping is also reflected in the fact that two different tests for hGH detection have been developed, each with their own dedicated WADA technical rules.[40]

Human Growth Hormone is a peptide with a short half-life period in blood, and low concentrations in urine, which complicates its detection in both of these matrices traditionally used in doping control.[41] However, the main challenge that anti-doping science faces with human Growth Hormone lies in distinguishing exogenously administered hGH from hGH naturally ('endogenously') produced by the human body. The secretion of hGH is pulsatile, which means that natural levels of hGH vary significantly, even within the course of 24 h. Moreover, there is a high interindividual and intraindividual variability in the secretion of hGH.

---

[37]Ibid., paras 127–137.

[38]See, for an overview of the scientific issues surrounding hGH already in 2006, Saugy et al. 2006, pp. i35–i39.

[39]A new version 2.3 of the Technical Document for Sport Specific Analysis has become effective on January 1, 2016, but the reference year of the document has not been updated.

[40]WADA hGH Guidelines, replaced as of 1 September 2015 by TD2015GH; World Anti-Doping Program Guidelines: Human Growth Hormone (hGH) Biomarkers Test for Doping Control Analyses, version 1.0, July 2015.

[41]Saugy et al. 2006, i35–i39, i37.

Hence, the overall concentration of hGH in a Sample cannot be used as a decisive criterion to confirm or refute the administration of exogenous hGH. However, administration of recombinant hGH has been shown to temporarily change the ratio between the different forms ('isoforms') in which hGH is circulating in the organism.[42]

This change in the ratio is used as the key determinant in the most common 'Isoform Test'.[43] The Isoform Test—often referred to as the 'direct approach'—was used in all cases brought before CAS so far. A new test based on biomarkers is available (the 'Biomarkers Test'), but is only gradually being introduced within the WADA-accredited laboratory network and,[44] to the best of the authors' awareness, has not yet been the object of the CAS scrutiny.[45] The two tests are not interchangeable—they exploit different analytical mechanisms and cover different windows of detection. Schematically, the hGH Isoform Test detects recombinant hGH during a short time window after its administration, while the Biomarkers Test targets modifications of human parameters induced by repeated use of hGH over time.[46]

3.3.2 The hGH Trilogy Before CAS Panels on the Decision Limits in the Isoform Test

In all three human Growth Hormone cases brought before CAS since 2013, the mechanics of the Isoform Test were at the core of the CAS proceedings. More specifically, the debate did not revolve around the validity of the analytical method itself, but rather around the 'decision limits', i.e. the ratios set in the relevant WADA Guidelines for WADA-accredited laboratories to determine whether to report a Sample positive for the presence of hGH (i.e. issue a so-called Adverse Analytical Finding).

---

[42]More precisely, recombinant hGH comprised almost exclusively of the '22-kDa' form, whereas the circulating hGH in human blood is present in various forms. When administration of hGH occurs, the proportion of 22-kDa in comparison with all other circulating forms is increased for a certain period of time; see WADA hGH Guidelines, Sect. 3.5.

[43]For a short description of the test, see CAS 2014/A/3488, *WADA v. Lallukka*, para 8, quoting CAS 2011/A/2566, *Veerpalu v. FIS*.

[44]Supporting document B to WADA Technical Document for Sport Specific Analysis (TD2014SSA), version 2.3, effective date 1 January 2016, n° 39.

[45]In the *NADA v. Sinkewitz* matter, the CAS panel refused to uphold the Athlete's request to have his Sample re-tested using Biomarkers Test (as opposed to the Isoform Test) on the basis that (i) it found that the Biomarkers Test was not more reliable, it just differed "in its scope of application" and (ii) "there is no right to be re-tested by using a testing method other than that provided by the applicable rule," CAS 2012/A/2857, *NADA v. Sinkewitz*, para 217.

[46]Supporting document B to WADA Technical Document for Sport Specific Analysis (TD2014SSA), version 2.3, effective date 1 January 2016, n° 39.

In 2013, the panel in the *Veerpalu* matter refused to uphold the Athlete's anti-doping rule violation, on the basis that the reliability of the decision limits had been insufficiently demonstrated by the Anti-Doping Organization. The *Veerpalu* award, rendered during the 2015 WADA Code review process, had considerable repercussions for the prosecution of hGH cases. Concretely, WADA commissioned new studies to be conducted on a larger amount of Samples with a view to confirming or adapting the Decision Limits. Meanwhile, in early 2014, before the results of the new studies could be published and the decision limits adapted in the WADA hGH Guidelines, a second CAS panel, in the *Sinkewitz* matter, considered that the presence of hGH can be established irrespective of the reliability of these decision limits.[47]

To reach these opposite conclusions, the two CAS panels apparently built their reasoning on diverging legal characterizations of the 'decision limits' needed to interpret the analytical results obtained through the Isoform Test.[48] The panel in *Veerpalu v. FIS* appeared to regard the test as a quantitative analysis in which decision limits, though set dynamically by WADA, have a legally decisive value. By contrast, the *Sinkewitz* panel regarded the decision limits are mere tools of interpretation. More specifically, the *Sinkewitz* panel insisted that since the decision limits are enshrined in WADA Guidelines, they only recommend to WADA-accredited laboratories when to report the ratios present in the Athlete's Samples as an Adverse Analytical Finding for hGH. The panel held that the ratio values found in a Sample can be shown by any other reliable means of evidence—including expert evidence—as indicative of the presence of exogenous hGH and thus of an anti-doping rule violation.[49]

When the *Lallukka* panel was called to decide on the third matter, it thus faced the difficult challenge of reconciling two apparently conflicting legal interpretations on the same issue in an evolving scientific landscape. In particular, the *Lallukka* panel at the time of the deliberation had the benefit of newly commissioned independent studies on the reliability of the decision limits triggered by the *Veerpalu* award, but meanwhile those decision limits had been deprived of decisive legal value by the panel in *NADA v. Sinkewitz*. The assessment in the *Lallukka* award thus addressed the re-calculated decision limits and removed the reservations raised in the *Veerpalu* matter with respect to their reliability. Simultaneously, however, the Panel adhered to the perception of the *Sinkewitz* panel, that the decision limits "merely constitute figures upon which reliance may be placed by means of evidence" and thus should not be treated as rules delimiting the scope of the prohibition, but only as evidence adduced by WADA to the effect that the Athlete's values in the Sample were such as to justify the conclusion that an anti-doping rule violation occurred.

---

[47]CAS 2012/A/2857, *NADA v. Sinkewitz*, para 192.

[48]See Rigozzi et al. 2014, pp. 54–56 for a discussion of the CAS panel's reasoning in the *NADA v. Sinkewitz* matter. Also available at www.wadc-commentary.com/sinkewitz/. Accessed on 16 February 2016.

[49]CAS 2012/A/2857, *NADA v. Sinkewitz*, para 193.

3.3.3 The hGH Isoform Test After WADA v. Lallukka: A Closed Debate or a Need for Rethinking the System?

The *Lallukka* matter and the findings of the award summarized above—at least on the face of it—removed a Damocles sword that had been hanging over the hGH Isoform Test since early 2013. The *Veerpalu* award and its refusal to recognize the reliability of the decision limits de facto put all results management for hGH findings on hold throughout the anti-doping movement. The *Sinkewitz* panel temporarily rescued the fate of pending hGH cases by denying any legally binding status to the decision limits. However, only the *Lallukka* panel had the full benefit of the additional studies and the revised decision limits and was thus able (on paper at least, see Sect. 3.5.4) to address the points that had led to the *Veerpalu* award. Thus, in a press release issued on 28 November 2014, WADA announced the *Lallukka* award as a ruling confirming that all concerns surrounding the hGH Isoform Test—in particular those raised in the *Veerpalu* award—were resolved, leaving no doubts regarding the validity and reliability of the newly published version 2.1 of the related WADA Guidelines.[50]

In the meantime, primarily in reaction to the *Veerpalu* award, a new provision had been introduced in the revised 2015 WADA Code (Article 3.2.1), with effect on 1 January 2015, that explicitly acknowledges the possibility for Athletes to challenge the reliability of analytical tools, including decision limits, but places on the Athlete the burden of proof on these issues.[51]

The combination of the *Lallukka* award and the introduction of Article 3.2.1 of the WADA Code removed two major obstacles to the implementation of the hGH Isoform Test. First, Anti-Doping Organizations can now again rely on the decision limits with confidence, and with the additional support of a CAS precedent. Second, the burden of proof has been shifted to the Athlete in the regulations implementing the WADA Code to show that these decision limits are not scientifically valid, which—given the significant resources needed to build a defence of this kind—should keep the anti-doping movement relatively safe from this type of challenge (see also Sect. 3.5.5).

---

[50]WADA Statement on the Juha Lallukka case, 28 November 2014. https://www.wada-ama.org/en/media/news/2014-11/wada-statement-on-the-juha-lallukka-case. Accessed 16 February 2016.

[51]Article 3.2.1 of the WADA Code reads as follows: "Analytical methods or decision limits approved by *WADA* after consultation within the relevant scientific community and which have been the subject of peer review are presumed to be scientifically valid. Any *Athlete* or other *Person* seeking to rebut this presumption of scientific validity shall, as a condition precedent to any such challenge, first notify *WADA* of the challenge and the basis of the challenge. *CAS*, on its own initiative may also inform *WADA* of any such challenge. At *WADA*'s request, the *CAS* panel shall appoint an appropriate scientific expert to assist the panel in its evaluation of the challenge. Within 10 days of *WADA*'s receipt of such notice, and *WADA*'s receipt of the *CAS* file, *WADA* shall also have the right to intervene as a party, appear amicus curiae or otherwise provide evidence in such proceeding".

However, neither of these advances resolves the fundamental issue that underlies all of these cases: the legal status of the Isoform Test within the WADA Code regime. In particular, the arbitrators in *WADA v. Lallukka* at no point discussed the opposing perceptions that led the previous CAS panels in the hGH Trilogy to their respective conclusions, nor did they set forth why one should be preferred over the other. Instead, the *Lallukka* panel appears to have tried to reach a ruling based on both approaches as two separate lines of reasoning, which results in even greater ambiguity surrounding the status of hGH in particular, and the structure of the WADA technical rules in general.

In a recent development, the hGH Guidelines have been replaced,[52] with effect on 1 September 2015, by a Technical Document (TD2015GH) with identical content (at least insofar as relevant for this article). This change in the type of document containing the rules governing Sample analysis and interpretation of results to report findings for hGH casts a new light onto the entire hGH Trilogy, bringing both clarification and new questions with respect to the merits of the CAS panels' approaches.

3.4 Attributing a Legal Status to Scientific Issues Under the WADA Code Regime

The CAS panels in both *NADA v. Sinkewitz* and *WADA v. Lallukka* relied on two initial findings that allowed them to bypass a more thorough analysis on the legal status of the Isoform Test within the WADA Code regime:

- WADA Guidelines are declared 'non-mandatory' under the WADA Code regime.[53] Hence, decision limits laid down in Guidelines have no legally binding status;
- The 'decision limits' in the hGH Isoform Test do not delimit the scope of the prohibition, i.e. they have no power to separate legally the prohibited from the non-prohibited.

Apart from this reference to the (declared) non-mandatory character of the WADA Guidelines, the panel's findings are detached from the mechanics of the WADA Code regime. This lack of systematic approach is regrettable, since it fails to create coherence and could leave the system vulnerable to further attacks, especially in view of the explicit mention of 'decision limits' as a possible object for challenge under the new Article 3.2.1 of the WADA Code.

---

[52]Of note, the Technical Document is still marked "draft" on the WADA website and the hGH Guidelines still marked "in force," but those mentions should not alter the effective date stated in the document itself, which is solely relevant legally speaking.

[53]See Purpose, Scope and Organization of the World Anti-Doping Program and the *Code*, 2015 WADA Code.

3.4.1 Threshold Substance, Non-threshold Substance, or….?

In order to assess the nature of the Isoform Test, the first question that deserves inquiry is whether human Growth Hormone must be considered a Threshold Substance within the meaning of the WADA Code regime. None of the CAS panels in the hGH Trilogy explicitly examined this issue, even though the point is essential to make a legal determination on the status of the 'decision limit' for the hGH Isoform Test.

Historically, the structure of the WADA Code regime is built on the distinction between Threshold Substances on the one hand, and Non-Threshold Substances on the other hand. These two categories form the basis for the document that describes the requirements on WADA-accredited laboratories when conducting Sample analysis, the International Standard for Laboratories (or 'ISL').[54] More specifically:

- For Non-Threshold Substances,[55] it is only necessary to confirm the identification of the Prohibited Substance in the Sample to report an Adverse Analytical Finding. The analysis is said to be 'qualitative'.[56]
- For Threshold Substances,[57] an Adverse Analytical Finding can only be reported if the Prohibited Substances is present in the Sample above a certain concentration. The analysis is 'quantitative': the laboratory must perform a quantification aimed at determining whether the substance is above the Threshold, which includes an uncertainty measurement. Threshold Substances are identified in the Technical Document on Decision Limits (TD2014DL).

This fundamental division is also reflected in Article 2.1.3 of the WADA Code for the standard violation of "Presence of a Prohibited Substance" in an Athlete's Sample. The provision sets forth both the rule of 'zero tolerance' and its limits: "Excepting those substances for which a quantitative threshold is specifically

[54]For more details, see Saugy et al. 2016.

[55]A Non-Threshold Substance is defined in the ISL as: "A substance listed on the *Prohibited List* for which the identification, in compliance with the Technical Document on the Identification Criteria for Qualitative Assays (TD IDCR), constitutes an *Adverse Analytical Finding*".

[56]Article 6.2.6.7 of the ISL: "The Laboratory is not required to quantify or report a concentration for an analyte of non-threshold *Prohibited Substances* in blood *Samples*".

[57]A Threshold Substance is defined in the ISL as: "An exogenous or endogenous *Prohibited Substance, Metabolite* or *Marker* of a *Prohibited Substance* which is analyzed quantitatively and for which an analytical result (concentration, ratio or score) in excess of a pre-determined Decision Limit constitutes an *Adverse Analytical Finding*. Threshold Substances are identified as such in the Technical Document on Decision Limits (TD DL)". Note that the WADA hGH Guidelines still incorporate the former (2012) version of the ISL's definition of Threshold Substance: "A substance listed on the TD DL for which the detection and quantification of an amount in excess of a stated threshold is considered an *Adverse Analytical Finding*".

identified in the *Prohibited List*, the presence of any quantity of a *Prohibited Substance* or its *Metabolites* or *Markers* in an *Athlete's Sample* shall constitute an anti-doping rule violation".

Outside the context of the Isoform Test, the term 'decision limit' thus has a well-established meaning for anti-doping analytics. The purpose of the 'Decision Limit'—a term defined under the ISL—is to harmonize the manner in which laboratories conclude that a substance is present above the Threshold.[58] The Decision Limit thus represents in reality a 'guard band', i.e. the Threshold plus a confidence interval that laboratories must include to report that the substance was present in the Sample above the Threshold.[59] Both the Thresholds and the related Decision Limits for Threshold Substances are specified in the Technical Document on Decision Limits (currently: TD2014DL).[60]

Even though the scientists in WADA-accredited Laboratories are the primary direct addressees of these rather technical rules, the legal implications of these rules should not be underestimated:

- No Adverse Analytical Finding can be reported for a Threshold Substance if a Sample does not meet the requirements of the Technical Document on Decision Limits[61];
- In the absence of an Adverse Analytical Finding, there can be no violation for Presence of a Prohibited Substance under Article 2.1 of the WADA Code; and
- Inversely, if the substance is present above the Threshold, an Adverse Analytical Finding must be reported and an anti-doping rule violation under Article 2.1 of the WADA Code is deemed to have been committed, irrespective of any other factual considerations (e.g. Athletes may not submit as a defence that they have naturally elevated endogenous levels).[62]

From a legal viewpoint, the Threshold thus acts as a standardizing mechanism in both directions: no prosecution is possible below the Threshold, but prosecution is

[58]The ISL defines Decision Limit as follows: "a concentration, accounting for the maximum permitted combined uncertainty, above which an *Adverse Analytical Finding* shall be reported".

[59]For more details, see Saugy et al. 2016.

[60]WADA Technical Document on Decision Limits for the Confirmatory Quantification of Threshold Substances (TD2014DL), version 1.0, effective date 1 September 2014.

[61]The Technical Document on Decision Limits explains the issue as follows: "This Technical Document shall be applied to the quantitative determination of a Threshold Substance in a *Sample* with particular regard to the decision limits (DL) that shall be applied to determine whether the result indicates an *Adverse Analytical Finding (AAF).*"

[62]In order to challenge a Threshold (assuming that challenge was considered admissible under Article 4 of the WADC), the Athlete would have to argue—and probably establish under Article 3.2.1 of the WADC—that the Threshold level does not exclude with sufficiently high confidence that the finding could result from endogenous production. By nature, the introduction of a fixed Threshold amounts to an acceptance that a certain percentage of Athletes might test positive based on their endogenous levels. See, for more details, Saugy et al. 2016, tbp.

unavoidable above the Threshold.[63] The stakes of determining whether hGH is a Threshold Substance are therefore high: if hGH is a Threshold Substance, the decision limit set for the Isoform Test would need to be characterized as an actual 'Decision Limit' within the meaning of the ISL and would thus truly define the scope of the prohibition, contrary to the CAS panels' most recent findings in the *Sinkewitz* and *Lallukka* matters.

The regulatory situation of hGH is ambiguous. Even though this is not explicit in the Prohibited List, it appears clear from the recent hGH cases that the object of the prohibition is perceived as being 'exogenous' hGH,[64] as opposed to hGH of any origin (exogenous or endogenous) above a certain level. However, the Technical Document on Decision Limits that should normally be the decisive document in this regard (see Sect. 3.4.1) obscures the legal situation rather than clarifies it. The Technical Document does mention hGH, but does not directly include the substance within the Table that defines the Decision Limits for Threshold Substances. Instead, a 'note' below the Table indicates that human Growth Hormone is also a Prohibited Substance for which a Decision Limit applies, but provides that such Decision Limit will be specified in "the corresponding WADA Guidelines or Technical Document" for the two currently existing tests (i.e. the Isoform Test and the Biomarkers Test, see Sect. 3.3.1).[65]

The functioning of the hGH Isoform Test itself does not provide clear-cut answers either: *a priori*, the purpose and mechanics of the test do not seem to point to hGH as a Threshold Substance. Clearly, the test does seek to determine whether exogenous hGH was actually present in the Athlete's organism at the time of Sample collection. It does so by trying to discriminate between the isoform ratio values proper to 'natural' occurrence of hGH, as opposed to the values indicative of exogenous administration of recombinant hGH.[66] In fact, since the concentration of hGH in the human body naturally fluctuates over time, it would be impossible to set a Threshold *stricto sensu* that would rely on the overall concentration of hGH in the Sample. On the other hand, the hGH Isoform Test is not purely qualitative either. It does include a form of 'cut-off'—the decision limit,

[63]This is assuming the Athlete cannot demonstrate a procedural defect in the manner in which the procedures were conducted in the particular matter (Article 3.2.2 or 3.2.3 of the WADA Code).

[64]See e.g., CAS 2014/A/3488, *WADA v. Lallukka*, para 15: "It is not disputed that exogenous hGH is a non-specified substance included in the category S2 (a) ("Peptide Hormones, Growth Factors and Related Substances") on the 2011 WADA Prohibited List".

[65]TD2014DL, note page 2 *in fine*: "Note: For detection of human growth hormone (hGH), the applicable values of $u_{c\ Max}$ and the corresponding DL will be specified in the corresponding WADA Guideline or Technical Document for the application of the hGH differential immunoassays and/or the hGH Marker Method for anti-doping analyses".

[66]As stated in TD2015GH, section 1.0, the test was "developed to distinguish between the proportions of hGH isoforms found under normal physiological conditions and those found after recombinant (rec) hGH injection".

formerly set in the WADA hGH Guidelines and newly in TD2015GH—that determines whether the ratio values detected in a Sample must be reported by anti-doping laboratories. It also involves an uncertainty measurement, which is usually the hallmark of Threshold Substances.[67]

In sum, hGH is currently in a regulatory limbo, in that the substance is treated much like a Threshold Substance, but without ever being explicitly qualified as such. This uncertainty likely arises from the sophisticated character of the Isoform Test, a test that seeks to differentiate exogenous from endogenous origin of a substance. From a functional perspective, a Threshold represents a standardized manner of drawing the line between doping 'relevant' and doping 'irrelevant' circumstances, when it is scientifically impossible or impracticable to demonstrate—directly or indirectly—whether a prohibited circumstance (e.g. an external administration) is the source of an analytical finding. In particular, endogenous production of a substance (unless it is triggered by use of a Prohibited Method) is accepted to fall outside the circumstances that anti-doping rules should target. Because of the standardizing effect of a Threshold (in particular, its irreducible potential to make Athletes with naturally exceptionally elevated levels test positive),[68] the proportionality principle commands that wherever technically feasible, analytical methods be implemented that discriminate between exogenous and endogenous origin of a substance, rather than to set norm beyond which the analytical findings are (irrefutably) deemed to be indicative of doping.[69] The drawback of tests of this kind is that they do not currently fit neatly within the historical binary structure of the ISL, a situation that will continue to produce diverging decisions if the situation is not recognized and clarified by CAS panels, or by restructuring and clarifying the ISL themselves.[70]

---

[67]TD2015GH, Sect. 3.3.2, footnote 5, whereby the uncertainty guard band is already incorporated, so that the Adverse Analytical Finding is "defined by the Threshold value itself, which constitutes the DL"; CAS 2014/A/3488, *WADA v. Lallukka*, para 14, quoting the laboratory's documentation package for the A-sample.

[68]See Saugy et al. 2016, tbp.

[69]For more details, see Viret 2016, p. 364.

[70]In fact, the section of the ISL on the validation of methods (ISL 6.4.1.1 (blood), by reference to ISL 5.4.4.1.2 (urine)) provides that: "For endogenous Threshold Substances, the *Athlete's Sample* will be deemed to contain a *Prohibited Substance* and the Laboratory will report an *Adverse Analytical Finding* if, based on any reliable analytical method the Laboratory can show that the *Prohibited Substance* is of exogenous origin". This provision, placed in the section of the ISL related to validation of methods, seems to encourage laboratories to develop methods that seek to determine the origin of the substance, but does not, in our view, create a possibility for the laboratory to report an Adverse Analytical Finding outside the requirements of the Technical Document on Decision Limits. For the analysis of a particular Sample, the definition of Threshold Substance and the fact laboratories are obliged under the ISL (section 6.2.6 "Documentation and reporting") to report an Adverse Analytical Finding only when they can establish that the Decision Limit set for the relevant Threshold Substance is exceeded should prevail.

3.4.2 What Legal Implications Do the Decision Limits Have in Practice?

If it cannot be determined whether hGH is a Threshold Substance *stricto sensu*, the real practical issue is ultimately whether a laboratory could produce an Adverse Analytical Finding irrespective of whether the decision limits set in WADA Guidelines are met, and thus whether a violation for Presence of a Prohibited Substance (Article 2.1 of the WADA Code) can truly be prosecuted regardless of the reliability of these limits. The legal implications of replacing, after the hGH Trilogy, the hGH Guidelines by a Technical Document (TD2015GH) must also be assessed. This assessment is of practical relevance in view of the fact that cut-off levels for other substances that can also be of endogenous origin (see e.g. human chorionic Gonadotrophin or 'hCG' that can indicate a pathology, see Sect. 3.4.3) are still enshrined in Guidelines only and may be equally replaced in future by a Technical Document.

The only rationale invoked by the CAS panels in the *Sinkewitz* and *Lallukka* matters for refusing to assign a legally binding value to the decision limits in the Isoform Test was a purely formal one. The CAS panels in the *Sinkewitz* and *Lallukka* matters relied exclusively on the fact that these decision limits are defined in 'WADA Guidelines'. Under the system of the WADA Code, Technical Documents are described as 'mandatory' and are declared integral part of the International Standard to which they relate, whereas Guidelines are described as 'non-mandatory'.[71] The two awards failed to take into account that the source of the reference for the Decision Limits itself is in the Technical Document on Decision Limits (see Sect. 3.4.1).

Even though the Technical Document on Decision Limits (TD2014DL) does not directly set the decision limits for hGH, it does give some valuable hints regarding its status under the WADA Code regime. In particular,

- It shows that in WADA's eyes hGH has a decision limit that at least deserves a mention within the Technical Document on Decision Limits established for Threshold Substances; and
- It shows that the value of a Decision Limit can be set indifferently in a Technical Document or in a Guideline, apparently at the sole discretion of WADA.

[71] Purpose, Scope and Organization of the World Anti-Doping Program and the *Code*, 2015 WADA Code: For International Standards, "Adherence to the *International Standards* is mandatory for compliance with the *Code*," as compared to 'Models of Best Practice and Guidelines', which "will be recommended by *WADA* and made available to *Signatories* and other relevant stakeholders, but will not be mandatory."

The same solution has been codified as a general rule in the 2015 ISL, which states for reporting an Adverse Analytical Finding for a Threshold Substance that the "value shall exceed the value of the relevant Decision Limit as specified in the Technical Document on Decision Limits or applicable Guidelines" (emphasis added).[72] The example of human Chorionic Gonadotrophin, which is not listed in the Technical Document on Decision Limits (TD2014DL), but nevertheless has a 'Decision Limit' set in the relevant Guidelines, shows that the alternative given in the ISL is far from hypothetical. As insignificant as it may appear at first sight, the recent amendment to the ISL thus has a considerable impact on the structure of the system, since it creates in reality an 'unofficial' third category of substances that have a Decision Limit within the meaning of the ISL, but are not considered Threshold Substances under the TD2014DL.[73] If the 'decision limits' set in those Guidelines are to be regarded as 'Decision Limits' under the ISL, this means that values below the Decision Limit cannot establish a violation on the basis of Article 2.1 of the WADA Code, but would need to be pursued for Use of a Prohibited Substance under Article 2.2, a provision that should require higher evidentiary efforts from the Anti-Doping Organization (at the very least, the Anti-Doping Organizations should be required to explain why the conditions for reporting an Adverse Analytical Finding could not been met).

The *Lallukka* award does not make it clear whether the skier was sanctioned for presence (Article 2.1) or for Use (Article 2.2) of a Prohibited Substance. WADA mentioned both legal foundations in its pleadings.[74] The CAS panel at no point explicitly determined which served as the basis for sanctioning the Athlete. Both the legal analysis and the dispositive part elude this question, by choosing wording such as "violated the applicable rule against doping"[75] or "is found guilty of an anti-doping rule violation."[76] It is to be assumed that the *Lallukka* panel either did not consciously consider the distinction, or did not see it necessary to reach a conclusion one way or another. By contrast, the *Sinkewitz* award—on which the *Lallukka* award relied for these aspects—clearly shows that the violation retained against Mr Sinkewitz was the presence of a Prohibited Substance, both in the legal analysis and in the dispositive part.[77] This means that the panels must have assumed that an Adverse Analytical Finding was present, and thus that such

[72]This language appears in Article 5.2.4.3.1.6 for urine and Article 6.2.4.2.1.6 for blood.

[73]The WADA Guidelines for Results Management, Hearings and Decisions (v. 1.0, October 2014), in their 'Template E: Notice of hCG finding', recommend the following wording to be notified to the Athlete: "the List sets a threshold for findings in relation to hCG". This statement is inaccurate, since there is no threshold set in the Prohibited List for hCG, nor even in the Technical Document on Decision Limits.

[74]CAS 2014/A/3488, *WADA v. Lallukka*, para 46.

[75]Ibid., para 114.

[76]Ibid., n° 3 of the operative part.

[77]CAS 2012/A/2857, *NADA v. Sinkewitz*, paras 173 & n° 3 of the operative part.

Adverse Analytical Finding can be reported irrespective of the decision limits. In fact, the *Sinkewitz* panel insisted on the use of the term "recommendation" to describe the effect of the decision limits for the laboratories.

It is highly questionable whether this description is accurate, in practice if not in law. As the panel in *Veerpalu v. FIS* stated, "the decision limits determine whether the recGH/pitGH ratios in Kit 1 and Kit 2 qualify as an [Adverse Analytical Finding]".[78] This extract was taken up, word for word, in the initial section of the *Lallukka* award.[79] The WADA hGH Guidelines for the Isoform Test, just like the equivalent provisions in the new Technical Document TD2015GH, consistently used the term "shall"—recognized to express an obligation under WADA technical rules[80]—in the section that instructs laboratories on how to interpret and report results depending on the ratio values obtained.[81] Decision limits thus at least seems binding on their main addressees, i.e. the laboratories. In fact, the newly introduced 2015 ISL provision mentioned above confirms that a laboratory is not authorized to report an Adverse Analytical Finding below the Decision Limit, irrespective of whether the Decision Limit is defined in a Guideline or in a Technical Document. This appears indeed the only solution capable of securing legal certainty and harmonized treatment of cases. If it were otherwise, laboratories would be left to assess, as a matter of scientific evidence, whether they can report the presence of exogenous hGH based on the ratio values detected in the particular Sample. As WADA pleaded in the *Veerpalu* matter, the calculation of the decision limits has been designed to guarantee a 99.99 % specificity of the hGH immunoassay test "in order to protect clean athletes".[82] Accordingly, if laboratories were to depart from an assessment based on these decision limits, possibly resorting to qualitative criteria, there would be no way of measuring the resulting risk of false positives. It is also very clear from all the expert testimonies that laboratories themselves perceive and treat the decision limit as a mandatory cut-off.[83]

---

[78]CAS 2011/A/2566, *Veerpalu v. FIS*, para 184.

[79]CAS 2014/A/3488, *WADA v. Lallukka*, para 9.

[80]Viret 2016, p. 639 and references.

[81]Specifically, section 7.1.2 provides: "The Confirmation Procedure shall produce an *Adverse Analytical Finding* if the analytical results (recGH/pitGH ratios) exceed the DL values for both kit '1' and kit '2'." If the DL is only exceeded for one kit, only an Atypical Finding can be issued (7.1.3). The Note 2 in that same section adds: "Therefore, the zone of analytical values considered compliant (negative) or not (*Adverse Analytical Finding*) with this decision rule would be defined by the threshold value itself, which constitutes the DL". World Anti-Doping Program Guidelines hGH Isoform Differential Immunoassays for anti-doping analyses, version 2.1, June 2014.

[82]CAS 2011/A/2566, *Veerpalu v. FIS*, para 199.

[83]Ibid., para 14. The initial laboratory report for the A Sample: "[…] The ratios are greater than the corresponding decision limits (DL) of 1.81 and 1.68, respectively. […] This constitutes an adverse analytical finding".

On the whole, the findings of the CAS panels in *WADA v. Lallukka* and *NADA v. Sinkewitz* that denied legally binding value to decision limits for the hGH Isoform Test appear not only detached from the mechanics of the WADA Code regime, but also from practical realities of the system. Of note, the panels themselves were not entirely consistent in their position that those decision limits "merely constitute figures upon which reliance may be placed by means of evidence to determine whether an anti-doping rule violation has or has not occurred in application of the rules".[84] While denying legal value to the decision limits and therefore declaring their reliability irrelevant, the panels nevertheless relied on these same decision limits to decide whether a case ought to be considered 'borderline' or not. However, without a determination on the reliability of these decisions limits, a 'borderline case' reasoning would seem deprived of any legal or indeed logical basis (this is assuming the CAS panel were in a position to determine what 'borderline' meant in this context, see Sect. 3.5.4).

The short-sightedness of the approach taken by the *Sinkewitz* and *Lallukka* panels in the hGH Trilogy to rely on the formal criterion of whether a decision limit is enshrined in a Guideline or in a Technical Document is evidenced by the subsequent transfer, only a few months after the *Lallukka* award, of the regulation of the hGH Isoform test from Guidelines into a Technical Document, without any substantive modification. If one were to follow the reasoning of the panels to its end, the consequence would be that, while Athletes such as Patrick Sinkewitz could previously be sanctioned if the presence of exogenous hGH could be established to the CAS panel's comfortable satisfaction, irrespective of whether the decision limits were met, this option would no longer be open today given that exactly the same decision limits are now enshrined in a Technical Document.

3.4.3 Need for Adapting the Legal Framework to Evolving Realities?

Beyond questioning the historical structure of the WADA Code, the hGH Trilogy also shows that causality can no longer totally be disregarded when dealing with substances that can be endogenously produced by the human body. Indeed, while the Adverse Analytical Finding traditionally relied on the mere presence of a substance (or its presence above a certain Threshold) in a Sample, the causes behind the analytical findings are necessarily relevant in a test that seeks to discriminate between the exogenous and endogenous origin of a substance.[85]

---

[84] Ibid., para 113.

[85] For more details, see Viret 2016, in particular p. 686 et seq.

The concern about the causes for the Adverse Analytical Finding, and thus indirectly the Athlete's conduct, appears between the lines in WADA's argument in the *Lallukka* award, in which it insisted that the ratios measured in the Athlete's Sample "can only be explained by the use of exogenous hGH".[86] The award also states that the values are "overwhelming evidence of administration of exogenous hGH, irrespective of whether the decision limits as set in WADA's Guidelines are reliable or not".[87] Thus, the CAS panels implicitly relativized the distinction between 'presence' and 'Use' (see Sect. 3.4.2). In fact, the panel in *NADA v. Sinkewitz* concluded its analysis with the statement that is was "convinced that the ratios found in the Respondent's [Mr Sinkewitz'] samples clearly indicate the presence of exogenous recGH and that those elevated ratios cannot be explained by natural sources but only by the administration of recGH".[88] This reference to the origin of the finding and the conduct attributable to the Athlete is extraneous to a violation under Article 2.1, which, precisely, excludes from legal scrutiny any consideration other than the presence of an Adverse Analytical Finding. Caution appears required here, since the prerequisites and the options offered to the Athlete are very different under the two types of violations. In particular, relying on causality issues in the context of an Adverse Analytical Finding is not an option open to the Athlete (e.g. the Athlete cannot invoke the origin of contamination to escape the finding of a violation under Article 2.1). Under these circumstances, it is questionable whether the option of evoking the causal chain of events behind the Adverse Analytical Finding should be opened to the Anti-Doping Organization, especially without adapting the regulatory framework.

Another illustration of this evolution, and of its potentially detrimental impact on the coherence of the system, can be found in the Guidelines governing human chorionic Gonadotrophin (the 'hCG Guidelines').[89] Elevated levels of hCG in men can indicate doping conduct, but also pathologies such as testicular cancer. HCG is not mentioned in the Technical Document on Decision Limits as a Threshold Substance, but the hCG Guidelines introduce a 'Decision Limit' (explicitly defined as in the ISL) above which laboratories shall report an Adverse Analytical Finding (see Sect. 3.4.2). In the section on results management, however, the hCG Guidelines invite Anti-Doping Organizations who receive a report of such an Adverse Analytical Finding to "alert the Athlete and advise that clinical investigations be performed within a reasonable time frame to exclude pathological

[86]CAS 2014/A/3488, *WADA v. Lallukka*, para 46.

[87]Ibid.

[88]CAS 2012/A/2857, *NADA v. Sinkewitz*, para 215.

[89]WADA Prohibited List 2016, class S2; WADA Guidelines for Reporting and Management of Urinary Human Chorionic Gonadotrophin (hCG) and Luteinizing Hormone (LH) Findings in Male Athletes, version 2.0, July 2015.

causes".[90] If the Athlete provides medical information "to support the claim that the result is due to a physiological or pathological condition, such information shall be taken into account and should lead the [Anti-Doping Organization] to stop the result management process of the case as an [anti-doping rule violation]". In addition, the hCG Guidelines provide that no Provisional Suspension shall be imposed during the course of the clinical investigations. A footnote adds that an Adverse Analytical Finding for certain forms of hCG "does not exclude the possibility of a pathological cause [...] it is a responsibility of the Athlete to provide medical information or clinical evidence demonstrating the [...] finding is the result of a pathological cause". Thus, the WADA hCG Guidelines not only set Decision Limits outside the scope of the TD2014DL, they also depart from the regime of proof mandated by the WADA Code (and imposed on Anti-Doping Organizations) on at least three aspects:

- Article 2.1.2 of the WADA Code explicitly provides that the presence of a Prohibited Substance in a Sample is 'sufficient proof' of a violation. The Adverse Analytical Finding is the report through which a laboratory identifies in a Sample the presence of a Prohibited Substance (WADA Code Appendix 1). The origin of the substance is only taken into account for determining the applicable sanction. The hCG Guidelines thus reintroduce an element of causation to the decision of whether to report the Adverse Analytical Finding at the level of the anti-doping rule violation already, which is at odds with the current system;
- Under Article 3.1 of the WADA Code, the elements of an anti-doping rule violation must be established by the Anti-Doping Organization. If, as the hCG Guidelines state, an Adverse Analytical Finding for hCG is not a sufficient indication of doping, but can result from other (non-prohibited) circumstances, no Adverse Analytical Finding should be generated in the first place, and the burden of proof should be on the Anti-Doping Organization to prove the Use of a Prohibited Substance occurred under Article 2.2 of the WADA Code, as opposed to a pathology. The hCG Guidelines seek to place on the Athlete a burden of proof that has no basis in binding WADA rules; and
- The hCG Guidelines provide that no Provisional Suspension shall be imposed during the investigations, which is contrary to Article 7.9 of the WADA Code, which imposes a mandatory Provisional Suspension upon notification of an Adverse Analytical Finding to an Athlete for a non-Specified Substance.[91]

The hGH Trilogy has the merits of underscoring that CAS panels are far from having built a coherent legal framework apt to respond to the new complexity of

---

[90]Of note, the WADA Guidelines for Results Management, Hearings and Decisions (v. 1.0, October 2014), have not—at the time of writing—been adapted to reflect the new hCG Guidelines. Template E: "Notice of hCG finding" still refers to report of an "Atypical Finding" in the recommended notice to be sent to the Athlete, whereas the new hCG Guidelines only provide for Adverse Analytical Findings to be reported in that context.

[91]Substances in class S2 of the Prohibited List (such as hCG) are not Specified Substances-specified (Article 4.2.2 of the WADA Code and preamble to the Prohibited List).

endogenously produced substances. The additional illustration of human chorionic Gonadotrophin demonstrates that solutions using Guidelines to reintroduce considerations on the causes behind analytical findings could not be implemented without the Anti-Doping Organizations putting themselves in contradiction with some of the most fundamental provisions of the WADA Code.

It would seem desirable for the anti-doping movement to initiate a thorough reflection on the manner in which to deal with similar situations. In this respect, it is useful to recollect a provision of the WADA Code that has been widely disregarded so far. Article 2.1.4 provides: "As an exception to the general rule of Article 2.1, the *Prohibited List* or *International Standards* may establish special criteria for the evaluation of *Prohibited Substances* that can also be produced endogenously". Surprisingly, this provision does not seem to have been discussed in the hGH Trilogy, even though it would seem to be the natural starting point for a coherent legal apprehension of the hGH Isoform Test and other tests involving some form of 'decision limits' to identify substances of exogenous origin. The introduction of Article 3.2.1 to the 2015 WADA Code, which presumes the scientific validity of decision limits "approved by WADA after consultation within the relevant scientific community and which have been the subject of peer review" should be viewed as an incentive to initiate such reflection and clarify the legal status of 'decision limits'. This is all the more so since, as acknowledged by the *Veerpalu* panel's ('dynamic approach'),[92] there is nothing in the current regime to prevent decision limits approved by WADA—whether they are enshrined in a Technical Document or in Guidelines—from being adjusted (i.e. increased or lowered) at any time based on the growing pool of data available as the number of hGH Isoform Tests conducted on Doping Control Samples increases.

3.5 Expert Evidence Before CAS Panels

3.5.1 Importance of Expert Evidence in Doping Disputes

As is often the case in doping cases, the outcome of the *Lallukka* award was entirely dependent on a scientific issue,[93] specifically whether the decision limits set for the Isoform Test are scientifically valid or whether the presence of exogenous hGH had been established irrespective of these limits.

In this context, the allocation of the burden of proof and the related standards of proof are decisive. Indeed, allocating the burden of proof to a party amounts to no less than making this party carry the risk of scientific uncertainty. Since the

[92] CAS 2011/A/2566, *Veerpalu v. FIS*, paras 113 and 205.

[93] See e.g., our comment of the *Chand* award in this volume.

issues in dispute are frequently those that have not yet achieved consensus within the scientific community or that have not been the object of sufficient studies, the party who bears the burden of proof faces a high hurdle. Overcoming this hurdle requires considerable resources and access to the best specialists in the field. Thus, proof in scientific matters almost necessarily means proof through expert evidence.

3.5.2 Who Acts as an Expert Before CAS?

The hGH Trilogy taken as a whole is a good illustration of the typical situation for involving experts in doping cases. On the one side, the Anti-Doping Organization appearing with its experts, frequently the director of the WADA-accredited laboratory that conducted the analysis or staff from other laboratories within the WADA-accredited network. On the other side, the Athlete, often relying on experts outside the scientific anti-doping community, or even appearing without experts at all for lack of financial resources, as was alleged in *WADA v. Lallukka*.

Under the Code of Ethics that WADA-accredited laboratories are required to follow (Annex B of the ISL), experts from WADA-accredited laboratories only intervene in a doping dispute if they are invited to do so by an Anti-Doping Organization.[94] Under these circumstances, it may be difficult for Athletes to find experts to match the high degree of specialization and proficiency that WADA-accredited laboratories personnel enjoy on analytical tests that they often contributed in developing, that they have implemented in their own laboratory and that they apply on a routine basis. This discrepancy is all the more consequential since CAS panels often attribute considerable value to the general professional credibility of the expert when evaluating expert evidence, especially when weighing conflicting expert opinions. In particular, CAS panels will typically not assign a lesser value to evidence given by experts within the laboratory network. On the contrary, their belonging to the 'insiders' of the anti-doping community is often viewed as enhancing the evidentiary value of their opinions.[95]

To remedy what could appear as a structural imbalance within the system, CAS panels can be encouraged to make increased use of the possibility offered to them under the CAS Code to appoint an expert.[96] A panel-appointed expert, as opposed

[94]Giraud et al. 2014, p. 335.

[95]Viret 2016, pp. 602–604 and 607.

[96]Article R44.3 of the CAS Code reads: "If it deems it appropriate to supplement the presentations of the parties, the Panel may at any time order the production of additional documents or the examination of witnesses, appoint and hear experts, and proceed with any other procedural step. The Panel may order the parties to contribute to any additional costs related to the hearing of witnesses and experts".

to a party's expert, carries the additional advantage that the CAS panel can involve both parties on an equal footing in defining the mission of the expert and can take into account the parties' respective financial positions in allocating the costs for the expertise.

3.5.3 Assessing Expert Evidence

The evaluation of expert evidence is a crucial step within the CAS panel's fact-finding analysis, especially since CAS proceedings do not include a preliminary 'admissibility' threshold for expert evidence.[97] Moreover, CAS proceedings typically involve party-appointed experts submitting opposing testimony in support of each side's arguments, so that CAS panels often need to assess which expert's testimony is more persuasive in order to make a final ruling on the dispute. This raises the issue of how CAS panels are to review and weigh expert evidence on the record. The *Lallukka* award contains a paragraph that seems to have developed in recent CAS practice as a standard statement to present the way in which CAS panels handle expert evidence:

> The Panel in the present case recognises that it is not its function to step into the shoes of scientific experts, or to seek to repeat the exercises carried out by those experts. It also recognises that any Tribunal faced with a conflict of expert evidence must approach the evidence with care and with an awareness as to its lack of scientific expertise in the area under examination. Bearing in mind the prescribed provisions as to the burden and standard of proof, the Panel considers that its role in applying the applicable standards as an appellate body is to determine whether the experts' evaluations (upon which WADA's case rests) are soundly based on the facts, and whether the experts consequent appreciation of the conclusion be derived [sic] from those facts is equally sound.[98]

Of note, this approach was initially developed in connection with Athlete Biological Passport cases,[99] to refute recurrent reproaches made by Athletes whereby CAS panels would in reality simply blindly defer to the opinion of the Anti-Doping Organizations' experts. The standard passage shows the need to strike a balance between the mission of the panel to adjudicate the case and its lack of specialist knowledge: legal hearing panels are not in a position to fully repeat an expert's assessment of the issues submitted to them, but their duty to retain the ultimate decision-making power does require them to exercise a certain level of control on expert opinions expressed before them.[100]

---

[97]See generally Rigozzi and Quinn 2014, pp. 7–12 for a discussion on the treatment witness and expert evidence in CAS proceedings.

[98]CAS 2014/A/3488, *WADA v. Lallukka*, para 97.

[99]See e.g., CAS 2010/A/2235 *UCI v. Tadej Valjevec & Olympic Committee of Slovenia*, Award of 21 April 2011, para 79; Viret 2016, p. 630 et seq.

[100]Viret 2016, p. 196 et seq.

A reservation must be made on the last aspect of the panel's statement, whereby "the Panel is bound to form a view as to which of possibly competing expert views it considers to be more persuasive".[101] While probably intended by the panel to underline the thoroughness with which it approached its mission, this statement is inaccurate and does not reflect the 'term sheet' of the judiciary in the fact-finding process. The specificity of the judiciary's mission is precisely that—contrary to the scientists—it is required to make a ruling that will put an end to the parties' dispute. This does not mean that, in order to do so, it is expected to form a position on an issue on which scientists themselves are unable to agree. A panel is never obliged to 'choose' among competing expert views if they do not feel in a position to do so, specifically if none of these views appears to reach the requisite threshold of persuasiveness. For this type of situations, the judiciary has been given a specific evidentiary instrument: the burden of proof. Thus, if the CAS panel is not able to make sense of conflicting expert opinions, or if the experts openly admit that the issue is scientifically unsettled, the burden of proof comes in and the party who carries that burden fails in its case.

3.5.4 Pitfalls to Be Avoided in Dealing with Science and Experts

Besides the evaluation of expert evidence, CAS panels must remain mindful of the proper task division themselves and the expert, as well as the scope of their competence to assess scientific issues without calling on an expert. As CAS proceedings aim at a fast resolution of the dispute, CAS panels tend to resort to their experience in doping matters to facilitate the evaluation of the evidence. While this is perfectly appropriate and even expected from a specialized arbitral tribunal, the *Lallukka* award illustrates some pitfalls that CAS panels should avoid, even if they are short on expert evidence from the parties' sides.

In the *Lallukka* matter, the CAS panel built the final part of its analysis on the merits on a comparison with the *Sinkewitz* case. The starting point was that the *Lallukka* panel considered the revised decision limit published in the new WADA hGH Guidelines to be "quite close" to those in the previous version, finding that the decision limits "did not vary in a magnitude that brings them anywhere near the ratio values found on the Athlete [i.e. Mr Lallukka]".[102] The panel went on to quote the *Sinkewitz* award whereby Patrick Sinkewitz' ratio values were not a borderline situation, and noted that "the ratio values found in the analysis of the Athlete's [Mr Lallukka's] samples are higher than those of Mr Sinkewitz, and significantly so". The CAS panel then presented the decisive extracts from the

[101]CAS 2014/A/3488, *WADA v. Lallukka*, para 97.

[102]Ibid., paras 100–101.

Sinkewitz award, in which experts appearing for the Anti-Doping Organization stated that Mr Sinkewitz' values were "particularly abnormal and clearly show an AAF and that recGH was administered". The *Lallukka* panel considered that the "findings in the *Sinkewitz* Case are pertinent and might be said to be applicable *mutatis mutandis* to the present dispute".[103]

The first pitfall concerns reliance on scientific issues determined in prior CAS awards, specifically in reference to expert evidence. It appears that the *Lallukka* panel relied on the similarity between the fact patterns of the two cases to apply findings of fact (as opposed to legal discussion) *mutatis mutandis* to Mr Lallukka. Thus, the panel—after describing the decisions limits as a matter of evidence—relied on evidence given in a different case, on a different Sample, collected from a different Athlete, to supports its findings that Mr Lallukka had administered hGH.

This approach appears rather questionable. If truly the presence of hGH in a Sample is an issue of fact that can be demonstrated by any reliable means of evidence, a CAS panel may not pray in aid expert evidence given in a different matter, and certainly not without giving the Athlete the opportunity to have those experts heard and to cross-examine them. Objectively, the panel was not in a position to determine whether these experts would have made the same statements with respect to Mr Lallukka's case. There may have been scientifically relevant differences between the two situations that the panel was unaware of, but that would have led experts to be less clear-cut or even to differ radically in their opinions.

A second pitfall that CAS panels should mind is the inconsiderate assessment of the scientific significance of figures or of differences between figures. CAS panels at times show a propensity towards acting as their own 'experts' in the scientific assessment of the case and of the relative importance of analytical values. As an example, one could doubt whether the CAS panel in *WADA v. Lallukka* was truly in a position, when faced with two pairs of ratio values, to determine whether one is 'significantly' higher than the other, or whether the case must be considered a 'borderline situation' (see Sect. 3.4.2). Similar reservations can be expressed with respect to the CAS panel's statements whereby the revised decision limits are "quite close" to those contained in the previous hGH Guidelines, or that those did not vary in a "magnitude that bring them anywhere near" the values found in the Athlete's Samples.

One must acknowledge that in this matter, the CAS panel did not receive the benefit of extensive scientific evidence submitted in support of the Athlete's position. Juha Lallukka mostly relied on the *Veerpalu* decision in his attempt to escape the finding of an anti-doping rule violation. The Athlete did not produce any further expert evidence of his own and did not elaborate on his scientific challenge, other than to dispute that the additional studies answered all points raised by the *Veerpalu* panel and to make some further assumptions regarding possible

[103]Ibid., para 106.

individual preconditions that could account for his high ratio values. The CAS panel was therefore placed in a delicate position, since it only had the benefit of written submissions and of expert evidence unrelated to the Athlete's individual circumstances. However, this situation should not justify drawing on expert evidence or scientific insights gained in prior CAS awards. In an extreme situation, this type of approach on the part of a CAS panel could represent an argument in favour of setting aside the CAS award before the Swiss Supreme Court for breach of the right to be heard (Article 190(2)(d) PILA).

More generally, neither the principle of *res iudicata* nor the rule of precedent apply to scientific findings. It is perfectly possible that the knowledge should evolve compared to the prior award or could not be transposed to a different set of facts. Arbitral tribunals under the Swiss law of arbitration applicable to CAS panels are under a duty, like judges in state courts, to call *ex officio* upon the services of an expert if they are confronted with issues that require specialist knowledge exceeding their competence.[104] The fact that CAS proceedings have traditionally relied on party-appointed experts would not appear to relieve a CAS panel from its duties in this regard. The same is true for specific CAS arbitrators who may already be familiar with scientific issues in anti-doping: this familiarity may assist them in understanding the parties' arguments and evaluate expert testimonies, but should not replace expert evidence altogether.[105]

3.5.5 Financial Aid for Athletes on Scientific Matters?

The *Lallukka* matter made it clear that Athletes need significant resources to challenge the scientific validity of the analytical tools used to charge them with anti-doping violations. This difficulty is likely to be exacerbated with the new provision introduced in the 2015 WADA Code that explicitly shifts the burden onto the Athlete in this respect (see Sect. 3.4.3). CAS proceedings in doping matters are designed to favour an expedited resolution of the dispute. However, speed should not be achieved at the expense of a thorough assessment of the case, especially if one of the parties is in a markedly less well-off position.

In *WADA v. Lallukka*, the CAS panel accepted the late filing of additional evidence by WADA, with the explanation that "documents filed are at the core of essential questions in these proceedings, as they directly address the findings of the *Veerpalu* case which form the Athlete's primary line of defence".[106] The CAS panel noted, as an important factor, that the Athlete failed to object to the

[104]See e.g. Poudret and Besson 2007, para 664.

[105]Viret 2016, pp. 625–626.

[106]CAS 2014/A/3488, *WADA v. Lallukka*, para 70.

production of this evidence and did not submit comments, in spite of being invited to do so.[107] The award reveals, also, that the fact that the Athlete did not comment on the additional evidence—and more generally his failure to substantiate further his challenges on the scientific aspects of the case—was probably related to the Athlete's lack of resources, as invoked by his counsel. As matters stand, the Legal Aid Guidelines adopted by the CAS do not appear to provide assistance in this type of situation. As per its wording, Article 6 of the Guidelines covers only the travel costs of an expert to a hearing, as opposed to the actual costs of obtaining expertise.[108] In cases where technical issues are pivotal, not being able to afford an expert to adequately defend one's case can raise questions in regards to the principle of equality of arms, which is protected under both Article 182(3) of the PILA and Article 6(1) of the ECHR.[109]

As just explained, this should not allow CAS panels to simply 'replace' the lack of expert evidence with their own assessment or to fill in the gaps with evidence obtained in previous purportedly similar matters. Instead, CAS panels need to become proactive when they are required to deal with specialized issues on which they have insufficient proficiency. Of note, in the *Veerpalu* matter, the only award of the hGH Trilogy in which a CAS panel refused to find sufficient evidence to support the Anti-Doping Organization's scientific case, the CAS arbitrators did adopt such proactive attitude, by asking questions and making orders for the production of evidence.[110] As mentioned above, the CAS Code does give panels the procedural tools to become proactive by ordering additional evidentiary measures, including the production of evidence under the control of the parties, or by appointing their own expert. The CAS Code also allows for a fair allocation of the costs, taking into account each party's financial situation (Articles R44.3 and R64.3 CAS Code).[111]

The panel's option of retaining an independent expert appears all the more recommendable when one considers the procedural framework of doping disputes

[107]Ibid., para 71.

[108]In fact, in *WADA v. Lallukka* (see para 33 of the award), the Athlete was initially granted legal aid that was in part to cover "the costs of any experts, witnesses, or interpreters in connection with a hearing, if necessary", but the Athlete's request for additional legal aid was denied (see para 42).

[109]Rigozzi and Robert-Tissot 2015, p. 74.

[110]CAS 2011/A/2566, *Veerpalu v. FIS*, paras 64–72.

[111]For more details on the implications of the new Article 3.2.1 of the WADA Code for the appointment of an expert by the panel, Viret M, CAS as the guardian of the validity of anti-doping science? A review of hGH cases through the prism of the revised 2015 World Anti-Doping Code, 23 July 2015. http://www.lawinsport.com/articles/item/cas-as-the-guardian-of-the-validity-of-anti-doping-science. Accessed 15 March 2016.

such as *WADA v. Lallukka*. In this case, the skier had already served almost two years of a provisional suspension[112] and been successful in two hearings at the national level. Hence, considering that this provisional suspension would normally be credited on any sanction that could be imposed,[113] in all likelihood what was at stake for the skier was, at most, a period of Ineligibility of approximately four months.[114] For Juha Lallukka, the cost–benefit analysis of whether to invest further resources to defend himself for a third time, this time against an even better-equipped opponent, must have been quite straightforward, in particular knowing that even if it had been an option for Mr Lallukka to make this investment at the CAS, he had not much to 'gain', besides clearing his name.

Thus the procedural framework of doping disputes can leave even an Athlete party with sufficient resources with little incentive to vigorously defend his position. In this context, a CAS panel could help to eliminate any potential doubts to the credibility of the CAS panel's finding by proactively appointing an expert. Specifically, this appointment can help alleviate doubts as to whether the decision was reached based on a full consideration of the issues. More generally, one may wonder whether CAS panels should continue to tolerate the practice of naming only the Athlete as a respondent in proceedings in which WADA (or another sports–governing body appealing) is in reality questioning the reasoning of the hearing panel constituted by the Athlete's National Anti-Doping Organization or other national sports organization, in application of the requirements of the WADA Code (Article 13.2.2). WADA named only the Athlete as a respondent, meaning that he alone would most likely be liable for the entire costs of the arbitration in case of a successful appeal (which was indeed the case in the *Lallukka* matter[115]). Considering the costs involved, there are good reasons to argue that the sports organization that rendered the supposedly 'flawed' decision under appeal (or on behalf of which that decision was rendered at the national level)[116] should

[112]The provisional suspension was imposed on 27 October 2011 and ended on 19 June 2013 by decision of the FINADA Supervisory Board (at para 24), 602 days. CAS 2014/A/3488, *WADA v. Lallukka*, n° 3 of the operative part.

[113]In application of Article 10.11.3 of the WADA Code (new numbering under the 2015 WADA Code), anti-doping regulations must provide that any period of Provisional Suspension served shall be credited against any period of Ineligibility subsequently imposed.

[114]The CAS panel in the *Lallukka* matter (unsurprisingly) settled on a sanction of a two-year period of Ineligibility starting from the notification of the CAS award, then deducted the 602-day provisional suspension that he already served, leaving Juha Lallukka with a period of Ineligibility just over four months long.

[115]CAS 2014/A/3488, *WADA v. Lallukka*, para 140.

[116]The same reasoning applies when the decision appealed is rendered by an independent national-level body. Insofar as both the Athlete and his National Anti-Doping Organization were the parties to the proceedings before the Finnish Sports Arbitration Board, an appeal filed by WADA against the decision ought to be directed against both parties to the prior proceedings.

systematically be named as a co-respondent.[117] An Athlete named as the sole respondent by WADA in CAS proceedings should also strongly consider asking for the relevant sport organization to be joined as a party to the CAS proceedings.[118] Participation of the sport organization that rendered the decision under appeal to compensate for any possible imbalance between WADA and the Athlete is all the more essential knowing that CAS awards are often used by subsequent CAS panels as precedent, but rarely do these panels consider whether the parties to the past dispute were on equal footing.

3.6 Conclusion—Outlook Beyond 2015

This article reviewed, through the prism of the hGH Trilogy, certain aspects of the World Anti-Doping Program that would deserve consideration if the system is to keep pace, in its regulatory framework, with evolving doping patterns.

With increasing abuse of doping agents that mimic substances naturally produced within the human organism, sophisticated analytical methods need to be developed that seek to discriminate between the endogenous and exogenous origins of these substances[119] As the hGH Trilogy shows, challenges for laboratories will in the future lie more in the interpretation of the results than in the underlying technology itself.[120] Moreover, for harmonization purposes and to avoid decisions

[117]When the CAS Code first came into effect, all appeal arbitration proceedings, thus effectively all doping disputes, were free-of-charge. However, successive revisions of the CAS Code have progressively narrowed the 'free-of-charge' rule to those cases that are both "exclusively of a disciplinary nature" and arising from a decision "rendered by an international federation or sports-body" (R65.1 of the 2016 CAS Code), thus cases such as *WADA v. Lallukka* that arose from a national-level decision are no longer free-of-charge. Mavromati and Reeb 2015, p. 640 explain that the original underlying motivation for providing cases free-of-charge in appeal cases, "was due to the fact that, at the time, the vast majority of appeal cases related to doping cases"; see also Rigozzi and Robert-Tissot 2015, pp. 73–74 for a discussion surrounding the evolution of the 'free-of-charge' rule at the CAS and implications on the validity of the arbitration agreement ("[i]t is a matter of common sense that a person cannot be compelled to arbitrate if she or he cannot afford to pay the costs related to the arbitration and is thus deprived of her or his fundamental right to have access to justice", thus "if an athlete can show that the compulsory arbitration mechanism is so expensive to actually prevent her or him from having access to justice, she or he could then seek to rescind the arbitration agreement."). There is the possibility to receive assistance with arbitration costs through legal aid (Guidelines on Legal Aid before the Court of Arbitration for Sport, 2013, Article 6), however, in the *Lallukka* matter, there is no indication in the award that the skier received legal aid that would cover arbitration costs, see CAS 2014/A/3488, *WADA v. Lallukka*, paras 33–34 and 42.

[118]In practice, the role of a joined sports organization could potentially be limited since it might itself disagree with the findings of its own tribunal in a prior instance, and often takes the position that it will defer to the findings of the CAS panel.

[119]Another illustration would be the Isotope Ratio Mass Spectrometry ("IRMS") method used for endogenous androgenic anabolic steroids.

[120]Giraud et al. 2014, p. 333.

made on an 'I-know-it-when-I-see-it' basis, these methods require WADA to set a number of technical 'limits' that so far have evaded a clear legal characterization and do not easily fit within the structure of a legal regime that was established to support the original 2003 version of the WADA Code.

Without truly rethinking the regulatory structure of the regime and the binary organization (quantitative versus qualitative analysis) of the International Standard for Laboratories, any attempt to introduce more flexibility may prove detrimental to the overall coherence of the system. In particular, it is currently not clear why certain Decision Limits should be set in binding Technical Documents and others only in non-mandatory Guidelines, nor whether WADA is truly free in its choice between these two types of instruments. Neither the *Sinkewitz* nor the *Lallukka* panels assessed the implications of this aspect of their reasoning when they relied on the non-mandatory character of the WADA hGH Guidelines to deny any legally binding character to the decision limit in the hGH Isoform Test. If the reasoning of these panels was followed, should WADA choose to transfer one and the same Decision Limit from a Guideline into a Technical Document (as occurred subsequently for the hGH Isoform Test), or the reverse, this would alter *ipso facto* the legal status of that Decision Limit and its meaning for the relevant case.

One could wonder whether a system can be considered proportionate in which scientific figures of similar nature can switch from a matter of fact to a matter of law (or vice versa) at the sole determination of one of the parties. Anti-doping regulators cannot have it both ways: if they wish to set strict limits beyond which an Athlete is not admitted to argue that no violation was committed, they must accept that they are themselves bound by these limits and cannot freely resort to other means of evidence whenever the reliability of the limits is challenged or the relevant limit not met in a particular matter.

Given that the overall mechanics of the system were never addressed upfront in the hGH Trilogy, it should not come as a surprise that they could support fundamentally diverging interpretations on the nature of the hGH Isoform Test and its related Decision Limits. Though the hGH Isoform Test appears formally reinstated in its credibility, it is only a matter of time until we see a similar debate arising again, possibly in connection with the hGH Biomarkers Test or another equally sophisticated method.

The new provision that introduced a presumption of the scientific validity of decision limits and analytical methods, in Article 3.2.1 of the WADA Code, will certainly influence the manner in which CAS panels will deal with the type of challenge that was at stake in the hGH Trilogy. In particular, the new provision should hopefully favour the appointment of experts by CAS panels. To this day, no challenge has been brought based on this new provision, so that one may need to await the next technological novelty in anti-doping analytical science to assess its true impact.

References

Giraud S, Joye C, Saugy M, Viret M (2014) Role of anti-doping laboratories in the fight against doping. CausaSport (Issue 4): 331–344

Mavromati D, Reeb M (2015) The code of the court of arbitration for sport: commentary, cases and materials. Kluwer Law International, Alphen aan den Rijn

Poudret J-F, Besson S (2007) Comparative law of international arbitration, 2nd edn. Sweet & Maxwell Ltd, London

Rigozzi A, Quinn B (2014) Evidentiary issues before CAS. In: Bernasconi (ed) International sports law and jurisprudence of the CAS: 4th CAS & SAV/FSA conference Lausanne 2012, Weblaw, Bern, pp 1–54

Rigozzi A, Viret M, Wisnosky E (2014) Switzerland: anti-doping reports. Int Sports Law Rev (Issue 3): 54–68

Rigozzi A, Robert-Tissot F (2015) "Consent" in sports arbitration: its multiple aspects: lessons from the Cañas decision, in particular with regard to provisional measures. In: Geisinger E, Trabaldo E (eds) ASA special series no. 41, pp 59–94

Saugy M, Robinson N, Saudan C, Baume N, Avois L, Mangin P (2006), Human growth hormone doping in sport. Br J Sports Med 40: i35–i39 (Suppl 1), i35–i39

Saugy M, Viret M, Giraud S (2016 tbp) Limits in anti-doping science. In: Bernasconi M (ed), Arbitrating disputes in a modern sports world—5th conference CAS & SAV/FSA Lausanne 2014

Viret M (2016) Evidence in anti-doping at the intersection of science and law. T.M.C Asser Press, The Hague

Author Biography

Marjolaine Viret is an attorney-at-law and postdoctoral researcher. She is currently collaborating on a research project supported by the Swiss National Science Foundation to create a commentary of the 2015 World Anti-Doping Code.

Emily Wisnosky is an attorney-at-law and doctoral researcher. She is currently collaborating on a research project supported by the Swiss National Science Foundation to create a commentary of the 2015 World Anti-Doping Code.

Chapter 4
The Sell-on Clause in Football: Recent Cases and Evolutions

Lucio Colantuoni and Willem-Alexander Devlies

Abstract The use of sell-on clauses is a regular practice in the world of football. Whenever a talented player is being transferred, several interested parties try to have a piece of the transfer fee, often by means of a sell-on clause. In its most common use, the sell-on clause is inserted in transfer contracts between two clubs, whereby the selling club, against a lower immediate transfer fee, retains the right to a certain percentage of a potential future transfer fee of the player to a third club. In this case both clubs enter into a partnership aimed at a win-win situation. In general, certain conditions need to be fulfilled to trigger the sell-on clause and this caused the occurrence of several disputes before FIFA and CAS, of which some will be discussed below. Among those, the case enrolled as 'CAS 2014/A/3508 *FC Lokomotiv v. Football Union of Russia & FC Nika*' will be discussed in more detail as it covers a series of interesting legal and practical issues and can be viewed as a recent leading case in that matter. However, the selling club is not the only interested party which may obtain a possible sell-on fee: the reality of football shows that even private investors could be interested in a return on a future transfer by retaining such type of percentage fees. This practice is prohibited now by recently implemented changes of the FIFA regulations, due to FIFA's combat against the so-called 'TPO—Third Party Ownership', but some comments should be drawn upon, as the practice of sell-on fees seems to be still legitimate

---

At the time of writing this chapter, Lucio Colantuoni (deceased) was Professor of Law at the Universita degli Studi di Milano.

L. Colantuoni
Sports Law Research Centre—Milano, Via Unione 8, 20122 Milan, Italy

W.-A. Devlies (✉)
Lovius, Brusselsesteenweg 62, 3000 Louvain, Belgium
e-mail: Willem.Devlies@Lovius.be

A. Duval and A. Rigozzi (eds.), *Yearbook of International Sports Arbitration 2015*,
DOI 10.1007/978-94-6265-129-6_4

after the new FIFA regulations and circulars, if the percentage is retained by the club (and/or by the player, this being even compulsory in some countries).

Keywords Football · Contracts · Sell-on clause · Transfers · FIFA—CAS jurisprudence · TPO · Percentage

Contents

4.1 Introduction

For over a decade, amateur and professional football clubs are inserting so-called 'sell-on' clauses in their transfer contracts, often in exchange of a lower immediate transfer fee or withdrawal of their training compensation rights, to secure potential profit of the resale of their promising former players in the future. In *Sport Club Internacional v. Bayer 04 Leverkusen,*[1] the CAS Panel described sell-on clauses and its *rationale* as follows: "Clauses providing for such kind of risk-sharing and of participation of a transferring club in possible, uncertain gains obtained by the new club in the event of a further transfer to a third club, are not uncommon in international transfer agreements of professional football players. The economic rationale of such clauses is, generally, that by agreeing into such arrangement, the transferring club accepts to receive, in a first place, a lower "first" transfer fee, with the expectation of receiving an additional "fee" if the recipient club will be able to transfer, with profit, the player to a third club".[2] Sell-on clauses are still regular practice in transfer agreements upon today and they can be used in relation to permanent transfers and/or to loans. The two clubs negotiating the deal have to decide what kind of transfer will trigger the sell-on fee and the figure of the sell-on fee (most commonly a certain percentage of the transfer fee received from a third club with possible minimum or maximum figures). The use of a sell-on clause

[1]CAS 2005/A/848, *Sport Club Internacional v. Bayer 04 Leverkusen*, Award of 23 February 2006.

[2]See also CAS 2005/A/896, *Fulham FC (1987) Ltd. v. FC Metz,* Award of 16 January 2006, para 57.

does not guarantee any profit, as the future of the player will always be uncertain. The most common wording of the sell-on clause in a transfer contract between Club A and Club B in relation to Player X can be summarised as follows: *In the event Player X is transferred from Club B to a third Club C, Club A has the right to receive ... % of the transfer fee received by Club B from Club C.* In practice, however, most sell-on clauses contain several variations or extra conditions upon which the sell-on clause shall be triggered, which leads in turn to many interpretation problems and regular disputes, as some clubs attempt not to comply with their payment obligation under the sell-on clause.

4.2 The Sell-on Clause in Football Transfer Contracts

4.2.1 Conditions and Peculiarities

The main condition to be fulfilled in order to trigger the sell-on clause is the transfer of the player to a third club. Without the player being transferred, no sell-on fee can be due. Although this condition might seem very simple and clear, it is often the main reason for disputes due to the different interpretation between the parties given to the word 'transfer'. This is because a transfer can both refer to a permanent transfer and/or a temporary transfer, i.e. a loan. Therefore, it is very important for the parties to be crystal clear in the wording of the sell-on clause and to specify whether or not the sell-on clause will be triggered in the event of a permanent transfer only or in the event of a loan as well. A second interpretation problem often occurs in relation to the words 'transfer fee' and/or 'transfer fee received' to calculate the sell-on fee. Is the percentage of the sell-on fee calculated on the transfer fee agreed in the contract with the third club or on the transfer fee actually received by the selling club? Is the sell-on fee due when the player was transferred for free or in exchange for another player? And which currency has to be applied? In case of breach, is the damages compensation relevant? Other problems occur when transfers go hand in hand with so-called 'participation agreements', by which the economic rights are being transferred for only 50 % to a third club, a regular practice for example in Italy. In many cases, parties often disputed the conditions which trigger the sell-on clause or the exact amount of the sell-on fee that had to be paid, and referred there disputes to FIFA or national dispute resolution bodies, of which some of them will be discussed below.

4.2.2 Recent FIFA and CAS Jurisprudence

4.2.2.1 Interpretation Issues: 'Transfer—Transfer Fee'

FIFA and CAS have resolved many disputes over the years in relation to the interpretation of the sell-on clause. Regarding the interpretation of the act of a 'transfer', different jurisprudence can be found within the FIFA and CAS decisions. In

Club Sekondi Hasaacas FC v. Club Borussia Mönchengladbach[3] for example, the sell-on clause only referred to the word 'transfer' without specifying the temporary or permanent character of it. The Sole Arbitrator found it was hardly imaginable that the mutual consent of the parties was to limit such right to a final transfer and to exclude any transfer, which was structured as a loan but was de facto in many ways similar and equivalent to a final transfer. In a recent decision,[4] the Single Judge of the FIFA PSC decided that, if the intention of the parties was to broaden the scope of the clause's applicability both to permanent transfers and loans, they would have explicitly included in its wording the precise kind of transfer, i.e. loan, that would have triggered as well the payment obligation. In *FC Metz v. Galatasaray SK,*[5] French club FC Metz and Turkish club Galatasaray SK concluded a transfer agreement regarding the French player Frank Ribéry (hereinafter the 'Player') on 31 January 2005. The transfer contract stipulated that the sporting rights of the Player would be assigned to Galatasaray SK until 30 June 2005 without any payment for this period and only as of 1 July 2005, Galatasaray SK would acquire the sporting rights permanently for an amount of € 2,000,000. The transfer contract further included a sell-on clause providing that Galatasaray SK will pay to FC Metz a percentage of 20 % on the amount of the transfer fee exceeding € 2,000,000 in the event of a future transfer of the player to a third club. In April 2005, both clubs signed an addendum to the transfer contract stipulating that in exchange for a bank guarantee, FC Metz would reduce its sell-on fee percentage from 20 to 11 %. Between 1 February 2005 and 13 June 2005, the Player played several matches for Galatasaray SK, until he complained with the club that he did not receive any salary or bonuses for the past 4 months. The Player filed a claim with FIFA on 14 June 2005 and the next day, the Player had signed an employment contract with French club Olympique Marseille. On 13 May 2006, the FIFA DRC accepted the claim of the Player and decided that Galatasaray SK had breached the contract without just cause. This decision was confirmed by CAS,[6] which decided that the Player had terminated his contract with just cause. It is important to note that in the Player's contract with Galatasaray SK, a penalty clause was stipulated that should the player desire to enter in a contract with another club, he would be able to terminate this contract unilaterally at any time after having paid € 10,000,000 to the club. In June 2007 the Player was transferred from Olympique Marseille to FC Bayern Munich for the amount of € 25,000,000 and in October 2007, FC Metz filed a claim with FIFA against Galatasaray SK for

---

[3]CAS 2007/A/1219, *Club Sekondi Hasaacas FC v. Club Borussia Mönchengladbach*, Award of 9 July 2007.

[4]FIFA PSC no. 1114580, decision of 20 November 2014. The Sell-on clause was formulated as follows: "[The Respondent] undertakes to ensure the 40 % (forty percent) of the economic rights of the [player] held by [the Claimant] in case of transfer of the [player] to any other organization".

[5]CAS 2009/A/1756, *FC Metz SASP v. Galatasaray SK*, Award of 12 October 2009.

[6]CAS 2006/A/1180, *Galatasaray SK v. Frank Ribéry & Olympique Marseille*, Award of 24 April 2007.

the amount of € 1,100,000 (11 % of 10,000,000) submitting that it had not been able to claim their sell-on fee due to misconduct of Galatasaray SK against the Player. The Single Judge of FIFA's PSC rejected the claim of FC Metz as it was of the opinion that also Galatasaray SK lost an opportunity (a transfer fee) in this matter, that FC Metz did not lose anything in this matter as it had gambled on a hypothetical gain, which lies in the nature of the sell-on clause, and that the misconduct of Galatasaray SK had no consequences on the transfer contract since this contract was absolutely independent from the employment contract of the Player. FC Metz appealed the case to CAS. On 12 October 2009, the CAS Panel rendered its arbitral award and decided as follows. According to the Panel, the sell-on clause provided for two conditions to be triggered: (i) the transfer of the player to a third club against payment of transfer compensation; and (ii) payment by this third club of transfer compensation exceeding € 2,000,000. These conditions are according to the Panel condition precedents as in Article 151 of the Swiss Code of Obligations (CO) that stipulates that "a contract which is dependent on the occurrence of an uncertain fact in order to be binding is deemed to be conditional".[7] The Panel further based its reasoning on Article 156 CO that reads "a condition is deemed to be fulfilled if its occurrence has been prevented by one party in bad faith" and which is based on the general principle of abuse of rights. According to Swiss authors, the application of Article 156 CO is submitted to five conditions: (i) the existence of a condition; (ii) the occurrence of this condition is prevented; (iii) a reprehensible behaviour of one of the parties to the contract or of a party entrusted with the benefit of the contract; (iv) the violation of the good faith principle by this party, on purpose or not; (v) a reasonable link between the behaviour of the preventing party and the non-occurrence of the condition.[8] The Panel consequently decided that these five conditions were met and that Galatasaray SK did not respect the principle of good faith, causing the termination of the contract by the Player with just cause, and, in turn, the loss of any profit expectation on a future transfer of the Player. Regarding the amount of the transfer fee on the basis of which the sell-on fee had to be calculated, the Panel emphasised that there was no clear evidence of the transfer value of the Player at that time, and therefore, referred to Article 42 CO, which gives discretion to the judge while having regard to the ordinary course of events and the measures taken by the damaged party.[9] Applying this principle, the Panel was of the opinion that the estimated transfer value was to be assessed at an amount of € 4,000,000, following which the amount of the sell-on fee of 11 % of the amount of the transfer fee exceeding € 2,000,000 (being € 2,000,000) was equal to € 220,000. Another famous case in this regard is the one of *Sevilla FC v. RC Lens.*[10] In 2007, the French club Racing Club de Lens

[7]CAS 2009/A/1756, *FC Metz v. Galatasaray SK,* paras 10–11.

[8]Ibid., paras 13–14.

[9]Ibid., para 24.

[10]CAS 2010/A/2098, *Sevilla FC v. RC Lens,* Award of 29 November 2010.

(hereinafter 'RC Lens') permanently transferred the Malian football player Seydou Keita (hereinafter the 'Player') to Spanish football club Sevilla FC (hereinafter 'FC Sevilla') for the amount of € 4,000,000. The transfer contract between RC Lens and FC Sevilla, included a sell-on clause, which stipulated as follows: "2.2.4—Profit-sharing. In case of resale of the player Seydou Keita by Sevilla FC to another club, Racing Club of Lens shall receive:—10 % of the capital gain between 4,000,000 Euro and 8,000,000 Euro.—15 % beyond 8,000,000 Euro.—These amounts may be cumulated". In 2008, the Player unilaterally terminated his employment contract with FC Sevilla in accordance with an indemnification clause[11] stipulated in his employment contract, providing for an indemnification in the amount of € 14,000,000 in the event of an early termination by the Player. The Player then signed a new employment contract with Spanish club FC Barcelona, which paid the full amount through the Spanish Football League to FC Sevilla. Following these events, RC Lens filed a claim with FIFA as it was of the opinion that the sell-on clause was triggered as a result of the Player's transfer to FC Barcelona, while FC Sevilla denied that any payment was due since no transfer occurred, as the Player merely terminated his contract by means of payment of the compensation provided for in the indemnification clause and, thus, there was no transfer agreement with FC Barcelona. In 2009, the Single Judge of FIFA's PSC[12] partially accepted the claim of RC Lens and ordered FC Sevilla to pay to RC Lens the amount of € 1,300,000 in accordance with the sell-on clause, as the Single Judge was of the opinion that the activation of the indemnification clause by the Player, bearing in mind that the amount of €14,000,000 was borne voluntarily by FC Barcelona, had to be considered as a transfer between FC Sevilla and FC Barcelona in the sense of the sell-on clause agreed between RC Lens and FC Sevilla. Both parties appealed the decision to CAS and in 2010 the CAS Panel decided to uphold the appeal of FC Sevilla and to set aside the FIFA decision. The CAS Panel was of the opinion that an interpretation dispute existed around the word '*resale*' stipulated in the sell-on clause. According to the Panel, the FIFA "Decision erred where it held that the transfer of the Player to FC Barcelona was a "transfer agreed between two clubs and a player for a specific amount", with the sole peculiarity that the 'specific amount' had been agreed only by FC Sevilla and the Player in the indemnification clause. With all deference, in the Panel's view, the Single Judge missed the point: the key aspect is not whether FC Sevilla agreed the measure of the amount to be paid by the Player in the event of termination of the Employment Contract, but whether FC Sevilla agreed to the termination of the Employment Contract. In the absence of this consent, the transfer of the Player to Barcelona cannot be equated to a sale".[13] Consequently, FC Sevilla did not have to pay any sell-on fee to RC Lens.

---

[11]In accordance with article 16 of the Spanish Real Decreto 1006/85, de 26 de junio 1985, por el que se regula la relaciõn laboral de los deportistas profesionales.

[12]FIFA PSC, decision of 9 December 2009.

[13]CAS 2010/A/2098, *Sevilla FC v. RC Lens*, para 88.

Apart from the interpretation of the word 'transfer/sale' in sell-on clauses, disputes also arise regarding the calculation basis of the sell-on fee, which is most of the time a percentage of the transfer fee received by the selling-club. An interesting case in relation to this issue is *Helsingborgs IF v. Parma FC S.p.A.*[14] Swedish football club Helsingborgs IF (hereinafter 'Helsingborgs IF') and the Italian football club Parma FC S.p.A. (hereinafter 'FC Parma') entered into a loan agreement during the summer window of 2007 in relation to the Kenyan football player McDonald Mariga (hereinafter the 'Player'). The loan agreement was concluded for the 2007/2008 Season and contained an option clause for a possible later definitive transfer of the Player, as well as a sell-on clause, which was stipulated as follows: "If Parma F.C. decides to take the option under the terms of the article 2, Parma F.C. undertakes to pay to Helsingborgs IF, in case of future transfer of the Player to another club, the net amount of 15 %—Transfer fee minus the net amount of € 2,000,000 (two million) paid under the terms of the article 3 before". In April 2008, FC Parma exercised the option and in February 2010, the Player was further transferred from FC Parma to FC Internazionale Milano (hereinafter 'FC Internazionale') for an alleged agreed amount of € 10,000,000, which lead to the triggering of the sell-on clause. However, on the same day, FC Parma and FC Internazionale entered into a co-ownership agreement for the Player by which FC Internazionale sold back 50 % of the economic rights of the Player for the amount of € 5,000,000 and only in June 2010, FC Internazionale purchased the remaining 50 % of the economic rights of the Player from FC Parma for the amount of € 4,200,000. Consequently, it was in dispute whether the 15 % sell-on fee had to be based on the agreed transfer fee of € 10,000,000 or the actual paid transfer fee of € 9,200,000. In January 2012, the Single Judge of the FIFA PSC[15] decided that the sell-on fee had to be calculated on € 9,200,000 as it was the transfer fee actually received by FC Parma. Helsingborgs IF filed an appeal with CAS and in February 2013, the CAS Panel decided to dismiss the appeal and to uphold the FIFA decision. The CAS Panel agreed with FC Parma that the amount of € 10,000,000 was only an indicative amount for the transfer of 100 % of the economic rights of the Player. The Panel considered that a sell-on fee is to be based on the amount actually received by a club for selling a player to a subsequent club and not on an indicative amount. Therefore, the 15 % sell-on fee had to be calculated on the amount of € 9.200.000, giving Helsingborgs IF the right to a total sell-on fee of 15 % x (€9,200,000–€ 2,000,000) being € 1,080,000.

Both of these interpretation issues will also be dealt with more detailed in the case of *FC Lokomotiv v. Football Union of Russia & FC Nika*[16] in the case commentary below.

---

[14]CAS 2012/A/2875, *Helsingborgs IF v. Parma FC S.p.A.*, Award of 28 February 2013.

[15]FIFA PSC no. 01121145, decision of 30 January 2012.

[16]CAS 2014/A/3508, *FC Lokomotiv v. Football Union of Russia & FC Nika*, Award of 23 March 2015.

4.2.2.2 Sell-on Clause in Combination with 'Participation Agreement'

As previously mentioned, it is common practice in some countries[17] that transfers of players go hand in hand with so-called 'co-ownership/participation' or 'sharing agreements'. When a player is transferred between two clubs, the clubs conclude a participation agreement simultaneously with the transfer agreement. In the transfer agreement, both clubs agree on a certain transfer fee for the player, whilst in the participation agreement, the buying club agrees to sell-back 50 % of the economic rights of the player to the selling club, by which both clubs own 50 % of the player's economic rights, but the buying club remains owner of 100 % of the player's federative rights. After a certain period of time, the clubs can agree to transfer the remaining 50 % of the player's economic rights for a certain amount. This situation leads to many disputes when a sell-on clause has been added to the transfer agreement, as it is often disagreed on which amount the sell-on fee needs to be calculated. In *Genoa Cricket and Football Club v. Club Atlético Peñarol*[18] for example, Italian football club Genoa Cricket and Football Club (hereinafter 'FC Genoa') and the Uruguayan football club Club Atlético Peñarol (hereinafter 'CA Peñarol') concluded a transfer contract in January 2011 in relation to the permanent transfer of the Spanish/Uruguayan football player Federico Martín Rodríguez Rodríguez (hereinafter the 'Player') from FC Peñarol to FC Genoa for the amount of € 4,000,000. The transfer contract also included a sell-on clause, which was stipulated as follows: "Genoa and Peñarol agree and commit that if, within 30 June 2015, in case of future transfer of the Player's sport performances and economic rights from Genoa to another Club for a total amount higher than € 4,000,000, Genoa will be obliged to pay to Peñarol a 10 % fee to be calculated upon the amount exceeding the above mentioned amount of € 4,000,000".

In the summer of 2011, the Player was permanently transferred from FC Genoa to Italian football club FC Bologna for an alleged transfer fee of € 6,000,000. In January 2013, CA Peñarol lodged a claim before FIFA alleging that FC Genoa did not complete the full payment of the € 4,000,000 transfer fee (which was due in several instalments) and requesting payment of the sell-on fee on the € 6,000,000 transfer of the Player to FC Bologna. FC Genoa did not respond to the claim and in June 2013, the Single Judge of FIFA's PSC[19] rendered its decision. The Single Judge accepted CA Peñarol's claim and ordered FC Genoa to pay the outstanding transfer fee amounts as well as the sell-on fee in the amount of 10 % x (€ 6,000,000–€ 4,000,000) being € 200,000. FC Genoa appealed the decision to CAS. During the CAS proceedings, FC Genoa argued that no sell-on fee payment was due because of the fact that the transfer agreement between FC Genoa and FC Bologna was combined with a so-called "sharing agreement", a construction

---

[17]Chile, Argentina and Uruguay for example, it also used to be in Italy.

[18]CAS 2013/A/3317, *Genoa Cricket and Football Club v. Club Atlético Peñarol*, Award of 26 May 2014.

[19]FIFA PSC no. 0613619, decision of 5 June 2013.

that—at the time—was widely used between Italian football clubs and regulated by the Italian Football Federation.[20] Following this sharing agreement, FC Genoa transferred the Player's registration to FC Bologna for an amount of € 6,000,000, whereas FC Genoa simultaneously acquired 50 % of the Player's economic rights by making a payment in the amount of € 3,000,000 to FC Bologna. In FC Genoa's view, once the sharing agreement expires, the Player's old club relinquishes its economic rights in the Player, which are then fully assigned to the club with which he is registered. If such is the case, the amount initially paid for the 50 % of the economic rights in the Player is not refunded and shall be counted against the total value of the transaction. According to FC Genoa, the sharing agreement with FC Bologna expired in July 2013, by which FC Genoa's sharing right had expired. As a consequence, the amount of € 3,000,000 became the final transfer fee paid by FC Bologna, which is less than the € 4,000,000 threshold that would have triggered the sell-on clause and, therefore, FC Genoa is not obliged to pay any sell-on fee in accordance with the sell-on clause. In May 2014, the Sole Arbitrator dismissed the appeal of FC Genoa and confirmed the FIFA decision. The Sole Arbitrator was of the opinion that the fact alone that FC Genoa was able to retain a proportion of 50 % of the Player's economic rights, while still being compensated with € 3,000,000, evidences that overall, the financial dimension of the transfer amounted to € 6,000,000 (equalling the amount which would mathematically correspond to 100 % of the economic rights of the Player). The fact that FC Genoa has eventually not been refunded the amount of € 3,000,000, constituted a risk which FC Genoa was willing to take, and of which it consequently also needs to bear the consequences. In this matter, the Sole Arbitrator stated that it is less decisive whether the clubs involved in a player's subsequent transfer may have concluded, in addition, a separate agreement concerning economic rights (in which the player's previous club is not involved in the first place). Rather, the only crucial factor is whether the subsequent transfer overall was, irrespective of its treatment from an accounting point of view, of an economic dimension which reaches the amount agreed upon in the sell-on clause. The Sole Arbitrator, interpreting the stipulated criteria of the sell-on clause in good faith, contented also that if an agreement between two clubs concerning economic rights were of relevance with respect to a previous club's entitlement to a sell-on fee, a club could easily circumvent its respective obligation.

Only one year later, CAS had to decide again in a similar case involving FC Genoa and the transfer of a player to FC Internazionale in combination with a sell-on clause and a participation agreement. In *Genoa Cricket and Football Club S.p.A. v. AC Sparta Praha,*[21] FC Genoa and the Czech football club AC Sparta

[20]Regulated at the time by Article 102bis "Diritto di partecipazione", Norme Organizzative Interne F.I.G.C.; however, since the 2015/2016 season, this regulation has been abolished by the Italian Football Federation.

[21]CAS 2014/A/3701, *Genoa Cricket and Football Club S.p.A. v. AC Sparta Praha*, Award of 11 May 2015.

Praha (hereinafter 'Sparta Praha') concluded a transfer agreement in January 2011 in relation to the permanent transfer of the Czech football player Juraj Kucka (hereinafter the 'Player') from Sparta Praha to FC Genoa for the amount of € 4,000,000. The transfer contract contained a sell-on clause that provided as follows:

> "Genoa and Sparta Praha agree and commit that, in case of future definitely transfer of the Player's sport performances and economic rights from Genoa to another club for a total amount higher than € 3.250.000,00 (including the possible loan fee for the loan of the player to the third club) Genoa will be obliged to pay Sparta Praha a 15 % fee to be calculated from the amount exceeding the abovementioned amount of € 3,250,000.00. Should the Bonus fee agreed under article 5), par. A) be due, the Parties agree that such a 15 % fee shall be calculated upon the final amount anyhow exceeding Euro 3,500,000.00."

In August 2011, as well as in the above mentioned case, FC Genoa and FC Internazionale concluded a transfer contract by which the Player was permanently transferred from FC Genoa to FC Internazionale as well as a participation or sharing agreement, by which it was agreed that FC Internazionale would pay a transfer fee of € 16,000,000, but FC Genoa would pay € 8,000,000 back to FC Internazionale at the same time. In this way, FC Internazionale paid an amount of € 8,000,000 to FC Genoa to acquire the federative rights and, eventually, held 50 % of the economic rights of the Player. On the same day, the Player was immediately loaned from FC Internazionale to FC Genoa, meaning that he was never physically transferred nor played for the *nerazzurri*. In June 2012, FC Internazionale and FC Genoa ended the participation agreement and the Player was permanently transferred back to FC Genoa for a transfer fee of € 13,000,000, whereof FC Internazionale paid back € 6,500,000. In this way, FC Genoa paid an amount of € 6,500,000 to acquire the federative rights as well as the remaining 50 % of the economic rights of the Player. In August 2013, Sparta Praha lodged a claim before FIFA against FC Genoa requesting FC Genoa to pay the amount of € 1,912,500, being 15 % sell-on fee based on the transfer fee paid by FC Internazionale to FC Genoa (€ 16,000,000) after deduction of the transfer fee paid by FC Genoa to Sparta Praha (€ 4,000,000). In April 2014, FIFA's Single Judge of the PSC[22] accepted Sparta Praha's claim and obliged FC Genoa to pay a sell-on fee in the amount of € 1,912,500 to Sparta Praha. The Single Judge was of the opinion that the sell-on clause was triggered by the permanent transfer of the Player from FC Genoa to FC Internazionale notwithstanding the fact that the Player actually never played for Internazionale due to the immediate loan of the Player to FC Genoa. As to the transfer fee to be taken into account, the Single Judge established that the participation agreement was not a part of the transfer of the Player from FC Genoa to FC Internazionale, but only from FC Internazionale back to FC Genoa and that the participation agreement nor the loan were part of the actual transfer, and therefore, the amounts of € 8,000,000 and € 6,500,000 should not be taken into account. In August 2014, FC Genoa lodged an appeal

[22]FIFA PSC, decision of 23 April 2014.

with CAS against the FIFA decision. According to FC Genoa, the true intention of FC Genoa and FC Internazionale was not to transfer the Player permanently but to merely transfer 50 % of the Player's economic rights while retaining his sporting rights. FC Genoa submitted that there were at least 4 compulsory conditions to be met to trigger the sell-on clause: (i) a permanent transfer of the Player; (ii) all sport performances shall be transferred from FC Genoa; (iii) all economic rights shall be transferred from FC Genoa; (iv) the total amount exceeds € 3,250,000. FC Genoa was of the opinion that none of the conditions were met. In May 2015, the CAS Panel partially upheld FC Genoa's appeal. According to the Panel, a definitive transfer must be distinguished from a definitive transfer with participation agreement; however, in both cases there is a definitive transfer of the player's sporting rights. Therefore, contrary to FC Genoa's arguments, the Panel found that the Player was transferred from FC Genoa to FC Internazionale on a permanent basis. The Panel was of the view that in order to trigger the sell-on clause there was no need for a 100 % transfer of the Player's economic rights as the sell-on clause does not make any reference to 100 % of such rights to be sold. Therefore, if together with the so-called federative rights only a portion of the economic rights is transferred, the sell-on clause is triggered. Having established that the sell-on clause was triggered by the transfer of the Player from FC Genoa to FC Internazionale, the Panel had to further decide on which amount the sell-on fee had to be calculated. In this respect, the Panel adhered to the view expressed in *Helsingborgs IF v. Parma FC S.p.A.*, insofar as it differs from the approach taken in *Genoa Cricket and Football Club v. Club Atlético Peñarol* both previously examined. On this basis, the Panel was of the opinion that the sell-on fee had to be calculated on the amount actually received by the club and not on the higher amount of the first definitive transfer with participation (€ 16,000,000) that was considered as only indicative. In this case the amount actually received by FC Genoa for the federative transfer of the Player from FC Genoa to FC Internazionale was € 8,000,000. Therefore, the Panel decided that FC Sparta Praha was entitled to a sell-on fee of € 712.500, being 15 % of (€ 8,000,000–€ 3,250,000).

It is remarkable to compare the two CAS decisions involving FC Genoa, in which the arbitrators concluded in a totally different way. Whilst in *Genoa Cricket and Football Club v. Club Atlético Peñarol* the Sole Arbitrator confirmed the FIFA decision and was of the opinion that the participation agreement should not be taken into account for calculating the sell-on fee as a percentage of the transfer fee received, the Panel in *Genoa Cricket and Football Club S.p.A. v. AC Sparta Praha* set aside the FIFA decision and concluded that the participation agreement has to be taken into account in relation to the actual transfer fee received. It has to be considered that CAS will normally decide on a 'case by case' approach, based on the evidence and substance of the specific file, although it can be highlighted that, the view of the Panel in *Genoa Cricket and Football Club S.p.A. v. AC Sparta Praha* seems to correspond with the CAS established jurisprudence[23] stating that,

[23] CAS 2012/A/2875, *Helsingborgs IF v. Parma FC*, para 73.

in general, the sell-on fee has to be calculated on the transfer fee actually received by the selling party. The authors of this article consider the Panel's view in the Sparta Praha case to be the more appropriate one, as the reasoning behind the sell-on clause is to share profit, which is only possible in relation to the amount of a transfer fee actually received by a club.

4.3 Case Commentary: CAS 2014/A/3508—Areas of Dispute

4.3.1 Factual and Procedural Background

An interesting award was rendered recently by CAS, dealing with several possible areas of dispute in relation to the sell-on clause. The case involved two Russian clubs and, therefore, the dispute was decided in first instance and appeal by the Football Union of Russia applying Russian law, before it was dealt with by CAS applying, subsidiarily, Swiss law. In December 2005, the Russian football club Lokomotiv Moscow (hereinafter 'FC Lokomotiv') and Russian football club FC Nika (hereinafter 'FC Nika') entered into an agreement for the permanent transfer of the Russian football player Denis Borisovich Glushakov (hereinafter the 'Player') from FC Nika to FC Lokomotiv for the amount of $ 300,000. The transfer contract between FC Lokomotiv and FC Nika contained the following sell-on clause: "FC Lokomotiv undertakes to pay FC Nika 15 % of the amount received for the transfer of D.B. Glushakov from FC Lokomotiv to another football club". In June 2006, FC Lokomotiv and Russian football club FC SKA Rostov-on-Don (hereinafter 'FC Rostov') entered into an agreement for the transfer of the Player from FC Lokomotiv to FC Rostov without payment of any transfer fee. In November 2006, the Player terminated his employment contract with FC Rostov and the next day, he signed again an employment contract with FC Lokomotiv. In February 2007, the Player was transferred on a loan basis from FC Lokomotiv to Russian football club OGU PFC Zvezda (hereinafter 'FC Zvezda'), from which he returned to FC Lokomotiv in December 2007 upon expiry of the loan. Finally, in June 2013, FC Lokomotiv entered into a transfer agreement with Russian football club FC Spartak Moscow (hereinafter 'FC Spartak') for the permanent transfer of the Player from FC Lokomotiv to FC Spartak for the contractual agreed amount of € 8,000,000. Following this transfer of the Player from FC Lokomotiv to FC Spartak, FC Nika contacted FC Lokomotiv regarding the sell-on clause, on the basis of which it claimed a sell-on fee equalling 15 % of the transfer fee received from FC Spartak. As FC Lokomotiv did not respond to such request, FC Nika filed a claim with the Dispute Resolution Chamber of the Football Union of Russia (hereinafter the 'FUR DRC'). In August 2013, the FUR DRC[24] accepted FC

[24]FUR DRC Resolution no. 112–13, decision of 22 August 2013.

Nika's claim and ordered FC Lokomotiv to pay FC Nika a sell-on fee in the amount of € 1,200,000, being 15 % of € 8,000,000. FC Lokomotiv in its turn filed an appeal against the decision of the FUR DRC with the Players' Status Committee of the Football Union of Russia (hereinafter the 'FUR PSC'). In December 2013, the FUR PSC[25] dismissed FC Lokomotiv's appeal and confirmed the FUR DRC decision. The FUR PSC was of the opinion that only the permanent transfer of the Player from FC Lokomotiv to FC Spartak triggered the sell-on clause, as the transfer of the Player from FC Lokomotiv to FC Rostov had to be considered as a loan and not a permanent transfer due to several circumstances such as the fact that no transfer fee was paid by FC Rostov whilst FC Lokomotiv had purchased the Player for $ 300,000 from FC Nika and the short term of the Player's stay with FC Rostov and his consequent return to FC Lokomotiv. FC Lokomotiv appealed the decision to CAS.

4.3.2 Decision of the Panel

FC Lokomotiv's principal submission was that the transfer of the Player from FC Lokomotiv to FC Rostov was a permanent transfer and not a loan as wrongly established by the FUR PSC, and therefore, triggered the sell-on clause. As no transfer fee was received, the sell-on fee was equal to zero euros and FC Nika's rights to claim a sell-on fee were consequently extinguished. Subsidiarily, Lokomotiv was of the opinion, in the event that the Panel would decide that the sell-on fee was triggered by the transfer of the Player from FC Lokomotiv to FC Spartak, that the sell-on fee should be calculated on the amount actually received by FC Lokomotiv in Russian roubles, being RUR 355,251,600 and not on the initially contractually agreed amount of € 8,000,000, which equals to a much higher amount in Russian roubles due to rate fluctuations. According to FC Nika on the other hand, there were two conditions to be fulfilled to trigger the sell-on clause: (i) the Player being transferred from FC Lokomotiv to a third club on a permanent basis, and (ii) Lokomotiv having received a transfer fee from a third club for the Player. Therefore, the question whether the transfer of the Player to FC Rostov was a permanent transfer or a loan was irrelevant, FC Lokomotiv did not receive a transfer fee and, therefore, the sell-on clause was not triggered as the second condition was not met. Only the permanent transfer of the Player to FC Spartak where FC Lokomotiv received a transfer fee triggered the sell-on clause. In March 2015, the Panel decided to partially uphold the appeal of FC Lokomotiv. The main issues to be resolved by the Panel, which applied the FUR regulations and, subsidiairily, Russian and Swiss law, were to establish what the conditions were for the sell-on clause to be triggered, whether the transfer from FC Lokomotiv to FC Rostov was

[25]FUR PSC Resolution no. 112–13K, decision of 5 December 2013.

a permanent transfer or a loan, and on what amount the sell-on fee had to be calculated.[26] First, the Panel was of the opinion that an interpretation problem existed between the parties about the true meaning of the sell-on clause and on what condition(s) it would be triggered. In this regard, the Panel did not agree with FC Nika and came to the conclusion that there was only one condition to be fulfilled to trigger the sell-on clause, this being a permanent transfer of the Player from FC Lokomotiv to a third club.[27] Therefore, following the first permanent transfer of the Player from FC Lokomotiv to a third club, even if there was no transfer fee received, the sell-on clause would be triggered and FC Nika's rights to a sell-on fee would be extinguished. Second, the Panel agreed with the FUR PSC that, although the transfer of the Player from FC Lokomotiv to FC Rostov was formalised as a permanent transfer, there were several circumstances, which indicated that the transfer was in reality a loan.[28] Consequently, the Panel concluded that FC Lokomotiv simulated a fictitious transfer, therefore, the simulated act (the permanent transfer) is without effect and the concealed act (the loan) is deemed valid.[29] On the basis of the foregoing, the Panel established that only the permanent transfer from FC Lokomotiv to FC Spartak triggered the sell-on clause. Finally, the Panel agreed with FC Lokomotiv that the sell-on fee should be calculated on the amount actually received by Lokomotiv, being RUR 355,251,600, and therefore, awarded FC Nika a sell-on fee in the amount of RUR 53,287,470.[30]

4.3.3 Commentary

4.3.3.1 Interpretation Principles

A difference in interpretation of the sell-on clause is a recurring cause for disputes between two parties having recourse to a sell-on clause. Therefore, it is always very important to be clear and unambiguous while drafting the clause and its conditions to be triggered. Many wordings can be confusing or misleading, especially in relation to the exact conditions to be fulfilled to trigger the sell-on clause and the exact amount of the payable sell-on fee. In the event of such interpretative disputes, the CAS has an established jurisprudence[31] in applying the interpretation

[26] CAS 2014/A/3508, *FC Lokomotiv v. Football Union of Russia & FC Nika*, para 169.

[27] Ibid., para 180.

[28] Ibid., para 194.

[29] Ibid., para 201.

[30] Ibid., paras 212–214.

[31] See for example: CAS 2004/A/642, *Hertha BSC Berlin v. G. & Club Atlético River Plate & RCD Mallorca*, Award of 1 March 2005; CAS 2005/A/871, *FC Rodopa v. Markovitch*, Award of 19 September 2006; CAS 2005/A/896, *Fulham FC v. FC Metz*; CAS 2010/A/2098, *Sevilla FC v. RC Lens*.

principles according to Swiss law.[32] Article 18(1) CO provides as follows: "When assessing the form and terms of a contract, the true and common intention of the parties must be ascertained without dwelling on any inexact expressions or designations they may have used either in error or by way of disguising the true nature of the agreement". On this basis, Swiss scholars[33] and case law[34] have indicated that the primary goal of interpretation is to ascertain the true common intentions (consensus) of the parties. Where a factual consensus cannot be proven, the declarations of the parties must be interpreted pursuant to the principle of good faith in the sense in which they could and should have been understood, taking into account the wording, the context as well as all circumstances. In addition to the wording of the contract, arbitrators can consider evidence of the circumstances in which the contract was concluded, the parties' respective interests, the purpose or objective of the contract, and usage in a specific industry. They can also consider the conduct and declarations of the parties before the contract was concluded, in particular their negotiations and subjective declarations of intent, as well as their conduct after the contract was concluded.

4.3.3.2 Aims and Conditions of the Sell-on Clause

The Panel reiterated the meaning and aim of the sell-on clause as it was already established by previous CAS jurisprudence.[35] According to this jurisprudence, sell-on clauses providing for such kind of risk-sharing and of participation of a transferring club in possible, uncertain gains obtained by the new club in the event of a further transfer to a third club, are not uncommon in international transfer agreements of football players. Their economic rationale is, generally, that by agreeing into such arrangement, the transferring club accepts to receive, in a first instance, a lower first transfer fee, with the expectation of receiving an additional fee if the recipient club will be able to transfer, with profit, the player to a third club. It does, however, not provide for a guarantee of an additional fee. In the present case, the Panel further established that it is indeed true that the idea of a sell-on clause is to share profit between two clubs where a potential higher transfer fee is obtained, but it cannot be accepted that a sell-on clause can only be triggered when the player is permanently transferred, with profit. After all, there is no guarantee that the player will be transferred to a third club for a higher amount than the transfer fee agreed upon between the first two clubs. It is possible that a player

[32]In the present case, the Panel applied Russian law on interpretation principles, in particular Article 431 of the Russian Civil Code, which applies the same principles.

[33]Wiegand (2015), para 7 et seq., ad Article 18 CO.

[34]SFT 4A_124/2014, decision of 7 July 2014, para 3.4.1.

[35]See for example: CAS 2005/A/848, *Internacional v. Bayer*; CAS 2005/A/896, *Fulham FC v. FC Metz*; CAS 2007/A/1219, *Sekondi Hasaacas FC v. Borussia Mönchengladbach*; CAS 2010/A/2098, *Sevilla FC v. RC Lens*.

could be transferred for a lower fee or no compensation, due to a long-term injury or lack of talent. As a conclusion, it can be accepted in general that the only condition to be fulfilled to trigger a sell-on clause is the permanent transfer of a player to a third club. If the player is permanently transferred to a third club for a lower transfer fee or no fee at all, the sell-on fee will still need to be calculated on this amount. Of course, it goes without saying that it depends on the drafting of the sell-on clause, as more conditions can be added in accordance to the parties' agreement.

4.3.3.3 The Simulated Transfer

Another interesting issue in the *FC Lokomotiv v. Football Union of Russia & FC Nika* case is the simulated transfer entered into by FC Lokomotiv to avoid having to pay the sell-on fee to FC Nika. The Panel was of the opinion that enough evidence existed to establish that the transfer of the player from FC Lokomotiv to FC Rostov was in fact a loan and not a permanent transfer, following which it did not trigger the sell-on clause.[36] In this respect, the Panel based its decision regarding simulation and its consequences on long-standing case law of the Swiss Federal Tribunal, which defines as simulated act as follows: "Within the meaning of article 18 of the Swiss Code of Obligations, a simulation exists when both parties agree that the legal effects corresponding to the objective meaning of their statement must not occur and that they have only wanted to create the appearance of a legal act towards third parties".[37]

4.3.3.4 Sell-on Fee—Calculation Basis

The last issue in the award concerned the amount on which the sell-on fee needs to be calculated once the conditions to trigger the sell-on clause are fulfilled. Also here, CAS is developing an established jurisprudence,[38] by which it is generally accepted that a sell-on fee is to be based on the transfer fee amount actually received by a club for selling a player to a subsequent club and not an indicative amount. It often happens that the parties of the transfer agreement agree on a certain transfer fee, but that on the date of the actual payment, another amount is being paid as the final transfer fee. In this particular case, FC Lokomotiv and FC Spartak agreed a transfer fee in euros, however, due to Russian legislation, the payment of the transfer fee was made in Russian roubles. For obvious reasons as argued by FC Nika, due to exchange rate fluctuations, this created a substantial

[36]CAS 2014/A/3508, *FC Lokomotiv v. Football Union of Russia & FC Nika*, paras 194–202.

[37]SFT, 4A_429/2012, decision of 2 November 2012. See also SFT 123 IV 61 at p. 68.

[38]See for example CAS 2007/A/1219, *Sekondi Hasaacas FC v. Borussia Mönchengladbach*; CAS 2014/A/3701, *Genoa Cricket and Football Club v. Sparta Praha.*

difference in value of the sell-on fee. The Panel, however, stated that this could not be taken into account and that the sell-on fee had to be calculated on the amount actually received by the club, being in Russian roubles. It is therefore important to clarify in the sell-on clause the exact criteria on which the sell-on fee should be calculated, including currency and/or exchange rate.

4.4 Sell-on Fees and Third Party Ownership (TPO)

In December 2014, FIFA's Executive Committee approved the implementation of article 18ter in the FIFA RSTP banning the third-party ownership (TPO) of players' economic rights, which came into force on 1 May 2015. According to Article 18ter(1) FIFA RSTP, "no club or player shall enter into an agreement with a third party whereby a third party is being entitled to participate, either in full or in part, in compensation payable in relation to the future transfer of a player from one club to another, or is being assigned any rights in relation to a future transfer or transfer compensation". This provision was implemented to protect the integrity of the competition and the independence of clubs and it was especially implemented against the influence of investment companies. In the new FIFA Regulations on Working with Intermediaries that came into force on 1 April 2015, a similar provision was implemented by Article 7(4) which stipulates that payments between clubs in relation to transfers shall not be paid to intermediaries and that intermediaries cannot own any interest in any transfer compensation or future transfer value of a player. Whilst FIFA prohibited investment companies and agents from having any interest in the future transfer value of players, there are no such provisions in FIFA regulations prohibiting clubs (and players themselves) from having a percentage in future transfer values of the said players. In some countries,[39] it is established by law that, in the event of a transfer of the player, a certain percentage of the transfer fee has to be paid to the player being transferred. Consequently and factually, with regard to clubs, this seems to confirm the use of sell-on clauses, by which clubs keep an interest in the future transfer values of their former players. Based on the wording of the new FIFA regulations, at least for clubs this practice seems not to fall under the scope of Article 18ter FIFA RSTP, so it is not to be considered as banned under new TPO rules.[40] However, FIFA informed its members by Circular no. 1502 of 28 September 2015 that, as of 1 October 2015, Article 4(2) of Annex 3 FIFA RSTP will be amended and clubs will be obliged to declare

---

[39]For example: Argentina (Article 8 CCT No. 577/2009) and Spain (Article 16 Resolución de 25 de septiembre de 2014, de la Dirección General de Empleo, por la que se registra y publica el Convenio colectivo para la actividad de fútbol profesional).

[40]And what about Agents, after the recent FIFA reform on Intermediaries? Interest in the transfer is banned, but a substantial percentage as "professional services" couldn't be equivalent? It will be interesing to follow the develpoments in practice and case law.

all sell-on fees in relation to transfers into the Transfer Matching System (TMS). Additionally, clubs will have the duty to declare in TMS any sell-on clause included in the transfer agreement that forms the basis of a specific transaction. This measure is intended to improve clarity and transparency as regards payments made in relation to an international transfer of a player. Equally, it will enhance legal security.

4.5 Conclusion

As said above, and commonly well known in the football industry, a so-called 'sell-on clause' is an additional clause to a contract negotiated between two clubs when a transfer of a player takes place (or, using a 'sale' terminology, that is often used in the common practice, when a club 'buys a player from another club'). It means that if and when the club, who 'buys' the player, will 'sell' him, the original club is entitled to a percentage of that transfer fee, being the so-called 'sell-on fee'.

These clauses are most common in transfers involving young players. This is because if the player happens to become very successful and the new signing club makes a subsequent and future big money transfer, then the original club who found and trained him can still profit from his success. This is a recurrent situation, and the 'weak club' has a legal way out in order to maximise return in the short and in the midterm. It is a commercial practice widely used by 'smaller clubs' that on a regular basis transfer promising young stars to 'bigger clubs'. For 'small clubs' keeping talented young players becomes more difficult when 'big clubs' take interest in those players. Often some transfer proposals are difficult to refuse and must be finalised in the interest of the financial management of the club, but such clauses can safeguard to some extent the longer-term economic returns for the club itself against missing out on the player's talents by granting a share of any future higher transfer fees. In this case, a sell-on clause could (or, better, should) be combined with a clear contractual provision, specifying at least the transfer fee returns: often, as in the *Sevilla* case examined, the parties are dividing the compensation to be paid by the new club into two components: a fixed amount (i.e. the transfer fee), payable upon the transfer of the player to the new club, and a variable, notional amount (i.e. the sell-on fee), payable to the old club in the event of a subsequent 'sale' of the player from the new club to a third club.

Those contractual agreements and specific clauses are often controversial due to a poor contractual drafting of the said clause or to pathological situations. As seen, most of the disputes arise from the interpretation of the term 'transfer' or 'sale', which can include (or not) loans. Other possible conflicts may arise on the amount of the transfer fee based on which the sell-on fee should be calculated, being the total fee or a fraction of it; very controversial in this regard was the peculiar situation in Italian football related to the so-called 'co-ownership/participation' (or *compartecipazioni/comproprietà*), which is still in use in some other countries.

However, it is a recurrent indication in the relevant jurisprudence of FIFA and CAS that a sell-on clause, normally referred to a 'resale' of a player, appears to apply not to any and all subsequent transfers of the player to a new club, but only to either of those transfers which are based on a mutual agreement or a contract. Therefore, where the right of the player to put an end to the employment agreement, and the corresponding obligation to pay an indemnity, is based on the legal consequences of a breach of contract and not on the mutual consent of the parties of the employment agreement itself and/or the termination of the employment agreement is the result of the exercise of a statutory right of the player, the transfer of the player occurs outside any contractual scheme. Consequently, the interpretation of a provision (the sell-on clause) contained in the transfer agreement and the calculation of the additional payment to be possibly made under it, does not include the amount received by the 'selling club' on the basis of an indemnification clause, because it is not considered a transfer fee, but a compensation for the damage sustained because of the unilateral breach by the player of the employment agreement. In other terms, the sell-on mechanism is not triggered.

The interpretation of the 'real and common intent of the parties', pursuant to the mentioned principles, beyond the literal meaning of the words used in the said sell-on clause, is used in order to determine its implications. The same principles are applied in the event of simulation acts, whereby clubs try to circumvent their payment obligation on the basis of the sell-on clause. This can occur as previously described in the *Lokomotiv* case, where a club simulates a permanent transfer for no transfer fee and then re-employs the player. In that way, the transfer would have triggered the sell-on clause, however, the sell-on fee would equal zero. To this respect, CAS has found that such a simulated act is without legal effects. Yet, it is the beneficiary of the sell-on fee who bears the burden of proving the existence of a simulation in order to safeguard the validity of the sell-on clause.

As far as TPO is concerned, it can be concluded that sell-on clauses do not fall under the scope of FIFA's TPO ban, as long as only clubs are involved. However, if one of the beneficiaries of the sell-on fee is a private investment company or an intermediary, the TPO ban will come into play. Therefore, FIFA recently amended the RSTP once again, obliging clubs to declare all sell-on fees included in transfer agreements into TMS, as more transparency will lead to stronger legal certainty.

In conclusion, are sell-on clauses to be considered legitimate and legally binding in general terms? Looking at the solid jurisprudence at FIFA and CAS level, together with the evolution of the FIFA Regulations, the answer is positive.

Acknowledgments We gratefully acknowledge the cooperation Luca Tettamanti for the case-law research and discussion of legal issues thereof.

Reference

Wiegand W (2015) Artikel 18 OR. In: Honsell H, Vogt NP, Wiegand P (eds) Basler Kommentar. Obligationenrecht I, Helbing Lichtenhahn Verlag, Basel

Chapter 5
CAS Provisional and Conservatory Measures and Other Options to Be Granted Interim Legal Relief

Ian Blackshaw and Thilo Pachmann

Abstract Article R37 of the CAS Code of Sports-related Arbitration empowers the CAS to grant provisional and conservatory measures for parties bound by the Code. When deciding whether to grant such measures, the CAS reviews whether (a) the relief is necessary to protect the applicant from irreparable harm, (b) the likelihood of success on the merits of the claim and (c) whether the interests of the applicant outweigh those of the respondent. Despite the fact that under the terms of Article R37 of the Code, the parties seeking provisional and conservatory measures expressly waive their rights to request the same type of measures from the ordinary competent courts, jurisprudence shows that state courts at least have parallel competence. First and foremost, the general exclusion of legal protection in advance is not valid as the CAS system does not offer a protection similar to the state courts. Additionally, state courts can usually act faster than the CAS. If third parties are affected, the CAS has no competence whereas state courts can order provisional measures against third parties. Contrary to provisional measures issued by state courts, there is no possibility to appeal provisional measures ordered by the CAS. However, once the CAS has issued its arbitral award, interim legal relief can be requested at the Swiss Federal Tribunal.

Keywords CAS · Preliminary measures · State courts' jurisdiction · International enforceability of provisional measures · R37 · CAS code

I. Blackshaw
Anglia Ruskin University, Cambridge, UK
e-mail: ian.blackshaw@orange.fr

T. Pachmann (✉)
Pachmann Rechtsanwälte, Zurich, Switzerland
e-mail: thilo.pachmann@pachmannlaw.ch

A. Duval and A. Rigozzi (eds.), *Yearbook of International Sports Arbitration 2015*,
DOI 10.1007/978-94-6265-129-6_5

Contents

5.1 Introductory Remarks

Like other arbitral bodies, such as the International Court of Arbitration of the International Chamber of Commerce, based in Paris, the CAS offers parties in ordinary and appeal arbitration proceedings, including cases coming before the CAS Ad Hoc Division, which sits during the Summer and Winter Olympic Games, the possibility of applying for and, in appropriate cases, being granted, within a short timeframe, certain protective measures, known as 'Provisional and Conservatory Measures', pursuant to the provisions of Article R37 of the CAS Code.[1]

---

[1]At the time of writing, the latest version of the CAS Code of Sports-related Arbitration dates from 1 March 2013, and Article R37 CAS Code reads as follow:

"No party may apply for provisional or conservatory measures under these Procedural Rules before all internal legal remedies provided for in the rules of the federation or sports-body concerned have been exhausted.

Upon filing of the request for provisional measures, the Applicant shall pay a non-refundable Court Office fee of Swiss francs 1000—without which CAS shall not proceed. The CAS Court Office fee shall not be paid again upon filing of the request for arbitration or of the statement of appeal in the same procedure.

The President of the relevant Division, prior to the transfer of the file to the Panel, or thereafter the Panel may, upon application by a party, make an order for provisional or conservatory measures. In agreeing to submit any dispute subject to the ordinary arbitration procedure or to the appeal arbitration procedure to these Procedural Rules, the parties expressly waive their rights to request such measures from state authorities or tribunals.

Should an application for provisional measures be filed, the President of the relevant Division or the Panel shall invite the other party (or parties) to express a position within ten days or within a shorter time limit if circumstances so require. The President of the relevant Division or the Panel shall issue an order on an expedited basis and shall first rule on the prima facie CAS jurisdiction. The Division President may terminate the arbitration procedure if he rules that the CAS clearly has no jurisdiction. In cases of utmost urgency, the President of the relevant Division, prior to the transfer of the file to the Panel, or thereafter the President of the Panel may issue an order upon mere presentation of the application, provided that the opponent is subsequently heard. When deciding whether to award preliminary relief, the President of the Division or the Panel, as the case may be, shall consider whether the relief is necessary to protect the applicant

As can be seen from the text of Article R37, which is set out in footnote no. 1, the kinds of preliminary measures that the CAS Arbitrators can issue in a given case are not specified or limited. Thus, the CAS has wide powers in this matter.

But traditionally in arbitral proceedings generally, these measures tend to fall into three broad categories as follows:

- measures to facilitate the proceedings, such as orders to safeguard vital evidence;
- measures aimed at preserving the *status quo* during the proceedings, such as those that preserve the object of the proceedings; and
- measures that safeguard the future enforceability of the decision, such as those concerning property.

For example, in the infamous '*Skategate*' case during the 2002 Salt Lake City Winter Games, an order was imposed on the judges not to leave the Olympic village before the CAS Ad Hoc Division had investigated the circumstances in which the disputed medal had been awarded.[2] In doping cases, orders have been made to preserve samples taken during a disputed doping control.

However, preliminary measures can never exceed the object of the dispute. Thus, such measures cannot be issued against anyone who is not a party to the dispute; or anyone else who is not bound by the arbitration agreement signed by the applicant seeking the preliminary measures.

5.2 Criteria for Granting CAS Provisional and Conservatory Measures

5.2.1 Overview

As will be seen from the abovementioned provisions of Article R37 of the CAS Code, when deciding whether to award any preliminary relief, the following considerations shall be taken into account:

- whether the relief is necessary to protect the applicant from irreparable harm;
- the likelihood of success on the merits of the claim; and
- whether the interests of the Applicant outweigh those of the Respondent(s).

Footnote 1 (continued)
from irreparable harm, the likelihood of success on the merits of the claim, and whether the interests of the Applicant outweigh those of the Respondent(s).

The procedure for provisional measures and the provisional measures already granted, if any, are automatically annulled if the party requesting them does not file a related request for arbitration within 10 days following the filing of the request for provisional measures (ordinary procedure) or any statement of appeal within the time limit provided by Article R49 of the Code (appeals procedure). Such time limits cannot be extended. Provisional and conservatory measures may be made conditional upon the provision of security."

[2]CAS ad hoc Division 02/004, *Canadian Olympic Association v. ISU*, Order of 14 February 2002.

According to CAS jurisprudence, these criteria need to be met cumulatively.

Hence, an Ad Hoc Panel sitting at the Salt Lake City Winter Olympics held that: "… each of these considerations is relevant, but any of them may be decisive on the facts of a particular case".[3]

In other words, the CAS must take all of the circumstances of the particular case into account, including the above criteria, when deciding whether or not to grant any preliminary relief.

However, before these criteria are discussed the applicant must meet the procedural matters. As Despina Mavromati & Matthieu Reeb point out[4]: "In the case of a request for provisional measures, the manifest lack of jurisdiction is apparent at the outset of the arbitration proceedings and the procedure is not set in motion. In these cases, the CAS Office sends a letter to the claimant/appellant". Hence, the authors will first discuss the procedural issues before coming to the criteria under which circumstances provisional measures are granted. Finally, some considerations on the enforcement of the arbitral awards are made.

5.2.2 Procedural Requirements

5.2.2.1 Time Limit

No actual time limit is laid down for the issuing of an Order for CAS Provisional and Conservatory Measures. Article R37 of the CAS Code merely provides for the Order to be issued "within a short time". In other words, urgently, which depends upon the requirements of each particular case. Such urgency is linked to the need to avoid the risk of irreparable harm being caused.

However, in deciding on the time limit for ordering provisional measures, it has been held that there is no urgency for a stay of execution where the applicant has contributed significantly to such urgency, by delaying the filing of the application for the provisional measures and by requesting the close to the expiration of the time limit.[5]

In cases of utmost urgency, it is possible for the CAS to issue an order for provisional measures based solely on the application—in other words, *ex-parte.*[6] In such cases, the CAS must give the other party an opportunity to be heard by filing a reply, but the deadlines for doing this are very short indeed—for example, three days.

---

[3]Ibid.

[4]Mavromati and Reeb 2015, p. 205. See also CAS 2011/A/2410, *A v. IF & G.*, Order of 23 May 2011, para 28.

[5]CAS 2008/A/1569, *Kurten v. FEI*, Order of 20 June 2008, para 6.4.2.

[6]See CAS 2008/A/ 1656, *PFC Botev 1912—Plovdiv AD v. BFU & Hristov*, Award of 18 November 2008, para 3.9.

In certain cases of utmost urgency, it might be reasonable to apply directly to the state court, as arbitral tribunals are sometimes even more reluctant than state courts to grant (*ex-parte*) provisional measures.

In the past, Swiss civil courts have quite often—and sometimes even within a day or two—ordered provisional measures in sporting matters. A Swiss civil court has, for example, accepted its competence for granting *ex-parte* provisional measures in a case against UEFA, due to the fact that the matter was of such urgency, that it was not timely for the parties to establish the competence of the CAS.[7]

The CAS will need to prove in the future that it is in a position to act as quickly and efficiently as state courts. Until this has been shown in reality, the legal protection through provisional measures by the CAS is not on an equal footing as the protection afforded through state courts.

5.2.2.2 Exhaustion of Remedies Before Sports Federation or Body

The CAS Code explicitly states in R37 that the prerequisite of granting provisional measures is the exhaustion of all legal remedies within the sports federation or body.

This procedural requirement outlined in the CAS Code is quite peculiar as the help of arbitral tribunals and other courts in matters of utmost urgency is in particular necessary if there is no time to exhaust all internal remedies of a sports federation or body. For this reason, it is necessary to take a short look back at how this rule developed and whether state courts offer more effective legal protection due to this requirement.

In the earlier CAS awards, the President of the Division or the Panel had to "first rule on the CAS jurisdiction".[8] In the 2010 revision of the CAS Code of Sports-related Arbitration, the following was added: "the Division President may terminate the arbitration procedure if he rules that the CAS has manifestly no jurisdiction". This phrase was retained in the 2013 revision, but manifestly was replaced by the word "clearly".

Akin to the exhaustion of legal remedies is the situation where a request for provisional measures is declared to be "premature"—that is, before the decision being appealed has become effective.[9] The development of this procedural requirement, hence, shows how reluctant the CAS takes on matters which are still in the hand of the sports federation or body.

Interestingly, no such rule exists before a Swiss state court. The question is only whether there is irreparable harm done if the Swiss state courts do not

[7]Schweizer 2011, ad Article 374 Swiss Code of Civil Procedure, para 10; also Civil Court of the Canton Tribunal Vaud MP 2011/22, *Y. SA v. UEFA*, Order of 27 September 2011, para IV.c).

[8]CAS 98/202, *Peristeri AC v. FIBA*, Order of 13 July 1998, see Reeb 2002, pp. 750–751.

[9]CAS 2012/A/2993, *Liberia Football Association v. Confederation Africaine de Football (CAF)*, Order of 30 November 2012, para 49.

intervene. However, if time allows and there are legal remedies within a Sports Federation available, it is certainly advisable to exhaust these legal remedies as a state court might rule that, due to the failure to act earlier, the plaintiff has forfeited the right to apply for provisional measures.

The fact that CAS requires the exhaustion of all legal remedies within a sports federation or body shows as well that the legal protection through provisional measures by the CAS is not yet on the same footing as the protection afforded through state courts.

5.2.2.3 Security

Again, under Article R37, provisional and conservatory measures may be made conditional on the provision of security by the party seeking them (para 4). Such security is often a financial guarantee to be given by the applicant seeking such measures against any possible loss suffered by the party subject to the restraining measures, in case the applicant is not ultimately successful in the proceedings. This happens in civil litigation quite often when an interim injunction is awarded by the court.

If such a request for security is made, the CAS Panel will usually issue what is known as an "Order on Request for Security for Costs".[10] The order on the security of costs can also be granted on article 183 para 1 of the PILA.[11]

5.2.2.4 Expedited Measures

Article R44(4) of the CAS Code provides, in addition, expedited measures to be ordered by the CAS, with the consent of the parties. This is a measure which is very valuable in relation to sporting disputes, where deadlines and time pressures often apply. For example, a sports person or a team, who has been denied eligibility to compete in a particular sporting event that is soon to take place, need to have their dispute settled very quickly if the possibility of competing is to remain open and not lost through any delay.

As mentioned, the expedited procedure cannot be imposed on the parties: both/all parties must consent for the CAS Panel to proceed in accordance with the provisions of Article R44(4).[12] This consent to an expedited CAS Arbitration Proceedings may be made expressly in advance in the corresponding Arbitration Clause, using such language as: "the procedures shall be conducted in an expedited manner".[13]

---

[10]CAS 2004/A/780, *Ch. Maicon Henning v. Prudentopolis SC & FIFA*, Order of 6 January 2005, para 7.2.

[11]CAS 2011/A/2360 & 2392, *English Chess Federation and Georgian Chess Federation vs. Fédération Internationale des Echecs (FIDE)*, Order of 27 June 2011, Order of 27 June 2011, para 2.2.

[12]CAS 2007/O/1440, *P. v. C.*, Award of 21 October 2008, para 3.22.

[13]CAS 2011/O/2627, *L. v. K.*, Award of 6 June 2012, paras 3.2 and 3.3.

5.2.2.5 "Stay of Execution"

Again, Article R48 of the Code also allows a party to obtain a "stay of execution" of the decision appealed against, provided a request to that effect is made at the time of filing the statement of appeal with the CAS and also reasons are given in support of such request. This measure is particularly apposite in appeals against bans for doping offences even though the CAS seems to be more reluctant to grant such a stay of execution[14] than the Swiss state courts.[15] But it has also been invoked in a variety of other cases, including a decision to have a football match played on neutral territory to avoid a risk of terrorism in the host club's country. If the request is not made at the time of filing the appeal, it is lost; the assumption being that there is no urgency, otherwise this would have been pleaded at the outset.

Apart from doping cases, applications for a stay of execution can also be made for all decisions of sports bodies, including, for example, decisions to change a result following a protest[16]; decisions to refuse the participation of a team owned by the same shareholder as another team[17]; and decisions to have a match played on neutral territory due to the risk of a terrorist attack in the host club's country.[18]

In another case, the CAS refused an application for a stay of execution of a decision of a sports federation, domiciled in Switzerland, which ordered the payment of a sum of money because the filing of an appeal on the merits of the case is sufficient to exclude enforcement of the debt by the Swiss Authorities.[19]

As a side note, it needs to be mentioned that it is advisable generally to request a stay of execution as the Swiss Federal Tribunal has held in a very surprising decision that an athlete loses the right to appeal after the ban or suspension has lapsed. This was true in the *Walilko* case. Igor Walilko, a twelve year old go-kart driver, was suspended for 24 months by the International Automobile Federation for doping. Walilko contested the ban at the CAS, which reduced his ban to 18 months. Walilko appealed to the Swiss Federal Tribunal requesting annulment of the ban. The appeal did not have (and was not requested to have) suspensive effect. As the ban ended during the time of the proceedings, the Swiss Federal Tribunal ruled that Walilko did not have any legitimate interest in the proceedings any more.[20]

---

[14]CAS 2000A/274, *Susin v. FINA*, Award of 19 October 2000, see Reeb 2002,p. 755; CAS 97/169, *Menegotto v. FIC*, Order of 15 May 1997, see Reeb 2002, p. 539.

[15]SFT 4P.148/2006, decision of 10 January 2007; SFT 4A_612/2009, order of 7 December 2010.

[16]CAS 98/190, *HC Prilly v. LSHG*, Order of 10 March 1998, see Reeb 2002, p. 747.

[17]CAS 98/200, *AEK Athenes & Slavia Prague v. UEFA*, Award of 20 August 1999, see Reeb 2002, pp. 38 and 42.

[18]CAS press release of 3 December 2003.

[19]CAS 2003/O/460, *Wüstenrot Salzburg v. Bukran*, Award of 16 June 2003, para 5.3, cited *verbatim* in CAS 2003/O/486, *Fulham v. OL*, Award of 15 September 2003, para 13.

[20]SFT 4A_636/2011, decision of 18 June 2012, para 2.3.2.

5.2.3 Substantial Criteria for Granting Provisional Measures

As already outlined, there are three criteria which need to be fulfilled to successfully request a provisional measure according to the CAS jurisprudence[21]: Irreparable harm, the likelihood of success on the merits and the balance of interests. These criteria are basically the same as in front of Swiss state courts.[22]

5.2.3.1 Irreparable Harm

In order to grant provisional measures, irreparable harm for the applicant must be anticipated. Irreparable harm is defined as a disadvantage that can at a later stage not be determined, measured or compensated.

Irreparable harm may be of a financial and/or moral nature. In this regard it needs to be noted that irreparable harm should only be determined in relation to the applicant and not its surroundings.[23] As it is difficult to establish the actual damage and its quantum, it is sufficient to establish the 'plausibility' of the irreparable harm. In certain cases, the mere possibility of irreparable harm being suffered by the applicant for provisional measures will be sufficient to satisfy this important requirement.[24]

The risk of irreparable harm must be specific and not based on general considerations, such as the young age of the applicant athlete or the risk that a sporting career may be adversely affected.[25] Hence, alleged damage to an applicant athlete's reputation should be supported by compelling facts in order to satisfy the requirement of irreparable harm. Moreover, risk of economic hardship is in most cases insufficient in so far as economic hardship is usually repairable.[26]

Generally speaking, the inability to participate in a major competition involves damage that is difficult to remedy. This is particularly true of the Olympic Games and the World Championships that only take place every four years.[27] In that case,

---

[21]CAS 2006/A/1137, *Cruzeiro Esporte Clube v. FIFA & PFC Krilja Sovetov*, Order of 17 August 2006; CAS 2007/A/1370, *FIFA v. Superior Tribunal de Justiça Desportiva do Futebol (STJD) & Confederação Brasileira de Futebol (CBF) & Mr Ricardo Lucas Dodô* & CAS 2007/A/1376 *WADA v. Superior Tribunal de Justiça Desportiva do Futebol (STJD) & Confederação Brasileira de Futebol (CBF) & Mr Ricardo Lucas Dodô*, Order of 10 December 2007.

[22]Article 261 et seq. Swiss Code of Civil Procedure.

[23]CAS 2012/A/2802, *Al-Masry FC v. EFA*, Order of 31 May 2012, para 6.5.

[24]CAS Ad Hoc Division OG 02/004, *Canadian Olympic Association v. ISU*, Award of 15 February 2002, see Reeb 2004, pp. 592–593.

[25]CAS 2010/A/2236, *D v. ADoP*, Order of 2 November 2010, para 6.4.

[26]CAS 2005/A/990, *Pobyedonostsev v. IIHF*, Order of 19 January 2006, para 8.2 (Award of 24 August 2006, para 7).

[27]CAS 2001/A/328, *F. v. ISOD, IPC, DS/USA*, Order of 3 August 2001, see iReeb 2004, pp. 633–634.

the applicant athlete argued that "the International Challenge Track and Field Championship is the sole event held this year in the Western Hemisphere for disabled athletes at which there will be a drug testing and at which disabled athletes will have the opportunity to establish world records; moreover this event has a financial interest for him". If there are no other issues involved this interest of the athletes usually outweighs the interest of the sports federation not to allow the athlete to participate in the major sporting event.

In football cases, the fact that a football club would be deprived of its right to register new players, nationally or internationally, until the end of the second period of registration was held to satisfy the requirement of irreparable harm, according to the definition of the Swiss Federal Tribunal.[28]

Quite surprisingly, the CAS has furthermore turned down the request of Michel Platini against the 90-day provisional suspension ordered by FIFA which did not allow him to participate during this time in the presidential elections of the FIFA. The reason given by the CAS Panel was that no irreparable harm was being caused. Obviously, the CAS Panel did not consider it as important enough for Michel Platini to be able to launch his candidature as FIFA president during this crucial time of the presidential elections. At least the CAS Panel did not allow FIFA to provisionally extend the 90-day provisional suspension for another 45 days.[29]

To sum it up, financial harm alone does usually not qualify as irreparable harm. Such irreparable harm is usually done in the case of a ban. Competitions usually are not postponed and cannot be repeated. Depending upon the importance of the competition, the harm caused to the athlete cannot be reversed. Therefore, in the case of a ban from competitions, the harm to the athlete has to be qualified as irreparable.

5.2.3.2 Likelihood of Success on the Merits

Provisional measures are only allowed if the applying party has a legitimate right for the preservation of which provisional measures are necessary. The party applying for provisional measures needs to plausibly convince the arbitration tribunal or the court, that it will win the main trial. Hence, the applicant for CAS provisional measures must, at least, establish a plausible case that the facts relied on and the rights the applicant tries to enforce exist and also that the material conditions for a legal action are fulfilled.[30]

---

[28]CAS 2006/A/1137, *Cruzeiro Esporte Clube v. FIFA & PFC Krilja Sovetov*, Order of 17 August 2006, para 8.4. See also SFT 126 I 207.

[29]CAS Media Release of 11 December 2015, "The 90-day provisional suspension imposed on Michel Platini remains in force, but FIFA is ordered not to extend it". Available at http://www.tas-cas.org/fileadmin/user_upload/Media_Release_Platini_FIFA_1112_final.pdf. Accessed 9 March 2016.

[30]CAS 2000/A/274, *Susin v. FINA*, see Reeb 2004, p.757; and CAS 2001/A/324, *Addo & Van Nistelrooij v. UEFA*, Order of 15 March 2001, see Reeb 2004, pp. 628 and 631.

Determining the likelihood of success on the merits is not an easy matter, but generally speaking, the greater the risk of irreparable harm being incurred by the applicant in the case, the lower the burden of establishing the chances of success and also satisfying the balance of interests requirement (see the following section).[31]

However, the request for provisional measures must be dismissed if the applicant, based on the undisputed facts of the case, is not able to satisfy the requirement of likelihood of success of the case on the merits.[32]

The success on the merits should be likely. However, where the resolution of the particular dispute depends upon the careful assessment of all the arguments and the evidence; this can only be made after a full procedure has been gone through and, therefore, it is not possible to express any further view on the merits of the dispute when dealing with an application for provisional measures at the outset of the proceedings. In such cases, it is sufficient that the likelihood of success on the merits of the case "cannot be denied" or "cannot be definitively discounted" at the time when the application is made for the provisional measures sought.[33]

As the threshold for the likelihood of success on the merits is much lower than winning the case on the merits afterwards, the applicant should usually be in a position to fulfil this criteria. The main claim only needs to be made probable.[34] Hence, the arbitrator deciding upon the request on provisional measures needs to take into consideration that the panel might accept the main claim in the future. This is only different in cases where the applicant has failed to fulfil some substantial formalities regarding the main claim. Almost only in such cases the request for a provisional measure can be declined based on non-existing chances on the merits.

5.2.3.3 Balance of Interests

The third criteria the applicant of a provisional measure has to meet is the balance of interests between all parties involved.

The essence of balancing the interests of the parties ("the balance of convenience principle" in Anglo-Saxon Common Law) lies in the fact that the interests of the party applying for the provisional measures must be assessed taking into account and striking a right balance with the interests of the party/parties who may be affected by those measures if granted.[35] The reason for this is that two possible outcomes must be considered. On the one hand, the party applying for provisional

[31]CAS 2011/A/2561, *FRB v. AIBA*, Award of 20 September 2011, para 6.11.

[32]CAS 2008/A/1677, *A. Enam v. Club Al Attihad Tripoli*, Order of 15 December 2008, paras 5.4. ff.

[33]CAS 2006/A/1141, *M. v. FIFA & FC Krijla Sovetov*, Order of 31 August 2006, para 7.3.

[34]See also in this regard the jurisprudence of the SFT 104 Ia 408, para 4.

[35]CAS 2001/A/324, *Addo & Van Nistelrooij v. UEFA*, see Reeb 2004, p. 631.

measures, which are not granted, wins the main trial. The award cannot be enforced due to not granting the provisional measures. On the other hand, the party opposing the provisional measures, wins the main trial, but is limited in its rights during the time of the legal process due to provisional measures being granted. Any provisional measure to be imposed must be assessed according to the principle of proportionality, taking into account the position of each party as well as the interests of third parties in both scenarios.

In one case, the CAS considered for example that the athlete's interest in being able to take part in a major competition, despite his suspension for doping, would outweigh the interests of the Federation, if the latter were not able to arrange a hearing before the start of the competition, and further considered that the Federation's interests "appear to be minimally affected" by the granting of a stay of execution of the suspension.[36] Even a rather short ban of four months affects very heavily the interests of a player which usually outweighs the interest of the sports federations or bodies: In the opinion of the CAS Panel "the deterrent effect of the sanction will not be undermined if its imposition is merely postponed and not cancelled".[37] These findings make sense as the result of an athlete can always be annulled in the aftermath, it will be never possible for the athlete to repeat the competition. Therefore, in most cases where athletes are involved (such as doping suspensions and transfer disputes), during the trial, the interest of the athlete should be rated high.

However, as regards anti-doping cases, the CAS, when weighing the balance of convenience, also considers the public interest in the fight against doping. As regards the interests of the International Federation (IF) to have its regulations correctly applied, the stay of the sanction does not prevent the CAS from re-imposing it at the end of the proceedings in the event that the appeal by the athlete is dismissed.[38]

In non-doping disciplinary cases, the risk of not being able to participate in the elections of an IF, for example, is generally considered to outweigh the interests of the IF in maintaining the *status quo*. Likewise, the risk that a National Federation (NF) may not be able to register athletes to competitions at the national or international level has been held to outweigh the interests of the NF in maintaining that situation.[39]

In football-related cases, as in doping-related cases, the interests of a Federation to see its regulations applied and its decisions enforced is not as important as the interests of another party risking irreparable harm as a result of the immediate execution of the decision.

[36]CAS 2001/A/238, *F v. ISOD, IPC, DS/USA*.

[37]CAS 2006/A/1137, *Cruzeiro v. FIFA & PFC*, paras 19 and 20.

[38]Ibid., para 8.5.

[39]CAS 2010/A/2500, *Amateur Boxing Association of Thailand v. AIBA*, Order of 15 July 2011.

There might also be situations where the request for provisional measures would affect third parties.[40] The ordering of a modification of a league standing as a provisional measure in football cases is likely to harm other teams as this could directly influence their capacity to play in the next year's competitions. As a result, the interests of one team in obtaining the provisional measures (especially, if this cannot change the team's position regarding relegation) does not seem to outweigh the interests of the other teams.[41]

Likewise, in a case in which a player is ordered to pay a specific sum to a club in financial difficulties, the risk that the appellant will not be able to recover that sum is considered to outweigh the club's interests in receiving immediate payment.[42] However, in this case, the player who requested a suspension of his payment duty offered to deposit the sum involved with the CAS until the final award was made. The fact that CAS granted such suspension of the payment duty shows that the willingness of the applicant to provide an adequate security for the possible damage of the counterparty can shift the balance of interest in favour of granting the provisional measure.

For all of these reasons it is much more likely that provisional measures are granted, if the current status is simply maintained, and no changes are ordered.

5.3 Enforcement of CAS Provisional and Conservatory Measures

As mentioned above, another important issue that needs to be addressed is the extent to which any preliminary measures granted can be legally enforced either by the CAS or with the assistance of the state authorities.

As explained, this is a controversial subject that would merit a lengthy article in its own right. Suffice to say that, in practice, the CAS measures carry a high degree of moral authority and, therefore, NFs and IFs tend to comply with them; and also through their own internal regularity mechanisms, they tend to ensure that sports persons under their jurisdiction also comply. Apart from this, failure to comply will weaken the position of the defaulting party in the subsequent proceedings. So, it is in that party's interest to conform.

As for non-voluntary enforcement by state courts, that, as mentioned, is a matter of local law. Whereas arbitral awards can be enforced in most states due to the

---

[40]CAS 2014/A/3471, *FC DNIPRO v. FFU,* Award of 18 February 2014, para 6.5. In this case, the Division President denied the request for provisional measures because it would affect third parties and it would not be possible to issue a decision affecting these parties without giving them the opportunity to be heard.

[41]CAS 2008/A/1525, *A.FC. v. HFF & O. FC*, Order on Request for Provisional Measures of 21 April 2008, para 78.

[42]CAS 2011/A/ 2603, *FC CFR 1907 Cluj SA v. RFF and SC Association FC v. Mateianu*, Award of 4 November 2011, para *7.9*.

Convention on the Recognition and Enforcement of Foreign arbitral Awards,[43] provisional measures do not qualify as awards in terms of Article 1 of the New York Convention. Additionally, *ex-parte* measures violate Article V of the New York Convention, as they do not grant both parties a fair hearing. For these reasons, provisional measures rendered by the CAS are not enforceable abroad. This means that a provisional measure rendered by the CAS in connection with an international competition held in a country other than Switzerland would not be enforceable in that country. This shows clearly how important the parallel competence of state courts is in urgent cases. Otherwise, the applicant would be completely in the hands of its counterparty which would not be acceptable in particular in cases of utmost urgency.

Judicial support becomes more problematic when the provisional measures are to be enforced outside Switzerland. For example, in Germany this is not a legal problem because Article 1041(2) & (3) ZPO allows German courts to authorise the enforcement of provisional measures ordered by an arbitral body with its seat outside Germany. But, in Italy, it is a problem, because Article 818 CPCI of the Italian law does not recognise the jurisdiction of arbitral bodies to grant provisional measures in the first place and will not, therefore, enforce them. As was stated above, legal enforcement of CAS Preliminary Measures depend upon the corresponding provisions of the applicable local law.

This renders it in our opinion evident that having to apply for provisional measures in an international setting at the CAS can lead to a severe disadvantage for the athlete, mainly due to lack of enforceability of preliminary measures granted by an arbitration tribunal. This disadvantage is especially obvious, when provisional measures allow the athlete to participate in a competition and such participation is not enforceable. An arbitration clause that obliges the athletes to mandatorily turn to CAS to request provisional measures would hence deprive the athletes of basic legal rights.

5.4 Waiver of State Courts' Jurisdiction?—Parallel Competence of State Courts

Furthermore, under the terms of Article R37 of the Code, the parties seeking CAS Provisional and Conservatory Measures "expressly waive their rights to request such measures from state authorities or tribunals"—in other words, from the ordinary competent courts.

The question is whether such a waiver is legally valid, given that, in effect, the parties are expressly agreeing to 'oust' (exclude) the jurisdiction of the courts, which, generally speaking, is contrary to 'public policy'.

[43]UNCITRAL, Convention on the Recognition and Enforcement of Foreign Arbitral Awards, 1958 ("New York Convention").

In general, such a waiver is valid only if the CAS offers a similar legal protection as state courts and if the CAS is effective and independent.[44] The later has already been established in Swiss jurisprudence as a Swiss court has held, in the past that, for such a waiver, first and foremost, the access to an independent and impartial judge has to be guaranteed.[45] This pre-condition already raises some serious issues for requests for provisional measures at the CAS. According to R37 of the CAS Code, the division presidents, which are chosen among the members of the International Council of Arbitration for Sport (ICAS), are the ones to decide. Unfortunately, all the members of the ICAS are selected by the sport organisations (International Sports Federations, National Olympic Committees, International Olympic Committee), even if certain ICAS members are chosen with the purpose of safeguarding the interests of the athletes. In certain cases, it would take a lot of time for the Appellant to finally end up with an impartial arbitrator.[46] In cases where urgent legal protection is needed, this is not acceptable. Until this issue is resolved, Swiss state courts have a parallel competence to deal with requests for provisional measures.[47]

A similar approach is taken in Germany. It should be noted that, in the well-known *Stanley Roberts v FIBA* case, a Munich Court (*Oberlandesgericht*) reviewed the matter of the abovementioned waiver from the point of view of Paragraph 1033 of the German Code of Civil Procedure, holding that the competence of CAS did not preclude the Court from granting provisional measures.[48] The court stated (in translation):

> Even though FIBA [the International Basketball Federation] contends that CAS, as an institutional arbitral tribunal, is capable of issuing a decision within 15 days, this very time-limit cannot always guarantee a sufficient protection, as for instance in the case of a directly upcoming competition. Considering that, as shown by daily practice, the state courts are in a position to issue preliminary orders within a timeframe of a few hours, it is out of the question that the interim measures orders by an arbitral tribunal are less effective in terms of enforceability than those ordered by state courts.

Further, the American swimmer, Gary Hall, obtained a temporary restraining order from the US District Court for the District of Arizona enabling him "to participate in any activities of FINA [the International Swimming Federation] or any of its member federations including international competition, as a competitor

[44] Rigozzi and Tissot 2012, para 29.

[45] Civil Tribunal of the Sarine, *X, Y, Z v Fédération Suisse de Basketball, City Fribourg Basketball Club*, Judgement of 20 June 1997, in Revue Fribourgeoise de Jurisprudence 1998, p. 51, at p. 56.

[46] Even though the CAS Code foresees extremely short deadlines for challenging the arbitrators such challenge becomes very difficult if the person(s) within the ICAS deciding upon the challenge of the arbitrator are potentially not impartial and not independent as well. This has led to a case where the appellant has requested that the Panel shall be composed by state courts. However, as the Panel was somehow composed the Swiss Federal Tribunal held that the appeal against the composition of the arbitral tribunal can only be filed against the final award; see SFT 4A_586/2014, decision of 25 November 2014.

[47] Civil Court of the Canton Tribunal Vaud, MP 2011/22, *Y. SA v. UEFA*, 27 September 2011, para VI.c).

[48] Cited in Martens 2001, p. 65.

until further notice of this court" despite the fact that he had already submitted an appeal, together with an application for provisional measures to the CAS against the decision of FINA to suspend him for doping.[49]

It also needs to be noted that the power of arbitral tribunals, such as the CAS, does not reach as far as the power of state courts. If a party were to violate an order issued by the arbitral tribunal, the arbitral tribunal would need the support of the state to enforce its order. A violation of the order granted by a state court, on the other hand, can directly include criminal sanctions against the parties and even third parties.

Swiss Law provides 'judicial assistance' for arbitral tribunals only pursuant to the provisions of Article 183(2) of the Swiss Private International Law Statute of 18 December, 1987, which states that, if the party concerned does not comply voluntarily, "the arbitration tribunal may call upon the assistance of the competent judge". Under Article 183 (3), the judge may "make the entry of provisional or conservatory orders subject to the receipt of appropriate security". Additional judicial support in Switzerland is available under Article 185 of that Statute.

Furthermore, such a waiver of jurisdiction of the courts is valid only if it is concluded by mutual agreement. The Swiss Federal Tribunal has stated that high level sport is characterised, nationally and internationally, through a very hierarchical structure, where athletes have no other choice than to accept the rules of the sports federations if they want to participate in competitions organised by those organisations.[50] Therefore, it can be concluded that all athletes are forced to enter into a contract with their sports association. The Swiss Federal Tribunal stated in the aforementioned ruling, that while the arbitration agreement is valid, the general exclusion in advance of legal means is not. This jurisprudence can be applied to *ex-parte* provisional measures as well, as the CAS system does not—due to its very nature—offer a similar protection as the state courts. For this reason, it is not possible to mandatorily renounce, in advance, the legal protection given by state courts in cases of urgency. Such a waiver would violate Article 27 (2) of the Swiss Civil Code.

The accepted view appears to be that state courts should only intervene, if the party applying for interim relief can establish that otherwise justice would be denied. However, due to the illegality of the waiver of state courts, it is accepted that the CAS and state courts have parallel competence to grant provisional measures.

5.5 Appeals Against Provisional Measures

Against provisional measures ordered by the CAS, there is basically no possibility to appeal before the Swiss Federal Court, as only final awards are admitted to appeal.[51] Only in the exceptional circumstances where the provisional measure de

[49]Cited in CAS 98/218, *Hall v. FINA*, Award of 27 May 1999.

[50]SFT 133 III 235, at p. 243.

[51]Article 77(1) a Swiss Federal Tribunal Court Act in connection with Article 190(2) PILA.

facto rules on the merits of the dispute and ultimately terminates the arbitration proceedings, the award on the provisional measure can be challenged before the Swiss Federal Tribunal.[52] This shows again that the legal protection given through provisional measures by the CAS is not on the same footing as the legal protection given through state courts.

Provisional measures issued by state courts can be appealed within 10 days before the competent cantonal court.[53] The reasons for an appeal are limited to a wrong application of the law and obvious misrepresentation of the situation.[54] An appeal has no suspensive effect; however, a suspensive effect can be granted. After the cantonal court, an appeal against the award on provisional measures has to be filed with the Swiss Federal Tribunal. However, the reasons for an appeal are restricted to violations of constitutional rights.[55] The legal protection regarding provisional measures are, hence, much more comprehensive before state courts than before CAS.

5.6 Provisional Measures in the Swiss Federal Tribunal

A final CAS award can be appealed before the Swiss Federal Tribunal. The reasons for contesting an award are very limited: only the violation of basic procedural rights and/or the violation of *ordre public* can be challenged.[56]

An appeal to the Swiss Federal Tribunal usually has no suspensive effect. However, it is possible to request a suspensive effect of the award[57] or even to request further provisional measures to maintain the current legal status and secure interests at risk.[58]

Such further provisional measures were requested by Claudia Pechstein, the famous German speed skater, who was suspended by the CAS for two years, due to anomalies in her blood. She appealed to the Swiss Federal Tribunal to lift the award of the CAS and she requested to be allowed to compete in a preparation event for the 2010 Olympics. As this was the last event to qualify for the Olympics, the Swiss Federal Court decided that the interests of Pechstein justified granting *ex-parte* provisional measures to compete in this event.[59] The disadvantage for Pechstein, if the provisional measure would not have been granted but she would have won the main case, was valued higher than the disadvantage for the

[52] SFT 4A_582/2009, decision of 13 April 2009, para 2.3.3.

[53] Articles 319a and 321 Swiss Code of Civil Procedure.

[54] Article 320 Swiss Code of Civil Procedure.

[55] Article 98 Swiss Federal Tribunal Court Act.

[56] Article 190(2) PILA.

[57] Article 103(3) Swiss Federal Tribunal Court Act.

[58] Article 104 Swiss Federal Tribunal Court Act.

[59] SFT 4A_612/2009, decision of 10 February 2010.

sports organisation and the other athletes if she competed but would lose the main case afterwards. The decision shows that the Swiss Federal Tribunal is free to grant provisional measures in order to maintain the current status until a final decision by the Swiss Federal Tribunal has been made.

However, only very few appeals to the Swiss Federal Tribunal are successful. In another case, the Swiss Football club FC Sion used players not eligible to play during two qualification games for the UEFA Europa League. As a disciplinary measure, both games against the opponents were qualified as a 0:3 loss. In consequence, FC Sion did not qualify for the UEFA Europa League. FC Sion appealed to the Swiss Federal Tribunal, asking to be reinstated into the competition. However, at the time of the decision, the UEFA Europa League was already over, and the Swiss Federal Tribunal ruled that it would not consider any measures or appeals as the competition was already over.[60]

5.7 Concluding Remarks

Provisional measures can be granted by the CAS or by the state courts. There is, basically, a parallel competence.

Depending upon the urgency of the matter, compliance by the opposing party, necessary knowledge of sports issues and the case in general, possible third party involvement and the scope of possible remedies, as well as the more comprehensive appeal possibilities in front of state courts, the parties need to decide beforehand whether they want to apply for the provisional measures offered by the CAS or by state courts.

As provisional measures awarded by the CAS are not generally enforceable by state courts, due to the lack of international conventions, in cross border situations, which very often arise in sports cases, it can be advisable to apply for provisional measures directly before the state courts. Moreover, state courts have more experience in issuing provisional measures in timewise extremely urgent situations. In other situations, the applicant may prefer to turn to CAS to request the provisional measure as the applicant trusts in the compliance of the sporting world with CAS awards.

References

Mavromati D, Reeb M (2015) The code of the court of arbitration for sport: commentary, cases, materials. Kluwer Law International BV, Alphen aan den Rijn

Martens D-R (2001) Übernahme von Dopingsperren anderer Verbände, OLG München: 26.10.2000 U (K) 3209/00. Zeitschrift für Sport und Recht (Issue 2) 65

[60] SFT 4A_134/2012, decision of 16 July 2012.

Rigozzi A, Tissot R (2012) La pertinence du "consentement" dans l'arbitrage du Tribunal Arbitral du Sport. Jusletter, 16 July 2012
Reeb M (2002) Digest of CAS Awards II 1998–2000. Kluwer Law International, The Hague
Reeb M (2004) Digest of CAS awards III 2001–2003. Kluwer Law International, The Hague
Schweizer P (2011) Procédure arbitrale. In: Bohnet F, Haldy J. Jeandin N, Schweizer P, Tappy D (eds) Code de procédure civile commenté, Helbing Lichtenhahn, Basel, pp 1429–1456

Chapter 6
The Basketball Arbitral Tribunal—An Overview of Its Process and Decisions

Erika Hasler

Abstract In the course of its almost ten years of existence, the Basketball Arbitral Tribunal has grown from an innovative if not experimental mechanism to resolve contractual disputes quickly and cost-effectively into a well-established international sports tribunal. BAT proceedings put the flexibility of international arbitration under the Swiss *lex arbitri* to the users' best advantage, while the tribunal's awards, mostly decided *ex aequo et bono*, have gradually built a jurisprudence distilling equitable principles in relation to recurrent issues in the context of professional sports contracts.

Keywords BAT · FIBA · Sports arbitration · Chapter 12 PILA · *ex aequo et bono* · SFT · NYC

Contents

The author would like to express her gratitude to Mr. Andreas Zagklis and Dr. Heiner Kahlert (then both) of the BAT Secretariat for their very helpful comments on a first draft of this article and for their answers to various queries on the workings of the tribunal. All mistakes or omissions are the author's alone.

E. Hasler (✉)
Lévy Kaufmann-Kohler, Geneva, Switzerland
e-mail: erika.hasler@lk-k.com

A. Duval and A. Rigozzi (eds.), *Yearbook of International Sports Arbitration 2015*,
DOI 10.1007/978-94-6265-129-6_6

6.1 Introduction

The Basketball Arbitral Tribunal (BAT), previously known as the FIBA Arbitral Tribunal or FAT, was established almost 10 years ago, in 2007, as an independent tribunal for the simple, quick and inexpensive resolution of contractual (i.e. non-disciplinary, non-technical and non-eligibility-related) disputes arising in the world of basketball.[1]

Seated in Geneva, Switzerland,[2] the BAT is composed of a President, Vice-President[3] and a roster of six arbitrators.[4] Its day to day work and the administrative aspects of proceedings are handled by the BAT Secretariat, based in Munich.

BAT arbitral proceedings are conducted under the BAT Arbitration Rules, the latest version of which was issued on 1 May 2014.[5] Furthermore, being all seated in Geneva in accordance with Articles 3.295 FIBA IR and 2.1 BAT Rules, BAT arbitrations are governed by the Swiss law of arbitration.

Switzerland has a dualist system for the law governing arbitration, meaning that international and domestic arbitrations are subject to two different regimes. International arbitrations are governed by Chap. 12 PILA (Articles 176–194), while domestic arbitrations are subject to the rules of Part 3 CCP (Articles

---

[1]See Article 3-289, under the heading Basketball Arbitral Tribunal (BAT), in Book 3, Chapter VII of the FIBA Internal Regulations (FIBA IR), further providing that FIBA, its Zones or their respective divisions cannot be directly involved in the disputes brought before the BAT. The name change (from FAT to BAT) was implemented on 1 April 2011, to better reflect the tribunal's independence from FIBA. Article 3-296 FIBA IR also stipulates that while the BAT's finances are guaranteed by FIBA, the tribunal is to be self-financing. For a comprehensive study of FIBA's dispute resolution mechanisms dealing with transfer and nationality disputes, disciplinary disputes, ad hoc (and technical) disputes as well as the BAT, see Zagklis 2013. On the FAT/BAT more specifically, see in particular Martens 2011 and Zagklis 2015b.

[2]See Article 3-295 FIBA IR.

[3]See Articles 3-297 and 3-298 FIBA IR on the roles of the BAT President and Vice-President, and Article 3-299 on the duties of the BAT President.

[4]The full list of BAT members and their profiles can be found at http://www.fiba.com/en/Module/c9dad82f-01af-45e0-bb85-ee4cf50235b4/4b2ba952-fe27-4a63-9f23-bc02e18215d8. Accessed 1 March 2016. The current President of BAT is Prof. Richard McLaren, a Canadian Barrister & Solicitor based in London, Canada, a member of the Faculty of Law, Western University Canada and CAS arbitrator with longstanding experience in sports law and dispute resolution. The six arbitrators currently on the BAT list are: Dr. Quentin Byrne-Sutton (Switzerland) (soon to be replaced by Ms Brianna Quinn, Switzerland & Australia); Prof. Dr. Ulrich Haas (Germany); Dr. Stephan Netzle (Switzerland); Raj Parker (England); Klaus Reichert, SC (Ireland); Annett Rombach (Germany). According to Article 3-299(b), BAT arbitrators are appointed by the BAT President "for a renewable term of two (2) years and shall have legal training and experience with regard to sport".

[5]The BAT Arbitration Rules are available at http://www.fiba.com/en/Module/c9dad82f-01af-45e0-bb85-ee4cf50235b4/3109bb9c-53bc-4cbc-99a8-a67e9f861277. Accessed 1 March 2016. According to Article 18.1 BAT Rules, the current version is applicable "to Requests for Arbitration received by the BAT Secretariat or by FIBA on or after [1 May 2014]". The previous versions of the FAT/BAT Rules were issued in 2007, 2009, 2010, 2011 and 2012.

353–399). Whether an arbitration is domestic or international depends on the domicile or habitual residence of the parties at the time of the conclusion of the arbitration agreement.[6] That said, the FIBA IR and the BAT Rules aim at eliminating this possible variance by stipulating that BAT proceedings "are governed by Chap. 12 [PILA], irrespective of the parties' domicile".[7]

Chapter 12 PILA is recognized for its liberal, arbitration-friendly character, and it is with these features in mind that the BAT seat was fixed in Geneva.[8] In particular, Chap. 12 stands out for its protectiveness of party autonomy, wide arbitrability of disputes, availability of provisional measures through arbitral tribunals, flexibility in matters of applicable law and hands-off approach to the review of arbitral awards by the courts.

By all standards, the BAT has been a successful 'experiment'. So much so that it is now a well-established arbitral institution and a significant presence in the landscape of sports dispute resolution.[9] More importantly, it has undeniably made a difference in the world of professional basketball, helping players, coaches and agents to keep clubs (and vice versa) to their contractual engagements.[10] A sports agent declared in 2011 that, by then, 99 % of his clients had a FAT/BAT clause in their contracts.[11] The BAT caseload statistics speak for themselves: from 2 requests for arbitration filed in 2007, the tribunal has gone on to register 150 in 2015, with the total number of requests filed adding up to 793 over that 9-year period.[12]

A further illustration of the interest of the BAT model is that it has recently been used as the template for a new arbitral institution, catering to parties in 'traditional' commercial disputes: the Court of Innovative Arbitration (COIA), created in 2015 and seated in Zurich, Switzerland.[13] The COIA shares many of the features of the BAT, and, like the BAT's, its stated goal is that of simplifying the

[6]Article 176(1) PILA.

[7]Articles 3-295 FIBA IR and 2.2 BAT Rules. The same wording is included in the BAT model clause as set out in Sect. 6.3 of the Preamble in the BAT Rules. This type of clause should satisfy the requirements of Article 353(2) CCP, which enables the parties to a domestic arbitration into opt out of the CCP regime and into Chap. 12 as the *lex arbitri*. That said, a BAT arbitration would generally be international within the meaning of Article 176(1) PILA in any event, at least so it would seem based on the actual experience so far, given that apparently there has been no BAT case involving Swiss-domiciled or Swiss-resident parties on either side, let alone on both (this can be verified the BAT website, where awards can be searched by the seat or domicile of the respondent, at http://www.fiba.com/bat/awards).

[8]Zagklis 2015b, p. 291. As reported ibid., in footnote 3, the BAT was the brainchild of Dirk-Reiner Martens, longstanding external counsel to FIBA and a well-known sports lawyer and arbitrator.

[9]As noted by Zagklis 2015b, p. 297, the BAT is now the second busiest sports tribunal after the CAS.

[10]See, e.g., Rosen 2011; Martens 2011, p. 57.

[11]Rosen 2011, quoting agent Brad Ames.

[12]Statistics available at http://www.fiba.com/en/Module/c9dad82f-01af-45e0-bb85-ee4cf50235b4/984a5df1-a490-49a5-8aa4-86d985e703d9. Accessed 1 March 2016.

[13]See http://coia.org/. Accessed 1 March 2016.

dispute resolution process while ensuring a fair outcome. It remains to be seen whether the COIA will be as successful as its basketball-specialized predecessor.

Meanwhile, notwithstanding its importance in contemporary sports arbitration, the BAT has been the object of surprisingly limited academic attention.[14] The YISA aims to fill that gap by launching a yearly digest of BAT jurisprudence, starting with its next (2016) issue. This article is but a prelude—a modest introduction to a more systematic and sustained study of basketball's arbitral *enfant prodige*.

In its first part, this introductory article provides an overview of BAT arbitration, covering the conduct of the proceedings from their commencement to the issuance of the award as well as the post-award phase and available remedies. The second part of the article focuses on selected aspects of the BAT's substantive jurisprudential output, with the aim of providing some insight into the actual results when disputes are decided according to the particular standard of *ex aequo et bono*.

6.2 BAT Arbitration—How Does It Work?

6.2.1 BAT Arbitration in a Nutshell

As just mentioned, the BAT was set up to offer simple, quick and inexpensive arbitration to resolve disputes arising in the dynamic environment of professional basketball. Accordingly, the BAT Arbitration Rules (BAT Rules),[15] which govern the proceedings before BAT tribunals, have a number of built-in features designed to facilitate the time- and cost-effective resolution of disputes.

In particular, the BAT Rules provide that, in the interest of speed, proceedings shall be conducted before a sole arbitrator (appointed by the institution from a closed list),[16] are subject to short time limits,[17] and, as a rule, limited to a single exchange of written submissions.[18] Hearings are held only if the arbitrator so decides after having consulted the parties.[19] Furthermore, the Rules stipulate that the proceedings shall in principle be conducted in English,[20] and that filings,

[14]For a list of the studies known to the author, please see the bibliographical references at the end of this article.

[15]The BAT Arbitration Rules currently in force are the 1st May 2014 version. They can be found on the BAT website at https://www.fiba.com/downloads/v3_expe/bat/BATArbitrationRules1May2014.PDF. Accessed 1st March 2016.

[16]BAT Rules, Preamble 0.2 and Article 8.1.

[17]BAT Rules, Preamble 0.2 and Article 7.

[18]BAT Rules, Preamble 0.2, and Article 12.1.

[19]BAT Rules, Preamble 0.2 and Article 13.1.

[20]Article 4 provides that: "1. The working language of the BAT shall be English. 2. Documents provided to BAT in a language other than English must be accompanied by a certified translation unless the Arbitrator decides otherwise. 3. The Arbitrator may decide, after consultation with the parties, to hold the proceedings in another language." .

notifications and communications, which must be in writing, can be made by email and fax.[21]

As to the merits, the BAT Rules[22] establish that, unless the parties have agreed otherwise, the dispute shall be decided *ex aequo et bono* rather than based on a specific national law, making it possible for arbitrators unfamiliar with the intricacies of different national legal systems to decide cases without the need for (costly and time-consuming) submissions and/or the involvement of experts on issues of local law.

The BAT Rules provide for the issuance of the final award within six weeks from the closing of the proceedings or the payment of the advance on costs, whichever occurs last.[23] To keep party costs under control, the Rules cap the contribution towards the prevailing party's "reasonable legal fees and other expenses incurred in connection with the proceedings" which the losing party will normally be ordered to pay.[24] Again to contain costs and for the sake of speed, only the dispositive part of the award (without the reasons) is issued, unless otherwise requested by a party, in cases where the amount in dispute is lower than € 30,000.[25] The same is true for cases valued between € 30,000 and € 200,000, if the respondent fails to pay its share of the advance on costs and the claimant so requests.[26]

Reportedly, the cumulative result of these features is that the average duration of BAT arbitrations is just above six months (2014 figures), and the cost/value ratio of cases a moderate 5.3 % (also in 2014).[27]

Finally, as discussed in more detail below, BAT awards are subject only to the limited legal remedies available under Chap. 12 PILA, and their enforcement can be sought via both the NYC and FIBA's ad hoc internal mechanism.

6.2.2 BAT Proceedings—Step by Step

BAT proceedings[28] are commenced with the filing of a request for arbitration, which should be accompanied or rapidly followed by payment of a 'non-reimbursable handling fee'. The amount of the handling fee depends on the monetary value

[21] Article 6.3 BAT Rules.

[22] Preamble 0.2, and Article 15.1 BAT Rules.

[23] Article 16.3 BAT Rules.

[24] Article 17.4 BAT Rules.

[25] Article 16.2.1(a) BAT Rules.

[26] Article 16.2.1(b) BAT Rules.

[27] For more details on these figures, see Zagklis 2015b, pp. 296–297.

[28] For a helpful overview of the main steps in a standard BAT arbitration, see the "Guide to Arbitration Procedures before the Basketball Arbitral Tribunal", available on the BAT website at http://www.fiba.com/en/Module/c9dad82f-01af-45e0-bb85-ee4cf50235b4/53eab3df-af21-4043-a4a6-5a264334ce65. Accessed 1 March 2016.

of the dispute, and can be calculated based on the scale set out in Article 17.1 BAT Rules.[29] Where the request for arbitration does not specify an amount, the fee is fixed by the BAT President based on the information available.[30] Failing payment of the handling fee, the arbitration will not proceed. If payment is still outstanding after the final time limit set by the BAT Secretariat to that effect, the request will be deemed withdrawn.[31]

The necessary contents of the request for arbitration are specified in Article 9.1 BAT Rules. To facilitate its filing and ensure that all the required elements are provided from the start, a pre-established template is available on the BAT website.[32] Should the request for arbitration as filed nonetheless be incomplete, the BAT Secretariat (or the arbitrator, once appointed) will invite the claimant[33] to provide the missing additional information or documents. Importantly, in view of the limitation to a single exchange of written submissions, the request must be accompanied by a copy of the contract containing the BAT arbitration clause and include a complete statement of the facts and legal arguments the claimant intends to rely on, as well as the (written) evidence in support and the relief sought.

The BAT Secretariat then forwards the request for arbitration to the BAT President for review. Provided he finds, on a *prima facie* basis, that there is a valid BAT arbitration agreement and that the request meets the requirements of the BAT Rules,[34] the BAT President proceeds to appoint an arbitrator from the BAT list.[35] According to Article 8.2 BAT Rules, "[b]efore proceeding with the arbitration, the [a]rbitrator shall send a written declaration of acceptance and independence to the BAT Secretariat. The parties shall be informed about the existence and content of such declaration". Article 8.3 BAT Rules specifies that the time limit to bring a challenge against the appointed arbitrator is "seven days after the ground for challenge has become known to the party making the challenge".[36] Meanwhile, the file is promptly transferred to the arbitrator.

---

[29]Counterclaims are also subject to payment of a non-reimbursable handling fee. See footnote 39 below.

[30]Article 17.1 BAT Rules. As currently set out in the BAT Rules, the non-reimbursable handling fee ranges between a minimum of € 1500 (for cases where the amount in dispute is less than € 30,000) and a maximum of € 7000 (for cases involving an amount in dispute above € 1,000,000).

[31]Article 9.2 BAT Rules.

[32]Available at http://www.fiba.com/bat/process. Accessed 1 March 2016.

[33]For the sake of simplicity, the singular (claimant, respondent, party etc.) will be used throughout this paper, it being understood that BAT proceedings can, and relatively often do, involve multiple parties on one or both sides.

[34]Article 11.1 BAT Rules.

[35]As provided in Article 8.1 BAT Rules, appointments are made on a rotational basis. See footnote 4 above on the current composition of the (closed) BAT list of arbitrators.

[36]Article 8.3 further provides that challenges are decided by the BAT President after having heard all the parties and the arbitrator. For an example where this procedure was followed, see BAT 0464/13, *Manakian v. FC Bayern München e.V.*, Award of 4 August 2014, paras 3–9.

Once the handling fee has been paid, the BAT Secretariat fixes the advance on costs, to be paid by the parties in equal shares (subject to a different decision by the arbitrator).[37] In addition, the Secretariat forwards the request for arbitration to the respondent and informs it of the time limit to file an answer, and of the appointment of the arbitrator.[38] As for the request, the BAT rules set out the required contents for the answer.[39] Most importantly, any defence against BAT jurisdiction must be raised in the answer at the latest. Once it has "entered an appearance" on the merits of the case, the respondent is precluded from raising a jurisdictional objection, including in annulment proceedings against the award (Article 186(2) PILA).

At this stage, it is useful to note that, although it contains no express provision on this point, the Swiss *lex arbitri* recognizes the possibility that proceedings may be conducted by default where the respondent refuses to take part in the arbitration despite being duly notified of its commencement.[40] Article 14.2 of the Rules expressly provides for the power of arbitrators to "proceed with the arbitration and deliver an award" in such cases, which are relatively frequent before the BAT.[41]

As to the BAT's jurisdiction, the respondent's default cannot be taken as a failure to object within the meaning of Article 186(2) PILA. Swiss law requires that the arbitrator ascertain his or her jurisdiction *ex officio*, based on the record as it stands.[42] Moreover, the arbitrator's authority to proceed with the case by default is

[37]Article 9.3.1 BAT Rules, which also provides that the advance on costs, as fixed by the Secretariat taking into account the amount in dispute and the complexity of the case, may be further adjusted in the course of the proceedings (see, e.g., BAT 0468/13, *Matic v. Club Sportif Municipal Targoviste*, Award of 4 February 2015, para 29).

[38]Article 11.2 BAT Rules.

[39]Article 11.2 BAT Rules. It should also be noted that if the answer contains a counterclaim, the corresponding handling fee will have to be paid by the respondent (Article 17.1 BAT Rules). Failing that payment, the counterclaim will be deemed withdrawn (see, e.g., BAT 0702/15, *Club Sportif Sagesse Beirut v. Kahzzouh*, Award of 7 October 2015, paras 26–27).

[40]SFT decision of 26 November 1980, *Semaine Judiciaire* 1982, p. 613, at p. 621. See also Kaufmann-Kohler and Rigozzi 2015, paras 6.18–6.20 with further references.

[41]For instance, among the published awards issued in 2015, the author has noted that the following were rendered by default: BAT 0712/15, *Hamilton v. Saski Baskonia SAD*, Award of 6 October 2015, para 17 and *passim*; BAT 0651/15, *Macvan v. Galatasaray Spor Kulübü Dernegi*, Award of 27 May 2015, para 5 and *passim*; BAT 0566/14, *Caracter v. Sichuan Jingqiang Blue Whale Pro Basketball Club*, Award of 27 January 2015, para 17 and *passim*. See also BAT 0664/15, *Funiciello v. El Jaish Sports Club and Taggard*, Award (previously issued without reasons) of 6 December 2015, paras 8, 9 and 11, 21, 25 and *passim*, recording that both respondents had failed to participate in the proceedings having led to the award without reasons. In BAT 0539/14, *Dragovic v. BC Spartak St. Petersburg*, Award of 12 October 2015, para 12 et seq., the respondent ceased to participate after filing its answer to the request for arbitration.

[42]SFT 120 II 155, 162, adding (at 165) that subject to good faith principles, the respondent can still intervene and challenge the arbitrator's jurisdiction at any later stage (until the rendering of the award). See also SFT 4A_682/2012, decision of 20 June 2013, para 4.4.2.1 with references. Ex multis, BAT 0651/15, *Macvan v. Galatasaray Spor Kulübü Dernegi*, para 15.

subject to a duty "to make every effort to allow the defaulting party to assert its rights".[43] Accordingly, the BAT Secretariat ensures that all procedural acts are notified to the respondent throughout the proceedings, and appropriate time limits are set for that party to react at each step, which will be duly recorded in the award.[44] On the merits—as with jurisdiction—the fact that the respondent is defaulting cannot be taken as an admission of the claimant's claims: the arbitrator should satisfy him- or herself that the claims are well founded in fact and in law.

Be that as it may, the arbitrator will not proceed with the arbitration until the full amount of the advance on costs is received by the BAT. When the respondent is defaulting and more generally if one party fails to pay its share, the other party may substitute for it.[45] If full payment of the advance is not made within the final deadline fixed to that effect by the BAT Secretariat, the request for arbitration is deemed withdrawn.[46]

Once the answer has been filed (in cases where both parties participate) or at any appropriate stage, the arbitrator may then in his/her discretion decide whether one or more further (exchanges of) submissions are necessary.[47] The arbitrator may issue orders requiring the production of documents, responses by one or all parties to specific questions, and more generally give any directions he or she deems appropriate for the conduct of the proceedings.[48] In fact, given that as a rule there is no hearing, BAT arbitrators tend to issue procedural orders calling for additional submissions or soliciting answers to specific questions relatively often.[49] Conversely, unsolicited submissions are not normally taken into account.[50] That said, all procedural steps and decisions in the arbitration are subject to the fundamental due process requirements of Article 182(3) PILA,

[43]Ex multis, see BAT 0651/15, *Macvan v. Galatasaray*, paras 24–25.

[44]The same is true if the default occurs not from the outset, but later in the proceedings, e.g. after the answer has been filed (see, e.g., BAT 0539/14, *Dragovic v. BC Spartak St Petersburg*, para 38 and *passim*).

[45]Article 9.3 BAT Rules.

[46]Article 9.3.4 BAT Rules.

[47]Article 12.1 BAT Rules (see also Article 3.1, providing in general terms that "the Arbitrator shall determine in his/her sole discretion the procedure in the proceedings before him/her").

[48]Article 12.2 BAT Rules. Note that Article 14.2 BAT Rules, enabling the arbitrator to proceed and deliver the award in proceedings by default, also applies "if any party fails to abide by an order of procedure or by directions given by the [a]rbitrator".

[49]For a few recent examples, see, e.g., BAT 0630/14, *Kaukenas v. BC Zalgiris Kaunas*, Award of 1 October 2015, paras 27–34; BAT 0468/13, *Matic v. Club Sportiv Municipal Targoviste*, Award of 4 February 2015, paras 20–25; BAT 0477/13, *Denson & Goldansky v. Ramat Hasharon BC*, Award of 3 February 2015, para 8.

[50]Article 12.1 BAT Rules. See however, for instance, BAT 0468/13, *Matic v. Club Sportiv Municipal Targoviste*, paras 27–30 and 59, where, given the specific circumstances, the arbitrator allowed the filing of unrequested submissions, noting that both parties had consecutively filed numerous documents, some of which unsolicited, but neither had complained of such submissions, and that "the principle of due process does not allow the arbitrator to disregard the parties' submissions easily".

prescribing that "the arbitral tribunal shall ensure equal treatment of the parties and their right to be heard in adversarial proceedings".[51]

Article 12.3 BAT Rules authorizes arbitrators to "attempt to bring about a settlement to the dispute". Under Swiss law, it is accepted that arbitrators may act as settlement facilitators.[52] Nonetheless, it is important that the parties agree to the arbitrator playing such a role and that the modalities of his or her intervention in that capacity take into account the need to preserve the parties' due process rights and the arbitrator's impartiality and independence.[53] BAT arbitrators have on several occasions either accepted the parties' invitation to act as settlement facilitators[54] or taken the initiative to offer their assistance in finding an amicable settlement.[55] Where the attempt is successful, the agreed settlement can be incorporated in an award by consent, as briefly discussed below.[56]

Article 183(1) PILA enables arbitrators to order provisional or conservatory measures, as reflected in the text of Article 10.1 BAT Rules,[57] with the specification, in Article 10.3, that any request for such measures "can only be brought together with or after the filing of the request for arbitration".[58] So far, it would

[51]On these requirements in Swiss-seated international arbitrations, see, e.g., Kaufmann-Kohler and Rigozzi 2015, paras 6.21–6.38, and Berger and Kellerhals 2015, paras 1115–1131. Note in addition that, as stated in Article 3.2 BAT Rules, the parties' due process rights must be exercised in good faith: if a party fails to raise "without undue delay [an] objection to a failure to comply with any provision of these Rules, or any other rules applicable to the proceedings, any direction given by the Arbitrator, or the conduct of the proceedings, [it] shall be deemed to have waived its right to object in that respect".

[52]See, e.g., Kaufmann-Kohler and Rigozzi 2015, para 1.28.

[53]Ibid., paras 1.29–1.30; Berger and Kellerhals 2015, para 171.

[54]See, e.g., FAT 0092/10, *Ronci & Coelho v. WBC Mizo Pecs*, Award of 15 October 2010, paras 26–27; FAT 0069/09, *Ivezic & Draskicevic v. Basketball Club Pecsi Noi Kosariabda Kft*, Award of 27 May 2010, para 24.

[55]See, e.g., BAT 0468/13, *Matic v. Club Sportiv Municipal Targoviste*, para 34; BAT 0421/13 *Berzins & Bill A. Duffy International Inc, db BDA Sports Management v. BC VEF Riga*, Award of 21 February 2014, para 21; BAT 0154/11, *Gloger & Bill A. Duffy International, Inc. v. Club C.B. Atapuerca*, Award of 17 August 2011, paras 24–27.

[56]See Sect. 6.2.3.

[57]Article 10.1 BAT Rules provides that "[u]pon request, the [a]rbitrator may make an order for provisional and conservatory measures. In cases of extreme urgency, such orders can be made ex parte." Although this point is still debated in comparative law, and in the silence of the PILA, Swiss commentators tend to agree that arbitrators may grant provisional measures *ex parte* where appropriate (see, e.g., Kaufmann-Kohler and Rigozzi 2015, para 6.124 and the references provided). Article R37 CAS Code also provides for *ex parte* interim measures "in cases of utmost urgency", and "provided the opponent is subsequently heard".

[58]Given that interim relief can only be ordered by the arbitrator (Article 10.1 BAT Rules) and after the filing of the request for arbitration (Article 10.3), there is no provision for a so-called "emergency arbitrator" in the BAT Rules (Article R37 CAS Code, for instance, allows parties to file requests for provisional measures prior to the filing of the request for arbitration, provided the latter is filed within 10 days, and orders for provisional measures can be ordered by the President of the relevant Division prior to the appointment of a panel).

seem that parties in BAT arbitrations have rarely made use of the possibility to request provisional measures from BAT arbitrators,[59] possibly (at least in part) in view of the already expedited nature of the proceedings.[60]

As mentioned above, the BAT Rules provide that in principle there will be no evidentiary hearing, unless the arbitrator decides otherwise after consultation with the parties.[61] This is in line with Swiss law, which recognizes that the parties' right to be heard under Article 182(3) PILA does not include an absolute right to an oral hearing.[62] The parties may ask for a hearing in the request for arbitration and the answer[63] or at a later stage in the proceedings. Where one party requests a hearing and the other objects, in order to decide in favour of the hearing, the arbitrator will need to be persuaded that receiving the testimony of the proffered witness(es) (or other evidence) in person or orally might change his or her opinion on the dispute, or assist

---

[59]The author is aware of the following awards mentioning that the parties had lodged requests for provisional measures (which were not granted in view of the requesting party's failure to establish the existence of a risk of irreparable harm, as one of the customary conditions to be met in order to obtain interim relief): BAT 0439/13, *Burns, Hart Sports Management and Players Group v. SS Sutor Srl*, Award of 19 March 2014 (paras 41–42 and 80–81); BAT 0449/13, *Steele, Greig and Slay v. SS Sutor Srl*, Award of 20 March 2014 (paras 57–58, 97–98); BAT 0463/13, *Johnson v. SS Sutor Srl*, Award of 20 March 2014 (paras 32–33, 71–72). While both the BAT Rules and the PILA are silent on the substantive requirements to be met for the granting of provisional measures by arbitrators, commentators note the emergence of transnational standards in this respect, as reflected for instance in the UNCITRAL Model Law on International Commercial Arbitration of 2006 (Article 17A) and the UNCITRAL Arbitration Rules of 2010 (Article 26(3)). This is also illustrated by the contents of Article R37 CAS Code, which was recently amended to codify the CAS's consistent practice in point (see in particular Kaufmann-Kohler and Rigozzi 2015, paras 6.119–6.120). All the aforementioned provisions refer to the following (in principle, cumulative) conditions: (i) a risk of serious or irreparable harm, (ii) a likelihood that the applicant will succeed on the merits, and (iii) a balancing of the parties' respective interests whereby the harm caused to the opponent does not outweigh the harm the applicant seeks to avert by requesting the measure(s).

[60]In principle, under the Swiss *lex arbitri* the courts retain their jurisdiction to order provisional measures, in parallel to that of the arbitrators. However, similar to Article R37 CAS Code, Article 10.4 BAT Rules purports to exclude the courts' jurisdiction to deal with requests for provisional measures, by stipulating that "[i]n agreeing to submit their dispute to these Rules, the parties expressly waive any right to request provisional or conservatory measures from any state court". The validity of such a waiver of the parties' right to access the courts is not undisputed in CAS appeals cases, primarily on the ground that consent to arbitration under the CAS Code is not consensual in those instances (see, e.g., Kaufmann-Kohler and Rigozzi 2015, paras 6.107–6.108). While the author is not aware, as yet, of any decision on the validity of Article 10.4's very similar waiver, it could be argued that the latter should be upheld in view of the consensual character of BAT arbitration, provided also that the BAT arbitrator is in a position to order the relief sought.

[61]According to Zagklis 2015b, p. 294, as of the time of his writing, the BAT had conducted five hearings in total.

[62]See, e.g., SFT 117 II 346, 348.

[63]See Articles 9.1 and 11.2 BAT Rules.

him or her in understanding the case.[64] This test will generally also involve a balancing of the overarching objectives of fairness and cost-effectiveness, which are both deeply ingrained in the BAT 'principles of procedure'.[65] As stipulated in Article 13.3 BAT Rules, the arbitrator can make the holding of a hearing conditional upon the payment of an additional advance on costs by one or both parties.[66] Moreover, pursuant to Article 13.2, the arbitrator is free to decide that the hearing will take place by telephone or video conference, and if it is to be held in person, where it shall take place.[67]

Once the arbitrator is satisfied that the parties' evidence and submissions on the record provide a sufficient basis for deciding the case, he or she will normally "declare the exchange of documents complete" and invite the parties to file "detailed accounts of their costs". Each party's cost submission will then be forwarded to the opposing side with an invitation to submit comments, if any, within a short deadline.

6.2.3 The Applicable Law and the Making of the Award

As noted above, one of the distinctive features of BAT arbitration resides in the applicable decisional standard on the merits. Indeed, the default solution under the BAT Rules is that the dispute will be decided not according to a particular law, but *ex aequo et bono* (often translated as "according to what is equitable and good").[68]

More precisely, Article 15.1 BAT Rules (as reflected in the BAT model arbitration clause)[69] provides that

> [u]nless the parties have agreed otherwise the Arbitrator shall decide the dispute *ex aequo et bono*, applying general considerations of justice and fairness without reference to any particular national or international law.

On the other hand, pursuant to Article 15.2 BAT Rules, if

---

[64]The process whereby the arbitrator reaches this conclusion is often referred to, in the Swiss jurisprudence on arbitration, as an 'anticipated assessment of the evidence' (*appreciation anticipée des preuves; antizipierte Beweiswürdigung*), which arbitrators are entitled to conduct in order to decide whether to admit evidentiary requests (including offers of evidence).

[65]See for instance the arbitrator's reasoning in BAT 0542/14, *Pancotto v. SS Felice Scandone Avellino SpA*, Award of 24 October 2014, paras 39–41, and BAT 0462/13, *Maresca v. Basket Juvecaserta srl*, Award of 13 June 2014, paras 37–40.

[66]For example, in cases BAT 0230/11, *Zouros v. BC Zalgiris Kaunas,* Award of 9 July 2012, and 0231/11, *Kantzouris v. BC Zalgiris Kaunas*, Award of same date, the arbitrator decided to make the respondent's request for a hearing by video conference conditional upon the payment of an additional advance of € 5000, to be paid by that party alone. The request for a hearing was subsequently withdrawn and the parties were given the opportunity to file additional written submissions instead.

[67]For instance, in BAT 0256/12, *Mr Coach and Agency v. Club*, Award of 13 December 2012, paras 18–22, the arbitrator, having heard both parties on the respondent's request for a hearing, decided that a hearing in person would be held in Munich.

[68]Black's Law Dictionary (2009), 9th ed.

[69]See also the BAT model clause at the beginning of the Rules, Preamble 0.3, providing, in fine, that the "arbitrator shall decide the dispute *ex aequo et bono*".

according to the arbitration clause the Arbitrator is not authorized to decide *ex aequo et bono*, he/she shall decide the dispute according to the rules of law chosen by the parties or, in the absence of such a choice, according to such rules of law he/she deems appropriate.

This wording is in keeping with Article 187(1) PILA[70] as it recognizes the autonomy of the parties to choose the rules governing the merits of their dispute (whether directly, as envisaged in Article 15.2, first limb, or indirectly, e.g. by reference to a set of arbitration rules containing a choice of law clause, as provided in Article 15.1) but also to the extent it provides that failing such a choice, it is for the tribunal to determine the applicable law.[71] Article 187(2) PILA further provides that the parties may "authorize the arbitral tribunal to decide *ex aequo et bono*", which is exactly what the BAT model clause and Article 15.1 BAT Rules do.[72]

In practice, the vast majority of BAT arbitrations are decided *ex aequo et bono*. In most cases this is so because the arbitration clause contains an express provision to that effect.[73] However, there are also cases where determining the *lex causae* requires a closer analysis of the parties' intent, for instance where the contract contains both a choice of law clause and an arbitration clause, each calling for the application of a different law. Indeed, it is not so rare for basketball contracts to incorporate a "classic" BAT arbitration clause providing that the arbitrator shall decide any dispute arising from or related to the contract *ex aequo et bono*, alongside a choice of law clause stipulating that the contract shall be "governed" or "construed, interpreted and enforced according to the laws of" a given country,

[70]Article 187(1) PILA reads as follows: "The arbitral tribunal shall decide the dispute according to the rules of law chosen by the parties or, absent such a choice, according to the rules of law with which the case has the closest connection".

[71]Although the language of Article 187(1) PILA is slightly more restrictive as it postulates that in such cases the arbitrator shall apply the so-called "closest connection" test to determine the applicable rules of law, rather than the ones he or she deems appropriate.

[72]As is systematically recalled under the heading "Applicable Law" in BAT awards decided *ex aequo et bono* (see, ex multis, BAT 0644/15, *Vougioukas v. Galatasaray Spor Kulübü Dernegi*, Award of 13 July 2015, paras 26–27) "[t]he concept of "équité" (or *ex aequo et bono*) used in Article 187(2) PILA originates from Article 31(3) of the *Concordat intercantonal sur l'arbitrage* [the Swiss statute that governed both international and domestic arbitration before the enactment of the PILA], under which Swiss courts have held that arbitration 'en équité' is fundamentally different from arbitration "en droit": "When deciding ex aequo et bono, the Arbitrators pursue a conception of justice which is not inspired by the rules of law which are in force, and which might even be contrary to those rules". In substance, it is generally considered that the arbitrator deciding ex aequo et bono receives 'the mandate to give a decision based exclusively on equity, without regard to legal rules. Instead of applying general and abstract rules, he must stick to the circumstances of the case at hand'" [references omitted]. In technical terms, and even though the two expressions are often used interchangeably, the decisional standard of *ex aequo et bono* should be distinguished from *amiable* composition (as recognised, e.g., under French law, pursuant to Article 1478 CCP). When acting as *amiables compositeurs*, arbitrators establish what the solution would be under the applicable (rules of) law and then adjust it if they consider the result to be unfair.

[73]Very often, the relevant contracts reproduce the BAT model clause, quoted in footnote 69 above.

or similar wording to the same effect.[74] In such cases, BAT arbitrators tend—where the contents of the relevant clauses and possibly other circumstances[75] so permit—to resolve the conflict by holding that

> the parties' common intention [in referring to a national law] was to account for the mandatory rules of local labour law […] to regulate such matters as working hours, safety, insurance, etc. as long as they did not become contentious, but that [as made clear by the terms of the relevant arbitration clause] any disputes deriving from the performance of the Parties' obligations under the contract would be decided *ex aequo et bono* if submitted to the [BAT].[76]

A similar approach, adopted in some other cases, has been formulated as follows:

> the parties did not intend to deviate from the principle that any dispute relating to the [contract] should be decided *ex aequo et bono*. The reference to [the relevant national law]

---

[74]See, e.g., FAT 0046/09, *Mahoric & Jakse v. BC Kyiv*, Award of 26 February 2010, paras 40–41 (choice of law clause providing that the contract "shall be governed by the laws of Switzerland"); FAT 0071/09, *Papadopoulos v. Fortitudo*, Award of 31 August 2010, paras 65–66 (choice of law clause providing that the contract "shall be construed, interpreted and enforced according to the laws of Italy"); FAT 0104/10, *Pavetic v. GS Trogylos Basket Priolo*, Award of 15 March 2011, paras 6, 53–55 (choice of law clause providing that the contract was to be "regulated by Italian and European Community law"); FAT 0118/10, *Bracey v. Achilleas Kaimakliou BC*, Award of 23 March 2011, paras 53–56 (choice of law clause providing that "[t]he laws of Cyprus shall govern this Agreement"); BAT 0631/14, *Valdeolmillos Moreno v. Comité Olìmpico Mexicano (COM, Asociación Deportiva Mexicana De Baloncesto (ADEMEBA), Liga Nacional de Baloncesto Profesional (LNBP), Instituto Veracruzano Del Deporte (IVD)*, Award of 30 October 2015, paras 87–89 (choice of law clause providing that the contract "shall be interpreted and enforced in accordance with the laws of Mexico"). For other similar examples, see FAT 0041/09, *Panellinios KAE BC v. Kelley*, Award of 12 November 2009, paras 55–59; FAT 0062/09, *Harper* et al. *v. Besiktas Jimnastik Kulübü*, Award of 26 March 2010, paras 51–54; FAT 0063/09, *Fisher & Entersport Management Inc. v. KK Vojvodina Serbijagas*, Award of 19 February 2010, paras 43–46; FAT 0082/10, *Benson & Paris v. Shanxi Zhongyu*, Award of 31 August 2010, paras 53–55; FAT 0083/10, *Ilievski v. KK Union Olimpija Ljubljana*, Award of 23 July 2010, paras 34–36; BAT 0139/10, *Sampson & Octagon v. Samahang Basketbol NG Pilipinas Inc.*, Award of 31 October 2011, paras 33–35; BAT 0172/11, *Jusup & Ivic v. KK Zadar*, Award of 6 October 2011, paras 45–47; BAT 0247/11, *Ignerski & Stanley v. Besiktas Jimnastik Kulübü*, Award of 3 September 2012, paras 53–56; BAT 0544/14, *Allred & Greig v. Halcones UV Promotora Deportiva A.C. & Halcones de Xalapa A.C.*, Award of 11 December 2014, paras 79–80; BAT 0562/14, *Zouros v. BC Zalgiris Kaunas*, Award of 3 March 2015, paras 48–49; BAT 0563/14, *White v. Guaiqueries De Margarita BBC*, Award of 30 April 2015, paras 39–40; BAT 0603/14, *Sarkis v. Amchit Club*, Award of 13 May 2015, paras 30–33; BAT 0702/15, *Club Sportif Sagesse de Beirut v. Khazzouh*, paras 45–48; BAT 0708/15, *Cousin Jr. & Fleisher v. BC Krasny Oktyabr*, Award of 5 January 2016, paras 31–33.

[75]One such circumstance is the fact that the parties have argued their case before arbitrator in reliance on *ex aequo et bono* principles rather than by reference to the law designated in the choice of law clause. At any rate, Swiss law admits that a choice of law clause can be concluded (or amended) by conduct (see, e.g., Kaufmann-Kohler and Rigozzi 2015, paras 7.27 and 7.76). See, for example, FAT 0046/09, *Mahoric & Jakse v. BC Kyiv*, para 41; BAT 0563/14, *White v. Guaiqueries De Margarita BBC*, paras 39–40; BAT 0702/15, *Club Sportif Sagesse de Beirut v. Khazzouh*, paras 45–48.

[76]FAT 0062/09, *Harper* et al. *v. Besiktas Jimnastik Kulübü*, paras 51–54; FAT 0071/09, *Papadopoulos v. Fortitudo*, paras 65–66; FAT 0082/10, *Benson & Paris v. Shanxi Zhongyu*, paras 53–55; FAT 118/10, *Bracey v. Achilleas Kaimakliou BC*, para 55; BAT 0172/11, *Jusup & Ivic v. KK Zadar*, paras 45–47; BAT 0247/11, *Ignerski & Stanley v. Besiktas Jimnastik Kulübü*, para 56; BAT 0702/15, *Club Sportif Sagesse de Beirut v. Khazzouh*, paras 45–48.

> may at best be understood as a declaration that the [contract] has validly been concluded and is binding under [the relevant law] but not as a choice of law. It does not in any way affect the Arbitrator's mandate to decide the dispute *ex aequo et bono*.[77]

In yet other cases, the arbitrator found that "the contents of the mission conferred upon him by the parties to the contract derive first and foremost from the part of the contract that is directly addressed to him, i.e. [the arbitration clause], which says that the 'arbitrator shall decide the dispute *ex aequo et bono*'", which however did not render void the provision stating that the contract was to be interpreted and enforced in accordance with a given national law. The arbitrator's competence being limited to the resolution of disputes "arising from or related to the present contract", the choice of law clause referring to national law remained applicable whenever an authority other than the BAT would be called upon to interpret or enforce the contract's provisions.[78] In general, the analysis and findings as to the *lex causae* in all these cases turned on the fact that the parties had expressly chosen BAT as the forum for the resolution of their contractual disputes and *ex aequo et bono* as the applicable standard before that forum in case of dispute.

Conversely, there have been a few instances where the parties, even though they opted for BAT arbitration, had exclusively chosen a national law as the law applicable to the merits, instead of retaining the default choice of ex aequo et bono. In such cases, BAT arbitrators have applied the law chosen by the parties, in accordance with their mandate under Article 15.2 BAT Rules (and Article 187(1) PILA).[79]

Finally, there have been a few cases where the parties had made no express choice of law but simply referred to arbitration in accordance with the BAT Rules. In such instances, the parties' agreement has been construed as incorporating a

---

[77]See, e.g., BAT 0708/15, *Cousin Jr. and Fleisher v. BC Krasny Oktyabr*, para 33; BAT 0603/14, *Sarkis v. Amchit Club*, paras 30–33; 0544/14, *Allred & Greig v. Halcones UV Promotora Deportiva A.C. & Halcones de Xalapa A.C.*, para 80.

[78]See, e.g., BAT 0631/14, *Valdeolmillos Moreno v. Comité Olímpico Mexicano (COM)* et al., para 89, referring to BAT 0107/10, *Kelati & Maravilla v. Olympiacos Piraeus BC*, Award of 13 April 2011, paras 46–47.

[79]See, e.g., FAT 0057/09, *Podkovyrov v. Slupskie Towarzystwo Koszykowki Sportowa Spolka Akcyjna*, Award of 15 March 2010, paras 40 and 46, where the arbitration clause provided that "[a]ll disputes should they arise shall be under Polish law and in the FIBA arbitral tribunal (FAT) courts" with no reference to *ex aequo et bono*, and the parties confirmed their preference for a decision based on Polish law; FAT 0034/09, *Tucker & Pro One Sports Management Inc. v. BC Kyiv*, Award of 3 May 2010, paras 58–60, where the parties provided, alongside a FAT arbitration agreement from which the mention of *ex aequo et bono* had been removed, for their contract to be "interpreted and enforced in accordance with the laws of Switzerland", or FAT 0095/10, *Shabalkin v. "Khimki" Basketball Club*, Award of 24 September 2010, paras 29 and 40, where the relevant agreement contained a provision for disputes to be "brought to [sic] Arbitration Court of FIBA", no mention of *ex aequo et bono*, and a clause referring to "the acting legislation of the Russian Federation" which was to govern sanctions "in the event of non fulfilment of the commitments envisaged [therein]". For a more recent example, see, e.g., BAT 0589/14, *Dean v. SS Felice Scandone SpA*, Award of 7 January 2015, paras 41 and 49, where the underlying contract contained a clause designating Swiss law as the *lex causae and* expressly excluding the arbitrator's power to decide *ex aequo et bono*.

choice of law in favour of *ex aequo et bono* principles, in view of the fact that the BAT Rules (selected by the parties to govern the arbitration) so provide.[80]

As to the making of the award, Article 189(1) PILA provides that the arbitral award "shall be rendered in conformity with the procedure and form agreed by the parties". Absent a specific agreement, Article 189(2) provides that the award "must be in writing, reasoned, dated and signed". Article 16.1 BAT Rules, which embodies "the procedure and form agreed by the parties" when they opt for BAT arbitration (absent any further specific agreement on this matter), follows Article 189(2)'s prescriptions, providing that the arbitrators shall issue "a written, dated and signed award with reasons". However, this general rule is subject to Article 16.2 BAT Rules, which reads as follows:

> 16.2.1 By agreeing to submit their dispute to arbitration under these Rules, the Parties agree that,
>
> (a) where the value of the dispute does not exceed € 30,000, the Arbitrator will issue an award without reasons
> (b) where the value of the dispute is between € 30,001 and € 200,000, and a Respondent fails to pay its share of an advance on costs, upon request by a Claimant, the Arbitrator may decide to issue an award without reasons and reduce the advance on costs [...]
>
> 16.2.2 If Article 16.2.1(a) applies or if the Arbitrator decides to issue an award without reasons in accordance with Article 16.2.1(b), the Arbitrator shall deliver reasons only if a party
>
> (a) files a request to that effect at any stage from when the Request for Arbitration is filed until no later than ten (10) days after the notification of the award without reasons; and
> (b) pays the respective advance on costs as determined and within the time limit set by the BAT Secretariat.

Article 16.2.1(a) of the BAT Rules was introduced in 2011, in response to demands by users involved in lower value cases, mostly female players and lower

[80]FAT 0075/10, *Tamir & Krayn v. Seastar Apoel Nicosia Basketball Club*, Award of 23 June 2010, para 40 ("any dispute [...] shall be submitted to the FIBA Arbitral Tribunal (FAT) in Geneva, Switzerland and shall be resolved in accordance with the FAT Arbitration Rules [...]"); FAT 0143/10, *Tapoutos v. Basketball Club PAOK KAE*, Award of 3 May 2011, para 37 (here, the arbitration clause simply provided for "arbitration by FAT of FIBA"). More recently, see, e.g., BAT 0477/13, *Denson & Goldansky v. Ramat Hasharon BC*, paras 26 and 32, where the contract provided that it was to be "governed by and interpreted in accordance to the FIBA Regulations, the FIBA Arbitral Tribunal [...]", and BAT 0539/14, *Dragovic v. BC Spartak St. Petersburg*, paras 42 and 47, where the contract stipulated that any dispute would be submitted to the BAT and "resolved in accordance with the [BAT] Arbitration Rules by a single arbitrator [...]".

division clubs, for whom reducing the costs of the proceedings would be critical in order to gain access to BAT arbitration.[81] Article 16.2.1(b) was added in 2014, giving the claimants in disputes of moderate value, where the claims are quite often not contested, the possibility to lower the cost of pursuing their case by requesting the issuance of the award without the reasons.[82] Overall, the changes introduced in Article 16.2 have significantly reduced the costs and length of BAT arbitral proceedings.[83]

As indicated in Article 16.1 last sentence, before signing the award, the arbitrator must submit the final draft to the BAT President for review.[84] In his 'scrutiny' of the award, the BAT President "may make suggestions as to [its] form", and "without affecting the arbitrator's liberty of decision, may also draw his/her attention to points of substance".[85]

At that stage, the BAT President also determines the costs of the arbitration,[86] which will be allocated by the arbitrator in the finalized award[87] taking into account the parties' relative success in the arbitration (i.e. "the relief(s) granted

[81] As noted by Zagklis 2015b, p. 297, "[t]he total costs for these cases have decreased by at least 30 % merely by applying a lower handling fee (€ 1500) together with a cap on the advance on arbitration costs (€ 5000). The arbitrator does not spend the time required to render a reasoned award unless a party requests a reasoned award and pays an additional advance on costs".

[82] Ibid. According to the same author, "this new rule will speed up BAT proceedings even more and further lower costs by requir[ing] fewer reasoned awards in situations in which the claim is uncontested".

[83] Ibid.

[84] Where the award is to be rendered without reasons, the arbitrator submits a standard summary form setting out the underlying reasons together with the unreasoned draft for the President's scrutiny.

[85] Similar provisions, calling for the scrutiny of the award by an internal institutional body prior to its issuance, can also be found in the CAS Code (Article R59(2), providing for scrutiny by the CAS Secretary General), and, in commercial arbitration, the ICC Rules of Arbitration (Article 33 entrusting the ICC Court with this task). Article 16.1 in fine also contains a provision allowing the BAT President to "consult with other BAT arbitrators on issues of principle raised in the award".

[86] The costs of the arbitration include "the administrative and other costs of BAT and the fees and costs of the BAT President and the Arbitrator" (Article 17.2 BAT Rules). As stated in the cost section of BAT awards, the BAT President fixes the arbitration costs by "taking into account all the circumstances of the case, including the time spent by the Arbitrator, the complexity of the case and the procedural questions raised". The decision on costs will be updated in Article 16.2 cases where a party subsequently requests the issuance of a reasoned award (to take into account the additional advance on costs paid for that purpose). Where the advances paid by the parties exceed the costs determined by the BAT President, the BAT will reimburse the excess in accordance with the arbitrator's decision on the relative allocation of the costs.

[87] Article 17.2 BAT Rules provides that "the final account of the arbitration costs may either be included in the award or communicated separately to the parties", however to the author's knowledge the latter possibility is rarely used.

compared with the relief(s) sought"), as well as their procedural conduct and financial resources.[88]

The award contains a final section (the so-called operative or dispositive part) setting out the arbitrator's decisions with regard to each of the parties' prayers for relief, the allocation of the arbitration costs and of the parties' legal expenses. Where Article 16.2.1 BAT Rules does not apply, the operative part of the award is preceded by a summary of the relevant facts and the proceedings, and sections presenting the parties' respective positions and arguments, evidence adduced and requests for relief, as well as the reasons for the arbitrator's determinations, including on jurisdiction and the applicable law.[89]

According to Article 16.6 BAT Rules,

> [i]f the parties reach a settlement after the [a]rbitrator has been appointed, the settlement shall be recorded in the form of a consent award if so requested by the parties and if the [a]rbitrator agrees to do so.

> It is generally accepted, including under Swiss law, that arbitrators can issue awards by consent (also referred to as awards "on agreed terms") setting out the terms of an amicable settlement reached by the parties, thereby providing them with an enforceable instrument to implement their agreement.[90] It is also generally recognized that the arbitrator should satisfy the parties' request for a consent award, unless the terms of the settlement breach fundamental rules of public policy.[91] Accordingly, when issuing an award by consent, BAT arbitrators ascertain the arbitrability of the underlying dispute in light of Article 177(1) PILA and verify that the parties' settlement does not contravene international public policy within the meaning of Article 190(2)(e) PILA.[92]

---

[88]See Article 17.3 BAT Rules. In setting out the exact amounts to be paid as a result of the determination and allocation of costs, the arbitrator takes into account the advances on costs paid by the parties. The non-reimbursable handling fee paid by the claimant (or counterclaimant), when (partially) successful, is considered as part of its legal fees and other expenses to which the other party shall (as a general rule) contribute in accordance with the allocation decided by the arbitrator. There have also been cases where the arbitrator decided, in view of the specific circumstances, not to apply the general rule, and thus that each party would bear its own costs (see, e.g., BAT 0468/13, *Matic v. Club Sportiv Municipal Targoviste*, paras 103–104).

[89]In Article 16.2.1 cases, where the award is rendered without reasons, the dispositive part is preceded by a paragraph stating that "[u]pon providing both parties with an opportunity to be heard, having ascertained his/her jurisdiction and considered the factual and legal arguments as well as the requests for relief submitted in this case, the Arbitrator decides as follows", and followed, after the indication of the seat, the date and the arbitrator's signature, by a "Notice about Request for Reasons" recalling Article 16.2.1's criteria and Article 16.2.2's requirements, and setting out the applicable advance on costs in case a party wishes to lodge a request for reasons.

[90]See, e.g., Kaufmann-Kohler and Rigozzi 2015, paras 7.105 and 7.109.

[91]Ibid., para 7.109, with further references.

[92]See, e.g., the awards in cases BAT 0243/11, *Court Side v. Kasnye Krylia Samara*, Award of 2 February 2012, para 11; BAT 0224/11, *Bavcic, MEGA Basketball LLC, BeoBasket Ltd. v. KK Union Olimpija Ljublijana*, and 0225/11, *Djordjevic, MEGA Basketball LLC, BeoBasket Ltd. v. KK Union Olimpija Ljublijana*, both of 9 March 2012, para 7.

Once it is finalized and signed, the award is notified to the parties by the BAT Secretariat, by email or fax enclosing a (pdf) copy of the signed original and indicating that "further copies will be forwarded by courier".

According to Article 16.4 BAT Rules, "BAT awards are not confidential unless ordered otherwise by the arbitrator or the BAT President". As reported by Zagklis, more than 90 % of BAT awards are posted on the FIBA website,[93] albeit sometimes in redacted form.[94]

In line with Article 190(1) PILA, Article 16.5 BAT Rules stipulates that the award is "final and binding" upon communication to the parties. Under Swiss law, the award acquires *res judicata* effect and becomes enforceable as from that moment.[95] The moment the award is communicated to the parties is also the starting point of the strict 30-day time limit for the filing of an action for annulment pursuant to Articles 190–192 PILA, as discussed in the following section.

6.2.4 Remedies Against BAT Awards

Pursuant to Article 16.5 BAT Rules, BAT awards are deemed made at the seat of the BAT, Geneva (regardless of where the proceedings were held and/or the award signed). For Swiss-seated tribunals like the BAT, the court having supervisory jurisdiction over the award is the SFT, Switzerland's Supreme Court. BAT awards are subject to the (limited) remedies available under Chap. 12 PILA. More specifically, the parties may seek the annulment of the award in accordance with Articles 190–191 PILA, unless they have expressly waived their right to do so pursuant to Article 192(1) PILA.[96]

---

[93]Zagklis 2015b, p. 294. The awards can be found at http://www.fiba.com/bat/awards. Accessed 1 March 2016.

[94]See, e.g., BAT 0213/11, *Player v. Club*, Award of 30 January 2013.

[95]Kaufmann-Kohler and Rigozzi 2015, paras 7.187–7.188; Berger and Kellerhals 2015, paras 1633 and 1637. In Switzerland, arbitral awards are deemed equivalent to a court judgment and immediately enforceable upon their issuance, without further formalities. In other words, there is no requirement to register or have a judgment entered upon the award by the local courts, as may be the case in other countries. Nevertheless, Article 193 PILA provides for the possibility to deposit the award with the Swiss court at the seat (in BAT's case this would be the Geneva court, namely the *Tribunal de première instance*) and/or request a(n optional) "certificate of enforceability" from the same court or the arbitral tribunal.

[96]Article 192 PILA reads as follows: "If none of them has its domicile, habitual residence, or a business establishment in Switzerland, the parties may, by an express statement in the arbitration agreement or by a subsequent written agreement, exclude any action for annulment in full or limit it to one or the other of the grounds listed in Article 190(2) PILA". For a detailed study of the waiver under Article 192(1) PILA, see Kaufmann-Kohler and Rigozzi 2015, paras 8.49–8.75. An agreement to waive the right to seek the annulment of the award does not affect a party's right to resist the enforcement of the award (indeed, if the award is to be enforced in Switzerland, Article 192(2) PILA provides that the NYC applies by analogy).

It is not so infrequent to come across Article 192(1) waiver agreements (also referred to as 'exclusion agreements') with respect to BAT awards.[97] This may be due to the fact that the original FAT model clause included such an agreement, at a time when FAT awards were subject to appeal before the CAS.[98] As the possibility to lodge appeals before the CAS was eliminated from the BAT Rules (in their May 2010 version), so was the waiver agreement regarding the annulment action before the SFT. The parties remain free to provide, in their contracts, for appeal before the CAS (whether instead or in addition to the annulment action before the SFT) and/or to waive their right to bring an annulment action, however, the default solution proposed in the BAT Rules has done away with these options.[99]

Assuming the right to seek the annulment of the award has not been waived, the time limit to bring the action is 30 days from the notification of the award.[100] In view of the fact that many BAT awards are issued without reasons by operation of Article 16.2.1 BAT Rules, it is important to note here that the SFT, faced with one such award in 2012 (in a case where the applicant had not made use of the possibility of requesting the issuance of the reasoned version), has clearly held that by agreeing that the award be issued without reasons, the parties do not waive their right to seek its annulment under Article 190(2) PILA.[101] Moreover, in cases subject to Article 16.2.1 BAT Rules, unless the applicant waives the right to request the reasons for the award, the 30 day time limit to file an application for annulment only starts running from the notification of the reasoned award.[102]

---

[97]The validity of one such agreement was upheld by the SFT in one of the two challenges against a BAT award that were brought before it: SFT 4A_232/2012, decision of 29 May 2012, para 2.

[98]See Preamble 0.3, and Article 18 of the FAT Rules in their versions of 15 March 2007, 9 December 2007, and 30 May 2009.

[99]For a recent example where the arbitration clause provided for appeal to the CAS and included a waiver of the action for annulment before the SFT, see BAT 0593/14, *Tomas v. Fenerbahce Spor Kulübü*, Award of 3 February 2015, para 21. For a case where the parties did not provide for appeal and nonetheless waived the action for annulment, see BAT 0539/14, *Dragovic v. BC Spartak St Petersburg*, para 42.

[100]Article 100(1) SCA. In this regard, it is important to note that under Swiss law, communication to the parties' counsel of record is considered equivalent to communication to the parties directly (see SFT 4P.273–283/1999, decision of 20 June 2000, para 5b), meaning that the time limit starts running from that moment.

[101]SFT 4A_198/2012, decision of 14 December 2012, para 2.2, albeit also noting that, realistically, the chances of success of the applicant would be considerably reduced in such a scenario.

[102]Article 100(1) SCA states that the time limit to bring an action for annulment runs from the notification of the "complete decision". That said, the parties can bring an action for annulment upon receipt of the sole operative part of the award, specifying that they will complete their application once the full decision is available. This possibility may be used, for instance, to request an immediate stay of the tribunal's award, which, as just noted, is binding and enforceable as from its notification, even if limited to the operative part (indeed, the *res judicata* effect and enforceability only attach to the operative part of the award in any event).

The limited (and exhaustive) grounds upon which the annulment of the award may be sought are set out in Article 190(2)(a)–(e) PILA, which reads as follows:

2. [the award] may only be challenged:

(a) if the sole arbitrator was not regularly appointed or the arbitral tribunal was not regularly constituted;
(b) if the arbitral tribunal wrongly accepted or denied jurisdiction;
(c) if the arbitral tribunal has ruled beyond the claims submitted to it or failed to decide one of the claims;
(d) if the principle of equal treatment of the parties or their right to be heard in adversarial proceedings has not been complied with;
(e) if the award is incompatible with public policy.

As is apparent from the above wording, Article 190(2) PILA's grounds are in essence directed at the procedural aspects of the arbitration, they do not go to the merits of the award itself, save where its result contravenes international public policy (Article 190(2)(e)), an exception which is interpreted very narrowly by the SFT.[103]

It should also be noted that the filing of an action for annulment does not entail an automatic stay of the enforceability of the award. If the applicant wishes to obtain such a stay, it must request an order to that effect from the SFT.[104] The requirements and related case law are quite strict.[105]

Finally, annulment under Article 190(2) PILA is by essence a 'cassatory' remedy, meaning that the SFT can only confirm or annul the award (in whole or in part), but not issue a new decision on the merits of the dispute in lieu of the tribunal.[106] There are only two exceptions to this principle: if the annulment action is brought on the ground that there was an irregularity in the appointment or composition of the tribunal (Article 190(2)(a) PILA) or that the tribunal lacked jurisdiction (Article 190(2)(b) PILA), the SFT can deal with that objection directly. It may thus uphold a challenge against an arbitrator, order his or her removal, and direct that a newly appointed arbitrator must rehear the case when the annulment is sought on Article 190(2)(a)'s ground, and, in cases brought under Article 190(2)(b) PILA, it may make a ruling on the arbitrator's jurisdiction (in addition to annulling or upholding the award).[107] Aside from these two scenarios, if the application for annulment is upheld, the SFT will normally remand the case to the arbitrator who rendered the award, for him or her to render a new decision. In so

[103]For a more detailed discussion of the contents and meaning of these grounds and the conduct of annulment proceedings before the SFT in sports matters, see Hasler and Hafner 2016, Sect. 17.2.2.4. See also Kaufmann-Kohler and Rigozzi 2015, paras 8.03–8.205; Berger and Kellerhals 2015, paras 1672–1880, and Rigozzi 2010.

[104]Article 103(1) and (3) SCA.

[105]For a discussion of the SFT's practice in this respect, see in particular Kaufmann-Kohler and Rigozzi 2015, paras 8.92–8.99, with further references.

[106]This is reflected by the fact that the provision governing the action for the annulment of awards in the SCA, Article 77, excludes the application of Article 107(2) SCA, which enables the SFT to rule on the merits upon annulment of a lower court's decision.

[107]SFT 136 III 605, 615–616.

doing, the arbitrator will have to take into account the reasons for annulment as set out in the SFT's decision.[108] In this regard, it is important to note that, because the defects that can be corrected by means of an action for annulment under Article 190(2) PILA are almost exclusively of a procedural nature, the parties may well end up with the exact same decision on the merits once the (procedural) defect(s) identified in the SFT's decision has/have been corrected.

In addition to the action for annulment, the SFT has held that the remedy of revision is available against international arbitral awards, even though the PILA does not mention it.[109] Revision is an extraordinary remedy, enabling the parties to request that the tribunal's decision be reconsidered even though it has become final. Given that it interferes with the fundamental principle of finality, revision is only available on very narrow grounds covering exceptional situations, namely when it is established that the award was influenced to the detriment of the requesting party by a crime or a felony,[110] or where the requesting party has discovered, after the issuance of the award, relevant and material (pre-existing) facts or conclusive evidence on which it was unable to rely in the course of the arbitration proceedings.[111] Requests for revision are naturally rare and, to the author's knowledge, none has been filed to date with regard to a BAT award.

6.2.5 The Enforcement of BAT Awards

BAT awards can be enforced under the NYC.[112] In this regard, one important issue needs to be highlighted: although employment disputes, which form the bulk of the BAT's docket, are arbitrable in Switzerland (under Chap. 12 PILA),[113] they are not in many other countries (in fact, this was one of the reasons for the choice of Switzerland as the seat of the BAT).[114] This may create difficulties at the enforcement stage, because Article V(2)(a) NYC provides that the recognition and enforcement of a foreign award may be refused by the courts of the countries under the laws of which the subject matter of the dispute is not arbitrable.

---

[108]SFT 4A_54/2012, decision of 27 June 2012, para 2.2.3 and the references.

[109]The SFT came to this conclusion in a 1992 decision (SFT 118 II 199). In that same decision, the SFT held that the revision of awards would be subject to the rules governing the revision of the its own decisions and that it would be the court of competent jurisdiction to deal with applications for the revision of awards rendered in Switzerland.

[110]Article 123(1) SCA.

[111]Article 123(2)(a) SCA.

[112]The seat of the BAT also determines the 'nationality' of BAT awards for the purposes of the NYC, meaning that they will be recognized and enforced as Swiss awards in other NYC countries.

[113]See Article 177(1) PILA, which provides that "any dispute involving a pecuniary [viz. economic] interest may be the subject matter of an arbitration".

[114]On this point, see, e.g., Martens 2011, p. 56, paras 3.2 and 7.

In reality, the NYC rarely—if ever—comes into play with regard to BAT awards, given that FIBA has addressed this and other potential hurdles in the enforcement process by setting up an ad hoc internal mechanism under Articles 3–300 to 3–302 FIBA IR.[115] Pursuant to Article 3-300, FIBA can impose sanctions on a party that fails to honour a BAT award, ranging from fines of up to CHF 150,000 to targeted bans (e.g. on international transfers for players, on the registration of new players for clubs, and on participation in the relevant international competitions for both players and clubs), it being understood that any such sanctions can be applied cumulatively and multiple times.[116]

In practice, the award creditor can file a request for sanctions against the recalcitrant debtor with FIBA, following which the award debtor is given an opportunity to be heard and (ideally) proceed to implement the award before the FIBA Secretary General takes a decision.[117] Decisions rendered pursuant to Article 3–300 FIBA IR can be appealed before the FIBA Appeals Panel.[118] For follow-up purposes, the BAT website includes a section entitled 'Sanctions' listing the clubs and players that have been sanctioned in accordance with Article 3–300 FIBA IR, and flagging those which are subject to pending sanctions.[119]

***

Having completed our overview of the BAT process, the second part of this article will focus on the merits, attempting to offer a sampling of the concrete reasoning and the decisions rendered by BAT arbitrators in accordance with the standard of *ex aequo et bono*.

6.3 BAT Arbitration—What Does It Mean?

6.3.1 Deciding Sports Disputes Ex Aequo et Bono

As explained by Martens,[120] the (relatively unusual) choice of providing for arbitration *ex aequo et bono* as the default rule in BAT arbitration was dictated by the

[115]Martens 2011, pp. 56–57.

[116]Article 3-300 FIBA IR. See also Articles 3-70 and 3-71 FIBA IR with regard to the licence restrictions that apply to sanctioned players and clubs. Article 3-300 in fine adds that the sanctions it provides for "can be extended, in FIBA's sole discretion, to natural or legal persons which are directly or indirectly linked to the first party, either from a legal or sporting perspective (e.g., different entity under a similar name, etc.)".

[117]Article 3-301 FIBA IR, adding that "upon request by FIBA, the national member federation to which [the award debtor] is affiliated shall actively and promptly take all necessary measures to ensure that [the award debtor] fully honours the BAT award within a time-limit fixed by FIBA. If a national federation fails to comply with the present Article, FIBA may impose disciplinary sanctions on [it] [...]".

[118]Article 3-302 FIBA IR.

[119]http://www.fiba.com/bat/sanctions. Accessed 1 March 2016.

[120]Martens 2011, p. 55.

overall objective of maximizing the speed of the decisional process whilst ensuring the fairness of the outcome. On the one hand, the reference to "considerations of justice and fairness" in lieu of a specific national law (which most often will be foreign to the arbitrator and/or at least one of the parties) simplifies the substantive legal framework, and on the other, it calls for a decision that is 'just', i.e. equitable and appropriate to the specific circumstances of the case to be decided. In essence, an *ex aequo et bono* decision will be based on the arbitrator's interpretation of the terms of the contract, which will also take into account the parties' overall relationship, respective situations and conducts, as well as any other relevant circumstances, in order to reach a fair and adequate solution in the dispute at hand.[121]

Although the BAT *ex aequo et bono* clause was initially "met with considerable skepticism in the legal profession",[122] it has quickly become the expected decisional standard for the tribunal's users.[123] It has also clearly achieved the desired result of allowing BAT arbitrators to decide the matters in dispute simply, efficiently and fairly, without having to deal with 'battles of legal experts', and extensive research in the intricacies of the multitude of different national laws they would otherwise be required to apply from one case to the next.[124]

Interestingly, while—as just seen—the very notion of a decision *ex aequo et bono* requires that disputes be determined on a case by case basis, as a specialized tribunal dealing exclusively (and on a large scale) with certain types of disputes, the BAT has developed a series of principles with regard to various recurrent concepts, arguments, claims and defences. In turn, the systematic publication of the awards rendered (to which the parties and arbitrators can then cite as 'persuasive authorities' on the same issues arising in later cases) has favoured the emergence of a consistent case law on several important questions. The existence and development of this body of jurisprudence contributes to the predictability (and therefore the efficiency) of the BAT system, ultimately enhancing legal security in the world of professional basketball.[125]

---

[121]Note that, as illustrated by the excerpts reproduced below, the relevant circumstances may also include general legal principles that are well established in the relevant context. In other words, a mandate to decide *ex aequo et bono* does not necessarily exclude that the arbitrator may consider the relevant or otherwise applicable legal rules (including, as the case may, general principles of law or trade usages); it only entails that the arbitrator is not bound to apply the law (as in arbitration 'ex lege'). For a study of the history, understanding and practice of *ex aequo et bono* in international commercial and investment arbitration, see Trakman 2012. On *ex aequo et bono* arbitration in Switzerland, see in particular Sykora (2011).

[122]Martens 2011, p. 55.

[123]As noted by Zagklis 2015b, p. 294 (footnote 19): "decisions rendered under *ex aequo et bono* principles have become so popular that parties only insisted on national law in about 3 % of the cases to date".

[124]Martens 2011, p. 55. It is also worth noting, as Martens does (ibid.), that the decisions rendered in many of the cases decided *ex aequo et bono* correspond by and large to the solution that would have obtained under the otherwise applicable national laws (were it not for the BAT clause). For a review of the outcome of some BAT awards rendered *ex aequo et bono* see, in addition to the discussion in the following section, Anthony 2013.

[125]For a perceptive study of the role of BAT jurisprudence in creating principles governing basketball contracts, see Zagklis 2015b, pp. 184-188.

The following section offers some illustrations of this phenomenon, one of the main areas of interest in the study of BAT arbitration. It features examples of substantive principles developed in the BAT case law (covering various issues, from the concept of 'guaranteed no-cut contracts' to the defence of hardship), captured in the form of direct quotations for the sake of brevity and immediacy. As stated at the outset of this paper, this first (and selective) compendium will be followed by a more systematic analysis of the BAT case law on various (other) issues, both procedural and substantive, which will be published in the form of a regular digest in the future issues of the YISA.

6.3.2 Examples from the BAT Case Law

6.3.2.1 The Concept of "Guaranteed no-Cut Contracts"

So-called no-cut or unconditionally guaranteed contracts are widely used (and particularly necessary) in basketball due to both the high rate of injuries for players and the high expectations of clubs when it comes to players' and coaches' performances. There are many variations as to how the "guaranteed no-cut" principle is expressed in basketball contracts, however some of the more common clauses in players' agreements are as follows:

> Contract Guarantee: Club agrees that this Agreement is unconditionally guaranteed contractual Agreement and that Player's Guaranteed Compensation and bonuses and the Agent Fee are fully guaranteed, due and payable, **including but not limited to in the event of Player's injury, illness, death, and/or lack of skill.**[126]

> [...] The Club agrees that this Agreement is a no-cut guaranteed agreement, and that the Club shall not have the right to suspend or release the Player in the event that **the Player does not exhibit sufficient skill or competitive ability, or in the event that an injury, illness or death shall befall the Player.** For the avoidance of doubt, in the event that the Player sustains an incapacitating injury or illness during the term of his Contract that renders the Player incapable of performing in some or all of the Club's remaining games or should the Club simply elect to replace Player with another player, Club agrees to meet all payment obligations to Player and Agent as though Player had performed in all games and met all obligations in this Agreement.[127]

> Club agrees that this Agreement is an unconditionally guaranteed contractual Agreement [...] The Club shall not have the right to suspend or release the Player in the event that **the Player does not exhibit sufficient skill or competitive ability, or in the event that an injury or illness shall befall the Player unless otherwise stated in the Agreement.** Accordingly, in such event, Club agrees to meet all payment obligations to the Player and Agent as though the Player had performed in all games and met all obligations in this Agreement. Without limiting any other rights of Player, if the Club rescinds this

[126]BAT 0284/12, *Appel & Wasserman Media Group v. Samsun Basketball Kulübü*, Award of 15 October 2012, para 7.

[127]BAT 0668/15, *Familia Basket Schio slr SSD v. Ogwumike*, Award of 26 August 2015, para 7.

Agreement without a legal cause, the Club is obligated to pay to the Player as an indemnity all salary compensation, benefits and bonuses contained in this Agreement. **This clause will operate even in case of injury, illness or lack of skills of the Player**."[128]

Similar wording is employed in the contracts of coaches:

> …the agreement is [sic] unconditionally guaranteed contractual Agreement and (…) the coach's guaranteed compensations and bonuses are net and fully guaranteed, due and payable, including but not limited to **in the event of Coach's injury, illness, death and/or lack of skill.** Thailand Basketball agrees that this agreement is a no-cut guaranteed agreement, and that Thailand Basketball shall not have the right to suspend or release the Coach **in the event that the Coach does not exhibit sufficient skill or competitive ability, or in the event that an injury, illness or death, occurred during the terms of this contract, shall befall the Coach.**[129]

> The guaranteed net Compensation above is vested in and owing to the Coach upon the completion of the execution of this Agreement and is **not contingent upon anything**. The Club agrees that this Agreement is a no-cut guaranteed agreement, and that the Club shall not have the right to suspend or release the Coach in the event that **the Coach's performance or the Club's performance is not satisfactory to the Club.** […] Should the Club elect to replace the Coach with another Coach at any time during the term of the Agreement, the Club shall continue to pay the Coach its (sic) guaranteed net Compensation […] for the full term of this Agreement at the times and the amounts specified above. In such an event **Coach shall be free to seek employment as a head coach with another club and shall be under no obligation to mitigate his damages** and should he be hired as a Head Coach the Coach's compensation with the new club shall reduce Club's obligation to pay the Coach its compensation and bonuses required herein by the amount the Coach receives as its compensation for its new club.[130]

> The CLUB GUARANTEE the AGREEMENT TO THE COACH, and all monies contracted as per Art. 3 and Art. 15 are hereby irrevocably guaranteed and shall be paid by the CLUB to both COACH and AGENT. THE CLUB CANNOT RESCIND THIS AGREEMENT AND SUBSTITUTE THE COACH, FOR **TECHNICAL REASONS OR POOR PERFORMANCES.**[131]

BAT arbitrators have interpreted the concept of a guaranteed contract as follows:

> "Guaranteed" means that the agreed salary payments are in principle due and cannot be reduced by the Club because the player is unable to provide his services because of sickness or injury or because the Player's performance did not meet the Club's expectations or because of lack of success of the Club's team…[132]

---

[128] BAT 0644/15, *Vougioukas v. Galatasaray Spor Kulübü Dernegi*, para 31.

[129] BAT 0429/13, *Coppa v. Basketball Sport Association of Thailand*, Award of 23 December 2013, para 56.

[130] FAT 0046/09, *Mahoric & Jakse v. Kyiv.*, para 5. See also FAT 0057/09, *Podkovyrov v. STKSSA*, para 5, where the contract expressly provided that all amounts were guaranteed (Article 3) but that the Club would have a right of termination "in case of 7 defeats on the way".

[131] BAT 0631/14, *Valdeolmillos Moreno v. Comité Olímpico Mexicano (COM) et al.*, para 10.

[132] BAT 0644/15, *Vougioukas v. Galatasaray Spor Kulübü Dernegi*, para 31.

> The purpose of Clause 9 of the Player Contract is to protect the Player's salary claims in certain cases where the Player does not perform as expected (or at all). Clause 9, first and second paragraph, makes clear that the Player's salary shall be fully guaranteed and cannot be affected by poor performance, diminished skills, injury or similar impairments to the Player's performance. The Club shall not be able to escape its payment obligations merely because it is unhappy with the Player's performance or because the Player no longer plays a role in its sporting strategy. The Player's right to demand payments on an accelerated basis in case of a unilateral rescission of the Player Contract flanks the salary guarantee that Clause 9 provides on behalf of the Player.[133]

However, and despite the broad wording of these contracts, it is generally recognized that they do not provide for full immunity for coaches or players in circumstances where their behaviour does not warrant protection:

> The guarantee of the salary is however not absolute but subject to certain explicit or implied exceptions: No salary can, e.g., be claimed in case of a justified termination of the Player Contract by the Club, which can also be concluded e contrario from Article 11, last sentence, of the Player Contract.
>
> Another exception concerns a player's duty to mitigate his damages. It has been consistent jurisprudence by the BAT based on generally accepted principles of the law of damages and also labour law that after an unjustified termination of the player contract by the club, the player has an obligation to take reasonable efforts to find a new club and that his alternative earnings shall be deducted from the compensation otherwise due by the club.[134]

In view of these stated exceptions, it is worth considering some common grounds for termination and the related BAT jurisprudence, as well as the BAT's approach to the concept of mitigation.

6.3.2.2 Common Grounds for Termination

a. Injury

Termination on the ground of injury is a very frequent scenario in BAT cases. The resulting awards have developed into a well-established case law, covering not only the principles to be applied to the termination of a contract following injury, but also the steps that both clubs and players are expected to take at the outset of their relationship in order to protect themselves.

As stated in the BAT 0502/14 award:

> The BAT already dealt with the issue of pre-existing injuries in several cases.[135] According to that jurisprudence, **the question who has to bear the consequences of an injury is a question of risk allocation. The Parties signed the Employment Contract as a guaranteed contract** (Clause 3.1: "The Club agrees that this Agreement is a no-cut

[133] BAT 0487/13, *KC Callero & Andrews v. SS Sutor Srl*, Award of 3 September 2014, para 66.

[134] BAT 0644/15, *Vougioukas v. Galatasaray Spor Kulübü Dernegi*, paras 32–33.

[135] Referring to BAT cases 0014/08, 0162/11, 0190/11, 0213/11 and 0318/12.

guaranteed agreement. – In case that Player gets injury during practising or games while carrying his obligations under this contract and that will bring him to being unable to perform in some or all rest games of the team, Club agrees to pay all salary as if Player would participate in all games.") **which assumes the Club to take the risk of any injury.**

However, risk allocation presupposes an informed decision by the Club when it accepts the Player, in other words a "guaranteed contract does not protect cheating".[136] In this context, **clubs are responsible to take reasonable measures to reduce the risk of undetected pre-existing injuries, e.g. by high standard medical examination consistent with best practice in the basketball industry**[137] and by **research of publicly available sources on the player's health condition.**[138] In the present case, the Club has not submitted evidence in regard to any specific questions asked to the Player. However, **Clause 1.4 of the Employment Contract provided the following obligation for the Player**:

"1.4 By signing this Contract **the Player is obliged to declare about current or previous injury or illness which might reduce his capability to perform at his best possible level.** The club does not fulfil its obligations (including financial one) for the consequences of the previous injuries or illnesses, that become apparent during the term of this contract including for the period of the player's disablement."

The Player's obligation under the Employment Contract to reveal – sua sponte – any significant and serious injury (Article 1.4. of the Employment Contract: "which might reduce his capability to perform at his best possible level") **is in line with BAT jurisprudence.**[139] According thereto **an injury is "significant and serious" within the above meaning if the Club would not have executed the contract had it known of the injury.**

According to general standards and in line with BAT jurisprudence, the **burden of proof for any fact lies with the party which derives its arguments from it.** In the present case the Club submits that it rightfully terminated the Employment Contract. Consequently, the **Club has to prove that the Player's [Player's body part] problems already preexisted when the Employment Contract was entered into, that the injury was likely to affect the Player's basketball performance during the term of the Employment Contract and that the Player knew of such significant and serious injury.**[140]

As is clear from the above, clubs will have a high burden of proof when it comes to justifying termination on the basis of an allegedly 'hidden' injury, as also noted in the following award:

---

[136]Referring to BAT 0154/11, para 77.

[137]Referring to BAT cases 0213/11, 0263/12 and 0318/12.

[138]Referring to BAT cases 0190/11 and 0213/11.

[139]Referring to BAT cases 0014/08, 0039/09, 0066/09, 0162/11 and 0213/11.

[140]BAT 0502/14, *Banic v. Unics Kazan Basketball Club*, Award of 30 April 2015, paras 80–83. See also BAT 0213/11, *Player v. Club*, para 97 et seq. (where a parallel was made with "*warranty issues that arise when goods are sold insofar as the respective duties and rights of the seller and the buyer. For example, what does it mean/contractually imply if a product is sold in the condition "as is", what is the responsibility of the seller for so-called "hidden defects", is the degree of responsibility different if the defect was known to the seller, what are the duties of the seller to inspect the goods upon delivery and what are the consequences if no inspection is made or if detected defects are not immediately invoked*").

> [...] the Respondent says that its position was justified as the Claimant had an injury which she hid. This is a very serious allegation and would require compelling proof that the Respondent had: (1) carried out a timely and thorough medical examination (consistent with best practice in the basketball industry) at which a series of specific questions had been put by the doctor or relevant practitioner; and (2) that the alleged injury complained of would not have been apparent to such a professional properly carrying out such an examination; and (3) answers given by the Claimant to the questions posed were knowingly incorrect and misleading.
>
> This is a heavy burden for any club and rightly so. A professional basketball club makes a significant investment in its players and it is therefore incumbent on a club to thoroughly examine a potential player as it is very well known (and reflected in virtually every professional basketball contract) that once the medical is passed, contract sums are usually guaranteed. This is the well-established practice and no well-informed club could be in any doubt about it. In short, if a club does not perform a thorough enough medical examination, then it must bear the later consequences.[141]

The award in BAT 0213/11 provides an example of the precautionary steps that have been recommended for clubs in BAT jurisprudence:

> [...] there is e.g. the possibility for the club to undertake basic research in advance regarding the player's playing history, particularly that of the prior season, to try and determine if the player has missed games, and, if so, whether it was for reasons of injury/illness, as well as to put precise oral and written questions to the player in that respect during the medical examination. Those questions can very easily be formulated to include soliciting information about any chronic or even isolated problems with muscles, tendons, and more generally articulations. A club may need to be even more cautious in this respect if a player has been on the circuit for many years and is of a certain age because that would tend to increase the risk of pre-existing medical conditions.
>
> If the club does not do its "homework" in advance in that respect and/or fails to undertake a thorough medical examination and within a procedure that obliges the player to carefully reflect upon prior injuries/illnesses, to make any corresponding disclosures and to sign his/her declaration in that connection, this may amount to a form of contributory fault/negligence which impacts the club's right to criticize the player's lack of candidness and characterise it as a breach of duty.[142]

Finally, it is important to note that in the event that a club intends to terminate a contract following an injury, it should do so without delay to ensure that the termination is deemed to have been in good faith:

> Indeed – given how simple it would have been to research her playing history and undertake a more in-depth medical examination in light of the clinical symptoms that appeared during the very first games – the Club's medical staff could not in good faith ignore the symptoms of a possibly serious underlying problem because the Club wished to benefit from the Player's skills on the court and at the same time deem the contractual guarantees

---

[141] BAT 0263/12, *Jujka and TP Sports Ltd v. Miejski Miedzyszkolny Klub Sportowy Katarzynki Torun "Energa"*, Award of 11 October 2011, paras 38–39.

[142] BAT 0213/11, *Player v. Club*, paras 109–110.

in case of injury to have become inapplicable. Nor could the Club blindly rely on the Player's explanations, except by being negligent.[143]

b. Other Grounds

There are, of course, other recurrent themes when it comes to the termination of a contract in basketball.

Insofar as clubs' termination of coaches and athletes are concerned, cases often arise in relation to an alleged lack of skill of the coach or player (that is not protected by an appropriate guarantee clause) and allegedly recurrent and/or serious breaches of the agreement by the coach or player.

When it comes to players and coaches terminating their contracts, the most obvious—and common—complaint is non-payment of salaries and other amounts.

Whether a party can immediately terminate a contract will, of course, depend on certain basic principles, such as: (i) whether the party has complied with its obligation to give notice of a breach and, if possible, to allow time for the breach to be rectified; (ii) if not, whether the breach is nevertheless sufficiently serious to warrant immediate termination; and (iii) whether the termination is in fact directly related to the alleged breach.

6.3.2.3 The Requirement to Give Notice

One of the clearest principles emerging from the BAT case law is that the parties must take a good faith approach to the termination of a contract.

Central to this question is whether the offending party has sufficiently been put on notice of the breach and, if possible, given an opportunity to rectify it prior to the contract being terminated:

> Furthermore it is a general principle of law – based on fairness – that alleged contractual breaches must normally be preceded by a formal notice of breach, which gives the other party a chance to conform its acts/behaviour and/or explain its position, before termination for cause can be resorted to; and it is a general principle in disciplinary matters that for reasons of fairness sanctions need to be foreseeable, progressive and proportional.[144]

---

[143] BAT 0668/15 and 0693/15 (consolidated), *Familia Basket Schio srl SSA v. Ogwumike & Sports International Group Inc. v. Familia Basket Schio*, para 82. See also BAT 0213/11, *Player v. Club*, para 111: "*Finally, it goes without saying that if a club discovers during the entry medical examination what it deems to be a problematic pre-existing medical condition, or at a later stage, i.e. after that examination, what it deems to be an unfairly undisclosed pre-existing medical condition of the player, the club must invoke this without delay to prevent being estopped from doing so; since it would be unfair to rely, on the one hand, on the possibility that the player may nevertheless be able to perform or become apt to play, and, on the other hand, reserve the possibility of invoking at a later stage the known medical problem*".

[144] BAT 0130/10, *Thomas et al. v. Baloncesto Fuenlabrada*, Award of 8 June 2011, para 145.

a. Notice Prior to a Club's Termination of a Coach or Player

In relation to the notice requirements imposed on clubs that wish to terminate a coach or player, it has been held that:

> [...] the Arbitrator finds that the less obvious, serious and damaging the alleged violations of the Player Contract by the Player are, the more the Club is required to notify and hear the Player before it takes the ultimate action and dismisses him prior to the agreed term of the agreement. There can be no question that the three reported incidents, which did not, on their own, justify a termination of the Player Contract, would have obliged the Club to timely notify and warn the Player and to hear him before it terminated the Player Contract. That did not happen. The Arbitrator finds that under the circumstances, the unilateral termination of the Player Contract was not justified.[145]

'Notice' requirements will often be expressly set out in the contracts themselves,[146] and are said to:

> [...] [echo] general principles of contract law – based on considerations of fairness – which require that before a contract is terminated for cause the other party must be given fair notice of the alleged breach/violation and be given the possibility of curing it, unless the breach is so serious that immediate termination is warranted.[147]

BAT arbitrators have also held that even where the underlying contract does not expressly require notice prior to termination, general considerations of fairness do:

> [...] even assuming that the Coach violated his professional duties, the early termination of a contract is only the last resort in case the relationship between the parties becomes unbearably distressed. If the misconduct is reparable, the party who is allegedly in breach of the contract must be warned and given an adequate opportunity to adjust its behaviour and to resume the execution of its contractual obligations. In the case at hand, no such warning has been issued by the Respondents. They did not provide any proof, either verbally or written, that they requested Claimant to return to Mexico and to continue to work as a head coach for the National Team.[148]

Furthermore, it is important to note that BAT arbitrators will generally prefer *contemporaneous* evidence that a coach or player was put on notice of alleged breaches in a timely fashion:

> [...] there is no contemporaneous evidence that during such period, i.e. between the end of September 2013 and February 2014, the HBF ever complained to the Coach or put him on notice that he was failing to perform any contractually specified or implied duties,

---

[145]BAT 0640/14, *Smith & Wasserman Media Group v. Galatasaray Spor Külübü Dernegi*, Award of 27 July 2015, para 48.

[146]See, for example BAT 0535/14, *Daniels v. Liaoning Hengye Basketball Club*, Award of 7 August 2014, para 33, where the Agreement in question stipulated that "*Club has the unilateral right to terminate the contract with the player if the player still violates any reasonable rules of Club and any rules of CBA League set by Chinese Basketball Association after Player and his Agent have previously been warned by Club two times in writing of same violation and given a chance to cure*".

[147]Ibid., para 34.

[148]BAT 0631/14, *Valdeolmillos Moreno v. Comité Olímpico Mexicano (COM) et al.*, para 111.

whether it be in relation to limited actions such as the participation in HBF board/committee meetings or broader tasks.[149]

Finally, it has been expressed (and is self-evident) that *written* notices should be served so as to make it clear to the offending party that the breach is serious and to provide proof of notice in any subsequent proceedings:

> [...] the Arbitrator would also like to point out that written, as opposed to oral, notices serve a purpose because they usually have more impact on the person receiving the warning and also serve as proof. In a context such as professional basketball, if clubs wish to ensure proof that notices/warnings have been given, they can serve written notices on the Player but also copy the Player's agents/representatives by email and/or fax/post.[150]

b. Notice Prior to Termination for Non-payment

Importantly, notice requirements are not solely aimed at clubs. Players and coaches will also be required to provide adequate notice prior to terminating a contract, in particular for non-payment. Often such warning requirements will be stipulated in the contract, for example in the following terms:

> In case of scheduled payments not being made to the Player or Agents by the Club within forty-five (45) days of the scheduled payment date, the Player will have right to request terminating this agreement unilaterally by serving a written notice to the Club. In case of the scheduled payments not being made within the next seven (7) days after such a written notice is received by the Club, the Player will have right to terminate this agreement unilaterally by serving the Club a final written notice of termination. In this case, the Player shall immediately be entitled to all salaries under this agreement and shall have no further obligations to the Club. The Club shall retain no rights to the Player except for the obligation to pay all salaries and earned bonuses under the terms of this agreement. Upon receipt of a request from the Turkish Basketball Federation to issue the Player's Letter of Clearance, the Club must authorize the federation to do so unconditionally within twenty four (24) hours without charging a transfer fee.[151]

In addition to the express terms of the agreement, it is clear from BAT jurisprudence that a player's termination on the basis of non-payment will be even more solid where he or she acts in a clear and fair manner:

> Those written communications in February-March 2013 establish that although the Claimants were systematic and rigorous in invoking and applying this particular term of article 5 of the Contract, they did so in a fair manner by making it clear from the outset that they intended to invoke it and by putting the Club on formal notice on three occasions in an explicit fashion (quoting the clause in question).

[149]BAT 0584/14, *Trinchieri v. Hellenic Basketball Federation*, Award 21 November 2014, para 73.

[150]BAT 0535/14, *Daniels v. Liaoning Hengye Basketball Club*, para 40. It has also been suggested that clubs ought to have players countersign written notices in order to prove that they have in fact been received (see BAT 0568/14, *Johnson v. Zhejiang Chouzhou Professional Basketball Club Company Ltd*, Award of 18 December 2014, para 89).

[151]BAT 0278/12, *Korstin v. Besiktas Jimnastik Kulübü Dernegi*, Award of 31 August 2012, para 47.

> Moreover by first putting the Club on notice that the Player would suspend his performance upon the delay in payment of the Agent's fee reaching 30 days and by actually enforcing that term (the Player stopped playing) before enforcing the right to terminate, the Claimants made it obvious that they were serious and that termination would follow if the payment was not received. Thus, in good faith the Club could and should have felt warned.[152]

With that said, it must be noted that when interpreting the notice requirements, the fact that a party has in the past accepted late payments will not necessarily constitute a waiver of his or her right to terminate the agreement for late payment, but rather be seen as a question of fact to be determined in light of the particular circumstances of the case.[153]

Finally, and while notice requirements may be enforced strictly,[154] BAT has also held that termination provisions referring to non-payment do not necessarily encompass situations where just "*any* payment was late by more than 30 days, no matter how substantial or insubstantial the outstanding amount".[155] Although such situations will be considered on a case by case basis, the general approach should take into account the parties' intentions:

> The Arbitrator is not convinced that the Parties indeed intended to allow for an early and immediate termination of the Coach Contract in case of payment default on the most negligible amount, as the wording of Clause 14 c) might suggest. Such understanding would run directly counter to the core premises of immediate contract termination for "just cause", against the background of which the termination options for a late or non-payment must be considered.[156]

6.3.2.4 Immediate Termination

The principle of *pacta sunt servanda* is an overriding consideration in any equitable review of the termination of a contract. Its significance has been expressed as

---

[152]BAT 0396/13, *Gaffney & Ayesa v. Club Joventut Badalona SAD*, Award of 16 October 2013, paras 74–75.

[153]See BAT 0278/12, *Korstin v. Besiktas Jimnastik Kulübü Dernegi*, para 49. To the contrary, see BAT 0720/15, *Millage v. Torku Konyaspor Basketbol Kulübü*, Award of 4 December 2015, paras 48–49.

[154]See, for example, BAT 0291/12, *Drucker & Beobasket Ltd v. Sutor Basket Montegranaro srl*, Award of 20 November 2012, paras 67–68: "*Article 7 of the Coaching Agreement entitles the Coach to terminate the Coaching Agreement with immediate effect after the Club's contractual payments were not received by the Coach within 30 days from the due date. [...] Then, the Coach must notify the Club that the Coaching Agreement would be deemed terminated if no payment was received within another 5 days. [...] The Arbitrator accepts that the Coach was not prohibited from sending his termination notice before the expiration of the 30-day time limit of Article 8 of the Coaching Agreement. However, also in that case, the termination notice could only lead to the termination of the Coaching Agreement if the due payments had not arrived at the Coach's bank account on or before 35 days upon the due date, i.e. on or before 14 January 2012. [...] The Agent's email of 3 January 2012 may have brought the Club to pay the due December 2011-salary. However, it did not terminate the Coaching Agreement*".

[155]BAT 0383/13, *Dikeoulakos* et al. *v. CSM Targoviste*, Award of 22 January 2014, para 78.

[156]Ibid., para 79.

follows:

> The principle of pacta sunt servanda is one of the leading principles in BAT jurisprudence. A signed contract is deemed valid and enforceable unless a party demonstrates (i) that it was in fundamental error regarding specific facts which must be considered in good faith to be an essential basis of the contract, (ii) that it was induced to enter into the contract by fraud of the other party, or (iii) that it signed the contract under duress from the other party.[157]

> It is a matter of universal acceptance that pacta sunt servanda, i.e., that parties who entered into contracts are bound by their terms. Observance of obligations entered into is a fundamental and integral matter common throughout all civilized nations and legal systems. Without such a principle, commerce, honesty, and the integrity of dealings would all but vanish. It is just and fair that when parties enter into the sort of contracts which they did in this matter, then the provisions of such contracts should be observed.[158]

BAT cases are therefore often decided by reference to this principle:

> The doctrine of pacta sunt servanda (which is consistent with justice and equity – parties who make a bargain are expected to stick to that bargain) – is the principle by which the Arbitrator will examine the merits of the claims.[159]

An exception to the *pacta sunt servanda* rule will obviously be where a party has committed a breach that is so serious as to render the continued performance of the contract impossible. That said, BAT arbitrators have consistently held that only a particularly serious breach of contract qualifies as "just cause" to immediately terminate the relationship between the parties:

> Early termination of a contract is the last resort if the relationship between contractual parties becomes distressed. In principle, therefore, an employment contract cannot be prematurely terminated based on a simple breach of obligation. Only a particularly serious breach of contract qualifies as "just cause".[160]

> […] it is up [to] the Respondents to demonstrate that the Coach violated his professional duties in a way that made it impossible for the Respondents to maintain the contractual relationship any longer.[161]

> In order to constitute a repudiatory breach of contract (and thus give rise to a right of termination on behalf of the aggrieved party), the Arbitrator considers that the breach must be fundamental (or constitute a breach of a fundamental term) and evince an intention, on the part of the party in breach, not to perform his obligations under the contract in some essential respect.[162]

---

[157]BAT 0318/12, *Hunter & Priority Sports and Entertainment v. Polisportiva Dinamo SRL*, Award of 15 October 2013, para 80.

[158]FAT 0065/09, *Mikhalevskiy v. Bikov*, Award of 12 April 2010, para 43.

[159]BAT 0650/15, *Jawai & Wasserman Media Group v. Galatasaray Spor Kulübü Dernegi*, Award of 30 July 2015, para 33.

[160]BAT 0631/14, *Valdeolmillos Moreno v. Comité Olímpico Mexicano (COM) et al.*, para 107 (referring to BAT 0383/13).

[161]Ibid., paras 106–107.

[162]BAT 0471/13, *Filipovski v. KK Union Olimpija Ljubljana*, Award of 28 April 2014, para 61.

6.3.2.5 Termination in Relation to the Specific Breach Relied upon

In addition to the requirement that only serious breaches allow for termination of a contract, it is also necessary for the party who terminated the agreement to establish that the breach in question was actually the motivating factor for the termination. This has been expressed by a BAT arbitrator as follows:

> [...] it would be necessary for the Respondent to demonstrate that:
>
> (i) the breach of contract was sufficiently serious so as to constitute a repudiatory breach of contract (in the sense of providing the aggrieved party with the right to terminate the contract); and
> (ii) the Contract was terminated on the basis of the Claimant's repudiatory breach of contract (and not for some other reason).
>
> [...] The Arbitrator also notes that the Termination Letter dated 28 April 2013 pursuant to which the Respondent terminated the Contract does not mention any of the Alleged Breaches (or indeed any misconduct on the part of the Claimant).
>
> Moreover, the Respondent has not provided any documentary evidence of notice being given to, or concerns being raised with, the Claimant in relation to any of the Alleged Breaches (or the Claimant's conduct more generally), despite being specifically requested for such evidence in the First Procedural Order. Therefore, based on the evidence before him, the Arbitrator accepts the Claimant's assertion that the Respondent first raised concerns in writing about the Alleged Breaches in its Answer, submitted in the course of these proceedings.
>
> In these circumstances, the Arbitrator finds that the Contract was not terminated on the basis of the Alleged Breaches committed by the Claimant (which in any event are not capable of constituting repudiatory breaches of contract).[163]

6.3.2.6 Ancillary Claims

BAT arbitrations often feature claims for payments in addition to the specified salary of the player or coach. In order to succeed with any such claims, parties will be required to produce directly relevant evidence and to specify and substantiate each of their claims. Furthermore, it should be kept in mind that BAT has established a particularly high threshold when it comes to amounts claimed for damages to a party's reputation.

a. Requirement of Specificity/Substantiation

For each and every claim of a party, the BAT requires: (i) directly relevant evidence; and (ii) specificity and substantiation.

[163] Ibid., paras 55 and 62–64.

This has been described as follows:

> In line with consistent jurisprudence of BAT, the claimant must prove the existence and the quantum of the damage claimed.[164]

By way of example, a 2014 case involved a request for a lump sum payment covering items as diverse as 'economic damages', 'employment damages', 'reputational damages' and 'tax damages'.[165] Despite being invited by the Arbitrator to "*'specify exactly' how the lump sum [was] calculated/composed in relation to the different heads of damages claimed*" the coach failed to do so. As a result, the BAT Arbitrator held that:

> This claim is unsubstantiated. In particular, Claimant has not submitted in what respect and in what amount he suffers damages. […] The same is true for all other heads of damages the Coach claims. […] Claimant alludes to certain types of damages allegedly incurred, but only in vague terms and in effect failing to specify the individual heads of damages or to provide any meaningful calculation.[166]

Furthermore, any claims submitted by the parties must be supported by clear and convincing evidence which proves not only the existence of the claim, but also the precise amounts in question.[167] That being said, there may be exceptions to this rule in situations where a party faces challenges in providing an exact calculation of damages:

> In that relation, it is noteworthy that it is not uncommon under rules and principles of damage law, to allow a judge or arbitrator some discretion in evaluating the quantum of the damage if the exact amount cannot be established because the nature of the damage or the circumstances render the proof particularly difficult, providing the claiming party substantiates the facts leading to the existence of the damage and gives certain indications as to the quantum.
>
> Furthermore, in keeping with the jurisprudence of the BAT, the Arbitrator finds that the ex aequo et bono clause in the Contract allows for a special indemnity to be fixed as compensation for damages, in order to adequately compensate a party that has convincingly evidenced the existence of damages, while at the same time its nature and/or the particular factual circumstances surrounding the damaging event(s) make the substantiation of the amount difficult or impossible.[168]

It is important to note, however, that even in circumstances where the arbitrator exercises his or her discretion, the amount fixed shall be compensatory rather than punitive and:

---

[164]BAT 0345/12, *FC Bayern München e.V. v. Foster*, Award of 20 March 2013, para 83.

[165]BAT 0631/14, *Valdeolmillos Moreno v. Comité Olímpico Mexicano (COM)* et al.

[166]Ibid., paras 118–122.

[167]See BAT 0502/14, *Banic v. Unics Kazan Basketball Club*, where the five invoices produced did not correspond to the timing of the player's medical treatment, nor to the amounts charged for it. The arbitrator held that he was "*not able to determine how the Player arrived at the amount claimed and whether he is entitled to any reimbursement. The Arbitrator finds that the claim for reimbursement of medical expenses is unsubstantiated and rejects the Player's request*" (paras 107–109).

[168]BAT 0334/12, *Scafati Basket v. Marigney*, Award of 27 March 2013, paras 78–79.

> [...] shall be determined with the aim of estimating an amount which is as close as possible to what the actual damage suffered was, bearing in mind all the relevant facts and evidence.[169]

b. Damages to Reputation

With respect to reputational damages claims, the BAT has established a high threshold, both in terms of the damage which can be held to be compensable and the evidence required to establish it.

As to the former, it has been stated that:

> In respect of Claimant's claim pertaining to immaterial damage, loss of reputation, honour and public image, the Arbitrator only notes as follows: In principle, national legislations are rather restrictive in awarding immaterial damages. The underlying idea is that – in principle – there is no rational standard for calculating such damages. Of course, there are plenty of exceptions to this rule. In particular inasmuch as fundamental legal interests are concerned (life, health, physical, safety, freedom of movement, sexual self-determination etc.), most jurisdictions will allow for some kind of compensation of immaterial damage.
>
> The Arbitrator finds that – absent any specific provision in the Contract and deciding ex aequo et bono – restrictive principles should apply when it comes to compensation of immaterial damages. In the case at hand, Claimant submits that he suffered damages in relation to his reputation, honour and public image. The Arbitrator finds that quite frequently unlawful behaviour of the contractual partner will result in a reputational damage. However, the damage to someone's reputation and honour must be of serious impact, beyond what is seen as normal, in order to qualify as existential impairment. [...]
>
> In any event, the Arbitrator finds that the Respondents' behaviour was not such as to have reasonably caused a serious impairment of Claimant's life that would warrant a compensation. Thus, the respective claim is dismissed.[170]

With respect to a club's claim for such damages,[171] another award held that:

> It is true that if the exact amount of damages cannot be established, the Arbitrator shall assess them in his discretion, but it is still up to the claiming party to demonstrate the facts leading to the asserted loss and give certain indications about the quantum of the loss. [...] the Arbitrator finds no documentary support of Claimant's allegation that the Club's image was affected and how such loss of reputation should be measured.[172]

---

[169] Ibid., para 86.

[170] BAT 0631/14, *Valdeolmillos Moreno v. Comité Olímpico Mexicano (COM) et al.*, paras 123–125.

[171] The club suggested that it suffered negative effects with respect to its "*image with the supporters, the media and the world of basketball*" (see BAT 0093/10, *ASD Pallacanestro Femminile Schio v. Braxton*, Award of 11 October 2010, paras 79–82).

[172] Ibid.

Such an approach has been followed in various other cases such as BAT 0298/12,[173] BAT 0212/11,[174] BAT 0584/14,[175] BAT 0543/14,[176] and BAT 0190/11.[177]

Finally, as shown in the award in FAT 0040/09, causation must be established before any claim for reputational damages can be accepted:

> With respect to the "punitive" damages requested by the Player as compensation for the possible negative effect on her reputation and contractual opportunities in Turkey caused by the article posted on Internet, the Arbitrator finds there is no evidence that the Club was involved in any manner with the publication of the article in question and cannot therefore in all fairness be deemed responsible. Accordingly, the corresponding claim for compensation by the Player is rejected.[178]

6.3.2.7 The Duty to Mitigate and Other Defences

Finally, it is worth noting two common responses to claims: (i) the duty to mitigate; and (ii) hardship or economic difficulties. While the former response is consistently upheld and applied by the BAT, the latter holds little weight as a justification for the failure to pay players and coaches.

---

[173]Where it was held at para 120 that: "*the Arbitrator finds that there is insufficient evidence of her image and reputation having suffered in a durable manner for any amount of compensation to be awarded in that connection*".

[174]Where it was held at para 49 that: "*The Claimant seeks image damages. The Arbitrator finds that this claim is not well founded. Apart from the fact that no proof has been adduced to support this claim, it is clear from the fact that the Claimant's reputation and skill have been recognised by Spartak Moscow for the 2011-2012 season that her reputation and image have not been adversely affected by the Respondent's actions*".

[175]Where it was held at para 83 that: "*With respect to the Coach claim for moral damages, the Arbitrator finds that the Coach has not established that his image or reputation suffered in any manner from his replacement by another coach, among others because it is frequent in team sports for a coach to be replaced for the sake of seeking new synergies, or proven the existence of any causality between the termination and any form of lost profit or other financial damage. Consequently, the claim for moral damages will be rejected*".

[176]Where it was held at para 52 that: "*With regard to the damages claimed by the Player for moral prejudice, the Arbitrator finds that no moral prejudice or corresponding financial damage have been established by the Player, and that the circumstances do not indicate any prejudice to her career or reputation was caused by the Club, bearing in mind also, once again, that the Player herself chose not to even try and find a new contract abroad*".

[177]Where it was held at para 87 that: "*The Club requests that the Player must pay a penalty at the discretion of the Arbitrator because he damaged the reputation of the Club when he constantly disregarded the Coach's instructions. However, the Club does not specify, let alone prove, the asserted reputational damage any further. The Arbitrator finds that this counterclaim is unsubstantiated and must be dismissed*".

[178]*Hornbuckle et al. v. Besiktas Jimnastik Kulübü*, Award of 29 October 2009, para 73.

a. The Duty to Mitigate

The duty to mitigate is one of the most clearly established principles in the BAT case law:

> […] according to the consistent jurisprudence of the BAT,[179] a player is under the duty to take all reasonable steps to mitigate the damage. Therefore, any other payments a player received (or might have – acting with due care – received) during the contractual period for which compensation is sought must be deducted from the amount claimed as damages.[180]

> […] a player or a coach whose contract has been prematurely terminated has an obligation to mitigate the damage of the Club. They must actively look out for a new source of income and may not remain passive.[181]

As to the duty of a player to mitigate her or his damages, the BAT has noted that:

> Another exception [to a guaranteed salary] concerns a player's duty to mitigate his damages. It has been consistent jurisprudence by the BAT based on generally accepted principles of the law of damages and also labour law that after an unjustified termination of the player contract by the club, the player has an obligation to take reasonable efforts to find a new club and that his alternative earnings shall be deducted from the compensation otherwise due by the club.[182] A player shall not profit from the early termination of the player contract but rather be put into the same economic situation as if that player contract would have correctly been fulfilled. The Arbitrator shall thus award the sum which would restore the injured party into the economic position that such party expected from performance of the contract. On the other hand, the injured party is obliged to mitigate the damage. In addition, any advantages which the injured party may have gained as a consequence of the breach (e.g. salaries otherwise earned) must be taken into account when calculating the compensation due.[183] The Arbitrator concludes that the Player must accept that the income he earned with [his new club] during the remaining season 2014/2015 shall be deducted from the compensation due by the Club. This alternative income concerns any earnings agreed between the Player and his new club, including bonus payments.[184]

BAT arbitrators will take into account various factors in assessing whether a player has adequately mitigated his or her position including (but not limited to): whether the player was under time pressure to conclude a new agreement due to the timing of the termination;[185] whether the player has provided sufficient infor-

---

[179] Referring to BAT 0129/10; FAT 0043/09.

[180] BAT 0155/11, *Kikowski v. KK Union Olimpija Ljubljana*, Award of 8 August 2011, para 8.

[181] See BAT 0257/12, *Orlando & DoubleB Management sas v. Besiktas Jimnastik Kulubu Dernegi*, Award of 3 August 2012, para 71.

[182] Referring to FAT 0005/08 p. 19; FAT 0014/08, para 68; FAT 0024/08, para 48–50; BAT 0237/11, para 56–59; BAT 0289/12, para 44; BAT 0535/14, para 53.

[183] Referring to FAT 0014/08, para 68.

[184] See BAT 0644/15, *Vougioukas v. Galatasaray Spor Kulübü Dernegi*, paras 33–34.

[185] See, for example, BAT 0501/14, *De Mondt & Stainier v. Kayseri Kaski Spor Kulübü*, Award of 14 August 2014; BAT 0497/13, *Jonusas & UAB East Players v. Basket Juvecaserta s.r.l.*, Award of 1 July 2014, para 65.

mation about his or her negotiations with other clubs and efforts to conclude a new contract (and, if so, what those efforts were);[186] and whether the player was forced for some reason to enter into a contract with inferior financial conditions or should have made greater efforts to conclude a contract with higher financial compensation.[187]

With regard to coaches, the BAT has recognized that "it may be more difficult for coaches to find alternative employment than for players".[188] BAT Arbitrators will, nevertheless, also look into factors such as: the timing of the termination (i.e. whether it is before the start of the season and, if not, the remaining time under the contract);[189] whether the coach has a "credible explanation" for agreeing to a significantly lower salary;[190] and whether the coach has submitted any evidence "to suggest that he attempted to obtain a higher salary".[191]

Finally, it is worth noting that even an express contractual provision suggesting that there is no duty to mitigate may not be accepted as binding by the BAT:

> This raises the question of whether the wording of a contract must always be decisive in determining the parties' respective rights and obligations or whether the circumstances surrounding its execution and performance as well as principles of fairness may sometimes lead to a different result.
>
> As noted in a prior BAT case (BAT 0421/13), in which a practically identical exclusion of the duty to mitigate and right to offset was contractually stipulated, in principle the clear wording of a contract is to be upheld.

[186]See, for example, BAT 0501/14, *De Mondt & Stainier v. Kayseri Kaski Spor Kulübü*. See also BAT 0303/12, *Markota & Xl Agency v. Union Olimpija Ljubljana*, Award of 8 May 2013, para 79: "*It is simply not sufficient for a player to spend well over half a professional season playing for the sake of playing, yet take no steps to mitigate his financial position*". See also BAT 0385/13, *Liatsos & Antoniou v. BC AEL Limassol*, Award of 22 January 2014, para 59.

[187]See, for example, BAT 0501/14, *De Mondt & Stainier v. Kayseri Kaski Spor Kulübü*; FAT 0024/08, *Sakellariou & Dimitropoulos v. Avellino*, Award of 11 May 2009, paras 48–49: "*In view of Claimant 1's admitted skills and potential, the Arbitrator holds that Claimant 1 should have made further efforts to find a new employment, even with terms substantially lower than in the Contract, instead of returning to an amateur level within less than one month after his release from the Contract. Indeed, Claimant 1 did not present any explanation why a promising young player receiving a monthly salary of EUR 4000 at the beginning of the season accepts shortly thereafter to join an amateur club and to render his services for more than six months in return of no salary at all*".

[188]BAT 0542/14, *Pancotto v. Felice Scandone SpA*, para 59. See also BAT 0631/14, *Valdeolmillos Moreno v. Comité Olímpico Mexicano (COM)* et al., para 115, referring to BAT 0256/12, para 170; BAT 0231/11, para 67: "*it is notoriously difficult for a (assistant) coach to find a coaching position during an ongoing basketball season*"; and BAT 0256/12, paras 169–170: "*mitigation is much more difficult for a coach than a player. A team needs many players, but only one head coach. Thus, Claimant 1 would certainly not find it easy to readily secure alternative employment*".

[189]BAT 0631/14, *Valdeolmillos Moreno v. Comité Olímpico Mexicano (COM)* et al., para 115.

[190]BAT 0542/14, *Pancotto v. SS Felice Scandone SpA*, para 58.

[191]Ibid., paras 58–59.

However, in many legal systems and to different degrees, a contractual clause which is unfair due to the circumstances in which it was negotiated or which produces unfair consequences due to changes in circumstances (under the principle "rebus sic stantibus") may sometimes be deemed invalid or its consequences tempered by the courts examining the circumstances. Furthermore, in a number of legal systems, e.g. under Swiss law, when interpreting a contractual provisions in light of all the circumstances, the wording of the contract is an important but not the only element which must be examined and weighed in seeking what the true intention of the parties was, i.e. in determining whether and in what manner there was a meeting of the minds.

In addition, in this case the parties to the Agreement expressly agreed that any dispute in front of the BAT must be decided "ex aequo et bono", which means that even if the wording of a contractual provision is clear, its content may nevertheless in certain circumstances be deemed intrinsically unfair and unjust.

Bearing in mind the foregoing legal context and principles, which assist the Arbitrator in his ex aequo et bono assessment of the case, the Arbitrator has some doubt regarding whether an advance, complete and unconditional exclusion of the duty to mitigate and of the right for a club to request the offset of any amounts earned by a player under a new contract with another club for the exact same period of time (the latter exclusion being much more far reaching), is in keeping with the rationale of an employment contract in the field of sport, in terms of basic fairness/balance of consideration.

Indeed, an employment contract of the sort is not a commercial contract entered into for pure profit; it is intended to ensure a fair remuneration in exchange for a player's duty to perform as best as possible as an athlete. Moreover, athletes often earn high salaries for their performance, and contracts such as the Agreement which are fully guaranteed already offer a significant degree of protection to the player. Therefore, unless the complete and unconditional exclusion of the duty to mitigate damages and of the right to set off duplicated earnings is interpreted to be a form of sanction for an abusive termination, it is not easy to consider that a clause of such type equitably fits with a contract of this nature.

Thus, the Arbitrator finds that, except where strong evidence is adduced that the parties to a fully-guaranteed player's contract discussed, understood and accepted all the consequences of such a far-reaching exclusion, it may not be automatically upheld as expressing the clear common intent of the parties, and its fairness may be evaluated ex aequo et bono in light of all the circumstances of the particular case, e.g. taking into consideration in what manner the contract was negotiated, in what manner it was terminated and by which party, in what financial and personal (for the player) position the respective parties were at the time, what financial and other impact the termination had on each of them, how easy it was/would have been for the player to find a new contract without suffering other possible consequences in terms of reputation/convenience, how much money is involved overall, etc.[192]

b. Defences Based on Economic Difficulties

Finally, in disputes arising from the non-payment of players, BAT arbitrators have shown an unwillingness to accept financial difficulties as a defence.[193]

---

[192] BAT 0535/14, *Daniels v. Liaoning Hengye Basketball Club*, paras 48–54.

[193] See, for example, BAT 0258/12, *Entersport v. Men's Basketball Club Dynamo Moscow*, Award of 25 June 2012, para 43: "*The alleged economic difficulties are certainly regrettable but they do not release the Club from its contractual obligations*", and BAT 0242/11, *Vrbanc v. KK Cibona Zagreb*, Award of 31 August 2012, para 48: "*financial difficulties faced by a club is no defence to a claim by a player for unpaid and overdue salary payments*".

Indeed, in a case in which the club's defence was based on financial hardship caused by the global economic crisis, the arbitrator held that this was neither unforeseeable when concluding a contract, nor was there any 'good faith' requirement for a player to reduce his salary where a club's financial situation had changed dramatically:

> With regard to the Respondent's submissions as to the application of the cited provisions of the [Greek Civil Code] in this case more generally, and again without needing to make formal findings on these points based on national law in light of his obligation to decide this dispute ex aequo et bono, the Arbitrator:
>
> - is not persuaded that a global financial crisis, a national recession, or financial difficulties particular to a specific person or organization, are necessarily extraordinary or unforeseeable; and
> - is not persuaded that any requirement of good faith between a player and his club would require the player to accept reduced payments or would excuse the club for making reduced payments simply because the club's financial circumstances had changed, even if they had changed dramatically.[194]

Further, the arbitrator held that it was not necessary to decide such cases on the basis of national law or the UNIDROIT Principles[195] as the BAT jurisprudence on the subject was both well-established and appropriate:

> It is well established in BAT jurisprudence that financial difficulties faced by a club provide no defence to a claim by a player for salary payments which are due and unpaid. The Arbitrator does not find that the Respondent's submissions on this point in relation to Greek law and other principles help him to reach a conclusion in this case which departs from the BAT jurisprudence. As explained above, the Arbitrator must decide this dispute ex aequo et bono, and that is what he has done. The Arbitrator finds that the existing BAT jurisprudence applies in this case. In disputes before the BAT, financial hardship – even if caused by a global or national financial crisis – is not a defence or answer to claims for amounts due and unpaid under contracts.[196]

Finally, BAT arbitrators have held that it is a player's right not to accept payment by instalments in such cases:

> The Respondent has proposed that it might pay the Claimant the money it owes him in instalments. The Arbitrator is unaware of any attempt having been made to do so to date. The Arbitrator notes the Claimant's statement that the letter in which that arrangement was proposed (i.e. the Respondent's response to the Procedural Order) was the first time the Respondent suggested such an arrangement in a lengthy period of correspondence, and that in the circumstances the Claimant declines to agree to such an arrangement. That is the Claimant's right.[197]

---

[194]See BAT 0314/12, *Papaloukas v. Olympiakos*, Award of 15 July 2013, para 76.

[195]UNIDROIT Principles of International Commercial Contracts 2010 (http://www.unidroit.org/english/principles/contracts/principles2010/integralversionprinciples2010-e.pdf.).

[196]BAT 0314/12, *Papaloukas v. Olympiakos*, paras 76–78.

[197]See BAT 0350/12, *Labovic v. BC Krasnye Krylia Samara*, Award of 10 June 2013, para 44. See also BAT 0166/11, *Fox v. BC Kalev Cramo*, Award of 17 August 2011, para 46.

With that said, one could imagine a situation in which a player's outright refusal to accept (only marginally) late payment by way of instalments could be held to be unreasonable in the circumstances. Thus, players should approach termination of a contract cautiously in such cases.[198]

References

Anthony SW (2013) Show me the money: examining FIBA's basketball arbitration tribunal and the impact of ex aequo et bono in international sports contract disputes. Resolved J Altern Dispute Resolut (Student Works Edition) 36–48

Berger B, Kellerhals F (2015) International and domestic arbitration in Switzerland. Staempfli, Bern

Kaufmann-Kohler G, Rigozzi A (2015) International arbitration—Law and practice in Switzerland. OUP, Oxford

Martens D-R (2011) Basketball arbitral tribunal, an innovative system for resolving disputes in sport (only in Sport?). ISLJ (1–2):54–57

Rigozzi A (2010) Challenging awards of the court of arbitration for sports. J Int Dispute Settl 1:217–265

Rosen DE (2011) For Americans overseas, a referee for paychecks. New York Times 5 February 2011

Sykora D (2011) Der schiedsgerichtliche Billigkeitsentscheid. Dike, Zurich

Trakman L (2012) Ex aequo et bono: basing decisions on that which is just and fair. Transnational Dispute Manage 9 (pages unnumbered)

Zagklis A (2013) Fast break: an overview of how the Fédération Internationale de Basketball handles disputes fairly, quickly, and cost-efficiently. In: Colucci M, Jones K (eds) International and Comparative Sports Justice, European Sports Law and Policy Bulletin vol 1, pp 113–128

Zagklis A (2015a) Lex sportiva—from theory to practice: lessons to be learned from the jurisprudence of the Court of Arbitration for Sport (CAS) and of the Basketball Arbitral Tribunal (BAT). In: Vieweg K (ed) Lex Sportiva. Duncker Humblot, Berlin

Zagklis A (2015b) Three pointer: an overview of how the basketball arbitral tribunal handles financial disputes. In: Panagiotopoulos DP (ed) Sports Law—Lex Sportiva—Lex Olympica and Sports Jurisdiction Experience—Development and Perspective (20th IASL Congress (2014)). EKEAD, Athens, pp 290–298

---

[198] For example see BAT 0383/13, *Dikeoulakos* et al. *v. CSM Targoviste*, para 79 (as discussed above).

Part II
Commentaries of CAS Awards

Chapter 7
CAS 2013/A/3365 *Juventus FC v. Chelsea FC* and *CAS 2013/A/3366 A.S. Livorno Calcio S.p.A. v. Chelsea FC*, Award of 21 January 2015

Antoine Duval

Abstract On 21 January 2015, the CAS rendered its award in the latest episode of the *Mutu* case. The core legal question raised concerned the interpretation of Article 14(3) of the FIFA RSTP, in their 2001 version, and more precisely whether, in the event a player is dismissed by his club for having consumed cocaine, the new club bears the duty to pay the compensation due by the player to his former club. Having won one of the most high profile cases in the history of the CAS, Chelsea FC has been desperately hunting for its money (as far as the US) since the rendering of the award. Thus, the English football club had the idea to turn against Mutu's first employers after his dismissal in 2005, Juventus and Livorno, with success in front of the FIFA DRC, but, as we will see, not before the CAS. This award is extremely important for lawyers involved in disputes arising out of transfers in football as it provides a robust justification for the need to take into account the EU law context of the adoption of the FIFA RSTP in interpreting their provisions.

Keywords CAS · *Bosman* ruling · EU law · FIFA RSTP · International sports law · *Lex sportiva* · Arbitration

Contents

Dr. A. Duval (✉)
T.M.C ASSER Institute for European and International Law, The Hague, The Netherlands
e-mail: a.duval@asser.nl

A. Duval and A. Rigozzi (eds.), *Yearbook of International Sports Arbitration 2015*,
DOI 10.1007/978-94-6265-129-6_7

7.1 Facts and Procedure of the Case

The *Mutu* saga is probably one of the best-known case in sports law (alongside the unbeatable *Bosman*[1] case and the up and coming *Pechstein*[2] one). It cumulates the glamour touch of a star's downfall due to a positive cocaine test and many important legal intricacies. The saga started in July 2004 with a private drug test conducted by Chelsea FC (hereafter Chelsea) on its players, including striker Adrian Mutu, who turned out to be positive to cocaine. The club issued a fine and a warning to its player. In October 2004, Mutu was again tested positive to cocaine, this time by the English FA. Upon this finding, and Mutu's admission of having ingested cocaine, Chelsea decided to terminate his contract on 28 October 2004. On 29 January 2005, the player was registered with AS Livorno Calcio (hereafter Livorno), before being transferred two days later to Juventus FC (hereafter Juventus). Indeed, Juventus had reached the quota of non-EU players it could recruit from outside Italy and used this strategy to circumvent the Italian rules applicable at that time.

Meanwhile, Mutu had challenged Chelsea's decision to terminate his employment contract in front of the FA's Appeals Committee (FAPLAC). In April 2005, the FAPLAC decided that Mutu had committed a breach of his employment contract without just cause. Mutu appealed this decision to the CAS without success.[3] In May 2006, Chelsea filed a complaint before the FIFA DRC to obtain compensation from the player due to the contractual breach without just cause. The FIFA DRC held in its decision of 26 October 2006 that it could not adjudicate the matter and that Chelsea had to turn to FAPLAC.[4] Chelsea appealed that decision to the CAS, which enjoined the DRC to decide on the matter.[5] Consequently, the DRC decided on 7 May 2008 to award € 17,173,990 in damages to Chelsea.[6] Unsurprisingly, Mutu decided to appeal the decision to the CAS. He was specifically contesting the amount of compensation awarded, but in its award of 31 July 2009 the CAS endorsed the DRC's decision.[7] It even held that Chelsea could have claimed higher damages, but decided it could not go *ultra petita* and award a higher sum to the club. Mutu had also unsuccessfully challenged the independence and impartiality of one of the CAS arbitrators due to his previous participation in

---

[1]CJEU, C-415/93, *Union Royale Belge des Sociétés de Football Association and other v. Jean-Marc Bosman and others*, ECLI:EU:C:1995:463.

[2]Oberlandesgericht München, 15 January 2015, Az. U 1110/14 Kart. See Duval and Van Rompuy 2016b.

[3]CAS 2005/A/876, *Adrian Mutu v. Chelsea Football Club Limited*, Award of 15 December 2005.

[4]FIFA DRC decision, 26 October 2006, http://www.fifa.com/mm/document/affederation/administration/106176_8523.pdf. Accessed 4 February 2016.

[5]CAS 2008/A/1644, *Adrian Mutu v. Chelsea Football Club Limited*, Award of 31 July 2009.

[6]FIFA DRC decision, 7 May 2007. See press release of FIFA, FIFA (2008) DRC reaches decision on Mutu. http://www.fifa.com/about-fifa/news/y=2008/m=8/news=drc-reaches-decision-mutu-850413.html. Accessed 4 February 2016.

[7]CAS 2008/A/1644, *Mutu v. Chelsea*.

the first *Mutu* case. Henceforth, he went on to contest the validity of the CAS award in front of the SFT mainly on the basis of an alleged lack of independence of this particular arbitrator. In its decision,[8] the SFT rejected Mutu's claims regarding the lack of independence of the arbitrator, a decision that has attracted criticisms in the literature.[9] Moreover, it also held that the amount of compensation awarded was not a restriction to free movement in the sense of the *Bosman* ruling and could not amount to an infringement of Mutu's personality rights. Indeed, the SFT found that: "This case is different from the matters which gave rise to the two precedents quoted, to the extent that the employees' freedom of movement, invoked by the Appellant, was not hindered at the end of the employment contract since after his suspension the player found a new employer in Italy, his immediate termination notwithstanding, without the new club having to pay a transfer fee to the Respondent".[10] Thereafter, Mutu decided to continue his legal fight at the ECtHR, where his case is still pending.[11]

Chelsea could rely on the final award giving it the right to collect damages against Mutu, but it still needed to get a hold on the money. To do so, it even asked (and obtained) the recognition and enforcement of the award in the United States, where Mutu was suspected of having some property.[12] Nevertheless, Mutu went on to play for smaller and smaller clubs, thus earning less and less, and Chelsea's hope of getting paid in full faded away. Thus, on 15 July 2010, five years after Mutu's move to Italy's Serie A, Chelsea decided to submit a petition to the FIFA DRC against Juventus and Livorno, asking the DRC to find them jointly liable with Mutu for the awarded compensation. The claim was based on Article 14(3) of the FIFA RSTP 2001, stating that: "If a player is registered for a new club and has not paid a sum of compensation within the one month time limit referred to above, the new club shall be deemed jointly responsible for payment of the amount of compensation". The FIFA DRC, in an unpublished decision issued in 2013,[13] followed Chelsea's suggested interpretation of Article 14(3) FIFA RSTP, finding that "under the clear wording of Article 14(3), the Player's New Club was automatically jointly

[8]SFT 4A_458/2009, decision of 10 June 2010. The translation used in the commentary is the one provided by Charles Poncet at http://www.swissarbitrationdecisions.com/sites/default/files/10%20juin%202010%204A%20458%202009.pdf. Accessed 4 February 2016.

[9]See von Segesser 2012 and Beffa 2011.

[10]SFT 4A_458/2009, para 4.4.3.1.

[11]See ECtHR, Request 40575/10, *Adrian Mutu v. Switzerland*, 13 July 2010. http://hudoc.echr.coe.int/eng?i=001-117165. Accessed 4 February 2016.

[12]United States District Court for the Southern District of Florida, No. 763, *Chelsea Football Club Limited v. Adrian Mutu*, 13 February 2012.

[13]See Chowdhury S, Adrian Mutu: Juventus and Livorno told to pay Chelsea compensation, 18 October 2013. http://www.bbc.com/sport/football/24587804. Accessed 4 February 2016. And John Shea, Initial considerations from the latest Adrian Mutu compensation ruling, 5 November 2013. http://www.lawinsport.com/blog/john-shea/item/initial-considerations-from-the-latest-adrian-mutu-compensation-ruling. Accessed 4 February 2016.

responsible for the payment of the Awarded Compensation due by the Player, should the latter fail to fulfil his obligations within a month of notification of the relevant decision".[14] In the DRC's opinion, the provision made "no distinction between the termination of the contract by a player without just cause and the termination of a contract by a club with just cause".[15] It also considered that "the registrations of the player with both [Appellants] were so closely connected that, given the exceptional circumstances of this specific matter, both Juventus and Livorno should be considered the player's new club in the sense of Article 14 of the Application Regulations".[16] Henceforth, both Juventus and Livorno decided to appeal the FIFA decision to the CAS, which in its award rejected the DRC's reasoning.

7.2 Interpreting Article 14(3) FIFA RSTP with a Little Help of EU Law

The whole case turns on the interpretation of the wording of Article 14(3) of the FIFA RSTP in its 2001 version. Does it entail that every club, whatever the circumstances, must pay compensation when it hires a player who bears the responsibility for the breach of his contract? Or, does it restrict this duty to the cases where the breach can be reasonably imputed to the will of the player to leave his former club?

7.2.1 Contractual or Quasi-statutory Interpretation?

In order to determine the interpretative tools to be used to ascertain the meaning of Article 14.3 FIFA RSTP, the Panel had first to clarify the legal nature of that provision under Swiss law. In other words, the question was whether Article 14(3) FIFA RSTP is to be interpreted according to "the general rules of interpretation of contracts" or in accordance with the interpretative methods "applicable to the interpretation of statutes and articles of by-laws of legal entities".[17]

Chelsea argued that Article 14(3) FIFA RSTP should be understood as a form of guarantee under Swiss law. As noted by the Panel, this would "require the existence of a contract between the relevant Parties".[18] However, the Panel did not con-

[14]CAS 2013/A/3365 & 3366, *Juventus FC & A.S. Livorno Calcio S.p.A v. Chelsea FC*, Award of 21 January 2015, para 39.

[15]Ibid.

[16]Ibid.

[17]Ibid., para 121.

[18]Ibid., para 128.

sider that there was a contractual relationship between the appellants and Chelsea.[19] Indeed, having recalled that under Swiss law an association and its indirect members are not bound by a contractual relationship, the Panel held that "[i]f there is no contractual relationship between an indirect member (i.e. any of the Parties) and a sport federation (i.e. FIFA), the conclusion should be the same as regards the relationship between two indirect members of the same federation".[20] Furthermore, the "[a]cceptance of general rules (such as FIFA Regulations) does not necessarily entail subjection to specific obligations when their scope must be determinable on the basis of minimum criteria" (as required under Swiss law with respect to contractual guarantees).[21] Thus, the Panel "[came] to the conclusion that the alleged guarantee cannot arise solely by virtue of the Appellants' indirect membership in the FIFA system, as claimed by Chelsea" and "[found] that the Appellants' putative liability based on Article 14.3 is not contractual in nature".[22] Instead, the interpretative questions raised by Chelsea's claim concerned exclusively the bylaws of a Swiss association: FIFA.

In order to interpret the FIFA RSTP, the Panel suggested four methods of interpretation under Swiss law:

- the literal interpretation ("interprétation littérale");
- the systematic interpretation ("interprétation systématique");
- the principle of purposive interpretation ("interprétation téléologique");
- the principle of so-called "compliant interpretation" ("interprétation conforme").[23]

The "starting point"[24] is the wording of the text, but there is in principle no hierarchy between these methods of interpretation. The Panel recalled that according to the SFT "[t]here is no reason to depart from the plain text, unless there are objective reasons to think that it does not reflect the core meaning of the provision under review".[25] Moreover, when asked to interpret a law, the SFT "adopts a pragmatic approach and follows a plurality of methods, without assigning any priority to the various means of interpretation".[26] However, the fundamental question is whether these methods should also be used to interpret the bylaws of a Swiss association. This question is key in the context of the CAS, as it is generally tasked with resolving disputes based on the interpretation of the private bylaws of SGBs, which are more often than not Swiss associations. Yet, in the majority of cases where this issue was problematized, CAS Panels have simply assumed that the

[19]Ibid., para 131.

[20]Ibid.

[21]Ibid.

[22]Ibid., para 136.

[23]Ibid., para 137.

[24]Ibid., paras 138–139.

[25]Ibid., para 139.

[26]Ibid.

four interpretative techniques mentioned above (or a slight variation thereof) were to be applied to interpret the bylaws of SGBs.[27] In the present case, the Panel decided to go one step further and to ground this assumption in a substantiated legal reasoning, thereby setting the scene for this award to become a reference point for future CAS jurisprudence. This interpretative choice is not obvious, a German Court, for example, has recently refused to apply the interpretative techniques used in the framework of German laws to the bylaws of the German Football Association (the DFB).[28]

Although it acknowledged that there is no consensus on the method to be used for the interpretation of the bylaws of Swiss associations, the Panel found that "[a] s regards the statutes of larger entities, it may be more appropriate to have recourse to the method of interpretation applicable to the law, whereas in the presence of smaller enterprises, the statutes may more legitimately be interpreted by reference to good faith".[29] Furthermore, it held that "FIFA's regulations have effects which are felt worldwide, and should therefore be subject to the more objective interpretation principles".[30] For the first time in the history of CAS, a Panel has provided a basic rationale for applying to private regulations interpretative principles that were developed in the context of national laws. The analogy drawn between the FIFA RSTP and Swiss law is telling. It speaks in favour of the recognition of the fact that FIFA (and other SGBs) have developed a form of transnational legal system that has very similar practical effects on its 'citizens' as national laws. This justification by a CAS panel of a key interpretative choice certainly supports the arguments of those who perceive the emergence of a *lex sportiva,*[31] or in the present case a *lex fifa.*[32] In the eyes of the CAS, the regulations of SGBs are closer, in terms of scope and complexity, to state law than to private contracts; they should thus be interpreted on the basis of the techniques that apply to the former. This has important legal consequences. For example, the recourse to

[27]See CAS 2002/O/373, *Canadian Olympic Committee (COC) & Beckie Scott v. International Olympic Committee (IOC),* Award of 18 December 2003, paras 46–47; CAS 2007/A/1363, *TTF Liebherr Ochsenhausen v. ETTU,* Award of 5 October 2007, para 12; CAS 2009/A/1810 & 1811, *SV Wilhelmshaven v. Club Atlético Excursionistas & Club Atlético River Plate*, Award of 5 October 2009, para 45; CAS 2010/A/2071, *Irish Football Association (IFA) v. Football Association of Ireland (FAI), Daniel Kearns and Fédération Internationale de Football Association (FIFA),* Award of 27 September 2010, para 20; CAS 2013/A/3151, *Jonathon Millar v. Fédération Equestre Internationale (FEI),* Award of 7 October 2013, para 71; CAS 2013/A/3047, *FC Zenit St. Petersburg v. Russian Football Union (RFU),* Award of 7 October 2013, para 71.

[28]See Hanseatisches Oberlandesgericht in Bremen, 30 December 2014, Az. 2 U 67/14. For more on this ruling see my commentary in this Yearbook.

[29]CAS 2013/A/3365 & 3366, *Juventus v. Chelsea,* para 143.

[30]Ibid., para 144.

[31]On *lex sportiva* see Latty 2007 and Duval 2013.

[32]Franck Latty was, to my knowledge, the first to make use of the concept of *lex FIFA*, see Latty 2011.

a purposive interpretation, typical of statutory interpretation, will imply that the meaning of the contested rule will be reconstructed with specific regard to the regulatory objective pursued by an SGB when adopting the rule in question.

7.2.2 EU Law as a Decisive Contextual Element to Interpret the FIFA RSTP

Following the methods set out above, the Panel first tried to interpret Article 14(3) FIFA RSTP on the basis of its wording. However, it came to the conclusion that the wording was ambiguous and therefore "it [was] necessary to look beyond the wording of this provision", adopting what it coined a "contextual approach".[33]

In short, "the context surrounding the implementation of the RSTP 2001 is of crucial importance in interpreting Article 14.3".[34] In the view of the Panel (and the appellants), the relevant context is constituted by the application of EU law to sport and especially the CJEU's ruling in the *Bosman* case.[35] Indeed, it is "[a]s part of the reform of the FIFA and UEFA rules following the Bosman decision, [that] FIFA adopted the RSTP 2001".[36] Thus, the requirements set by the CJEU's jurisprudence in sports matters are decisive to define the purpose of the provisions of the FIFA RSTP. The rejection decision[37] adopted by the European Commission in its competition law investigation of the FIFA transfer regulations was also deemed an essential element in this context.[38] Specifically, the Panel referred to the Commission's view "that the limitations on unilateral termination introduced by the new FIFA Regulations would help improve the production and distribution of sport entertainment, since they would preserve the integrity of competitions".[39]

In the present case, the Panel considered that the notion and pursuit of "contractual stability [that] is at the centre of the debate".[40] In a nutshell, the key question was: Does the paramount objective of contractual stability justify that Article 14(3) FIFA RSTP be interpreted so as to find Juventus and Livorno jointly liable for Mutu's breach of contract? In this regard, Chelsea contended that Article 14(3) FIFA RSTP "is designed to protect contractual stability by means of a deterrent,

[33]CAS 2013/A/3365 & 3366, *Juventus v. Chelsea*, para 148.

[34]Ibid., para 149.

[35]On the *Bosman* ruling and its aftermath see Weatherill 2003 and Van den Bogaert 2005.

[36]CAS 2013/A/3365 & 3366, *Juventus v. Chelsea*, para 151.

[37]European Commission, Rejection Decision, Case IV/36 583, *SETCA & FGTB v. FIFA,* 28 May 2002. http://ec.europa.eu/competition/antitrust/cases/dec_docs/36583/36583_54_3.pdf. Accessed 4 February 2016.

[38]CAS 2013/A/3365 & 3366, *Juventus v. Chelsea*, para 156.

[39]Ibid., para 157.

[40]Ibid., para 158.

namely by ensuring that the parties who benefit from the player's breach—the player himself and his New Club—are not allowed to enjoy that benefit without paying compensation to the player's former club",[41] while Juventus and Livorno argued that "Article 14.3—and FIFA regulations in general—are not meant to protect a club's bad investment".[42] Which of these two interpretations does EU law support? That was the question.

For the Panel, "the Player was the author of his misfortune, but the Club was not required to terminate his employment if they still valued his services and preferred to hold him to his contract". Instead, "[t]he Club was entitled, not obliged, to dismiss him" and that "makes all the difference in terms of assessing the position of his subsequent employer(s) under the FIFA regulations, read in light of their object and purpose".[43] As "Chelsea put an end to the Player's Employment Contract, no issue of contract stability, whose purpose was to safeguard the functioning and regularity of sporting competition, was at stake".[44] Thus, "it strains logic for the club now to contend that the Appellants somehow enriched themselves by acquiring an asset (the player) which it chose to discard".[45] Or in other (similar) words, it seems "incongruous for Chelsea to try to seek an advantage from the fact that the New Club benefits from the Player's services, whereas Chelsea was no longer interested in his service".[46] Moreover, the Panel found it "hard to understand how, in the name of contract stability, Chelsea's claim of € 17,173,990 against the Player is to be borne jointly and severally by the New Club, which has never expressed a specific agreement in this regard, had nothing to do with the Player's contractual breach, and was not even called to participate in the proceedings, which established the Awarded Compensation".[47] Hence, "Chelsea's conduct appears to have had no other purpose than to increase its chances for greater financial compensation" and the Panel "does not see the connection between the damage being claimed and the interest of protecting legitimate contractual expectations".[48] In short, the interpretation of Article 14(3) FIFA RSTP supported by Chelsea does not fit the fundamental objective of this provision, as derived from its legislative context (including the *Lethonen*[49] case of the CJEU and the Commission's rejection decision in the competition law complaint against the FIFA transfer system).

---

[41]Ibid., para 159.

[42]Ibid., para 160.

[43]Ibid., para 161.

[44]Ibid., para 163.

[45]Ibid.

[46]Ibid., para 166.

[47]Ibid., para 165.

[48]Ibid., para 168.

[49]CJEU, C-176/96, *Jyri Lehtonen and Castors Canada Dry Namur-Braine ASBL v. Fédération royale belge des sociétés de basket-ball ASBL*, ECLI:EU:C:2000:201.

Interestingly, the Panel also recognized that "[t]here must be a balance between the players' fundamental right to free movement and the principle of stability of contracts, as supported by the legitimate objective of safeguarding the integrity of the sport and the stability of championships".[50] In the present case, "[i]f the New Club had to pay compensation even if it is established that it bears no responsibility whatsoever in the breach of the Employment Contract, the player would be hindered from finding a new employer".[51] Indeed, "it is not difficult to perceive that no New Club would be prepared to pay a multi-million compensation (or transfer fee), in particular for a player who was fired for gross misconduct, was banned for several months, and suffered drug problems".[52] In short, "Chelsea's interpretation of Article 14.3 would bring the matter back into pre-Bosman times, when transfer fees obstructed the players' freedom of movement".[53] Had Chelsea's interpretation prevailed, "the balance sought by the 2001 RSTP between the players' rights and an efficient transfer system, which responds to the specific needs of football and preserves the regularity and proper functioning of sporting competition would be upset".[54] Consequently, this interpretation was deemed "incompatible with the fundamental principle of freedom to exercise a professional activity and [...] disproportionate to the protection of the old club's legitimate interests".[55] Thus, the Panel concluded that "Article 14.3 does not apply in cases where it was the employer's decision to dismiss with immediate effect a player who, in turn, had no intention to leave the club in order to sign with another club and where the New Club has not committed any fault and/or was not involved in the termination of the employment relationship between the old club and the Player".[56]

The decision to interpret the FIFA RSTP as if it were a statute is clearly not anodyne. It leads the CAS to give a prominent place to the CJEU's case law and to FIFA's agreement with the EU Commission in cases in which the wording of the FIFA RSTP is unclear. The Panel, thus, recognized that an interpretation of the FIFA RSTP that runs contrary to the requirements imposed by EU law on FIFA is in principle not tenable.

---

[50]CAS 2013/A/3365 & 3366, *Juventus v. Chelsea*, para 169.

[51]Ibid, para 172.

[52]Ibid.

[53]Ibid, para 174.

[54]Ibid.

[55]Ibid.

[56]Ibid, para 177.

7.3 Beyond the Mutu Case: How Much Contractual Stability is Compatible with EU Law?

This award is of great interest, not so much for its solution, but for the method used to reach it. The CAS had already in the past based its interpretation of the FIFA RSTP on their legislative history and especially on their being the result of a negotiation with the EU Commission in the aftermath of the *Bosman* ruling.[57] It is the first time, however, that it does so in such length and depth. In previous cases, a CAS Panel would, for instance, purport to reconstruct the legislative history of the FIFA RSTP by merely referring to FIFA's Circular Letter no 769.[58] By following this approach in the *SV Wilhelmshaven* case, the CAS was by and large ignoring the case law of the CJEU, and it should not come as a great surprise that a German Court later blocked the enforcement of the award.[59] The *Wilhelmshaven* case is a timely reminder for other CAS Panels that the FIFA RSTP must be interpreted in conformity with EU law and especially the case law of the CJEU on free movement of workers. Ignoring the potential reach of EU law is not an option, as CAS awards would face the risk of seeing their validity contested in front of

---

[57]For example: "It must be remembered that the FIFA Regulations have been issued to regulate the legal and economic aspects of the transfer of players in accordance with the principle of free movement of workers as established by the EC treaty and substantiated by the European Court of Justice in its ruling of 15 December 1995 (case C-415/93), thereby taking the specific needs of professional football into account. In this context, any provisions in the FIFA regulations affecting the player's freedom of movement should be interpreted narrowly." CAS 2004/A/691, *FC Barcelona SAD v. Manchester United FC*, Award of 9 February 2005, para 38; "However, the principle behind Article 5 para 5 of the Application Regulations is clear: the free movement of workers within the EU/EEA must not be restricted by the imposition of a requirement for the payment of sums by way of compensation for training and education in respect of a player to whom the training club does not offer a contract. In such a case, the failure to offer a contract is an important factor in the assessment of compensation. The compensation payable should not be of such an amount as would impede the player's ability to move to a new club." CAS 2006/A/1125, *Hertha BSC Berlin v. Stade Lavallois Mayenne FC*, Award of 1 December 2006, para 25; "Finally, because of the potentially high amounts of compensation involved, giving clubs a regulatory right to the market value of players and allowing lost profits to be claimed in such manner would in effect bring the system partially back to the pre-Bosman days when players' freedom of movement was unduly hindered by transfer fees and their careers and well-being could be seriously affected by them becoming pawns in the hands of their clubs and a vector through which clubs could reap considerable benefits without sharing the profit or taking corresponding risks. In view of the text and the history of Article 17 para 1 of the FIFA Status Regulations, allowing any form of compensation that could have such an effect would clearly be anachronistic and legally unsound." CAS 2007/A/1298, 1299 & 1300, *Wigan Athletic FC & Webster v. Heart of Midlothian*, Award of 30 January 2008, para 81.

[58]CAS 2009/A/1810 & 1811, *SV Wilhelmshaven v. Excursionistas*, paras 46–49.

[59]See Hanseatisches Oberlandesgericht Bremen, 30 December 2014, Az. 2 U 67/14 and my commentary in this yearbook.

national courts or the EU Commission.[60] At a time when "Global Legal Pluralism"[61] seems to be a prevailing characteristic of our transnational legal environment, this opening of the CAS towards the impact of EU law on the *lex sportiva* is a sign of its willingness to dialogue and peacefully interact with another, influential, transnational legal order, regime or system.

The decision of the CAS to properly acknowledge the legislative history of the FIFA RSTP and in particular the crucial role played by EU law in their inception, if it is espoused by other CAS Panels, as it should, is susceptible to substantially influence the future interpretation of the FIFA RSTP. Restrictions imposed by the FIFA RSTP on the free movement of players must be justified by a legitimate objective recognized by the CJEU and be proportionate to attain this objective. In the present case, the interpretation of Article 14(3) FIFA RSTP promoted by the DRC ran counter to this requirement as it is not truly aimed at an acceptable legitimate objective and certainly not a proportionate mean to attain contractual stability. This reasoning could also put into question previous interpretations of other provisions included in the FIFA RSTP. It is especially true of the interpretation of Article 17(1) FIFA RSTP, which foresees that in the event of termination of a contract without just cause, the party in breach shall pay compensation.[62] The central interpretative conundrum concerns the evaluation of the amount of compensation due.[63] The provision itself provides only vague legal guidelines to calculate this compensation. Thus, CAS Panels have proceeded on a case-by-case basis in defining the appropriate method to evaluate the amount due. In the *Webster* case, based on the legislative history of the FIFA RSTP and its need to be interpreted in conformity with EU law, the CAS Panel confined the compensation awarded to the club to the outstanding wages owed to the player.[64] This decision faced a lot of criticisms from FIFA[65] and the clubs[66] and was later overturned by another CAS

---

[60]Duval 2015.

[61]Schiff Berman 2012.

[62]Article 17.1 FIFA RSTP (version 2015) stipulates, in case a contract is terminated without just cause, that "1. [i]n all cases, the party in breach shall pay compensation. Subject to the provisions of Article 20 and Annexe 4 in relation to training compensation, and unless otherwise provided for in the contract, compensation for the breach shall be calculated with due consideration for the law of the country concerned, the specificity of sport, and any other objective criteria. These criteria shall include, in particular, the remuneration and other benefits due to the player under the existing contract and/or the new contract, the time remaining on the existing contract up to a maximum of five years, the fees and expenses paid or incurred by the former club (amortised over the term of the contract) and whether the contractual breach falls within a protected period."

[63]Czarnota 2013.

[64]CAS 2007/A/1298, 1299 & 1300, *Webster v. Heart*, para 86.

[65]See FIFA (2008) FIFA Dismayed with CAS Decision. http://www.fifa.com/about-fifa/news/y=2008/m=1/news=fifa-dismayed-with-cas-decision-682195.html. Accessed 4 February 2016.

[66]See European Club Association (2009) ECA: FIFA's Article 17 'goes too far' in removing protection for club. http://www.e-comlaw.com/world-sports-law-report/article_template.asp?Contents=Yes&from=wslr&ID=1097. Accessed 4 February 2016.

Panel in the *Matuzalem* award.[67] Since then, a stable and predictable method to calculate the compensation due is missing. CAS Panels have adopted club-friendly interpretations of the (relatively large) amounts for which players have been deemed liable under Article 17(1) FIFA RSTP.[68] In the *Mutu* award under commentary, the Panel was conscious of the potential repercussions of its reasoning with regard to the interpretation of Article 17(1) FIFA RSTP. In its conclusion, the award clearly stated that "[t]hese findings do not compromise contractual stability, as a player will still be dissuaded from unilaterally breaching his contract (in some other way than terminating it), because he will then face the burden of a potential compensation awarded in favour of his previous club". It also added that "[t]he prospect of having to pay a high compensation may actually serve as a broader deterrent for players willing to put an end to their employment contracts than if a New Club were to be found jointly and severally liable".[69] The Panel seems to endorse the view that the current jurisprudence on the compensation due on the basis of Article 17(1) FIFA RSTP would be in line with an EU law conform interpretation. Yet, this view is contested, many EU law scholars dissent and it has been convincingly argued that the way the compensation is calculated in case of a breach of contract tips the balance too far on the side of contractual stability, to the detriment of the fundamental right to free movement of the players. For some, it is therefore incompatible with the letter and spirit of EU law as applied to the transfer system in *Bosman* and thereafter.[70]

7.4 Conclusion: Interpretation Matters!

This award is not to be overlooked by sports arbitration practitioners or scholars. For some legal theorists, interpretation is crucial in defining the practical meaning of the law.[71] Judges are often called to offer a fitting interpretation of the rules in a particular case constellation.[72] While courts are traditionally portrayed as the *bouche de la loi*, in practice, they frequently act as relatively autonomous interpreters involved in a constructive decision-making operation, for which they are engaging in constrained interpretation of the text of the law.[73]

[67]CAS 2008/A/1519 & 1520, *FC Shakhtar Donetsk v. Mr. Matuzalem Francelino da Silva & Real Zaragoza SAD & FIFA*, Award of 19 May 2009.

[68]See Czarnota 2013 and Zimmerman 2015.

[69]CAS 2013/A/3365 & 3366, *Juventus v. Chelsea*, para 177.

[70]See recently Parrish 2015 and Pearson 2015.

[71]See Venzke 2013.

[72]On the idea of the interpretative fit see Dworkin 1977.

[73]In other words: "Chaque interprète, quelle que soit sa position dans la chaîne discursive, est à la fois libre et contraint: libre en raison de la polysémie virtuelle et de la texture ouverte des termes du langage ordinaire, contraint par la structure, discursive et juridique, du champ concerné." Ost and Van de Kerchove 2002, p. 445.

The CAS is acting as the functional equivalent to a national judge in transnational sporting disputes. Its judicial practice is not dissimilar to that of a national judge, especially in appeal cases. CAS panels refer to previous case law and are bound to interpret rules in the form of the SGBs' regulations. Hence, it is crucial that they explain and justify, as the Panel did in the award commented here, the interpretative techniques they rely upon to concretize the regulations of the SGBs in particular cases. It is undoubtedly telling that in this award the arbitrators decided to have recourse to the same techniques as used for the interpretation of Swiss laws. Such techniques emphasize the wording of the rule, but equally its legislative context. Adopting this approach amounts to putting the private transnational lawmaking of SGBs on par with that of national states. By the same token, it implies that legal practitioners will need to look closely at (but also have access to) the legislative processes that led to the adoption of a specific sporting regulation (e.g. the FIFA RSTP or the WADC), in order to construct convincing legal arguments regarding its interpretation. This is not an unproblematic development. SGBs, as should be obvious after the recent FIFA and IAAF scandals, lack the democratic foundations of (many) national governments when they promulgate regulations. Hence, this also highlights the need to develop transparent and inclusive processes to underpin the adoption of these regulations. Such a participative legislative process was, albeit in a convoluted way, followed in the case of the FIFA RSTP, which are the result of a complex negotiation amongst a diverse set of football stakeholders under the umbrella of the European Commission in the aftermath of the *Bosman* ruling.[74] As we have argued, this particular legislative context was decisive for the outcome of the latest *Mutu* case, and could potentially lead to further inflexions in the interpretation of the FIFA RSTP by CAS panels.

References

Beffa L (2011) Challenge of international arbitration awards in Switzerland for lack of independence and/or impartiality of an arbitrator—is it time to change the approach? ASA Bull 29:598–606

Czarnota P (2013) FIFA transfer rules and unilateral termination without "Just Cause". Berkeley J Entertain Sports Law 2:1–47

Duval A (2013) *Lex Sportiva*: a playground for transnational law. Eur Law J 19:822–842

Duval A (2015) The court of arbitration for sport and EU law: chronicle of an encounter. Maastricht J Eur Comp Law 22:224–255

Duval A (2016a) The FIFA regulations on the status and transfer of players: transnational law-making in the shadow of Bosman. In: Duval A, Van Rompuy B (eds) The legacy of Bosman: revisiting the relationship between EU law and sport, Springer, T.M.C. ASSER Press, The Hague, pp 81–116

[74]Duval 2016a.

Duval A, Van Rompuy B (2016b) Protecting athletes' right to a fair trial through EU competition law: the *Pechstein* case. In: Paulussen C et al (eds) Fundamental rights in international and European law, Springer, T.M.C. ASSER Press, The Hague, pp 245–278

Dworkin R (1977) Taking rights seriously. Harvard University Press, Cambridge

Latty F (2007) La Lex Sportiva: Recherche sur le droit transnational. Martinus Nijhoff Publishers, Leiden

Latty F (2011) La Lex FIFA. In: Maisonneuve M (ed) Droit et Coupe du Monde, Economica, Paris, pp 9–27

Ost F, Van de Kerchove M (2002) De la pyramide au réseau? Pour une théorie dialectique du droit. Facultés universitaires Saint-Louis, Bruxelles

Parrish R (2015) Article 17 of the FIFA Regulations on the Status and Transfer of Players. Compatibility with EU law. Maastricht J Eur Comp Law 22:256–282

Pearson G (2015) Sporting justifications under EU free movement and competition law: the case of the football 'transfer system. Eur Law J 21:220–238

Schiff Berman P (2012) Global legal pluralism. A jurisprudence of law beyond borders. Cambridge University Press, Cambridge

Van den Bogaert S (2005) Practical regulation of the mobility of sportsmen in the EU post Bosman. Kluwer Law International, The Hague

von Segesser G (2012) Equality of information and impartiality of arbitrators. In: Wautelet P, Kruger T, Coppens G (eds) The practice of arbitration: essays in honour of Hans van Houtte. Hart Publishing, Oxford, pp 45–51

Venzke I (2013) How interpretation makes international law: on semantic change and normative twists. Oxford University Press, Oxford

Weatherill S (2003) "Fair Play Please!": recent developments in the application of EC law to sport. Common Market Law Rev 40:51–93

Zimmerman M (2015) Vertragsstabilität im internationalen Fussball. Dike Verlag, Zürich

Chapter 8
CAS 2014/A/3486, *MFK Dubnica V. FC Parma*, Award of 2 February 2015

Roy Levy

Abstract The case centres around a request for training compensation for a player who played 65 matches in the 'A' team of a Slovak club before he was transferred to an Italian club at the age of 20 years. As the player moved within the EU, special FIFA provisions apply which require that in order to be eligible to receive training compensation, the old club must offer the player a new contract by registered mail at least 60 days before the expiry of the existing contract. The main issues in dispute between the parties were (i) if the old club had sent a new employment contract to the player by registered mail, and (ii) when the training of the player had ended. Further, this seems to be only the third time that a CAS Panel had to deal with the exclusion of evidence based on Article R57(3) CAS Code. Recently, also the Swiss Federal Tribunal—as the court of 'supervisory jurisdiction' dealing with appeals against CAS awards—decided on the legality and scope of this provision, expressing a different opinion from that of the CAS. This is why this article discusses the Panel's discretion to exclude evidence in depth.

Keywords Training compensation · Exclusion · Evidence · Development · Article R57(3) CAS Code · FIFA · CAS

Contents

R. Levy (✉)
Probst Partner, Zurich, Switzerland
e-mail: roy.levy@probstpartner.ch

A. Duval and A. Rigozzi (eds.), *Yearbook of International Sports Arbitration 2015*,
DOI 10.1007/978-94-6265-129-6_8

8.1 Facts and Procedure

8.1.1 The Parties

MFK Dubnica (hereinafter 'Dubnica') is a football club with its registered office in Dubnica, Slovak Republic. At the time the CAS award was rendered the 'A' team of Dubnica played in the second highest football league in the Slovak Republic. Dubnica is registered with the Slovak Football Association, which in turn is affiliated to FIFA.

FC Parma (hereinafter 'Parma') is a football club with its registered office in Parma, Italy. At the time the CAS award was rendered the 'A' team of Parma played in the highest football league in Italy. Parma is registered with the Italian Football Association, which in turn is affiliated to FIFA.

8.1.2 The Facts

The goalkeeper, Mr Pavol Bajza, born on 4 September 1991 (hereinafter the 'Player') was registered with the Slovak Football Association as a "non-amateur" with Dubnica on 6 August 2007 (at the age of 15). In the season 2009/2010, more specifically on 11 July 2009, he made his first appearance in the 'A' team of Dubnica in the First League in the Slovak Republic, but only as a substitute goalkeeper. On 27 February 2010, i.e. when the Player was 18 years old, he played his first match in the 'A' team and was fielded in all 14 games of the second part of the 2009/2010 season.

On 1 February 2010, the Player and Dubnica signed a professional employment contract for a period of two and a half seasons, i.e. valid until 30 June 2012.

In the 2010/2011 season, the Player remained the first choice goalkeeper and played 18 matches in the 'A' team. During the second half of the season, he was replaced by a more experienced goalkeeper. At the end of this season, Dubnica was relegated to the second highest football league in Slovak Republic.

At the start of the 2011/2012 season, the Player again became the first choice goalkeeper of Dubnica and played all 33 matches throughout this season.

Dubnica claimed to have sent the Player, on 13 March 2012, a contract offer by registered mail—an important fact which was disputed by Parma.

On 30 June 2012 the Player's original employment contract with Dubnica expired. On 20 August 2012 (at the age of 20) the Player was officially registered with Parma. On 31 August 2012, Dubnica requested Parma to pay training compensation on behalf of the Player the amount € 300,000, which request remained unanswered by Parma.

Dubnica then filed its claim with the FIFA DRC and the latter concluded that Dubnica had failed to prove that it had complied with Article 6 para 3 of Annexe 4 of the FIFA RSTP, which provides that an employment offer must be made by registered mail at least 60 days before the expiry of the contract.[1]

Following the FIFA DRC decision Dubnica filed an appeal with the CAS.

8.1.3 The Arguments

8.1.3.1 Dubnica's Arguments

According to Dubnica's submission, it had offered a professional contract to the Player on various occasions since 2011 and had sent a letter to the Player by registered mail with a "new professional contract proposal", the delivery of which was accepted by the Player. Dubnica—who bore the burden of proof—claimed to have complied with all the prerequisites of the FIFA RSTP, and filed the following documents to corroborate its position:

- A letter dated 13 March 2012, addressed to the Player, stamped by Dubnica and signed by the Chairman of the Board of Directors of Dubnica, which read

  > "Subject sending the Professional Player Contract.
  > Please find attached to this letter the proposal of the new Professional Player Contract since your valid Professional Player Contract expires on 30 June 2012".

- A professional player contract dated 13 March 2012, stamped by Dubnica and signed by the President and another member of the Board of Directors of Dubnica, for the seasons 2012/2013 and 2013/2014.
- An undated 'Postal Receipt' bearing the name of Dubnica as sender and the name and address of the Player, including the filing number 135.
- An undated 'Bulk Posting Form' bearing the name of Dubnica as sender, the name and address of the Player, the place of delivery, the 'Certificate of posting' number "(68 78 62) 135" with date "13/3".
- Finally—which is essential for the case at hand—a letter dated 24 September 2013, i.e. after the FIFA DRC decision was rendered, from the Director of Regional Headquarters of *Slovenska Posta*, which provides as follows: "Following your application of 12 September 2013 for the provision of information concerning the delivery of the registered mail, certificate of posting no. RR

[1]The FIFA DRC decision was rendered on 31 July 2013.

68 786 213 5 SK, posted on 13 March 2012, place of posting: Nova Dubnica, to the addressee: Pavol Bajza, [address], we hereby inform you that the mail in question was delivered on 15 March 2012. The mail was accepted by the authorized recipient".

Dubnica argued that it sufficiently proved to have offered the Player a professional contract via registered mail at least 60 days before the expiry of his current contract, as provided by the FIFA RSTP. Since Dubnica complied with the requirements, it maintained that the burden of proof shifted to Parma to prove that the envelope was empty.[2]

In the hearing before the CAS, the Player confirmed that the alleged correspondence of Dubnica of 13 March 2012 was addressed to his home address and permanent residence. He explained that Dubnica owed him € 5000 for outstanding remuneration and that Dubnica never offered him an extension of his contract at the premises of the club. The Player stressed that he also never received such an offer by registered mail, but that his mother—living in the same house—had received something by regular post. His mother told him about a received envelope only on 20 July 2012.[3]

With respect to Parma's argument that the training of the Player was terminated before he transferred to Parma, Dubnica argued that Parma did not provide any evidence that the Player had already concluded his training and, with reference to jurisprudence of the FIFA DRC and CAS, that the requirements to consider a Player's training terminated are very high. Hence, the amount of the training compensation should not be reduced.[4]

8.1.3.2 Parma's Arguments

Parma argued that Article 6(3) of Annex 4 to the FIFA RSTP must be applied as written, otherwise it would be nearly impossible for a club interested in retaining the services of a player to examine whether the requirements of this provision are complied with. Parma maintained that Dubnica filed new evidence—mainly the letter from the Director of Regional Headquarters of "Slovenska Posta" dated 24 September 2013—which it could have gathered and presented before the FIFA DRC already. Parma requested the Panel to exclude such evidence based on Article R57(3) CAS Code.[5] But even in case the newly filed evidence would be permitted, according to Parma's opinion, Dubnica did not prove that it made a contractual offer to the Player in compliance with Article 6(3) of Annex 4 to the FIFA RSTP. Dubnica did not provide any paper trail of the contractual offer, no

---

[2]CAS 2014/A/3486, *MFK Dubnica v. FC Parma*, Award of 2 February 2015, para 37.

[3]Ibid., para 78.

[4]Ibid., para 37.

[5]Ibid., para 38.

exchange of emails, text messages or any other written correspondence related to the negotiations.[6] Further, Parma argued that Dubnica failed to provide a proof of delivery. A legal act which does not come to the attention of the addressee cannot be considered a contractual offer in the first place.[7]

With regard to the completion of the Player's training before his 21st birthday, Parma claimed that pursuant to CAS jurisprudence a player that regularly plays in the 'A' team of a club is to be deemed as having completed his training. By becoming the substitute goalkeeper of the 'A' team of Dubnica on 11 July 2009, it must be considered that the Player completed his training on that day. Alternatively, his training was completed when he became the first goalkeeper on 27 February 2010. Further Parma argued that the CAS jurisprudence differentiates between the training of a player and the development of a player.[8]

As to the calculation of an alleged training compensation, Parma maintained that Dubnica would—if at all—only be entitled to € 96,438, alternatively to € 128,082 and more alternatively to € 239,451.[9]

8.1.4 The Law

Article 20 of the FIFA RSTP provides:

> Training compensation shall be paid to a player's training club(s): (1) when a player signs his first contract as a professional and (2) each time a professional is transferred until the end of the season of his 23rd birthday. The obligation to pay training compensation arises whether the transfer takes place during or at the end of the player's contract. The provisions concerning training compensation are set out in Annexe 4 of these regulations.

Annex 4 to the FIFA RSTP provides
Article 1 Objective

> A player's training and education takes place between the ages of 12 and 23. Training compensation shall be payable, as a general rule, up to the age of 23 for training incurred up to the age of 21, unless it is evident that a player has already terminated his training period before the age of 21. In the latter case, training compensation shall be payable until the end of the season in which the player reaches the age of 23, but the calculation of the amount payable shall be based on the years between the age of 12 and the age when it is established that the player actually completed his training.

Article 6 Special provisions for the EU/EEA

> 3. If the former club does not offer the player a contract, no training compensation is payable unless the former club can justify that it is entitled to such compensation. The former club must offer the player a contract in writing via registered post at least 60 days before

[6]Ibid.

[7]Ibid.

[8]Ibid.

[9]Ibid.

the expiry of his current contract. Such an offer shall furthermore be at least of an equivalent value to the current contract. This provision is without prejudice to the right to training compensation of the player's previous club(s).

8.1.5 The Merits

First, the CAS Panel discussed Parma's request, based on Article R57(3) CAS Code, to exclude the evidence submitted by Dubnica which was not part of the proceeding before the FIFA DRC.

With regard to the question whether or not training compensation was due, the Panel found that the main issues to be resolved were the following:

1. Is Dubnica entitled to receive training compensation from Parma in respect of the Player?
2. Did the Player complete his training prior to his registration with Parma?
3. To what amount of training compensation is Dubnica entitled, if any?
4. Is any interest payable?

8.1.5.1 The Exclusion of Evidence Pursuant to Article R57(3) CAS Code

Article R57 CAS Code provides, in its first paragraph, that "[t]he Panel has the full power to review the facts and the law. […]. Paragraph 3 then reads [t]he Panel has the discretion to exclude evidence presented by the parties if it was available to them or could reasonably be discovered by them before the challenged decision was rendered […]". This para 3 was introduced in the latest amendment of the CAS Code and entered into effect on 1 January 2013. The Panel held before the amendment of Article R57 the CAS jurisprudence was clear regarding the interpretation of Article R57 CAS Code[10]:

> […] There is a long line of CAS awards, even going back many years, which have relied on article R57 of the CAS Code to firmly establish that the CAS appeals arbitration allows a full de novo hearing of a case, with all due process guarantees, which can cure any procedural defects or violations of the right to be heard occurred during a federation's (or other sports body's) internal procedure. Indeed, CAS appeals arbitration proceedings allow the parties ample latitude not only to present written submissions with new evidence, but also to have an oral hearing during which witnesses are examined and cross-examined, evidence is provided and comprehensive pleadings can be made.[11]

[10]Ibid., para 49.

[11]CAS 2009/A/1880 & 1881, *FC Sion & E. v. Fédération Internationale de Football Association (FIFA) & Al-Ahly Sporting Club*, Award of 1 June 2010, para 18.

The CAS Panel then asked the question if the newly amended Article R57(3) CAS Code has any influence on this long line of CAS jurisprudence. It noted that the *de novo* basis of review is, in essence, the foundation of the CAS appeals system and the standard of review should not be undermined by an overly restrictive interpretation of Article R57(3) CAS Code.[12] The Panel found that according to this provision it is entirely free to accept or reject any such evidence, and doing so should not disrupt the fundamental principle of *de novo* review. However, the Panel also noted that "[...] the discretion to exclude evidence should be exercised with caution, for example, in situations where a party may have engaged in abusive procedural behaviour, or in any other circumstances where the Panel might, in its discretion, consider it either unfair or inappropriate to admit new evidence".[13]

With respect to the letter dated 24 September 2013 from the Director of the Regional Headquarters of *Slovenska Posta*, which was filed after the FIFA DRC decision was rendered, the Panel understood that Dubnica attempted to collect additional evidence to support its position, which was completely in line with the arguments and evidence already presented during the proceedings before the FIFA DRC. The Panel found that Dubnica neither engaged in abusive procedural behaviour, nor did the Panel consider it unfair or inappropriate to admit the new evidence. Consequently, it admitted the new evidence.

8.1.5.2 Was Dubnica Entitled to Receive Training Compensation from Parma?

Turning to the question whether training compensation was due, the Panel found, first of all, that Article 6(3) of Annex 4 to the FIFA RSTP is a *lex specialis* to Article 20 of the FIFA Regulations. The requirements for a training compensation pursuant to Article 6(3) are

i. an offer in writing for a new contract 60 days before the expiry of the current contract;
ii. a notice of the offer sent by registered mail;
iii. financial terms in the offer that are at least as favourable as those in the current contract.

The CAS had no doubt that the first and the last requirements were fulfilled. With regard to the disputed question as to whether or not a notice of the offer was sent to the Player by registered mail, the Panel held that the content of the letter dated 24 September 2013 of the Director of Regional Headquarters of *Slovenska Posta* in conjunction with the 'Postal Receipt', the 'Bulk Posting Form', the letter dated 13 March 2012 and the professional player contract, all regarding the same registration number of the registered mail and the same date of dispatch, constituted

[12] CAS 2014/A/3486, *MFK Dubnica v. FC Parma*, para 51.

[13] Ibid., para 53.

sufficient evidence to prove that Dubnica sent the Player a contractual offer via registered mail on 13 March 2012, which offer was delivered at the home address of the Player on 15 March 2012, i.e. 107 days before the expiry of the employment contract.[14]

Further, the Panel found that even if the Player had no knowledge of the content of the delivery made on 15 March 2012, the fact that a delivery was made at his home address resulted in a shift of the burden of proof to the Player, who would then have to establish that this letter did not contain a contractual offer from Dubnica.[15]

With regard to Parma's argument that there was no paper trail of the alleged negotiations (no exchange of emails, text messages or any other correspondence) and therefore it was not demonstrated that a contractual offer was made, the Panel deemed it very likely that no negotiations took place since it was clear from the beginning that the Player was not interested in staying with Dubnica. However, this is not relevant with respect to the requirements of Article 6(3) of Annex 4 of the FIFA RSTP, as the only question is whether it can be proven that a contractual offer was actually made despite the fact that the Player was not interested in entering into a new contract.[16]

Consequently, the Panel concluded that Dubnica had complied with the prerequisites of Article 6(3) of Annex 4 of the FIFA RSTP.[17]

8.1.5.3 Did the Player Complete His Training Prior to His Registration with Parma?

Article 6(2) of Annex 4 to the FIFA RSTP provides that a training compensation is due, "unless it is evident that a player has already terminated his training period before the age of 21".

First, with respect to the burden of proof whether or not the Player has terminated his training, the Panel referred to FIFA circular letter no. 801, which states in relevant part

> The Committee was asked to determine what triggers the end of a player's training and/or education. It maintained that it is a question of proof, which is at the burden of the club that is claiming this fact. A player who regularly performs for the club's 'A' team could be considered as having accomplished his training period. This may certainly signal that the formation of a player has been completed but there may be other indications hereto. The decision on this will have to be taken on a case-by-case basis. This principle will also apply to apprentice professionals or players under a scholarship agreement.

[14] Ibid., para 79.
[15] Ibid., para 81.
[16] Ibid., para 85.
[17] Ibid., para 90.

Hence, the Panel found that the burden of proof lied with Parma.[18]

Then the Panel summarized the pertinent CAS case law and held that according to a certain line of CAS jurisprudence a player that regularly plays in the 'A' team of a club is deemed to have completed his training.[19] However, according to another line of CAS jurisprudence, this does not constitute the only decisive factor for the completion of the player's training. There are further factors that are generally taken into consideration.[20]

Consequently, the Panel noted that playing for the 'A' team of a club is only one factor (albeit an important one) to consider. Another important factor is the level of the relevant league, since it is much harder for a player to reach the 'A' team of a club which plays in a top league than one that plays in a less developed league [sic].[21] The Panel then concluded that although in the 2009/2010 season the Player played 14 games in the 'A' team of Dubnica which played at the time in the First League in the Slovak Republic, he had not terminated his training as the Slovak league is not one of the top leagues in Europe and the Player was only 18 years old at the time.[22] According to the Panel, also the 2010/2011 season was not the end of the Player's training period, although he played the entire first part of the season in the 'A' team of Dubnica, as (i) the Slovak league was still not one of the top leagues in Europe, (ii) the Player was subsequently replaced by a more experienced goalkeeper and (iii) he was not included in the national team of the Slovak Football Association.[23]

In the opinion of the Panel, the turning point came in the 2011/2012 season, when the Player played all 33 matches throughout the season in the 'A' team. Although, due to the relegation of Dubnica, the Player only played in the second Slovak league, he attracted the attention of a club like Parma, playing in one of the top European leagues. These aspects were decisive for the Panel to conclude that the Player terminated his training at the beginning of the 2011/2012 season.[24]

Finally, the Panel noted that some CAS cases suggest that there is a difference between the "training" and the "development" of a player.[25] This Panel however found that although there may be such a distinction *as a matter of fact*, in the sense that a football player does not stop learning and might still improve as a

---

[18]Ibid., para 95.

[19]CAS 2003/O/527, *Hamburger Sport-Verein e.V. v. Odense Boldklub*, Award of 21 April 2004; CAS 2006/A/1029, *Maccabi Haifa FC v. Real Racing Club Santander*, Award of 2 October 2006.

[20]See Sect. 8.2.3 of this Article; CAS 2006/A/1029, *Maccabi Haifa v. Santander*, para 20 et seq.; CAS 2008/A/1705, *Neue Grasshopper Fussball AG Zurich v. Club Alianza de Lima*, Award of 18 June 2009, para 9.4.

[21]CAS 2014/A/3486, *MFK Dubnica v. FC Parma*, para 100.

[22]Ibid., para 102.

[23]Ibid., para 103.

[24]Ibid., para 104.

[25]CAS 2006/A/1029, *Maccabi Haifa v. Santander* and CAS 2011/A/2682, *Udinese Calcio S.p.A. v. Helsingborgs IF*, Award of 23 May 2012.

player after the end of his training period, the FIFA RSTP suggest otherwise. The FIFA RSTP define 'training compensation' as "the payments made in accordance with Annexe 4 to cover the **development** of young players" (emphasis added). Hence, according to the Panel, the training compensation may also refer to the period in which the young player's skills are still in the process of development, which has to be determined on a case-by-case basis.[26]

8.1.5.4 To What Amount of Training Compensation Was Dubnica Entitled, if Any?

The provisions on how to calculate the training compensation can be found in Articles 4–6 of Annex 4 to the FIFA RSTP. The general rule to calculate the training compensation due to a player's former club is to take the costs that would have been incurred by the new club if it had trained the player itself. This general provision, however, is subject to numerous exceptions, especially with respect to transfers inside the territory of EU/EEA.[27]

Referring to FIFA's annual circular letters regarding the categorisation of clubs, the Panel calculated that Dubnica was entitled to a training compensation in the amount of € 219,897.

8.2 Commentary

8.2.1 The Exclusion of Evidence Based on Article R57(3) CAS Code

The case at hand entails a few interesting legal issues. First of all, it seems to be only the third time that the CAS had to deal with a request under the new Article R57(3) CAS Code, which provides that the Panel has the discretion to exclude evidence which was not submitted in the first instance proceeding although it was available or could have reasonably been discovered at that stage.[28] Since its introduction, a number of authors have commented on this provision. The Panel's

---

[26] CAS 2014/A/3486, *MFK Dubnica v. FC Parma*, para 106.

[27] Article 6 of Annexe 4 to the FIFA RSTP.

[28] The other two were: CAS 2013/A/3286-3294, *SC FC Sportul Studentesc SA v. Romanian Football Federation & several players*, Award of 7 March 2014; and CAS 2014/A/3518, *Zamalek Sporting Club v. Accra Hearts of Oak Sporting Club*, Award of 31 October 2014. See Kitching J, Not comfortably satisfied? The upcoming Court of Arbitration for Sport case of the thirty-four current and former players of the Essendon football club, 4 September 2015. http://www.asser.nl/SportsLaw/Blog/post/not-comfortably-satisfied-the-upcoming-court-of-arbitration-for-sport-case-of-the-thirty-four-current-and-former-players-of-the-essendon-football-club-by-james-kitching. Accessed 10 January 2016.

interpretation, affirming that the discretion granted by Article R57(3) should be exercised with caution, for example in situations where a party may have engaged in abusive procedural behaviour or where it would be unfair or inappropriate to admit new evidence, is in line with the commentaries. As will be shown, in its own commentary, the CAS is even more restrictive in the interpretation of this provision, whereas the SFT seems to give it a much wider scope. Reason enough to take a deeper look at Article R57(3) CAS Code.

When this new provision was introduced into the CAS Code, many authors (including the author of this article) were of the opinion that this is a very delicate rule because it could be in contradiction to the principle of *de novo* review in CAS proceedings.[29] The CAS Code establishes the *de novo* principle as follows: "The Panel has full power to review the facts and the law. It may issue a new decision which replaces the decision challenged or annul the decision and refer the case back to the previous instance".[30] In order for the CAS to fully review the facts and the law, the parties must be able to submit all the evidence (and arguments) they deem necessary to support their position. Excluding a party's evidence in the CAS proceedings could be regarded as a violation of the right to be heard, and may constitute a ground to appeal the CAS award before the Swiss Federal Tribunal based on Article 190(2)(d) or (e) of the PILA.[31] Further, the *de novo* principle has a curing effect, in the sense that it heals procedural mistakes made by the previous instance.

It has to be taken into account that often times, the first instances in sports arbitration proceedings are internal judicial bodies of the sports organization itself, and not professional independent arbitral tribunals. These internal judicial bodies are not considered independent and an athlete or a club may have good reasons not to submit certain evidence due, for instance, to perceived bias on the part of an arbitrator, the possibility of negative repercussions, etc.[32] Hence, the review of the decisions rendered by such bodies before the CAS shall be a comprehensive one; i.e. one without limitations. Or, as the CAS itself put it in an earlier decision "the virtue of an appeal system which allows for a full rehearing before an appellate body is that issues of the fairness or otherwise of the hearing before the tribunal of first instance fade to the periphery (…)".[33] Rightly, the recently published com-

---

[29]Levy R, The new CAS Rules—what you need to know, 27 May 2013. http://www.lawinsport.com/blog/roy-levy/item/the-new-cas-rules-what-you-need-to-know. Accessed 10 January 2016. See also Rigozzi et al. 2013a, b, p. 1036 para 4.

[30]Article R57(1) CAS Code.

[31]Del Fabro 2015, p. 1153.

[32]Levy 2013.

[33]CAS 1998/A/208, *N., J., Y., W. v. FINA*, Award of 22 December 1998.

mentary to the CAS Code, written by the Secretary General and a Legal Counsel of the CAS, clarifies and limits the use of Article R57(3) CAS Code[34]

> From all the above, it is clear that the full power of review, as a well-established principle in appeals before the CAS, should be preserved to the extent that the previous instance is not an independent arbitral tribunal but the internal body of a sports federation. The newly inserted third paragraph of Article R57 CAS Code should therefore be interpreted in such a way as not to circumvent the core principle of the Panel's full power of review. This is possible if CAS Panels reserve the application of this provision to exceptional circumstances and as a safeguard in order to avoid abusive conduct by one of the parties: the control of good faith should therefore be the key element prior to the application of Article R57 paragraph 3, and in this way the award will not risk violating Article 190 paragraph 2 (d) PILA.

In other words, the CAS's commentary of the Code suggests not to make use of Article R57(3) CAS Code if the previous instance was an internal judicial body of a sports organization—even if the new evidence is filed in an abusive manner, or in bad faith. The exclusion of evidence should only be a legitimate procedural measure if the following two (cumulative) prerequisites are fulfilled:

(i) the previous instance was an independent arbitral tribunal, i.e. not an internal judicial body of a sports organization, and
(ii) the filing of the new evidence is abusive or in bad faith.

In any event, the general rule should always be for the Panel to have the full power of review and only in exceptional circumstances to apply Article R57(3) CAS Code.

If the future CAS Panels will apply the formula proposed in the CAS's commentary, the scope of application of Article R57(3) CAS Code will be very limited since many decisions which are appealed to the CAS were taken by an internal judicial body of a sports organization. In an earlier publication, Mavromati even considered that this would limit excessively the scope of the provision, rendering its application *de facto* impossible.[35] According to the author of this article, the necessity of this provision can be questioned if its application is limited to such a narrow scope. Would the Panel not be allowed to exclude evidence which was submitted in an abusive manner or in bad faith, based on general legal principles anyway, even without the provision of Article R57(3) CAS Code? Although the CAS Code does not stipulate for all the parties to act in good faith, this fundamental principle is enshrined in the Swiss Constitution,[36] the Swiss Civil Code[37] and the Swiss Code of Civil Procedure[38] (Swiss law governs the procedure before CAS as the *lex arbitri*). Further, the IBA Rules on the Taking of Evidence in International

[34]Mavromati and Reeb 2015, Article R57, para 53.

[35]Mavromati 2014, p. 56.

[36]Article 9 Swiss Constitution.

[37]Article 2(1) CO.

[38]Article 52 Swiss Code of Civil Procedure.

Arbitration (hereinafter "IBA Rules") provide in their Preamble that the taking of evidence shall be conducted on the principle that each party shall act in good faith. The IBA Rules are designed to supplement the legal provisions and the institutional, ad hoc or other rules that apply to the conduct of the arbitration (i.e. the IBA Rules may supplement the CAS Code).[39] Further, the IBA Rules provide that "[i]f the Arbitral Tribunal determines that a Party has failed to conduct itself in good faith in the taking of evidence, the Arbitral Tribunal may, in addition to any other measures available under these Rules, take such failure into account in its assignment of the costs of the arbitration [...]".[40] One of the measures which the Arbitral Tribunal may take is the exclusion of evidence according to Article 9(2) IBA Rules.[41] Consequently, if the scope of Article R57(3) CAS Code is to be limited to abusive behaviour and bad faith, the author of this article suggests that it would not have been necessary to introduce it in the first place as the exclusion of evidence could have been based on general principles of law and the IBA Rules.

It seems that the initial reason for the insertion of Article R57(3) CAS Code was to put pressure on the parties to act with the proper diligence already in the first instance proceedings. The CAS presumably had experiences where parties may not have taken the first instance proceedings as seriously as the CAS proceeding and only started collecting all the evidence once the CAS proceeding had started. "This may engender substantial delays in the process of the case before the CAS, delays that could otherwise have been avoided if the case had been rightly dealt with (and all evidence had been presented) already at the previous instance".[42] While it is understandable that the CAS is not very happy about this phenomenon, it is just as understandable that prospective appellants may not want to make huge efforts for a proceeding before an internal judicial body of a sports organization which they do not expect to take an independent decision in the matter, or where they anticipate that making such efforts will not make a difference to the outcome. "Let's save our resources for the CAS proceeding" is an often heard sentence from these appellants. It would seem that the CAS wanted to change this attitude with the introduction of Article R57(3) CAS Code, but is now realizing that this would not be appropriate for the above-mentioned reasons, and is, thus, drastically narrowing the scope of this rule.

In fact, there could be another reason why the scope of this provision must be restricted. Most appeals to the CAS are appeals against decisions taken by federations which are based in Switzerland (there are about 60 international sports federations having their seat in Switzerland). These federations have the legal form of an association. It is established CAS jurisprudence that an appeal against a

[39]Preamble para 1 IBA Rules on the Taking of Evidence in International Arbitration.

[40]Article 9(7) IBA Rules on the Taking of Evidence in International Arbitration.

[41]Zuberbühler et al. 2012, Article 9 para 18. Article 9(2) contains a catalogue of provisions allowing the arbitral tribunal to limit or exclude certain evidence. Bad faith is not explicitly mentioned, but this catalogue is not exhaustive, i.e. there may be other reasons to exclude evidence.

[42]Mavromati and Reeb 2015, Article R57, para 46.

decision of a sports federation based in Switzerland is an appeal pursuant to Article 75 CO which provides: "Any member who has not consented to a resolution which infringes the law or the articles of association is entitled by law to challenge such resolution in court within one month of learning thereof. (Emphasis added)".[43] The fact that each member has the right to challenge a decision taken by the association *in court* means that the member has the statutory right to bring the case together with all its arguments and evidence to an independent and impartial tribunal. This may also be an arbitral tribunal as long as it is independent and impartial, however, an internal judicial body of a sport organization is not sufficient to meet this requirement.[44] Hence, the parties must have the right to bring forward all arguments and evidence they wish before an independent and impartial arbitral tribunal.

Interestingly, the SFT commented on the legality and the scope of Article R57(3) CAS Code in a recent appeal against a CAS award.[45] In summary, the SFT upheld the discretion of the CAS to stipulate in the CAS Code a provision which allows the Panel to exclude certain evidence, without restricting the application of such provision like the CAS commentary did.[46] The CAS award appealed before the SFT was the first one which excluded evidence pursuant to Article R57(3) CAS Code.[47] The appellant argued that the arbitrator's restrictive interpretation of Article R57(3) of the CAS Code amounted to introducing an impermissible limitation upon his power of review, which violated the requirements of Article 6(1) of the European Convention of Human Rights (fair trial) and was a violation of procedural public policy pursuant to Article 190(2)(e) PILA. According to the SFT, the concept of procedural public policy does not necessarily oblige an arbitral tribunal to consider all aspects of a case with full power of review. Once it is clear that the parties have waived their right to submit their dispute to a state court by

[43] CAS 2013/A/3139, *Fenerbahçe SK v. Union des Associations Européennes de Football (UEFA)*, Award of 5 December 2013, para 104 et seq.; CAS 2013/A/3140, *A. v. Club Atlético de Madrid SAD & Real Federación Española de Fútbol (RFEF) & Fédération Internationale de Football Association (FIFA)*, Award of 10 October 2013, para 8.6; CAS 2008/A/1639, *RCD Mallorca v. The Football Association (FA) & Newcastle United*, Award of 24 April 2009, para 28 et seq.; CAS 2011/A/2360 & 2392 *English Chess Federation and Georgian Chess Federation v. FIDE*, Award of 3 July 2012, para 93 et seq.

[44] SFT 127 III 429; Riemer 1990, Article 75, para 85; Sprecher 2015, para 7.2.2.

[45] Upon request, the CAS did not provide the author of this article with a copy of the CAS award as the appeal to the SFT was partially upheld and thus the case has to be reopened, meaning that it is currently pending and confidential. From the SFT decision, one can deduce that it is about an appeal of a (Romanian) football club against nine of its players who successfully requested payment of outstanding salaries.

[46] SFT 4A_246/2014, decision of 15 July 2015. See for an English summary of the judgment, Vosser N and Boehm H, Swiss Supreme Court partially grants petition to set aside CAS award, 26 August 2015. http://www.swlegal.ch/getdoc/c4dc5bf7-6a8a-4dd8-8390-8541c97f3093/2015_Nathalie-Voser_Hannah-Boehm_Petition-to-set-a.aspx. Accessed 10 January 2016.

[47] CAS 2013/A/3286 & 3294, *SC FC Sportul Studentesc SA v. Romanian Football Federation et al.*

agreeing to arbitration, it is admissible that they limit the arbitral tribunal's power of review with regard to the subject matter and/or depth of its review, either directly or by their choice of arbitration rules.[48] This rather lenient approach of the SFT is in line with its earlier jurisprudence where it stated that the arbitral tribunal has the right to exclude evidence if the latter is not submitted in compliance with the applicable formal rules.[49]

To conclude, it is interesting to notice that the CAS is restricting its own discretion in the application of Article R57(3) CAS Code, while the SFT, the court with supervisory jurisdiction over CAS awards, has adopted an approach that leaves room for giving a much wider scope to this provision.

8.2.2 The Requirement to Submit a Contract Offer by Registered Mail

In the interest of predictability of legal decisions, it is unfortunate that the CAS did not have to decide if the requirement to send the contract offer by registered mail is a formal prerequisite or if training compensation is also due if it can be proven by other means that a contract offer was made on time. In an earlier CAS award, however, the Panel held that the requirement of a transmission by registered mail has been foreseen by FIFA as a way to provide evidence and not as a condition of validity. "It has been recognized in the past, both by the FIFA DRC and by CAS, that when FIFA amended Article 6 para 3 of Annex 4 of the Regulations, and notably introduced the formal requirement of the "registered letter", its objective was to make it easier for the former club to discharge its burden of proof and to get a training compensation. However, there are still other ways to prove that an offer was sent, be it through witnesses or fax receipts, for instance".[50]

If the player is an amateur player and not a professional, the rules which the CAS applies are even less strict. The CAS concluded that in order to justify entitlement to training compensation for an amateur player, the training club should at least show a *bona fide* interest in retaining the services of the player for the future. At the same time, in order to encourage player training, the Panel considered that

[48]Nevertheless, the SFT partially set aside the CAS award for another reason. It held that the sole arbitrator had violated the appellant's right to be heard by failing to address material arguments raised by it; SFT 4A_246/2014, para 7.2.2.

[49]SFT 4P.196/2003 of 7 January 2004, para 4.1; Jermini and Gamba 2013, Article 15 para 11.

[50]CAS 2010/A/2316, *Stoke City FC v. Brescia Calcio* (date unknown), para 71; CAS 2009/A/1757, *MTK Budapest v. Inter Milan,* Award of 30 July 2009; FIFA DRC decision, 23 January 2013, para 24. See Chantler M, Training compensation in football, 4 May 2013. http://www.lawinsport.com/blog/mills-reeve/item/training-compensation-in-football. Accessed 10 January 2016.

compensation should be granted whenever it would appear contrary to common sense to conclude that the training club was not at all interested in keeping the player.[51] In fact, as made clear by Article 6(3) of Annex 4 to the FIFA Regulations and underlined in the CAS jurisprudence, a claim to training compensation may be retained even if a professional contract has not been offered.[52] Indeed, it would be unreasonable to require a club to offer a professional contract to every young amateur player in order to avoid the risk of losing any entitlement to training compensation.

To conclude, it seems that even if Dubnica could not prove that it sent the new contract by registered mail, it would still be entitled to training compensation if it could prove by other means that it made an offer to the Player before the deadline. In the opinion of the author of this article, the earlier CAS Panels were right in considering the provision that an employment offer must be made by registered mail not to be a legal requirement but rather a recommended way of delivery in order to prove that the contract was sent to the player before the expiry of the deadline of 60 days.

8.2.3 When Has the Player's Training Ended?

Another disputed issue in the reviewed award was when the training of the Player had ended. The Panel did not apply the approach which can be found in some CAS jurisprudence, namely to deem the training of a player to have ended once he plays regularly for the 'A' team.[53] The Panel followed the FIFA circular letter, which suggests that a case-by-case assessment should be conducted, which may be influenced by many factors, not just if the player plays in the 'A' team. Such other factors may be, according to CAS jurisprudence[54]

a) The player's value to a club (reflected in the salary, loan fee, transfer value, etc.);
b) The player's public notoriety at national and international level;
c) The player's position at the club (captain, regular player);
d) Level of games;
e) The player's regular inclusion in the national team.

---

[51] CAS 2014/A/3486, *MFK Dubnica v. FC Parma*, para 69.

[52] CAS 2006/A/1152, *ADO Den Haag v. Newcastle United FC*, Award of 7 February 2007, para 8.16; CAS 2009/A/1757, *MTK Budapest v. Inter Milan*, para 7.13.

[53] CAS 2003/O/527, *Hamburger Sport-Verein e.V. v. Odense Boldklub*; CAS 2006/A/1029, *Maccabi Haifa FC v. Real Racing Club Santander.*

[54] CAS 2006/A/1029, *Maccabi Haifa FC v. Real Racing Club Santander*, para 20 et seq.; CAS 2008/A/1705, *Neue Grasshopper Fussball AG Zurich v. Club Alianza de Lima*, para 9.4.

The advantage of applying such a flexible approach is that the Panel can, by considering a number of different factors, reach a fair assessment of the situation. On the other hand, applying a rigid approach would be beneficial for the legal predictability of training compensation cases. Considering various factors increases the discretion of the Panel and, with that, the decision may be less predictable and less understandable for the parties.

The Panel in the case at hand found that the decisive moment to consider the training of the Player to have ended, was the moment he played all 33 games of the 2011/2012 season in the 'A' team, although the club only played in the second highest Slovak league at the time. The Panel mentioned several times in the award that the Slovak league was not one of the top leagues in Europe and, therefore, it is easier to get into the 'A' team than in one of the top leagues. This is true and when looking at each season separately, the Panel's arguments make perfect sense. However, following the line of argumentation of the Panel, one could just as well consider the training of the Player to have ended the previous season (2010/2011). As the Panel noted, the Player played from 27 February 2010 (during the 2009/2010 season) until the 18th round of the subsequent 2010/2011 season, and was fielded in 32 successive matches as the starting goalkeeper of the 'A' team of Dubnica in the highest football competition in Slovak Republic (in this season Dubnica played in the first league). During the second half of the 2010/2011 season, the Player was replaced by a more experienced goalkeeper, and at the end of that season Dubnica was relegated to the second highest league.[55]

So eventually, boiling the Panel's arguments down to their essence, the Panel found that playing 32 successive matches (over two seasons) in the 'A' team in the highest national league did not end the training of the Player, but playing all 33 matches in one season in the 'A' team in the second highest league did end the training of the Player. Looking at the case from that perspective gives the decision a bit of an arbitrary touch, and could have saved FC Parma € 60,000, the amount which it paid for training compensation for season 2010/2011.[56]

The Panel's view that the difference between training and development of a player is only a factual one ("as a matter of fact"[57]), is not in line with previous CAS jurisprudence[58] and neither serves the legal predictability nor the parties' satisfaction. Although it did not change anything in the case at hand, and although arbitral tribunals are different than state courts, it is unfortunate when Panels do not consider themselves bound by previous CAS jurisprudence without providing clear and specific reasons for departing from previous case law. The parties should be able to rely on CAS case law in a proceeding before the CAS.

[55]CAS 2014/A/3486, *MFK Dubnica v. FC Parma*, para 8.

[56]Ibid., para 118.

[57]Ibid., para 106.

[58]See CAS 2011/A/2682, *Udinese Calcio v. Helsingborgs* and CAS 2006/A/1029, *Maccabi Haifa v. Santander*.

The actual amount of the training compensation was calculated properly by the Panel and thus there is no need to discuss that aspect in detail.[59]

8.3 Conclusion

Overall, the Dubnica award is well reasoned. In this author's view, the issue about the exclusion of evidence was handled well and the Panel's argumentation is perfectly in line with the opinion of the CAS commentary. The Panel was also right to deem the new employment contract to have been sent by registered mail, since the evidence was overwhelming in its entirety. On the other hand, the reasoning with respect to the question of the moment when the training of the Player had ended, was not convincing. In the interest of legal predictability and practicability for the clubs to calculate training compensation, it would be desirable if a CAS Panel could establish at least a few binding criteria which would help the parties to assess when a player's training has ended. Also with respect to the difference between training and development, the Panel did not help to solve future disputes on training compensation by stating an opinion which runs counter to past CAS awards.

References

Del Fabro M (2015) Ein Streifzug durch die Anfechtungsklage nach Art. 75 ZGB. Aktuelle juristische Praxis 24:1140–1159

Jermini C, Gamba A (2013) Art. 15. In: Zuberbühler T, Müller K, Habegger P (eds) Swiss Rules of International Arbitration, Commentary, 2nd edn. Schulthess, Zurich, pp 185–195

Mavromati D (2014) The panel's right to exclude evidence based on article R57 para. 3 CAS code: a limit to CAS' full power of review? CAS Bulletin (Issue 1) 48–56

Mavromati D, Reeb M (2015) The code of the court of arbitration for sport, commentary, cases and materials. Kluwer Law International BV, Alphen aan den Rijn

Riemer HM (1990) Berner Kommentar, Band I, 3. Abteilung, 2. Teilband. Stämpfli, Bern

Rigozzi A, Hasler E, Noth M (2013a) Sports arbitration under the CAS rules. In: Arroyo M (ed) Arbitration in Switzerland. A Practitioner's Guide. Kluwer Law International BV, Alphen aan den Rijn, pp 885–1083

Rigozzi A, Hasler E, Quinn B (2013b) The 2011, 2012 and 2013 revisions to the code of sports-related Arbitration. Jusletter. 3 juin 2013

Sprecher T (2015) Die Anfechtung von Vereinsbeschlüssen. In: Kunz P, Arter O, Jörg F (eds) Entwicklungen im Gesellschaftsrecht X. Stämpfli, Bern, pp 148–176

Zuberbühler T, Hofmann D, Oetiker C, Rohner T (2012) IBA rules of evidence, commentary on the IBA rules on the taking of evidence in international arbitration. Schulthess, Zurich

[59] CAS 2014/A/3486, *MFK Dubnica v. FC Parma*, paras 109 et. seq.

Chapter 9
TAS 2011/A/2578, *OGC Nice Côte d'Azur & Yannick Dos Santos Djalo v. FIFA*, Order on Provisional Measures of 11 October 2011 and CAS 2013/A/3647, *Sporting Clube de Portugal SAD v. OGC Nice Côte d'Azur* & CAS 2013/A/3648, *OGC Nice Côte d'Azur v. Sporting Clube de Portugal SAD & FIFA*, Award of 11 May 2015

Wouter Lambrecht

When two dogs fight over a bone a third party carries it away.
—Dutch proverb.

Abstract This case evidences why clubs ought to be extremely diligent when negotiating the transfer of a player, even more so when such negotiations take place under severe time pressure to beat the closing of a transfer window. Following a hectic day of negotiating and re-negotiating a player's transfer and employment contracts, OGC Nice failed to upload the necessary documents in TMS in due time for the ITC to be requested. Faced with this emergency, OGC Nice requested an exception to the FIFA transfer rule, but such exception was denied by the FIFA PSC Single Judge. In turn, also the CAS rejected the joint request of the player and OGC Nice for provisional measures by which they sought his registration outside the transfer window. In the absence of both payment of his salary and integration with the team, the player finally terminated his

Views expressed in the present text are those of the author only and the author alone and do not necessarily reflect those of ECA or any other institution to which the author may belong.

W. Lambrecht (✉)
Attorney-at-law, Head of Legal at the European Club Association, Nyon, Switzerland
e-mail: wouter.lambrecht@ecaeurope.com

W. Lambrecht
FIFA Dispute Resolution Chamber Member, Zurich, Switzerland

W. Lambrecht
Mediator at the Court of Arbitration for Sport, Lausanne, Switzerland

A. Duval and A. Rigozzi (eds.), *Yearbook of International Sports Arbitration 2015*,
DOI 10.1007/978-94-6265-129-6_9

contract with OGC Nice, subsequently joining the former club's big rivals Benfica SL via a free transfer. Unhappy with the unsuccessful transfer to OGC Nice, and even more so with the free transfer of the player to their rivals, Sporting Clube de Portugal initiated an action, seeking payment of the transfer amount as per the contract as well as additional damages for loss of chance and damages for sporting loss. The CAS panel had to evaluate how to apply the conditions precedent in the transfer contract, whether there was any contributory negligence to be taken into account, and after doing so finally ordered OGC Nice to pay Sporting Clube de Portugal a significant amount of money… this for a player from whose sporting performances it never benefitted.

Keywords Transfer contract · Lack of ITC · Provisional registration/measure · Conditions precedent · Damages · Contributory negligence · Loss of chance

Contents

9.1 Facts

The origins of this case go back to the last day of the European summer transfer window in 2011, more precisely 31 August 2011. During the month of August, OGC Nice Côte d'Azur ('OGC Nice') and Sporting Clube de Portugal ('Sporting') entered into negotiations for the transfer of the professional player Yannick Dos Santos Djalo ('Player'), who was to join the first-mentioned Club. After having agreed on the terms of the contract and following several exchanges on 31 August, a final transfer contract was exchanged at 03:32 PM via email. This contract was made subject to several conditions precedent, i.e. the signing of the employment contract, the issuance of the ITC, as well as approval of the employment contract by the French Football Association. The contract also provided for a sell-on clause granting 50 % of any future transfer fee to Sporting. At 04:00 PM, the Player and his agent arrived at the club to finalize the employment contract that had been discussed earlier with OGC Nice. However, both parties failed to reach agreement on the amount of salary in that, what the Club had intended to be a gross amount, the Player wanted the same amount net. Due to its financial constraints, OGC Nice at first considered the negotiations terminated. However, later that day and after an away game of OGC Nice in Toulouse, the Club's President returned to Nice and restarted negotiations with the Player at around 10:30 PM. As a result of these re-negotiations, new terms were agreed upon by means of a new salary and additional bonuses that would cover the difference between the parties. In this respect, 10 % of a future sell-on fee was awarded to the Player but, given this development, OGC Nice wanted to re-negotiate Sporting's participation in a future transfer down from 50 % (as mentioned in the originally agreed transfer contract) to 40 %. These changes to the transfer contract were discussed between both clubs from 10:30 PM to 11:45 PM, and at 11:50 PM a draft of the amended agreement was sent by OGC Nice to Sporting. This draft included a new clause shifting the burden upon Sporting to undertake all necessary steps to obtain the ITC required for the qualification of the Player. Sporting then sent the signed transfer agreement to OGC Nice at 11.59 PM, but when OGC Nice received it and uploaded the relevant documents in the FIFA TMS, the deadline for requesting the ITC had already passed. As the French Football Federation ('FFF') was prevented from requesting the ITC via TMS, OGC Nice asked the FFF to request,[12] it from FIFA and petition for an exception. The FIFA administration refused to grant such an exception to OGC Nice, a decision later confirmed by the Single Judge of FIFA's Players' Status Committee in a ruling dated 23 September 2011. In the meantime, the Player had been training with OGC Nice and had participated in some friendly games.

9.2 TAS 2011/A/2578—Request for Provisional Measures

9.2.1 Request

Following the refusal of the Single Judge to allow for an exception, OGC Nice and the Player lodged a joint complaint with the CAS on 28 September, seeking the following provisional measures:

> to order FIFA to deliver the ITC for the Player in favour of OGC Nice pending a decision on the merits of the appeal
>
> Alternatively
>
> to order FIFA to immediately take any necessary measures allowing the Player to play for OGC Nice pending a decision on the merits of the appeal.

[1]TAS 2009/A/1828 & 1829, *Olympique Lyonnais v. US Soccer Federation*, Award of 18 March 2010.

[2]Simon 2014, pp. 80–84.

9.2.2 Argumentation by the Parties

In support of its case, OGC Nice relied, amongst others, on the following arguments:

OGC Nice had signed and recruited the Player for his well-known offensive qualities and depriving the Club from the services of the Player would have an impact on its competitiveness in the French League 1. Its lack of competitiveness could contribute to its relegation to a lower division, in addition and particularly noting that OGC Nice was ranked no 17 in the League, a situation that was created by the absence of the Player.

Besides, OGC Nice argued that the uploading of the documents into TMS had been a laborious and slow process, that they had initiated the uploading prior to midnight, and, therefore, that denying the registration of the Player with OGC Nice constituted 'excessive formalism' which would be contrary to Swiss law and, possibly, even to the European Convention of Human Rights in that the rules (transfer window) were being applied with a rigour that served no interest warranting protection.

From his side, the Player invoked that he was suffering sporting damages since he was left without either a club or a contract, and thus without salary and that, as a consequence thereof, his sporting career was suffering.

9.2.3 Assessment by the Panel

In assessing the request, the CAS evidently recalled the main three conditions that would have to be met for provisional measures to be granted; i.e. irreparable harm, likelihood of success and balance of interest. Whereas most CAS orders on provisional measures deem these conditions to be cumulative,[3] this particular decision reads

> [t]hese conditions are in principle cumulative but the CAS should, however, have a degree of latitude to appreciate more generally the situation by keeping in mind the three conditions without it being necessary or useful to apply strict conditions which could lead to more difficulties rather than to a real legal security.[4]

---

[3]See CAS 2007/A/1677, parties and date unknown; CAS 2009/A/1918, *Jakub Wawrzyniak v. Hellenic Football Federation (HFF),* Order of 13 August 2009.

[4]Free translation. The original (TAS 2011/A/2578, *OGC Nice Côte d'Azur & Yannick Dos Santos Djalo v. FIFA*, Order of 11 October 2011, para 5.3) reads: "[c]es conditions sont en principe cumulatives, mais le TAS doit toutefois "disposer de la latitude nécessaire pour apprécier globalement la situation à l'aide des trois critères susmentionnés sans qu'il soit nécessaire, ni utile, de prévoir des conditions strictes qui pourraient donner lieu à plus de difficultés que de véritable sécurité juridique" (TAS 2008/A/1552 voir également CAS 2007/A/1396 & 1402, ordonnance du 5 mars 2008 et CAS Ad Hoc OGW Salt Lake City 004, décision du 14 février 2002).".

Keeping the above in mind, the CAS held that the argument of 'competitiveness' lacked pertinence as OGC Nice failed to prove that its poor ranking was due to the absence of the Player. At the same time, the CAS noted that OGC Nice had another five strikers at its disposal and that, therefore, being deprived of the services of one player could not be considered as something that would constitute 'irreparable harm'.[5] As to the Player, the CAS held that the contract had validly been entered into and that, as such, he should benefit from its terms whilst also keeping in mind that the upcoming winter transfer window (three months hence) meant that he would not be deprived unduly or for an excessively long time from playing football.[6] As to the chances of success, the CAS noted that OGC Nice's own negligence had caused the ITC request to be made outside the prescribed period by disrespecting the relevant provisions of the FIFA RSTP. Besides, the CAS held that OGC Nice could have uploaded the employment contract, the proof of identity, and the first transfer contract well before midnight since these documents had been at its disposal well before that time, thus allowing enough of a window for an ITC request to be made. In fact, the CAS noted that the 'proof of identity' was only uploaded after midnight.[7] Although not directly addressed as such, in terms of balance of interest the CAS held that allowing an exception in favour of OGC Nice would violate the principle of equality which forms the cornerstone of the TMS system in that the rules ought to be applied in a strict and equal manner in relation to all clubs worldwide. OGC Nice's negligence ought, therefore, not to be accepted as valid grounds to put in question the working of the TMS, which actually seeks to make the transfer system more credible and transparent; hence, there could be no question of 'excessive formalism'[8]; as was withheld in a case brought to CAS' attention just shortly after the introduction of FIFA TMS.[9]

Thus, by its order of 11 October 2011, the Panel rejected OGC Nice's and the Player's request for provisional measures.

9.2.4 Commentary

It is quite clear to everyone involved in the world of football that transfers and all related administrative formalities should occur within the set time frame and within the relevant transfer windows. However, room for manoeuvring and case-by-case assessment and appreciation does appear to exist within the context of

---

[5]TAS 2011/A/2578, *OGC Nice* et al. *v. FIFA*, paras 5.5–5.6.

[6]Ibid., paras 5.9–5.10.

[7]Ibid., paras 5.11–5.12.

[8]Ibid., paras 5.14–5.15.

[9]TAS 2011/A/2351, *Calcio Catania v. FIFA*, Order of 16 March 2011.

Article 6 of Annex 3 of the FIFA RSTP.[10] This article basically allows the FIFA Administration to deal with a validation exception, such as the issue of requesting the ITC only a few minutes after the fixed deadline. Due to a lack of (accessible) case law, it is unclear under what circumstance FIFA allows such validation exception but it is understood that FIFA is very reluctant in doing so.[11] It could be argued that those cases in which clubs had already started inputting the relevant data into TMS prior to the deadline but were unable to complete the process before the deadline, and this for reasons beyond their control, should benefit from this exception. However, it should be admitted that the failure to upload the documents in this case was not due to unforeseen circumstances. Be that as it may, one could, for example, imagine that a temporary breakdown of the FIFA TMS website or an interruption in Internet access would trigger a validation exception, especially if such events occur on the side of the 'selling club' which, as per the FIFA RSTP, is obliged to counter-match the information in TMS before an ITC can be requested.

An exception to this extent was granted to a Belgian club in a case[12] where they had uploaded all necessary information into the TMS but were prevented from requesting the ITC due to the counter-party club not having uploaded the necessary information. The latter club had been unable to do so within the deadline due to the time that was lost in requesting a new TMS password and subsequent internet problems the club had encountered. In addition, the strict application of the transfer windows and the possibility to request an ITC via FIFA may, and possibly ought to, also be put in question, given the tenor of Article 6 of the FIFA RSTP.[13] According to this article, players whose contract has expired prior to the end of a

[10]Annex 3, Article 6 FIFA RSTP 2015: "1. Upon request, the relevant department will deal with any validation exceptions and, if need be, refer the matter to the competent decision-making body, i.e., the Players' Status Committee, its single judge, or the DRC or a DRC judge, as the case may be, for a decision, except for the so-called "player confirmation", which needs to be dealt with by the association concerned (cf. Annexe 3, Article 5.2 para 1). 2. Upon request, the relevant department will deal with any validation warnings and, if need be, refer the matter to the competent decision-making body for a decision.".

[11]Goal, FIFA block Grosskreutz move to Galatasaray, 2 September 2015. http://www.goal.com/en/news/11/transfer-zone/2015/09/02/14993882/fifa-block-grosskreutz-move-to-galatasaray. Accessed 10 January 2016. Mirror, Everton refused clearance by FIFA for Odjidja-Ofoe loan move, 7 September 2012. http://www.mirror.co.uk/sport/football/transfer-news/everton-refused-clearance-by-fifa-for-vadis-1311277. Accessed 10 January 2016. Skysport, Fulham winger Bryan Ruiz denied move to La Liga side Levante, 11 February 2015. http://www.skysports.com/football/news/11095/9710288/ruiz-not-heading-to-levante. Accessed 10 January 2016.

[12]FIFA TMS Decision, no 45131, 9 February 2012, unpublished.

[13]Article 6(1) FIFA RSTP 2015: "Players may only be registered during one of the two annual registration periods fixed by the relevant association. As an exception to this rule, a professional whose contract has expired prior to the end of a registration period may be registered outside that registration period. Associations are authorised to register such professionals provided due consideration is given to the sporting integrity of the relevant competition. Where a contract has been terminated with just cause, FIFA may take provisional measures in order to avoid abuse, subject to Article 22.".

transfer window may be registered outside the transfer windows; the same holds true for those players who have terminated their contract with just cause. In theory, each transfer (contract) of (for) a player goes hand in hand with the requirement that the selling club and the concerned player terminate their employment relationship by means of a mutual agreement. As such, the relevant employment contract would expire prior to the end of a registration period, implying that Article 6 FIFA RSTP could be invoked in these kinds of cases and where an ITC has been requested just outside the transfer window period. Moreover, lacking payment and/or the registration of a player, thus preventing him from playing, a professional player could theoretically terminate his contract with just cause,[14] which in turn, as per Article 6 FIFA RSTP, would allow him to register himself with a third new club outside the transfer window.

Applied *in casu*, OGC Nice was effectively prevented from registering the Player due to its late ITC request, but the Player could with perfect reason have been registered with a third new club following the termination of his contract with OGC Nice for just cause, and this prior to the opening of the winter transfer window.

9.3 CAS 2013/A/3647 Sporting V. OGC Nice & CAS 2013/A/3648 OGC Nice V. Sporting & FIFA

9.3.1 Events Following the Request for Provisional Measures

As seen above, on 11 October 2011, the CAS rejected the request for provisional measures. Shortly thereafter, OGC Nice requested the FFF to formally deny the request for admission of the Player's employment contract (homologation) and subsequently also withdrew its appeal to the CAS. OGC Nice informed the Player that his contract had never entered into force and that it could potentially enter into a new transfer and employment contract with the Player in the winter transfer period. The Player from his side sought integration with the squad and payment of his salary but, in the absence of both, he finally terminated his contract with just cause on 25 November 2011. Sporting and OGC Nice exchanged several emails

[14]For example: FIFA DRC Decision, no 7121165, 20 July 2012, paras 17–20. In addition, the DRC was eager to emphasize that it is the responsibility of the engaging club, i.e. Club A, to ensure that the player is properly registered with his new club in order to be able to provide it with his services. Since the engaging club is the one supposedly interested in acquiring the rights of the player and in benefiting from his services, it is also expected from it that it acts accordingly in view of obtaining the player's ITC and his subsequent registration. […]. Having established that Club A is to be held liable for the non-execution of the employment contract at the basis of the present dispute, without just cause, the DRC began to establish the consequences of such breach.

during the month of November to execute the transfer during the winter period but, meanwhile and strangely enough, Sporting and the Player had also signed an official termination agreement on 11 October. In January 2012, the Player signed an employment contract with SL Benfica and joined the latter club on a free transfer. In February 2012, Sporting lodged a claim with the FIFA PSC against OGC Nice claiming the transfer fee, its rights due as per the sell-on clause, as well as compensation for damages to its sporting image as a result of the Player's joining their rivals on a free transfer.

By its decision dated 19 March 2014, the FIFA PSC awarded Sporting the transfer fee plus interests, whilst all further claims were dismissed. This decision was subsequently appealed to the CAS by both clubs.

9.3.2 Argumentation by the Parties

Article 2 of the first as well as of the re-negotiated transfer contract reads as follows:

> This agreement is subject to the following conditions:
>
> a. The signing of an employment contract between OGC Nice and the player.
> b. The issue of the player's international transfer certificate by the Portuguese football association.
> c. The approval by the new club's football association of the contract between OGC Nice and the player.

It should come as no surprise that the argumentation of both Parties in the dispute are linked to this very article, i.e. whether the conditions precedent under letter (b) and (c) prevented the contract from entering into force or whether OGC Nice's conduct had actually prevented the fulfilment of such conditions.

9.3.2.1 Sporting

In its statement before FIFA and the CAS, Sporting developed three main lines of argumentation.[15]

First, according to Sporting, the contract *had* entered into force, and this irrespective of whether the conditions precedent were met or not. More precisely, Sporting relied on Article 151(2) of the Swiss CO which reads: "[T]he contract takes effect as soon as [the relevant] condition precedent occurs, **unless the Parties clearly intended otherwise**" (emphasis added). Given that the Player had started his training and played friendly matches with OGC Nice, Sporting argued

[15] CAS 2013/A/3647 *Sporting Clube de Portugal SAD v. OGC Nice Côte d'Azur* & CAS 2013/A/3648 *OGC Nice Côte d'Azur v. Sporting Clube de Portugal SAD & FIFA*, Award of 11 May 2015, paras 80–86 and 100.

that the transfer contract had been executed by OGC Nice and that, as such, "the Parties had clearly intended otherwise" within the meaning of Article 151(2) CO.

Second, Sporting stated that, in any case, OGC Nice was responsible for the non-completion of the transfer in the summer period as well as in the winter period and that OGC Nice had breached Article 152(1) CO which stipulates: "[U]ntil such time as the condition precedent occurs, the conditional obligor must refrain from any act which might prevent the due performance of his obligation". The acts concerned were the negligent behaviour on 31 August 2011, the withdrawal of the appeal against FIFA's decision to deny the ITC, lack of integration of the Player by OGC Nice, the request directed at the FFF not to homologate the contract, and the non-performance of the transfer during the winter period. Similar to what was mentioned in the CAS order on provisional measures, Sporting argued that OGC Nice could have prepared the FIFA TMS instruction already in the afternoon of the 31st of August with the first transfer contract and all other relevant documents, and that the new contract could have been uploaded at a later moment.

Third, Sporting also put forward that OGC Nice had acted in bad faith and, as such, violated Article 156 CO which reads: "A condition is deemed fulfilled where one of the parties has prevented its fulfilment by acting against good faith".

9.3.2.2 OGC Nice

According to OGC Nice,[16] the contract was made subject to three specific conditions precedent, two of which never occurred. The ITC was never issued and the FFF did not approve the employment contract, implying that the transfer contract never entered into effect. In this respect, OGC Nice relied on the very notion of the condition precedent in itself which is reflected in Article 151 CO.[17]

Besides, OGC Nice put forward that letting the Player train with the team could not be seen as a clear indication or intent of executing the contract without the conditions precedent having been fulfilled. It merely acted in good faith, hoping to have a fit player should the ITC be issued after the 1st of September.

As to Article 152(1) CO, OGC Nice put forward that this article only contains a negative obligation in that it only obliges the Parties to refrain from any acts that could jeopardize the fulfilment, thus not imposing positive obligations to satisfy the conditions.

Furthermore, OGC Nice argued that Article 156 CO did not apply since there was no bad faith on its part. OGC Nice alleged that it had done everything it possibly could have done to upload the documents as soon as possible and that, in any case, Sporting was to be blamed too since it had displayed a lack of sense of urgency on the 31st of August in exchanging documents.

---

[16]Ibid., paras 64–71.

[17]Article 151 CO: "1. A contract is conditional if its binding nature is made dependent on the occurrence of an event that is not certain to happen. 2. The contract takes effect as soon as this condition precedent occurs, unless the parties clearly intended otherwise".

Finally, OGC Nice further argued that it had even offered to execute a transfer during the winter period despite there being no obligation to do so. More precisely, it had acted in complete good faith notwithstanding the fact that it had been clear to all parties that the transfer had to be executed during the summer.

9.3.3 Assessment by the Panel

9.3.3.1 Intention of the Parties Prompting the Conditions Precedent

> "The contract takes effect as soon as this condition precedent occurs, unless the parties clearly intended otherwise" – article 151(2) CO

The Panel recalled the general rule that a contract that was made subject to a condition precedent does not take effect if the condition precedent is not fulfilled, whereas "the exception that the Parties intended otherwise refers to situations in which Parties actually intended that rights and obligations should arise already before the condition is fulfilled".[18] Keeping in mind the arguments of both Parties, the Panel had to evaluate whether letting the Player train with the team shortly after the 1st of September constituted such an exception whereby rights and obligations arose. In doing so, the Panel felt that allowing a player to train with "his future club" cannot be seen as behaviour that would allow one to conclude that the OGC Nice had "consciously waived" the conditional nature of transfer contract. According to the Panel, Sporting did not submit convincing evidence that this sensible approach on the part of OGC Nice represented a form of amendment to the transfer contract. As such, the Panel held that there was no clear intention on the part of OGC Nice to execute the contract irrespective of the conditions precedent.[19]

9.3.3.2 Did OGC Nice Fail to Take the Necessary Actions to Trigger the Condition?

Whereas a plain reading of Article 152(1) CO only refers to a negative obligation to refrain from specific acts, the Panel stressed that this very article also contains a positive duty to act in good faith in order to safeguard the fulfilment of a condition.

> However, under Swiss law it is recognized that in addition to the negative aspect, Article 152 para. 1 CO also establishes positive duties of the parties to do what is appropriate to safeguard the prospect of fulfilment *(cf. Matt, Der bedingte Vertrag in schweizerischen und liechtensteinischen Privatrecht,* ZStP Nr. 260, page 374*)*. In this respect, the provision requires the parties to act positively in a way that is expected from them in good faith

[18]CAS 2013/A/3647 & 3648, *OGC Nice v. Sporting* et al, para 102.

[19]Ibid., para 103.

> *(Ehrat, Felix R. Art. 152 und Art 156, in: Honsell Heinrich, Vogt Nedim Peter, Wiegand Wolfgang, Basler Kommentar I, OR Art. 1-529, 5. Aufl., Basel 2011).*[20]

Keeping this in mind, the Panel analysed all the relevant acts and omissions which had taken place in order to establish whether or not OGC Nice had undertaken the necessary steps to safeguard the fulfilment of the conditions precedent.

The Panel started by recalling the facts that took place on the 31st of August and noted that OGC Nice had tried to finalize and upload all documents on time and that the last document was uploaded only four minutes after the deadline, which was not an undue delay.[21] As such, OGC Nice had acted in good faith, in spite of the fact that, according to the Panel, the late return of the President from the away game (which led to a delayed restart of the negotiations) contributed to the risk and events that occurred later that day.

Next, the Panel turned its attention to OGC Nice having withdrawn its appeal from the CAS following the denial of provisional measures. According to the Panel, it would have been prudent to continue this appeal since the Panel deciding on the provisional measures had, when doing so, not been aware of all the fact-specifics of the case, e.g. that the Player had wanted a net, rather than a gross salary, which in turn led to the transfer contract having to be re-negotiated at the last minute. Such an argument could, according to the Panel, have been presented with some chance of success.[22]

Next, the Panel noted that following the negative decision on the request for provisional measures, OGC Nice no longer allowed the Player to train with the team, nor did it pay him any salary, following which the Player terminated his contract. According to the Panel, the transfer contract, contrary to the more established practice, did not contain a specific clause that obliged the parties to execute the transfer during the summer transfer window of 2011. Moreover, according to the Panel, the discussions that took place between OGC Nice and Sporting after the 1st of September actually indicated that both parties were interested, to a certain extent, in implementing the transfer agreement during the winter period. As such, OGC Nice should have safeguarded that possibility by agreeing to an interim solution with the Player rather than provoking him to terminate the contract by not integrating him into the team and not paying him.[23]

Finally, the Panel also noted that OGC Nice, having indicated to Sporting its interest in concluding the transfer in the winter, did not try to convince the Player to sign a new employment contract and to complete the transfer in winter.

As such, the Panel concluded that

> Nice did not do all that could have been expected from it in good faith to safeguard the fulfilment of the condition precedent. Although the above acts or omissions might not,

[20]Ibid., para 105.

[21]Ibid., para 108.

[22]Ibid., para 109.

[23]Ibid., para 110.

> taken in isolation, justify this conclusion, the Panel considers that, cumulatively, they support their conclusion that Nice did not do all that could have been reasonably expected.[24]

9.3.3.3 Bad Faith by OGC Nice?

Having ruled a violation of the Club's positive duties under Article 152(1) CO, the Panel also examined whether OGC Nice's acts or omissions amounted to a demonstration of bad faith by which it prevented the condition from being enacted. In this respect, the Panel recalled that a violation of Article 156 CO required more than Article 152, in that the party preventing the fulfilment must have acted against good faith in an obviously wilful manner.

Since the Panel only found a violation of Article 152 CO by assessing all individual acts and omissions together whereas, individually, these could not be judged to be severe, the Panel held that such acts could not be considered to be impediments to the fulfilment of the condition and evidence of bad faith. More precisely, the Panel stated that OGC Nice had protected its own interests by acting in the way it did.

> The element of protecting primarily [one's] own interest does not generally speak for bad faith within the meaning of article 156 CO *(EHRAT, Felix R. Art. 152 und 156, in: Honsell Heinrich Vogt Nedim Peter, Wiegand Wolfgang, Basler Kommentar I, OR, Art. 1-529, 5. Aufl., Basel 2011, page 869).*[25]

9.3.4 Damages

9.3.4.1 General

Although OGC Nice did not in bad faith prevent the conditions from being fulfilled, it failed, according to the Panel, to take the necessary steps to make their fulfilment possible.

Having established that Swiss law was applicable to the dispute, the Panel held as follows:

> it is admitted that the consequences of non-compliance with the duties arising out of Article 152 are an obligation to compensate the damages caused. This means Nice would be liable for damages under Article 97 et seq. CO [...].[26]

In establishing the damages, the Panel specified

> Compensation for breach of an obligation shall generally be based on the principle of positive interest meaning that the amount shall be determined that puts the injured party in the position that the same party would have had the obligation been performed properly [...].[27]

[24]Ibid., para 112.

[25]Ibid., para 115.

[26]Ibid., para 117.

[27]Ibid., para 118.

In relation to the principle of positive interest, Sporting claimed the payment of the transfer fee as well as compensation for the loss of chance to benefit from an additional amount of money as per the sell-on clause in the contract. Besides, Sporting had also claimed damages for loss of sporting image due to the Player's having joined their great rivals Benfica SL.

As to the transfer fee claimed by Sporting:

> Had the obligation to safeguard the fulfilment been executed properly, the condition could have been fulfilled in the winter transfer window and the transfer fee would have been paid. The Panel considers that a causal link between the potential fulfilment of [OGC] Nice's obligation under Article 152 para. 1 CO and the fulfilment of the condition can be established. In such a case, Sporting would have received a transfer compensation of € 1,000,000. Consequently, [OGC] Nice is generally liable for damage of € 1,000,000.[28]

As to the damages claimed under the sell-on clause, the Panel stated that, in order to award damages for loss of chance, there ought to be a logical nexus between the damage allegedly suffered and the lost chance.[29] While the CAS has upheld such a claim in the past, more precisely in the award rendered in the matter CAS 2009/A/1756 *FC Metz SASP v. Galatasaray SK*, Sporting's claim in the case under review was not upheld by the Panel for lack of a logical nexus, and this irrespective of whether under Swiss law such a loss of chance would justify a compensation. With regards to the claim for damages resulting from a loss in sporting image, the Panel rejected this argument since OGC Nice could not influence the choice of the Player's next club once the latter became a free agent, in addition to which it doubted that the evidence provided was sufficient to establish actual loss of image.[30]

9.3.4.2 Contributory Negligence?

Having established the damages as per the principles of positive interest, the Panel had to analyse whether Sporting's behaviour had contributed to OGC Nice's non-compliance with Article 152 CO.

Similar to contract law in many other jurisdictions, Swiss law, pursuant to Article 44 CO,[31] in effect provides that compensation may be reduced if there are circumstances attributable to the injured party that helped to give rise to, or increase, the damage. In this respect, the Panel took into account that Sporting had signed a formal termination agreement on 11 October, at a time when the contractual situation of the Player with OGC Nice and his registration was very unclear

[28] Ibid.

[29] Ibid., para 119.

[30] Ibid., para 120.

[31] Article 44(1) CO: Where the injured party consented to the action which caused the loss or damage or circumstances attributable to him helped give rise to or compound the loss or damage or otherwise exacerbated the position of the party liable for it, the court may reduce the compensation due or even dispense with it entirely.

and uncertain. Although the Panel recognized that Sporting had been obliged to terminate the agreement with the Player as per the transfer contract, it decided that the club could have acted more prudently by doing so at a later stage and linking such termination to the actual registration of the Player with OGC Nice. Had Sporting done so, it could, according to the Panel, have retained the federative rights of the Player and kept alive the possibility to later on transfer the Player to OGC Nice or to a third club for a transfer fee.

Besides, the Panel also took into account that Sporting could have done more prior to, and during, the winter transfer window, not only by contacting the Player to clarify his intentions but also by contacting OGC Nice to see whether the latter wanted to change the terms of the contract, other than merely urging them to complete the transfer during the winter transfer window. As such, and although "the Panel considered the acts and omissions of Nice more severe than the circumstances attributable to Sporting", the acts and omissions of Sporting justified a reduction of the compensation by 20 %, in line with Article 44(1) CO.[32] Hence, the Panel ruled that OGC Nice was liable to Sporting for damages in the amount of € 800,000.

9.3.5 Commentary

In essence, there was only one winner in this transfer saga, more precisely the third club, which managed to sign a talented player on a free transfer… in this specific case SL Benfica.

> When two dogs fight over a bone a third party carries it away.

The Player was prevented from playing competitive football for 5 months, OGC Nice had to pay € 800,000 in damages for a player from whose playing services it never benefitted, while Sporting received less than it initially had in mind when entering into the transfer contract… Moreover, it is unclear how much OGC Nice had to pay to agents and to the Player pursuant to the latter's termination of the employment contract with just cause. From a sensible point of view, the decision reached by the Panel appears to be correct and fair. That said, it is somewhat odd that the Panel, when assessing whether or not a violation of Article 152(1) CO had occurred, took into account the omissions of both OGC Nice and Sporting during the winter period. More precisely, by this time, the Player was no longer contractually bound to either club, so it is unclear how a new transfer agreement could have been agreed to and/or concluded between them. Neither of them had any rights anymore with regards to the Player, including the so-called federative rights. As to Sporting's claim to damages for loss of chance in relation to the sell-on clause, it is interesting to compare the reasoning of this Panel to the reasoning

[32]Ibid., para 124.

of the Panel in the case of *FC Metz v. Galatasaray*.[33] Similar to Sporting, FC Metz claimed damages for loss of chance as per a sell-on clause and this following the unilateral termination of the employment contract by the player with just cause, e.g. non-payment of salary.

With respect to the claim, the following can be ascertained from the case abstract of the award[34]:

> If the parties to a transfer contract have signed a sell-on clause which makes the payment of a percentage of any transfer compensation paid by a third party for a player conditional upon the fulfilment of conditions […] the parties must act in a loyal way and according to the rules of good faith to fulfil said conditions.
> In case of violation of these requirements, for instance if one party breaches the employment contract it concluded with the player, causing the loss of any transfer expectation, the conditions are deemed to be accomplished anyway, according to art. 156 CO.
> It follows that the third party is entitled to receive the amount agreed in the sell-on clause.

Whereas the non-payment of salary in the case of FC Metz was considered a violation of Article 156 CO in terms of the entitlement as per the sell-on clause, with all due consequences and damages payable by Galatasaray to Metz, the Panel in the case of OGC Nice and Sporting felt that there was no logical nexus and even put in question whether, under Swiss law, loss of chance would justify a compensation. Besides, it should also be noted that if the transfer contract between the Parties had contained an additional condition precedent, requiring for the ITC to be issued before the 1st of September 2011, the outcome of this case might have been entirely different… More precisely, the CAS Panel held that on 31 August 2011, OGC Nice had done all that could in good faith be expected of it to safeguard the fulfilment of the condition. This once again teaches us that the careful drafting of a contract is extremely important. Possibly this is what Real Madrid and Manchester United did in relation to the (failed) transfer for the player David De Gea in the summer transfer window 2015…

Finally, it is noted that the English Premier League ('PL') has introduced a specific procedure[35] for national transfers, on the transfer deadline day, by means of which the PL acknowledges reality in that it is not always for clubs to get a deal completed and provide all the necessary documents on the transfer deadline day in due time. A specific 'Transfer Deadline Deal Sheet' was drafted and allows a club to confirm to the PL that a deal has been reached for the transfer of a player. This document needs to be received by the PL before the transfer deadline and once the sheet arrives, clubs have an additional two hours to submit all the necessary documents and paperwork after the window closes. This is something which FIFA TMS may want to explore in the future…

---

[33]CAS 2009/A/1756, *FC Metz SASP v. Galatasaray SK*, Award of 12 October 2009.

[34]Available on the CAS website, in the Archives section: http://www.tas-cas.org/en/jurisprudence/archive.html. Accessed 10 January 2016.

[35]Premier League, Guide to transfer deadline day summer 2015, 16 September 2015. http://www.premierleague.com/en-gb/news/news/2015-16/sep/010915-guide-to-transfer-deadline-day-summer-2015-16.html. Accessed 10 January 2016.

Reference

Simon G (2014) L'admissibilité des appels formés par les clubs contre les décisions relatives aux transferts internationaux des footballeurs. CAS Bull (2):80–84. http://www.tas-cas.org/fileadmin/user_upload/Bulletin_2014_2.pdf

Chapter 10
CAS 2014/A/3832 & 3833, *Vanessa Vanakorn v. Fédération Internationale de Ski (FIS)*, Award of 19 June 2015

Jack Anderson

Abstract Vanessa Vanakorn's participation in the women's grand slalom at the 2014 Winter Olympics was tainted by controversy. Allegations of the manipulation of her qualification results surrounded the skier's presence at Sochi where she represented Thailand, finishing last in her chosen event. Subsequently, the governing body for the sport, the International Ski Federation, suspended Vanakorn for four years for various breaches of the FIS's betting and anti-corruption regulations. Vanakorn appealed to CAS. The CAS award presents some interesting discussion on legal technicalities such as the standing of an athlete in such a case and on the applicable standard of proof to be used by the investigating body. In substantive terms, the CAS award also revealed that what had happened in the qualification process was not, on the evidence presented, an occasion of result manipulation and, at best, was an incident of questionable "field of play" management. In sum, Vanessa Vanakorn, a celebrated classical musician by profession, successfully defended her amateur sporting reputation at CAS and thus can call herself, for now and ever more, an Olympian.

Keywords Match-fixing · Result manipulation · Skiing · Legal standing · Standard of proof · Field of play

Contents

J. Anderson (✉)
School of Law, Queen's University, Belfast BT7 1NN, UK
e-mail: jack.anderson@qub.ac.uk

A. Duval and A. Rigozzi (eds.), *Yearbook of International Sports Arbitration 2015*,
DOI 10.1007/978-94-6265-129-6_10

10.1 Introduction

Dopers apart, the Olympics has a colourful history of cheating. Arguably the most audacious example occurred at the 1976 Olympics when, in the fencing rotation of the modern pentathlon, Russia's Boris Onischenko was found to have wrapped an intricate wiring system into the leather handle of his épée enabling him, at the press of a button, to manipulate the electronic scoreboard so as to a register a 'hit' on his opponent without ever having to make contact with that opponent. Probably the most shameful example of cheating was at the 2000 Paralympics in Sydney when Spain won gold at the basketball tournament. The classification in question—intellectual disability—required that squad members have an IQ of less than 75. Only two of the 12 members of the team had the level required. One of the most recent instances of cheating came during the group stages of the women's doubles badminton tournament at the London Olympics of 2012. Players from China and South Korea attempted to lose in order to manipulate the subsequent knockout draw. The farce began when Chinese top seeds Wang Xiaoli and Yu Yang showed little interest in beating Korea's Jung Kyung-eun and Kim Ha-na to finish top of their group. Coming second would have meant avoiding compatriots and second seeds Tian Qing and Zhao Yunlei at least until the final. The Koreans responded in kind deliberately knocking the shuttle cock out of play or into the net, much to the crowd's derision.

The participants in all three examples were subsequently disqualified for, and disgraced by, their actions, but of enduring interest is the motivation underpinning all three. First, in 1976 Onishchenko was a three-time world champion and twice Olympic silver medallist but he was considerably older, at 38, than his opponents. Accordingly, he was desperate for one last chance to win Olympic gold, which would secure his continued preferential treatment in his day job as a member of the Red Army.[1] The origins of the Spanish scandal of 2000 appeared to lie in Spanish Paralympic sports administrators' desire fraudulently to secure greater state funding for their sport by linking it to the reflected national glory for Spain of success at the Games; indeed, Spain had their most successful Paralympics in Sydney, winning 107 medals to finish third in the medals table after Australia and Britain.[2] The action of the Chinese and Korean badminton pairs was, more

[1]See generally Burnton S, 50 Stunning Olympic moments No. 18: Boris Onischenko Cheats, GB Win Gold, 14 March 2012. http://www.theguardian.com/sport/london-2012-olympics-blog/2012/mar/14/50-stunning-olympic-moments. Accessed 18 January 2016.

[2]Despite immediate suspicion in the Spanish media, the scandal was only fully revealed in the months after the 2000 Paralympics by a whistle-blower on the team who felt shamed by the episode. See Tremlett G, The Cheats, 16 September 2004. http://www.theguardian.com/sport/2004/sep/16/gilestremlett.features11. Accessed 18 January 2016. Subsequently, the head of the Spanish Federation for Mentally Handicapped Sports at the time was found guilty of fraud and ordered by a Madrid court to return the government subsidies which the federation received for the Paralympians. See Tomlinson S, Man that Led Shameful Spanish Basketball Team who Pretended to be Disabled to Win Paralympic Gold Found Guilty of Fraud, 14 October 2013. http://www.dailymail.co.uk/sport/othersports/article-2459172/Spanish-basketball-team-pretended-disabled-win-Paralympic-gold-guilty-fraud.html. Accessed 18 January 2016.

straightforwardly, a desire, supported by their coaches, to give themselves a better chance to win the competition by taking an easier path to the final.

The various motives outlined above can be easily understood (if not followed) by anyone who has participated *at an* Olympics: Onischenko's desperation to make the most of what was likely a unique, final opportunity to compete and medal at an Olympics; the Spanish athletes' aim to bask in the glory, nationally, reputationally and financially of being a member of a successful Olympian team; the adherence by the Chinese and Korean badminton teams to the letter if not the spirit of the Games in seeking a better path to the final. It is therefore wholly unsurprising that such motives can also be identified in athletes seeking to qualify *for an* Olympics. This contribution focuses on one such qualification process and namely the process by which Vanessa Vanakoron was permitted to take to the starting gate at the women's grand slalom skiing event at the Winter Olympics of 2014 held in Sochi, Russia.

10.2 Case History and Context

Sixty seven competitors finished the women's grand slalom event at Sochi in mid-February 2014. In last place, representing Thailand and a full 50s behind the gold medallist Tina Maze of Slovenia, was Vanessa Vanakorn. Slovenia features heavily in this story because Vanakorn qualified for Sochi through four hastily staged races in Krvavec, Slovenia, just days before the deadline for Olympic qualification in January 2014. Subsequently, in March 2014, the Ski Association of Slovenia (SAS) reviewed the four races and forwarded a report to the International Ski Federation (FIS).[3] On 6 November 2014, a FIS hearing panel (FIS HP) found to its comfortable satisfaction that the results of the four races that took place on 18 and 19 January at Krvavec were manipulated to Vanakorn's advantage and thus in breach of various regulations in the FIS's Betting and Anti-Corruption Violation Rules (FIS BAC Rules). The FIS HP banned Vanakorn from skiing at FIS-sanctioned events for 4 years. On 18 November 2014, the FIS Council, acting on the FIS HP's Decision, annulled the four race results. Accordingly, without the points earned in the Slovenian races, Vanakorn should not, as the FIS informed the IOC, have been deemed eligible to participate at the 2014 Winter Olympics at Sochi. Vanakorn appealed both FIS decisions to CAS in December 2014 and the matter was heard in Lausanne on 3–4 March 2015.

Before that CAS award is analysed, two points of context are noteworthy, both of which ensured that Vanakorn's lengthy ban garnered significant media attention.

First, Vanessa Mae was born in 1978 in Singapore to Thai and Chinese parents and moved to England at the age of four after her mother married a British lawyer.

[3]FIS or Fédération Internationale de Ski is the governing body for the sports of Alpine skiing, Cross-Country skiing, Ski Jumping, Nordic Combined, Freestyle skiing and Snowboarding at the worldwide level, and has its registered office in Oberhofen/Thunersee, Switzerland.

She is a violin virtuoso and was a child prodigy in classical music. At just eight, she became the youngest pupil at the Central Conservatory of Music in Beijing. At 13, she released her first album, *Violin*, and became the youngest soloist to record both Beethoven and Tchaikovsky concertos. She has since amassed worldwide record sales in excess of 10 million. She claims to have skied from a young age but only began to take it seriously from 1999 onwards when, on meeting her current partner, a ski instructor, she began to ski more frequently. In 2010, Mae, a British citizen, announced an ambition to represent her step-father's country of birth (Thailand and thus taking his name, Vanakorn) as a downhill skier at the 2014 Winter Olympics in Sochi, Russia.[4]

The idea of a world famous violinist and enthusiastic if amateur skier seeking Olympic glory piqued the interest of the media. This interest intensified when the FIS HP found that, in their view, Vanakorn had, in effect, cheated and possibly even bought her way to Olympic qualification. The alleged manipulation of results by Vanakorn also fed into the wider concerns in international sport and law enforcement about match-fixing and match manipulation with reports emanating from Slovenia that the initial report by SAS on the four races at Krvavec in January 2014 had also been forwarded to the national police.[5]

This wider global concern about match-fixing in sport was epitomised in 2014 by the launch in September of the Council of Europe's Convention on the Manipulation of Sports Competitions.[6] Article 3(4) of that Convention, which defined the 'Manipulation of Sports Competitions' appeared, at first instance, perfectly to encapsulate Vanakorn's misconduct on the ski slopes of Slovenia in January 2014

> Manipulation of Sports Competitions means an intentional arrangement, act or omission aimed at an improper alteration of the result or the course of a sports competition in order to remove all or part of the unpredictable nature of the aforementioned sports competition with a view to obtaining an undue advantage for oneself or for others.[7]

Nevertheless, when the CAS Panel released its award in June 2015, it concluded largely in favour of Vanakorn, annulling the FIS HP's decision to impose a

---

[4]Craig O,Vanessa-Mae: I Want to be an Olympic Skier, 8 August 2010. http://www.telegraph.co.uk/news/celebritynews/7932222/Vanessa-Mae-I-want-to-be-an-Olympic-skier.html. Accessed 18 January 2016.

[5]Telegraph Sport & Press Agencies, Vanessa Mae was Allowed to Ski at 2014 Winter Olympics after Results Fiddled, 11 July 2014. http://www.telegraph.co.uk/sport/othersports/winter-olympics/10962001/Vanessa-Mae-was-allowed-to-ski-at-2014-Winter-Olympics-after-results-fiddled.html. Accessed 18 January 2016.

[6]Details of Treaty No. 215, *Council of Europe Convention on the Manipulation of Sports Competitions*, available at http://www.coe.int/en/web/conventions/full-list/-/conventions/treaty/215. Accessed 18 January 2016.

[7]See similarly the definition used in Article 2.2 of IOC's Code on the Prevention of the Manipulation of Competitions as approved by the IOC Executive Board on 8 December 2015 and available at http://www.olympic.org/Documents/Commissions_PDFfiles/Ethics/olympic_movement_code_on_the_prevention_of_the_manipulation_of_competitions-2015-en.pdf. Accessed 18 January 2016.

four year ban by observing

> 148. The Panel emphasizes that it fully supports the fight against match-fixing/result manipulation/corruption, which is a major threat to sport, and considers that such fight must be conducted relentlessly by the various sports bodies, at national and international level.
> 149. However, in the case at hand, there is no reliable and convincing evidence which links the Appellant herself to corruption for having intervened directly (or indirectly) in manipulating the results.
> 150. The way the organisation and the running of the Competitions were handled exposes itself to criticism. There are some doubts on certain sequences of events, which remain unclear, but for corruption to occur, there must be deliberate circumvention of the law and illegal acts, which were not demonstrated by FIS to the comfortable satisfaction of the Panel in the case at hand.[8]

The reasons why the appointed CAS Panel (chaired by Prof Dr Martin Schimke of Germany as supported by a Canadian attorney, Patrice Burnet, and an English solicitor, Mark Hovell) held largely in favour of Vanakorn—a concurrent appeal by Vanakorn against the FIS Council's decision of 18 November was dismissed—are now examined.

10.3 Facts and Procedure

Vanakorn's life-long passion and profession lies in classical music but, as noted earlier, she viewed skiing as her life-long hobby. Typical of a high achiever professionally, she aimed high in her ambitions for her favourite pastime, seeking international recognition. Realistically she knew that she would never likely qualify for a British Olympic team, which, for the 2014 Winter Games, had strict selection criteria based around eligible participants achieving a top-30 place in the FIS World Cup standings during the qualification period—at the time Vanakorn was ranked at 3166 in the world in giant slalom.[9] Moreover, 'enthusiastic amateurs' had effectively been prohibited from competing at the Winter Olympics following a change to the rules emanating from the 'Eddie the Eagle' phenomenon at the 1988 Winter Games.

Eddie Edwards was a British skier who in 1988 became the first competitor to represent Britain in Olympic ski jumping. He finished last in the 70 and 90 m events but his enthusiasm, quirky personality and 'underdoggedness' ensured him a celebrity status. The Olympic authorities were not as impressed. In response, and partly because of safety concerns for participants—the conditions for the 90 m jump at the 1988 Games were quite windy and there were genuine concerns for

[8]CAS 2014/A/3832 & 3833, *Vanessa Vanakorn v. Fédération Internationale de Ski (Vanakorn v. FIS)*, Award of 19 June 2015.

[9]Williams O, Violinist Vanessa Mae set to Compete at Winter Olympics, 20 January 2014. http://www.bbc.co.uk/sport/winter-olympics/25802907. Accessed 18 January 2016.

Edwards' safety on landing—the so-called 'Eddie the Eagle Rule' was established by the IOC in 1990, meaning an athlete had to be in the top 30 % of international competitors, or the top 50, whichever was fewer.[10] The rule meant, for instance, that Edwards would never again compete at an Olympic Games.

Nevertheless, while attending the 2009 Ski World Championships in Val d'Isère, Vanakorn noticed that there was an exception to the above rule for 'exotic' skiers, i.e. an exception to promote the participation of skiers from nations which could be considered 'developmental' in terms of skiing tradition and resources. In brief, under the applicable Olympic qualification rules for Sochi 2014, countries with no skier ranked in the world's top 500 (Thailand had no such skier) could still send one man and one woman to the Games—to compete in slalom and giant slalom—if those athletes met a second set of criteria; namely that "those athletes came within a maximum of 140 FIS points (the lower the points, the better the ranking) through competing at sanctioned FIS competitions in the respective events on the Olympics FIS points List published on 20 January 2014".[11]

On 6 and 7 January 2014, Vanakorn competed in two FIS races at Funaesdalen in Sweden accumulating FIS points of 193.45 and 218.63, respectively, followed by a competition in Italy on 11 January in which her FIS Points stretched to 269.44 and thus well outside the 140 FIS Points threshold for Olympic qualification.[12] Undeterred, Vanakorn instructed her coach and agent to organise four giant slalom competitions before the 20 January cut off point. Vanakorn's coach and agent arranged the races in Slovenia, obtained the backing of the Thai Olympic Committee and asked the FIS officially to record the races on its FIS race Calendar for that month. Bizarrely (and there is much that was bizarre about the events of January 2014 in Krvavec) one of the races was listed as the 'Thai Junior National Championships'. As it happens, Vanakorn, at the time aged 35, making her 18 years older than the majority of the entrants, finished last but as she was the only one of the six, eventual finishers in that national junior championship who had Thai citizenship, she was declared champion.[13]

At the end of the four races at Krvavec, Vanakorn managed to achieve just below 140 FIS Points and thus qualified for the Sochi Games. In March 2014, however, the executive of the Alpine Sub-Committee of SAS began to carry out a review of the Krvavec races. On 11 July 2014, the SAS decided to suspend 4 named individuals involved in the organisation of the races. Further, on receipt of the SAS's report, the FIS initiated a disciplinary hearing against the four named individuals and others involved in the organisation of the races and including Vanakorn. On the grounds of the manipulation of race results and "complete

[10]Pye S, Reappraising Eddie 'the Eagle' Edwards, 4 February 2014. http://www.theguardian.com/sport/2014/feb/04/reappraising-eddie-eagle-winter-olympics-ski-jumping. Accessed 18 January 2016.

[11]CAS 2014/A/3832 & 3833, *Vanakorn v. FIS*, para 11.

[12]Vanakorn's race history can be found through the search facility at http://data.fis-ski.com/global-links/search-a-athlete.html. Accessed 18 January 2016.

[13]CAS 2014/A/3832 & 3833, *Vanakorn v. FIS*, para 14.

disregard" for the integrity of sport, this FIS HP barred Vanakorn from any participation in FIS-sanctioned events for four years and further referred the matter to the FIS Council, recommending to the Council that the results of the Krvavec races be expunged and any points awarded to participants be deleted. On 18 November 2014, the FIS Council duly followed the HP's recommendation, further noting that Vanakorn should not have taken part in the 2014 Sochi Games and that the IOC should be informed in order to take further action, including barring Vanakorn from participation at future Games.[14]

On 1 December 2014, Vanakorn filed a statement of appeal to CAS pursuant to her right of appeal under Article 9 of the FIS BAC Rules and in line with Articles R47 and R48 of the CAS Code.[15] The preliminaries to be considered by the CAS Panel (on jurisdiction, admissibility and scope of review and applicable law) were largely uncontroversial,[16] save in one point raised, in a relatively mean spirited manner, by the FIS. The FIS argued that Vanakorn lacked legal interest (*intérêt à agir*) in, and thus the standing (*locus standi*) to, objecting to their decisions on two grounds.[17] First and with particular relevance to the FIS HP's decision, the FIS pointed out that Vanakorn had decided to stop ever competing again in FIS-sanctioned competitions even on becoming re-eligible to compete on serving her ban. Moreover, and with particular regard to the FIS Council's Decision, given she did not win a medal at the Winter Olympics of 2014, the determination by the FIS Council that she should not have participated at Sochi "could no longer have any practical relevance in view of the lapse of time".[18]

At the hearing, Vanakorn confirmed that she did in fact intend to resume her skiing career and therefore her interest in appealing against her existing four year ban imposed by the FIS HP was evident. The CAS Panel agreed and similarly they concurred that, if the core element of the FIS Council Decision was confirmed (the deletion of the results of the Krvavec race) this would have an impact on her career accumulation of FIS points, crucial to her prospective qualification for races and competitions. Most importantly, on the issue of legal standing, the Panel

[14]Ibid., paras 26–27.

[15]There were two separate filings, against the FIS HP (CAS 2014/A/3832) and the FIS Council Decision (CAS 2014/A/3833). With agreement by the parties, the CAS Office consolidated the proceedings.

[16]For example, pursuant to Article R57 of the CAS Code, the Panel noted that the matter would be considered *de novo*, *Vanakorn v. FIS*, para 67 and pursuant to Article R58 of the CAS Code, the Panel deemed that the applicable regulations in case at hand were primarily the FIS rules and, subsidiarily, Swiss law, *Vanakorn v. FIS*, paras 68–70. The FIS regulations in question satisfied the legal basis requirement pursuant to CAS jurisprudence on establishing a clear, predictable connection between the incriminated behaviour and sanction, see CAS 2014/A/3832 & 3833,*Vanakorn v. FIS*, paras 84–88 and citing *inter alia* CAS 2007/A/1363, *TTF Liebherr Ochsenhausen v. ETTU*, Award of 5 October 2007.

[17]Citing CAS 2010/A/2091, *Dennis Lachter v. Derek Boateng Owusu*, Award of 21 December 2011, para 13 and CAS 2009/A/1880 & 1881, *FC Sion & E. v. Fédération Internationale de Football Association (FIFA) & Al-Ahly Sporting Club*, Award of 1 June 2010, para 152.

[18]CAS 2014/A/3832 & 3833, *Vanakorn v. FIS*, para 64.

highlighted that Vanakorn could, as with virtually all athletes sanctioned on similarly grounds, "avail herself of a legal interest to rehabilitate her reputation which can be deemed tarnished by the FIS HP Decision concluding and declaring that she was either an active or knowing participant in a manipulation".[19]

10.4 Parties' Submissions and Arguments

Vanakorn's submission can be distilled into four points.[20]

First, she argued that given the seriousness of the allegations—the manipulation of competition results—the standard of proof "must come very close" to the criminal standard of beyond a reasonable doubt and accordingly hearsay evidence and indirect proof should not be admissible.

Second, she argued that it is accepted and frequent practice for beginners or novices to lower their FIS points average by selecting and even organising their 'own' FIS races. These "easy" races, she admitted, may even be specifically "tailored" to the needs of an individual racer. Further, Vanakorn also acknowledged that it is "natural" that those who need the race will pay the expenses of the organising local ski association or ski club. All of the above, Vanakorn boldly stated, is exactly what she, with the backing of the Thai Olympic Committee did at Krvavec in January 2014 and it was, she reiterated, a practice "not only common, but…definitely not against the FIS rules and regulations".[21]

The third plank of her argument moved to a denial of some of the key allegations made against her by various witnesses at the Krvavec races. These allegations, relating to some if not all of the four races, were threefold in nature and alleged: (a) that Vanakorn started outside of the starting gate and thus manipulated her finishing time; (b) that there were doubts regarding the number of competitors who were officially listed as competing in and/or their registered finishing times and those who actually competed the course in real time; and (c) that Vanakorn had asked, even ordered, some of the participants, who she had paid to compete, to ski slowly. All three contentions were forcefully denied by Vanakorn who questioned the reliability of the witnesses and pointed out to the Panel that the registration of the timing or finishing position of other participants in the races in which she competed was not her responsibility and was not, in any event, of any advantage to her.

The final argument made by Vanakorn was one in which she alluded, somewhat conspiratorially, to the fact that the initial SAS investigation was tainted by the

[19]Ibid., para 63.

[20]Ibid., para 72.

[21]Ibid.

fact she appeared to be an innocent victim of 'political manoeuvring' or jealousy between various clubs on the SAS Alpine Committee. There were also suggestions by Vanakorn that the FIS had subsequently and unduly influenced witnesses to the proceedings.[22]

The FIS's response was threefold in nature.[23]

First, the FIS highlighted to CAS that the various circumstances surrounding the organisation of the Krvavec races, although not clear violations of the rules, must objectively be considered as unusual and highly suspicious. The FIS's 'suspicions' related to the extremely hurried organisation of the races, which resulted in the race taking place in foggy weather conditions not normally considered safe for FIS races. In fact, the fog on the course was so dense that, according to the FIS "it was not possible to control whether the competitors passed all the gates correctly". The effective mislabelling of one of the races as a National Junior Championship also illustrated, according to the FIS, that the spirit of its rules, and the integrity of its sport, were stretched to their limits in the effort to lower Vanakorn's points total to an average of 140.

The FIS then went on to argue that certain practices at Krvavec did however stray into race manipulation contrary to FIS BAC Rules, including the orders to certain participants to slow down and the 'phantom' or inaccurate recording of participants' finishing positions and times.[24] Arguably, the most serious allegation directed against Vanakorn was witness evidence to the effect that she was seen to have started from outside the starting gate on at least two occasions and that the starting wand appeared deliberately to have been left open and then triggered manually only when Vanakorn was already on the course. The manual triggering of the starting gate, it was suggested, indicated that the irregular start took place with Vanakorn's knowledge.[25] All of the above, the FIS submitted, was reinforced by the fact that a number of the officials on duty at Krvavec had been sanctioned by the FIS HP because they disregarded their duties as chief of race, referee, starter, time keeper, technical delegate and members of the race jury. These officials, the FIS observed, had not challenged that FIS HP decision.

[22]These allegations were dismissed summarily by the CAS Panel—Ibid., paras 99–102. No convincing evidence was supplied to support the accusations and in any event the Panel noted that any procedural irregularities that might have occurred previously would be largely cured by the *de novo* powers of the Panel pursuant to Article R57 CAS Code.

[23]CAS 2014/A/3832 & 3833, *Vanakorn v. FIS*, para 73.

[24]And specifically a violation of Article 3.2.1 of the FIS BAC Rules: "Fixing or contriving in any way or otherwise improperly influencing, or being a party to fix or contrive in any way or otherwise improperly influence, the result, progress, outcome, conduct or any other aspect of an Event or Competition."

[25]An irregular start constituted a violation of Article 613.5 of the International Ski Competition Rules (ICR). Under Article 205 ICR all participants are taken to have constructive knowledge of all ICR rules and technicalities, including those relating to proper starting procedures.

10.5 Panel's Rationale and Award

Before assessing the substantive issue of whether or not to annul the various FIS decisions declaring that Vanakorn had been involved in the manipulation of results, the Panel had to deal briefly (and usefully) with the applicable standard of proof in 'integrity' cases of this kind.[26] According to Article 4(1) of the FIS BAC Rules, the applicable standard of proof was that of 'comfortable satisfaction' which the regulation went on to interpret as a "standard which is greater than the mere balance of probability but less than proof beyond a reasonable doubt". The CAS Panel at hand noted that, although 'comfortable satisfaction' is a standard that is widely applied by CAS Panels in disciplinary as well as in match-fixing/corruption proceedings,[27] the Panel still had to "more precisely determine the standard of proof within this bandwidth given the application of the typical standard applicable in civil proceedings ('balance of probability') and of the one applicable in criminal proceedings ('proof beyond reasonable doubt') can lead to very important different conclusions depending on the facts, and the available evidence, of a particular case".[28]

In its analysis of the present case and with regard to the standard of proof and the assessment of evidence, the Panel was guided by three principles

- Corruption is, by its nature, concealed as the parties involved will seek to use evasive means to ensure that they leave no trail of their wrongdoings[29];
- The paramount importance of fighting corruption of any kind in sport also considering the nature and restricted powers of the investigation authorities of the governing bodies of sport as compared to national formal interrogation authorities[30];
- In assessing the evidence the Panel would bear in mind that the athlete had been charged with serious offences… [and thus]… the Panel…considered that it needed to have a high degree of confidence in the quality of evidence.[31]

The CAS Panel then moved to consider whether Vanakorn was, as the FIS alleged, either an active and knowing participant in the manipulation of results or, at the very least, whether as a FIS competitor she ought to have known that the Krvavec races were being manipulated for her benefit.[32] The Panel quickly identified the

---

[26]CAS 2014/A/3832 & 3833, *Vanakorn v. FIS*, paras 89–98.

[27]Citing CAS 2009/A/1920 *FK Pobeda and others v. UEFA*, Award of 15 April 2010, para 85; CAS 2010/A/2172, *Oriekhov v. UEFA*, Award of 18 January 2011, para 53; CAS 2011/A/2426, *Amos Adamu v. FIFA*, Award of 24 February 2012, para 88 and CAS 2011/A/2490, *Daniel Köllerer v. Association of Tennis Professionals and others*, Award of 23 March 2012, paras 85–87.

[28]CAS 2014/A/3832 & 3833, *Vanakorn v. FIS*, para 93.

[29]Ibid., para 96, citing CAS 2010/A/2172, *Oriekhov v. UEFA*.

[30]Ibid., citing CAS 2009/A/1920, *FK Pobeda v. UEFA*.

[31]Ibid., para 98, citing CAS 2011/A/2490, *Köllerer v. ATP*.

[32]Ibid., paras 103 et seq.

four key accusations against Vanakorn: the suspicious circumstances surrounding the organisation of the Krvavec races[33]; the irregular starts[34]; that some participants were asked to ski slowly[35]; and the manipulation of the results lists.[36]

On the first point, the Panel noted that, although there were some unusual circumstances surrounding the holding of the Krvavec races—most egregiously the labelling of one race as the Thai Junior National Championships—nothing in the organisational process violated the FIS rules, as the FIS itself had admitted. Moreover, the Panel noted that, although the FIS nevertheless considered the organisation of Krvavec races as violating the 'spirit of sport', it was of the view that "if anything had to be blamed in the case at hand, it is rather the system put in place by FIS to organise competitions and not [Vanakorn] for having 'used' it for her own benefit".[37] In this, the Panel went on to observe that it had learned that it is common that some non-European national federations ask and pay ski clubs or other national federations to organise races for them and sometimes to do so for the specific benefit of an individual racer and that this practice "is part of the DNA of the FIS race sanction system".[38]

Furthermore, and using an estoppel-based argument, the Panel stated that the FIS was at all times well aware of the holding of the Krvavec races; had in part facilitated them in advance by publishing their occurrence on its website on 14 January 2014; and had appointed a Technical Delegate to oversee the races, who testified that he did not witness any irregularities. This led the Panel to conclude that since the FIS had given "its imprimatur to the event and the way it was to be organised, it can hardly blame [Vanakorn] for using the existing rules to her advantage".[39]

As regards the irregular starts, the Panel stated that the evidence from witnesses was inconsistent. At most Vanakorn testified that she may on one occasion have opened the starting wand unintentionally but that she had nevertheless always followed the starter's instructions.[40] Consequently, the Panel was not comfortably satisfied that Vanakorn had in fact committed any irregular start. Moreover, the Panel was not in any event convinced that an irregular start could qualify or equate to a charge of result manipulation or match-fixing. The matter was, at best, the

[33]Ibid., paras 104–115.

[34]Ibid., paras 116–123.

[35]Ibid., paras 124–126.

[36]Ibid., paras 127–129.

[37]Ibid., para 109.

[38]Ibid., para 110.

[39]Ibid., para 111.

[40]Ibid., para 121. The starter did not give any testimony at CAS.

Panel held, a 'field of play' issue for the Technical Delegate to resolve,[41] and from which CAS Panels generally abstain.[42]

Inconsistencies in witness evidence also led the Panel to dismiss the allegations against Vanakorn as regards the suggestion that some participants had been asked to ski slowly. There was no evidence to suggest that Vanakorn personally or her entourage had approached the other participants. There was some evidence that the starter had warned at least one participant to slow down but this may have been a warning given the bad weather conditions. Overall, the Panel did not have the necessary confidence in the evidence given by the FIS to conclude that any instructions given to ski slowly were imparted for the purpose of manipulating race results.[43]

Finally, there were the allegations against Vanakorn that 'mistakes' on the results list were deliberate manipulations made in order to have a favourable impact on the calculation of Vanakorn's FIS Points.[44] The Panel was comfortably satisfied that the results lists of the race did contain some errors but that these were merely administrative in nature and not the consequence of any manipulation by the organisers and/or Vanakorn's entourage.

In conclusion therefore, the Panel held that it was not comfortably satisfied that either Vanakorn personally or any member of her entourage fixed, contrived or otherwise improperly influenced the organisation or outcome of the Krvavec races and thus the FIS HP's decision of 6 November for breach of FIS BAC Rules made against Vanakorn was annulled.[45] As regards the FIS Council decision of 18 November 2014, the Panel noted that on the same date the FIS Council had held that the chief of Krvavec race, the referee, the starter, the technical delegate and chief of timing had all been sanctioned. The FIS Council, as permitted to do so under its FIS BAC Rules, had exercised its discretion to declare the results of the Krvavec races so tainted by maladministration that all accompanying results and qualification points therefrom should not stand. The CAS Panel, noting that none of the officials involved had challenged the FIS Council's decision against them,

[41]Ibid.

[42]See for example, CAS 2010/A/2090, *Aino-Kaisa Saarinen & Finnish Ski Association v. FIS*, Award of 7 February 2011, para 35. Abstinence by CAS from ruling on field of play decisions is not a matter of jurisdiction, but of arbitral self-restraint. The rationale for such self-restraint includes supporting the autonomy of officials; avoidance of the interruption to matches in progress; seeking to ensure the certainty of outcome of competition; the relative lack of perspective and/or experience of appellate bodies compared with that of match officials. In sum, the doctrine at any rate applies to prevent rewriting the results of the game or of sanctions imposed in the course of competition. The doctrine is disapplied upon proof that decisions otherwise falling within its ambit were vitiated by bias, malice, bad faith, arbitrariness or legal error. No evidence of bad faith in this respect was given, see CAS 2014/A/3832 & 3833, *Vanakorn v. FIS*, para 133.

[43]Ibid., para 126.

[44]Ibid., para 127.

[45]Ibid., paras 130–133 and 147.

and recognising that Vanakorn personally was not guilty of any manipulation, agreed that the FIS Council had reasonably exercised its discretion in this regard and thus Vanakorn's appeal is this respect was dismissed.[46]

10.6 Commentary and Conclusion

In overall review, there are two technical points of interest from the Vanakorn CAS award.

The first relates to an athlete's legal interest or standing in challenging a disciplinary sanction and particularly, but not exclusively, one which is of serious consequence, as relating to, for instance, doping or match-fixing. There is a tendency to think of the athlete and the accompanying sanction solely in terms of the direct professional and economic impact—as in the athlete's ineligibility to compete and earn (prize) money from their trade. And yet, the reputational impact (and indirect economic impact in terms of losing sponsors, etc.) on a professional sports person of, in effect, being tarnished with the accusation of fraudulent work practices ought not to be underestimated. Moreover, neither should the reputational impact on an amateur athlete of being labelled a cheat—and the Vanakorn award is a rare example of an amateur athlete pursuing a CAS appeal—be forgotten.[47] This is why, in considering Vanakorn's standing to take the case, the Panel's reference to an athlete's "legal interest to rehabilitate her reputation" is noteworthy and welcome.[48] Indeed, the reaction of another participant at the Sochi Games—Claudia Pechstein—to allegations of doping has illustrated starkly to the International Skating Union (ISU) and to CAS itself how powerfully motivating an athlete's interest in rehabilitating their reputation can be, to the extent that the legal basis of global sport's system of dispute resolution is now being challenged in national courts.[49]

The second technical point of interest is the Panel's elaboration and guidelines on the use of the 'comfortable satisfaction' standard of proof. Although, as the Panel notes, the hybrid standard is used widely by international governing bodies and CAS Panels in disciplinary as well as in match-fixing/corruption proceedings, the exact location of the term in the bandwidth between the normal civil and

[46]Ibid., paras 134–140 and 147.

[47]Although technically an amateur athlete, Vanakorn is an extremely wealthy professional violinist and reportedly had the capacity to pay more than £135,000 (€180,000) in legal costs to successfully appeal to CAS. See Hope N, Vanessa-Mae: IOC rule that skier can be called an Olympian, 4 January 2016. www.bbc.co.uk/sport/winter-sports/35218889. Accessed 18 January 2016.

[48]CAS 2014/A/3832 & 3833, *Vanakorn v. FIS*, para 63.

[49]CAS 2009/A/1912, *P. v. International Skating Union (ISU) & CAS*, Award of 25 November 2009, as reviewed by David McArdle in McArdle 2013. See also Duval and Van Rompuy 2016.

criminal standards of proof has always been somewhat elusive. The Vanakorn Panel's guidelines in this regard are again noteworthy and welcome.[50]

The key substantive question in this CAS case was however less technical and, in some ways, very straightforward: how was it possible for a ski racing novice, in her mid-thirties and without any prior competitive ski or other competitive sport history, to accomplish the qualifying standard for the Olympic Winter Games only a few months after beginning training?[51] Vanakorn's first officially listed race on the FIS's website was at the New Zealand championships in August 2013—she did not finish. Between then and Krvavec she raced a further 10 times. She registered FIS points in eight of those 10 races with an average of just over 253 FIS Points—way outside the 140 qualification cut off for the Sochi. Further, the momentum gained by Vanakorn from her 'success' at Krvavec meant that within a year of skiing competitively in the giant slalom, her world ranking fell from 3166 in the various FIS points lists for 2013/2014 to a low of 1785 in the 2014/2015 equivalents.[52]

The FIS's blunt reply to the above question was that Vanakorn and her entourage had likely used her private wealth to cheat, manipulating results, fixing races and paying off organisers, officials and other competitors along the way. The FIS's attitude in this regard can be seen as analogous to the reaction to the aforementioned behaviour of the Spanish 'Paralympic' basketball team and sports administrators of 2000, who, blinded by the prospect of Olympic glory, trampled on the integrity of their sport. In addition, the FIS's reaction to what they perceived as an attack on the integrity of their sport, and their imposition of a lengthy ban, must also be understood in light of what might be called the 'moral panic'[53] that became associated with match-fixing in sport globally in 2014—and has also been alluded to earlier in this piece. The most welcome aspect of this CAS award is therefore that the Panel did not 'panic' and on undertaking a meticulous review of the evidence pared down the events at Krvavec to their nub in order to assess whether with comfortable satisfaction such events could be deemed, as the FIS held them to be, manipulative in purpose, nature and outcome.

The evidence did not support the FIS's contention. In the Panel's opinion the events at Krvavec could not be equated to or conflated with match-fixing. At most, some administrative errors and field of play violations occurred for which the officials in charge (who were likely 'smitten'[54] and thus distracted by the presence of

---

[50]CAS 2014/A/3832 & 3833, *Vanakorn v. FIS*, paras 96–98.

[51]Ibid., para 104.

[52]At the time of writing, 15 January 2016, Vanakorn's FIS Points average is 249.29. She is ranked 2969th in the world. Vanakorn's race history can be found through the search facility at http://data.fis-ski.com/global-links/search-a-athlete.html. Accessed 18 January 2016.

[53]This term used in sociological and criminological research refers generally to an extreme social response (usually played out in the media) to the belief that the moral condition of society is facing an acute threat from a particular social condition or recent social phenomenon or the immoral, socially deviant behaviour of a specific group of persons.

[54]CAS 2014/A/3832 & 3833, *Vanakorn v. FIS*, para 145.

a world famous musician) had been sanctioned and the race results duly expunged from FIS records. Vanakorn, similar in age to Onishchenko at the Montreal Games of 1976, shared his desire for one final chance at being an Olympian but there the analogy ended. She did not cheat to realise her objective. She did not, for example, have an 'Onischenko wire' in the handle of her ski pole through which she should raise or lower the starting gate on demand. In fact, although it was obvious that the Krvavec races were organised for the sole purpose of allowing Vanakorn to qualify for the Olympics at short notice, FIS regulations permitted such events.[55] Further, no other competitor at the Krvavec races appeared to have been paid to compete (slowly or otherwise). The only payments that the Panel found to have been made were to the amount of € 6055 which Vanakorn paid to the local ski club for the organisation of the races—an amount which the Panel deemed 'not unreasonable'.[56]

Reasonable though the payment may have been, the Panel admitted the fact that such a practice existed was still somewhat surprising, observing

"In contrast to most other competitions and sports, where approaching and/or paying organisers may create a suspicion of wrongdoing, in the present case, as the system is built around such possibilities, these simple facts can certainly not be an indication of wrongdoing, let alone conclusive evidence of corruption or illegal activity. The Panel wonders whether the FIS should consider exercising enhanced oversight over such races".[57]

The analogy here is similar to the aforementioned debacle at the women's badminton competition at the London Olympics. There, the faulty design of the group stages was a factor in the abject displays of the Chinese and Korean teams—echoing the infamous Germany v Austria game at the FIFA World Cup of 1982 which saw Algeria eliminated at the first group stage. In short, the fundamental *cause* of the farrago at the 1982 World Cup, the 2012 London Olympics and on the ski slopes at Krvavec lay with the poor regulatory oversight and foresight of the governing body; and the *effect* of this poor oversight and foresight would ultimately impact most adversely on the integrity of the sport as a whole and less on the individuals who exploited it. In this, a lasting outcome of the Vanakorn award may be the tightening up of the regulations permitting skiers from 'developing' nations appearing at the Olympics, thus echoing the fallout from the behaviour of the Spanish Paralympic basketball team of 2000, which led to the withdrawal of intellectual disability classifications for the Athens and Beijing Paralympics to the detriment of hundreds of innocent Paralympians globally.[58] Cheating in sport—be it doping, fixing, etc.—is rarely a victimless crime.

---

[55]Ibid., para 144.

[56]Ibid.

[57]Ibid., para 110.

[58]The tightly regulated classification returned, in part, for London 2012; see Jinkinson B and Hammond C, How the Paralympics Checks Intellectual Disability, 30 August 2012. http://www.bbc.co.uk/news/magazine-19371031. Accessed 18 January 2016.

Finally, given that the FIS Council's decision was upheld by CAS and the points associated with the Krvavec races wiped from the record books, it remained open for the IOC to declare that Vanakorn should not have competed at the Sochi Games. Possibly fearing another CAS application,[59] but likely in an effort to draw a line under the matter that had dragged on for two years, the IOC announced in January 2016 that it had decided not to annul Vanakorn's Sochi results. Vanakorn expressed delight at the news and, undaunted, said that she expected to return to competitive skiing in March 2016 with the long-term ambition of qualifying for the 2018 Winter Olympics in PyeongChang, South Korea.[60]

In conclusion then, in mid-January 2014 Vanessa Vanokorn was a world famous violist and an enthusiastic amateur skier. 1 month, € 6000, 4 Slovenian slaloms and 2 further runs at Sochi later, she was, and now will be forever, an Olympian. To paraphrase Pierre de Coubertin from all those years ago; it is the taking part that counts.

References

Duval A, Van Rompuy B (2016) Protecting athletes' right to a fair trial through EU competition law: The *Pechstein* Case. In: Paulussen C et al (eds) Fundamental rights in international and European law, Springer, T.M.C. ASSER Press, The Hague, pp 245–278

McArdle D (2013) CAS 2009/A/1912–1913 *Pechstein v International Skating Union*. In: Anderson J (ed) Leading cases in sports law, Springer, T.M.C. ASSER Press, The Hague, pp 209–225

[59]CAS 2014/A/3832 & 3833, *Vanakorn v. FIS*, para 64.

[60]Hope N, Vanessa-Mae: IOC rule that skier can be called an Olympian, 4 January 2016. http://www.bbc.co.uk/sport/winter-sports/35218889. Accessed 18 January 2016.

Chapter 11
CAS 2015/A/3874, *Football Association of Albania v. UEFA & Football Association of Serbia*, Award of 10 July 2015 and CAS 2015/A/3875, *Football Association of Serbia v. UEFA*, Award of 10 July 2015

Andreas Zagklis

Abstract In cases CAS 2015/A/3874 and CAS 2015/A/3875, the Court of Arbitration for Sport dealt with the disciplinary consequences of the violent incidents which led to the Serbia versus Albania qualifier for UEFA EURO 2016 being abandoned. The CAS Panels in charge of these cases decided upon numerous procedural and substantive arguments raised by the national associations involved and UEFA. This match will not only be remembered for the drone device which was remotely controlled to fly low over the pitch carrying a banner with nationalistic symbols; it will be equally referenced in the future for the legal presumption used by the majority of the CAS Panel in case 3874 in order to determine that the Albanian FA was strictly liable for the operation of the drone. Equally, the CAS awards provide useful guidance to match officials and event organisers on how to react in cases of violent incidents and match interruptions. Communication with the teams and clear instructions are key to the event organiser being in a position to draw consequences from the teams' refusal to continue the match. The 3874 award also adds a valuable summary and in-depth analysis on the interpretation of the term 'directly affected party' in the UEFA Statutes, being the party with a right to file an appeal against a UEFA decision. From a case-management perspective, the uninformed reader may wonder whether the CAS Appeals Division President, when deciding to appoint the same President of the Panel to two cases so closely connected, should also make use of the discretion embedded in Article R52 and consolidate the proceedings.

Keywords Football · Disciplinary · Directly affected party · Consolidation · Match forfeit · Violence · Racism · Strict liability

A. Zagklis (✉)
Martens Rechtsanwälte, Munich, Germany
e-mail: a.zagklis@martens-lawyers.com

A. Duval and A. Rigozzi (eds.), *Yearbook of International Sports Arbitration 2015*,
DOI 10.1007/978-94-6265-129-6_11

Contents

11.1 Introduction

The CAS has received approximately 4000 cases in its 30 years of existence. The *corpus* of CAS jurisprudence is without doubt rich and is growing on a daily basis, especially regarding disciplinary matters. Together with it, the quality and sophistication of parties' pleadings before CAS is ever increasing and CAS Panels are often called to address multiple defences and complex argumentations, while trying to identify the facts relevant to the resolution of the dispute. In less than a decade, the responsible user of CAS has seen the task of following the development of the jurisprudence become a serious challenge.

The present commentary will try to address such a need by including a summary-style presentation of the cases' factual and procedural backgrounds (which are virtually identical—see Sect. 11.2 below) and a selection of main issues that are useful both for future reference and for reflection (see Sect. 11.3 below). Naturally, the selection is subjective and not exhaustive; the intention is not to "rehear" the case but to approach the issues at times through the eyes of the arbitrators and at times through those of counsel.

11.2 Summary of Facts and Procedure

11.2.1 Facts

This summary is based on the findings of the CAS Panels in cases CAS 2015/A/3874, Football Association of Albania v. UEFA & Football Association of Serbia (hereinafter 'the 3874 case' or 'the 3874 proceeding'), and CAS 2015/A/3875, Football Association of Serbia v. UEFA (hereinafter 'the 3875 case' or 'the 3875 proceeding').

On 14 October 2014, Serbia hosted Albania in Belgrade for a match of Group I of the Qualifying Round for the UEFA EURO 2016. The Football Association of Albania (hereinafter 'FAA') and the Football Association of Serbia (hereinafter 'FAS') had agreed—in view of the strained relationship between the two countries—that no tickets for this game were to be sold to Albanian supporters. Accordingly, the FAA only invited approximately 100 persons to attend the match, in particular FAA representatives, staff and sponsors.

From the beginning, the match was dominated by incidents related to the rivalry between the two countries. Notably, during the pre-match ceremony when the Albanian anthem was played as well as during the match itself, Serbian supporters sang various chants including (in Serbian) "Kill, kill the Albanians" and "Kill and slaughter them until there are none left". During the match, Serbian supporters *inter alia* displayed various banners containing references to Kosovo. Further, they burned a NATO flag, threw burning flares and a firecracker onto the field and tried to disturb Albanian players during the match with a laser pointer. Following these incidents, the referee decided to stop play on the 42nd minute.

Whilst the game was stopped, a drone appeared above the playing field. It carried a banner on which the map of 'Greater Albania' was pictured, an area comprising the territory of Albania, various parts of Serbia, Montenegro, F.Y.R. of Macedonia, Kosovo and northern Greece. The banner also pictured several Albanian nationalistic symbols. When the drone descended towards the pitch, a Serbian player reached for the banner and began pulling the drone down by the cords from which the banner hung. Two Albanian players approached him and snatched the banner from his hands.

At this point a greater chaos erupted across the playing field. The CAS Panels summarised the incidents as follows:

> One of the invading Serbian supporters was observed to take hold of a plastic chair (which appertained to one of the security stewards around the field), and to then run with it to the rim of the center circle, and then use the chair to hit one of the Albanian players, Mr. Bekim Balaj, on the shoulder. This same Serbian supporter then attempted to tackle Mr. Balaj, but instead took down the Albanian captain, Mr. Lorik Cana, who had intervened, apparently to prevent an escalation of the scuffle. As they fell to the ground, a security steward was seen to run towards them and, with his fist seen to be clenched, to throw punches. Although it is disputed between the Parties whether the punches were aimed at the Albanian player or the Serbian supporter, the Panel has reached the view, on the basis of a close examination of the evidence that the steward was trying to hit the Albanian player.
>
> In other parts of the playing field the following facts were observed: (i) a Serbian supporter punched the Albanian player, Mr. Mergim Mavraj; (ii) a Serbian substitute player punched the Albanian player, Mr. Ermir Lenjani, in the face; (iii) a Serbian substitute player punched the Albanian player, Mr. Orges Shehi; (iv) a notorious Serbian supporter, Mr. Ivan Bogdanov, accompanied by other supporters, walked calmly around the field waiving and clapping his hands to incite the crowd (Mr. Bogdanov is recognised as an individual who took center stage in, and faced criminal charges for, incidents that occurred in 2010 during the 2012 UEFA European Championship qualifier match between Italy and Serbia); and (v) a Serbian supporter reached the Albanian bench area and attacked a member of the Albanian delegation.
>
> The Serbian supporters were observed to throw objects, including chairs, at the Albanian side's bench from the stands.

> Throughout these events the Match stoppage continued. Due to the chaos and massive disorder, the Match Referee ordered, with the aim of securing the players' safety, all the players to head back into the locker rooms.[1]

While the Albanian players were leaving the field, objects were thrown at them and some Serbian supporters physically attacked them. One of the most notorious supporters of the Serbian team, after taking part in the attack, calmly sat down on the field next to a corner flag, whilst the security personnel did not intervene. Further, one of the security stewards waived his arms up and down towards the crowd as though to encourage it to chant louder. Several Albanian players got injured in the course of these incidents.

Thereafter, a crisis meeting was held, including inter alia the referee, several UEFA officials as well as the captains of the teams and representatives of the involved Football Associations. The group was discussing whether to resume the match. The UEFA officials and the referee, encouraged by the UEFA Match Centre in Nyon, wanted to resume the match, once safety was ensured. When notifying this to the team captains, the Albanian captain declared that his team was neither mentally nor physically prepared to restart the match. He signed a declaration to this effect, which was prepared by the UEFA Match Delegate. The typed text of the declaration reads: "I, Lorik Cana, captain of the Albanian National Team declare that my team, after what happened around the 40th minute of the first half of the match Serbia versus Albania on 14 October 2014 my team is physically and mentally not able to restart the game. And they feel not safe at all. I told this to the referee and the delegate, in the presence of my President mr Duka" (sic). To this, Mr. Cana, added in handwriting prior to signing the document: "the physical injuries of many of my players, don't allow us to keep playing, and we were even attacked by the securities of the stadium".

Subsequently, the referee decided to abandon the match.

The device controlling the drone could not be found, even though the police searched the Albanian players and staff as well as their belongings and locker rooms after the match abandonment.

11.2.2 Procedure

At the first UEFA-internal instance, the UEFA Control, Ethics and Disciplinary Body (hereinafter 'CEDB') dealt with the disciplinary violations of FAA and FAS separately and, on 23 October 2014, took the following decisions:

(a) FAA: The CEDB sanctioned the FAA with a 0:3 forfeit of the match for refusing to continue to play. Further, the CEDB imposed a fine of € 100,000

[1] *CAS 2015/A/3874, Football Association of Albania v. UEFA & Football Association of Serbia, Award of 10 July 2015, paras 18–21; CAS 2015/A/3875, Football Association of Serbia v. UEFA, Award of 10 July 2015, paras 16–19.*

on the FAA for the drone incident. The Panel considered itself comfortably satisfied that one or several supporters of the FAA had controlled the drone.

(b) FAS: The CEDB sanctioned the FAS for the above described behaviour of Serbian players and supporters and also for insufficient organisation of the match. The sanctions included deducting three points in the UEFA EURO 2016 Qualifying Round; a sanction of two UEFA competition matches as host association behind closed doors; and a monetary fine of € 100,000.

The FAA, as well as the FAS, appealed these decisions before the second UEFA-internal instance, the UEFA Appeals Body (hereinafter 'UEFA AB'). The FAA requested in its appeal the lifting of the sanctions related to the drone incident or, alternatively, that the sanctions be considerably reduced. Also, it requested the UEFA AB to order that the FAS (and not the FAA) lose the match with a 0:3 forfeit and that further sanctions be inflicted upon the FAS for racist and discriminating behaviour in relation to the chants. The FAS on its side requested the lifting of the fine of € 100,000 as well as the tree point deduction but did not contest the order to play its next two UEFA competition matches as host association behind closed doors. After having heard both appeals in a single proceeding, the UEFA AB issued a single decision dated 2 December 2014 (hereinafter 'UEFA AB Decision') rejecting both appeals and confirming both CEDB decisions.

On 30 December 2014, the FAA challenged the UEFA AB Decision before the CAS, thus initiating the 3874 proceedings. On the same day, the FAS also challenged the UEFA AB Decision before the CAS, thus initiating the 3875 proceedings. Subsequently, the FAS intervened in the 3874 proceedings, requesting CAS—like the Respondent UEFA—to dismiss the appeal. The Panel accepted FAS as an Intervening Party in the 3874 proceedings. Conversely, the FAA did not intervene in the 3875 proceedings. With respect to the constitution of the CAS Panels, UEFA nominated the same arbitrator in both proceedings. The FAS and the FAA nominated different arbitrators in the 3874 and 3875 proceedings, respectively. The President of the Appeals Arbitration Division (hereinafter 'the Division President') decided to appoint the same President of the Panel in both cases. Three days before the hearing, the FAA requested to be provided by the CAS with the submissions filed by UEFA and FAS in the 3875 case proceeding; the Panel rejected the motion and reserved its right to provide the reasons for its decision in the final award.

By arbitral award dated 10 July 2015, the CAS partially upheld the FAA's Appeal in the 3874 case. The Panel dismissed the Appellant's request to impose sanctions on the FAS for racist and discriminating behaviour due to lack of standing. It confirmed the fine of € 100.000 imposed on the FAA. Lastly, it ruled that the match shall be deemed to have been forfeited by the FAS by the score of 0:3. The FAS also challenged the UEFA AB Decision before the CAS. By arbitral award dated 10 July 2015, CAS rejected the appeal in the CAS 3875 case and confirmed the UEFA AB Decision.

11.3 Comment

The commentary will focus on the following selected issues, as they were addressed by the CAS Panels in the 3874 and/or the 3875 case.

- Case management: two separate CAS appeal proceedings (see Sect. 11.3.1 below)
- Standing to appeal and the notion of 'directly affected party' (see Sect. 11.3.2 below)
- Strict liability and the notion of 'supporter' (see Sect. 11.3.3 below)
- Host team's and UEFA's duties for order and security at UEFA competitions (see Sect. 11.3.4 below)
- Refusing to play or being responsible for a match not being played in full (see Sect. 11.3.5 below)

11.3.1 Case Management: Two Separate CAS Appeal Proceedings

The procedural trajectory of this dispute, from the CEDB through to the UEFA AB and CAS, is quite noteworthy. Although UEFA opened separate disciplinary proceedings against FAA and FAS, and two separate CEDB decisions were issued, upon appeal the UEFA AB decided to hear both cases (and the various witnesses) in one hearing for reasons of procedural economy. It also issued one decision for both appeals. At the third instance, the cases were split again and they remained as such until the end of the CAS proceedings, leading to the issuance of two final CAS awards.

It is pertinent at this point to look at Articles R50(2) and R52(4) of the CAS Code, which provide in relevant part as follows:

> R50 […]
> When two or more cases clearly involve the same issues, the President of the Appeals Arbitration Division may invite the parties to agree to refer these cases to the same Panel; failing any agreement between the parties, the President of the Division shall decide.
> […]
> R52 […]
> Where a party files a statement of appeal in connection with a decision which is the subject of a pending appeal before CAS, the President of the Panel, or if he has not yet been appointed, the President of the Division, may decide, after inviting submissions from the parties, to consolidate the two procedures.

The CAS Code gives the Division President certain tools so as to make the resolution of an appeals' dispute more efficient. These tools, which may even be imposed on the parties,[2] could be categorised as follows:

[2]Mavromati and Reeb 2015, p. 446, para 16.

(a) appointing the same President of the Panel;
(b) referring the cases to the same Panel;
(c) consolidating the proceedings.

The main criterion to be considered when exercising the discretion embedded in the CAS Code is set out in the text of the provisions ('same issues', for referral to the 'same Panel'; same 'decision', in order 'to consolidate'). A leading commentary on the CAS Code provides further criteria, drawing an analogy to other arbitration rules[3]: the identity of the parties, of the applicable rules and of the underlying legal relationship. Another leading commentary points out the potential difficulty of consolidating two cases when the parties have already nominated an arbitrator.[4] In the author's opinion, depriving a party from the right to appoint *on its own* an arbitrator is a serious intervention in the arbitral process.

In the matters at hand, and since the awards are silent on this issue, it is unknown whether UEFA requested that the CAS follow the same procedural approach as the UEFA AB and conduct one proceeding or if the CAS, on its own initiative, invited the parties to express an opinion on a possible consolidation.

Ultimately, one can only assume that the problem of party-appointed arbitrators in consolidated cases, especially when these cases are so high profile, heavily controversial and with evident political importance for the appealing parties, played an important role. Hence, instead of forcing the FAA and FAS to jointly choose an arbitrator, the Division President preferred to take a conservative—and sensible—decision of allowing the cases to proceed separately and be heard by panels that were by 2/3 the same.

The procedural issues that emanated from such decision would be revealed one-by-one as the case advanced. First, the parties were faced with an important dilemma: to intervene or not to intervene in the 'other' proceeding?

The FAS decided to intervene in the 3874 proceeding and was accepted by the Panel as an intervening party; the FAA decided not to intervene in the 3875 proceeding but requested a copy of the submissions filed in the other case, in order to ensure that both the FAA and—mainly—the arbitrator nominated by it in the 3874 case had the same information as the other two members of the Panel, who were sitting on both cases. As reflected in the 3874 award, the Panel dealt with these matters in an elegant way, refusing to order the document production, as the request came late in the process, and providing the FAA with assurances that the members of the Panel who were on both cases would decide "based exclusively on the evidence and arguments submitted in the [3874] case".[5]

---

[3]Ibid., p. 464, para 17.

[4]Rigozzi et al. 2013, p. 1011, para 10.

[5]CAS 2015/A/3874, *Football Association of Albania v. UEFA & Football Association of Serbia*, para 90.

This statement, and the fact that at the hearing "counsel for [FAA] stated that he trusted the President's indication", can be seen as one of the advantages of the closed list of CAS arbitrators: parties and counsel can form their own opinion on whether a certain CAS arbitrator, with proven record of independence and impartiality in dozens of CAS cases over a longer period of time, will stick to his duties and deliver justice as demanded by the CAS Code. Nevertheless, it is true that the circumstances of these parallel proceedings rightfully raised concerns regarding the principle of 'equality of information'[6] among the arbitrators, a principle confirmed in ICC arbitrations.[7]

As it is common in arbitration, however, and with the proceedings remaining separate, the question 'who can be bound by the CAS award' still required a solution: would the Panel in the 3874 case have been able to issue the same holding, imposing sanctions on the FAS, in the event that the FAS had not intervened?[8] And even if the FAS intervened in the CAS 3874 proceedings, is it a desirable result to have the same party being sanctioned for the same match through two different CAS awards?

The above questions show that the non-consolidation of the proceedings can have very serious consequences, sometimes negative, which cannot be cured by the Panel's authority to remit the case back to the previous instance with binding instructions and the power of *res judicata* on certain findings.

One needs to recognise that these possible negative consequences are difficult for the Division President to predict at the outset of the case. For this reason, in the author's opinion R52(4) rightfully allows also the President of the Panel, once appointed, to take a decision on consolidating the proceedings.

To conclude, it seems that in cases with so many similarities, especially when the same decision is being challenged by two appeals filed on the same day, the Division President's decision to appoint the same President of the Panel is a very prudent approach that can correct multiple procedural disadvantages in the course of the proceedings. When to take the extra step of proposing or even imposing consolidation, requires of course a particularly fact-sensitive evaluation.

---

[6] *See* also von Segesser 2010, pp. 49–50.

[7] The ICC Court may not confirm an arbitrator or may accept a challenge if the arbitrator concerned might have had, because of his or her involvement as arbitrator in a previous or other case, access to information which the other arbitrators did or do not have. Voser N, Swiss Federal Tribunal rejects arbitrator challenges, 1 July 2010. http://www.swlegal.ch/Publications/Arbitration-Case-Digest/Swiss-Federal-Tribunal-rejects-arbitrator-challeng.aspx. Accessed 15 February 2016.

[8] In such a situation, were the CAS Panel in the 3874 case to follow the opinion of the Panel in CAS 2011/A/2551, *Fenerbahce SK v. UEFA & Turkish Football Federation*, Award of 18 June 2012, it would likely have decided to dismiss the FAA's appeal as regards the 0:3 forfeit and additional sanctions over the FAS, on the basis that "it is precluded from taking a decision which would directly affect the situation of a third party in such a way without that party being able to present its position.".

11.3.2 Standing to Appeal and the Notion of 'Directly Affected Party'

The legal debate on who can be recognised as a 'directly affected party' has its roots in Article 62(2) of the UEFA Statutes, which provides as follows:

> Right to Appeal
> Only parties directly affected by a decision may appeal to the CAS. However, where doping-related decisions are concerned, the World Anti-Doping Agency (WADA) may appeal to the CAS.

First comes the need to identify the legal nature of the problem. The title of the provision ('Right to Appeal') which follows para 1 of the same Article entitled 'Jurisdiction', has led various CAS Panels and counsel to deal with the matter as 'standing to sue/to appeal', which is under Swiss law a matter belonging to the merits of the dispute. It would be interesting, however, to see this point argued also as a question of scope of the arbitration agreement included in the UEFA statutes, specifically as a question of jurisdiction *ratione personae*. Interestingly in the 3874 matter, where FAA tried to have FAS sanctioned under the harsh provisions of racist behaviour, the Panel followed the usual path of standing but also mentioned that one of the main issues it had to decide was

> (A) whether the Appellant's request to sanction the FAS under Article 14 DR for racist and discriminatory chants is an admissible appeal, or whether the Appellant lacks standing to sue in that regard;[9] (emphasis added).

This was unfortunately—because there is no issue of admissibility, clearly—a consequence of the UEFA AB decision, declaring the same head of FAA's appeal as 'inadmissible' and leading the parties, in their respective submissions before CAS, to refer to the FAA appeal being 'inadmissible, for lack of standing'.

Although the award does not contain the usual 'Admissibility' section where the timeliness and formal completeness of the appeal is examined, the Panel approached the matter carefully in the section of the merits. The analysis has two focal points

(a) The provision itself provides the first defining factor: the party must be directly affected by the *decision* and not by the conduct giving rise to the disciplinary proceedings. Thus, the fact that the FAA and its players may have been the victim of the opposing side's conduct was irrelevant.
(b) The words 'directly affected' are to be interpreted 'in a restrictive manner', as was previously held in the CAS 2008/A/1583 & 1584 matter. The right to appeal belongs only to the addressee of the disciplinary measure or to a directly affected party,

[9] *CAS 2015/A/3874, Football Association of Albania v. UEFA & Football Association of Serbia*, para 164.

> …as opposed to [a party] "indirectly affected" by it, the latter encompassing the situation in which a third party is only affected due to its status as a competitor of the addressee of the measure taken by UEFA.

Despite this statement, a few paragraphs later the CAS Panel supports its position that the FAA is not a directly affected party as follows:

> […] the Appellant is not "directly affected" by the measures that may have been reasonably applicable for an infringement of Article 14 DR (see supra at para 49). In this respect, taking into consideration that this would have been the first violation of Article 14 DR committed by the FAS, the Panel is of the opinion that, under Article 14 paras. 2 and 3 DR, the appropriate punishment would have been within the range between the sanction provided for a first offence ("a minimum of a partial stadium closure") and the sanction applicable for a second offence ("one match played behind closed doors and a fine of € 50,000") with no room for additional disciplinary measures under Article 14 para 4 DR (which in the Panel's view would not be appropriate for a first offense, absent any evidence of truly extraordinary circumstances). The Panel observes that a sanction ranging between a partial stadium closure and a match behind closed doors and a fine would not have given any **advantage** to the Appellant. In fact, paradoxically, it might have even been detrimental to the Appellant (as a match behind closed doors could benefit one of the Appellant's competitors, which would have the opportunity to play in Serbia without any Serbian spectators present).[10] (emphasis added)

Even if the CAS Panel simply wanted to show the remoteness of FAA's legal interest and did not intend to imply that the existence of an "advantage" for the competitor would *ipso facto* raise him to the status of a 'directly affected party', the above analysis demonstrates the difficulties that the provision creates.

Indeed, combining the criterion of 'reasonably applicable measures' with the broad list of sanctions listed in Article 6 of the UEFA Disciplinary Regulations, ranging from a warning to a ban on all football-related activities, makes it almost impossible to determine with legal certainty the number of potential persons with a right to appeal.

The author shares the CAS Panel's opinion that the anti-doping regulatory regime has long established similar restrictive approaches with regard to the right of appeal of the co-competitor(s) and that "such a procedural situation is not inappropriate as it is commonplace in other sporting matters".

The FAA's argument that UEFA could 'bury' a violation may have some merit, since the disciplinary inspectors represent UEFA[11] and are not independent from it, at least not to the extent that WADA is towards the International Federations and the National Anti-Doping Organisations. But the need for clarity is much bigger than the theoretical danger pointed out by the FAA: the debate around the notion of the 'directly affected party' has created enough disputes to date so that an amendment of the rules could be considered. Using the valuable input provided

[10] Ibid., para 181.

[11] Article 25(2) UEFA Disciplinary Regulations.

by the CAS jurisprudence,[12] a provision similar to that adopted by WADA[13] that lists the persons entitled to appeal against a decision of UEFA generally—or of the UEFA AB in particular—would be a welcome development.

11.3.3 Strict Liability and the Notion of 'Supporter'

The so-called drone incident did not only bring about turmoil on the football pitch and headlines in the media around the world. It gave rise to a high-level legal debate, as presented in the 3874 award.

The parties did not take issue with the application of the principle of strict liability in disciplinary matters. It remained common ground that the national associations and clubs must be held responsible for the behaviour of their supporters. The CAS Panel confirmed that this principle is a cornerstone in the fight of the football authorities against hooliganism.[14]

The key question was rather different: how far can this (strict) liability extend?

The FAA challenged the UEFA AB's conclusion that it was comfortably satisfied that the drone carrying the Albanian nationalistic banner was controlled by an Albanian supporter: no Albanian fans were in the stadium, the police searched the Albanian delegation for the drone's operating device to no avail, and there was no proof Albanian fans were in the vicinity.

The Panel followed the approach taken by previous panels, i.e. that the term 'supporter' is an open concept which is intentionally undefined and which must be assessed from the perspective of a reasonable and objective observer.[15] CAS jurisprudence has even held that it is not necessary for supporters to be in the stadium, or to be in sight.[16]

Turning to the present case, the majority of the Panel decided to follow a 'presumptive approach' which led to the conclusion that it was 'highly likely' that Albanian supporter(s) deployed the drone and banner. The 3874 award refers to a series of factual parameters that support this conclusion, such as the nature of the symbols and words depicted on the banner; the fact that the Albanian players reacted protectively towards the banner; and the fact that the banner gave rise to strongly negative feelings on the part of the Serbian players, staff and spectators in the stadium.[17]

---

[12]From the most recent jurisprudence: CAS 2015/A/4151, *Panathinaikos FC v. UEFA & Olympiacos FC*, Award of 26 November 2015, paras 134–139.

[13]Similar to Article 13(2)(3) World Anti-Doping Code ('Persons Entitled to Appeal'), ed. 2015.

[14]CAS 2015/A/3874, *Football Association of Albania v. UEFA & Football Association of Serbia*, para 187.

[15]Ibid., para 189.

[16]CAS 2013/A/3139, *Fenerbahçe SK v. UEFA*, Award of 5 December 2013.

[17]CAS 2015/A/3874, *Football Association of Albania v. UEFA & Football Association of Serbia*, paras 195–198.

Besides the factual elements, which indeed pointed in the direction of a hidden Albanian supporter,[18] the use of a presumption which is not expressly provided for in the applicable rules is quite an exceptional step.

In the author's opinion, the drone incident tested the limits of the strict liability rules in the UEFA Disciplinary Regulations. There is no doubt that supporters are very rarely personally identified and even more rarely proven to be supporters of one or the other team. The theoretical risk of sabotage by an opponent's supporter, no matter how unlikely, exists always and not only in case that the 'unruly supporter' is not in the stadium; it can therefore not be used against the presumption used by the Panel. Furthermore, it is true that Swiss law allows the use of presumptions based on reasonable and objective criteria, as long as they are rebuttable.

The CAS Panel had thus the difficult task to justify that in the exceptional circumstances of this case a combination of strict liability with the use of an—unwritten—presumption was required. In the eyes of an external reader this approach could be from a sporting perspective appropriate, because the sport should not appear to be toothless before such innovative types of misconduct. On the other hand, the absence of a written presumption may not only surprise an affected party by exposing it to responsibility it was not aware it had, but makes it even more difficult to rebut the presumption. The rebuttal of a presumption is a big hurdle when trying to prove a negative and especially when the same (high) standard of 'comfortable satisfaction' continues to apply.[19] Be that as it may, in this case, the FAA did not manage to rebut the presumption, which the majority of the Panel found to be applicable. Therefore, the FAA was sanctioned for the drone incident.

---

[18]After the end of the proceedings and issuance of the awards, the self-proclaimed drone operator Ismail Morina, an Albanian citizen domiciled at the time in Italy, described in an interview to the New York Times how he piloted the drone from a church tower neighbouring the football stadium in Belgrade. For the online version of the interview Montague J, Ending an Albania-Serbia Game and Inciting a Riot, With a Joystick, 10 August 2015. http://www.nytimes.com/2015/10/08/sports/soccer/as-albania-faces-serbia-meeting-the-drone-pilot-who-ended-their-last-match.html?_r=0. Accessed 30 October 2015.

[19]The introduction of a lower standard for the rebuttal of a presumption would be an important balancing factor. For example, the presumption that WADA-accredited laboratories conduct sample analyses in accordance with the applicable rules can be rebutted if it is proven, by balance of probabilities (i.e. by a lower standard than that of 'comfortable satisfaction' which is required for anti–doping organisations to establish a violation), that a departure from the applicable standards occurred, which could reasonably have caused the Adverse Analytical Finding (Article 3(2) World Anti-Doping Code).

11.3.4 Host Team's and UEFA's Duties for Order and Security at UEFA Competitions

The strict approach taken by the Panel in the 3874 case in relation to the FAA's liability was followed also in the 3875 case, where FAS was found to have violated its duties as match organiser.

In this respect, it is relevant to quote Article 16(1) of the UEFA Disciplinary Regulations

> 1 Host associations and clubs are responsible for order and security both inside and around the stadium before, during and after matches. They are liable for incidents of any kind and may be subject to disciplinary measures and directives unless they can prove that they have not been negligent in any way in the organisation of the match. (emphasis added)

After citing the incidents that took place in the stadium and which clearly constitute violations of the above provision, the CAS Panel applied both *quantitative* and *qualitative* criteria to arrive at the conclusion that the FAS was negligent in the organisation of the match

(a) approx. 15 % of the available stewards were not deployed at all, while the vast majority of those deployed were stationed outside the stadium. The same is true for almost 90 % of the police forces, which intervened only after the match was interrupted. Therefore, the security measures were not sufficient for such a high-risk match.

(b) The record was incomplete as regards the hiring, selection and training of the security personnel, meaning that the FAS was unable to demonstrate that it lacked any negligence with respect to the behaviour of the stewards. Therefore, the security measures were not adequate for such a high-risk match.

In a consistent manner, the Panel applied its hard line approach also with regard to UEFA's responsibility, drawing attention to the fact that UEFA seemed to have somewhat underestimated, when drawing the qualifying groups, the high risks posed by a match between Serbia and Albania; and failed to raise any objections as to the Serbian security measures prior to the match. This finding certainly increases the level of pre-game diligence that a competition organiser needs to demonstrate, regardless if the regulations it has enacted place all the responsibility on the host team.

These circumstances would be considered as—the only—mitigating factors that the Panel allowed itself to consider when it came to determining the sanction applicable to the FAS.

11.3.5 Refusing to Play or Being Responsible for a Match not Being Played in Full

One of the most interesting sections of the award in the 3874 case is that addressing the question of which national association, the FAA or the FAS, should be held responsible for the match not having been played in full.

Procedurally, it was mentioned *supra* (Sect. 11.3.1) that the Panel had 'free hands' to reach a conclusion and impose it in a binding manner on the parties since all three involved entities were parties to at least one of the two proceedings, and in particular the proceeding dealing with the abandonment of the match.

What also merits some attention, and it seems to have played an important role here, is the fact that the CAS Panel on the one hand heard the case *de novo* but on the other hand had before it less (or less direct) evidence than the UEFA AB.

Indeed, the 3874 award contains numerous references[20] to (and lengthy quotes of) statements made by the parties' officials and their counsel, the match officials and also by UEFA AB members. None of the match officials testified at the CAS hearing. This is an indication that on this particular topic the bulk of the evidentiary measures took place in the previous instance as the CAS Panel did not have the chance to see all the witnesses being examined before it or to question them itself. Of course, the arbitral tribunal is largely left in the hands of the parties as regards the witnesses and experts they decide to call. In this case, however, it would have been very difficult for the Panel to decide the questions posed to it, if it had not ordered UEFA to produce the audio recordings of the UEFA AB hearing and subsequently the FAA and FAS to transcribe any parts of the recordings they intended to rely on. Still, the Panel had an uphill battle to evaluate the probative value of the various statements on file.

From a regulatory perspective, Article 27.01 of the Regulations of the UEFA European Football Championship 2014–2016 and Article 21(1) of the UEFA Disciplinary Regulations provide as follows:

> If an association refuses to play or is responsible for a match not taking place or not being played in full, the UEFA Control and Disciplinary Body takes a decision in the matter.
> and
> If a match cannot take place or cannot be played in full, the member association or club responsible forfeits the match.

The above provisions seem to create an interesting 'one-way' mechanism, namely that if the match cannot take place or cannot be played in full, then there must be one party responsible, in fact solely responsible, and the applicable sanction on such party can only be a forfeit of the match. This position was supported

---

[20] E.g. "The Panel has also had regard to the testimony of the other UEFA officers offered at the UEFA Hearing" (CAS 2015/A/3874, *Football Association of Albania v. UEFA & Football Association of Serbia*, para 216); "(ii) a preponderance of the testimony at the UEFA Hearing indicated that…" (CAS 2015/A/3874, *Football Association of Albania v. UEFA & Football Association of Serbia*, para 222).

also by UEFA, which rejected that there could be a shared responsibility between national associations under said rules, equating the situation to the 'flipping of a coin' (i.e. either the FAA or the FAS must be held responsible and, accordingly, either national association must lose the match by a forfeit of 0:3).

The parties argued extensively on this point and the Panel, with a finding that was essentially an *obiter dictum* since it proved not to be applicable to this case, noted

> The Panel is of the view that, in principle, there may be situations where a shared responsibility should be attributed to both clubs or associations and that, were such the case, the adjudicatory body might have a discretion under Swiss law in interpreting and applying the UEFA rules so as to devise a fair and reasonable solution to a specific case (for example, a 0-0 result or a match replay with or without spectators). However, for the reasons set out below (see infra at para 239 et seq.), the Panel is of the opinion that the point does not arise in the present case, where the responsibility for the match not being played in full is to be attributed to one national association.[21]

The CAS Panel went on to disagree with the conclusion reached by the UEFA AB, i.e. that the statement signed by the Albanian team captain was the decisive element for the non-continuation of the match. Instead, the Panel considered that, for there to be a refusal to resume play, there must first have been a clear, direct and unconditional order that the match must be resumed. Since the referee's decisions "regarding facts connected with play"—to which the decision to resume play belongs—benefits from a significant degree of protection under standing CAS jurisprudence for "field of play" calls, these decisions must be precise and free from ambiguity in the perception of the concerned athletes or teams.

In this case, the Panel emphasised that the referee's instruction was conditional, by referring to his testimony before the UEFA AB

> The Panel notes that the Match Referee is a native English speaker and a highly experienced referee, and that he appears to have chosen his words with very great care. He was asked directly whether he personally ordered the teams to continue the Match. The Panel notes that he did not say that he so ordered. Rather, he repeatedly offered an answer in the passive tense, and in a manner that indicates that a person other than him may have issued an instruction, or perhaps a suggestion. He told the UEFA Appeals Body that both "teams <u>were told</u> that they must return to the field of play and continue the game <u>once the safety was ensured</u>" (emphasis added). Three points may be noted with respect to the formulation of his words: first, he does not state that he told the teams they must return; second, the formulation chosen is not of an order being given; and third, such direction as was given was conditional on safety being "ensured". There is no evidence before the Panel that the Match Referee ever told the teams that safety had been ensured.[22] (emphasis in the original)

Since there was no refusal by the FAA, the Panel had to determine which party, the FAA or the FAS, was responsible for the match not being played in full and what the applicable consequences should be.

---

[21] *CAS 2015/A/3874, Football Association of Albania v. UEFA & Football Association of Serbia, para 210.*

[22] Ibid., para 228.

The Panel's analysis was then focused on identifying the incident, among the many that occurred, that was *casually linked* to the abandonment of the match.

The drone incident was not deemed to be the decisive factor because, when it occurred (42nd minute), the match had already been stopped due to the unruly behaviour of the fans in the stadium, who had thrown objects at Albanian players and staff before the Match began, and continued to do so once it had started. On the contrary, the Panel found that the factors that led the Match to not being played in full were created by the Serbian supporters, who sung chants that were "offensive and imbued with racist and discriminatory content"; threw objects on the pitch, including coins, bottles and chairs; invaded the pitch; attacked the Albanian players by tackling, kicking and throwing punches. In these circumstances, the fears of the Albanian players were "entirely reasonable and understandable". Thus, the Panel concluded that

> [...] the Match stoppage and the eventual Match Referee's abandonment of the Match were proximately caused by the security lapses of the Match organizers and the intolerable and outrageous acts of violence exerted on the Albanian players by the Serbian supporters and by at least one security steward. For these acts the FAS bears the exclusive responsibility in accordance with the UEFA rules. The drone incident certainly did not assist in calming matters down, but in all the circumstances it is these other appalling acts of behaviour which are the significant factors in causing the Match to be abandoned.

As a result, and since the rules allowed no discretion to the Panel, FAS was sanctioned with a 0:3 forfeit of the match in the 3874 case in addition to the deduction of 3 points which was confirmed in the 3875 case. The Panel interestingly noted that, in order to preserve the FAS's right to be heard, it would have remitted the case back to the UEFA AB "so as to allow FAS to set forth its defence as to the proportionality of the sanction" however it did not do so because "a referral back to the previous instance would serve no purpose, as the FAS would not be in a position to obtain a different sanction for its responsibility in causing the abandonment of the Match".

References

Mavromati D, Reeb M (2015) The code of the court of arbitration for sport: commentary, cases, materials. Kluwer Law International BV, Alphen aan den Rijn

Rigozzi A, Hasler E, Noth M (2013) Sports arbitration under the CAS rules. In: Arroyo M (ed) Arbitration in Switzerland. A practitioner's guide. Kluwer Law International BV, Alphen aan den Rijn, pp 885–1083

von Segesser G (2010) Equality of information and impartiality of arbitrators. In: Wautelet P, Kruger T, Coppens G (eds) The practice of arbitration, essays in honour of Hans van Houtte. Hart Publishing, Oxford and Portland, pp 45–51

Chapter 12
CAS 2014/A/3759, *Chand v. AFI & IAAF*, Award of 24 July 2015

Marjolaine Viret and Emily Wisnosky

Abstract Dividing competitions into male and female categories is a hallmark of most sports. So is the near-unassailable autonomy of sports organizations to regulate participation in their sport. Spanning 161-pages, and still only described as an "interim award," the Chand award illustrates the complexity of attempting to fit into a traditional legal framework the highly charged ideological and ethical issues raised when sports organizations exercise this autonomy to "police" the male versus female divide. This comment analyses track-and-field athlete Dutee Chand's challenge to the validity of the IAAF's Hyperandrogenism Regulations, which excluded women whose testosterone levels fell within the "normal" male range from competition. In particular, Ms Chand challenged their scientific validity, discriminatory effect and proportionality, in addition to alleging a similarity to a doping sanction. While primarily focused on the legal questions that arise from the CAS award, this comment also addresses the bigger picture, in particular the dilemmas of organized sport caught between its ambition to strive for the limits of human performance and the need to secure a level playing field.

Keywords Burden of proof · Standard of proof · Validity of sports rules · Proportionality · Discrimination · Interim award · Anti-doping · Eligibility rules · Hyperandrogenism

M. Viret (✉) · E. Wisnosky
School of Law, University of Neuchâtel, Avenue du 1er-Mars 26,
2000 Neuchâtel, Switzerland
e-mail: marjolaine.viret@unine.ch

E. Wisnosky
e-mail: emily.wisnosky@unine.ch

A. Duval and A. Rigozzi (eds.), *Yearbook of International Sports Arbitration 2015*,
DOI 10.1007/978-94-6265-129-6_12

Contents

12.1 Introduction

In mid-2015, a panel of the CAS assessed the status of female athletes in athletic sports affected by a health condition referred to as 'hyperandrogenism'. Dutee Chand, a young Indian female athlete ('Ms. Chand' or the 'Athlete'), challenged the validity of the International Association of Athletics Federations ('IAAF')'s Regulations Governing Eligibility of Females with Hyperandrogenism to Compete in Women's Competition ('Hyperandrogenism Regulations' or 'Regulations').

The Regulations describe the criteria and procedure for identifying situations of hyperandrogenism among female athletes in athletics, and for dealing with these situations. Schematically, the Regulations provide that an athlete is eligible for women's competition if her androgen levels are below the 'normal male range', which is defined as having total testosterone levels measuring less than 10 nmol/L.[1] If her total testosterone levels are greater than or equal to 10 nmol/L, the athlete may still be eligible to compete if she is able to establish, by a balance of probabilities, that she "derives no competitive advantage from having androgen levels in the normal male range".[2] The Regulations stipulate that the athlete may be required to submit to a 'full' medical examination at an IAAF-approved facility,[3] designed to verify the degree of virilization of the athlete. The stakes for female athletes identified as suffering from hyperandrogenism are high, since under the Regulations they can potentially be banned from competition unless and until they undergo medical treatment to reduce their testosterone level below the "admissible" threshold.

Of note, it was not disputed in this case among the parties that Ms. Chand is a woman. Nor was it suggested that she ever took exogenous testosterone (or any other substance prohibited by the relevant anti-doping rules).[4] Generally speaking,

[1]Hyperandrogenism Regulations, Article 6.5(i).

[2]Hyperandrogenism Regulations, Article 6.5(ii).

[3]According to the Regulations, the "full" examination will normally include the following tests: "physical, laboratory (including genetic testing), imaging and psychological assessment". (Article 5.29).

[4]CAS 2014/A/3759, *Chand v. IAAF,* Award of 24 July 2015, para 36.

the background presented in the *Chand* award regarding the details of the athlete's actual medical situation was tenuous; accordingly, the CAS panel conducted its assessment under the assumption of her being genuinely an athlete with hyperandrogenism within the meaning of the IAAF Regulations.

The *Chand* panel embarked on an ambitious analysis of the validity of a set of highly controversial regulations, largely without the comfort of a set of facts relating to a concrete dispute. Ms. Chand challenged the Regulations' validity on the bases of unlawful discrimination, lack of scientific validity, breach of proportionality and conflict with the World Anti-Doping Code ('WADA Code'). In a 161-page award commented on hereinafter, the CAS panel reported the testimony of over 15 witnesses, heard over the course of a four-day hearing, and reviewed numerous scientific reports relating to the topic of hyperandrogenism. Highlighting the legal and scientific complexity of the issues, the CAS panel was not satisfied that the evidence it heard in the case was sufficient to uphold the validity of the Regulations. Notwithstanding this finding, the award does not put a definitive end to the dispute. In a somewhat unusual move, the CAS panel issued a decision referred to as an 'interim award' instead of a final award, leaving the door open for the IAAF to submit further evidence to prove its case within two years.

In this comment, we first summarize the background (2) and proceedings at the CAS (3), before turning to the merits of the case (4). The Section discussing the merits breaks down the award into five topics: the requests for relief and the reach of the CAS' ruling in this respect (4.1), the 'preliminary' issues considered by the CAS panel, including on evidence (4.2), the assessment of scientific validity, discrimination, and proportionality (4.3); the Athlete's challenge that the Regulations served as an impermissible disguised doping sanction (4.4); and the CAS panel's decision to issue an "interim," rather than "final" award (4.5). For each of these five Sections, we present the CAS panel's reasoning, followed by a comment specific to the topic, before concluding with general remarks regarding the challenges involved in imposing norms on the human body within organized sport.

12.2 Background

In this case, Ms. Chand, a young female athlete,[5] already successful in the sport of athletics at the junior level,[6] was prohibited from further participation in competition ostensibly due to high, naturally occurring testosterone levels in contravention of the applicable rules.

---

[5]Ibid., paras 7 & 8. Dutee Chand, born in 1996, was a resident athlete at the National Institute of Sports in India, operated by the Sports Authority of India, a public body unaffiliated with the IAAF.

[6]Ibid., para 1. She won numerous junior athletic events both at the national level in India, and at the international level, taking the gold medal in two events at the Asian Junior Track and Field Championships in May 2014.

In Summer 2014, Ms. Chand underwent two medical examinations. The first examination was conducted at the request of the Athletics Federation of India (AFI) Medical Commission.[7] The second, more comprehensive, examination took place at a training camp of the Sports Authority of India.

The motivation for the first medical examination, which took place in June 2014, remained disputed. According to Ms. Chand, the doctor performing the examination (the AFI Chairperson) told her that it was conducted as part of a "*high performance profile*" that the AFI was creating for her, and they needed to check to make sure that she did not have any "diseases".[8] According to the AFI Chairperson, however, the examination (including the ultrasound) was conducted because Ms. Chand (and another female athlete) had complained of "chronic abdominal pains".[9] At the same time, the AFI Chairperson also reported that "several participants" at a recent athletics event had "expressed concerns" to the AFI about Ms. Chand's appearance and her eligibility to compete in female events, but denied that these concerns in any way motivated the first examination.[10]

Following the first examination, the AFI sent an email to the Sports Authority of India, expressing "*definite doubts*" about Ms. Chand's gender.[11] It reminded the Sports Authority of India of past hyperandrogenism cases that "*brought embarrassment to the fair name of sports in India*".[12] Accordingly, it recommended that the Sports Authority of India urgently perform a "*gender verification test*" on Ms. Chand, given that she was scheduled to compete in the World Junior Athletic Championships in less than a month.[13]

The second examination appeared more intrusive than the first. Ms. Chand described the experience as "*humiliating,*" reporting that she was subject to questions by a male doctor about "her body hair, menstrual cycle, surgical history and her hobbies".[14]

On 13 July, following the second examination and just five days before the World Junior Athletics Championship, Ms. Chand was notified by the Sports Authority of India that she was not permitted to participate in the imminent Championship, nor in the upcoming Commonwealth Games. The reason provided for her exclusion was that "her '*male hormone*' levels were too high".[15] According to Ms. Chand, this decision left her shocked and devastated.[16]

[7]Ibid., para 11.

[8]Ibid., para 11.

[9]Ibid., para 12.

[10]Ibid., para 12.

[11]Ibid., para 13.

[12]Ibid., para 13.

[13]Ibid., para 14.

[14]Ibid., para 373. According to the Athlete, this second exam included "blood tests, clinical tests by a gynaecologist, karyotyping, an MRI examination and a further ultrasound examination". Ibid., para 15.

[15]Ibid., para 16.

[16]Ibid., para 374.

Two days later, on 15 July, the Sports Authority of India spoke publicly about Ms. Chand's case. It issued a statement whereby an "unnamed female athlete had been subjected to a gender test".[17] Despite the fact that Ms. Chand's name was not mentioned in the press release, from 15 July onwards, numerous articles appeared in the Indian press "speculating that the Athlete had been made to undergo tests to determine her gender".[18] The following day, on 16 July, the Sports Authority of India issued a press release clarifying that the test was not in fact a "gender verification test," which test had been abandoned by the International Olympic Committee ('IOC') and IAAF, but a hyperandrogenism test, which rendered her ineligible for competition in the female category.[19] Nevertheless, Ms. Chand reported "severe distress" as a result of the media speculation, saying that it "humiliated and '*shamed*'" her and her family.[20] She said that even in her rural village she was unable to escape the "intense and invasive media attention" and the "cruel questions" posed to her by reporters made her feel "like a student who had failed her exams".[21]

Over a month later and upon reviewing Ms. Chand's medical records from the second examination conducted by doctors affiliated with the Sports Authority of India, the AFI reached a decision to suspend Ms. Chand. Ms. Chand met with the AFI and the Sports Authority of India on 14 August, after which the Sports Authority of India transferred Ms. Chand's medical reports to the AFI.[22] According to a letter sent by the Director General of the Sports Authority of India to the President of the AFI on 22 August, the Sports Authority of India's medical examination established that Ms. Chand suffered from hyperandrogenism, and recommended that she be "*excluded from participation in women's events till her hyperandrogen level is brought down to permissible limits*".[23] The letter continued to state that AFI was yet to notify Ms. Chand of her "*disqualification*" and suggested *inter alia* that the AFI communicate a "*deep regret for the fact that [the Athlete] was not clearly told about the tests beforehand and the information was not kept confidential*".[24]

On 26 August, the AFI wrote to the Sports Authority of India (reportedly enclosing copies of the IAAF Regulations Governing Eligibility of Athletes who have Undergone Sex Reassignment to Compete in Women's Competition rather

[17] Ibid., para 17.

[18] Ibid., para 18.

[19] Ibid., para 19.

[20] Ibid., para 374.

[21] Ibid., para 374.

[22] Ibid., para 23.

[23] Ibid., para 24.

[24] Ibid., para 25.

than the IAAF's Hyperandrogenism Regulations).[25] The AFI letter noted that the AFI had "not compromised the confidentiality of the Athlete's case".[26]

Finally, on 31 August, the AFI sent Ms. Chand a letter (the "Decision Letter") informing her that she was "provisionally suspended from participating in any athletics events with immediate effect".[27]. Ms. Chand responded on 18 September, pleading the AFI to reconsider its decision and allow her to compete without undergoing medical intervention. She also requested that the AFI keep her medical records confidential and not share them with the IAAF or any other organization without her consent.[28] If the AFI were to decide not to withdraw the suspension, Ms. Chand asked for their support in her appeal at the CAS.[29]

12.3 CAS Proceedings

Ms. Chand filed an appeal before the CAS against the AFI's Decision Letter on 26 September 2014, naming both the AFI and the IAAF as respondents.

Ms. Chand requested a public hearing in her case. On 6 October, Ms. Chand's legal representative communicated to the CAS Court office that Ms. Chand did not agree to confidential arbitration proceedings (save for her personal medical records), highlighting the important issues of "*public interest and general application*" raised by this case.[30] On 22 January 2015, Ms. Chand filed an application for a public hearing, requesting also that the submissions made by the parties be publicly accessible. The IAAF and AFI objected to this request. The CAS denied the request, relying on the lack of agreement by the parties and the relevant articles of the CAS Code (R44.2 and R57).[31]

In addition to her request for a public hearing, Ms. Chand also applied for provisional relief that would allow her to compete in athletics event pending the CAS

[25]Ibid., para 26.

[26]Ibid., para 26.

[27]Ibid., paras 27 & 28. As reported in the award, the text of the Decision Letter read in relevant part: "*Based on your medical reports received from Sports Authority of India and a copy of the same has already been handed over to you by SAI in person, you are hereby provisionally stopped from participation in any Competition in athletics with immediate effect.* To be eligible for participation, you are further advised to follow the annexed IAAF guidelines". (para. 27). Ms. Chand stated that the letter incorrectly enclosed the IAAF Sex Reassignment Regulations rather than the Hyperandrogenism Regulations (para. 28).

[28]Ibid., para 29.

[29]Ibid., para 29.

[30]Ibid., para 77.

[31]Ibid., para 91.

panel's decision on the merits. The Athlete premised her request for provisional relief on the irreparable harm she might face should she give into pressure that her major sponsor was placing on her to drop her appeal and instead undergo medical treatment.[32] The IAAF, without prejudice to its position, voiced that it had no objection to Ms. Chand competing at the national level until the end of the CAS proceedings, and confirmed that the AFI was of the same mind.[33] In light of the IAAF and AFI's lack of objection, the CAS wrote to the parties stating that Ms. Chand "was permitted to compete at all national level events pending the issuance of a Final Award in the proceedings".[34] The AFI also confirmed by letter that it would permit the Athlete to compete in national and state level events pending the outcome of the case.[35]

The hearing was held from 23 to 26 March 2015. On the final day of the hearing, the CAS panel (noting the agreement of the parties' counsel) directed that Ms. Chand was permitted to compete in the "Asian Athletics Championships" in June 2015, which directive was confirmed in writing on 10 April 2015.[36]According to the CAS panel, the AFI "took a largely passive stance" in the proceedings.[37] The panel noted, in particular, that "[i]t did not file any written submissions in the proceedings, nor was it represented at the hearing".[38]

12.4 Discussion of the Merits

12.4.1 Request for Relief

12.4.1.1 CAS Award

According to the CAS award, Ms. Chand submitted two requests for relief, namely that

(a) *[T]he Hyperandrogenism Regulation[s] be declared invalid and void; and*
(b) [T]he Decision Letter be set aside and she be declared eligible to compete.[39]

The CAS award does not appear to include a mention of the "request for relief" on part of the IAAF.

The CAS panel reported that the parties during the course of the hearing "reached agreement that if the Panel were to invalidate the Hyperandrogenism Regulations, then the IAAF would communicate the outcome of the judgment to

[32]Ibid., para 82.
[33]Ibid., para 84.
[34]Ibid., para 85.
[35]Ibid., para 85.
[36]Ibid., para 102.
[37]Ibid., para 435.
[38]Ibid., para 430.
[39]Ibid., para 104.

all of its member federations, who would then be required to amend their national implementing rules accordingly to reflect the invalidity of the Regulations. In light of that agreement, the parties agreed that it is unnecessary for the Panel to make a formal ruling upon request (b)".[40]

In light of the panel's decision that only the Athlete's first request for relief was to be addressed, the award focuses on the question of whether the Hyperandrogenism Regulations must be declared "*invalid and void*".[41]

12.4.1.2 Comments

As a result of the panel limiting its inquiry to the 'abstract' prayer of relief directed at the validity of the Hyperandrogenism Regulations, the CAS award remains mostly detached from the particular circumstances surrounding Ms. Chand's exclusion from competition. More generally, the factual background before the panel seemed rather scarce. In particular, it was not established that the Athlete's total testosterone levels were in fact greater than the maximum level of 10 nmol/L authorized by the Hyperandrogenism Regulations, nor did she undergo the three-step screening process foreseen in the Regulations to determine if she was hyperandrogenic.[42] Thus, this appeal proceeded on the 'assumption' that she was in fact in contravention of the Regulations. Consequently, much of the CAS panel's analysis (bordering on all of the analysis) was done on a hypothetical basis, with the Athlete's particular circumstances playing a very minor role.

As a consequence, the award bears a strong resemblance to an advisory opinion, rather than the resolution of a concrete dispute. The instrument of the advisory opinion was abandoned in the 1 January 2012 revision of the CAS Code, to avoid sport federations using it as a means to receive legal opinions (which in practice were treated as though they had a binding effect) on existing disputes, thus bypassing adversarial proceedings.[43] Awards of the type rendered in the *Chand* matter would seem to reintroduce this instrument through the backdoor. Even though Ms. Chand evoked her personal situation to exemplify the harm and distress caused to athletes like her, no attempt was made to determine the exact regulations applicable to her case (i.e., the Regulations themselves or another national set of regulations), nor was there any plea before the CAS panel to explore whether Ms. Chand had been treated in compliance with applicable rules, an argument that might have led to the Decision Letter being invalidated without

[40]Ibid., para 105.

[41]Ibid., para 104.

[42]Ibid., para 36.

[43]See, e.g., Mavromati and Reeb 2015, pp. 603–604. In the US law context, it has been said that the "adversarial nature" of the dispute is diminished when parties lack "such a personal stake in the outcome of the controversy as to assure that concrete adverseness which sharpens the presentation of issues". U.S. Supreme Court, *Baker v. Carr*, 369 U.S. 186 (1962), at 204.

even having to assess the validity of the Hyperandrogenism Regulations. With its 161-pages devoted—in vain—to reaching a final decision working through unresolved issues, the *Chand* award highlights the difficult position hearing panels are placed in when asked to reach legal conclusions on a 'dispute' in an unsettled scientific, legal, and ethical context, especially when the interests on the side of the individual(s) concerned are discussed in the abstract and not supported by relevant factual evidence of injury.

Beyond the effect that removing the 'concrete' prayer for relief from the panel's consideration had on the nature of the dispute, it also raises questions as to what (if any) legal effect the CAS award had vis-à-vis Ms. Chand. To the extent that the Athlete sought to return (free and clear) to competition, one fails to see a justification for her choice to formally abandon her request to invalidate the Decision Letter. As the outcome of the dispute revealed, this choice opened the door to two years of legal uncertainty stemming from the CAS panel's decision to issue an interim award (See Sect. 12.4.5.2, below). Had the prayer for relief directed at the Decision Letter been maintained/set aside, the CAS panel would have been forced to issue a final ruling on the validity of the actual decision made against Ms. Chand, regardless of whether the IAAF should subsequently come up with additional evidence to support its Regulations.

The case illustrates the considerable faith that CAS panels place in sport organizations to accept CAS decisions, as well as in the authority of these organizations to enforce it by 'sports-internal' means. This approach that resembles a form of informal dispute resolution, verging on mediation, is reflected in the dispositive part of the award, and the lack of regard given to the enforceability of its wording. The CAS panel merely expresses its views on the validity of a set of sports regulations, trusting that sports governing bodies will comply with their promise to implement the CAS ruling, and impose its respect on their member federations in a manner that would require the latter to review and withdraw any decisions already issued that could conceivably be in conflict with the invalidated Regulations. The effectiveness of this approach is all the more questionable when—as was the case with Ms. Chand—an athlete's participation in national level sport also falls under the purview of government agencies that operated under their own hyperandrogenism regulations and fall entirely outside of the jurisdiction of the IAAF. Without a binding decision ordering the invalidation of the Decision Letter and absent more clarity on the legal relationships among the parties and the applicable rules, one can only assume that the Athlete would be forced to rely on the willingness of the AFI to spontaneously withdraw this Decision Letter to resume competition in the long term.[44]

[44]According to the *Chand* award, the AFI issued a letter that permitted her to compete in national- and state level competitions in the short term, i.e. "pending the determination of her appeal by the CAS". CAS 2014/A/3759, *Chand v. IAAF*, para 86.

12.4.2 Evidentiary Issues and Deference to the Sports Organization's Discretion

12.4.2.1 CAS Award

In what it qualified as a 'preliminary issue,' the CAS panel asked each of the parties to "clarify their position in relation to the burden and standard of proof".[45] The relevant section of the award further included the parties' positions regarding whether the IAAF was entitled to expect from the CAS panel a 'deference' or the benefit of a 'margin of appreciation' in the assessment of the validity of its rules.

12.4.2.2 Athlete's Position

Ms. Chand "accepted that [she] bore the onus of establishing that the Hyperandrogenism Regulations breach[ed] higher-ranking rules (namely the IAAF Constitution, the IOC Charter and the laws of Monaco)" to the balance of probability standard.[46] Per the specific question of discrimination, according to the *Chand* panel, Ms. Chand accepted that she bore "the burden of proof in establishing unlawful discrimination".[47] In her view, if she established "a *prima facie* discriminatory effect," the burden would then shift to the IAAF to "justify" this discrimination, a task which entails establishing "that the discriminatory measure is a necessary and proportionate means of achieving a legitimate aim".[48] The Athlete submitted that IAAF's justification must be established to a "comfortable satisfaction" standard.[49] The Athlete also contended in her appeal brief that the burden ought to be on the IAAF to establish the scientific validity of its Hyperandrogenism Regulations to the comfortable satisfaction of the panel. However, the CAS panel noted that, the Athlete changed her stance during the hearing by "expressly accepting" that she bears the "burden of proof on the issue of scientific basis and that the standard of proof is the balance of probabilities".[50]

With respect to the CAS panel's authority to review the case, the Athlete contended that, per CAS jurisprudence, the IAAF "is not entitled to any special deference or margin of appreciation in defending the Hyperandrogenism Regulations," since the "critical question is whether a lower-ranking rule conflicts with a higher-ranking rule".[51]

---

[45]Ibid., para 106.
[46]Ibid., para 106.
[47]Ibid., para 107.
[48]Ibid., para 107.
[49]Ibid., para 107.
[50]Ibid., para 442.
[51]Ibid., para 108.

12.4.2.3 IAAF's Position

The IAAF agreed "that the Athlete bears the onus of establishing that the Hyperandrogenism Regulations are invalid".[52] It also agreed that if "the Regulations are *prima facie* discriminatory, the burden shifts to the IAAF to justify that discrimination".[53]

However, the IAAF held a different view as to the level of scrutiny to which its "sporting imperative[s]" should be open. According to the award, the IAAF "accept[ed]" that "its view of what constitutes a sporting imperative, and its assessments of necessity and proportionality, must be honestly and reasonably held".[54] The IAAF further submitted that "the judgment of a sports governing body must not be interfered with unless it is shown to be '*evidently and grossly disproportionate*' (FIFA & WADA, CAS 2005/C/976 & 986, para 143) or '*irrational or perverse or otherwise outside the margin of discretion*' available to the regulator (Sheffield United v FAPL, FAPL Arbitration Award, 3 July 2007, para 38)".[55] Thus, the IAAF concluded that "the burden is on the Athlete to show that a reasonable person acting in good faith could not take the view that the eligibility rule is necessary and appropriate" or alternatively, "even if the IAAF bears the burden of establishing the validity of the Regulations, in light of the broad margin of appreciation that regulators enjoy in this context, the IAAF says that it has to do no more than persuade the Panel that the assumptions underlying the Hyperandrogenism Regulations are supported in good faith by competent scientists".[56]

12.4.2.4 The CAS Panel's Analysis

The CAS panel found that "the Athlete bears the burden of proving that the Hyperandrogenism Regulations are invalid",[57] setting forth the following framework:

> If the Athlete establishes that the Hyperandrogenism Regulations are *prima facie* discriminatory by reference to a higher-ranking rule or otherwise, on the balance of probabilities, the burden shifts to the IAAF to establish that they are justifiable as reasonable and proportionate, that is, to justify the discrimination. The requisite standard to justify

---

[52]Ibid., para 109.

[53]Ibid., para 109.

[54]Ibid., para 110.

[55]Ibid., para 110.

[56]Ibid., para 111.

[57]Ibid., para 443. According to the CAS panel at para 441, "[t]he parties agreed that the Athlete bore the burden of proving that the Hyperandrogenism Regulations are invalid. The parties also agreed that, once a *prima facie* case of discrimination is established, the burden shifts to the party responsible for the discriminating measure to justify the discriminatory effect".

discrimination of a fundamental right, which includes the right to compete as recognized in the Hyperandrogenism Regulations, should be to a level higher than that of the balance of probabilities.[58]

In spite of this initial statement, the CAS panel concluded that "[t]he standard of proof for each issue is the balance of probabilities",[59] referencing two previous CAS cases.[60] The panel, however, added the following: "[T]he Panel accepts that the requisite standard to justify discrimination of a fundamental right, including the right to compete that is recognised in the Hyperandrogenism Regulations themselves, requires the IAAF to overcome positively the onus to establish that justification".[61]

As to the scientific validity of the foundations for the Regulations, the CAS panel noted that the Athlete accepted bearing the burden of proof in this respect, to a balance of probability.[62]

The CAS panel did not explicitly address the issue of deference in this section of the award.

12.4.2.5 Comments

12.4.2.5.1 Burden and Standard of Proof in Science-Related Domains

CAS panels must make a determination on the burden of proof with respect to the various issues at stake, as well as on the requisite standard of proof. The *Chand* case illustrates the strong influence that this determination can exert on the outcome of a dispute when sufficient scientific evidence does not exist in support of either party's claim.

The CAS panel's reasoning is difficult to reconstruct and the system of proof envisaged by the CAS panel is certainly not straightforward. To support its determinations, the CAS panel referred to two CAS awards that required the panel to delve into scientific issues:

[58]Ibid., para 443.

[59]Ibid., para 447.

[60]Ibid., para 446. The *Chand* panel mentioned the *Pistorius* matter, in which the panel found that the "standard of proof is clearly not 'beyond a reasonable' doubt", rejecting that it could "in that Panel's view, be any of the possible intermediate standards that are discussed from time to time in connection with, for example, the disciplinary processes of professional or regulatory bodies". It also noted that the *Pistorius* panel applied the balance of probabilities standard, and also that the *Veerpalu* panel applied the comfortable satisfaction standard. See CAS 2008/A/1480, *Pistorius v. IAAF*, Award of 16 May 2008; See also CAS 2011/A/2566, *Andrus Veerpalu v. International Ski Federation (FIS)*, Award of 25 March 2013.

[61]CAS 2014/A/3759, *Chand v. IAAF*, para 447.

[62]Ibid., para 442.

In *Veerpalu v. FIS*,[63] the issue at stake was the reliability of the decision limits used in the human Growth Hormone (hGH) doping test to decide whether an athlete illegitimately used exogenous hGH. The panel in *Veerpalu v. FIS*, like the panels that followed in the trilogy of hGH cases brought before CAS,[64] showed the difficulties in determining a range of normal ratios of naturally occurring hGH with a degree of reliability sufficient to justify the harsh consequences imposed on athletes sanctioned for an anti-doping rule violation. The *Veerpalu* panel found that the scientific validity of the decision limits was for the anti-doping organization to prove, to the comfortable satisfaction of the hearing panel.

In *Pistorius v. IAAF*,[65] Oscar Pistorius—a double amputee and track runner—claimed the right to compete in IAAF track events alongside "able-bodied" athletes. The IAAF refused to accept his participation at those events, relying on a newly introduced rule prohibiting use of technical devices giving the athlete an advantage over other competitors. The IAAF claimed that Mr. Pistorius' prosthesis would in fact confer him such an advantage. After Mr. Pistorius underwent a series of performance tests, the CAS panel—based on the expert evidence—found that the state of scientific evidence produced by the IAAF did not allow for a sufficiently satisfying conclusion that Mr. Pistorius was enjoying an overall net advantage over able-bodied competitors, and granted him the right to compete at IAAF-sanctioned events. The CAS panel considered that the burden of establishing the advantage conferred by the prosthesis was on the IAAF, but that the standard burden of proof outside disciplinary matters should be by a mere balance of probabilities.

The award does not describe how exactly the CAS panel in *Chand v. IAAF* drew inspiration from the two cases. Unlike the panel in the *Chand* matter, the panels in the two precedents—*Veerpalu v. FIS* and *Pistorius v. IAAF*—reached a clear position on the applicable burden and standard of proof. In doping matters, panels are assisted by the fact that the WADA Code provides guidance on most aspects of proof. Nevertheless, the uncertainty of CAS panels when dealing with issues of scientific evidence is also palpable in those cases.[66]

The above ambiguities are all the more critical since these disputes more often than not revolve around matters that are not precisely settled within the scientific community or not sufficiently explored to allow for definitive scientific

---

[63]CAS 2011/A/2566, *Andrus Veerpalu v. FIS*. See also the authors discussion of the hGH trilogy in XR to Lallukka Article.

[64]CAS 2012/A/2857, *Nationale Anti-Doping Agentur Deutschland v. Sinkewitz*, Award of 24 February 2014, CAS 2014/A/3488, *WADA v. Lallukka*, Award of 20 November 2014; See also Rigozzi et al. 2015b; see also Viret M, CAS as the guardian of the validity of anti-doping science? A review of hGH cases through the prism of the revised 2015 World Anti-Doping Code, 23 July 2015. http://www.lawinsport.com/articles/item/cas-as-the-guardian-of-the-validity-of-anti-doping-science. Accessed 1 May 2016.

[65]CAS 2008/A/1480, *Pistorius v. IAAF*.

[66]See section "A Presumption of Scientific Validity of Analytical Tools" in Viret M, CAS as the guardian of the validity of anti-doping science? A review of hGH cases through the prism of the revised 2015 World Anti-Doping Code, 23 July 2015.

conclusions. The burden of proof[67] with respect to the scientific issues—along with the related standard—thus becomes the decisive factor that will make a party prevail or lose its case. By allocating the burden of proof on these issues, the CAS panel thus can predefine the outcome of a dispute with quasi-certainty. In all three cases compared above, the CAS panel ended up having to rule on the merits falling back on the burden of proof, finding against the party that had not discharged its burden. Symptomatically, hardly any of the scientific issues discussed in the *Chand* award were satisfactorily resolved in the CAS panel's eyes: neither the Athlete nor the IAAF were able to discharge their burden on the respective issues that had been allocated to them. It is only because the IAAF bore the burden on the very issue that the CAS panel ultimately deemed decisive that they failed to prevail (see Sect. 12.4.3.2.2).

It thus seems essential that CAS panels develop a firm and well-reasoned practice as to who bears the burden of proof when it comes to the scientific validity of evidentiary methods, or the reliability of the foundations that support a sports rule; and this whether the stakes involved are an ineligibility for participation in sport or an actual disciplinary sanction.

12.4.2.5.2 Need to Distinguish Evidence on Facts and the Scientific Foundations of a Regulation

A preliminary aspect that would merit thorough discussion when allocating the burden and standard of proof is that science can serve two functions in a sports dispute:

- The issue at stake can be a fact of the case requiring scientific knowledge or the scientific reliability of the evidentiary method used to establish those facts (e.g., the scientific validity of the analytical method used to detect a doping substance); or
- The issue at stake can be the solidity of the scientific foundations allegedly supporting a sports regulation (i.e., whether an eligibility requirement rests on a sound scientific basis).

CAS panels do not currently seem to distinguish clearly between the two types of issues; rather, they apply the same reasoning based on burden and standard of proof to both. While similar considerations may apply to both types of issues, the nature of these issues is intrinsically different. The former are clearly issues of fact, whereas the latter relate to the validity of a regulation, i.e., ultimately an issue of legal appreciation of the case.

When it comes to proving facts of the case through scientific evidence, the CAS jurisprudence in disciplinary matters appears more or less settled on the view that the burden of proof is on the sports organization to establish the factual prerequisites for the disciplinary offence.[67] There also appears to be a general view that the

---

[67]For more details, see Viret 2016, Sects. 3.1.2.3 and 7.3.3.2.2.2.

standards of proof must be differentiated, in that the standard for establishing elements of the offence must be the "comfortable satisfaction" standard, whereas elements that the person concerned by the proceedings must adduce for their defence must only be proved by a balance of probability. Outside disciplinary matters, the same allocation of the burden of proof should continue to prevail as soon as the rule or measure in dispute aims at restricting the Athlete's rights or otherwise affects their legitimate interests by creating distinctions among them.[68]

Similar considerations must, in our view, be transposed to the scientific soundness of sports regulations. Leaving aside possible "presumptions" explicitly introduced in the rules (and their legal admissibility),[69] the validity of the scientific foundations for sport regulations is part of the justification that sports organization must be able to adduce each time they purport to impose restrictions on athlete rights. Thus, in the *Chand* case, the scientific validity of the Regulations ought to be treated as a prerequisite for demonstrating that the discrimination is justified by legitimate goals. More precisely, the scientific validity must be demonstrated to establish the aptitude of the rule to achieve the legitimate goals it claims, within the proportionality assessment. While this does not represent a burden of proof *stricto sensu*, the sports organization carries the risk that no such scientific foundations can be demonstrated, since in that event the CAS panel will have to conclude that there is no indication that the regulations were apt to achieve their goal.

In sum, the manner in which the CAS panel in the *Chand* award appeared to simply endorse the Athlete's 'concession' made at the oral hearing that she had the burden of proof with respect to the lack of scientific validity of the Hyperandrogenism Regulations appears questionable. It is part of the mission of the adjudicatory body to allocate the burden of proof among the parties; all the more so when it comes to assessing the legal validity of a regulation, as opposed to establishing facts of the case. While parties may accept that certain facts of the case are undisputed, thereby de facto removing these issues from the scope of proof, the same ought not to be open to them for matters that relate to the proportionality of the regulations applied. Only the CAS panel can decide what will prevail in case it cannot be satisfied of the scientific validity of these foundations, regardless of the parties' respective positions.

12.4.2.5.3 Deference of a CAS Panel to Sports Organization's Discretion

The issue of deference is much discussed in CAS case law, particularly the question of whether sports organizations are entitled to a certain level of discretion based on their autonomy, in spite of the power of the CAS panel to review

[68]As described above, the standard of proof is less straightforward. In the *Pistorius* matter, the CAS panel considered that the standard should be by a balance of probability outside disciplinary matters.

[69]The 2015 WADA Code enshrines a new provision (Article 3.2.1) that explicitly presumes the scientific validity of the analytical tools used to produce analytical findings in Doping Control.

a dispute de novo on issues of fact and of law (Article R57 of the CAS Code). Despite the frequency with which it arises, the issue of deference is seldom accompanied by extensive analysis.

The *Chand* panel did not make explicit its findings on the issue of deference. However, the panel implicitly rejected the notion that it might interfere with a regulation only if it is "evidently and grossly" disproportionate.[70] This interpretation is in sync with recent CAS case law considering this issue in the anti-doping context. For anti-doping sanctions, the clear trend is that CAS panels will not defer to decisions made by the hearing panels of sports federations on the issue of proportionality, though that was not always the case. In the *Hardy* award, decided in 2010, the CAS panel proposed that the findings of a lower hearing body as to the proportionality of a sanction should not be interfered with unless they are "evidently and grossly" disproportionate to the offence.[71] This decision is still regularly relied upon by parties wishing to limit the CAS panel's power of review. CAS panels since the *Hardy* award, however, have consistently reached the conclusion that there is no true deference beyond the traditional self-restraint of a judicial body reviewing a well-reasoned decision rendered by a previous, specialized, hearing body.[72]

One exception tolerated by CAS panels relates to decisions issued by panels within a sports organizations composed of members with a certain level of scientific or specialized expertise. Even in this context, however, the CAS practice seems to be moving away from their past self-restraint on specialized issues. Recently CAS panels, for example the panel in the *Veerpalu* matter, have shown little hesitation to address even very technical and scientific issues.[73]

12.4.3 Scientific Validity, Discrimination, and Proportionality

12.4.3.1 CAS Award

The reasoning of the CAS panel with the goal of determining the validity of the Hyperandrogenism Regulations forms the essential part of the legal analysis in the

[70]For example, when discussing the framework of its proportionality analysis, the panel implicitly rejected the IAAF's argument that the Regulations should only be invalid should they be considered "evidently and grossly" disproportionate by finding that the principle of proportionality "applies notwithstanding the wide discretion given to a Federation to determine its affairs and regulations" Ibid., para 230.

[71]CAS 2009/A/1870, *WADA v. Hardy*, Award of 21 May 2010, para 125.

[72]CAS 2012/A/2804, *Kutrovsky v. ITF*, Award of 3 October 2012.

[73]Other recent examples include the CAS 2013/A/3437, *International Shooting Sport Federation (ISSF) v. WADA*, Award of 18 December 2014, where the panel found unconvincing the reasoning of WADA's Therapeutic Use Exemption (TUE) panel regarding the performance-enhancing effect of a substance on an athlete's body; and CAS 2014/A/3751, *XX v. WADA*, Award of 10 February 2015, where the CAS panel overturned a diagnosis made by a medical professional.

award. It is therefore useful to give the reader an overview of the entire reasoning, while keeping in mind that only a small (final) part of the reasoning ultimately proved relevant to the *ratio decidendi*.

12.4.3.1.1 Scientific Validity

The CAS panel's discussion surrounding the scientific validity of the Regulations focused on two key questions: (i) whether testosterone enhances performance (via the increase in lean body mass); and (ii) whether there is "a difference between exogenous and endogenous testosterone" in this respect.[74]

According to the panel, the parties agreed that lean body mass "contributes to strength and ultimately to sports performance",[75] but disputed the role of (endogenous) testosterone in developing lean body mass. The panel noted that one scientific study presented in the case, as interpreted by one of the Athlete's experts, suggested no correlation between testosterone and lean body mass, while "many studies" have found a correlation.[76] The Athlete's expert, a "renowned specialist" in human growth hormone, suggested that the difference in lean body mass (in post-puberty) men and women, is "not directly attributable" to testosterone since "growth hormone […] is also very influential".[77] However, the CAS panel placed more weight on the "scientific evidence" submitted by the IAAF than the "professional experience and hypothesis" relied upon by the Athlete,[78] concluding that the Athlete's evidence fell short of discharging her burden in this respect.

Another issue for discussion was whether testosterone is "an appropriate differentiating factor" between male and female athletic performance.[79] The IAAF's position was that while there "may be other contributing factors […] testosterone remains the most suitable".[80] The Athlete attempted to rebut this position by providing examples of "outliers", i.e., elite women athletes who are completely insensitive to testosterone,[81] and male athletes with "low levels of testosterone".[82] The CAS panel acknowledged that these outliers were "not sufficiently explained by the scientific evidence adduced",[83] but nevertheless concluded that the Athlete did not discharge her burden on this point either.[84]

---

[74]CAS 2014/A/3759, *Chand v. IAAF*, para 454.

[75]Ibid., para 454.

[76]Ibid., para 455.

[77]Ibid., para 460.

[78]Ibid., para 460.

[79]Ibid., para 462.

[80]Ibid., para 469.

[81]Ibid., para 464.

[82]Ibid., para 466.

[83]Ibid., para 472.

[84]Ibid., para 472.

As to the question of whether endogenous and exogenous testosterone impact lean body mass "and by extension sports performance" alike, the panel was not convinced by the Athlete's arguments. In the panel's view, "no single study has established, to an appropriate level of certainty, a scientific basis to come to a definitive conclusion one way or the other".[85] It then summarized the findings of the studies submitted and related expert testimony. In particular, it noted that of the women (over 30, according to a different section of the award[86]) that underwent "treatment" under the Hyperandrogenism Regulations, all experienced a decrease in performance, but the panel did not find that these results constituted a "scientifically based study," thus it was unable to draw any conclusions from the data. Since it had found that the Athlete bore the burden of proof (see Sect. 12.4.2.5.1, above), the panel concluded that the "Hyperandrogenism Regulations are reasonably based on such scientific and medical data and opinion as were available to the IAAF".[87]

12.4.3.1.2 Discrimination

Ms. Chand submitted that the Hyperandrogenism Regulations violate the antidiscrimination provisions "in the Olympic Charter, the IAAF Charter and international human rights law," since they discriminate on two bases: (i) a natural physical trait; and/or (ii) sex.[88]

Ms. Chand argued that the Hyperandrogenism Regulations are discriminatory because they prohibit participation in sports based on naturally occurring testosterone levels, while other physical traits do not lead to a similar prohibition. She described any performance-enhancing benefits from testosterone as a "natural genetic gift, which should not be viewed differently from other natural advantages derived from exceptional biological variation".[89] Noting that there is no other naturally occurring physical trait that serves as a basis to prohibit participation in sport, she maintained that there is "no principled or permissible reason for prohibiting a female athlete from competing because of an unusual natural genetic trait, even if that trait confers an advantage over fellow female competitors who lack that trait".[90]

The CAS panel noted that the parties were not in dispute that the Hyperandrogenism Regulations are "*prima facie* discriminatory" on two grounds. The first grounds applies between female and male athletes, namely it is "*prima facie* discriminatory to require female athletes to undergo testing for levels of endogenous testosterone when male

85 Ibid., para 474.
86 Ibid., para 248(d).
87 Ibid., para 488.
88 Ibid., para 112.
89 Ibid., para 113.
90 Ibid., para 113.

athletes do not".[91] The second applies among female athletes, since the rules place "restrictions on the eligibility of certain female athletes to compete on the basis of a natural physical characteristic".[92]

The CAS panel then turned to the consequences of this conclusion. According to the CAS panel, the "IOC Charter, the IAAF Constitution and the laws of Monaco" all prohibit discrimination and these "provisions are higher-ranking rules that prevail".[93] Thus, the CAS panel concluded that unless the "Hyperandrogenism Regulations are necessary, reasonable and proportionate," they would be invalid due to inconsistency with these higher-ranking rules.[94] The CAS panel explained that this approach is "consistent with the countervailing requirements for sport and is recognized in a wide range of domestic and international laws, including laws directed to the prohibition of discrimination generally".[95]

12.4.3.1.3 Proportionality

In the section of the award presenting the submissions of the parties, the CAS panel noted that "[t]he issue of proportionality arises both as a freestanding ground of challenge and in relation to the specific question of whether the IAAF can justify the discriminatory effect of the Hyperandrogenism Regulations […]".[96] Since the parties did not make submissions as to the laws of Monaco regarding proportionality, the panel held that: "the detrimental impact of a measure must be proportionate, in that it must not exceed that which is reasonably required in search of the justifiable aim".[97] At the outset of its analysis, it then reiterated that the "IAAF bears the burden of establishing on the balance of probabilities that the Hyperandrogenism Regulations are a proportionate means of achieving the legitimate objective of ensuring fairness in athletics competition".[98]

Ms. Chand submitted that the "harm caused by the application of the Hyperandrogenism Regulations is grossly disproportionate to any benefits the rules are designed to achieve".[99] In particular, Ms. Chand listed the following

[91] Ibid., para 448.

[92] Ibid., para 448.

[93] Ibid., para 449.

[94] Ibid., para 449.

[95] Ibid., para 450.

[96] Ibid., para 229.

[97] Ibid., para 230. Supporting its proposed framework, the CAS panel noted that "[t]his principle applies notwithstanding the wide discretion given to a Federation to determine its affairs and regulations. The Panel accepts the legitimate objective of the IAAF to organize competitive athletics to ensure fairness in athletic competition. It is legitimate and necessary to divide athletes into male and female categories. This is because male athletes have such an advantage over female athletes that competition between the sexes is not fair".

[98] Ibid., para 501.

[99] Ibid., para 231.

"harms" caused by the Hyperandrogenism Regulations: "(a) stigmatisation of female athletes caught by the Regulations; (b) serious damage to the self-esteem and gender-identity of female athletes with hyperandrogenism; (c) female athletes undergoing medical tests without fully informed consent; and (d) female athletes undergoing unnecessary medical procedures with serious long-term side effects".[100] In addition, she highlighted harm that female athletes incur from procedures that are not kept confidential, alluding to "numerous examples" of leaked identities to the press.[101] She referenced her own case as a "good illustration of the harm that the Hyperandrogenism Regulations are apt to cause".[102] In particular, she stressed the harm that she suffered from the leak of investigation to the press, and the harm she might have incurred had she undergone medical intervention.[103]

The IAAF focused its submissions on the manner in which the Hyperandrogenism Regulations respond to its "legitimate objective of protective fairness in competitive athletics by ensuring that elite female athletes are able to compete on a level playing field".[104] The IAAF, according to the award, sees the Hyperandrogenism Regulations as "necessary and proportionate means" to achieve this legitimate objective.[105] It proposed as a proper balance that the "restriction on a hyperandrogenic athlete's ability to compete must be weighed against the "*need to be fair...to the vast majority of female athletes who are within the (much lower) normal female range*".[106] More specifically, the IAAF's expert "stated that if women are to be treated as a '*protected class*' in athletics competitions for reasons of fairness, then the IAAF must police the sex divide '*to safeguard the promise of fair competition offered by the division of disciplines into sex-specific events*".[107] The IAAF saw it as an "*ethical obligation*" to maintain these categories of competition, given testosterone's performance-enhancing effects.[108]

The IAAF rejected the Athlete's submission that the Hyperandrogenism Regulations impermissibly discriminate based on sex, "because of the absence of any equivalent eligibility restriction on male athletes with unusually high endogenous testosterone".[109] In support of its stance, the IAAF pointed to its expert's tes-

[100]Ibid., para 231.
[101]Ibid., para 236.
[102]Ibid., para 240.
[103]Ibid., para 240.
[104]Ibid., para 242.
[105]Ibid., para 242.
[106]Ibid., para 244.
[107]Ibid., para 244.
[108]Ibid., para 244.
[109]Ibid., para 247.

timony, who stated "that he is unaware of any evidence of a strong correlation between male athletes with exceptional [...] testosterone levels and enhanced performance in sport".[110] He also noted that, unlike female athletes who "supported a regulation for hyperandrogenism," there is no similar support to be found for such a regulation in male competitions.[111]

In addition, the IAAF responded to a number of "disadvantages and risks identified by the Athlete".[112] Of note, it emphasized that the Hyperandrogenism Regulations do not raise doubts about the gender of those under its ambit, rather it "expressly acknowledge[s] the femaleness of the Athlete".[113] In addition, it rejected other arguments suggesting that the Hyperandrogenism Regulations stigmatize athletes, coerce medical intervention, circumvent informed consent to medical treatment, improperly propagate a western conception of femininity, breach confidentiality of the hyperandrogenic cases, noting that there have been over 30 cases, and no one knows the identity of these athletes.[114]

The CAS panel began its analysis by recognizing that the IAAF was in an "invidious position of having to reconcile the existence of a binary male/female system of athletics categorisation with the biological reality that sex in humans is a continuum with no clear or singular boundary between men and women".[115] The CAS panel accepted that this was a challenging endeavor that the IAAF undertook with good faith and diligence, endeavoring to "create a system of rules that are fair, objective and founded on the best available science".[116] It then turned to the practical application of the Hyperandrogenism Regulations, accepting that they "are administered in confidence and with care and compassion".[117] In support of this finding, it noted that athletes are given the "benefit of the doubt" although acknowledging that "this is not expressly reflected in the text of the Regulations".[118] The panel further noted that the Hyperandrogenism Regulations sometimes serve to reveal a "medical condition that requires treatment, which the IAAF then provides, to the benefit of the athlete concerned".[119] Finally, it acknowledged that the IAAF was open to the possibility of updating the Regulations to "protect the rights of the athletes who are subject to their provisions".[120]

---

[110]Ibid., para 247.

[111]Ibid., para 247.

[112]Ibid., para 248.

[113]Ibid., para 248(a).

[114]Ibid., para 248.

[115]Ibid., para 504.

[116]Ibid., para 505.

[117]Ibid., para 507.

[118]Ibid., para 507.

[119]Ibid., para 507.

[120]Ibid., para 507.

The panel then evaluated IAAF's "legitimate objective" in adopting the Hyperandrogenism Regulations. According to the CAS panel, the IAAF adopted the Regulations "to provide for fair competition and a level playing field within the female category".[121] It accepted that this was a legitimate objective. It also emphasized that the purpose of the Hyperandrogenism Regulations is not to "police the male/female divide".[122] The panel finally accepted that "levels of endogenous testosterone are a key biological indicator of the differences between male and females", but then reemphasized that testosterone levels are not being used for that purpose in the Hyperandrogenism Regulations. Rather, they are being used to create a "new category of ineligible female athletes within the female category".[123] Thus, in the CAS panel's view, its next step was to evaluate whether the Hyperandrogenism Regulations were an "effective and proportionate means of achieving that purpose".[124] The CAS panel held that this analysis was necessary for two reasons: (i) "the significant detrimental consequences for hyperandrogenic athletes"; and (ii) the Hyperandrogenism Regulations are discriminatory, both on the basis of sex and among females on the basis of a natural trait.[125]

The panel highlighted two key detriments that athletes experience due to the Hyperandrogenism Regulations. First, it found that it is "antithetical to the fundamental principle of Olympism" to prevent "some women from competing at all as a result of the natural and unmodified state of their body".[126] Second, it found that "conditioning their right to compete on undergoing medical intervention" is also antithetical to the fundamental principles of Olympism.[127] Again, the CAS panel reframed its analysis, stating that in light of these significant detriments, the Hyperandrogenism Regulations are only valid if "it is clearly established to be a necessary and proportionate means of achieving fair competition".[128]

In the eyes of the CAS panel, the "underpinning" of the Hyperandrogenism Regulations was that "some members of the female class have a competitive advantage over other members of the female class that is similar to the performance advantage enjoyed by male athletes".[129] The CAS panel saw in this "underpinning" an implicit assumption that "hyperandrogenic females enjoy a *significant performance advantage* over their nonhyperandrogenic peers, which outranks the influence of any other single genetic or biological factor, and which is of

[121] Ibid., para 508.
[122] Ibid., para 510.
[123] Ibid., para 511.
[124] Ibid., para 508.
[125] Ibid., para 508.
[126] Ibid., para 513.
[127] Ibid., para 513.
[128] Ibid., para 513.
[129] Ibid., para 517.

comparable significance (if not identical magnitude) to the performance advantage that males typically enjoy over females".[130]

The CAS panel found that the IAAF was unable to establish to the requisite standard of proof that the degree in performance enhancement going ahead with testosterone levels above the threshold set in the Regulations is significant. The CAS panel reasoned that this question was not answered by simply pointing to the difference in performance advantage between men and women, since there were other factors besides testosterone "that may also contribute to the significant male athletic advantage over females".[131] The CAS panel also found a study suggesting that the "over-representation of hyperandrogenic females in elite female population"[132] unpersuasive. It surmised that it provided "indirect evidence" that high levels of endogenous testosterone could enhance athletic performance, but emphasized that this study does not speak to the degree of the advantage.

Moreover, the CAS panel was not convinced that the medical examination provided for in the Regulations serve the purpose of adequately assessing the degree of the effect of testosterone on athletes' performance. The Hyperandrogenism Regulations only prohibit participation after both testosterone levels are tested, and a subsequent medical examination is conducted. The purpose of this medical assessment is to "give an assessment of the likely effect of the testosterone on the athlete's body".[133] However the CAS panel found that "[i]n light of the paucity of data concerning the magnitude of the performance advantage that hyperandrogenic females typically derive from enhanced androgen levels" the IAAF has not established that its medical examination enables "a reliable conclusion to be reached as to the degree of competitive advantage that results from a level of endogenous testosterone over 10 nmol/L in an athlete".[134]

Thus, the CAS panel found that it was "unable to conclude that the Hyperandrogenism Regulations fulfill their stated purpose," but allowed that this conclusion might be "because available data are not yet available".[135] Noting that IAAF carried the onus, to establish that the Hyperandrogenism Regulations fulfilled their stated purpose, it held that "[t]he IAAF has not established, on the balance of probabilities that the Hyperandrogenism Regulations apply only to exclude female athletes that are shown to have a competitive advantage of the same order as that of a male athlete".[136]

[130]Ibid., para 517.

[131]Ibid., para 520.

[132]Ibid., paras 523–524.

[133]Ibid., para 530.

[134]Ibid., para 530.

[135]Ibid., para 531.

[136]Ibid., para 531.

12.4.3.2 Comments

It is obvious from the award that the CAS panel extended ample efforts to reach a solution that would do justice both to the sports organization's concern to guarantee a level playing field in its sport, and to the harsh consequences entailed for female athletes.

Nevertheless, the case is a textbook example of the complexity created when CAS panels premise their analysis on the parties' submissions, without clearly delineating whether these submissions relate to the facts of the particular case, the general scientific background, the contents of the law, or the legal appreciation of the case. This complexity is all the more regrettable given that the CAS panel ultimately based its decision on a criterion (lack of proof that testosterone levels above the threshold give female athletes a competitive advantage over their opponent to a degree comparable to those of male athletes) that none of the parties specifically pleaded, nor perhaps even anticipated. Three aspects of the shortcomings that excessive reliance on the parties' submission creates are analyzed below.

12.4.3.2.1 Deference to the Parties' Agreement Beyond the Facts of the Dispute

Throughout its analysis, the CAS panel relied on the parties' positions and concessions to determine how issues should be solved, or whether an issue required addressing at all. This approach in effect prevented the CAS panel from setting out a clear legal framework for its analysis and results in a certain opacity in reading the award. To add to the opacity, the CAS panel did not adhere to a strict separation between factual background and legal analysis, as would normally be the case (and be desirable) for CAS awards. Instead, the award may discuss the same issue in part along with the "Parties' Submissions" and in part in the section on the merits. Likewise, the factual background of the case and the panel's findings can appear within the same section of the award.[137]

The deference to the parties' agreement on issues of law is apparent in the determination of the discriminatory nature of the Regulations, an issue solved in only three paragraphs in the part of the award devoted to the merits.[138] The panel

[137]The "Factual Background" section of the award was subdivided into three parts: (i)"Background Facts", (ii) "The Issues", and (iii) "The relevant regulations". The material in the "Background Facts" was true to its name, but the "Issues" section, while summarizing legal issues, also included "important facts about this particular case" that were not in dispute. Ibid., para 36. Background facts of the case were also presented under the section heading "[t]he circumstances of the Athlete's suspension", within the "Submissions of the Parties" section. This section, as mentioned above, also included findings made by the panel. As an additional example, the *Chand* panel made findings as to the legal framework it applied to the proportionality analysis in the award, para 230, which was also within the "Submissions of the Parties" section of the award.

[138]Ibid., paras 448–450. The CAS panel also addressed this issue in the "Submissions of the Parties" section, paras 117–118.

consistently used the terminology "accepts" in the context of fundamentally legal issues, i.e., the existence of discrimination (e.g., "the Athlete accepts that she bears the burden of proof in establishing unlawful discrimination"[139] or "[t]he IAAF accepts that the Hyperandrogenism Regulations are a sex-based eligibility restriction and therefore *prima facie* discriminatory on grounds of sex"[140]). This usage raises questions as to the legal relevance of the statements. Technically, the parties 'power to concede' certain aspects of their case pertains only to issues of fact, while issues of law are left for CAS panels to identify, discuss, and decide.[141] With respect to discrimination, however, the panel continued, interpreting the IAAF's 'acceptance' as a 'concession' that established the sex-based eligibility restriction was discriminatory. Moreover, the CAS panel did not analyze the contents of the laws of Monaco (declared applicable in addition to IAAF rules) on this issue, but simply noted that the Athlete "contended, and the IAAF did not submit to the contrary, that the IOC Charter, the IAAF Constitution and the laws of Monaco all provide that there shall not be discrimination".[142] It is thus unclear whether the arbitrators conducted a genuine reasoning on the issue of discrimination or whether they simply endorsed the parties' converging views.

Another aspect on which the CAS panel simply appeared to endorse a party's concession—this time on part of the Athlete—is the Athlete bearing the burden of proof with respect to the 'scientific validity' of the Hyperandrogenism Regulations. As previously explained, the burden of proof—assuming showing the validity of a regulation can be described as a burden of proof—for the validity of a legal regulation must be allocated by the CAS panel, not as a result of the parties' concessions (see Sect. 12.4.2.5.1). In the *Chand* award, however, the CAS panel gave no explanations to support its finding that the scientific validity for the Regulations was for the Athlete to disprove, other than to note that the Athlete had accepted this burden during the oral hearing.

12.4.3.2.2 Artificial Separation Between Scientific Validity and Proportionality Assessment

The panel's reliance on the Athlete's acceptance at the oral hearing of her carrying the burden of proof for the scientific validity of the Hyperandrogenism Regulations resulted in a seemingly artificial divide in the award between the assessment of 'scientific validity' of the foundations for the Regulations on the one hand, and their justification and proportionality on the other hand. It is nevertheless useful to examine both limbs of the assessment jointly, given the intrinsic connection between the two (see also Sect. 12.4.2.5.1).

[139]Ibid., para 107.

[140]Ibid., para 117.

[141]See, e.g., our discussion on the distinction between facts and law in Rigozzi et al. 2015a, para 6.

[142]CAS 2014/A/3759, *Chand v. IAAF,* para 449.

Under the first limb (i.e., scientific validity), the CAS panel posed the question of whether "there is a scientific basis in the use of testosterone as a marker for the purposes of the Hyperandrogenism Regulations".[143] On this issue, the burden of proof was on the Athlete (per her own acceptance) to show that there is no such scientific basis. The CAS panel thus found that testosterone can indeed be used as a marker, since the scientific evidence available was insufficient to shift the balance to either side, i.e. the so that the Athlete had not discharged her burden to a balance of probability.[144]

Under the second limb (i.e., justification for discriminatory effect/proportionality), the CAS panel assessed whether the testosterone marker as used in the Hyperandrogenism Regulations is a proportionate means of ensuring the stated objective of a level playing field. The CAS panel determined what they found to be the decisive factor, i.e., whether testosterone above the 10 nmol/L threshold gives female athletes a competitive advantage so significant that it outranks any other genetic or biological characteristic.[145] For this aspect, the burden of proof was declared (and accepted by the parties) to be on the IAAF. Since there was not sufficient scientific evidence available on this point either, the IAAF failed to discharge its burden, so the CAS panel had to declare that they could not uphold the validity of the Regulations.

In sum, without delving into the intricacies of the scientific issues considered, the outcome of the assessment was rather predictable if one considers the two limbs of the assessment as a whole. Since the CAS panel already had to fall back on the burden of proof with respect to whether endogenous testosterone levels are a reliable marker altogether for determining male versus female performance, it comes as little surprise that the IAAF was not able to discharge its burden that an elevated level of testosterone creates a sufficiently significant impact on such performance.

From a perspective of legal technique, the distinction between (i) whether testosterone is a relevant marker of performance, and (ii) whether the testosterone threshold set reflects a sufficiently significant performance advantage, appears rather artificial. Both aspects account jointly for the scientific foundations of the Hyperandrogenism Regulations. The fact that the former was affirmed and the latter denied is not solely related to the fact that there was insufficient scientific evidence on both issues, but that the Athlete happened to "accept" the burden of

---

[143]Ibid., para 499.

[144]Ibid., para 499: Note that the CAS panel erroneously declared itself "satisfied, to the requisite standard of proof, that there is a scientific basis in the use of testosterone as a marker". This is plainly in contradiction with the allocation of the burden of proof and the assessment that the CAS panel conducted: the assessment was whether the Athlete could establish that there is no such scientific basis.

[145]Ibid., para 517: In the words of the CAS panel: the "premise underpinning the Hyperandrogenism Regulations is therefore that some members of the female class have a competitive advantage over other members of the female class that is similar to the performance advantage enjoyed by male athletes".

proof on the 'scientific validity'. It is not clear how the CAS panel decided to draw the line between aspects that should be discussed as part of the scientific validity, as opposed to the aspects that should fall within the justification assessment. An imaginable reason for the line drawn is that it allowed the CAS panel to uphold at least the general pillars of the Hyperandrogenism Regulations (i.e., use of the testosterone marker), while still ruling in favor of the Athlete's participation in competition (i.e., lack of sufficiently demonstrated significance of the threshold set).

On a final note, the finding that the validity of the Hyperandrogenism Regulations could not be upheld based on the evidence on the record ended the CAS panel's inquiry, precluding the need to examine further elements of whether the discrimination was permissible. However, as discussed separately (see Sect. 12.4.5, below), the panel in the *Chand* award decided to issue an interim award seeking further evidence from the IAAF as to the question of proportionality, specifically as to the degree of advantage that testosterone affords hyperandrogenic athletes. Should the IAAF meet this burden, they would then demonstrate that the testosterone threshold set forth in the Regulations is apt to fulfill its goals. This would not necessarily mean, however, that the other limbs of the proportionality analysis are also fulfilled (see Sect. 12.4.3.1.3, above). In particular, the CAS panel would then still need to examine the questions of necessity, i.e., whether there are no equally effective but less intrusive means to achieve the same result. In other words, it is entirely possible that the IAAF could submit within the next two years sufficient evidence to discharge its burden of proof to the effect that the current testosterone threshold creates a sufficiently significant performance advantage, but the CAS panel would still refuse to uphold the validity of the Hyperandrogenism Regulations for reasons of unjust discrimination.

12.4.3.2.3 Failure to Look into the Ultimate Foundations for the Regulations

An aspect that is only addressed between the lines in the CAS award is the question of the justification for the male versus female separation as the key divide in athletics. The CAS panel was adamant that it was not in dispute among the parties that segregating males and females into separate categories is "appropriate" and that there "should be an objective criterion or criteria to police this divide".[146] It observed that "[i]t is clear that this may require policing and give rise to difficult decisions when nature does not divide into these categories so simply".[147]

Had the CAS panel not limited itself to the parties' dissenting points to guide its analysis, it might have usefully explored the implications of the separation itself and of its current modalities. Indeed, even if the CAS panel insisted that the Hyperandrogenism Regulations do not police the male versus female divide but create a form of 'third category' that does not fall within either category, the

[146]Ibid., para 510.

[147]Ibid., para 514.

justification for the Hyperandrogenism Regulations is ultimately conditioned by the need to remedy to the shortcomings inherent in the IAAF's choice to rely on a segregation between male and female as *a summa divisio*, and to use as a distinguishing criterion whether a person is a female as a matter of law. The panel continued that "there is no evidence before the Panel that legal recognition as a female varies in most countries other than reference by the parties to the fact that there are a small number of countries where a person's status as a male or female is determined exclusively by a process of self-identification".[148]

All these issues of law that constitute the very pillars for the need for a Hyperandrogenism Regulations were treated by the CAS panel as within the "context of accepted facts".[149] This view appears untenable. Whether the Regulations rely on the legal characterization of gender (or a different criterion), the applicable law to determine whether an athlete is male or female, and what this means in terms of different legal systems across the world, all these issues are not set of facts that parties to an individual dispute can simply agree upon. These issues are for the CAS panel to assess. It seems understandable that the CAS panel would not want to step into a minefield as treacherous as the justification for the male versus female divide in athletics. However, this point might well have led into farther-going reflection and it is unfortunate that it was not well identified as problematic in the award.

A system that seeks to police a divide that is based on an issue of law (whether someone is a female "as a matter of law") through a corrective factor that relies on a fact (the person's level of testosterone) is bound to create incoherence and injustice at the fringes. This is especially the case if the corrective factor acts to exclude athletes from the category into which they fit as a matter of law, without offering them the option to compete in the category in which the corrective factor would place them. Assuming that there is no prospect that gender be abandoned altogether as the primary division in athletics, it would be worthwhile exploring to what extent a definition of 'gender' specific to sport—comparable to the 'sports nationality' used for participation in international sport—could not ultimately do greater justice to the singularity of human bodies. Other alternative solutions, including abandoning the divide between male and female altogether, have been proposed in the past.[150] The IOC issued a statement after holding a Consensus Meeting on Sex Reassignment and Hyperandrogenism of its Medical & Scientific Commission in November 2015, recommending that "to avoid discrimination, if not eligible for female competition the athlete should be eligible to compete in male competition" (see also Sect. 12.4.5.2).[151]

---

[148]Ibid., para 510.

[149]Ibid., para 509.

[150]For an overview and references, see Sánchez et al. 2013.

[151]IOC (2015) IOC Consensus Meeting on Sex Reassignment and Hyperandrogenism November 2015. http://www.olympic.org/Documents/Commissions_PDFfiles/Medical_commission/2015-11_ioc_consensus_meeting_on_sex_reassignment_and_hyperandrogenism-en.pdf. Accessed 14 April 2016.

12.4.4 No Disguised Impermissible Doping Sanction

The CAS panel dismissed the Athlete's argument that the Hyperandrogenism Regulations operate as impermissible "disguised doping rules"[152] that impose "a doping sanction on female athletes who fall foul of the endogenous testosterone limit".[153]

12.4.4.1 CAS Award

12.4.4.1.1 Athlete's Position

Ms. Chand submitted that the Hyperandrogenism Regulations are incompatible with the WADA Code in two respects: (i) they have the effect of impermissibly adding endogenous testosterone to the prohibited list enacted by the WADA applicable in doping matters, and (ii) they serve as an unauthorized additional sanction to those provided in Article 10.

Suggesting that the Hyperandrogenism Regulations "share the same rationales and consequences as the rules on exogenous testosterone"—i.e., protecting a level playing field in sports—the Athlete contended on the first aspect that the Regulations represented a breach of the IAAF's obligations under Article 23.2.2 of the WADA Code. This provision requires Signatories to implement a series of WADA Code Articles "without any substantive changes," among those Article 4.3.3, which states that WADA's Prohibited List is final and cannot be challenged.[154]

As to the second aspect, the Athlete focused on the similar consequences and perception of the Hyperandrogenism Regulations, compared to the WADA Code sanctioning regime. She characterized the Hyperandrogenism Regulations as effectively imposing a "lifetime ban from all athletic competition" on those athletes who decline "the medical interventions necessary to resume competing".[155]

While the Athlete acknowledged that the Hyperandrogenism Regulations contained aspects of both an eligibility rule and a sanction, she argued that two factors—"consequences of their application and athletes' general perception"—meant they "should be treated as a disciplinary sanction".[156] She submitted that the "fact

[152]Ibid., para 358.

[153]Ibid., para 357.

[154]Ibid., para 358.

[155]Ibid., para 359.

[156]Ibid., para 362. In support of her position, she referenced two previous CAS cases that struck down (ostensibly eligibility) rules that impermissibly interfered with the substance of the WADA Code: CAS 2011/O/2422, *USOC v. IOC*, Award of 4 October 2011 and CAS 2011/A/2658, *BOA v. WADA*, Award of 30 April 2012.

that the consequence of exceeding the 10 nmol/L testosterone threshold—a lifetime prohibition on competing—is more severe than the available sanction for a first doping offence" per the WADA Code.[157]

12.4.4.1.2 IAAF's Position

The IAAF submitted that Hyperandrogenism Regulations are properly characterized as an eligibility rule, not as a disciplinary rule. The IAAF distinguished the rules discussed in the CAS cases cited by the Athlete in support of her position, suggesting that they were "clearly doping-related" as they "sought to remedy what was perceived to be an excessively lenient approach under the WADA Code".[158] In contrast, the Hyperandrogenism Regulations are, according to the IAAF, "entirely different in character" in that they "do not add a further punishment on top of the prescribed WADA Code sanctions for an anti-doping rule violation; nor do they create a new anti-doping rule violation".[159] Instead, the IAAF insisted that the Hyperandrogenism Regulations "establish an eligibility condition equivalent in character to a boxing weight-limit".[160] In support of this characterization, it argued that "[e]xceeding the specified level of testosterone is not treated as doping or any other form of misconduct. On the contrary, as soon as an athlete meets the eligibility criteria she is permitted to compete".[161]

12.4.4.1.3 The CAS Panel's Analysis

The CAS panel held that the Athlete failed to meet her burden to establish "that the Hyperandrogenism Regulations are a disguised doping sanction that is incompatible with the provisions of the WADA Code".[162] The panel noted that this issue was only addressed "briefly" during the hearing, and noted that the Athlete's counsel "conceded that this ground was the weakest aspect of the Athlete's case" and was addressed "only briefly" at the hearing.[163]

In the panel's view the Athlete confounded anti-doping sanctions and eligibility rules. Eligibility rules, as described by the CAS panel, are those that "establish objective conditions that regulate the ability of individual athletes to participate in particular categories of athletics competition".[164] While these

[157] CAS 2014/A/3759, *Chand v. IAAF*, para 362.

[158] Ibid., para 365.

[159] Ibid., para 365.

[160] Ibid., para 365.

[161] Ibid., para 365.

[162] Ibid., para 541.

[163] Ibid., para 540.

[164] Ibid., para 542.

> may operate to prevent a particular individual from competing in a particular category (or, in some cases, in any category). … [eligibility rules] do not involve any element of punishment or censure; they are not framed in terms of 'violations' of prohibited conduct; and they do not serve any retributive or deterrent purpose.[165]

Anti-doping sanctions, in contrast, "seek to punish and deter certain prohibited conduct, namely the deliberate or inadvertent ingestion of performance enhancing substances".[166] The CAS panel emphasized that anti-doping regulations only limit the "distorting effect" of exogenous substances, thus 'endogenous doping' would be an oxymoron.

In support of its finding that the Hyperandrogenism Regulations were an eligibility rule and not a form of anti-doping control, the CAS panel listed the following factors:

- *Wording*: They are not framed in sanctioning terms, i.e., "prohibited conduct and sanctions for corresponding 'violations'".[167]
- *Effect*: They do not "impose penalties on athletes who have particular levels of naturally occurring testosterone" nor do they "involve any reprimand or censure," noting in particular the requirement for the confidentiality of the outcomes of any examination conducted under the Hyperandrogenism Regulations.[168]
- *Operation*: The panel acknowledged that the Hyperandrogenism Regulations do prevent athletes with testosterone levels above a certain threshold from competing, however: "those individuals can immediately resume competing as soon [as] they meet the eligibility criteria".[169]

The CAS panel also remained unpersuaded that the Hyperandrogenism Regulations effectively added endogenous testosterone to WADA's Prohibited List. In support of this position, it listed categories of substances and methods prohibited, and then concluded that "[t]he Hyperandrogenism Regulations do not purport to modify, supplement or expand that list in any way".[170]

12.4.4.2 Comments

The CAS panel rejected Ms. Chand's argument that the Hyperandrogenism Regulations serve as an disguised doping sanction. However the discussion leaves untouched the deeper issue of whether sports organizations can target via eligibility rules circumstances related to performances of the human body that they are not allowed to address as part of their anti-doping efforts.

---

[165]Ibid., para 542.

[166]Ibid., para 543.

[167]Ibid., para 544.

[168]Ibid., para 544.

[169]Ibid., para 544.

[170]Ibid., para 545.

12.4.4.2.1 No 'Impermissible' Doping Sanction

In support of her argument, the Athlete referenced two cases in which a purported eligibility rule was found to be invalid on the basis that it impermissibly interfered with the WADA Code: *USOC v. IOC*[171] and *BOA v. WADA*.[172] In the *USOC v. IOC* case, the US Olympic Committee challenged an IOC regulation that prohibited athletes from participating in the next edition of the Olympic games, if they had committed an anti-doping rule violation implicating an ineligibility period of six months or longer. The CAS panel in *USOC v. IOC* held that this rule, which the IOC argued was an "eligibility rule," was "properly characterised" as a disciplinary measure.[173] Moreover, since the rule imposed additional punishment on conduct already sanctioned under the WADA Code regime, it was in conflict with the provision of the WADA Code that precludes sports organizations from adopting rules that effectuate a substantive change to the WADA regime, and was therefore invalid. The *BOA v. WADA* award treated a similar rule adopted by the British Olympic Association with—broadly—identical reasoning and outcomes.[174]

The scope of the Hyperandrogenism Regulations creates a convincing distinguishing factor between the situation before the *Chand* panel on the one hand, and the rules that were subjected to the CAS panels in the *USOC* and *BOA* cases on the other hand. In both of the *USOC* and *BOA* CAS awards¸ the disputed rules targeted the very same behavior that had been established to violate the WADA Code. In contrast, the disputed rules in *Chand v. IAAF* targets a biological 'trait' in Athletes, which as the *Chand* panel correctly highlighted, technically falls outside the scope of anti-doping regulation. Thus, no issue of *ne bis in idem* nor double jeopardy arises, since there is no direct conflict with the WADA Code in the sense of imposing additional consequences for a conduct already punished as constitutive of doping.

In the *Chand* matter, the circumstances that led to her coming under the scrutiny of sports authorities under the Hyperandrogenism Regulations, did not—and could never—lead to her being suspected of doping. Anti-doping rules do not target endogenous production of a substance by the human body, quite to the contrary.[175] Considerable resources are invested in ensuring that sports organizations

[171]CAS 2011/O/2422, *USOC v. IOC*.

[172]CAS 2011/A/2658, *BOA v. WADA*.

[173]CAS 2011/O/2422, *USOC v. IOC,* para 8.19.

[174]In CAS 2011/A/2658, *BOA v. WADA*, the rule at issue was a BOA bye-law, declaring that athletes who committed an anti-doping rule violation would be ineligible for consideration as a member of the Great Britain Olympic Team. The *BOA v. WADA* CAS panel at para 8.39, found that the bye-law had the "effect of changing the sanctions and their effect", thus the BOA (like the IOC), was also in breach of its duty to implement Article 10 without substantive change.

[175]There may exceptions in which the endogenous production is artificially altered through use of a Prohibited Method, i.e. as may occur through blood transfusion.

are able to appropriately discriminate, at the level of detection, between the presence of exogenously administered and endogenously produced testosterone.[176]

12.4.4.2.2 The Ultimate Issue—Extension of the Control on Human Performance

In spite of the fact that they target different circumstances, clear parallels can be drawn between the underlying policy justifications for the Hyperandrogenism Regulations and for anti-doping regulations. Creating 'equal chances' (*Chancengleichheit*) among competitors is one of the major rationales of the fight against doping and has inspired many aspects of the WADA Code.[177] Likewise, the *Chand* award refers on multiple occasions to the Hyperandrogenism Regulations' "legitimate objective of protecti[ng] fairness in competitive athletics by ensuring that elite female athletes are able to compete on a level playing field".[178] It is also notable that the discourse surrounding the application of the Regulation uses terminology borrowed from the WADA Code. Throughout the *Chand* award, the Hyperandrogenism Regulations are described in terms encountered also in connection with doping offences.[179]

With respect to the nature of the consequences resulting from the application of the Hyperandrogenism Regulations, the *Chand* panel found that these Regulations "do not impose penalties" nor do they "involve any reprimand or censure." This may be true insofar as no direct blame is placed on the athlete for being above the applicable threshold, nor is there a direct moral reproach involved in the ban from competing.[180] The reproach behind the Hyperandrogenism Regulations is more subtle, and results from the options offered to the athlete to be admitted back to competition. The Hyperandrogenism Regulations delineate the manner in which an athlete can "fix" her abnormal characteristic (i.e., by undergoing medical treatment to bring back her testosterone levels below the threshold) in order to resume participation in her athletic discipline, which colors the Regulation system with an

[176]This is currently achieved through a combination of analytical methods described in the WADA Technical Document on Endogenous Anabolic Androgenic Steroids (TD2014EAAS), with the key method if Isotope Ratio Mass Spectrometry (IRMS), an analytical methods used to differentiate exogenous from endogenous origin of a substance (TD2014IRMS).

[177]Kaufmann-Kohler G, Rigozzi A and Malinverni G (2003) Legal opinion on the conformity of certain provisions of the draft World Anti-Doping Code with commonly accepted principles of international law, para 28. https://wada-main-prod.s3.amazonaws.com/resources/files/kaufmann-kohler-full.pdf. Accessed 20 February 2016.

[178]CAS 2014/A/3759, *Chand v. IAAF,* para 242.

[179]As way of examples, when Ms. Chand was prohibited from competing, the panel described it as "provisionally suspended" Ibid., para 27; and the AFI speaks of notifying the Athlete of her "disqualification" Ibid., para 24.

[180]Compare in CAS 2011/O/2422, *USOC v. IOC,* para 8.15: "[o]nce the [Regulation] is used to bar the participation of an athlete, the effect of the Regulation is disqualification … and would be undeniably disciplinary in nature".

undesirable hue. The Regulations exercise a form of coercion on the athlete: if she fails to undergo medical treatment, she is to blame for her predicament. This is exacerbated by the extremely sensitive and emotionally charged context of gender identity in which the Regulations operate.

In sum, if one can agree with the CAS panel's reasoning that the Hyperandrogenism Regulations do not amount to an impermissible 'additional' doping sanction, one should still acknowledge that they affect athletes in a manner that is comparable to the finding of a doping offence. The CAS panel, however, failed to enter this deeper debate of whether sports organizations are free to decide which traits inherent to the diversity of human bodies can lead to exclusion from sport.

There are good reasons for which anti-doping regulations are confined to circumstances of exogenously administered substances and methods. It is generally accepted in the context of anti-doping that athletes cannot be made responsible for substances naturally produced by their body. The substances are part of their natural characteristics that may in fact account for an important part of their talent and success in their sport. Thus, the WADA Code relies on an athlete's "personal duty to ensure that no Prohibited Substance enters his or her body" (Article 2.1.1), and provides that special criteria be established "for the evaluation of Prohibited Substances that can also be produced endogenously" (Article 2.1.4) to delimit the anti-doping rule violation.

The Hyperandrogenism Regulations extend the prerequisites for participating in organized sport to inborn characteristics. Here, an entire category of female athletes is expected to undergo (potentially) serious treatment altering their hormonal system without clear medical indication, only to be allowed to exercise their sports activities, based on a characteristic that has not even been clearly established to make a significant difference in their performance, at least not compared to other natural interindividual variability. As acknowledged in the award, these forced interventions on a human body are in conflict with the "spirit of sport" and the essence of Olympism identified in the WADA Code as the intrinsic value of sport, which the WADA Code describes specifically as "the pursuit of human excellent through the dedicated perfection of each person's natural talent" (preamble to the WADA Code).

Nor does the CAS panel's reliance on the significance of the degree of performance enhancement derived from a natural trait provide any further level of comfort. The CAS panel concluded that the Regulations would be justified only if the IAAF could establish that the degree of performance enhancement was significant, which is a risky path to take. If one accepts the discretion of sports authorities to go down this path no principle emerges from the *Chand* award that would guide when efforts to standardize human performance should cease. Even if one accepts that testosterone levels might be the 'best' indicator of exceptional sports performance, it does not follow that it is the only significant indicator. Indeed, if the 'significance' of the trait is the justifying factor, one fails to see why the CAS panel's reasoning should not also prohibit from competition athletes with other rare naturally occurring traits that significantly contribute to performance, such as aerobic capacity (VO_2 max),[181] red blood cell count[182] or even the length of an achilles tendon;[183] traits that have all contributed to writing the legends of modern sport.[184]

It is hardly imaginable that this sort of logic, i.e., culling the (naturally occurring) outliers for the sake of 'fair' sport, could be extended to the men's division without drastically altering the conception of 'sport'. In the CAS panel's reasoning one is not far from perceiving behind the focus on hyperandrogenism a form of 'idealized' view that men are inherently superior to women in athletics, and that a woman is supposed to produce the level of performance that a 'standard' woman body is expected to deliver. Viewed from this angle, it is not surprising that the Regulations are often perceived to be unfairly repressive for female athletes. As previously discussed (see Sect. 12.4.3.2.3), at no point did the CAS panel question the fundamental pillar for the Hyperandrogenism Regulations, which is the divide between male and female categories and the fact that this divide is fixed by the person's gender as a matter of law.

12.4.5 Rendering of an 'Interim' Award

12.4.5.1 CAS Award

At the end of its analysis, the panel reached the conclusion that the IAAF had "not discharged its burden of establishing that the criteria in the Hyperandrogenism

---

[181]Tour de France champion cyclist Chris Froome recently released biometric data relating to his aerobic capacity, i.e., VO_2 max, that according to Phillip Bell, a scientist involved in the test, placed him "close to what we believe are the upper limits for VO_2 peak in humans". Austen I, Chris Froome releases test results but does little to silence his critics, 3 December 2015. http://www.nytimes.com/2015/12/04/sports/cycling/chris-froome-releases-test-results-but-does-little-to-silence-his-critics.html?_r=0. Accessed 14 April 2016.

[182]Finnish cross-country skiing legend, Eero Mäntyranta, a 7-time Olympic medallist who placed in over 500 races, was reported to have a genetic mutation causing a hypersensitivity to EPO that led to a red blood cell count "measured up to 65 percent higher than that of an average man". Epstein 2013, p. 284. It should also be noted that the UCI previously did enforce a "no-start rule" that prohibited a rider from competition for 15 days if certain blood parameters exceeded a set threshold. The rule was designed to reduce the health-risk from EPO use among cyclists and was repealed after a test for exogenously administered EPO and the athlete blood passport program was introduced. Marty D, Nicholson P and Haas U (2015) Cycling independent reform commission: report to the president of the Union Cycliste Internationale. http://www.uci.ch/mm/Document/News/CleanSport/16/87/99/CIRCReport2015_Neutral.pdf. paras 102–103 & 117. Accessed 14 April 2016.

[183]Part of the success of Donald Thomas, a high jumper from the Bahamas, who advanced to the finals in the World Championships within eight months of starting his high-jumping career, has been attributed to his "uncharacteristically long" achilles tendons. Length (and stiffness) of achilles tendons are said to be important for jumping. Epstein 2013, p. 32.

[184]This is all the more true given that the case did not address the (almost inevitable) possibility that the relative significance of testosterone compared to other factors underlying exceptional 'performance' is likely to vary significantly across the many disciplines falling under the umbrella of athletics.

Regulations are necessary and proportionate to pursue the legitimate objective of regulating eligibility to compete in female athletics to ensure fairness in athletic competition".[185] Hence, the panel continued by stating that they were "unable to uphold the validity of the Regulations".[186] In light of its findings, the panel decided to issue a decision referred to an 'interim award'.

In its operative part, this interim award declares the Hyperandrogenism Regulations "suspended" for a period of two years. Within this period, the IAAF will be entitled to "submit further written evidence to the CAS concerning the magnitude of the performance advantage that hyperandrogenic females enjoy over other females as a result of their abnormally high androgen levels".[187] If the IAAF does opt to submit further evidence, "the Panel will issue further directions enabling the Athlete to respond to that evidence and listing the matter for a further hearing for the Panel to consider whether that evidence is sufficient to establish the validity of the Regulations".[188] In the event no evidence were to be filed within the two-year window, or in the event that the IAAF should declare at any time to the CAS office that it does not intend to file any such evidence, the Hyperandrogenism Regulations "shall be declared void".[189]

12.4.5.2 Comments

The logical outcome of the CAS panel's findings that it was unable to uphold the validity of the Regulations based on the evidence on the record would have been for the panel to prepare a final award. The legal consequences drawing from the application of the burden of proof should put an end to the dispute. However, the panel took a surprising and unusual option, by rendering a decision they referred to an 'interim award' instead.

From a perspective of legal technique, it is not clear what the award is intended to amount to under general principles of international arbitration. The solution chosen by the CAS panel seems to have emerged in a completely unanticipated manner. None of the parties sought an interim award in the request for relief, nor are there any indications that the parties even contemplated this option. Clearly, the CAS panel did not intend for this 'interim award' to be 'final' insofar as the IAAF was invited to file further evidence. Further, the CAS panel kept open the option to convene a new hearing—demonstrating that the arbitrators assumed the CAS panel would remain formally constituted until one of the options described in the dispositive part of the award concretizes.

---

[185] CAS 2014/A/3759, *Chand v. IAAF*, para 536.

[186] Ibid., para 548.

[187] Ibid., para 548.

[188] Ibid., para 548.

[189] Ibid., para 548.

An 'interim award' is typically a decision rendered in the course of the proceedings, to address a procedural objection or resolve a preliminary issue before addressing the merits of the matter (e.g., a ruling on jurisdiction). In its substance, the dispositive part of the *Chand* award resembles more closely a form of order granting provisional measures (suspension of the prohibition to compete and the validity of the Regulations), coupled with an evidentiary measure taken on the panel's own initiative, i.e., a request for additional evidence directed at the party bearing the burden of proof.

While these two options are theoretically available to arbitration panels under the Swiss *lex arbitrii* applicable in CAS arbitration, in this matter the time limit (two years) could arguably be regarded as constituting a denial of justice. Indeed, if the award is truly to be characterized as an 'interim award' as described by the CAS panels, no appeal against this award is admissible before the Swiss Supreme Court under the Swiss Private International Law Act (Article 190 para 3).[190] The award does not acquire a *res iudicata* effect and cannot be enforced, even though it binds the panel itself (as opposed to a mere procedural order).[191]

Seen from this perspective, the interim award seems difficult to reconcile with the principle of legal certainty that judicial decisions are to bring in a concrete dispute opposing parties with an interest in the outcome. In particular, even though the decision was largely presented in the media as a victory for the affected athlete,[192] in reality it leaves Ms. Chand in a legally questionable state of limbo during the two years following the award.

One fails to see why the CAS panel—insofar as they considered having the power to make findings with respect to the validity of the Regulations themselves—could not have simply declared the current regulation null and void. After all, the CAS Code provides for a clearly delineated time limit during which evidence must be provided. The IAAF could in any event enact a new set of regulations relying on new evidence, either before or after the (somehow arbitrary) two-year time limit set by the *Chand* panel.

The IOC's reaction to the interim award rendered in the *Chand* matter shows that little progress was made in resolving the dispute over the validity of the Hyperandrogenism Regulations. In November 2015, the IOC Medical & Scientific Commission reaffirmed its position by insisting on the need to have rules in place "for the protection of women in sport and the promotion of the principles of fair competition." The statement also encourages the IAAF, with support of other

---

[190]Only an appeal for grounds of irregular composition of the tribunal or lack of jurisdiction could be filed, which would not be of relevance for the present matter.

[191]Kaufmann-Kohler and Rigozzi 2015, paras 7.105–7.106.

[192]See, e.g., Branch J, Dutee Chand, Female sprinter with high testosterone level, wins right to compete, 27 July 2015. http://www.nytimes.com/2015/07/28/sports/international/dutee-chand-female-sprinter-with-high-male-hormone-level-wins-right-to-compete.html. Accessed 14 April 2016; Grégoire M, Réhabilitation de Dutee Chand: "Une victoire pour toutes les femmes de l'athlétisme", 28 juillet 2015. http://www.liberation.fr/sports/2015/07/28/rehabilitation-de-dutee-chand-une-victoire-pour-toutes-les-femmes-de-l-athletisme_1355262. Accessed 14 April 2016.

sports organizations, "to revert to CAS with arguments and evidence to support the reinstatement of its hyperandrogenism rules." The statement immediately attracted criticism—both as to the modalities of its adoption and as to its contents—on part of circles close to Ms. Chand's defence and opposed to hyperandrogenism regulations.[193] The CAS award does not seem to have altered either camp's position. This may be in part a side effect of the panel's decision to opt for an interim award, but also demonstrates more generally the limitations on the power of law and judicial authorities to resolve disputes of such ethical and ideological dimension.

12.5 Conclusion

In the *Chand* award, both the case of *Veerpalu v. FIS* and *Pistorius v. IAAF* were cited as precedents in connection with proof (see Sect. 12.4.2.5.1). Issues related to burden and standard of proof often form the core aspects of disputes related to the requirements for participating in sports competition, especially when these conditions depend on the stated goal of organized sport to operate based on a level playing field. The parallel between these cases can be expanded into a broader reflection on difficulties of setting up regulations that seek to categorize or constrain the athlete body, or indeed the human body in general. Together, the three cases demonstrate the limits of the input that scientific state of knowledge can provide when it comes to drawing the line between normality and abnormality in human physiology for purposes of meeting the Olympic ideals in sport.

The three types of disputes reflect different facets of elite sport struggling with creating a level playing field in the face of the singularity of the human organism. Doping cases such as the *Veerpalu* matter generally illustrate the concern of the regulators in sport to prevent an 'average' athlete from gaining an illegitimate advantage over his or her opponent by 'artificial' means. The *Pistorius* matter brings into the spotlight attempts for allowing athletes with an initial handicap to compensate that handicap through means of technology, while avoiding that this compensation should ultimately result in giving the athlete an unfair edge over nonhandicapped competitors. The *Chand* award, finally, raises the issue of an athlete's intrinsic right to exploit a superior natural physical ability or characteristic, versus the concern to guarantee a minimum degree of uncertainty on the outcome of a competition within a category of competitors.

Boundaries between natural assets, medically indicated interventions and improper human enhancement are extremely difficult to set, and always involve

[193] Kidd B, Karkazis K and Mitra P, Open letter to Thomas Bach and Members of the IOC, 9 February 2016. http://www.sportsintegrityinitiative.com/wp-content/uploads/2016/02/open-letter-ioc-12-feb-2016-1.pdf. Accessed 14 April 2016.

a component of value judgment or considerations of sports policy. Notably, in the *Chand* case, the assessment was conditioned from the outset by the seemingly unshakeable assumption—shared by all parties—that the distinction between male and female is to remain the *summa divisio* in athletics. Likewise, in the case of Oscar Pistorius, the whole debate was implicitly overshadowed by the image of a future cyborg-athlete whose performance would be primarily achieved through technological enhancement, thus destroying the myth of victory obtained through sweat and tears, supported by the Olympic spirit and the motto "citius, altius, fortius."

References

Epstein D (2013) The sports gene: inside the science of extraordinary athletic performance. Penguin, New York

Kaufmann-Kohler G, Rigozzi A (2015) International arbitration: law and practice in Switzerland. Oxford University Press, Oxford

Mavromati D, Reeb M (2015) The code of the Court of Arbitration for Sport: commentary, cases and materials. Kluwer Law International, Alpen aan den Rijn

Rigozzi A, Viret M, Wisnosky E (2015a) Breaking down the process for determining a basic sanction under the 2015 World Anti-Doping Code. Int Sports Law J 15:3–48

Rigozzi A, Viret M, Wisnosky E (2015b) Switzerland: anti-doping reports. Int Sports Law Rev (3) 54–56

Sánchez F, José Martínez-Patiño M, Vilain E (2013) The New Policy on Hyperandrogenism in Elite Female Athletes is not about "Sex Testing. J Sex Res 50:112–115

Viret M (2016) Evidence in anti-doping at the intersection of science & law. T.M.C. Asser Press, The Hague

Author Biography

Marjolaine Viret is an attorney-at-law and post-doctoral researcher. She is currently collaborating on a research project supported by the Swiss National Science Foundation to create a commentary of the 2015 World Anti-Doping Code.

Emily Wisnosky is an attorney-at-law and doctoral researcher. She is currently collaborating on a research project supported by the Swiss National Science Foundation to create a commentary of the 2015 World Anti-Doping Code.

Chapter 13
CAS 2014/A/3474, *Clube de Regatas do Flamengo v. Confederaçao Brasileira de Futebol (CBF) & Superior Tribunal de Justiça Desportiva (STJD)*, Award of 5 October 2015

Juan de Dios Crespo and Paolo Torchetti

Abstract The jurisdiction of the Court of Arbitration for Sport is established in Article R47 of the CAS Code. The early jurisprudence established that Article R47 required that federative statutes explicitly recognize CAS jurisdiction to retain competence as an appeal court over their decisions. Here the CAS has consistently applied the doctrine of direct jurisdiction. Since the development of that jurisprudence, the doctrine of indirect jurisdiction has developed, namely in the *Pizarro* and *Flamengo* cases. Indirect jurisdiction is established in the CAS where national federation rules refer to or incorporate applicable international federation rules that explicitly recognize the jurisdiction of the CAS where the subsidiary regulations do not. The doctrine of indirect jurisdiction, however, does have some outer limits where it has not been recognized as applicable to appeals of the decisions regarding Financial Fair Play licensing decisions nor to decisions of the Fédération Internationale de l'Automobile. This article seeks to review the jurisprudence of the CAS with respect to its jurisdiction, demonstrate that the traditionally rigid interpretation of its jurisdiction has evolved in order to recognize the principle of indirect jurisdiction, and that in some cases CAS jurisdiction is recognized where a complex set of regulations requires a sophisticated analysis such as in the *Flamengo* case.

Keywords Jurisdiction · CAS · Direct jurisdiction · Indirect jurisdiction · *Pizarro* and *flamengo* cases · Financial fair play · Fédération internationale de l'automobile · Sports arbitration

J. de Dios Crespo · P. Torchetti (✉)
Ruiz-Huerta and Crespo Abogados, Valencia, Spain
e-mail: ptorchetti@ruizcrespo.com

J. de Dios Crespo
e-mail: jddcrespo@ruizcrespo.com

A. Duval and A. Rigozzi (eds.), *Yearbook of International Sports Arbitration 2015*,
DOI 10.1007/978-94-6265-129-6_13

Contents

13.1 Introduction

Traditionally the CAS has held that a jurisdictional clause delineating its authority to resolve a legal dispute requires its explicit recognition. Ideally, jurisdictional clauses would clearly set out in unambiguous terms which arbitral panel has authority to resolve a particular dispute.

Unfortunately, there are countless examples within the international sports law context where jurisdictional clauses do not clearly identify the competent arbitral panel. The clause may be worded unclearly or in an unintelligible manner. It is also possible that national and international federation rules may contradict each other, making it difficult to understand which judicial body has jurisdiction. In some cases, the complex and fractioned world of the international sports pyramid contributes to the confusion.

The result is that the legal basis conferring jurisdiction on the CAS may not always be so direct. It may be necessary to review and apply several federation statutes to determine the appropriate jurisdiction. In this sense, the doctrine of indirect jurisdiction generally refers to those cases where there is no explicit jurisdictional clause in the relevant statute but where jurisdiction of the CAS is recognized by reference to another statute. It is this reference to another external statute that ultimately recognizes the indirect jurisdiction of the arbitration panel.

Most recently the CAS had the opportunity to consider this issue of indirect jurisdiction in CAS 2014/A/3474, *Clube de Regatas do Flamengo v. Confederaçao Brasileira de Futebol ('CBF') & Superior Tribunal de Justiça Desportiva ('STJD').*

In this case, the player Andre Clarindo Dos Santos received a one match suspension for his behaviour in the final of the 2013 Copa do Brasil. Santos subsequently played in the next match and the Brazilian authorities sanctioned his club, Flamengo, for fielding an ineligible player. Flamengo appealed the national decision to the CAS, despite the incidence that the CFB statutes do not explicitly confer appeal jurisdiction to the Lausanne-based arbitration body. In rendering the decision, the CAS Panel decided that appellate jurisdiction can be conferred on the CAS in cases where the national statutes do not directly refer to CAS appeal process, but where national statutes indirectly incorporate international federation statutes that refer to the appeal powers of the CAS.

The result is that in this case Flamengo successfully argued that the doctrine of indirect jurisdiction is indeed a legitimate method in recognizing an appeal route to the CAS. This doctrine, however, is not universally applicable and depends on the precise wording of both the national and international federation rules.

Therefore the purpose of this work is to analyze various jurisdictional clauses and the CAS jurisprudence regarding jurisdiction. The authors will discuss the concept of direct and indirect jurisdiction within the context of several federative rules with concrete examples. In addition, the authors will discuss these principles within UEFA's Licensing and Financial Fair Play Regulations as well as the jurisdiction of the CAS to hear appeals concerning decisions of the Fédération Internationale de l'Automobile ('FIA').

The conclusions reached by the authors are that the doctrine of indirect jurisdiction will only confer appellate jurisdiction of the CAS in sporting disputes where national federation rules refer to or incorporate applicable international federation rules that explicitly recognize the jurisdiction of the CAS where there is no other appeal route. This is an evolution from the original jurisdictional awards issued by the CAS that have required that the federative statutes explicitly, in no uncertain terms, recognize the jurisdiction of the CAS. This evolution is clearly a response to the increasing complexity of international sports law where the regulation of sporting activities is regulated by many complicated and sometimes contradictory statutes.

Finally, we note that many of the issues that arise in connection with jurisdictional clauses contained in statutes and regulations may also arise when analyzing arbitration clauses inserted in private contracts. Although the issues may be analogous, for the sake of parsimony, this paper will exclusively deal with jurisdictional clauses contained in statutes and regulations; it will not consider contractual arbitration clauses unless otherwise stated.

13.2 The Starting Point: Article R47 of the CAS Code

Article R47 of the CAS Code sets out the CAS' jurisdiction to hear appeals[1]

> "R47 Appeal
> An appeal against the decision of a federation, association or sports-related body may be filed with CAS if the statutes or regulations of the said body so provide or if the parties have concluded a specific arbitration agreement and if the Appellant has exhausted the legal remedies available to him prior to the appeal, in accordance with the statutes or regulations of that body.
> An appeal may be filed with CAS against an award rendered by CAS acting as a first instance tribunal if such appeal has been expressly provided by the rules of the federation or sports-body concerned."

Clearly, the CAS Code contemplates the jurisdiction of CAS to hear appeals against the decisions of federations ("(a)n appeal against the decision of a federation, association or sports-related body may be filed with CAS"). The issue that arises is how specific the wording of the federation's statutes must be in order to confer jurisdiction on the CAS. The wording that "the statutes or regulations of the said body so provide or if the parties have concluded a specific arbitration agreement" leaves room for interpretation. If the jurisdictional clause in the statutes of federation refers to the CAS for a particular type of dispute, that will be end of the inquiry. This is direct jurisdiction.

As demonstrated in the jurisprudence, however, the question as to what includes the "statutes or regulations of said body" is hardly determinative as federation statutes can incorporate the rules of other federations or associations, and sometimes those regulations can be contradictory. This is the source of the tension between direct and indirect jurisdiction as described below.

13.3 Direct Jurisdictional Clauses in Theory

Ideally a jurisdictional clause will leave little to interpretation and be particularly specific to remove all ambiguity. Theoretically speaking, a perfectly direct jurisdictional clause of a federation will contain three elements to ensure that the appeal route over a sports-related dispute is clear: the designated arbitral body, the scope of the dispute submitted to arbitration and (as the case may be) the determination of the parties who have standing (to sue or be sued).

[1]Article R47, CAS Code.

13.3.1 Identify the Arbitral Body

Most importantly an effective jurisdictional clause will unambiguously designate a specific arbitral or judicial body with jurisdiction over the dispute. The clause must be clear and specific in the sense that it will identify one specific body, and, where relevant, it will state whether the designated body is to act as the first instance or appellate body.

An example of an ambiguous jurisdictional clause is one that conjunctively identifies two potential judicial bodies to hear a dispute simultaneously without explaining, which retains jurisdiction over the first instance hearing. Such a clause can be cured by ensuring that the wording specifically identifies which arbitral panel is the first instance decision-maker and which performs the appeal function. Precision in the drafting of jurisdictional clauses is essential to ensure that the appeal route is clear. Federations or associations should only refer to the exclusive power of one judicial body to hear appeals.

An example of a jurisdictional clause that clearly identifies which arbitral tribunal retains jurisdiction is Rule 61 of the Olympic Charter[2]

> "61 Dispute resolution
> 1. The decisions of the IOC are final. Any dispute relating to their application or interpretation may be resolved solely by the IOC Executive Board and, in certain cases, by arbitration before the Court of Arbitration for Sport (CAS).
> 2. Any dispute arising on the occasion of, or in connection with, the Olympic Games shall be submitted exclusively to the Court of Arbitration for Sport, in accordance with the Code of Sports-Related Arbitration."

This clause provides that the IOC Executive Board has the initial jurisdiction to entertain disputes relating to the application and interpretation of the Olympic statutes and that the CAS has exclusive jurisdiction to hear appeals against those decisions. Although the language of paragraph 1 of Rule 61 may appear to limit the ability to appeal a decision of the IOC Executive Board, in previous cases the IOC has not challenged the authority of the CAS. The CAS itself has previously held that it does have jurisdiction to hear appeals under Rule 61 of the Charter, as reasoned by the Panel in CAS 2012/A/2913, *Mu-yen Chu & Chinese Taipei Olympic Committee v. International Olympic Committee*:[3]

> In particular, the Appellants refer, for the purposes of Article R47 of the Code, to Rule 61 of the Olympic Charter, whose para. 2 provides that "any dispute arising on the occasion of, or in connection with, the Olympic Games shall be submitted exclusively to the Court of Arbitration for Sport (CAS), in accordance with the Code of Sports-Related Arbitration", and to the email sent by the IOC on 30 August 2012 (§ 24 above). The Respondent, while submitting that the present dispute is not covered by any arbitration clause, expressly declared that it "accepts arbitration and does not oppose CAS jurisdiction". The jurisdiction of CAS was further confirmed by the parties' signing the Order of Procedure.

[2]Rule 61, Olympic Charter.

[3]CAS 2012/A/2913, *Mu-yen Chu & Chinese Taipei Olympic Committee v. IOC*, Award of 15 March 2013.

In turn, Article R47 of the CAS Code applies and the jurisdiction of the CAS as the arbiter of disputes regarding the Olympic Charter is established.

It must be noted, however, that in practice the IOC, technically speaking, does not oppose the jurisdiction of the CAS as the review panel of a decision of the IOC Executive Board. It appears that this "non-opposition" has been interpreted by the CAS as the IOC not refusing jurisdiction where this approach has shaped the jurisprudence. An example is where the decision of CAS 2012/A/2913 grants jurisdiction of the CAS over IOC Executive Board decisions, not as a matter of an automatic right in applying the jurisdictional clause following an analysis of the jurisdictional clause, but merely because the IOC has not opposed its jurisdiction.

The authors are of the opinion that the Olympic Charter grants the CAS the jurisdiction to review decisions of the IOC Executive Board concerning "any dispute arising on the occasion of, or in connection with, the Olympic Games" whether or not the IOC technically submits as the wording of Rule 61 is clear.

13.3.2 Scope of the Dispute

Second, a well-drafted jurisdictional clause will clearly identify the scope of the dispute to be arbitrated. Due to the general nature of Article R47 of the CAS Code, this limitation must be found in the relevant federation or association rules.

Rule 61(2) of the Olympic Charter attempts to identify the scope or type of disputes that are subject to CAS jurisdiction in that the issue must arise "on the occasion of, or in connection with, the Olympic Games."[4] The wording is quite broad and may present some difficulties with respect to defining what is "in connection with the Olympic Games".

A good example of a jurisdictional clause with a well-defined scope is the one that clearly identifies the types of disputes subject to arbitration. Although, in general, the FIFA Statutes are not drafted in very clear terms. Articles 22, 23 and 24 of the FIFA RSTP clearly identify which disputes are to proceed to the Players' Status Committee and which are to be heard by the Dispute Resolution Chamber, by specifically distinguishing between disputes that relate to the solidarity mechanism, training compensation and other employment disputes of an international dimension.

As the jurisdiction of the CAS regarding the decisions of FIFA judicial bodies is clear, the appeal routes in these cases are equally clear. Although this is an obvious and well-settled example, the jurisdictional clauses of FIFA do provide a clear model for other federations and associations to follow.

[4]Rule 61, Olympic Charter.

13.3.3 Standing to Appeal

Finally, a well-drafted jurisdictional clause will clearly identify not only the appropriate arbitral panel and the scope of the dispute, but also the type of dispute and who retains standing to appeal the decision.

The Fédération Internationale de Natation ('FINA') provides an example of a particularly well-drafted jurisdiction clause. The FINA Constitution outlines which internal panel hears which type of dispute. General governance disciplinary decisions are taken by the FINA Executive and are appealed to the FINA Bureau[5] whereas specific disciplinary infractions are handled by the FIFA Disciplinary Panel.[6] The FINA Doping Panel[7] and the FINA Ethics Panel[8] make decisions regarding the FINA Doping Control (DC) Rules and the FINA Ethics Code, respectively.

The FINA Constitution then goes on to unambiguously specify the appeal route for each type of hearing and issue. Decisions of the Doping Panel, the Disciplinary Panel or the Ethics Panel are appealed "directly to CAS."[9] For greater specificity, the FINA Constitution in order to avoid confusion regarding the appeal of a decision of the FINA Bureau, which is an additional appeal step for disciplinary proceedings, determines the following:[10]

> An appeal against a decision by the Bureau, the FINA Doping Panel, the Disciplinary Panel or the Ethics Panel shall be referred to the Court of Arbitration for Sport (CAS), Lausanne, Switzerland, within the same term as in C 12.11.3. The only appeal from a decision of the Doping Panel, the Disciplinary Panel or the Ethics Panel shall be to the CAS. The CAS shall also have exclusive jurisdiction over interlocutory orders and no other court or tribunal shall have authority to issue interlocutory orders relating to matters before the CAS. Decisions by the CAS shall be final and binding, subject only to the provisions of the Swiss Private International Law Act, section 190.

Finally, with respect to the parties to the dispute, the FINA Constitution grants "Member, member of a Member or individuals" standing before the CAS to sue such decisions. A member is defined as a "Member Federation—(which) means the national federations affiliated to FINA in a country or Sport Country recognized by FINA."[11] This definition confers the ability of not only member national federations but also national sub-associations, clubs who are members of Members according to national federation rules and athletes the standing to appeal. Ultimately there is little ambiguity in the FINA jurisdictional clause to the

---

[5]Article C12.3, FINA Constitution.

[6]Arts C12.11.1 and C12.6, FINA Constitution.

[7]Article C12.5, FINA Constitution.

[8]Article C12.7, FINA Constitution.

[9]Article C12.11.2, FINA Constitution.

[10]Article C12.11.4, FINA Constitution.

[11]Article C3.14, FINA Constitution.

CAS as it defines the appropriate arbitral panel, the scope and type of dispute and who has standing to appeal the decision.

The ability to limit what person or organization can appeal a decision to the CAS, however, is complicated by national and international federation rules granting the standing to appeal to 'affected parties'.

The Canadian system provides a relevant example. The Sport Dispute Resolution Centre of Canada ('SDRCC') hears the appeals against decisions of Canadian national sporting federations and decisions of the SDRCC involving sanctions for doping can be appealed to the CAS.[12] The Canadian Sport Dispute Resolution Code ('SDRCC Code') grants 'affected parties' the right to be notified of disputes heard by the SDRCC and the subsequent ability to participate in proceedings.[13] The SDRCC Code identifies an 'affected party' as "a Person who may be adversely affected by a decision of the [SDRCC], such as losing a previously granted status or privilege."[14] Therefore, an athlete who may lose his or her position on a Canadian national team due to the successful appeal of a doping sanction by another athlete indeed retains standing to appeal the decision before the SDRCC and eventually to the CAS.

Ultimately, effective jurisdiction clauses must identify who has standing to sue in an appeal before the CAS. The unambiguous identification of the relevant parties to the dispute, including the definition of 'affected parties' can only serve to ameliorate the predictable jurisdiction of the CAS, otherwise identified as 'direct jurisdiction'.

13.4 Established CAS Jurisprudence

As mentioned above, Article R47 of the CAS Code determines that "an appeal against the decision of a federation, association or sports-related body may be filed with CAS if the statutes or regulations of the said body so provide." Historically the CAS jurisprudence has determined that despite the clarity of the FIFA statutes described above, national federations must clearly adopt the CAS' jurisdiction in their regulations to be subject to its competence.

As the recent *Flamengo* case has revisited this issue of jurisdiction and applied the principle of indirect jurisdiction, it is worth identifying how the CAS has interpreted and applied the concept of its jurisdiction in football cases.

---

[12] Article 6.21(h), SDRCC Code.

[13] Article 6.12, SDRCC Code.

[14] Article 1.1(a), SDRCC Code.

13.4.1 Direct Jurisdiction: Expressly Recognized

Historically, the CAS has consistently affirmed that in order for it to have jurisdiction to hear an appeal of the decision of an international or national federation or association it must be expressly recognized in the statutes or regulations of the sports federation or association.

One of the earlier CAS decisions affirming the concept of direct jurisdiction was the 2002 decision in *Besiktas v. FIFA & SC Freiburg*.[15] Besiktas filed an appeal with the CAS against a decision rendered by the FIFA Special Committee before FIFA had stated in the Circular 827 that the CAS would hear appeals against its decisions. The articles of the FIFA Statutes had not yet been amended to expressly recognize jurisdiction of the CAS. Instead, the FIFA Statutes only recognized the Arbitration Tribunal for Football (TAF). The 2002 Panel was clear in their ruling that, as the jurisdiction of the CAS was not established that it had no power to hear the appeal.

The CAS had a further opportunity to consider its jurisdiction with respect to the FIFA regulations and the rights of appeal to the CAS that were introduced in 2004. In *Ismailia Sporting Club v. Confédération Africaine de Football*, the Panel noted that the existence of the FIFA regulations (containing the arbitration clause) in and of itself was not sufficient and that the jurisdiction of the CAS had to be explicitly recognized by the football federation's regulations[16]

> It is only with the implementation by the individual confederations of the new FIFA statutes into their individual statutes, that the CAS can be held to have jurisdiction. The FIFA rules that came into force on 1 January 2004 do not constitute per se a basis for arbitration. Instead, they constitute an instruction to introduce a regulation providing for CAS arbitration. This was implemented by the coming into force of the new C.A.F. regulations on 1 September 2004. It follows that the Court of Arbitration for Sport has no jurisdiction with regard to the decision of the C.A.F. Appeal Committee and that therefore, it cannot proceed with the present arbitration.

In 2004, the CAS reasoned that the FIFA rules recognizing CAS jurisdiction must be specifically incorporated in the relevant federation's rules in order for the CAS to have jurisdiction to hear appeals against that federation's decisions. The famous Ashley Cole case of 2005 applied the exact same reasoning. The Panel declared in no uncertain terms that "in order for the CAS to have jurisdiction to hear an appeal, the statutes or regulations of the sports-related body from whose decision the appeal is being made, must expressly recognize the CAS as an arbitral body of appeal."[17] The Panel ruled that as rule 63 of the regulations of the Football

[15]TAS 2002/O/422, *Besiktas v. FIFA & SC Freiburg*, Award of 10 March 2003.

[16]CAS 2004/A/676, *Ismailia Sporting Club v. Confédération Africaine de Football (CAF)*, Award of 15 December 2004, paras 2.6 and 2.7.

[17]CAS 2005/A/952, *Ashley Cole v. Football Association Premier League*, Award of 24 January 2006, para 7.

Association Premier League ('FAPL') stated that the decisions of the appeal board were final, the CAS had no jurisdiction to hear an appeal.

The Cole Panel also determined that the reference to the FIFA Statutes at the time did not recognize the jurisdiction of the CAS as "the FIFA Statutes do not contain any mandatory provision that obliges the Respondent to allow" where "the CAS jurisprudence suggests that if the FIFA Statutes did compel the Respondent to provide for a right of appeal from its decisions, no right of appeal to the CAS would exist until the Respondent had made provision for this right in its statutes or regulations."[18] The Panel specifically stated that the regulations must make "direct reference" to the jurisdiction of the CAS.[19]

The CAS continued to apply this concept of direct jurisdiction whereby mere membership in FIFA was only an invitation to accept CAS jurisdiction (*point de départ à une procédure d'arbitrage*) and not explicit acceptance. In the award of *A. v. Caykur Rizespor Kulübü Dernegi & Turkish Football Federation (TFF)*, the CAS ruled that as the issue at appeal was a domestic Turkish contractual matter and not a disciplinary matter involving FIFA, and as the regulations of the TFF did not recognize the jurisdiction of the CAS in domestic Turkish contractual matters, the CAS had no jurisdiction to hear the appeal of a decision of the TFF.[20] The award in *Telecom Egypt Club v. Egyptian Football Association* did the same where it reasoned that mere general 'recognition' was not sufficient to establish jurisdiction.[21]

Ultimately the concept of the necessity of a direct jurisdictional clause to establish CAS competence is a well-entrenched principle in the interpretation of Article R47 of the CAS Code. The early cases from 2002 to 2008 clearly apply this principle, and the CAS has also more recently applied this principle in 2010.[22] Despite this overwhelming jurisprudence, the CAS has held that in certain cases it can have, what the authors term—indirect jurisdiction.

13.4.2 The Pizarro Decision: Indirect Jurisdiction

This doctrine of indirect jurisdiction of the CAS was previously applied in the case of *Claudio Pizarro v. Federación Peruana de Fútbol*.[23] The *Pizarro* case involved the appeal rights of the player Pizarro against the decision of the Peruvian Football

[18]Ibid., para 10.

[19]Ibid., para 14.

[20]CAS 2008/A/1602, *A. v. Caykur Rizesport Kulübü Dernegi & Turkish Football Federation (TFF)*, Award of 20 February 2009.

[21]CAS 2009/A/1910, *Telecom Egypt Club v. Egyptian Football Association (EFA)*, Award of 9 September 2010, para 31.

[22]CAS 2010/A/2170, *Iraklis Thessaloniki FC v. Hellenic Football Federation* and CAS 2010/A/2171, *OF IFC v. Hellenic Football Federation*, Awards of 23 February 2011.

[23]CAS 2008/A/1617, *Claudio Pizarro v. Federacion Peruana de Futbol*, Award of 15 April 2009.

Federation ("PFF") to suspend him for 18 months for unruly behaviour after the night of a national team match.[24] In essence, the rules of the PFF did not explicitly provide for the appeal jurisdiction of the CAS to review such disciplinary decisions, but the disciplinary regulations of the PFF did refer to and incorporate the FIFA Statutes. The player sought to have the PFF decision overturned before the CAS.

In its decision, the CAS ruled that as the PFF strictly complies with FIFA provisions on the transfer of players, the regulations regarding the participation of players in the selection of international events for the national team and countless other obligations, the PFF must also have observed FIFA regulations incorporating into its rules the right to appeal to the CAS.[25] The CAS explained that as the PFF reference to the FIFA Statutes was exhaustive the right to appeal to the CAS, which forms part of those statutes, was not excluded.[26]

The Panel concluded that the FIFA Statutes were applicable to the PFF which enabled the appeal to the CAS.[27]

13.4.3 *Indirect Jurisdiction Explained*

As a result, CAS jurisprudence recognized that the incorporation or reference to an international federation's regulations that clearly provide for an appeal to the CAS by a national federation is sufficient to satisfy the requirement of Article R47 of the CAS Code to the effect that "an appeal against the decision of a federation, association or sports-related body may be filed with CAS *if the statutes or regulations of the said body so provide*" (emphasis added).

This is precisely what is meant by indirect jurisdiction. Jurisdiction to be heard before the CAS on appeal can be established, under specific circumstances, in cases where a federation did not directly recognize the CAS but referred to other statutes which did. This principle has been most recently applied in the CAS award of *Flamengo v. CBF & STJD.*

13.5 *Flamengo v. CBF & STJD*: The Award

Santos, the former Brazilian international who plays predominantly as a left-back, has been no stranger to controversy. In July 2014, after Clube de Regatas do Flamengo accumulated a mere 7 points in 11 games, Santos was attacked by a

[24]Ibid.

[25]Ibid., para 109.

[26]Ibid., para 113.

[27]Ibid., para 116.

Flamengo fan following his performance in Flamengo's 4-0 loss against Porto Alegre's Sport Club Internacional, and ended up in hospital.[28]

Santos, however, has also been the subject of controversy in the legal field, in relation to the doctrine of CAS indirect jurisdiction, as set out in the *Flamengo v. CBF & STJD* award.

This case is the appeal of a decision taken by the STJD of Brazil filed by Flamengo further to Article R47 of the CAS Code. The decision of the three-member CAS Panel is relatively recent as it was heard in Lausanne in June 2014 and released in October 2015.[29]

13.5.1 The Facts of the Case

Despite winning the 2013 Copa do Brasil for Flamengo played against Club Atletico Paranaense ('Paranaense') at the Maracana Stadium, Santos was sent off the pitch by the referee during the closing minutes of the second leg of the final. Santos did not compete in Flamengo's subsequent match, the 37th round of the Brazilian National Championship (the 'Brasileirao') played on 1 December 2013. It is worthy to note that the Brasileirao is not the same competition as the Copa do Brasil (in which Santos had been sent off, as just mentioned).

After Flamengo's 37th Brasileirao match on 2 December 2013, the prosecutor of the STJD condemned Santos' actions in the Copa do Brasil final, and several days later the Disciplinary Commission of the STJD suspended Santos for one match for his unsporting behaviour. Santos played in Flamengo's next match after the suspension was levied against FC Cruzeiro on 7 of December 2013. That match was Flamengo's final Brasileirao match and obviously not a match involving the Copa do Brasil competition.

After the Prosecutor of the STJD denounced Flamengo for fielding an ineligible player, Santos, in the match against FC Cruzeiro, the Disciplinary Commission of the STJD decided that Flamengo has violated Article 214 of the Brazilian Code of Sport Justice ('CBJD'). As a result the STJD imposed the following sanctions on Flamengo: (a) the deduction of 3 points applied to its standing in the Brasileirao; (b) elimination of the point obtained in the match against FC Cruzeiro; a fine of 1000 reiais. The loss of 4 points resulted in Flamengo losing five places in the final standings of the Brasileirao, which made it fall to 16th place, barely avoiding the relegation zone.

Flamengo appealed the decision of the STJD to the CAS requesting that (a) the CAS recognize its jurisdiction in the matter; (b) an order for provisional measures

[28]Coombs D, Former Arsenal signing Andre Santos attacked by fan in Brazil, 20 July 2014. http://www.hitc.com/en-gb/2014/07/20/former-arsenal-signing-andre-santos-attacked-by-fan-in-brazil/page/1/. Accessed 17 November, 2015.

[29]CAS 2014/A/3474, *Clube de Regatas do Flamengo v. Confederaçao Brasileira de Futebol (CBF) & Superior Tribunal de Justiça Desportiva (STJD)*, Award of 5 October 2015.

be issued, staying the STJD decision; (c) the STJD decision be eventually set aside; and (d) Flamengo be absolved of any violation of Article 214 of the CBJD. The STJD and CBF naturally opposed this appeal.

In issuing its award the CAS ruled that

- the CBF may be sued in this appeal while the STJD cannot;
- Santos was not suspended for the Brasileirao (37th round) match held after the final of the Copa do Brasil;
- Santos was ineligible to play in the final match of the Brasileirao; and
- Flamengo is to be sanctioned for fielding an ineligible player.

This CAS decision addresses several important and interesting issues that provide practitioners with some guidance. The significance of the decision is that the jurisdiction of the CAS can be established by incorporation of, or reference to other statutes, and not necessarily only by explicit wording in the statute itself.

13.5.2 Indirect Jurisdiction of the CAS in Flamengo

As a preliminary matter, the CAS Panel considered whether the jurisdiction issue was a procedural or substantive matter. The CAS jurisprudence on this very issue is inconsistent where some CAS cases have treated it as a procedural matter[30] and others have decided that jurisdiction is a substantive issue to be decided within the context of the merits of the appeal.[31] The Panel in the *Flamengo* award noted that most recently the CAS has applied the reasoning of the Swiss Federal Tribunal and that jurisdiction is a substantive issue to be addressed within the merits of the decision.[32]

With respect to the merits of the jurisdictional question, the appellant Flamengo argued that the CAS retains jurisdiction to hear the appeal of decisions of the STJD and the CBF. It noted that Article 1(2) of the CBF statutes stipulates that "all members, organs and parties of the CBF, as well as clubs… must observe and comply, in Brazil, all statutes, regulations, directives, decisions and the Code of Ethics of the Federation Internationale de Football Association—FIFA."

In addition, Flamengo noted that as there is no national arbitral tribunal in Brazil, Article 68(3) of the FIFA Statutes is triggered: "instead of recourse to ordinary courts of law, provisions shall be made for arbitration. Such disputes shall be taken to an independent and duly constituted arbitration tribunal recognized under the rules of the Association or Confederation or to CAS." Therefore, Flamengo

[30]CAS 2008/A/1639, *RCD Mallorca v. The Football Association (FA) & Newcastle United*, Award of 24 April 2009; CAS 2007/A/1329, *Chiapas FC v. Cricuma Esporte Clube* and CAS 2007/A/1330, *Chiapas FC v. R.*, Awards of 5 December 2007.

[31]CAS 2008/A/1517, *Ionikos FC v. C.*, Award of 23 February 2009.

[32]CAS 2009/A/1869 (parties and date unknown).

argued that by reference Article 67(1) and 67(2) of the FIFA Statutes indeed to confer indirect jurisdiction on the CAS to hear appeals against decisions of the STJD and the CBF.

The CBF took the opposite position rejecting the doctrine of indirect jurisdiction, arguing that that the CAS has no jurisdiction to hear this dispute as the relevant Brazilian sporting statutes do not provide for an express appeal route against decisions taken by the STJD to the CAS.

In rendering its decision, the "Panel observed that it is consistent CAS jurisprudence that Article 67(1) of the FIFA Statutes does not by itself grant jurisdiction to CAS as a final instance in national matters."[33] In this sense the Panel explicitly noted the *ratio* in CAS 2011/A/2483 that proclaims that "the regulations of FIFA ...need to be adopted in the federation's rules either word by word or by reference to apply to domestic matters."

On this issue, the CAS Panel did in fact recognize that the CAS has indirect jurisdiction to hear appeals of the CBF. The Panel accepted the argument put forth by the Appellant that Article 1(2) of the CBF statutes does indeed include a reference to the FIFA Statutes where "all members, organs and parties of the CBF, as well as clubs ... must observe and comply with FIFA Statutes." The Panel also went as far to say that "the implementation of article 1(2) of the CBF Statutes went further than to merely recognizing CAS in accordance with article 68(1) of the FIFA Statutes, but required all members of the CFB to comply with the statutes and regulations of FIFA."[34] Therefore, as the FIFA Statutes include the arbitration and appeal clauses in Article 67, those appeal rights secured in the FIFA Statutes form part of the legal appeal route for decisions taken by the CBF.

The Panel also found that Flamengo had exhausted all available national remedies, in compliance with Article R47 of the CAS Code, and that the CAS had jurisdiction to deal with the question as to whether Santos was ineligible to compete when he was fielded by Flamengo in the final match of the Brasileirao.

13.5.3 Merits of the Flamengo Decision

In addition to the jurisdictional issue, the *Flamengo v. CBF & STJD* Panel decided several other issues worth mentioning.

Relying on a domestic Brazilian sporting statute, the respondents argued that the issue before the Panel is "inarbitrable" because it is in "consideration of matters related to the sports discipline and competition." Here the Panel did not apply the traditional jurisprudence of the CAS regarding 'field of play' issues and characterized this dispute as a disciplinary case. In this sense, it noted that the

[33] CAS 2014/A/3474, *Flamengo v. CBF & STJD*, Award of 5 October 2015, para 88.

[34] Ibid., para 92.

regulation that the respondents were relying on did not specifically exclude the arbitration of disciplinary cases and that the issue before the Panel was 'arbitrable'.[35]

Both the CBF and the STJD took the position that neither of them had standing to be sued. The Panel followed CAS established jurisprudence that determines that the STJD is an arbitral tribunal that "forms an integral part of the CBF and that the STJD has therefore no standing in and of itself."[36] On the other hand, the *Flamengo* Panel held that the CBF did have standing to be sued.

With respect to the actual merits of the decision regarding Santos' suspension, the Panel was required to consider whether Santos was automatically suspended for the next (37th) round of the Brasileirao following the sending off in the final Cup match; if Santos was ineligible to compete in the final round of the Brasileirao; and whether Flamengo was guilty of fielding an ineligible player in the final match of the season.

With respect to the automatic suspension issue, the Panel found that the general rule is that a player is automatically suspended in the subsequent match in the same competition from which he was sent off. In this case, Santos could not serve the suspension in the same competition (Copa do Brasil) and as clearly set out in the relevant Brazilian statutes an automatic suspension cannot be served in another competition.[37] This implies that the application of a suspension to another competition requires an express decision by the relevant body. As no such decision had been issued before the penultimate (37th round) match of the Brasileirao, Santos was not suspended at that point. The Panel concluded that the suspension operated with immediate effect the day after it was rendered by the STJD and that Santos was ineligible to compete in the last match of the Brasileirao.

Article 214 of the CBJD applies a sanction to Brazilian clubs who use ineligible players in a match. Flamengo argued that by not fielding Santos in the penultimate match and consulting the online registry prior to the last match, it was diligent and that the Panel ought to mitigate the penalty in the circumstances. The Panel ruled that there was no doubt that Article 214 was violated and that mitigating or aggravating circumstances were not present.[38]

13.5.4 Conclusions Regarding Flamengo

The significance of the *Flamengo* award lies in the subsequent recognition of the doctrine of indirect jurisdiction, which was previously set out in the *Pizarro* case. As we can see, the doctrine of indirect jurisdiction is applicable where there is no

[35]Ibid., para 125.

[36]Ibid., para 143.

[37]Ibid., paras 162–165.

[38]Ibid., paras 216–220.

direct recognition of the jurisdiction of the CAS, but where such jurisdiction recognized by a national association's rules indirectly refer to or incorporate an international federation's jurisdictional clause providing for CAS arbitration.

The general principle that we can draw from the jurisprudence is that the relevant rules must refer to or incorporate the specific jurisdictional clause providing for arbitration in order to find that the CAS has indirect jurisdiction to hear the appeal of a federation's decision. In this sense, the incorporated statutes cannot distinguish between doping issues and other issues, identifying the CAS as the competent appeal panel for one, but not the other types of issues.

In order to further illustrate this jurisprudence and the application of the doctrine, the authors will now consider other areas where these issues arise, including appeals against Financial Fair Play licensing decisions (6.) and against decisions of the Federation International de l'Automobile (7.).

13.6 Indirect Jurisdiction of the CAS in UEFA FFP Matters

The introduction of UEFA's FFP Regulations ('FFP Regulations') has triggered the development of a new area of jurisprudence in the world of football law. Several appellants have attempted to use the doctrine of indirect jurisdiction to appeal against a decision of a national association to deny the issuance of a UEFA license, without success.

As a result, it is worthy to note the application of this doctrine within the context of UEFA licensing decisions. The lesson to be learned within this context is that licensing decisions made specifically by UEFA can be appealed to the CAS because the relevant UEFA statutes explicitly provide for this appeal route. On the other hand, the decisions taken by national football associations may not be appealed unless the national football federation statutes explicitly provides for CAS jurisdiction or if the UEFA licensing statutes are referred to and incorporated into the national football association regulations.

Here we see the limits of the applicability of the doctrine of indirect jurisdiction as it is applied in practice to the ability of European clubs to appeal licensing decisions.

13.6.1 Context: The Delegation of Licensing Decisions to National Associations

Clubs in UEFA member associations that wish to compete in either the Champions or the Europa League must fulfil the substantive requirements of the FFP Regulations. Article 4.01(c) of both the UEFA Champions League Regulations

('CLR')[39] and the UEFA Europa League Regulations ('ELR')[40] specifically requires that prospective clubs have obtained a license issued by the competent NFA in accordance with the UEFA FFP Regulations. The language of these provisions is clear in that the UEFA CLR and UEFA ELR specifically delegate the initial licensing functions to "the competent national body in accordance with the UEFA Club Licensing and Financial Fair Play Regulations."

The UEFA FFP Regulations require that, within each member association, there are two decision-making bodies in charge of determining whether a club has satisfied the licensing requirement, a First Instance Body and an Appeals Body.[41] The First Instance Body makes its decision based on the documents submitted to it by the predetermined deadline.[42] The Appeals Body serves as a review court, which can consider the evidence submitted to the First Instance Body as well as submissions made once the appeal has been lodged.[43]

Once these remedies have been exhausted within the national UEFA member association, however, it is unclear whether the CAS has jurisdiction to hear an appeal against the final decision. The general thrust of the jurisprudence is that it depends on the specific language of the national association's jurisdictional clause. As we see below, some associations have directly recognized the appellate jurisdiction of the CAS for FFP licensing decisions, while others have not. In this sense, these jurisdictional decisions of the CAS with regard to national licensing decisions have demonstrated the outer limits of the application of the doctrine of indirect jurisdiction.

13.6.2 Context: Powers and Decisions of UEFA

In addition to the licensing process delegated to national football associations, UEFA retains general powers of enforcement both inside and outside the licensing process. In cases where "there is any doubt as to whether a club fulfils the admission criteria defined" by the FFP Regulations the UEFA General Secretary can refer the case to the UEFA Club Financial Control Board ('CFCB').[44] These investigations can be carried out at any time, even after the end of the competition. Therefore, the UEFA CFCB can exercise its power both within and outside the licensing process.

These decisions are enforced by two UEFA bodies where the UEFA CFCB is split into two units, the Investigatory Chamber, which is responsible for

[39]Article 4.01(c), UEFA CLR.

[40]Article 4.01(c), UEFA ELR.

[41]Article 7(1), FFP Regulations.

[42]Article 7(2), FFP Regulations.

[43]Article 7(5), FFP Regulations.

[44]Article 4.01(c), UEFA CLR; Article 4.01(c), UEFA ELR.

monitoring and investigations, and the Adjudicatory Chamber, which is tasked with reviewing the positions of the parties and passing judgement in individual cases. Once the Investigatory Chamber has concluded its investigation, it has the following options: a) dismiss the case; b) conclude with a settlement agreement; c) apply disciplinary measures limited to a warning, a reprimand or a fine; d) refer the case to the Adjudicatory Chamber.[45]

The Adjudicatory Chamber operates much like an arbitration or judicial body where a binding decision is issued. Here the parties can submit written representations,[46] a hearing may be convened in order to present evidence,[47] interested parties may be given intervener status,[48] and the Adjudicatory Chamber shall deliberate and issue a judgment[49] where it can either dismiss the case, accept or reject the club's admission to a UEFA club competition, impose disciplinary measures or uphold, reject, or modify a decision of the CFCB Investigatory Chamber.[50]

As clearly indicated in the arbitration clause of the FFP Procedural Rules, decisions of the UEFA CFCB Adjudicatory Chamber can be appealed to the CAS as Article 34(4) of the FFP Procedural Rules directly confers unequivocal and exclusive jurisdiction by providing that "Final decisions of the CFCB may only be appealed before the Court of Arbitration for Sport (CAS) in accordance with the relevant provisions of the UEFA Statutes."[51]

This direct jurisdiction has been recognized in the jurisprudence relating to FFP licensing cases, i.e. inter alia, FC Petrolul Ploiesti v. UEFA;[52] Beşiktaş JK v. UEFA;[53] Bursaspor Kulübü Dernegi v. UEFA;[54] Györi ETO v. UEFA[55] and Málaga CF SAD v. UEFA.[56]

13.6.3 No Indirect Jurisdiction: Rayo Vallecano and Parma FC

Decisions applying FFP Regulations made by the Appeals Body of national federations may not necessarily be appealed where such decisions could be final. The

[45] Article 13(2), FFP Procedural Rules.

[46] Article 20, FFP Procedural Rules.

[47] Arts 21 and 23, FFP Procedural Rules.

[48] Article 22, FFP Procedural Rules.

[49] Arts 24 and 25, FFP Procedural Rules.

[50] Article 27, FFP Procedural Rules.

[51] Article 34(2), FFP Procedural Rules.

[52] CAS 2013/A/3453, *FC Petrolul Ploiesti v. UEFA*, Award of 20 February 2014.

[53] CAS 2012/A/2824, *Besiktas JK v. UEFA*, Award of 31 October 2012.

[54] CAS 2012/A/2821, *Bursaspor Kulübü Dernegi v. UEFA*, Award of 10 July 2012.

[55] CAS 2012/A/2702, *Göry ETO v. UEFA*, Award of 8 May 2012.

[56] CAS 2013/A/3067, *Málaga CF SAD v. UEFA*, Award of 8 October 2013.

ability to appeal depends on the specific wording of the national federations' arbitration clauses.

Rayo Vallecano finished in 8th place in the 2012/2013 edition of *La Liga* and had qualified to compete in the UEFA Europa League, as Málaga Club de Fútbol which finished seventh, was refused a UEFA License due to FFP irregularities. Coincidentally, Rayo Vallecano suffered overdue payables and was also refused a UEFA license by both the First and Second Instance Licensing Committees of the Real Federación Española de Fútbol ('RFEF') under the RFEF Club Licensing Regulations.

The club appealed this decision to the CAS.[57] The initial application to provisionally suspend the sanction pending but the final result of the case was rejected on the basis that CAS jurisprudence indicates that economical or financial damage per se cannot constitute irreparable harm.

As the arbitration clause of the RFEF Statutes stipulates that "the RFEF recognizes the jurisdiction of the Court of Arbitration for Sport (CAS) exclusively in those disputes which may arise *between the RFEF, FIFA, and/or UEFA*" there is no direct arbitration clause referring disputes between clubs and the RFEF to the CAS. The Panel considered the CAS Code and determined that neither the arbitration clause in the RFEF statutes nor the UEFA clause generally recognizing CAS jurisdiction was sufficient to refer the dispute to Lausanne.[58]

Unsurprisingly, the Panel also noted that if UEFA wishes to have FFP licensing decisions made by national Football Associations reviewed by the CAS it is up to UEFA to ensure that the member's arbitration clause explicitly confers jurisdiction.

A similar decision was reached in *Parma FC v. FIGC & Torino FC*.[59] The Federazione Italiana Giuoco Calcio ('FIGC') refused Parma FC a UEFA license, prohibiting it from competing in the Europa League for overdue payables because Parma FC had not paid personal income tax deductions on payments from October and November 2013 to ten of its players. The club appealed the second instance decision of the Alta Corte di Giustizia Sportiva which confirmed the first instance decision. The CAS held that there was no jurisdictional clause in its favour and that the decision of the Alta Corte di Giustizia Sportiva was final for three reasons.

First, Articles 4.21 and 6.9 of the Italian UEFA Club Licensing Manual[60] explicitly grant the Alta Corte di Giustizia Sportiva the exclusive jurisdiction to hear Italian licensing appeals. Second, the general clause recognizing the jurisdiction of the CAS contained in the Manual is not sufficient to trump the appeal route provided for a specific category of disputes (relating to the refusal or withdrawal of licenses), whereby jurisdiction is exclusively devolved to another body, i.e. the

[57]CAS 2013/A/3199, *Rayo Vallecano de Madrid SAD v. RFEF*, Award of 22 October 2013.

[58]Ibid., paras 5.5–5.7.

[59]CAS 2014/A/3629, *Parma FC v. FICG & Torino FC*, Award of 31 October 2014.

[60]FIGC Manuale delle Licenze UEFA.

Alta Corte.[61] Third, the same reasoning applies to Article 59 of the UEFA Statutes. Following established CAS jurisprudence, the reference to the general jurisdiction of the CAS in this provision is not sufficient to confer jurisdiction because it only constitutes an instruction for the national associations to introduce a regulation providing for CAS arbitration, but is not in itself part of the national (in this case, FIGC) regulations. The Panel explained that if FIGC rules do not comply with UEFA Statutes it is for UEFA and the FIGC to ensure such compliance.

13.6.4 Direct Jurisdiction: The Romanian Football Federation

On the other hand, some national federation licensing regulations do grant direct jurisdiction to the CAS in the review of a national licensing decision. The CAS heard appeals and issued awards concerning the decision of the Romanian Football Federation in *S.C. F.C. Universitatea Cluj S.A. v. Romanian Football Federation (RFF) & Romanian Professional Football League (RPFL)*.[62]

In this case, it was clearly established that the relevant Romanian federation rules recognize the jurisdiction of the CAS to hear such appeals. This is not an indirect use of jurisdiction rather a direct application where the RFF and the RPFL have, on the contrary, explicitly provided for the jurisdiction of the CAS.[63]

Therefore, the precedent has been set; clubs do not have the ability to challenge domestic licensing committee decisions implementing UEFA FFP standards unless the domestic football association explicitly agrees to allow the review. The incorporation of FFP principles to domestic licensing procedures is not sufficient in the eyes of the CAS and the particular jurisdictional appeal clause to the CAS must be directly adopted or incorporated. The applicability of the indirect jurisdiction of the CAS has been limited in this context as some European national football associations do not explicitly recognize the jurisdiction of the CAS either by incorporation or reference.

13.7 Indirect Jurisdiction of the CAS in Decisions of the FIA

Similar arguments have been made to apply the doctrine of indirect jurisdiction in favour of the CAS in order to review decisions of the Fédération Internationale de l'Automobile ('FIA'). The legal landscape of professional motor racing subject

[61] FIGC Manuale delle Licenze UEFA, Article 7.10 and Annex L.01 A.

[62] CAS 2013/A/3194, *SC FC Universitatea Cluj SA v. RFF & RPFL*, Award of 18 November 2013.

[63] Ibid., para 37.

to the jurisdiction of the FIA presents particular issues that are not present in the world of football, mainly because the FIA does not operate on the same federative basis as other associations, and as the seat of the FIA is located in Paris, France.

13.7.1 FIA: The Legal Landscape

The final judicial chamber within the FIA is the International Court of Appeal ('ICA'), meaning that the issuance of an ICA decision amounts to the exhaustion of internal remedies within the meaning of Article R47 of the CAS Code. The jurisdictional clause for appeals against decisions of the FIA is found in Article 15 of its Judicial and Disciplinary Rules

> For the avoidance of doubt, nothing in these rules shall prevent any party from pursuing any right of action which it may have before any court or tribunal, subject at all times to such party having first exhausted all mechanisms of dispute resolution set out in the Statutes and regulations of the FIA.

This jurisdictional clause is particularly broad as it confers the ability to lodge an appeal before "any court or tribunal" so long as all internal dispute resolution mechanisms have been exhausted. There is, however, no direct or explicit reference to have a decision of the FIA ICA heard on appeal before the CAS.

On the other hand, the FIA is part of and has accepted the general pyramid structure of the international sports landscape for two reasons. First, the FIA is a member of the IOC, the Association of IOC Recognized International Sports Federations ('ARISF') and is recognized by SportAccord. As mentioned above, Rule 61 of the Olympic Charter recognizes the jurisdiction of the CAS. In addition, Article 7A.4.4 of SportAccord Statutes determines that member associations' regulations "must also contain a specific provision recognizing the exclusive jurisdiction of the Court of Arbitration for Sport, in Lausanne, Switzerland". This provides certain context that the FIA does operate in the international sports pyramid world.

Second, the FIA does indeed have an office in Geneva, Switzerland. The CAS, by virtue of its location in Switzerland, could be an appropriate venue to resolve an appeal against ICA decisions as Article 26 of the FIA Statutes explicitly determines that the ICA is subject to the jurisdiction of Swiss Law

> The International Court of Appeal shall be entrusted with judging definitively any dispute or conflict resulting from the application of the present Statutes, of the Statutes of the body governed by Swiss law, of the International Sporting Code, and more generally of the rules and regulations decreed by the FIA, with settling any dispute relating to FIA activities, and with hearing any litigation which may be submitted to it by the President of the FIA.

Ultimately, there are some arguments to suggest that the FIA must be subject to the indirect appeal jurisdiction of the CAS by virtue of incorporation and reference to other statutes.

13.7.2 No Indirect Jurisdiction of the CAS for Decisions of the FIA

The CAS Panel in CAS 2015/A/3872, *Sheikh Khalid Al Qassimi & Abu Dhabi Racing Team v. FIA*, Qatar Motor and Motorcycle Federation, & Nasser Al-Attiyah did not agree with these arguments and refused to hear an appeal against a decision of the FIA ICA.

Here Al Qassimi and Al-Attiyah were competing in the 2014 Dubai International Rally as part of the 2014 FIA Middle East Rally Championship. Al-Attiyah complained to the race stewards that Al Qassimi violated certain racing regulations. The stewards did not agree and Al-Attiyah appealed to the FIA ICA, which did find that Al Qassimi violated racing regulations and granted certain sporting results to Al-Attiyah. Al Qassimi appealed this decision of the ICA to the CAS.

The Panel observed that "CAS decisions have consistently affirmed that in order for the CAS to have jurisdiction to hear an appeal, there must exist a specific arbitration agreement between the parties, or else the jurisdiction of the CAS must be expressly recognized in the statutes or regulations of the sports-related body."[64] The CAS Panel ruled that the general recognition of the IOC and SportAccord did not suffice and that it is necessary for a jurisdictional clause to confer appeal jurisdiction to the CAS. As Article 15 of the FIA Judicial and Disciplinary Rules does not do so, nor do the aforementioned rules incorporate a CAS arbitration clause contained in another statute, the CAS does not have jurisdiction to hear appeals against the FIA ICA's decisions. The general effect of the award is that belonging to the Olympic Movement, ARISF and SportAccord is not sufficient to confer jurisdiction upon the CAS. In relation to the incidence of the fact that the FIA has a seat in Geneva, the Panel concluded that Swiss Law, although favourable towards sport arbitration, cannot create a right to arbitration on its own without a clear arbitration provision.

13.8 Conclusion

As seen above, the early CAS jurisprudence clearly established that Article R47 of the CAS Code required that the statutes of a sports-governing body explicitly recognize CAS jurisdiction in order for the latter to be competent to hear appeals against the sports-governing body's decisions. In this sense, the CAS has consistently applied the doctrine of direct jurisdiction.

[64] CAS 2015/A/3872, *Sheikh Khalid Al Qassimi & Abu Dhabi Racing Team v. FIA, Qatar Motor and Motorcycle Federation & Nasser Al-Attiyah*, para 31.

More recently, the so-called doctrine of indirect jurisdiction has developed, namely in the *Pizarro* and *Flamengo* cases, where jurisdiction will be conferred on the CAS by national federation rules that refer to or incorporate the applicable international federation rules which explicitly recognize the jurisdiction of the CAS.

This jurisprudence goes further than the earlier awards, which required that a federation's statutes explicitly, in no uncertain terms, recognize the jurisdiction of the CAS. This evolution is clearly a response to the increasing complexity of international sports law, which entails that sporting activities are now regulated by numerous complex and sometimes contradictory statutes and other rules.

Nevertheless, the doctrine of indirect jurisdiction does have some limitations as we have seen within the context of the application of the UEFA FFP Regulations and the regulations of the FIA. In this sense, we can observe that although indirect jurisdiction is an argument available to establish CAS jurisprudence, the relevant statute must wholly and fully incorporate the entirety of the other federation's regulations, or specifically incorporate the appeal regulation recognizing the CAS.

In any event, it is interesting to note that the jurisdiction of the CAS in the world of sports law has not yet been entirely consolidated. There are still issues that are not subject to CAS jurisdiction and disputes that will never be heard by a truly international arbitral panel. If the CAS is to further establish its jurisdiction over the entire world of sports law, its recognition must be expanded.

Chapter 14
CAS 2014/A/3730, *FK Bohemians Praha v. FA Czech Republic*, Award of 22 December 2015

Marketa Haindlova

Abstract The dispute described below related to the interpretation of a FACR ("the Respondent") rule indicating that the last two clubs of the Czech second division are to be relegated to the third division at the end of a season. In order to fill the resulting two vacant spots, two clubs are promoted from the third division. FK Bohemians Praha ("the Appellant") claimed that in case of such vacancy, promotion shall be offered to the teams ranked second, third, or fourth. If these teams refuse promotion, the team ranked on the penultimate position in the Czech second division shall not be relegated. In the Respondent's view, by contrast, the relevant rule provides that the promotion shall be offered to any further team of the third division according to its position. The Appellant filed a motion to the FACR Appeal Committee. The Appeal Committee held that it lacked jurisdiction and this decision was challenged before CAS. The CAS Panel held that the argument of the champion not being entitled to promotion was not raised before the FACR's Appeal Committee and therefore could not be the subject of the decision. As the Appellant did not challenge the champion's promotion at the Respondent's level, the Panel could not rule on this issue. Finally, the champion of the third division, contrary to what the Appellant contended, was promoted to and competed in the 2014/2015 season of the Czech second division. The Appellant's appeal invoking that the champion had refused promotion was therefore groundless.

Keywords Football · Applicable law · CAS jurisdiction · Right to due process

M. Haindlova (✉)
Markéta Haindlová—Advokátní Kancelář, Prague, Czech Republic
e-mail: marketa.haindlova@centrum.cz

A. Duval and A. Rigozzi (eds.), *Yearbook of International Sports Arbitration 2015*,
DOI 10.1007/978-94-6265-129-6_14

Contents

14.1 Facts and Procedure

14.1.1 The Facts

The award commented here concerns a dispute between a Czech professional club FK Bohemians Praha (the "Appellant"), which is a member of the Football Association of the Czech Republic, and the latter (the "Respondent" or "FACR"), which is the national football association of the Czech Republic, affiliated to FIFA.

In the sporting season 2013/2014, the Appellant played in the Czech second division, organized by the Respondent, and known, at the time, as the Druhá League. At the end of the 2013/2014 season, the Appellant was penultimate in its league. Pursuant to the relevant regulations of the Respondent, a club ranked on the penultimate position of the second league is to be relegated to the third league, which, contrary to the first and second leagues, is for nonprofessional teams.

The third league consists of the so-called Bohemian Football League (Česká fotbalová liga, CFL) and the Moravian-Silesian Football League (Moravskoslezská fotbalová liga, MSFL). The league assembly and, with it, the draw for the CFL (and MSFL) 2014/2015 season was held, and the Appellant was among the teams foreseen to compete in the CFL. The Appellant, however, was of the opinion that it was not to be relegated to the CFL, and should rather have remained in the second league, given that the teams of the CFL that had ended the 2013/2014 season on a rank allowing them to be promoted to the second league had, as the Appellant contended, refused such promotion.

Nevertheless, the Appellant was not permitted to participate in the league assembly and draw for the second league's 2014/2015 season, on the ground that it had been relegated to, and was to participate in, the third league.

Consequently, the Appellant filed a motion with the Respondent's Appeal Committee, requesting a review of the procedure applied by the steering body of the competitions and its inclusion into the draw for the second league's 2014/2015 season. The Appeal Committee rendered its decision on the same day (the "Challenged Decision") and held that it lacked competence to consider the Appellant's motion.

14.1.2 The Parties' Arguments Before the CAS

14.1.2.1 The Appellant's Statement of Appeal

In its statement of appeal filed on 28 August 2014, the Appellant challenged the decision of the Appeal Committee FACR, considering that it violated the applicable FACR regulations and laws of the Czech Republic, but also the fundamental principles of the organization of sports competitions and the principles of fair play, which national sports associations such as the FACR ought to observe and comply with.

In its appeal brief, the Appellant requested the CAS: to set aside the decision taken by the Respondent's Appeal Committee, dismissing its application for the revision of the procedure of the governing body of the competition and placement of the member of FACR (the Appellant) in the balloting for the Czech Football League, and to replace the aforementioned decision and reinstate the Appellant in the balloting for the Second division of the Czech Football League for the following sporting season. Furthermore, the Appellant asked that the Respondent be ordered to pay compensation to it, in an amount of no less than CZK 15,000,000.

In the alternative, the Appellant requested the CAS to fully accept its appeal against the Decision of the Appeal Board of the Respondent and, as a consequence, to adopt an award annulling said decision and remitting the case to the Appeal Board (pursuant to Article R57 of the CAS Code); to fix a sum of 10.000 CHF to be paid by the Respondent to the Appellant, as a contribution to its legal fees and costs; and to condemn the Respondent to the payment of the whole CAS administration costs and the Arbitrator(s) fees.

The Appellant submitted that the CAS had jurisdiction to decide the dispute on the basis of Articles 3 and 29 of the Statutes of the Respondent, in connection with Article 66(1) of the FIFA Statutes. The Appeal Committee of the Respondent in its Challenged Decision wrongfully denied its competence to hear the Appellant's motion. The Appellant argued that the Challenged Decision violated the applicable regulations of the Respondent, the applicable laws of the Czech Republic as well as fundamental principles of the organization of sports competitions and the principles of fair play. The refusal of the Appeal Committee of the Respondent to hear the appeal of the Appellant constitutes a denial of the Appellant's right to due process and right to equal treatment as well as a violation of the principle of a two-instance process, pursuant to the Statutes of the Respondent.

The second league and the third league competitions are organized in accordance with the Respondent's Competition Regulations and are managed by the relevant governing body which is the League Assembly. Throughout the history of the Respondent, the League Assembly determining the teams which were to participate in the second (and first) league was held before the balloting caucus for the third league took place. However, at the end of the 2013/2014 season, the Respondent for the first time held the balloting caucus for the third league before the League Assembly with the balloting caucus for the second league.

The Appellant was included in the balloting caucus for the third league although a team who had finished the 2013/2014 CFL competition on the first rank, as well as other teams that according to the applicable regulations would have had the right to be promoted to the second league, had refused promotion. In view of this, the Appellant considered that it should have remained in the second league.

The Appellant sent a note to the Respondent pointing out that the rules of the Competition Regulations which were in force at that time had not been followed and that the conduct of the Respondent damaged the Appellant. The League Assembly which would determine the participants of the 2014/2015s league season should take place in accordance with the relevant regulations of the Respondent and in accordance with the otherwise applicable law. Although invited to attend, the Appellant was not admitted to the League Assembly and the reason provided to the Appellant's representative was that the Appellant had been relegated to the third league.

According to the Appellant, the valid version of Article 5(8)(b) of the Competition Rules of the Respondent provided that if the first four teams of the third league did not want to be promoted to the second league, the team which ranked on the higher relegation place (i.e., the penultimate position) in the second league would not be relegated. Nevertheless, Article 5(8) of the Competition Rules was amended on July 18, 2013 without any accompanying statement and without informing the relevant stakeholders. Pursuant to Article 5(8)'s new version, the governing body of the competition has to offer the other (lower ranked) teams from the appropriate competition (CFL, MSFL) the opportunity of being promoted if the higher ranked teams refuse to be promoted. The Appellant contended that such (unexpected and unannounced) amendment of the Competition Rules contravened the general principles of good faith, legal certainty and security, and is intolerable within the sphere of sports law.

Furthermore, not only the champion of the CFL 2013/2014 sporting season, but also the other CFL clubs which had ended right behind it, had rejected promotion, thus the Appellant should have remained in the second league. In addition, because of the Respondent's noncompliance with its own rules and the Appellant not being placed in the second league, the Appellant suffered damage which the Respondent must compensate.

14.1.2.2 The Respondent's Answer

On 28 November 2014, the Respondent filed its answer and requested the CAS to dismiss the appeal, to order the Appellant to pay the costs of the arbitration in full and CHF 10,000 to cover the Respondent's legal fees and out-of-pocket expenses.

The Respondent did not object to the competence of the CAS to hear the matter, and agreed that pursuant to Article R58 of the Code, the dispute was to be determined in accordance with Czech law.

The Respondent confirmed that the Appellant had finished the 2013/2014 season of the second league in the penultimate position.

According the Respondent's Statutes,[1] the Executive Committee of the Respondent is competent to adopt, amend, and issue the Respondent's rules and regulations. Any amendments to the Competition Rules and other regulations are published on the Respondent's website. Further, all key documents of the Respondent are published in hard copy format from time to time, as part of the Set of Regulations that can be purchased by any of its members.

The Respondent also agreed with the Appellant that Article 5(8)(b) of the Competition Rules was the key provision for the purposes of the present dispute. However, in contrast to the Appellant's contentions, the Respondent noted that the version of Article 5(8)(b) that was valid since at least the 2007/2008 sporting season provided that if the CFL team that according to its rank is entitled to promotion to the second league rejects promotion, the managing authority of the league will offer promotion to other teams in the CFL. In 2013, the Executive Committee of the Respondent adopted an amendment to Article 5(8)(b) of the Competition Rules which was published on the Respondent's website and became part of the Respondent's Set of Regulations. Nevertheless, because of widespread criticism by members of both the first and second league, the Executive Committee reviewed its decision and decided not to adopt that particular amendment of the Competition Rules. The Respondent properly published the final wording of Article 5(8) of the Competition Rules on its official website. According to the Respondent, at the League Assembly, where a representative of the Appellant was present, the potential amendment of Article 5(8) was discussed and the members were informed and assured that the rules for promotions to both the first and second league were not changed. This question of a potential amendment of Article 5(8) of the Competition Rules was discussed again during another League Assembly and it was confirmed again that the relevant rule would not be changed (that League Assembly was also attended by a representative of the Appellant).

The Respondent underscored that the Appellant was invoking an obviously invalid wording of the Competition Rules that had been published on the Respondent's official website purely by mistake. Indeed, the Respondent pointed out that the same website contains numerous references to the fact that the change of the Competition Rules upon which the Appellant was relying had not been adopted.

Because the Appellant had finished the 2013/2014 season in the penultimate position of the second league, it attended the drawing caucus for the third league. In contrast to what the Appellant explained, the champion of the CFL was in fact promoted and played in the second league.

According to the Respondent, the Challenged Decision was correct and had been issued in compliance with the Respondent's bylaws, and the Appellant has not proven any damage under Czech law.

[1] Statutes of FACR passed by the General Assembly of FACR on 7 June 2014.

14.1.2.3 The Appellant's Second Brief

According to the Appellant, as Article 29(2) of the Statutes of the Respondent calls for the application of the FIFA provisions and since the FIFA Statutes contain a choice of Swiss law, the case was to be determined by applying Swiss law. The Appellant agreed on the applicability of Czech law only to extent that it does not contravene any legal provision provided by the Swiss legislation which has to be applied mandatorily.

In accordance with Article 12 of the Respondent's Statutes, the Appeals Committee of the Respondent would have been competent to rule on the merits of the motion submitted by the Appellant. In the Appellant's opinion, when discussing the Appellant's motion, the Appeals Committee violated the procedural rules of Article 3(1) of the Appeal and Review Rules of the Respondent as it did not invite any representative of the League Assembly or the Steering Committee (the governing body of the competition) to discuss the motion.

The relevant Competition Rules which were applicable at that time were disregarded and instead of those, a new wording was applied, despite the fact that it had not been properly approved and issued, and therefore had not entered into force. Not only was the wording of Article 5(8) of the Competition Rules to which the Appellant referred published on the Respondent's website, but it was also included in the printed Set of Regulations. The version to which the Respondent referred was uploaded on the day when the Appeal Committee discussed the Appellant's motion.

Even if one was to accept that Article 5(8) of the Competition Rules was modified, one would have to note that the Executive Committee of the Respondent would not have been entitled to adopt such change, as the Competition Rules could not be amended during the sporting year (modified in September when the sporting season had already started). Hence, the relevant applicable version of the Competition Rules was the version to which the Appellant referred, and not the one invoked by the Respondent.

In mid-2014, the champion of the CFL published on its website a thanking note for its fans, but also informed that it was impossible to fulfil the licensing criteria required to be admitted to the second league. In addition, other public media sources reported on the rejection of CFL clubs that would have been eligible for promotion. For this reason, a situation arose where it would have been required to apply the applicable provision under the Competition Rules and decide that the Appellant should not be relegated to the third division.

The Appellant had no other choice than applying for the CFL 2014/2015 season as the drawing caucus for the forthcoming CFL season was held on 21 June 2014, while the League Assembly took place four days later. The Appellant claimed that the scheduling the caucus to CFL competition prior to the League Assembly with caucus for the first and second league was supposed to force the Appellant to apply to the CFL in order to avoid any risk of sanctions under Article 5(3) of the Competition Regulations, and then on the basis of such "fake" application to the

CFL rule on the Appellant's exclusion from the second league on the grounds it had already applied for another category.

The Appellant claimed that the damage it had suffered consisted primarily of the withdrawal of major sponsorship contracts. Sporting loss derived from its undue relegation, resulting in the diminishment of the value of its players (which were now playing in the third instead of the second league). Furthermore, having violated its obligations as an association in relation to the Appellant as a member, the Respondent was to be held liable for its breach and the damage suffered by the Appellant.

In order to be in a position to prove its contentions, the Appellant requested that the Respondent be ordered to produce certain evidence, including the relevant notification by the Respondent of the amendment of the Competition Rules, the description of the licensing procedure applied to the champion of CFL for the 2014/2015 sporting season, the evaluation results of this champion's application, in particular in respect of financial criteria and infrastructure requirements, and the relevant licensing material. The Appellant also requested (1) an explanation by the Respondent's licensing manager as to whether the champion of CFL complied with the relevant criteria, and (2) an explanation by the Respondent as to any potential financial support it had provided to the champion of CFL.

In its conclusions, the Appellant reiterated the prayers for relief it had made in the appeal brief, but omitted its alternative request to the effect that the CAS fully uphold its appeal against the Challenged Decision and, as a consequence, adopted an award annulling the said decision and remanding the case back to the Appeal Board of the Respondent (pursuant to Article R57 of the CAS Code).

14.1.2.4 The Respondent's Rejoinder

In its response to the Appellant's reply brief, the Respondent argued that the dispute was to be determined by applying Czech law, as there was no valid reason for the case to be settled by application of Swiss law.

The Respondent's position was that the Challenged Decision complied with the relevant regulations. The Appeal Committee duly concluded that it had no competence, the champion of CFL was duly promoted to the second league, and Article 5(8)(b) of the Competition Rules was not valid in the wording invoked by the Appellant.

The Appeal Committee had no competence to hear the Appellant's motion as the conditions of Article 12 of the FACR Statutes were not fulfilled. The Appeal Committee was right to determine that the Appellant only challenged the course of action taken by the competition's management body, and it did not challenge a decision of the management body of the competition, nor did it challenge the schedule of competition in itself. Pursuant to Article 12(2) of the FACR Statutes, however, the competence of the FACR Appeal Committee covers only decision-making as to whether the schedules for the competitions of all classes and the decisions of the management bodies are in accordance with the Competition Rules and the schedules for the relevant competitions.

The Respondent should have contested the competition schedule of the second league which was issued on the League Assembly with drawing caucus after the submission of the Appellant's motion. The Respondent, however, did not contest the competition schedule of the second league.

The review procedure which the Appellant chose to initiate is an extraordinary legal remedy with strict conditions and is limited exclusively to the review of decisions made by bodies of the district/regional football associations. In the case at hand, however, no decision of a body of a district/regional football association was made and, subsequently, challenged by the Appellant in its motion.

Given that the Appellant's action was not brought against a concrete steering committee decision, it was not an appeal within the meaning of Article 12 of the FACR Statutes or other applicable rules.

The champion of CFL duly and successfully completed the licensing procedure, it duly and timely submitted an application for the 2014/2015 sporting season and it duly attended the League Assembly with drawing caucus for the second league 2014/2015 season. For these reasons, it is irrelevant what statements were expressed on this team's website or by other media. The winner of the respective lower competition gained the requested license in accordance with the Licensing Manual and signed up to second league. Therefore, in the Respondent's view, the Appellant's appeal was meritless.

The Appellant should have known that Article 5(8)(b) of the Competition Rules was in force almost during the entire sporting season 2013/2014, in the same wording as in the previous seasons. Therefore, the Appellant should have known that the teams finishing on the last and penultimate positions would not remain in the second league and were automatically relegated to the third league.

In contrast to what the Appellant contended, the drawing caucuses for the third league were always, at least in the last three sporting seasons, held before the drawing caucuses for the first and second league took place.

Any decision about the damages sought by the Appellant would be beyond the scope of the Panel's review. Further, the Appellant failed to prove the applicable law, the breach of any of the Respondent's obligations, the existence, and quantum of the damages claimed, as well as the causal link.

14.2 Commentary

14.2.1 The Applicable Rules of Law

Pursuant to Article R58 of the CAS Code, the dispute must be decided "according to the applicable regulations and, subsidiarily, to the rules of law chosen by the parties or, in the absence of such a choice, according to the law of the country in which the federation, association or sports-related body which has issued the challenged decision is domiciled or according to the rules of law the Panel deems appropriate. In the latter case, the Panel shall give reasons for its decision".

As seen above, the Appellant held that Czech law was to be applied to the extent it did not contravene any mandatory provision of Swiss law, while the Respondent contended that the dispute was to be decided pursuant to Czech law.

The case at hand was about a dispute between the Respondent and one of its members, concerning the latter's promotion or relegation with respect of competitions organized under the auspices of the Respondent. The applicable regulations in the sense of Article R58 of the Code are, therefore, the statutes and regulations of the Respondent.[2] Thus, the Panel held that the dispute was to be determined by applying the statutes and regulations of the FACR and, given that there was no express choice of law by the parties, Czech law.[3]

14.2.2 Merits of the Dispute: The Appellant's Request for Setting Aside the Challenged Decision and for Its Reinstatement in the Balloting for the Second League

Pursuant to Article R57 CAS Code, the Panel has full power to review the facts and the law. It may issue a new decision which replaces the decision challenged or annul the decision and refer the case back to the previous instance.[4] The Appellant had the burden of demonstrating, in particular, that it was entitled to request reinstatement in the balloting for the second division, that the Challenged Decision was rendered in violation of the applicable statutes and regulations of the Respondent and must therefore be set aside, and that it suffered a damage in the amount of CZK 15,000,000 for which the Respondent was to be held liable.[5]

Article 2(2)(c) of the Respondent's Statutes provides that the Respondent pursues its objectives, among others, by adopting and issuing rules and regulations to organize and conduct competitions, including the competition rules, competition charts, registration rules, transfer rules, and disciplinary code. Pursuant to Article 10(8)(d), the FACR Executive Committee is the competent body to adopt and issue the FACR rules and regulations, including amendments thereto.[6]

---

[2]CAS 2008/A/1482, *Genoa Cricket and Football Club S.p.A. v. Club Deportivo*, Award of 9 February 2009; CAS 2006/A/1180, *Galatasaray SK v. Frank Ribéry & Olympique de Marseille*, Award of 24 April 2007; CAS 2013/A/3228, *Evgeny V. Levchenko v. Russian Football Association (RFA)*, Award of CAS 15 January 2014.

[3]CAS 2014/A/3730 FK, *Bohemians Praha v. FA Czech Republic*, 22 December 2015, para 78.

[4]Ibid., para 79.

[5]Ibid., paras 80 and 81.

[6]Ibid., para 82.

It was not disputed by the parties that the FACR Executive Committee issued the Competition Rules; the Appellant finished the 2013/2014s league competition on the penultimate position; as a rule, the last two clubs of the second league are to be relegated to the third division at the end of a season; in order to fill the resulting two vacant spots, one club is promoted from each CFL and MSFL to the second league.[7]

The parties were, however, in disagreement as to what rule shall apply in case of any extraordinary vacancy in the second league, e.g., if a team cannot be promoted or rejects promotion from the lower league, although it would have, according to its position at the end of a season, qualified for such promotion. They further disagreed as to whether the Appellant was, as a consequence of one such (alleged) extraordinary vacancy, to be reinstated in the second league for the 2014/2015 season.[8]

The Appellant lodged its motion with the Respondent's Appeal Committee. In that motion the Appellant wrote that, "as is evident from public sources, at least six teams of CFL refused advance to the second league… In view of the above, the Appellant is of the opinion that the procedure of the managing authority violated the rules of FACR, because in a situation where the first four CFL teams clearly refused promotion to a higher class of competition (to the second league) it is necessary to apply the above cited provisions of the Competition Rules of football, therefore decide that the Appellant, which was placed on the higher elevation spot in the second league chart, is not relegated".[9]

In line with its aforementioned motion, in its appeal brief, the Appellant explained that "the champion of CFL, despite having succeeded on the field on gaining the right to promote to the Czech second division at the end of the sporting season 2013/2014, did not manage to fulfil the economic criteria set forth by the Respondent in order to be included in the Czech second division and therefore was compelled to reject being promoted. The team that was ranked second in the CFL at the end of the sporting season 2013/2014 was the subsequent club entitled to substitute the champion. However, this team for the same reasons as the champion also refused the possibility to be promoted to higher division, as was published in the local press and duly notified by both clubs to the Respondent. Accordingly, in the light of applicable regulations at that stage, the Appellant was entitled to maintain its position in the Czech second division due to the express refusal of the CFL champion and the team that was ranked second behind it".[10]

The Panel, thus, noted that the Appellant's motion to the FACR's Appeal Committee, as well as its appeal brief, were submitted on grounds that not only the

[7]Ibid., para 83.

[8]Ibid., para 84.

[9]Ibid., para 85.

[10]Ibid., para 86.

champion of CFL, but also the teams having ranked behind the champion on second, third, and fourth position had rejected promotion to the 2014/2015s league competition. The Appellant therefore argued that in such case of a vacancy, pursuant to Article 5(8)(b) of the Competition Rules, the Appellant should not have been relegated to the third league, but remained in the second league.[11]

It was only in its second brief before the CAS that the Appellant contended that it would have been impossible for the champion of CFL "to have complied with the licensing criteria required for participating in the Czech second division and that the champion's sudden compliance with those criteria could only be due to external (illegal) aid from the Respondent".[12]

In other words, the Appellant's motion for reinstatement which led to the Challenged Decision was based solely on the Appellant's assumption that the champion of CFL, as well as other clubs ranked behind the champion, had *refused* to be promoted to the second league, but not on the ground that the champion should not have been promoted as it had not fulfilled the relevant criteria. The argument of the champion not being entitled to promotion was, thus, not addressed by the FACR's Appeal Committee and, as a consequence, was not (and could not be) the subject of the Challenged Decision. In light of the above, the Panel held that it could not rule on this issue. The Appellant did not challenge the champion's promotion at the Respondent's level. The CAS acting as an appeal body has no competence to determine, as a first instance legal body, licensing issues of the Respondent. Any ruling by the Panel on the issuance of a license to the champion of CFL would be ultra petita and would, most importantly, violate the champion's right to be heard given that that team was not a party to the CAS proceedings and, thus, not in a position to present and defend its position.[13]

For the sake of completeness, the Panel nonetheless considered the Appellant's explanations according to which the champion of CFL should not have been granted a license. In this context the Panel, first, concluded that the Appellant's complaint according to which the champion should not have been promoted to the second league as it had not fulfilled the relevant criteria and that, instead, the Appellant should have remained in the second league, is to be seen as an appeal in a licensing matter.[14]

The Panel also considered whether the Appellant by lodging such an appeal would have followed the appropriate legal path within the Respondent's review process and whether pursuant to the regulations of the Respondent the Appellant would have had a right to lodge an appeal against the grant of a license to another team. In analyzing these questions, the Panel first noted that in accordance with

[11]Ibid., para 87.

[12]Ibid., para 88.

[13]Ibid., para 89.

[14]Ibid., para 91.

Article 7 of the FACR's Licensing Manual, a complaint in respect to the issuance of a license must be filed by means of an appeal with the Licensing Tribunal. The Appellant, however, chose to lodge its motion with the Respondent's Appeal Committee. While this inappropriate choice of legal remedy may not, per se, necessarily preclude the Appellant from an appeal to the CAS, the Panel also noted that, in accordance with Article 7(4) of the Licensing Manual, an appeal in a licensing matter may be lodged only by a license applicant who has not been granted the license by the Licensing Commission (the applicant itself) or a licensee whose license has been revoked by the Licensing Commission or the Respondent's Licensing Manager.

Against this background, the Panel concluded that the Appellant did not fulfil any of these criteria. The Appellant was not the applicant in respect of the license granted to the champion of CFL. The Appellant did not complain about any withdrawal of a license that had been granted to it, and the Appellant is, obviously, not the Respondent's Licensing Manager. In sum, the Panel noted that the rules of the Respondent did and do not allow a third party, such as the Appellant, to lodge an appeal against the grant of a license to another club.[15]

As to the question whether Article 5(8)(b) of the Competition Rules was relevant in the present appeal proceedings, the Appellant explained that in case of a vacancy Article 5(8)(b) of the Competition Rules provides that "to the second league shall advance the team that was ranked second in the CFL or MSFL, depending on which of these competitions the team whose place was vacated in the second league belongs to territorially. If the second-ranked team is not interested in the advancement to the higher league, the governing body will, in turn, offer the possibility to advance to the team that has ranked third and then to the team that has ranked fourth. If even these teams will not have interest in the progress, the team which in the second league ranked on higher relegation place, does not get relegated".[16]

The Respondent, on the other hand, explained that in such case the applicable wording of Article 5(8)(b) would read like that "to the second league shall be promoted, the team that ranked second in either the CFL or MSFL, depending on to which of these leagues the team whose place in the second league became vacant belongs territorially. If this team is not interested in such promotion, the managing authority of the league will offer promotion to other teams in the relevant league (CFL or MSFL), consecutively according their positions".[17]

The Appellant claims that in case of such vacancy, promotion shall be offered to the teams ranked second, third or fourth in either the CFL or MSFL. If these teams decline promotion, the team ranked on the penultimate position in the second league shall not be relegated. In the Respondent's view, however, the relevant rule provides that the team ranked on the penultimate position shall not benefit

[15]Ibid., paras 92–96.

[16]Ibid., para 98.

[17]Ibid., para 99.

from any such vacancy and, therefore, the promotion shall be offered to any further team of the third league according to its position.[18]

For its part, the Panel noted that Article 5(8)(b) of the Competition Rules is to be applied only if and when there is an actual vacancy. In other words, if the teams having ranked first in the CFL and MSFL both advance to the second league, Article 5(8)(b) of the Competition Rules does not have to be applied.[19]

The Panel held that the Respondent had provided sufficient evidence demonstrating that the champion of CFL had been promoted and actually participated in the 2014/2015s league competition. Consequently, the Panel found that there was no need to fill a vacancy in the second league in accordance with Article 5(8)(b) of the Competition Rules.[20]

14.3 Conclusion

In sum, the Panel held that, first, the present appeal was an appeal against the Respondent's Challenged Decision, the subject matter of which was the Appellant's request to be reinstated in the second league in accordance with Article 5(8)(b) of the Competition Rules on ground that the champion of CFL, as well as the other clubs ranked behind the champion, had refused promotion to the second league. Nevertheless, as had been established, the champion, contrary to what the Appellant contended, was promoted to and participated in the 2014/2015s league competition. The Appellant's appeal invoking that the champion had refused promotion was, therefore, groundless, and Article 5(8)(b) of the Competition Rules did not apply.

Second, the Panel held that the Appellant's challenge of the grant of a license to play in the second league to the champion could not be heard in these CAS appeal proceedings.

Third, even if one assumed that the appeal was also about a challenge of the grant of a license to the champion of CFL, it would have to be dismissed as the Respondent's regulations would not entitle the Appellant to challenge the grant of a license to another club.

For these reasons, the Appellant's requests that the Panel set aside the Challenged Decision and reinstate the Appellant in the second league were to be dismissed and, especially, the Panel found that the Appellant's appeal was unfounded and thus to be dismissed entirely.

Finally, more than one year after the commencement of this arbitration, the CAS ruled that the appeal of the Czech football club against the decision of the

---

[18]Ibid., para 100.

[19]Ibid., para 101.

[20]Ibid., para 102.

Appeal Committee of the Czech Football Association was dismissed. Therefore, the decision of the Appeal Committee of the Czech Football Association was confirmed. The Appellant was ordered to bear the entire costs of the arbitration and to pay CHF 5000 to the Respondent, as a contribution towards its legal and other costs incurred in connection with the CAS proceedings.

Part III
Commentaries of Decisions of National Courts

Chapter 15
Oberlandesgericht Bremen, 2 U 67/14, *SV Wilhelmshaven v. Norddeutscher Fußball-Verband e.V*, 30 December 2014

Antoine Duval

Abstract At the very end of 2014, the Oberlandesgericht (OLG) Bremen rendered an important judgment in the dispute opposing a German club, the SV Wilhelmshaven e.V., to its regional association, the Norddeutscher Fußball-Verband e.V. The decision, which has been appealed to the Bundesgerichtshof (BGH), was not as commented as the nearly simultaneous judgment of the OLG München in the *Pechstein* case. Nonetheless, it entails important considerations regarding FIFA's training compensation system and its private enforcement mechanism of CAS awards and FIFA decisions. In this commentary, I will first summarize the facts and the procedure of the case, and then discuss its impact on the compatibility of FIFA's training compensation system with EU law. Finally, I will show how this ruling might put into question the internal enforcement system established by FIFA to bypass the traditional procedure of recognition of international awards.

Keywords CAS · FIFA · EU law · Sports law · Bosman · Training compensation · Lex sportiva

Contents

A. Duval (✉)
T.M.C ASSER Institute for European and International Law,
The Hague, The Netherlands
e-mail: a.duval@asser.nl

A. Duval and A. Rigozzi (eds.), *Yearbook of International Sports Arbitration 2015*,
DOI 10.1007/978-94-6265-129-6_15

15.1 Facts and Procedure of the Case

The case involves the move of an Argentinean player, holder of an Italian citizenship, to the SV Wilhelmshaven and the training compensation due to his former youth clubs back in Argentina based on the FIFA RSTP. The player, born in 1987, was an amateur player with two Argentinean clubs: Club Atlético Excursionistas from 20 March 1998 to 7 March 2005, and Club Atlético River Plate from 8 March 2005 until 7 February 2007. From 8 February 2007 to 30 June 2007, he signed a fixed-term professional contract with SV Wilhelmshaven, which was later extended for one season.

Back then, SV Wilhelmshaven was playing in the Regional League Nord (fourth tier of German football) and was therefore considered as a club of category 3 for the purpose of the application of the FIFA RSTP. In June 2007, Excursionistas and River Plate initiated proceedings with the FIFA DRC claiming € 100,000 and 60,000 respectively in training compensation. These claims were granted (partially for River Plate which obtained € 57,500) by the DRC in two concomitant decisions on 5 December 2008.[1]

SV Wilhelmshaven decided to appeal the DRC's decisions to the CAS. A hearing in front of a sole arbitrator was held on 26 August 2009 and the final award rendered on 5 October 2009.[2] The arbitrator confirmed the DRC decisions awarding the claimed compensations to both Argentinean clubs and rejected all the objections raised by SV Wilhelsmshaven.

The club, however, continued stubbornly to refuse to pay the training compensations. Henceforth, on 13 September 2011, FIFA's disciplinary Committee sanctioned SV Wilhelmshaven with a fine of CHF 22,500 and imposed a payment deadline of 30 days. In case the club refused to abide by the deadline, its first team would face a 6 points penalty. In light of SV Wilhelmshaven's non-compliance with this decision, FIFA called on the Deutsche Fußball Bund (DFB) to enforce the sanction and secure the payment of the fines. On 9 March 2012,

[1]Decision of the FIFA DRC, *River Plate v. SV Wilhemshaven*, 5 December 2008. http://www.fifa.com/mm/document/affederation/administration/drctraining/128921a.pdf. Accessed 10 January 2016. Decision of the FIFA DRC, *Excursionistas v. SV Wilhelmshaven*, 5 December 2008. http://www.fifa.com/mm/document/affederation/administration/drctraining/128921b.pdf. Accessed 10 January 2016.

[2]CAS 2009/A/1810 & 1811, *SV Wilhelmshaven v. Club Atlético Excursionistas & Club Atlético River Plate*, Award of 5 October 2009.

the DFB dutifully implemented FIFA's request, a decision which was later confirmed by its internal tribunal (DFB-Sportgericht) on 14 November 2012. 6 points were deducted from the ranking of SV Wilhelmshaven's first team in the Season 2011/2012. Furthermore, the club's financial account with the DFB was debited with the requested € 21,150. Nevertheless, the club kept on refusing to pay the training compensations awarded by the DRC and the CAS.

On 15 August 2012, FIFA again asked the DFB to deduct 6 more points from SV Wilhelmshaven's first team's total for the Season 2012/2013. Given that, in the meantime, the club had been relegated at the end of the 2011/2012 season to a lower league, the Norddeutscher Fussball Verband (NFV) was competent to implement the latest round of sanctions. It did so on 23 August 2012 and its internal tribunal later confirmed the validity of this decision on 1 October 2012. Concurrently, on 5 October 2012, a new decision of the FIFA DC requested the relegation of the club. SV Wilhelmshaven appealed the decision to CAS, which confirmed FIFA's disciplinary decision on 24 October 2013.[3] The forced relegation was definitely ratified by the board of the NFV on 7 December 2013 and validated by its internal tribunal on 20 February 2014.

Thereafter, the club decided to challenge the implementation of the FIFA sanctions by the DFB and the NFV in front of the Landgericht (LG) Bremen. On 25 April 2014, the LG simply rejected the claims of the club and considered that the CAS award, not challenged by the club in front of the SFT, was a valid legal basis for the sanctions and that the DFB and NFV were bound by their statutes to enforce FIFA's disciplinary decisions.[4] The club swiftly appealed the ruling to the OLG Bremen, which in its decision of 30 December 2014 overruled the LG. It held that the CAS award was contrary to EU law and, therefore, could not constitute a valid ground for the FIFA sanctions. Thus, the NFV should have refused to implement those sanctions. The OLG's decision touches upon two important legal questions: the compatibility of FIFA's training compensation rules with EU law and the duty of German (national or regional) football associations to implement the disciplinary sanctions issued by FIFA. It has been appealed to the highest German civil court, the BGH, which is due to decide on the matter in 2016.

[3]CAS 2012/A/3032, *SV Wilhelmshaven v. Club Atlético Excursionistas*, Award of 24 October 2013.

[4]LG Bremen, 12 O 129/13, *SV Wilhelmshaven v. Norddeutscher Fußball-Verband e.V*, 25 April 2014. See Heermann 2014.

15.2 The Compatibility of FIFA's Training Compensation System with EU Law

The first aspect of the case that is of interest to international and European sports (and particularly football) lawyers is the one regarding the compatibility with EU law of FIFA's training compensation system as enshrined in the FIFA RSTP. It is well known that the current FIFA training compensation system was put in place in the aftermath of the CJEU's *Bosman*[5] ruling. Yet, its compatibility with EU law was never really tested in front of courts.

15.2.1 The FIFA RSTP's Training Compensation System

I will first focus on FIFA's training compensation regime enshrined in Article 20 of the 2015 version of the FIFA RSTP.[6] It must be recalled that the predecessor of the current FIFA RSTP was adopted after nearly 2 years of negotiations between the European Commission, UEFA, FIFA and FIFPro.[7] The negotiations ended early 2001 with the adoption of a set of principles meant to serve as a blueprint for the drafting of new FIFA transfer regulations.[8] Concerning training compensations, the principles stipulated that "in the case of players aged under 23, a system of training compensation should be in place to encourage and reward the training effort of clubs, in particular small clubs".

Article 20 of the FIFA RSTP, transposing this principle, reads as follows:

> "Training compensation shall be paid to a player's training club(s): (1) when a player signs his first contract as a professional, and (2) each time a professional is transferred until the end of the season of his 23rd birthday. The obligation to pay training compensation arises whether the transfer takes place during or at the end of the player's contract. The provisions concerning training compensation are set out in Annexe 4 of these regulations".

Hence, Article 20 establishes two different scenarios giving rise to a right to a training compensation: the signing of a first professional contract and each transfer

[5] CJEU, C-415/93, *Union Royale Belge des Sociétés de Football Association and others v. Bosman and others*, ECLI:EU:C:1995:463.

[6] If not indicated otherwise I refer to the 2015 version of the FIFA RSTP. http://resources.fifa.com/mm/document/affederation/administration/02/70/95/52/regulationsstatusandtransfer_2015_e_v051015_neutral.pdf. Accessed 10 January 2016.

[7] On these negotiations see Irving 2002. See also the work of Borja García on the informal agreement between the EU Commission and UEFA and FIFA: García 2007, 2011.

[8] European Commission, IP/01/314, Outcome of discussions between the Commission and FIFA/UEFA on FIFA Regulations on international football transfers, 5 March 2001. http://europa.eu/rapid/press-release_IP-01-314_en.htm. Accessed 10 January 2016.

until the end of the season of the player's 23rd birthday. The key to understanding how this duty to pay a training compensation operates in practice is only to be found in Annex 4 of the FIFA RSTP. Article 1(1) of Annex 4 qualifies the scope of the obligation to pay a training compensation. It states that:

> "A player's training and education takes place between the ages of 12 and 23. Training compensation shall be payable, as a general rule, up to the age of 23 for training incurred up to the age of 21, unless it is evident that a player has already terminated his training period before the age of 21. In the latter case, training compensation shall be payable until the end of the season in which the player reaches the age of 23, but the calculation of the amount payable shall be based on the years between the age of 12 and the age when it is established that the player actually completed his training".

Pursuant to Article 2(2) of Annex 4, a training compensation is not due when "the former club terminates the player's contract without just cause (without prejudice to the rights of the previous clubs)", or when "the player is transferred to a category 4 club, or if a professional reacquires amateur status on being transferred".[9]

To calculate the amount of training compensation due, every football association that is a member of FIFA is "to divide [its] clubs into a maximum of four categories in accordance with the clubs' financial investment in training players".[10] For each category the training costs are equivalent to "the amount needed to train one player for one year multiplied by an average "player factor", which is the ratio of players who need to be trained to produce one professional player".[11] The training compensation is meant to cover "the costs that would have been incurred by the new club if it had trained the player itself".[12] Thus it is calculated "by taking the training costs of the new club multiplied by the number of years of training, in principle from the season of the player's 12th birthday to the season of his 21st birthday".[13] The training costs for players for the seasons between their 12th and 15th birthdays, however, are always based "on the training and education costs of category 4 clubs".[14]

Following the negotiations with the European Commission, FIFA carved out a specific provision for players moving from one association to another inside the territory of the EU (including the associations based in states party to the European Economic Area). This provision stipulates that "[i]f the player moves from a lower to a higher category club, the calculation shall be based on the average training costs of the two clubs".[15] On the other hand, if the player moves from

[9]Article 2(12) Annex 4 FIFA RSTP.

[10]Article 4(1) Annex 4 FIFA RSTP.

[11]Ibid.

[12]Article 5(1) Annex 4 FIFA RSTP.

[13]Article 5(2) Annex 4 FIFA RSTP.

[14]Article 5(3) Annex 4 FIFA RSTP.

[15]Article 6(1)(a) Annex 4 FIFA RSTP.

a higher to a lower category, "the calculation shall be based on the training costs of the lower category club".[16] Moreover, "the final season of training [in the sense of Article 1(1) Annex 4] may occur before the season of the player's 21st birthday if it is established that the player completed his training before that time".[17] Finally, "[i]f the former club does not offer the player a contract, no training compensation is payable unless the former club can justify that it is entitled to such compensation".[18]

The FIFA framework applicable to training compensations is not easy to navigate and many of its provisions have been refined by the jurisprudence of the CAS and FIFA DRC.[19] Some economists have been pointing out the need to introduce mechanisms to compensate for the "muscle drain"[20] generated by the dramatic economic imbalances between clubs and leagues across the world. In this regard, the FIFA rules were labelled an "important role model".[21] Yet, the compatibility of this complex regulatory structure with EU law has never been tested in front of national or European courts. This makes this challenge by the SV Wilhelmshaven so interesting.

15.2.2 The Compatibility of FIFA's Training Compensation System with EU Law: Many Questions

In its *Bosman* ruling, the CJEU famously held that the aim of "encouraging the recruitment and training of young players must be accepted as legitimate".[22] It added, "that the prospect of receiving transfer, development or training fees is indeed likely to encourage football clubs to seek new talent and train young players".[23] Nevertheless, it concluded that "because it is impossible to predict the sporting future of young players with any certainty and because only a limited number of such players go on to play professionally, those fees are by nature contingent and uncertain and are in any event unrelated to the actual cost borne by clubs of training both future professional players and those who will never play

[16]Article 6(1)(b) Annex 4 FIFA RSTP.

[17]Article 6(2) Annex 4 FIFA RSTP.

[18]Article 6(3) Annex 4 FIFA RSTP.

[19]See De Weger 2008, pp. 117–133 and Bakker 2008.

[20]Andreff 2006, pp. 325–330.

[21]Ibid., p. 329.

[22]CJEU, C-415/93, *Union Royale Belge Stés de Football Association et al. v. Bosman et al.*, para 106.

[23]Ibid., para 108.

professionally".[24] Hence, receiving such fees could not be "a decisive factor in encouraging recruitment and training of young players or an adequate means of financing such activities, particularly in the case of smaller clubs".[25] As a final nail into the coffin of training compensations, at least it was thought at that time, the Court explicitly followed its Advocate General in holding that "the same aims can be achieved at least as efficiently by other means which do not impede freedom of movement for workers".[26]

In the aftermath of the *Bosman* ruling, FIFA simply disregarded the proposals made by Advocate General Lenz when suggesting alternative financing mechanisms to support the training of players.[27] Instead the FIFA training compensation system as it stands nowadays is a stark rebuttal to the CJEU's stand in *Bosman*. In fact, it pretends to do the impossible in the eyes of the Court: calculating realistically the costs of training a player in a specific club in order to offer an objective benchmark for the training compensations.[28] This scheme is an updated version of FIFA's proposals as endorsed by the EU Commission in its informal agreement with FIFA and UEFA in 2001. Nevertheless, the Commission's endorsement is not binding on the Court, and many prominent authors have expressed scepticism as to the compatibility of the FIFA RSTP with EU law.[29]

A real life legal test in front of the CJEU is yet to occur, though it came close to it in the recent *Bernard* case.[30] In its ruling, the CJEU reaffirmed that "the objective of encouraging the recruitment and training of young players must be accepted as legitimate".[31] It also recognized that "the clubs which provided the training could be discouraged from investing in the training of young players if they could not obtain reimbursement of the amounts spent for that purpose where, at the end of his training, a player enters into a professional contract with another club".[32] Thus, it held "that a scheme providing for the payment of compensation for training where a young player, at the end of his training, signs a professional

---

[24]Ibid., para 109.

[25]Ibid.

[26]Ibid., para 110.

[27]Opinion of Advocate General Lenz in case C-415/93, para 239.

[28]This was always the key (and controversial) question for the assessment of the compatibility of training compensations with EU law. In other words: "The question of the necessity of payments on the occasion of the transfer of a player depends essentially on the amount of the payment and hence on the basis of calculation. Objective criteria are thus needed, which ought to be based primarily on the costs of training". Egger and Stix-Hackl 2002, p. 89.

[29]For a leading EU law scholar it is "far from clear that the Commission's "compromise" agreement with football governing authorities is fully compatible with EC law". Weatherill 2003, p. 71. See also Drolet 2006.

[30]CJEU, C-325/08, *Olympique Lyonnais SASP v. Olivier Bernard and Newcastle UFC*, ECLI:EU:C:2010:143. On this case see Pijetlovic 2010, Weatherill 2010, Hendrickx 2010 and Lindholm 2010.

[31]CJEU, C-325/08, para 39.

[32]Ibid., para 44.

contract with a club other than the one which trained him can, in principle, be justified by the objective of encouraging the recruitment and training of young players".[33] However, to be proportionate, the scheme must take "due account of the costs borne by the clubs in training both future professional players and those who will never play professionally".[34] In the *Bernard* case, the French system in place at the time of the dispute, and since then replaced, was deemed incompatible with EU law as the amount of the compensation was not directly correlated with the costs of training the player. What would be the CJEU's assessment if it were confronted with the FIFA RSTP? Would it conclude that the training compensations as calculated by FIFA constitute an unlawful restriction of the free movement of the players, or would it deem them justified? Which are the training costs to be taken into account? Those of the old club or those of the new club? Many were prompt to see, in the *Bernard* judgment, a "significant step forward"[35] in the recognition of the compatibility of the FIFA system with EU law.[36] The present SV Wilhelmshaven case is a good opportunity to test this assumption.

15.2.3 The Compatibility of FIFA's Training Compensation System with EU Law: Some Answers in the SV Wilhelmshaven Case

SV Wilhelmshaven had argued in front of the CAS that the FIFA RSTP was contrary to the right to free movement of workers under EU law insofar that it would impose in case of a transfer of a European citizen from Argentina to Germany that the training compensation be based only on the training costs saved by the German club. However, the single arbitrator, relying on previous CAS awards, held that "such argument would have been available to the individual Player, not to the Appellant".[37] This interpretation goes against the well-established case law of the CJEU,[38] as noted by the OLG Bremen.[39] Consequently, the CAS also declined to

[33]Ibid., para 45.

[34]Ibid.

[35]A phrase used by UEFA's Head of European Affairs, see Zylberstein 2010.

[36]"Prima facie, it appears that Article 20 and Annex 4 of the FIFA Regulations satisfy the general criteria of the judgment in *Bernard*". Pijetlovic 2010, p. 867.

[37]CAS 2009/A/1810 & 1811, *SV Wilhelmshaven v. Excursionistas & River Plate,* para 42. Referring to CAS 2004/A/794 (parties and date unknown) and CAS 2006/A/1027, *Blackpool F.C. v. Club Topp Oss*, Award of 13 July 2006, para 41.

[38]"Whilst the rights deriving from Article 48 of the Treaty are undoubtedly enjoyed by those directly referred to—namely, workers—there is nothing in the wording of that article to indicate that they may not be relied upon by others, in particular employers". CJEU, C-350/96, *Clean Car Autoservice Gmbh v. Landeshauptmann von Wien*, ECLI:EU:C:1998:205, para 19.

[39]OLG Bremen, 2 U 67/14, *SV Wilhelmshaven v. Norddeutscher Fußball-Verband e.V*, Decision of 30 December 2014.

recognize the applicability to the case at hand of Article 6 of the Annex 4 FIFA RSTP. It considered that "[t]he title of this provision clearly suggests that its scope is narrowly circumscribed within a limited geographic area, *i.e.* the EU/EEA territory".[40] Furthermore, the arbitrator considered "that Article 6 of Annex 4 to the FIFA Regulations is nothing more than the codification of the system agreed upon by the European authorities and put into place to govern the transfer of a player moving from one association to another inside the territory of the EU/EEA".[41] Thus, he saw "no reason to depart from the unambiguous wording of Article 6 of Annex 4 to the FIFA Regulations, which is obviously not applicable in the case of a player moving from a country outside the EU/EEA to a country within the EU/EEA".[42] On this exact point, the OLG Bremen begged to differ.

The OLG was not convinced by the distinction between intra-EU and extra-EU transfers made in Article 6 Annex 4 FIFA RSTP. Under the CJEU's jurisprudence, the right to free movement is also enjoyed by EU workers moving from a non-EU state to an EU Member state.[43] Hence, in the view of the OLG, not only could the club legitimately invoke the right to free movement of its player, but it was also right to consider that Article 6 Annex 4 FIFA RSTP should have been applicable to an EU citizen moving from Argentina to Germany. Consequently, the German judges held that the non-application of Article 6 Annex 4 FIFA RSTP and the imposition of the calculation method foreseen in Articles 4 and 5 Annex 4 FIFA RSTP were contrary to the player's free movement rights under EU law.[44]

Nonetheless, the OLG Bremen also acknowledged that the FIFA training compensation rules were in principle supporting "the objective of encouraging the recruitment and training of young players".[45] Furthermore, at least Article 6 (1)(b)

[40]CAS 2009/A/1810 & 1811, *SV Wilhelmshaven v. Excursionistas & River Plate*, para 46.

[41]Ibid., para 49.

[42]Ibid.

[43]In this regard, the OLG refers to CJEU, C-122/96, *Stephen Austin Saldanha and MTS Securities Corporation v. Hiross Holding AG,* ECLI:EU:C:1997:458.

[44]"Die hier vorgenommene Entschädigung orientiert sich somit nicht an den für die Ausbildung bei den argentinischen Vereinen angefallenen Kosten, sondern nimmt einen Ausgleich in Höhe des pauschal eingeschätzten Aufwands vor, der dem übernehmenden Verein im Hinblick auf diesen Spieler erspart worden ist. Durch die Bemessung der Abfindung an der wirtschaftlichen "Wertigkeit" des Kontinentalverbandes des übernehmenden Fußballklubs sowie an dessen "Wertigkeit" innerhalb seines Verbandes orientiert an der Spielklasse, in der sich der Verein befindet, findet letztlich eine Abfindung nach dem Wert des Spielers statt, den dieser unter pauschalierter Einschätzung der wirtschaftlichen Leistungsfähigkeit des übernehmenden Vereins für diesen hat. Für den Senat unterscheidet sich diese Art der Abfindung nicht entscheidend von den Abfindungsregeln, die der EuGH in der Bosman-Entscheidung und in der Entscheidung Olympique Lyonnais als nach Article 45 AEUV (bzw. Article 48 EG-Vertrag a.F.) mit dem Recht auf Freizügigkeit nicht vereinbar eingestuft hat". OLG Bremen, 2 U 67/14, para II.1.h).

[45]Ibid.

of Annex 4 FIFA RSTP is deemed suitable to attain this objective and compatible with EU law.[46] The key point being for training compensations to cover only the real costs incurred to train the player,[47] this is what the CAS and the DRC had failed to take in account in the calculation of the training compensation owed by the SV Wilhelmshaven.[48] For FIFA's training compensation system overall, this case is rather comforting.[49] In line with the CJEU's *Bernard* ruling, the German court found that the current rules applicable to EU players moving inside the EU territory are aimed at attaining a legitimate objective (encouraging the training of players) and proportionate to this objective as long as the training compensations are calculated (at least partly) based on the costs sustained by the training club. The aspect of the CAS and DRC's interpretations of the FIFA RSTP which the OLG Bremen found to be clearly in breach of EU law is limited to cases involving EU nationals moving from outside the territory of the EU to an EU member state. Hence, the *SV Wilhelsmhaven* case is actually less a threat to FIFA's post-*Bosman* training compensation scheme, than to its private enforcement system of CAS awards.

15.3 The Challenge to the Private Enforcement System of CAS Awards by FIFA

One of the many reasons for the popularity of the CAS is the ability of SGBs to self-enforce CAS awards without the need for further formal recognition by the public authorities. As we will see, this ability is put into question by the OLG Bremen's ruling.

[46]"Soweit in Article 6 Ziff. 1.b) bei einem Wechsel des Spielers von einem Verein der höheren in eine niedrigere Kategorie die Entschädigung gemäß den Trainings–kosten des Vereins der tieferen Kategorie bemessen wird, handelt es sich um eine Regelung, die zu einer Erleichterung des Vereinswechsels führt, also gegenüber der an sich erforderlichen Orientierung an den Kosten des ausbilden–den Vereins im Hinblick auf Article 45 AEUV eine Besserstellung des Spielers enthält und daher insoweit unbedenklich ist". Ibid.

[47]"Transferentschädigungen erfüllen mithin die Funktion des Ersatzes von Ausbildungskosten nur dann, wenn sie sich an den tatsächlichen angefallenen Ausbildungskosten orientieren und nicht am Marktwert des fertigen Spielers". Ibid.

[48]"Die hier vorgenommene Entschädigung orientiert sich somit nicht an den für die Ausbildung bei den argentinischen Vereinen angefallenen Kosten, sondern nimmt einen Ausgleich in Höhe des pauschal eingeschätzten Aufwands vor, der dem übernehmenden Verein im Hinblick auf diesen Spieler erspart worden ist". Ibid.

[49]In this regard, I differ from the more critical assessment of the EU law analysis used by the OLG provided in Orth and Stopper 2015, pp. 54–56.

15.3.1 The Private Enforcement System of CAS Awards by FIFA

The CAS was not always a successful arbitral venue, it is only after the entry into force of the World Anti-Doping Code and the decision of FIFA to enable appeals against its internal decisions to the CAS that the "Supreme Court of World Sport" really took off. Appeals of FIFA decisions constitute an important share of the CAS caseload. This is most likely a byproduct of the economic dominance of football in global sport. The CAS attractiveness is also probably correlated to the comparative advantage of CAS (and FIFA) proceedings over recourse to civil courts in contractual disputes involving clubs and/or players.[50] Indeed, in any CAS procedure involving a FIFA decision, the final award will enjoy the support of FIFA at the enforcement stage.[51] This system has been deemed "significantly more effective, quicker and less expensive than the recognition and enforcement of an arbitral award under the NYC".[52] This principle is enshrined in Article 64 of the FIFA Disciplinary Code, which foresees:

1. Anyone who fails to pay another person (such as a player, a coach or a club) or FIFA a sum of money in full or part, even though instructed to do so by a body, a committee or an instance of FIFA or a subsequent CAS appeal decision (financial decision), or anyone who fails to comply with another decision (non- financial decision) passed by a body, a committee or an instance of FIFA, or by CAS (subsequent appeal decision):
   a) will be fined for failing to comply with a decision;
   b) will be granted a final deadline by the judicial bodies of FIFA in which to pay the amount due or to comply with the (non-financial) decision;
   c) (only for clubs:) will be warned and notified that, in the case of default or failure to comply with a decision within the period stipulated, points will be deducted or relegation to a lower division ordered. A transfer ban may also be pronounced;
   d) (only for associations) will be warned and notified that, in the case of default or failure to comply with a decision within the period stipulated, further disciplinary measures will be imposed. An expulsion from a FIFA competition may also be pronounced.
2. If a club disregards the final time limit, the relevant association shall be requested to implement the sanctions threatened.
3. If points are deducted, they shall be proportionate to the amount owed.
4. A ban on any football-related activity may also be imposed against natural persons.
5. Any appeal against a decision passed in accordance with this article shall be lodged with CAS directly.

A forerunner of this provision was first introduced in Article 70 of the FIFA Disciplinary Code in 2005.[53] Back then it did not mention directly the enforce-

[50] De Weger 2008, p. 39.

[51] According to Ulrich Haas citing the FIFA Disciplinary Committee this enforcement mechanism would fail in less than one per cent of cases. See Haas 2014, p. 13.

[52] Ibid.

[53] Article 70 FIFA DC (version 2005).

ment of CAS awards but only of FIFA decisions. Already in 2006, the CAS decided that it could also apply to CAS awards.[54] Thereafter, the provision was modified to explicitly include CAS awards in 2007.[55] Finally, it was again changed in 2011 to the current formulation of Article 64 FIFA DC. This final change reflected the will of FIFA to clearly exclude from the scope of this provision the awards which were adopted pursuant to the ordinary procedure of the CAS.[56]

This system is based on a gradual pressure exercised by the FIFA Disciplinary Committee on the debtor, starting with fines and points deductions and ending with bans and relegations. Such a private system of enforcement, which circumvents the national civil law procedures, is a peculiar attribute of the sporting society, but it is not exclusive to it.[57] Yet, it challenges one of the core pillars of the political theory underlying the sovereignty of the nation state, its monopoly on force.[58] Though, the force exercised by FIFA is merely of symbolic nature, and can be challenged in front of national courts in our transnational age it plays a role that is functionally equivalent to the police powers of states. This *de facto* power of FIFA is not uncontroversial, and has been attacked before the SFT in the past.[59] The case in question involved a Spanish football club, Rayo Vallecano de Madrid SAD, which challenged the dismissal by the CAS of an appeal it had lodged against a decision of the FIFA Disciplinary Committee aimed at enforcing a previous decision by the FIFA PSC.[60] The club argued in front of the SFT that the

[54]A Panel held that "although CAS is assuredly not "a body of FIFA", its awards are to be considered, under the FIFA Statutes and from its perspective, to have the same effect as a decision issued by a body of FIFA. As a result, the failure to comply with a CAS award, in addition to the possible enforcement proceedings available at State level, exposes a party affiliated with FIFA also to a possible disciplinary proceeding, in accordance with Article 70 FDC. Any different interpretation would seriously impair the efficiency and effectiveness of the FIFA disciplinary system: appeal to the CAS is intended to secure an external review of the FIFA decisions, and cannot be construed as a way to obtain per se, even on the basis of frivolous appeals, an immunity from the disciplinary sanctions for non-compliance with obligations imposed by FIFA rules", CAS 2005/A/957, *Clube Atlético Mineiro v. Fédération Internationale de Football Association (FIFA)*, Award of 23 March 2006, para 26.

[55]The new provision was enshrined in Article 71 FIFA DC, which became Article 64 FIFA DC in 2009.

[56]Haas 2014, p. 15.

[57]As shown, for example, by the study on diamond dealers in New York by Lisa Bernstein, see Bernstein 1992.

[58]Max Weber famously held that "a state is a human community that (successfully) claims the monopoly of the legitimate use of physical force within a given territory".

[59]See SFT 4P.240/2006, decision of 5 January 2007. See also Haas 2014, pp. 14–15.

[60]More factual details on the case can be found in the CAS award, see CAS 2006/A/1008, *Rayo Vallecano de Madrid SAD v. Fédération Internationale de Football Association (FIFA)*, Award of 21 August 2006.

adoption (and/or the threat) by FIFA of sanctions meant to enforce a financial claim between two private parties would be incompatible with the ban on private enforcement, pertaining to the fundamental principle of the monopoly of the state on enforcement, which forms part of public policy,[61] thus constituting a violation of Article 190(2)(e) PILA. The SFT dismissed the claim. It left open the question whether such a monopoly of the state on enforcement is actually part of substantive public policy.[62] Instead, it simply held that "on closer inspection" FIFA was not in practice imposing a forced execution of a monetary claim.[63] This was supported by the fact that FIFA lacked the ability to use the procedural tools available to the state, as for example the seizure and commercialization of assets.[64] Hence, it qualified the decision of the FIFA DC, and the ensuing CAS awards, as a sanction derived from the rights of the association to discipline its members.[65] It is recognized that a Swiss association can impose sanctions on its members to ensure the respect of the rules it deems necessary to attain its purpose.[66] This is an elegant way to avoid dealing with an extremely complex and controversial issue: the public-like enforcement power of private associations in the sport sector. The difficulty of this circumvention is reflected in the decision of the SFT. The Court acknowledges that the members of FIFA are not entirely free to join (or resign)

[61]"Die Beschwerdeführerin rügt eine Verletzung des Ordre public nach Article 190 Abs. 2 lit. e IPRG. Die Aussprechung bzw. die unmittelbare Androhung von schwerwiegenden Sanktionen durch die Beschwerdegegnerin im Rahmen der "Vollstreckung" einer finanziellen Forderung zwischen Personen des Privatrechts (vorliegend die Beschwerdeführerin und der brasilianische Club) verstosse gegen das Verbot der privaten Zwangsvollstreckung, welches Teil des fundamentalen und dem Ordre public zuzurechnenden Prinzips des Vollstreckungsmonopols des Staates sei". SFT 4P.240/2006, para 4.

[62]Ibid., para 4.2.

[63]"Denn—richtig besehen—geht es beim angefochtenen Schiedsspruch und dem Beschluss der FIFA-Disziplinarkommission nicht um die Zwangsvollstreckung einer Geldforderung". Ibid., para 4.2.

[64]"Die Beschwerdegegnerin masst sich aufgrund des Beschlusses ihrer Disziplinarkommission nicht etwa die dem Staat zur Vollstreckung von Geldforderungen zur Verfügung stehenden Zwangsmassnahmen an, wie die Pfändung und Verwertung nach dem Schuldbetreibungs–und Konkursrecht". Ibid.

[65]"Der angefochtene Schiedsspruch betrifft keine Zwangsvollstreckung, sondern Sanktionen auf vereinsrechtlicher Grundlage. Es ist im schweizerischen Vereinsrecht anerkannt, dass die Verletzung von Mitgliedschaftspflichten Sanktionen wie Vereins—oder Verbandsstrafen zur Folge haben kann[...]". Ibid.

[66]"Wenn ein privater Verein (wie vorliegend die Beschwerdegegnerin) zur Erreichung seines Zwecks Regeln und Bestimmungen aufstellt, denen sich seine Mitglieder unterwerfen, ist es grundsätzlich zulässig, dass er Sanktionen vorsieht, um die Verpflichtungen der Mitglieder abzusichern". Ibid.

from FIFA, as it is in a monopoly position.[67] Nonetheless, *in fine*, the judges endorse the legality of the private power of FIFA and deny that it might conflict with the monopoly on enforcement of the state and therefore public policy within the meaning of Article 190(2)(e) PILA.[68] Hence, this decision left untouched the practical contradiction at play between public and private enforcement in sports cases.

In fact, a few years later, in 2012, the private enforcement issue popped up again in the *Matuzalem* case,[69] although this time around it was not the principle of private enforcement that was challenged, but the scope of the sanctions FIFA can impose on the basis of its private enforcement system. In 2009, Matuzalem was found in breach of his contract by the CAS and ordered to pay a substantial compensation of € 11,858,934 to his former club Shakhtar Donetsk.[70] As he did not abide with the CAS award, Matuzalem was sanctioned on 31 August 2010 by the FIFA Disciplinary Committee and threatened with a lifelong ban from any football-related activity.[71] The CAS confirmed the sanction and Matuzalem appealed the award to the SFT. The appellant argued that the threat of a lifelong ban was contrary to his freedom to exercise a profession enshrined in Article 27(2) of the Swiss Constitution and an excessive restriction of its legal personality contrary to Article 27 CC.[72] In a nutshell, the SFT found that the threat of an unlimited occupational ban constitutes a substantial restriction to the Appellant's freedom and disregards the limits to contractual commitments enshrined in Article 27(2) CC.[73] Henceforth, the award is declared contrary to substantive public policy as provided under Article 190(2)(e) PILA. This is the first award in Switzerland to be overturned by the SFT on the basis of being contrary to substantive public policy.[74] It highlights both the risks of allowing private enforcement and the existence of some legal checks to control these risks under Swiss law. In other words, FIFA's private enforcement system is allowed to operate by the SFT only if it inflicts proportionate and reasonable sanctions to clubs, players or national associations.

---

[67]"Die Mitglieder unterwerfen sich solchen Sanktionsmöglichkeiten freiwillig, auch wenn—wie die Beschwerdeführerin mit einer gewissen Berechtigung geltend macht—bei der dominanten Stellung, wie sie die Beschwerdegegnerin im Fussball einnimmt, die Möglichkeit des Austritts für einen Fussballclub, der an Meisterschaften mitspielen möchte, kaum in Frage kommt". Ibid.

[68]Ibid.

[69]Haas 2014, pp. 18–20. See also specifically on this case Levy 2012 and Steingruber 2012.

[70]See CAS 2008/A/1519 & 1520, *FC Shakhtar Donetsk (Ukraine) v. Mr. Matuzalem Francelino da Silva (Brazil) & Real Zaragoza SAD (Spain) & FIFA*, Award of 19 May 2009.

[71]For more details see CAS 2010/A/2261 & 2263, *Mr. Matuzalem Francelino da Silva (Brazil) & Real Zaragoza SAD (Spain) v. FIFA*, Award of 29 June 2011.

[72]SFT 138 III 322, 327–328 (para 4.2).

[73]Ibid., para 4.3.5.

[74]Burger 2012.

This autonomous enforcement system with its embedded checks and balances is now under challenge by the OLG Bremen in the SV Wilhelmshaven case.

15.3.2 The OLG Bremen's Challenge to FIFA's Private Enforcement System

In principle, SV Wilhelmshaven is no member of FIFA and cannot be directly sanctioned by it. Yet, FIFA can get to it through Wilhelmshaven's membership in German football associations, in particular the DFB and the NFV. If the DFB or (indirectly) the NFV were to refuse to implement a decision of the FIFA Disciplinary Committee, they would in turn face the risk of being themselves sanctioned by FIFA. This could, for instance, result in the German national team being barred from entering the FIFA World Cup—obviously an unacceptable outcome for the DFB, which is thus obliged, in practice, to implement the sanctions imposed by FIFA (and the same is true of the NFV).

Nevertheless, since the OLG Bremen's ruling in the *SV Wilhelmshaven* case, the DFB and NFV are stuck in a perverse situation. A legal catch-22 for which there is no satisfying way out. Indeed, the OLG considered, and here the whole EU law and private enforcement puzzle comes together, that due to the fact that the CAS award was contrary to EU free movement rights, its enforcement through the private power of the NFV is contrary to EU law.[75] This is a remarkable statement.[76] The CJEU itself has never qualified the free movement rights as being part of the so-called 'European public policy', though in light of their importance for the European Union it is most likely that it would if asked.[77] Furthermore, the OLG did not stop there, it also claimed that the NFV misused its power to sanction its members by assuming that it did not have the competence to review the decision handed out by the FIFA Disciplinary Committee.[78] This is a dangerous legal move for FIFA.

---

[75]"Der verfügte Zwangsabstieg ist rechtswidrig und damit unwirksam, weil er als Beugemittel zur Durchsetzung von gegen den Kläger gerichteten Zahlungsansprüchen dient, deren vom CAS bestätigter Ausspruch durch die Verbandsgerichtsbarkeit der FIFA mit Article 45 AEUV nicht vereinbar ist. Ihre zwangsweise Durchsetzung über die Strafgewalt des Beklagten verstößt damit gegen zwingende Normen des EU-Rechts, was von dem Beklagten zu beachten ist". OLG Bremen, 2 U 67/14, para II.1.h.

[76]Heavily criticized by Orth and Stopper, who considered instead that the sanction is "self-executing". See Orth and Stopper 2015, p. 52.

[77]See Duval 2015.

[78]"Die Rechtswidrigkeit der Vereinssanktion folgt aber auch bereits daraus, dass der Beklagte eine Disziplinarentscheidung getroffen hat in der irrigen Annahme, bloßes Vollzugsorgan der FIFA-Disziplinarkommission zu sein und zu einer inhaltlichen Überprüfung der "umzusetzenden" Entscheidung nicht berechtigt zu sein, und damit seine Strafgewalt nicht wirksam ausgeübt hat". OLG Bremen, 2 U 67/14, para II.1.h.

Instead of recognizing that national associations, be it the DFB or the NFV, were bound to enforce FIFA's decision implementing a CAS award,[79] it endowed them with a duty to review the award on the face of its compatibility with German (and thus European) mandatory rules. This is based, firstly, on the Court's unwillingness to recognize that SV Wilhelmshaven has submitted freely to the jurisdiction of FIFA and the CAS.[80] Indeed, the OLG's finding in this regard is that SV Wilhelsmhaven's consent can neither be grounded in its membership of the DFB and then NFV,[81] nor in the readiness of the club to turn to FIFA and later the CAS in this dispute.[82] In the latter case, the OLG Bremen uses a very similar argument than the one employed by the OLG München in its *Pechstein* ruling to justify the refusal of the recognition of the CAS award.[83] It finds that SV Wilhelmshaven had no real alternative but to go to FIFA and the CAS as the DFB (and the NFV) believed it would be automatically bound by their decisions.[84] In the *Pechstein* ruling, the Munich court had found similarly that Claudia Pechstein was forced to go to the CAS, if she wanted to preserve her chances to participate in the Olympics.[85] In any event, the OLG Bremen believes that the DFB's (and NFV's) duty to check the compatibility of CAS awards (and FIFA decisions) with German (and

---

[79]The view eloquently defended by Orth and Stopper 2015, pp. 52–53.

[80]Ibid., para II.1.i).

[81]Ibid., para II.1.i)aa) and cc).

[82]See ibid., para II.1.i)bb).

[83]OLG München, Az. U 1110/14 Kart, *Claudia Pechstein v. DESG and ISU*, 15 January 2015. See the commentary by Mathieu Maisonneuve in this volume.

[84]"Gegen eine Unterwerfung des Klägers durch Teilnahme an den ihn betreffen—den Verfahren vor der FIFA wendet dieser zutreffend ein, dass ihm letztlich keine andere Möglichkeit blieb, als seine Interessen in diesen Verfahren zu vertreten. Da nach Auffassung des DFB sowie des Beklagten der DFB und die ihm angeschlossenen Verbände an die Entscheidungen der Verbandsgerichtsbarkeit der FIFA gebunden und ohne eigene Prüfungskompetenz verpflichtet sind, die Entscheidungen der FIFA gegenüber ihren von den Entscheidungen betroffenen Mitgliedern im Wege von Vereinsstrafen umzusetzen, musste sich der Kläger an den Verfahren vor der FIFA beteiligen, um seinen Argumenten Gehör verschaffen zu können". OLG Bremen, 2 U 67/14, para II.1.i)bb).

[85]"Es kann dahinstehen, ob die Klägerin durch die Anrufung des CAS, dessen Zuständigkeit die Beklagte zu 2. nicht in Frage stellte, oder durch die Unterzeichnung dessen Order of Procedure eine neue Schiedsvereinbarung mit der Beklagten zu 2. traf. Auch darin läge lediglich eine Perpetuierung des Missbrauchs der marktbeherrschenden Stellung der Beklagten zu 2. Denn der Klägerin stand keine andere aussichtsreiche Möglichkeit zu Gebote, ihre Zulassung zu den damals bevorstehenden Olympischen Winterspielen vom 12. bis zum 28. Februar 2010 in Vancouver zu erreichen, als diese durch die kartellrechtswidrige Schiedsvereinbarung vom 2. Januar 2009 vorgegebene Vorgehensweise. Eine Anrufung der schweizerischen Gerichte war angesichts des Stands der schweizerischen Rechtsprechung, wie sie auch später in den Entscheidungen des schweizerischen Bundesgerichts zum Spruch des CAS zum Ausdruck kam, nicht erfolgversprechend. Auch die Beantragung einer auf ihre Zulassung gerichteten einstweiligen Verfügung bei einem deutschen Gericht wäre nicht zuletzt wegen der Unwägbarkeiten in Bezug auf die Beurteilung deren internationaler Zuständigkeit kein hinreichend sicheres Mittel gewesen". OLG München, Az. U 1110/14 Kart, para B.II.2.b).

European) mandatory rules derives from Article 17a(2) DFB-Statutes,[86] which stipulates that:

> "The DFB recognizes the Court of Arbitration for Sport (CAS) seated in Lausanne (Schweiz) as an independent court for international disputes and subject itself to the decisions of the CAS unless they conflict with national or international mandatory laws, or FIFA and UEFA Regulations provide for an exception".[87]

The wording of this provision was considered clear ("eindeutig"[88]) by the Court. In its view the DFB (and its affiliate the NFV) should have conducted a proper check of the compatibility of the controversial award with German mandatory laws including the EU free movement rights. This interpretation is not uncontroversial, and some voices are contesting in Germany the solution adopted by the OLG.[89] The good news for FIFA's private enforcement system is that the DFB can relatively easily amend the text of this provision. The bad news is that even if it does, the OLG Bremen does not seem convinced that the club should be bound, via the national associations, by FIFA and CAS's decisions, due to the *de facto* forced nature of FIFA's jurisdiction and CAS arbitration. Thus, if this view were to be upheld by the BGH, the DFB and the NFV would be left hanging between a rock and a hard place. Moreover, it is questionable whether the national associations dispose of sufficient legal expertise and competence to review the compatibility of CAS awards with EU law. Would these decisions then be appealable in front of the German courts? It is hard to imagine how such a check is supposed to operate in practice without putting a heavy burden on the federations and drastically delaying the resolution of the dispute.

15.4 Conclusion

The OLG Bremen's decision is more specific and less accessible than the *Pechstein* ruling.[90] It tackles EU law considerations as well as civil law questions. Moreover, the final result is rather specific to the German context, as it is at least partially dependent on the interpretation of the statutes of the DFB. Yet, its practical and theoretical importance should not be underestimated. The case indirectly challenged, even before the *Pechstein* ruling, the consensual nature of the

[86]See OLG Bremen, 2 U 67/14, para II.1.j).

[87]Translation by the author. The original indicates: "Der DFB anerkennt den Court of Arbitration for Sport (CAS) mit Sitz in Lausanne (Schweiz) als unabhängige richterliche Instanz in internationalen Streitigkeiten und unterwirft sich den Entscheidungen des CAS, soweit zwingendes nationales oder internationales Recht nicht entgegensteht oder die FIFA—oder UEFA-Reglemente Ausnahmen zulassen".

[88]OLG Bremen, 2 U 67/14, para II.1.j).

[89]Orth and Stopper 2015, pp. 54–53.

[90]To my knowledge only two German commentaries have been published so far: Orth and Stopper 2015 and Meier 2015.

jurisdiction of the CAS (and FIFA). Additionally, it threatens one of the core conditions for the success of the CAS: the private enforcement of CAS awards by the SGBs.

The EU law part of the ruling is fairly traditional in its reasoning. It relies heavily on the existing jurisprudence of the CJEU in the *Bosman* and *Bernard* cases and is relatively favourable to the training compensation system put in place by FIFA. Indeed, the negative conclusion of the OLG should not distract from the fact that it recognizes, for the first time, the compatibility of parts of the FIFA RSTP with EU law. Its final conclusion that the CAS award in the *SV Wilhelmshaven* case contradicts EU law is based solely on the fact that the CAS refused to acknowledge the right of the club to rely on the EU-specific provisions of the FIFA RSTP in the framework of the transfer of the Italo-Argentine player. In sum, this case is rather a peculiar exception. FIFA should feel comforted that its training compensation system is compatible with EU law.

With the much-discussed *Pechstein* ruling, this case highlights the current distrust of German courts towards the CAS. In general, it seems doubtful that this suspicion is entirely misplaced. There is something fundamentally wrong with an arbitral institution when its panels consistently enforce an interpretation of EU law that runs entirely contrary to the interpretation proposed by the CJEU. If it is not done in purpose, then it betrays a profound lack of expertise regarding EU law, which is bound to create problems at the stage of enforcement of CAS awards. Similarly, the lack of independence of the ICAS flagged in the *Pechstein* ruling is not an imaginary flaw of the CAS, but a key structural default that should trigger an in-depth reform of the institution.[91] In the *SV Wilhelmshaven* case, as well as in the *Pechstein* one, the OLG acknowledged that CAS arbitration is forced arbitration. Therefore, it is impossible to rely on consent to justify a limited review of the compatibility of the CAS awards with fundamental rules of law. The CAS, due to the intensity of private power exercised by the SGBs on the athletes and the clubs, must abide by stricter standards of review than usual commercial arbitration. As such this does not threaten the survival of the CAS, which indeed fulfils a crucial function for global sport.[92] Instead, it takes the CAS seriously by requiring that it be reformed to ensure its independence, and that it abides by EU law standards.[93] Yet, the automatic check of CAS awards by national SGBs promoted by the OLG Bremen is certainly not a sustainable legal solution. It risks prolonging disputes indefinitely and bestows national SGBs with a legal responsibility that they are not equipped to shoulder. In this regard, a more structural approach, focused on improving the functioning of the CAS itself is clearly preferable.

---

[91]Duval and Van Rompuy 2016.

[92]On this crucial function see the chapter by Jan Paulsson in this volume.

[93]For a similar demand, see Duval 2015.

At the time of writing, the *SV Wilhelmshaven* case is still pending before the Bundesgerichtshof (BGH), the highest German civil court. With this and the *Pechstein* case on its plate, the BGH will fundamentally shape the future of sport's private dispute resolution mechanisms. Broadly speaking the BGH needs to decide whether the CAS can continue to operate as it does and whether its awards deserve a wide scope of deference or not.[94] The BGH could also, if it is asked—or even *ex officio* if it feels the need—refer a preliminary question to the CJEU on the compatibility of the FIFA training compensation system with EU free movement rights. This would probably be a definitive way to settle a question, which has been left hanging since the *Bosman* ruling, now 20 years ago.

References

Andreff W (2006) International labour migration. In: Andreff W, Szymanski S (eds) Handbook on the economics of sport. Edward Elgar, Cheltenham, pp 325–330

Bakker M (2008) The training compensation system. Int Sports Law J (1–2):29–36

Bernstein L (1992) Opting out of the legal system: extralegal contractual relations in the diamond industry. J Legal Stud 21:115–167

Burger L (2012) For the first time, the supreme court sets aside an arbitral award on grounds of substantive public policy. ASA Bull 30:603–610

De Weger F (2008) The jurisprudence of the FIFA dispute resolution chamber. T.M.C. Asser Press, The Hague

Drolet J-C (2006) Extra time: are the new FIFA transfer rules doomed? Int Sports Law J (1–2):66–73

Duval A (2015) The CAS and EU law: chronicle of an encounter. Maastricht J Comp Eur Law 22:224–255

Duval A, Van Rompuy B (2016) Protecting athletes' right to fair trial through EU competition law: the Pechstein case. In: Paulussen C et al (eds) Fundamental rights in international and European law: public and private law perspectives, Springer, T.M.C. Asser Press, The Hague, pp 245–278

Egger A, Stix-Hackl C (2002) Sports and competition law: a never-ending story? Eur Comp Law Rev 23:81–91

García B (2007) UEFA and the European union: from confrontation to co-operation? J Contemp Eur Res 3:202–223

García B (2011) The 2001 informal agreement on the international transfer system. Eur Sports Law Policy Bull 2:17–29

Haas U (2014) The enforcement of football-related arbitral awards by the court of arbitration for sport (CAS). Int Sports Law Rev 14:12–29

Heermann P (2014) Landgericht Bremen kann FIFA-statuten nicht materiell-rechtlich prüfen. CausaSport (2):181–183

Hendrickx F (2010) The bernard-case and training compensation in professional football. Eur Labour Law J 1:380–397

Irving J (2002) Red card: the battle over european football's transfer system. Univ Miami Law Rev 56:667–725

Levy R (2012) Swiss federal tribunal overrules CAS award in a landmark decision: FIFA vs Matuzalem. Int Sports Law J (3–4):35–38

[94] In favour of such a hands-off approach, see Orth and Stopper 2015.

Lindholm J (2010) Case C-325/08, Olympique Lyonnais SASP v. Olivier Bernard and Newcastle United UFC, judgment of the court of justice (Grand Chamber) of 16 March 2010, not yet reported. Common Market Law Rev 47:1187–1197

Meier P (2015) Ein Urteil mit Sprengkraft? CausaSport (1):62–68

Orth J, Stopper M (2015) Entscheidungsvollzug in der Verbandspyramide und Ausbildungsentschädigung. Zeitschrift für Sport und Recht (2):51–56

Pijetlovic K (2010) Another classic of EU sports jurisprudence: legal implications of Olympique Lyonnais v Olivier Bernard and Newcastle UFC (C-325/08). Eur Law Rev 35:857–868

Steingruber A-M (2012) Matuzalem: CAS award set aside on the ground of public policy. Int Sports Law J (3–4):39–44

Weatherill S (2003) "Fair Play Please!": recent developments in the application of EC law to sport. Common Market Law Rev 40:51–93

Weatherill S (2010) The Olivier Bernard case: how, if at all, to fix compensation for training young players? Int Sports Law J (1–2):3–6

Zylberstein J (2010) The Olivier Bernard judgment: a significant step forward for the training of players. Eur Sports Law Policy Bull 1:51–68

Chapter 16
Oberlandesgericht München, *Az. U 1110/14 Kart, Claudia Pechstein v/ International Skating Union (ISU)*, 15 January 2015

Mathieu Maisonneuve

Abstract CAS arbitration is fundamentally a forced arbitration. In the first instance, Ms Claudia Pechstein brought an action against the ISU before a German tribunal, which held that arbitration agreements were null given the absence of free consent of the athletes. On appeal, in a resounding ruling rendered on 15 January 2015, the *Oberlandesgericht* of Munich held that arbitration agreements imposed by sports institutions on their members constituted an abuse of dominant position. Contrary to the Swiss Federal Tribunal, the German Court considered, at least in appearance, the CAS as structurally favourable to sports governing bodies. Consequently, the Court refused to recognize the arbitral award in which the CAS had confirmed the sanction for doping imposed by the ISU on Ms Pechstein on the grounds that the award violated international public policy. Beyond this particular case, the ruling has led to an overall reflection on the CAS's independence; for instance, by putting an end to the system of the closed list of arbitrators.

Keywords CAS · Competence-competence · Forced arbitration · Arbitration agreement · Free consent · Competition law · Abuse of dominant position · Independence · ICAS · Violation of international public policy

Contents

With the help of Jonas Knetsch, Law Professor at the University of Reunion Island, and Jessica Betti, Law and economics student, to whom the author addresses his sincere thanks.

M. Maisonneuve (✉)
Saint Joseph University, Beirut, Lebanon
e-mail: mathieu.maisonneuve@univ-reunion.fr

A. Duval and A. Rigozzi (eds.), *Yearbook of International Sports Arbitration 2015*,
DOI 10.1007/978-94-6265-129-6_16

16.1 Introduction

It is rather uncommon for a court ruling dealing with the CAS's organization and functioning to be entitled to anything more than a few lines in the news. It is just as unusual that a ruling rendered by any other court than the SFT actually puts into question, to a great extent, the CAS's very future. The ruling rendered by the regional Court of Appeal of Munich (*Oberlandesgericht München*, OLG) on 15 January 2015 in the case involving Ms Claudia Pechstein against the International Skating Union (ISU) is, at least from this perspective,[1] of rare interest as regards international arbitration in sports-related matters.[2]

16.2 Facts and Proceedings

The facts underlying this case are quite exceptional since Ms Pechstein is not just any athlete. She is one of the most successful champions in the history of the Olympic Games. From Albertville in 1992 to Turin in 2006, she won nine medals, among which are five gold medals at the winter games, in long track speed skating. On 1 July 2009, the ISU banned her from all competitions for a duration of two years for a doping offence. Not as a result of a doping control having detected the presence of prohibited substances in her system, as is customarily the case, but as a result of anomalies which were revealed in her biological passport, suggesting she was doped.

The ensuing lawsuits were bound to be just as exceptional. First of all, Ms Pechstein challenged the sanction imposed before the CAS. Since her appeal failed,[3] she then asked, in vain, the SFT to annul the award rendered[4] in that dispute. The athlete could have left it at that. However, after her request for the revision of the award (where she argued that a new diagnostic method would establish that she suffers from blood anomalies) was also denied[5] by the SFT, she decided to appeal before other courts, namely before the ECtHR, where she brought an action against Switzerland, on November 11, 2010, invoking a violation of Article 6(1) and (2) of the ECHR; and before the German courts, in order to obtain compensation for damages she suffered supposedly unlawfully.

---

[1]Lemouton F-G, Le TAS, forcé de se réformer, 14 April 2015. http://www.lequipe.fr/Tous-sports/Article/Le-tas-force-de-se-reformer/45824. Accessed 1 February 2016.

[2]For an English translation see Duval A, The Pechstein Ruling of the OLG München, 6 February 2015. http://ssrn.com/abstract=2561297. Accessed 1 February 2016. In the present commentary, all the citations of the OLG's ruling comes from this translation.

[3]CAS 2009/A/1912, *P. v. International Skating Union (ISU) & CAS*, Award of 25 November 2009, available on the CAS's online database.

[4]SFT 4A_612/2009, decision of 10 February 2010.

[5]SFT 4A_144/2010, decision of 28 September 2010.

In a judgment released on 26 February 2014,[6] which attracted a great deal of attention, the local Court of Munich (*Landgericht München*, LG) did not remain indifferent to some of Ms Pechstein's arguments. Notably, the LG considered, just as she had claimed, that CAS arbitration clauses are void, at least in cases where they purport to bind professional athletes, on the grounds that the latter's consent was not free. This factual observation was not new given the situation of structural inequality in which the athletes find themselves towards sports governing bodies.[7] However, the legal consequence drawn from such a finding was, as radical as it was original. These elements posed a serious threat to the future of the CAS's system, even if, in the present ruling, the LG has recognized the litigious award but only for reasons related to the merits of the case. Ms Pechstein had failed to object to the arbitral tribunal's lack of jurisdiction in due course, i.e. during the arbitral proceedings, a conduct that was deemed contrary to procedural good faith.

The OLG, which was seized with a challenge against the LG's ruling, confirmed the German courts' jurisdiction to rule on Ms Pechstein's petition. In its opinion, assuming a valid arbitration agreement binding Ms Pechstein to the ISU actually existed, it would only cover appeals against the latter's decisions, but not possible actions for compensation.[8] The fact that the Munich higher court went beyond a *prima facie* examination of its own jurisdiction should come as no surprise given the traditional hostility of German law towards the negative effect of the principle of competence-competence.[9]

Above all, the OLG confirmed the invalidity of the CAS arbitration clause (3.1), though based on a different reasoning than that adopted by the LG. This time round, the court refused to recognize the CAS award (3.2), opening the way to a reassessment by the German courts of the sanction imposed by the ISU. Although the decision commented could potentially inspire other national jurisdictions, it does not seem to be the case in France, essentially for procedural reasons.

16.3 Commentary

16.3.1 The Invalidity of CAS Arbitration Agreements

Doctrinal doubts as to the validity of the CAS arbitration clause have been around for quite some time.[10] In this regard, the LG's ruling in 2014 constituted a first judicial shot. The OLG decision, rendered in 2015, constitutes a second one.

[6] See in particular Maisonneuve 2014, p. 670 and Flecke and Granier 2014, p. 480.

[7] Same observation, see in particular Pinna 2004, p. 38; Rigozzi 2005, p. 179; Latty 2007, p. 535 et seq.; Zen-Ruffinen 2012, p. 489 et seq.

[8] OLG München, Az. U 1110/14 Kart, *Claudia Pechstein v. DESG and ISU*, 15 January 2015, paras 20 et seq.

[9] Gaillard 1999, p. 396.

[10] See in particular Baddeley 1996, p. 135 and Netzle 1998, p. 45.

Yet, the approach adopted by the latter court is different from that of the former one. Contrary to the LG, the OLG held that "arbitration agreements between a dominant organizer of international sports competitions and the athlete taking part in these competitions are not per se invalid due to the lack of free will of the athlete".[11] While the statement is clear, the underlying legal reasoning is not so obvious. As far as we can analyze the ruling, it seems that the OLG has implicitly privileged the return to a stricter legal orthodoxy.

In other words, in order to be valid, one's consent does not need to be in principle perfectly free. It must only be free of defect, in particular of duress within the meaning of German law.[12] The fact that a professional athlete consents to an arbitration agreement is economically necessary since it conditions his or her entry into a competition. However, in this case, that condition has not been regarded as a sufficient factual constraint to vitiate one's consent.[13]

There is no doubt as to the higher court's willingness not to condemn in principle the forced nature of arbitration in sports-related matters. Before negating the reasoning of the lower court, it asserts, in fact, that

> sound and weighty arguments speak in favour of avoiding to leave to the many potentially competent national courts the duty to deal with disputes arising between athletes and international federations in the framework of international competitions, and instead to refer them to a single sports tribunal. In particular, a uniform competence and procedure can preclude that similar cases be decided differently, and therefore safeguard the equal opportunities of athletes during the competitions.[14]

On this issue, the ruling rendered by the OLG echoes the SFT's case law.[15] Just as the latter, the court was fully aware that the athletes' consent to CAS arbitration was considerably constrained. As the SFT, the Court considers that the compelling nature of this arbitration is fundamentally a good thing. Unlike the LG, the Court refuses, in particular for reasons of expediency, to consider that arbitration clauses in favour of the CAS would be void because they are de facto imposed. Just as the tribunal did, the Court considers that the structural imbalance between sports governing bodies and athletes does not necessarily have to remain without legal effect.

But while the only consequence the SFT expressly derived from this situation is the non-enforceability of the waiver of the action for annulment against the CAS's awards, the OLG went further by drawing conclusions as regards the validity of the arbitration agreement itself.

According to the OLG, sports governing bodies are in a dominant position. As a consequence, it is necessary to ascertain that they do not take advantage of this situation by forcing professional athletes to resort to the CAS in the event of a dispute with the latter. Despite their usual associative status, it is manifest that sports

---

[11]OLG München, Az. U 1110/14 Kart, *Claudia Pechstein,* para 90.

[12]para 123 (1) BGB.

[13]OLG München, Az. U 1110/14 Kart, *Claudia Pechstein*, para 92.

[14]Ibid., para 89.

[15]In particular SFT 133 III 235.

governing bodies are associations of undertakings or undertakings, in the eyes of the European Union law,[16] and are in a monopolistic situation, or at least, in an oligopolistic position in their respective markets.

The OLG's reliance on German competition law[17] deserves to be fully approved. First of all, because competition law is more 'international' than the resort to other mechanisms of protection of parties, who are said to be weak. For instance, we could have considered the mechanism of qualified lesion in German law.[18] In this case, it is not just about knowing whether German athletes can benefit from a specific legal protection against the CAS but also to consider whether the arbitration system in sports-related matters, which is based on the principle of universality, is not, at the very least in its current state, contrary to a rule known by many national legal systems: the prohibition of the abuse of a dominant position.

In addition, reliance on competition law has the advantage, compared to other legislations throughout the world, for instance statutes governing consumer protection against unfair terms,[19] that it covers both amateur and professional athletes. And last but not least, the rules keeping abuses of dominant position in check rely on a logic of proportionality which is adapted to CAS arbitration,[20] just as the notion of 'unconscionability'[21] does in American law or the prohibition against excessive commitments does in Swiss law.[22] The CAS system pursues perfectly legitimate objectives, in particular that of ensuring the equal treatment of athletes in the settlement of sports disputes. However, it ought to be ensured that the system does not go beyond what is necessary to reach that objective or that the system does not violate unnecessarily any fundamental rights.

That sports governing bodies compel athletes, who depend upon them, to submit to arbitration rather than to the state courts is a good thing. But forcing the athletes to submit to an arbitration institution which is detrimental to their interests is another situation altogether.

Is it the CAS's case? The question could seem outdated. Since 2003,[23] the SFT has constantly maintained that the CAS offers adequate guarantees of independence and impartiality. In fact, this is still a topical issue, namely because the SFT's rulings in this respect have never won the unanimous support of legal practitioners and/or academic writers.[24] Given the SFT's benevolence towards the CAS, a sec-

[16]See General Court, T-193/02, *Laurent Piau v. Commission*, ECLI:EU:T:2005:22; CJEU, C-519/04, *David Meca-Medina and Igor Majcen v. Commission,* ECLI:EU:C:2006:201; CJEU, C-49/07, *MOTOE v Elliniko Dimosio*, ECLI:EU:C:2008:376.

[17]Referring to para 19 GWB [German Act against Restraints of Competition].

[18]Referring to para 138 BGB.

[19]CJEU, C-168/05, *Elisa María Mostaza Claro v. Centro Móvil Milenium SL*, ECLI: EU:C:2006:675.

[20]In this sense, see Maisonneuve 2011, paras 752 et seq.

[21]Maisonneuve 2005.

[22]Article 27 of the Swiss Civil Code.

[23]SFT 129 III 445.

[24]In particular Zen-Ruffinen 2012 and Rigozzi 2013, p. 304 et seq.

ond look by a significant foreign court was to be expected. It could have helped to close the debate. On the contrary, it has relaunched it.

Contrary to the SFT, the OLG considered that the CAS was structurally biased in favour of sports governing bodies due to the latter's "decisive influence on the selection of the persons acting as CAS arbitrators".[25] The OLG considers that this decisive influence mainly derives from Articles R33, S6 and S4 of the CAS Code. According to Article R33, parties to the dispute can only choose as arbitrators individuals who are registered on the CAS list of arbitrators. Pursuant to Article S6, these individuals are registered on this closed list by the International Arbitration Council in sports-related matters. And, Article S4 provides that the *ICAS* "is composed of twenty members, experienced jurists appointed in the following manner: four members are appointed by the International Federations (IFs), three by the Association of Summer Olympic (ASOIF), and one by the Association of the Winter Olympic Ifs (AIOWF), chosen from within or outside their membership. Four members are appointed by the Association of the National Olympic Committees (ANOC) chosen from within or outside its membership, four members are appointed by the International Olympic Committee (IOC), chosen from within or outside its membership, four members are appointed by the twelve members of the ICAS listed above, after appropriate consultation with a view of safeguarding the interests of the athletes, four members are appointed by the sixteen members of ICAS listed above, chosen from among personalities independent of the bodies designating the other members of the ICAS."

In other words, the only individuals who are likely to intervene as arbitrators before the CAS are admittedly selected by a distinct body, other than sports governing bodies, namely the ICAS. However, 12 out of the ICAS's 20 members are directly appointed by sports governing bodies and the eight remaining members are appointed by the first 12 members, that is to say indirectly appointed by sports governing bodies According to the OLG, "these provisions regulating the selection of the potential CAS arbitrators favour the sports associations in disputes against athletes, thus embedding a structural imbalance that is threatening the neutrality of the CAS".[26]

In the OLG's view, the decisive influence of sports governing bodies on the selection of individuals who are likely to sit as arbitrators in CAS Panels would incidentally result from the President of the Appeals Arbitration Division's authority. He can solely select in each case the president of the three arbitrator's panel or, if applicable and no agreement has been reached between the parties, the sole arbitrator. If we follow the previous reasoning: the President of the Appeals Division is appointed by the ICAS, that is to say indirectly appointed by sports governing bodies. In the OLG's opinion, this appointment is likely to reduce the athletes' trust in the independence and impartiality of the arbitral tribunal in charge of judging them.

---

[25]OLG München, Az. U 1110/14 Kart, *Claudia Pechstein*, para 95.

[26]Ibid., para 104.

These provisions of the CAS Code were obviously known to the SFT. So how can one explain that, despite the analysis of identical elements, the OLG has reached a different conclusion as regards the independence and impartiality of the CAS?

If the two courts' conclusions differ, it is simply because they analyzed the CAS's independence and impartiality from two different angles: the SFT analyzed the individual point of view whereas the OLG analyzed the collective angle. The former focused on verifying whether the CAS was not depending on any international sports governing bodies which could have been likely to be a party to the litigation before it, whereas the second questioned the CAS's independence with regard to international sports governing bodies as a whole.

This analysis is relevant. Admittedly, international sports governing bodies do not form an indivisible whole. However, they do share sufficient elements to be compared: first of all, they share common interests, within the Olympic movement, but they also have more or less the same understanding of the system which is symbolized by the principle of autonomy within the sporting world. The structural risk does not reside only in the fact that a person appointed as an arbitrator in a given arbitration owes his or her inclusion in the CAS's list to sports governing bodies, nor in the fact that the institution has a particular connection with the CAS. The risk would come from the fact that the individuals who are likely to be appointed as arbitrators share, a priori, the same views as these sports governing bodies.

The personal independence of CAS arbitrators is not at issue and is not what is being questioned here. Instead, the main purpose of the OLG is to point out that the selection method to get on the CAS's list of arbitrators is inappropriate since arbitrators might be perceived as sharing the sports governing bodies' views. Though they are not deemed subject to controls nor any commanded assignments, arbitrators who are carried away by the same music might suddenly start whistling to the same tune. Of course, the interest of federations and the athletes' global interest can go together. However, they cannot be linked during a trial. In almost any dispute (save for rare exceptions), there are necessarily two competing interests: on the one hand the institutional interest and on the other hand the personal interest.

As the OLG summarized it, the decisive influence which sports governing bodies have on the composition of the CAS,

> creates the risk that the persons included on the CAS arbitrators list predominantly or even entirely favour the side of the sporting associations over the athletes. This is also true concerning the arbitrators that are not suggested by the sporting association, but are selected in view to protect the interest of athletes or on the basis of their independence, as they are designated by ICAS members chosen by the sporting associations. A balanced influence of the parties on the composition of the arbitral tribunal that would be needed to safeguard its independence is thus not provided. Such a structural deficiency threatens the neutrality of the arbitral tribunal; this is independent of the fact whether the persons included on the CAS list of arbitrators are in any way linked to the sports associations, as this would actually open the possibility to challenge their nomination. Even when the personal integrity of the persons included on the CAS list is not affected, there is a potential

risk that arbitrators share the worldview of the sports associations rather than the one of the athletes.[27]

The OLG's assessment as regards the CAS's independence and impartiality could seem to rely on a rather hypothetical reasoning: sports governing bodies would have a natural tendency to appoint, as members of the ICAS, individuals who share their views; these same individuals would, in turn, appoint further members who also share their views; then the ICAS, as a whole, would appoint on the CAS's arbitrator's list, members who would preferably think along the same lines, which would be detrimental to athletes.

Obviously, there is no certainty. Nevertheless, it is completely plausible and this mere possibility is, in itself, a problem. CAS arbitration is not quite like ordinary arbitrations since it is a forced arbitration. An arbitration imposed by sports institutions on athletes. While it is undoubtedly opportune to put up with it, it is just as opportune to remain even more demanding towards this type of arbitration.

The principle of equal treatment of competitors before the courts certainly demands to subject them to a "worldwide sport's supreme court"[28] such as the CAS. However, the principle of justice imposes to ensure athletes are not being diverted from national jurisdictions against their own interest, in the interest of sports governing bodies. Especially as sports disputes frequently involve fundamental rights.

In principle, the SFT follows this same line of thought. However, to this date, it has only had a limited impact on its case law. Specifically, it is by reference to these principles that the SFT has excluded the validity waiver of the action for annulment against CAS awards[29] even though Article 192(1) of the Private International Law Act (PILA), providing for such waiver, seems to apply to sports arbitration just as it applies to all other types of arbitration.

Failing to submit CAS awards to an extensive control, as called for by legal doctrine,[30] it was at least necessary to go further by requiring an exemplary independence from the CAS. This is the solution followed by the OLG, by expressly resorting to the 'theory of appearance', well known to the ECHR[31] and which is epitomized in the English adage 'justice must not only be done, it must also be seen to be done'.

Not only the organization and functioning of CAS must not favour sports institutions over athletes, but they should be such as to never even allow for any doubts to be raised. Doubts are like a slippery slope for the recognition of CAS awards.

---

[27]Ibid., para 106.

[28]According to president J.-A. Samaranch's expression, quoted by Mbaye in Reeb 2002, p. X.

[29]SFT 133 III 235.

[30]In this sense, see in particular Rigozzi 2005, p. 732.

[31]See for instance ECtHR, no 29369/10, *Morice v. France*, decision of 11 July 2013, para 98.

16.3.2 The Non-recognition of the CAS Awards

Compared to the first instance ruling, the decision handed down by the OLG is paradoxically rather good news, both for Ms Pechstein and the CAS.

In first instance, Claudia Pechstein's claim had been successful on the principle since the court judged that the arbitration agreement which establishes the competence of the CAS was void. But, the LG had held that the award ought to be recognized by reference to the principle of procedural good faith, which requires the aggrieved party to complain about an alleged procedural irregularity as early as possible during the arbitral procedure, noting that Ms Pechstein had failed to do so in the present case. On appeal, Ms Pechstein benefited this time from a favourable ruling both in principle *and* in practice.

The 1958 Convention on the recognition and enforcement of foreign arbitral awards (New York Convention), to which Germany is a party, provides for the possibility to refuse the recognition of an award that violates the public policy of the country where recognition is sought. In European Union countries, unlike in Switzerland, competition law forms part of public policy. By basing this ruling on the existence of an abuse of a dominant position, the court used a different reasoning than that of the LG, which had solely based itself on the absence of freedom, and could therefore have refused to recognize the award. As much as it may be possible to link the grievance of lack of jurisdiction to the plaintiff's behaviour, it is hardly conceivable to make the country's public policy depend on an individual's procedural conduct.

Moreover, the OLG pointed out that in this case, Ms Pechstein's behaviour could have been explained by any other reason than that of bad faith. Indeed, the judgment underlines the fact that given the time lapse between the suspension's delivery and the beginning of the Olympic Games in Vancouver, Ms Pechstein had no other credible choice but to hope for a favourable award.[32]

Would the OLG have reached the same outcome on the basis of any other grounds for refusal as listed by the New York Convention? For instance the invalidity of the arbitration agreement? Probably not. It is often assessed under the law to which the parties have subjected the case or under the law of the country in which the award was rendered. In this case, it was assessed under Swiss law. Independently from the principle of procedural good faith, it was difficult to refuse the recognition of the Peichstein's award on this ground. According to the SFT's jurisprudence,[33] arbitration agreements in favour of the CAS are perfectly valid.

Though Ms Pechstein is probably delighted with the judgment delivered by the OLG, it would be unwise to claim victory yet. The refusal to recognize the CAS award does certainly open the door to a retrial on the grounds of the ISU's

[32]OLG München, Az. U 1110/14 Kart, *Claudia Pechstein*, para 137.

[33]For instance SFT 133 III 235. See also STF 4A_548/2009, decision of 20 January 2010, para 4.1 and STF 127 III 123, para 4.1.1.

suspension inflicted upon her. However, there is no guarantee that the German courts, assuming the OLG's judgment will not be overruled by the German Supreme Court (*Bundesgerichtshof*), will judge it illegal.

Be that as it may, the judgment rendered by the OLG is not such bad news for the CAS compared to the decision rendered in first instance. On February 26, 2014, by condemning the principle of forced arbitration imposed on athletes by governing sports bodies, the LG was threatening the CAS's very foundations. On January 15, 2015, by placing itself in the field of competition law, the OLG only sanctioned some of the CAS system's imperfections: "the imposition of an arbitration clause by the organizer of international sporting competitions is not per se an abuse of a dominant position".[34]

Will the CAS be compelled to reform in order to secure the recognition of its awards in Germany? Nothing is so sure. First of all, the ISU has filed an appeal before the Supreme Court. Second, the new German anti-doping law enacted on December 10, 2015 contains a para (11) which expressly allows sports governing bodies to subordinate the athlete's participation to a competition which they organize to the acceptance of an arbitration clause.[35]

In case the OLG's decision would neither be overruled nor thwarted by a valid legislative provision, only two amendments to the CAS Code would be sufficient to ensure the recognition of CAS awards in Germany.

The first would consist in cutting the umbilical cord structurally linking arbitrators to sports institutions. Three options can be considered in this regard

Option A would be to put an end to the sports governing bodies' power of making direct and indirect appointments of the ICAS's members who then register arbitrators on the CAS list. However, one question remains: to whom should this power be given?

Option B would be to consider an equal representation within the ICAS in which: half would be appointed by sports governing bodies and the other half would be appointed by the states, on the same model as the foundation board of the World Doping Agency (WADA) and its executive committee. However, it may not be sufficient. The Court of Appeal of Munich rather seems to consider designating authorities which would be specifically representative of the athletes' interests.[36]

Option C, which is expressly considered by the court,[37] would be to put an end to the closed list system. The parties would then be free to choose their arbitrators provided they meet some general competence requirements, i.e. parties would not be compelled to choose an individual selected by the ICAS.

Would the CAS awards' coherence suffer from it? It is true that the existence of the CAS's jurisprudence is a fundamental requirement of the CAS system, which

[34] OLG München, Az. U 1110/14 Kart, *Claudia Pechstein*, para 88.

[35] Gesetz gegen Doping im Sport, *BGBl*, 2015 I, p. 2210.

[36] OLG München, Az. U 1110/14 Kart, *Claudia Pechstein*, para 112.

[37] Ibid.

is largely justified by the idea of equality of competitors before the court, and a closed list might be needed in theory to ensure the minimum knowledge base of potential arbitrators. However, the effectiveness of this procedure is dubious.

Of the approximately 300 individuals who constitute the CAS list, few are in practice, fine connoisseurs of the CAS's jurisprudence. *Ex ante* information of potential arbitrators is, in any case, less efficient than information given a posteriori, be it by the intermediary of the CAS's court office which provides them with the relevant legal precedents or by the opportunity given to its secretary general to "draw the attention of the Panel to fundamental issues of principle".[38] In addition, the disappearance of the closed list of arbitrators could be counterbalanced, as proposed by A. Rigozzi,[39] by the creation of a list of presidents from which the panel president would necessarily be selected or, when appropriate, the sole arbitrator. Nevertheless, in order to comply with the requirements imposed by the OLG's ruling, it would be appropriate that members of that list should not be designated, even indirectly, by sports governing bodies. At the very least, one should connect option C with option B.

Concerning the second necessary amendment to the CAS Code: it consists in ending the suspicion nourished by athletes, even wrongly, as to a possible bias of either the presidents who chair the CAS panels or the sole arbitrators appointed by the president of the CAS's Appeals Arbitration Division.

De facto, if the ICAS's composition is modified so as not to depend upon sports governing bodies, suspicion would vanish. However, as considered above, a rotating list of presidents could also remediate the issue. The presidents or, if need be, the sole arbitrators would no longer be chosen at (almost) the sole discretion of the president of the CAS Appeals Arbitration Division, but in turns, in a pre-established order, subject to their availability or their proficiency in the arbitration's language.[40] Such rotating lists already exist, namely within the sports dispute resolution centre of Canada (SDRCC).[41]

Equal representation within the ICAS, opening of the list of arbitrators of the CAS, creation of a rotating list of presidents: These proposals are amongst the minimal reforms which we can consider as appropriate even though they could finally not be or no longer be legally necessary for the survival of the CAS.[42]

In the press release issued after the OLG ruling,[43] the CAS pointed out that the Munich's Court of Appeal had considered the Code's version in force in 2009, and that since then substantial changes had occurred. It is perfectly accurate, at least from a formal point of view, to state that one of these modifications deals with

---

[38]Arts R46 and R59 of the CAS Code.

[39]Rigozzi 2005, para 575.

[40]In this sense, Rigozzi 2005, Ibid.

[41]See Article 6(8) of the Canadian Sport dispute resolution code.

[42]For further analysis, see Zen-Ruffinen 2012, p. 489 et seq.

[43]See the CAS press release of March 2015 on the Pechstein ruling of the OLG. http://www.tas-cas.org/fileadmin/user_upload/CAS_statement_ENGLISH.pdf. Accessed 1 February 2016.

articles of the code on which the OLG based its conclusion on the existence of a structural disadvantage to the detriment of athletes. Since January 1 2012, the ICAS' duty to nominate an important share of the CAS list of arbitrators on the basis of proposals made by sports governing bodies has disappeared. Despite being insufficient, this is a substantial achievement. In its ruling, the OLG merely refers to the link between the ICAS members and sports governing bodies, via the influence of the latter on the designation of the former.[44] Based on the letter of the Code, the link remains intact. However, factually, the ICAS has recently opened itself to more diverse profiles.

In the same press release, the CAS also correctly argued that, given its universal vocation, it was hardly feasible that its rules satisfied the requirements of all the different national courts which could be called upon to recognize and enforce its awards. However, in this case the commented ruling raises a more general question: do international sports governing bodies take advantage of their dominant position by imposing athletes to resort to the CAS? As far as the OLG is concerned, the answer goes without a doubt: "the reason why athletes accept to subject their disputes with sports associations to an arbitration tribunal, the composition of which is mainly determined by sports associations, is solely linked to the monopoly position of the sports associations. If the athlete could participate to the World Championship while agreeing to the competence of a neutral arbitration tribunal, we can safely assume that only this arbitration clause would be agreed upon to the detriment of the arbitral tribunal structurally favourable to the sports associations".[45]

Although the ruling appears to be strongly argued, the answer given by the OLG can be debatable. That being so, the question raised by the Munich Court is a general question, which the CAS cannot simply brush aside. Indeed, the notion of abuse of a dominant position derived from competition law is, despite variations, well known in most countries of the world. The OLG's reasoning on the basis of German competition law could equally have been made (and upheld) on the grounds of European Union law.[46] The question raised deserves better than a simple denial.

Will this denial be dealt with by the European Court for Human Rights? In parallel to the damages claims brought before the German jurisdictions, Ms Pechstein has brought an action before the ECtHR, asking the latter to condemn Switzerland.[47] In her opinion, the Swiss confederation failed to fulfil its obligations set out in Article 6(1) of the ECHR by refusing, via the SFT, to annul the CAS award confirming her suspension for doping even though the CAS would not constitute an independent and impartial tribunal. Nevertheless, the ECtHR will

---

[44]OLG München, Az. U 1110/14 Kart, *Claudia Pechstein*, para 106.

[45]Ibid., para 113.

[46]In this sense, see Duval and Van Rompuy 2016.

[47]Req. no 67474/10 lodged on 11 November, 2010; also see req. no 4575/10 lodged on 13 July 2010, *Adrian Mutu c. Suisse*.

only adopt a position on this last question if it considers beforehand that the claimant had not renounced, by accepting the arbitration, to invoke formally the guarantees of Article 6(1) ECHR. Insofar as such a renunciation must be "free, legal and unequivocal"[48] in order to produce its effects, doubts are allowed as regards the CAS clause's ability to exempt it from complying with the guarantees provided by Article 6(1) ECHR. In its ruling, the OLG came down in favour of the clause's conformity to the ECHR.[49] However, if the ECtHR happened to hold a different position, another ruling in sports-related matters might make the future headlines.

References

Baddeley M (1996) Le sportif, sujet ou objet? La protection de la personnalité du sportif. Revue de droit suisse (2):135–252

Duval A, Van Rompuy B (2016) Protecting athletes' right to a fair trial through EU competition law: The *Pechstein* Case. In: Paulussen C et al (eds) Fundamental rights in international and European law. Springer, T.M.C. ASSER Press, The Hague, pp 245–278

Flecke G, Granier T (2014) Chronique de Jurisprudence Etrangère: Allemagne. Revue de l'Arbitrage (2):475–500

Gaillard E (1999) L'effet négatif de la compétence-compétence. In: Haldy J, Rapp J-M, Ferrari P (eds) Études de procédure et d'arbitrage en l'honneur de Jean-François Poudret. Faculté de droit de Université de Lausanne, Lausanne, pp 387–402

Latty F (2007) La Lex sportiva. Recherche sur le droit transnational. Martinus Nijhoff, Boston

Maisonneuve M (2005) Le droit américain de l'arbitrage et la théorie de l'*unconscionability*. Revue de l'Arbitrage (1):101–114

Maisonneuve M (2011) L'arbitrage des litiges sportifs. LGDJ, Paris

Maisonneuve M (2014) Commentary on *Landesgericht* München I, 26 février 2014, Claudia Pechstein c/ International skating union (ISU), Urteil Az. 37 O 28331/12. Revue de l'Arbitrage (3):667–698

Netzle S (1998) Jurisdiction of arbitral tribunals in sports matters: arbitration agreements by reference to regulations of sports organisations. ASA Special Series (11):45–58

Pinna A (2004) Les vicissitudes du Tribunal arbitral du sport. Gazette du Palais (140–141):31–45

Reeb M (2002) Digest of CAS awards II 1998–2000. Kluwer Law International, The Hague

Rigozzi A (2005) L'arbitrage international en matière de sport. Helbing & Lichtenhahn, Bruylant, LGDJ, Basel

Rigozzi A (2013) L'importance du droit suisse dans la résolution des litiges sportifs internationaux. Revue de droit suisse (I):301–325

Zen-Ruffinen P (2012) La nécessaire réforme du Tribunal Arbitral du Sport. In: Rigozzi A, Sprumont D, Hafner Y (eds) Citius, Altius, Fortius, Mélanges en l'honneur de Denis Oswald. Helbing Lichtenhahn, Bâle, pp 483–537

[48]ECtHR, no 1643/06, *Suda v. Czech Republic*, decision of 28 October 2010, para 48 (free translation).

[49]OLG München, Az. U 1110/14 Kart, *Claudia Pechstein*, para 92.

Chapter 17
Sports Arbitration Cases Before the Swiss Federal Tribunal in 2015—A Digest

Erika Hasler and Yann Hafner

Abstract This digest provides an overview of the legal framework governing actions for the annulment of arbitral awards before the SFT and a discussion of the requirements and other practical issues that should be kept in mind in that context, with particular emphasis on the aspects relevant to sports disputes. It then summarizes the decisions issued by the SFT in its capacity as the court of supervisory jurisdiction over sports-related arbitral awards rendered in Switzerland in the course of the year 2015.

Keywords SFT · CAS · Annulment · Revision · Remedies against arbitral awards · *Lex arbitri* · Chapter 12 PILA · Part 3 CCP · SCA

Contents

E. Hasler (✉)
Lévy Kaufmann-Kohler, Geneva, Switzerland
e-mail: erika.hasler@lk-k.com

Y. Hafner
Chaire de droit du sport II, University of Neuchâtel, Neuchâtel, Switzerland
e-mail: yann.hafner@unine.ch

A. Duval and A. Rigozzi (eds.), *Yearbook of International Sports Arbitration 2015*,
DOI 10.1007/978-94-6265-129-6_17

17.1 Introduction

This is the first installment of the YISA's new annual digest of the SFT's case law in sports arbitration cases. It is meant as a complement to the commentaries and articles examining CAS awards and other sport-related arbitral and court decisions in the Yearbook. The SFT's case law is of significance in this context as the Lausanne-based Supreme Court is entrusted with supervisory jurisdiction over the two most important arbitral institutions in the field of sports, the CAS and the BAT.

Contrary to the other contributions in the YISA, ours does not provide an analysis or commentary of the relevant decisions (there are other, excellent sources offering that type of content[1]). Instead, in the following pages we will provide a concise and practice-oriented overview of the governing legal framework, followed by structured summaries of the SFT's decisions on sports matters rendered in the period under review (1st January to 31 December 2015).

Our aim in preparing this contribution was to help interested practitioners gain an overall grasp of the SFT's annual jurisprudential output in sports-related arbitral matters and efficiently navigate the relevant issues and developments. We hope to have achieved that purpose and will gladly receive any feedback from readers that will help us improve the digest's future editions.

17.2 The Legal Framework Governing Remedies Against Sports Arbitral Awards in Switzerland

17.2.1 Overview

As most modern arbitration laws, Switzerland's PILA has opted for the seat of the arbitration as the connecting factor to determine the law governing the arbitration, or *lex arbitri*. The two major arbitral institutions in the realm sports, the CAS and the BAT, are both seated in Switzerland[2] and thus subject to the Swiss law of arbitration.

Switzerland has a so-called dualist system in relation to the *lex arbitri*, meaning that the governing legal regime will differ depending on whether the arbitration is

[1] See, in particular, the sources cited in footnote 15 below.

[2] According to Article R28 CAS Code "the seat of CAS and of each [CAS panel] is Lausanne, Switzerland". Article 2.1 BAT Arbitration Rules stipulates that "the seat of the BAT and of each arbitral proceeding [...] shall be Geneva, Switzerland [...]".

domestic or international. Domestic arbitrations are subject to Part 3 CCP (Articles 353–399), whereas international arbitrations are governed by Chapter 12 PILA (Articles 176–194). The relevant factor to determine whether an arbitration is domestic or international is the parties' domicile or habitual residence at the time the arbitration agreement was concluded. As provided in Article 176 PILA, an arbitration will be international and thus subject to Chapter 12 "if, at the time the arbitration agreement was entered into, at least one of the parties had neither its domicile nor its habitual residence in Switzerland".[3] That said, even when all the parties to the arbitration agreement are domiciled or habitually reside in Switzerland, Article 353(2) CCP enables them to opt out of the domestic regime and submit their arbitration to Chapter 12 PILA.[4] In fact, the possibility to opt into the PILA regime for domestic arbitrations was introduced primarily to deal with the risk of unequal treatment in sports cases. Indeed, given the high number of international sports federations seated in Switzerland, it could occur relatively easily that disputes with athletes or other sports persons fall under the domestic arbitration regime (apart from the cases involving Swiss nationals, it is not so infrequent for foreign athletes to be domiciled in Switzerland) even in cases having a purely international subject matter (e.g., relating to an international competition having taken place outside Switzerland). The inequality between these cases and those (arising from perfectly similar situations) subject to Chapter 12 PILA results from the fact that the domestic arbitration regime is more protective for the applicant.[5] The idea in adopting Article 353(2) CCP was thus to encourage sports federations to include express provisions opting out of the CCP (and into Chapter 12 PILA) in their regulations and for parties to sports-related contracts to agree to make use of the same possibility. It would appear that so far (the CCP, including

[3]Article 353(1) CCP states "[t]he provisions of [Part 3 CCP] apply to the proceedings before arbitral tribunals seated in Switzerland, unless the provisions of [Chapter 12 PILA] apply". The CCP, i.e., the first Swiss federal act governing civil procedure (which until then was governed by cantonal laws), entered into force on 1st January 2011, replacing, in as far as arbitration was concerned, the intercantonal treaty of 1969, often referred to by its abridged name, the *Concordat*.

[4]Article 353(2) CCP reads: "[t]he parties may exclude the application of [Part 3 CCP] by making an express declaration to this effect in the arbitration agreement or a subsequent agreement, and instead agree that the provisions of [Chapter 12 PILA] apply. The declaration must be in the form specified in Article 358 [CCP]". The reverse (opting out of the PILA and into the CCP regime) is also possible, pursuant to Article 176(2) PILA. For a discussion of the requirements for the valid conclusion of such an opt-in/opt-out agreement, see Kaufmann-Kohler and Rigozzi 2015, paras 2.36–2.46.

[5]This point was specifically addressed in the Government's message accompanying the Draft Bill for the CCP (Feuille fédérale/Bundesblatt 2006, p. 7000). In particular, Article 393 CCP provides for wider annulment grounds against awards, notably Article 393(e), under which the award may be set aside for arbitrariness (whereas the corresponding ground under Chapter 12 PILA - Article 190(2)(e) - refers to the much narrower notion of violation of international public policy). For a summary of the main differences between Chapter 12 PILA's and Part 3 CCP's regime governing arbitration, with specific regard to the admissibility of the annulment action and the available grounds, see Kaufmann-Kohler and Rigozzi 2015, paras 8.08–8.10; 8.16–8.17. For an example where an athlete benefited from the (then even) more protective domestic regime, see SFT 4P.148/2006, decision of 10 January 2007 (dealing with cyclist Danilo Hondo's challenge against a CAS award).

Article 353(2), came into force in 2011) not many federations have done so. That said, we note that the BAT Rules stipulate in Article 2.2 that "the tribunal's proceedings are governed by Chapter 12 PILA, irrespective of the parties' domicile".

Be that as it may, the majority of sports arbitrations are international and thus subject to Chapter 12 PILA, which is why we will focus on the international arbitration regime in this digest, referring to domestic arbitration only when necessary in light of a particular case.[6]

Within Chapter 12 PILA, remedies against arbitral awards are governed by Articles 190–192 PILA. Article 190(1) PILA provides that awards are final as from their notification, Article 190(2)(a)–(e) PILA sets out the (limited) grounds upon which the annulment of awards may be sought, while Article 190(3) specifies that preliminary awards are only subject to restricted grounds for annulment but must be challenged immediately, and Article 191 PILA establishes that the SFT has the exclusive jurisdiction to deal with annulment proceedings, which are to be conducted in accordance with Article 77 of the Supreme Court Act (hereinafter SCA).[7] Finally, Article 192(1) PILA enables the parties (provided they are not seated in Switzerland) to agree to waive their right to seek the annulment of the award (on all or some of Article 190(2)(a)–(e)'s grounds).

In addition to annulment, the remedy of revision is available against arbitral awards rendered in Switzerland. Chapter 12 PILA is silent in this regard, but the SFT decided in its landmark *Perrodo* judgement of 1992 that this was a *lacuna* to be filled by judicial means.[8] By contrast, Part 3 CCP expressly provides for the revision of domestic awards in its Articles 396–399.[9] Under both the international and the domestic regime, the SFT has jurisdiction to hear requests for the revision of arbitral awards. Revision is an exceptional remedy, allowing for the reconsideration of a decision definitively vested with *res judicata* effect on the basis of very specific and narrow grounds. These grounds are set out in Article 123 SCA, which may be translated in relevant part as follows:

(1) The revision of a decision may be requested when criminal proceedings establish that it was influenced to the detriment of the party seeking its reconsideration by a crime or a felony, even if no conviction ensued. If criminal prosecution is not possible, proof [of the crime of felony] can be brought by other means.
(2) Revision may also be requested:

   a. [...] when the party seeking the reconsideration of the decision has subsequently discovered relevant facts or conclusive evidence on which it was unable to rely

[6]As it happens, all the sports-related SFT decisions issued in the period under review dealt with international arbitration awards.

[7]Note however that under Article 390 CCP, the parties may agree to derogate from the rule establishing the SFT's jurisdiction and provide for annulment proceedings to be brought before the cantonal court at the seat of the arbitration. In that case, the proceedings are governed by the relevant provisions of the CCP.

[8]SFT 118 II 199, 203. In so doing, the Court established the provisions governing the revision of its own decisions were to apply by analogy.

[9]For detailed commentary of the grounds for annulment of Article 393(a)–(f), see e.g., (in French), Schweizer Ph (2011) Article 393 CCP. In: Bohnet F et al. (eds) Code de procédure civile commenté. Helbing Lichtenhahn, Basel.

in the previous proceedings, to the exclusion of facts or evidence that came into existence after the decision […]

The time limit to apply for the revision of the decision is 90 days from the time when the applicant becomes aware of the relevant grounds.[10] For cases brought on the basis of Article 123(2)(a) SCA, the absolute time limit is 10 years after the decision was rendered. If the request for revision is successful, the SFT annuls the award and refers the case back to the original arbitral tribunal, or possibly—given the long period of time that may have elapsed—to a newly constituted one.

There are a few well-known cases of revision proceedings involving sports awards. For instance, in 2010, Claudia Pechstein unsuccessfully sought the revision of the CAS award confirming her two year ban for blood doping, relying on new medical evidence pursuant to Article 123(2)(a) SCA.[11]

Rigozzi has noted that the SFT's jurisdiction to hear requests for the revision of awards is not mandatory. Indeed the CAS has entertained at least two requests for revision of its own awards.[12]

To our knowledge, there were no publicly known decisions dealing with the revision of sports arbitral awards in the period under review. Accordingly, the following overview will focus on the procedural aspects of annulment proceedings, many of which apply mutatis mutandis to revision proceedings.

The SFT is the highest ranking court in Switzerland. Consequently, its decisions on the annulment (or revision) of awards are subject to no further review and can only be challenged, by means of an action against Switzerland, before the ECtHR.[13]

In 2015, the SFT rendered 54 decisions on actions for annulment against arbitral awards. Of these, 18 related to sports awards (17 CAS and 1 ad hoc award).

The SFT's decisions are available on the Court's website,[14] and are reproduced (entirely or in excerpted form), compiled and commented upon in a number of

[10]See Article 124(1)(d) SCA. See Kaufmann-Kohler and Rigozzi 2015, para 8.215, for a discussion of the possibility of filing an application under Article 121(a) SCA, which covers cases where "the provisions relating to the constitution of the [tribunal] or the challenge of [an arbitrator] were not complied with" in the arbitration and is subject to a different, shorter time limit of 30 days.

[11]SFT 4A_144/2010, decision of 28 September 2010.

[12]CAS 2010/A/1270, *D. Meca Medina & I. Majcen v. FINA*, unreported award, and CAS 2008/A/1557, *FIGC, Daniele Mannini, Davide Possanzini and CONI v. WADA*, Award of 27 July 2009, applying by analogy the rules developed by the SFT under Article 123 SCA.

[13]Two cases currently pending against Switzerland in relation to arbitral proceedings concern sports disputes: these are the *Mutu* and *Pechstein* complaints, both filed in 2010 and still pending before the ECtHR (docket numbers 40575/10 and 67474/10, respectively).

[14]www.bger.ch. Accessed 4 February 2016. Decisions are generally posted online (in most cases, redacted so as to conceal the parties' names and other personal information) a few days after they have been notified to the parties. Decisions that are slated for inclusion (usually in excerpted version) in the Court's official reports, which are equally accessible on the Court's website, are marked with an asterisk upon posting. Once published in the official reports, their docket number (e.g., for the *Matuzalem* case, SFT 4A_558/2011) is replaced by the official reports' reference number (i.e., for that same case, SFT 138 III 322, where 138 stands for the 138th (yearly) volume in the collection—started in 1875—, III for the relevant part in that volume and 322 for the page number where the decision can be found).

regular digests,[15] some of which are specifically devoted to sports arbitration cases.[16] In recent years, English translations of the SFT's decisions relating to international arbitration, including sports arbitration, have also been published or made publicly available by specialist practitioners.[17]

In the following paragraphs, we will focus on the legal framework governing annulment proceedings against international arbitral awards before the SFT, as well as the main procedural and practical issues parties and their counsel should be aware of in that context. We will briefly discuss, in particular, the admissibility of the action (as well as the formal requirements for the application; see Sects. 17.2.2.1—17.2.2.2 below), its nature and consequences (see Sects. 17.2.2.3, **17.2.2.5** and 17.2.2.6), the scope and contents of the available grounds for annulment (see Sect. 17.2.2.4) and the SFT's power of review (see Sect. 17.2.2.3).

All of these aspects should be kept in mind by applicants and respondents in drafting their submissions to the SFT.[18]

---

[15]The quarterly journal of the Swiss Arbitration Association (ASA Bulletin) publishes several SFT decisions (including those relating to sports arbitration cases) in each issue. In addition, see e.g., in English, Xavier Favre-Bulle's Case Notes on International Arbitration, appearing once a year in the Revue Suisse de droit international et européen (RSDIE/SZIER), and the comprehensive review published in the proceedings from the annual conference "New Developments in International Commercial Arbitration", held in November of each year, edited by Christoph Müller, Sébastien Besson and Antonio Rigozzi (featuring Luca Beffa's review, referenced in this digest's bibliography, in the 2015 edition); in French, see Pierre-Yves Tschanz's and Isabelle Fellrath's yearly digest in the Revue de l'arbitrage, and Pierre-Yves Gunter et al's digest, published once a year in the Paris Journal of International Arbitration/Les Cahiers de l'arbitrage; in German, see, eg, Bernhard Berger's contribution, entitled *Die Rechtsprechung des Bundesgerichts zum Zivilprozessrecht, Teil 3., Schiedsgerichtsbarkeit*, and published once a year in the Zeitschrift des Bernischen Juristenvereins (ZBJV/RSJB). On a more frequent basis, see the very useful newsletters on arbitration cases issued by Nathalie Voser et al. (http://www.swlegal.ch/Publications/Arbitration-Case-Digest.aspx. Accessed 4 February 2016); Frank Spoorenberg et al. (http://www.taverniertschanz.com/en/publications/publication/Arbitration/29.html. Accessed 4 February 2016) and Hansjörg Stutzer et al. (http://thouvenin.com/publications/. Accessed 4 February 2016). All of the foregoing publications cover both commercial and sports arbitration.

[16]In addition to the SFT decisions reproduced in the CAS Bulletin (published twice a year and available at http://www.tas-cas.org/en/bulletin/cas-bulletin.html), see e.g., in English, Luca Beffa's and Olivier Ducrey's yearly *Review of the Case Law of the of the Swiss Federal Tribunal Concerning Sports Arbitration* in the sports law journal CausaSport; in English and French, see also Antonio Rigozzi's and Ullrich Haas's *Chronique de jurisprudence en matière d'arbitrage sportif*, published in the Paris Journal of International Arbitration/Cahiers de l'arbitrage; and in French, Mathieu Maisonneuve's, Sébastien Besson's, Franck Latty's and Marc Peltier's *Chronique de jurisprudence arbitrale en matière sportive* (covering also SFT decisions), published annually in the Revue de l'arbitrage.

[17]See in particular the *Swiss International Law Reports* series by Paolo Michele Patocchi and Matthias Scherer; and Charles Poncet's translations, available online at http://www.swissarbitrationdecisions.com/. Accessed 4 February 2016.

[18]For excellent practical advice on how to draft an application for annulment, see Arroyo 2013b, paras 60–81.

17.2.2 The Action for Annulment Against International Arbitral Awards Before the SFT

As indicated above, annulment proceedings against arbitral awards before the SFT are governed primarily by Article 77 SCA,[19] which forms part of Chap. 3 of the SCA, covering "civil law appeals", i.e., judicial recourses against decisions in civil matters, which include arbitral awards. Article 77 SCA sets out a specific regime for challenges against international arbitral awards, essentially by carving out some of the other SCA provisions that apply to civil law appeals in general[20] and by referring to Articles 190–192 PILA as far as the grounds for annulment and other specific issues are concerned.[21]

17.2.2.1 Admissibility

To be admissible, an action under Article 77 SCA must be directed against an arbitral award (as opposed to other types of decisions) (a.), and not be covered by an exclusion agreement within the meaning of Article 192(1) PILA (d.).[22] The party bringing the action must have standing to do so (c.), ensure it files its request within the applicable time limit (b.), rely (exclusively) on one or more of the grounds for annulment listed in Article 190(2)(a)–(e) PILA, and adequately substantiate its complaint (f.). The SFT has not yet had to decide whether the threshold amount in dispute set out in Article 74(1) SCA applies to arbitration matters (e.).

a. *Decisions subject to annulment*
   The action for annulment pursuant to Articles 190–192 PILA can be brought only against arbitral awards, which are not defined in the PILA.[23] According to

---

[19]In free translation, Article 77 SCA reads as follows: "*1.* A civil law appeal is admissible against decisions by arbitral tribunals: a. in international arbitration, pursuant to the requirements of Arts 190 to 192 PILA; b. in domestic arbitration, pursuant to the requirements of Arts 389 to 395 of the CCP. *2.* Arts 48(3), 90 to 98, 103(2), 105(2) and 106(1), as well as Article 107(2) SCA, to the extent that this latter provision entitles the SFT to rule on the merits of the dispute, are not applicable in such cases. *3.* The SFT shall review only the grounds that the applicant has raised and substantiated".

[20]See Article 77(2) SCA.

[21]See Article 77(1)(a) SCA. For domestic arbitral awards, see Article 77(1)(b) SCA, referring to Articles 389–395 CCP.

[22]Article 192(1) PILA provides that "[i]f none of them has its domicile, habitual residence, or a business establishment in Switzerland, the parties may, by an express statement in the arbitration agreement or by a subsequent written agreement, exclude any action for annulment in full or limit it to one or the other of the grounds listed in Article 190(2) [PILA]" (free translation). On this provision, see the reference given in footnote 53 below.

[23]Article 188 PILA states that arbitrators may render "partial awards", without defining this particular type of decision, and Article 189 PILA merely provides that awards "shall be rendered in conformity with the procedure and form agreed by the parties" (including by reference to a set of arbitration rules), or, absent an agreement, that they shall be made by a majority or by the presiding arbitrator, in writing, and be reasoned, dated and signed.

the SFT, to qualify as an award (which by statute is deemed equivalent to a domestic court judgment), a decision must be issued by an arbitral tribunal, which must be independent and impartial within the meaning of Articles 30(1) Swiss Federal Constitution[24] and 6(1) ECHR, on the basis of an agreement between the parties that validly ousts the jurisdiction of the courts.[25]

This means in particular that decisions rendered by the internal judicial bodies of SGBs, which lack the requisite independence (even if they are denominated 'arbitral tribunal'), cannot be challenged before the SFT.[26] Similarly, the decisions issued by arbitral institutions (which are not arbitral tribunals) in the course of the proceedings (e.g., decisions on the appointment of, or challenges against arbitrators) are not normally subject to annulment before the SFT.[27] A party aggrieved by one such decision must await the first award rendered by the arbitral tribunal in the disputed composition in order to seek its annulment by reference to the underlying institutional decision.[28] Procedural orders by the arbitrators (including orders on provisional measures) which, by their nature, do not bind the tribunal and can therefore be revoked or amended in the course of the proceedings are not awards and thus also not subject to an annulment action before the SFT. Be that as it may, the SFT's case law shows that the question whether a particular decision constitutes a challengeable award is to be determined on the basis of its content rather than its form or denomination.[29]

Furthermore, Swiss law distinguishes between final, partial and preliminary arbitral awards. The distinction must be kept in mind as it affects both the timing and the grounds upon which the annulment action may be brought.[30] Final awards (i.e., decisions which by ruling on matters of substance or procedure bring the arbitration to an end) and partial awards (i.e., decisions that, without putting an end to the proceedings in their entirety, rule definitively on certain

---

[24]Article 30(1) FC provides that "[a]ny person whose case falls to be judicially decided has the right to have their case heard by a legally constituted, competent, independent and impartial court. [...]".

[25]With regard to CAS awards, see, e.g., the discussion in SFT 119 II 271 *Gundel*.

[26]See, e.g., the discussion in SFT 4A_374/2014, decision of 26 February 2015, para 4.3.2.1 (summarized in Sect. 17.3.5.4 below), with further references.

[27]See however, with regard to decisions issued by the CAS Court Office and the President of a CAS division, SFT 4A_600/2008, decision of 20 February 2009, SFT 4A_126/2008, decision of 9 May 2008, and SFT 4A_282/2013, decision of 13 November 2013. On this issue, see in particular the discussion in Kaufmann-Kohler G. and Rigozzi A. (2015) International Arbitration—Law and Practice in Switzerland, para 8.24.

[28]Note however that not only must the parties wait until the first award rendered by the tribunal to challenge the decision as to its composition, if that award is not the final award, but only a preliminary or partial award, they also must not wait until after the time limit to challenge that particular award, or else they will be precluded from contesting it (including the decision on the tribunal's composition that is "subsumed" in it) at a later stage. See the following paragraph and the references given in footnote 29 below on this issue.

[29]See, e.g., SFT 136 III 597, 599; SFT 140 III 520, 523.

[30]For a more detailed discussion on these issues, see, e.g., Kaufmann-Kohler and Rigozzi 2015, paras 8.18–8.27; Berger and Kellerhals 2015, paras 1680–1696; Arroyo 2013b, paras 16–24.

claims) can be challenged on all the grounds set out in Article 190(2) PILA [letters (a)–(e)], and the challenge must be brought within 30 days from the date of notification of the award. Preliminary awards, which include awards upholding jurisdiction,[31] must also be challenged within 30 days from their notification (i.e., without awaiting the final award), but the challenge can only be brought on the grounds set out in letters (a) and (b) of Article 190(2) (i.e., as discussed in more detail below, irregular constitution or composition of the tribunal and incorrect decision on jurisdiction).[32] However, as recently clarified by the SFT, the grounds contained in letters (c)–(e) of Article 190(2) PILA (decision *infra*, *extra* or *ultra petita*; violation of the parties' right to be heard and to equal treatment; award contravening public policy) can be relied upon, in the context of a challenge based on letter(s) (a) and/or (b), if and (only) to the extent they are directly related to the composition or the jurisdiction of the tribunal.[33]

b. *Time limit to bring the action*
The time limit to file an annulment action is 30 days "from the notification of the [award] in full".[34] This means that when, as is relatively frequent in CAS arbitration,[35] the tribunal issues the dispositive part of the award first and then notifies the full decision with the reasons at a later stage, the time limit only runs from the latter event.[36] The same is true for BAT awards in the instances envisaged in Article 16.2.1 BAT Rules.[37]

---

[31]An award denying jurisdiction is of course a final award.

[32]This is expressly stated in Article 190(3) PILA.

[33]See SFT 140 III 520 (relating to a CAS award), para 2.2.3, referring to SFT 140 III 477, rendered on the same day and deciding this particular issue.

[34]Article 100(1) SCA.

[35]For a recent example of this scenario, see SFT 4A_126/2015, decision of 14 April 2015 (summarized in Sect. 17.3.1.1 below), para 1.4.

[36]See Arts R46(2) and R59(3) CAS Code. On the other hand, the party wishing to seek the annulment of the award is free to file the action upon receipt of the sole operative part, reserving its right to supplement its filing once the grounds for the award are made available. This possibility may be useful, for instance, to seek an immediate stay of the award pending the annulment action (on the—strict—requirements for obtaining a staying order from the SFT see Sect. 17.2.2.3 below).

[37]Art 16.2.1a) BAT Rules provides that where the value of the dispute does not exceed € 30,000 the award will be issued without reasons. Article 16.2.1b) BAT Rules stipulates that the arbitrator may decide to the same, upon request by the claimant, in cases where the amount in dispute is comprised between € 30,001 and 200,000, if the respondent fails to pay its share of the advance on costs (which will also allow for a reduction of the overall advance). In both scenarios, the parties have a time limit of 10 days from the award's notification to request that the reasons be issued. Where these BAT rules apply, the SFT will consider that the challenge is admissible (subject to any other requirements) against an unreasoned award upon expiry of the time limit to request the reasons (SFT 4A_198/2012, decision of 14 December 2012, clarifying also that a failure to request reasons did not amount to a waiver of the right to seek the annulment of the award, even though the absence of reasons would make it considerably more difficult for the SFT to review the decision and thus for the applicant to succeed in its request for annulment).

Importantly, the time limit to file an application for annulment cannot be extended.[38] With regard to its computation, the time limit starts to run on the day after notification.[39] If the 30th day thereafter falls on a Saturday, Sunday or official holiday, the time limit will expire on the first following business day.[40] It should also be noted that the running of time limits before the SFT is stayed *ex lege* during certain annual holiday periods.[41]

While it is clear that notification is the event that triggers the running of the time limit to bring the action for annulment, the manner in which awards should be notified is not determined in the PILA or the SCA. The modalities for notification are thus left to party autonomy, meaning that they are often regulated by the applicable arbitration rules.[42] For instance, the CAS Code provides in Article R31(2) that "[a]ll arbitration awards, orders and other decisions made by CAS and the Panel shall be notified by courier and/or by facsimile and/or by electronic mail but at least in a form permitting proof of receipt".[43] Articles R46(3) and R59(4), as amended in the 2016 edition of the Code, further specify that the award is subject to "recourse pursuant to Swiss law within 30 days from the notification of the *original* award". The addition of the language just quoted in 2016 reflects the SFT's determination in a 2011 ruling (confirmed in the subsequent case law), that Article 100(1) SCA's time limit with respect to CAS awards only begins to run with the notification of the original award by post, even though the parties receive an advance copy by fax (or email), given that the Code requires that the award be both signed and notified by a means permitting proof of receipt.[44] Conversely, in a more recent sports case where the award under challenge was rendered in ad hoc (not CAS) proceedings, the SFT found that the application for annulment had been filed belatedly because the time limit had started to run with the notification of the advance copy of the award by email (as required by the applicable UCI regulations and in line with the practice followed for the other official communications in the course of that arbitration), and not from receipt of the original by post the following day.[45] To our knowledge, this question has not yet arisen

[38]Article 47(1) SCA. It can, however, be reinstated in very exceptional circumstances (Article 50(1) SCA), where the applicant or its counsel were prevented from complying with the time limit through no fault of their own, and provided a reasoned request for reinstatement is filed, together with the application for annulment, within 30 days from the time when the relevant impediment ceases.

[39]Article 44(1) SCA. This is so even if that day is a non-working day, e.g., a Sunday (see, e.g., Arroyo 2013b, para 33).

[40]Article 45 SCA.

[41]That is, from the 7th day before Easter up to and including the 7th day thereafter, from 15 July up to and including 15 August, and from 18 December up to and including 2 January (Article 46 SCA).

[42]SFT 4A_392/2010, decision of 12 January 2011, para 2.3.1.

[43]For a critical reading of this wording (as amended in 2013) in light of the SFT's prior case law, see Kaufmann-Kohler and Rigozzi 2015, para 8.38.

[44]SFT 4A_392/2010 of 12 January 2011, para 2.3.2, ASA Bulletin 2012, p. 397.

[45]SFT 4A_609/2014, decision of 20 February 2015, para 2.3; ASA Bulletin 2015 pp. 373–377.

with respect to a BAT award, which, according to the BAT Rules, "shall be [notified] in writing, including telefax and e-mail",[46] but must also be signed.[47] It is also worth noting that (absent any agreement to a different effect) the notification of the award to the parties' counsel of record is deemed made to the parties themselves and therefore effectively triggers the running of the time limit.[48] Finally, to comply with the time limit, the application must be filed, on or before the expiry of the time limit, directly with the SFT in Lausanne, or with a Swiss (or Liechtenstein) post office, or with a Swiss diplomatic or consular office abroad.[49]

c. *Standing*
According to Article 76(1) SCA, a party may file an application for annulment only if he or she "(a) has taken part in the [arbitral] proceedings or was denied access to such proceedings; and (b) is directly affected [by the award] and has an interest worthy of protection in its annulment". As interpreted by the SFT, the requirements for standing under Article 76(1) are that the applicant (i) has participated in the arbitration or was precluded from doing so; (ii) is directly affected by the award because it impacts his or her protected interests, and (iii) has a present, personal interest in the annulment. The first limb of Article 76(1)(a) SCA is aimed at avoiding the interference of third parties in the annulment proceedings, while the second limb provides for an exception to that rule which may be relevant in sports cases. In doping disputes, for instance, a person having a personal interest in the outcome of the case, such as a competitor of an athlete accused of doping, will likely not have been able to participate in the arbitration,[50] but would in principle have standing to request the annulment of the award before the SFT under Article 76(1)(a) SCA. The requirement for an 'interest worthy of protection' under Article 76(1)(b) SCA is understood to be met when the annulment of the award would protect the applicant from pecuniary or moral harm directly resulting from it.[51] The requirement for a 'present, personal interest',

[46]BAT Rules, Article 6.3.

[47]BAT Rules, Article 16.1.

[48]The fact that the award is separately served on the parties, if such service occurs at a later date, will not have the effect of 'restarting' the running of the time limit. See, e.g., Kaufmann-Kohler and Rigozzi 2015, para 8.38 and the references; Arroyo 2013b, para 33.

[49]Article 48(1) SCA. If the request for annulment is sent from a non-Swiss (or Liechtenstein) post office, it will be deemed timely filed only if it can be shown that it transited via the Swiss postal system prior to the expiry of the time limit (see Kaufmann-Kohler and Rigozzi 2015, para 8.40 and the references). A filing by fax directly to the SFT will not suffice to meet the time limit. On the possibility to file the request for annulment by email, see the information and instructions available on the SFT's website, at http://www.bger.ch/fr/index/juridiction/jurisdiction-inherit-template/jurisdiction-elektronische-beschwerde.htm. Accessed 4 February 2016. See also Arroyo 2013b, para 47. For an example where a submission by e-mail was deemed in admissible as it did not comply with the SFT's technical requirements, see SFT 4A_596/2015, decision of 9 December 2015, p. 2.

[50]See Article 13.2.3 WADA Code.

[51]SFT 4A_126/2015, decision of 14 April 2015, para 4.1 (summarized Sect. 17.3.1.1 below).

which is not expressly mentioned in Article 76(1) SCA but is set forth in the SFT's case law, may give rise to difficulties in cases resulting from a disputed sports ban. If the ban period imposed by the award expires before the filing of the application for annulment, the application will be inadmissible for lack of a current personal interest in obtaining the annulment. If the ban expires once the application has been filed but while the SFT proceedings are still pending, the application will be deemed to have become 'without object'. In both these cases, however, the ban can be shown to continue to produce consequences for the athlete (e.g., due to its stigmatizing character) notwithstanding its expiry. In particular, in doping cases, the ban will be considered to produce continuing consequences for the sanctioned athlete, and thus establish the existence of a current personal interest as required by the SFT's case law, because it would constitute an aggravating circumstance in case of a subsequent offense.[52]

d. *No waiver of the right to seek the annulment of the award*
As mentioned above, under Article 192(1) PILA, the parties may waive their right to seek the annulment of the award (altogether or only with respect to certain grounds).[53] In accordance with that provision, such an 'exclusion agreement' can only be made (i) if none of the parties has its domicile, habitual residence, or a business establishment in Switzerland, and (ii) by an express statement in the arbitration agreement or a subsequent written agreement. Moreover, in the well-known *Cañas* decision, the SFT has ruled that exclusion agreements contained in sports regulations are unenforceable due to the non-consensual nature of the athletes' acceptance of the relevant clauses, which are imposed by SGBs as a condition for participating in the sport.[54] On the other hand, BAT arbitration clauses relatively frequently include an exclusion agreement.[55] Because the disputes submitted to BAT are of a commercial nature and the waiver is freely entered into by the parties in concluding the contract, provided that it meets the other requirements for its validity, it will normally operate to render an application for annulment against the award inadmissible.[56]

---

[52]SFT 4A_576/2012, decision of 28 February 2013, para 2, ASA Bulletin 2014, p. 543.

[53]For a detailed analysis of the waiver of annulment under Article 192(1) PILA, see Kaufmann-Kohler and Rigozzi 2015, paras 8.49–8.75.

[54]SFT 133 III 235. In any event, with respect to CAS appeals cases, due to the fact that they often involve an international federation or other SGB, many of which are seated in Switzerland, issues relating to exclusion agreements do not arise very frequently.

[55]This may in part be due to the fact that the first editions of the BAT (then called FAT) Rules, in 2007 and 2009, included a model arbitration clause containing an exclusion agreement. At the time, the clause provided for appeal to CAS as the suggested remedy against FAT awards. In the later versions of the Rules (from 2010 onwards), the reference to CAS appeal was withdrawn from the model clause and so was the exclusion agreement in relation to the annulment action before the SFT, presumably so as not to encourage the parties to indiscriminately waive any and all remedies against the award.

[56]Indeed, in one of the two cases relating to BAT awards that have been dealt with by the SFT so far, the Court upheld an exclusion agreement and thus declared the application for annulment inadmissible (SFT 4A_232/2012, decision of 29 May 2012).

e. *Amount in dispute*
The SFT has not yet ruled on the applicability to arbitration of Article 74(1) SCA,[57] which provides that recourses against decisions in civil matters (as are arbitral awards) in pecuniary disputes are "admissible only if the amount in dispute is at least: "(a) 15,000 CHF in employment […] matters; (b) 30.000 CHF in all other cases".[58] With the exception of football disputes, where the amounts at stake are often quite high, this threshold could create problems in CAS appeals or in BAT cases.[59] For instance, in CAS appeals cases, the relief sought is unquantified when it is a request for the annulment or confirmation of an SGB's decision imposing a ban. So far, the issue could be left undecided, either because the application was deemed inadmissible for other reasons, or because the case involved monetary sanctions in addition to the ban which were higher than the threshold and/or because it was possible to quantify the financial impact of the ban for the athlete and again the amount so established was above Article 74(1)(b)'s threshold.[60]
The manner in which the amount in dispute should be calculated is set out in Article 51 SCA. Specifically, the Court will look at the totality of the claims before the arbitral tribunal,[61] and where the parties' prayers for relief in the arbitration did not seek the payment of a determined amount, Article 51(2) SCA provides that the SFT will fix the amount in dispute on the basis of its own assessment.

f. *'Rügeprinzip' and 'substantiation requirement'*
Only the annulment grounds listed in Article 190(2)(a)–(e) PILA can be raised against an arbitral award. Moreover, Article 77(3) SCA provides that the SFT only reviews the grounds which the applicant raises in express terms (the so-called *Rügeprinzip* or *Rügepflicht*, which, put differently, means that the SFT will not examine *ex officio* whether the award falls foul of one or the other of the grounds for annulment listed in Article 190(2) PILA). In addition, the SFT regularly recalls that applicants are also subject to a 'substantiation requirement'

[57]Article 74 SCA is not in the list of provisions that are "carved out" from the rules governing arbitration by Article 77(2) SCA.

[58]Article 74(2) SCA then goes on to qualify this rule by adding that the application is admissible irrespective of the amount in dispute if it raises "a legal question of principle", an exception that is interpreted strictly by the SFT (see Corboz 2014, paras 30–46). Be that as it may, scholars agree that Article 74(1)(b) SCA should not apply to arbitration. See, e.g., Berger and Kellerhals 2015, para 1799, and Kaufmann-Kohler and Rigozzi 2015, paras 8.42–8.47.

[59]Notably, the BAT Rules include several provisions tailored to cover cases where the amount in dispute is less than € 30,000 (see e.g., Articles 9.3.1, 16.2.1 and 17). That said, most BAT cases involve employment disputes, which are subject to the lower threshold of CHF 15,000 under Article 74(1)(a) SCA.

[60]See, e.g., SFT 4A_10/2009, decision of 8 July 2009, para 3.1.

[61]In SFT 4A_112/2014, decision of 28 April 2014, para 1.1, the SFT noted that the amount in dispute in annulment proceedings against a final award corresponds to the total of the claims submitted to the tribunal for determination in the award. In that case, the relevant amount for purposes of Article 51(1) SCA was the last amount claimed by the applicant and disputed by the respondent before the arbitrator, not the difference between that claim and the amount actually awarded by the arbitrator.

(*Substantiierungspflicht*), meaning that they must discuss and explain the alleged violation in some detail. If the application does not meet the *Rügeprinzip* and substantiation requirements, i.e., it merely criticizes the legal reasoning or conduct of the arbitral tribunal, without explaining how the alleged mistakes or defects amount to violations covered by Article 190(2)'s grounds, the SFT declares it inadmissible.[62] Finally, it should also be noted that when the award relies on several alternative or subsidiary reasons, each one of them must be impugned in the application for annulment, failing which the application will also be deemed inadmissible.

17.2.2.2 Requirements as to the Contents of the Application (and Other Written Submissions Before the SFT)

Submissions to the SFT must be written in one of the Court's official languages, namely German, French or Italian.[63] If a submission is filed in a foreign language, the SFT will grant an additional time limit for the relevant party to provide a translation into one of the official languages.[64] Moreover, pursuant to Article 42 SCA, submissions to the SFT must be signed,[65] state the relief sought, the grounds invoked and the evidence relied upon, which must be attached to the brief, together with a copy of the challenged award.[66] The parties must also submit a power of attorney authorizing their counsel to act on their behalf in the proceedings.[67] Again, if any of these formal requirements are not satisfied in the initial submission, the SFT will grant an additional time limit for the relevant party to remedy the defect(s).[68]

17.2.2.3 Nature and Effects of the Action for Annulment; SFT's Power of Review

The annulment action pursuant to Articles 190–191 PILA is, in principle, merely 'cassatory' in nature, meaning that the SFT can only confirm or vacate (in full or in part) the award; it cannot issue a ruling on the merits replacing the

[62] See, e.g., in the period under review, SFT 4A_36/2015, decision of 26 January 2015, para 2. and SFT 4A_174/2015, decision of 30 June 2015.

[63] The parties are free to use each a different official language in their submissions (see, e.g., SFT 4A_684/2014, decision of 2 July 2015, para 1), in which case the SFT will issue its decision in the language of the application.

[64] See e.g., SFT 4A_70/2015, decision of 29 April 2015, para C.

[65] Pursuant to Article 40 SCA, only lawyers admitted to a Swiss bar or lawyers authorized to practice in Switzerland under an international treaty may represent parties before the SFT. Hence, counsel signing the parties' submissions must meet these requirements.

[66] Article 42(1)–(3) SCA.

[67] Article 40(2) SCA.

[68] Article 42(5) SCA.

annulled award.[69] This should be kept in mind in drafting the prayers for relief in the application for annulment. Indeed, there would be no point in asking the SFT, for instance, to impose a higher sanction than that set in the award or to order the payment of damages which were not awarded by the panel, as the corresponding prayer for relief will simply be declared inadmissible.[70]

Similarly, in accordance with Article 105(1) SCA, the SFT grounds its decision on the facts as established by the arbitral tribunal in the award, which it cannot (subject to very limited exceptions)[71] review and rectify. The application for annulment should again be drafted taking this aspect into account. For instance, the applicant should refrain from supplementing or amending the factual submissions made in the arbitration as recorded in the award. Any such new or amended factual allegation will be discarded as inadmissible.[72]

On the other hand, the SFT has full power to review the parties' legal arguments and the tribunal's reasoning, meaning that it can base its decision on different legal considerations than those set out in the parties' submissions and in the award. This also means that the parties may further develop their legal arguments (provided they had already raised them in the arbitration), to the extent they may serve to support the application in accordance with the grounds set out in Article 190(2) PILA and in the light of the award rendered by the arbitrators.

Finally, it is important to note that the filing of the application for annulment does not have the effect of automatically staying the enforceability of the award.[73] As stated in Article 190(1) PILA, the award is final (i.e., binding and enforceable) as from its notification. Exceptionally, upon request by a party, the SFT can order the stay of a challenged award.[74] If the stay is granted, the award is not enforceable as long as the stay is maintained, but remains final, is still binding and has *res judicata* effect (albeit subject to dismissal of the action by the SFT).

[69]Article 77(2) SCA excludes the application of Article 107(2) SCA, which empowers the SFT to decide on the merits of the dispute. There are two specific exceptions to this rule, as will be seen in Sect. 17.2.2.6 below.

[70]See, e.g., Kaufmann-Kohler and Rigozzi 2015, para 8.120 and the references.

[71]In particular, subject to the facts themselves having been established in violation of one or more of Article 190(2) PILA's grounds (discussed in the following section), which is to be demonstrated by the party seeking a review of such facts, including by showing that the relevant allegations had already properly been put before the arbitrators.

[72]See, e.g., SFT 4A_684/2014, decision of 2 July 2015, para 2.4.

[73]Article 77(2) SCA excludes the applicability of Article 103(2) SCA (which provides for the automatic staying effect of appeals in civil matters) to annulment proceedings against awards.

[74]See Article 103 SCA (the stay also be granted *ex officio*, but that is an extremely rare occurrence). On the (strict) requirements applied by the SFT for the granting of a stay of enforceability, see Kaufmann-Kohler and Rigozzi 2015, paras 8.95–8.97 [for the period under review, the stay of enforceability was granted in only one of the four cases in which it was requested (SFT 4A_246/2014, decision of 15 July 2015, para C. The other cases where the request was unsuccessful were SFT 4A_634/2014, decision of 21 May 2015; SFT 4A_70/2015, decision of 29 April 2015; SFT 4A_374/2014, decision of 26 February 2015)]. The request for a staying order can only be filed together with or after the application for annulment (not before). Upon request by the opposing party, the SFT can make the order conditional upon the posting of security.

17.2.2.4 Grounds for Annulment (Article 190(2)(a)–(e) PILA)[75]

Under *Article 190(2)(a) PILA*, the award may be annulled in case of 'irregular constitution of the arbitral tribunal'. This ground covers situations where the tribunal's appointment was not in accordance with the parties' agreement[76] or where the arbitrator(s) did not satisfy an essential requirement agreed upon by the parties, or lacked independence or impartiality, which are statutory requirements.[77] It is important to note that, to the extent a party becomes aware of any such ground, it must raise it immediately in the arbitral proceedings and maintain it throughout, notwithstanding an institutional decision rejecting the objection, in order to be able to rely on it at the annulment stage. In other words, the right to seek the annulment of the award on the basis of Article 190(2)(a) PILA may be waived by the parties, including by conduct.[78]

Article 190(2)(b) PILA provides that the award may be annulled when the tribunal incorrectly accepted or denied jurisdiction. This ground covers challenges to the validity of the arbitration agreement as to form or substance, including the arbitrability of the dispute, as well as the capacity of the parties to enter into such an agreement and to be parties to the arbitration. In particular, Article 190(2)(b) PILA encompasses disputes as to the parties' consent to arbitration and the determination of the arbitration agreement's scope *ratione personae*, *ratione materiae* and *ratione temporis*. Importantly, as reflected in Articles 186(2) PILA,[79] R39(2) and R55(1) CAS Code and 11.2 BAT Rules,[80] an objection going to the tribunal's jurisdiction must be raised immediately in the arbitration. If a party considers that the tribunal lacks jurisdiction, e.g., because that party did not validly consent to arbitration, but fails to object in a timely fashion—e.g., because it proceeds to make filings on the merits of the case—it will be deemed to have definitively waived its jurisdictional objection (a situation referred to by the German word *Einlassung* in the SFT's case law[81]).

[75]For a detailed discussion of each of the grounds for annulment under Article 190(2) PILA, see, e.g., Kaufmann-Kohler and Rigozzi 2015, paras 8.130–8.205; Berger and Kellerhals 2015, paras 1702–1788; Arroyo 2013a, paras 12–233. See also, in French, Bucher 2011, paras 40–158 (regular updates of this commentary are made available online by the author, at http://www.andreasbucher-law.ch/NewFlash/bis.html. Accessed 4 February 2016), and in German, Göksu 2014, paras 2028–2148. The corresponding (but more extensive) grounds with respect to domestic awards are listed in Article 393(a)–(f) CCP.

[76]See, e.g., SFT 4A_282/2013, decision of 13 November 2013, paras 3–4.

[77]See, e.g., SFT 136 III 605 (i.e., the landmark *Valverde* decision), 608–615 (para 3).

[78]Ibid., para 5.3.2; SFT 4A_282/2013, decision of 13 November 2013, para 5.3.

[79]Article 186(2) PILA provides that "a jurisdictional defence must be raised prior to any defence on the merits".

[80]These rules are all to the effect that a defence of lack of jurisdiction must be raised at the latest in the respondent's answer to the request for arbitration or statement of appeal.

[81]For an example of decision dealing with this issue in the period under review, see SFT 4A_634/2014, decision of 21 May 2015, para 3.

Pursuant to Article *190(2)(c) PILA*, the award is subject to annulment if the tribunal "has ruled beyond the claims submitted to it [decision *extra* or *ultra petita*], or failed to decide one of the claims [decision *infra petita*]". The "claims submitted" to the tribunal for the purposes of this provision are the parties' prayers for relief.[82] With regard to challenges on the *infra petita* ground, it should be noted that they may have little prospect of success against CAS or BAT final awards, which normally include in their dispositive section a closing sentence to the effect that "all other motions or prayers for relief", or "any other or further reaching prayers for relief are dismissed". Indeed, the SFT generally accepts that such a statement is sufficient to rule out a finding that the award was rendered *infra petita*.[83] An award will be deemed *ultra petita*, with regard to monetary claims, if the amount awarded by the tribunal exceeds the total of the quantified claims made by the parties. More specifically with regard to sports matters, it may be worth noting that in CAS appeals cases, an award imposing a disciplinary sanction higher than that sought before the panel will not be considered *ultra petita* if the sanction is not higher than that imposed by the lower instance decision.[84]

The annulment ground covered by Article *190(2)(d) PILA* is the violation of fundamental principles of procedure, namely the parties' right to "equal treatment [and] to be heard in adversarial proceedings", as set out in Article 182(3) PILA.[85] Alleged violations of the principle of equal treatment are rarely upheld by the SFT, which adopts a pragmatic approach in dealing with this guarantee. On the one hand, the SFT has held that some disparity in the tribunal's treatment of the parties may be dictated by the circumstances,[86] and on the other, it tends to require that the incriminated conduct by the arbitrators results in an actual disruption of the equality of arms between the parties (i.e., that one of the parties will be put at a disadvantage in the defense of its case).[87] In other words, not any difference in the treatment of the parties will justify an annulment of the award. The second limb of Article 190(2)(d) PILA is two-pronged: it guarantees both the parties' right to be heard, i.e., the right to present one's case, and the adversarial principle, i.e., the opportunity to rebut the opponent's case. Although violations of the parties' right to be heard are

---

[82]The reference here is to substantive prayers for relief, not procedural ones.

[83]With regard to a CAS award, see, e.g., SFT 4A_314/2012, decision of 16 October 2012, para 5. For a critical view of this jurisprudence, see, e.g., Kaufmann-Kohler and Rigozzi 2015, para 8.161.

[84]SFT 4A_682/2012, decision of 20 June 2013, para 5.

[85]Article 182 PILA lays down the general principles governing the procedure in Swiss-seated international arbitrations. It reads as follows: "1. The parties may, directly or by reference to arbitration rules, determine the arbitral procedure; they may also submit it to a procedural law of their choice. 2. Where the parties have not determined the procedure, the arbitral tribunal shall determine it to the extent necessary, either directly or by reference to a law or to arbitration rules. 3. Whatever procedure is chosen, the arbitral tribunal shall ensure equal treatment of the parties and their right to be heard in adversarial proceedings".

[86]See Kaufmann-Kohler and Rigozzi 2015, para 6.25, referring to an SFT decision of 11 May 1992, para 5a. In other words, the right to equal treatment is not absolute: it does not require identical treatment of the parties, but only that similar situations are handled in a similar manner by the tribunal.

[87]For an example relating to a BAT award where this ground was invoked (but deemed to have been waived by conduct), see SFT 4A_198/2012, decision of 14 December 2012, para 3.2.

often invoked, they are rarely successful before the SFT,[88] which has developed a number of interpretive rules limiting the scope of this guarantee. In particular, the parties' right to adduce evidence is circumscribed to that which is capable of proving facts that are relevant and material to the outcome of the dispute, and which are not already proven by other evidence on record. In addition, arbitral tribunals are empowered to refuse to take evidence offered by the parties if they consider, based on a so-called 'anticipated assessment', that such evidence would not change their opinion on the relevant matter(s). Finally, the tribunal's reliance on a legal norm or theory that was not invoked by the parties does not result in a breach of their right to be heard (by operation of the *jura novit curia* principle), unless it can be shown that the application of the relevant norm or theory takes the parties by surprise as it could not possibly have been anticipated by them (so-called 'surprise effect').[89]

In spite of the aforementioned limitations, the SFT will uphold a request for annulment based on Article 190(2)(d) if the applicant demonstrates that the tribunal has failed to take into consideration factual or legal submissions which were duly presented, relate to material aspects of the case and could have influenced its outcome.[90] In this regard, the SFT's case law often refers to the arbitrators' "minimal duty to examine and address the pertinent issues", holding that a failure to comply with this obligation amounts to a so-called 'formal denial of justice'.[91]

Again, a party who considers that the tribunal has infringed its right to equal treatment and/or to be heard in adversarial proceedings must raise the corresponding objection forthwith, giving the tribunal an opportunity to remedy the defect. If the tribunal fails to do so, the aggrieved party must maintain its objection, on pain of preclusion at a later stage. Indeed, the SFT has often underscored that the parties' procedural conduct is subject to the principle of good faith, meaning that the applicant may be estopped from relying on a ground for annulment if it has not raised the relevant objection in due course, or confirmed it at any appropriate juncture in the proceedings.[92]

---

[88]See, e.g., Dasser and Roth 2014, p. 464, showing that although Article 190(2)(d) PILA is the most frequently invoked ground, it was admitted in only 5.5 % of the SFT's annulment decisions rendered between 1989 and 2013.

[89]For a critical analysis of the relevant case law, see Kaufmann-Kohler and Rigozzi 2015, paras 8.183–8.184. For an example of decision dealing with this particular ground in the period under review, see SFT 4A_634/2014, decision of 21 May 2015, para 4. The surprise effect was found to be established (i.e., the parties' right to be heard breached with regard to a legal argument) in a decision dealing with a CAS award in 2009 (SFT 4A_400/2008, decision of 9 February 2009).

[90]In other words, the tribunal is not required to consider each and every argument brought forward by the parties, to the extent any such argument is devoid of relevance. For a detailed discussion of the SFT's approach to this aspect of the parties' right to be heard, see Kaufmann-Kohler and Rigozzi 2015, para 8.181. The only decision (partially) annulling a CAS award in the period under review upheld a complaint made in reliance on this particular ground (SFT 4A_246/2014, decision of 15 July 2015, para 6.3).

[91]See, e.g., the *Cañas* decision, SFT 133 III 235, 248, with further references.

[92]This also means that if a party declared at the end of the hearing that it was satisfied with the conduct of the proceedings, it will in principle be precluded from raising Article 190(2)(d) PILA's ground against the award (see, e.g., in the period under review, SFT 4A_544/2014, decision of 24 February 2015, summarized in Sect. 17.3.4.6 below).

In accordance with *Article 190(2)(e) PILA*, an award can be set aside if it contravenes public policy. The SFT's case law distinguishes between procedural and substantive public policy. This distinction aside, the SFT has acknowledged time and again the difficulty of giving an exact and comprehensive definition of public policy for annulment purposes.[93] In its current case law, the Court provides an abstract definition which it then illustrates (as far as the substantive facet of public policy is concerned) with a non-exhaustive (and evolving) list of examples. The relevant passage in its decisions is generally set out in the following terms:

(1) procedural public policy guarantees the parties' right to an independent decision, made in accordance with the applicable procedural law and based on the facts submitted and relief sought from the arbitral tribunal; there is a violation of procedural public policy when fundamental and generally recognized principles are breached, giving rise to an intolerable conflict with one's sense of justice, such that the decision appears contrary to the values accepted in a state abiding by the rule of law.[94]
(2) On the other hand:

   a. an award breaches substantive public policy when it violates fundamental principles of substantive law in such a serious way that it is no longer consistent with the legal system and the accepted set of values; among such principles, one finds inter alia the *pacta sunt servanda* maxim (i.e., the doctrine of the sanctity of contracts), the rules of good faith, the prohibition against abuse of rights, the prohibition against discriminatory or spoliatory measures, and the protection of persons lacking legal capacity.[95]

---

[93]See, e.g., the landmark *Tensacciai* case, SFT 132 III 389. As noted in this decision (at para 2.2.2), one of the difficulties in defining public policy within the meaning of Article 190(2)(e) PILA is to determine its source: here, the STF underscored that public policy as a ground for annulling an international arbitral award is not domestic (i.e. the lex fori's) public policy. The notion of public policy under Article 190(2)(e) PILA is disconnected from a particular domestic law, and instead reflects the fundamental values that, without necessarily being universal, are common to the nations belonging to a given civilization.

[94]One of the fundamental and generally recognized norms which form part of procedural public policy within the meaning of Article 190(2)(e) PILA is the principle of *res judicata*. Indeed, the only award that has been annulled on the ground of a breach of procedural public policy to date was that rendered by the CAS in the *Atlético Madrid* case, which the SFT found to conflict with a prior judgment on the same issue and vested with *res judicata* effect (SFT 136 III 345). A violation of procedural public policy has been (unsuccessfully) invoked in 2 cases in the period under review (SFT 4A_246/2014, decision of 15 July 2015; SFT 4A_374/2014, decision of 26 February 2015, summarized in Sect. 17.3.5 below).

[95]The only award annulled for breach of substantive public policy pursuant to Article 190(2)(e) PILA, so far, was also a CAS award, namely the one issued in the landmark *Matuzalem* case. In that instance, the fundamental principle which the SFT found to have been violated by the tribunal's decision was the prohibition against "excessive contractual undertakings" pursuant to Article 27(2) CC (i.e., advance agreements waiving or restricting one's freedom or economic livelihood to such an extent that they breach the law or are to be deemed *contra bonos mores* or unconscionable). A violation of substantive public policy has been (unsuccessfully) invoked in 4 cases in the period under review (SFT 4A_568/2015, decision of 10 December 2015, SFT 4A_634/2014, decision of 21 May 2015, SFT 4A_426/2014, decision of 6 May 2015, SFT 4A_70/2015, decision of 29 April 2015), summarized in Sect. 17.3.5 below).

In spite of these open ended definitions, the SFT underscores that public policy within the meaning of Article 190(2)(e) PILA is a very narrow concept, meaning that the chances of obtaining the annulment of the award on this ground are extremely limited.[96] In particular, the SFT regularly recalls that an award can be set aside under Article 190(2)(e) PILA only if its actual result (as embodied in the dispositive part) contravenes public policy. In other words, if the reasons underlying the award violate public policy but its outcome is still compatible with the relevant set of recognized fundamental values, the award will stand.

As seen above (Sect. 17.2.2.1(a) in fine), the admissibility of one or the other of the grounds just examined will depend on the type of award at stake. If the award sought to be annulled is final or partial, all of the above grounds may be relied upon in the application. If the challenged award is preliminary, interim or interlocutory in nature, the application will be admissible only if it is based on Articles 190(2)(a) and/or (b) PILA. The grounds in Articles 190(2)(c)–(e) can be relied upon only to the extent that they are directly and strictly related to the composition and/or jurisdiction of the tribunal (i.e., the grounds set out in Articles 190(2)(a) and (b) PILA).

17.2.2.5 Procedure Before the SFT[97]

Annulment proceedings before the SFT are generally 'documents only'.[98] Provided the applicant has paid the advance on costs as fixed by the Court[99] and the application for annulment is not manifestly inadmissible, the SFT will forward a copy thereof to the respondent and the arbitral tribunal, inviting them to file an answer, respectively, observations, within 30 days.[100] The respondent's answer

[96] In the SFT's own words, "l'annulation d'une sentence arbitrale international pour ce motif de recours est chose rarissime" and "il doit […] être clair dans l'esprit de quiconque conclut une convention d'arbitrage donnant lieu à l'application [of Chapter 12 PILA], que ses chances de succès seront extrêmement minces le jour où il voudra attaquer une sentence arbitrale en invoquant le motif de recours prévu à l'Article [190(2)(e) PILA]" (see ATF 136 III 389, 391–392).

[97] For detailed descriptions of the manner in which annulment proceedings are conducted before and handled within the SFT, see, e.g., Arroyo 2013b, paras 50–54; Kaufmann-Kohler and Rigozzi 2015, paras 8.76–8.129.

[98] Requests for the holding of a public hearing will be denied in most cases. For a sports-related example, see SFT 4A_612/2009, decision of 10 February 2010, para 4.2, being one of the SFT rulings issued in the *Claudia Pechstein* case.

[99] For an examination of the SFT's practice with respect to the costs of the proceedings before it, see Kaufmann-Kohler and Rigozzi 2015, paras 8.100–8.108, with further references.

[100] Contrary to the time limit for filing the application, the one for the respondent's answer and tribunal's observations can be extended upon a reasoned request. However, where no such request is made and the submission is untimely, it will be deemed inadmissible and disregarded by the SFT. For an example in a sports case in the period under review, see SFT 4A_374/2014, decision of 26 February 2015, para 3, where the Court found that the respondent's answer was filed one day late, which in turn meant that the applicant's reply and the respondent's rejoinder (to the extent they were responsive to points contained in the answer) were not taken into consideration and the parties' costs were assessed accordingly.

and the tribunal's observations, if any,[101] will be forwarded to the applicant, who will be granted a short time limit to file an optional reply. If the applicant does file a reply, the respondent will be entitled to file a rejoinder (and the tribunal additional observations).

17.2.2.6 Consequences of the SFT's Decision[102]

a. *Successful application*

   If the SFT upholds the application for annulment, given the cassatory nature of the proceedings under Article 77 SCA, its decision will generally contain a declaration that the award is annulled and the case remanded to the arbitral tribunal for it to render a new award. The tribunal can only reconsider the portions of its original award which are affected by the annulment decision, and, while the SFT does not give instructions to the arbitrators, in re-deciding the relevant matters the tribunal will be bound by the reasons set out in the Court's decision.[103]

   The SFT can also only partially annul an award, to the extent that the relevant part(s) are autonomous and severable from the rest. Indeed, in the only case where the application for annulment was successful in the cases under review in this digest, the SFT issued a partial annulment decision.[104]

   The rule that the SFT will only (fully or partially) 'annul and remand' an award if the application is successful is subject to two exceptions: (i) if the SFT concludes that the tribunal wrongly upheld or denied its jurisdiction (i.e., where the SFT upholds an application based on Article 190(2)(b) PILA), the operative

[101]It is relatively rare for arbitral tribunals to submit observations in annulment proceedings in commercial arbitration cases. Conversely, the CAS (more precisely, the CAS Secretary General on behalf of the panel that rendered the award) systematically submits observations before the SFT. Indeed, the SFT's decisions in the period under review note that the CAS has submitted observations in 8 of the 9 cases where the application was considered on the merits (in the 8 other cases where the application was declared inadmissible or withdrawn, there was no possibility to file observations in any event). In the proceedings against the award issued in the only non-CAS (ad hoc) arbitration that concerned a sports dispute in that same period, the arbitral tribunal also filed observations before the SFT (SFT 4A_609/2014, decision of 20 February 2015, para B.).

[102]Generally on this question see Arroyo 2013b, paras 55–59; Berger and Kellerhals 2015, paras 1824–1832; Kaufmann-Kohler and Rigozzi 2015, paras 8.119–8.125.

[103]See, e.g., Kaufmann-Kohler and Rigozzi 2015, para 8.123 and references, Arroyo 2013b, para 57.

[104]SFT 4A_246/2014, decision of 15 July 2015, para 8 (summarized in Sect. 17.3.4.2 below). Here the Court noted that the principles developed in its case law with regard to the partial annulment of awards could be applied by analogy in the situation at hand, where each of the three applicants had originally brought a separate claim against the respondent (before the DRC), and the cases had been joined upon appeal before the CAS. Accordingly, the SFT annulled the award only to the extent it related to the claims of three of the nine applicants, and confirmed the remainder of the panel's decisions (see paras 1. and 2. in the dispositive part of the SFT decision).

part of its decision will include a declaration to that effect;[105] (ii) where the application was brought on the basis that an arbitrator or the tribunal lacked independence and/or impartiality (Article 190(2)(a) SCA), the SFT can also directly order the removal of the disqualified arbitrator(s).[106]
Again, the parties' prayers for relief should be drafted in keeping with the above mentioned principles and practices.

b. *Unsuccessful application*
If the SFT rejects the application for annulment, the award is confirmed, it continues to be binding and deploy *res judicata* effect, and it definitively becomes final (pursuant to Article 190(1) PILA) and enforceable.[107]
In closing this section on the legal framework and practical aspects of annulment proceedings, it bears to note that applications for annulment against arbitral awards are rarely successful before the SFT.[108] Accordingly, applicants will be well advised to carefully consider the contents of the award in the light of both (1) the (very limited) available grounds for annulment, and (2) the likely costs of the proceedings.[109]
This statement, as well as the foregoing analysis, will now be illustrated by reference to the actual decisions rendered by the STF in the past year. In the following section, we summarize (under the heading of the annulment ground(s) invoked in the applications) the decisions handed down by the SFT in sports arbitration matters between 1 January and 31 December 2015. As mentioned, only one of the 18 applications for annulment brought during that period was successful and resulted in the partial annulment of the award (on the ground of a violation of the applicants' right to be heard; SFT 4A_246/2014, decision of 15 July 2015, see Sect. 17.3.4.2 below).

17.3 Summaries of the SFT's Decisions Rendered Between 1 January and 31 December 2015

In the period under review, the SFT rendered 18 decisions in total with respect to sports matters. We have summarized below the decisions that contain actual holdings on the merits of the annulment action, as opposed to those that are limited to

[105]Where applicable (i.e., if the award is annulled because the arbitrators incorrectly found they had jurisdiction over the dispute), the SFT may still remand the case to the tribunal for it to issue a final decision on the costs of the arbitration.

[106]See, e.g., SFT 4A_126/2015, decision of 14 April 2015, para 4, summarized in Sect. 17.3.1.1 below.

[107]Arroyo 2013b, para 58; Berger and Kellerhals 2015, para 1824.

[108]See, e.g., Dasser and Roth 2014, p. 466, concluding that approx. 7 % of the applications filed between 1989 and 2013 had succeeded in securing the annulment of the award, noting also that, however, challenges against sports awards tend to be more successful than those concerning commercial arbitration awards, with a success rate of approx. 10 % in the same period of time.

[109]For a detailed discussion of the costs of the proceedings in annulment actions under Article 77 SCA, see Kaufmann-Kohler and Rigozzi 2015, paras 8.100–8.108.

dispositive procedural determinations, namely where the application was found to be inadmissible,[110] or orders recording the withdrawal of the application.[111]

17.3.1 Article 190(2)(a) PILA—Irregular Constitution of the Arbitral Tribunal

17.3.1.1 SFT 4A_126/2015, Decision of 14 April 2015

Underlying facts, proceedings and decision(s)
This case concerned a former Olympic athlete who challenged both the IOC decision denying her request to have her samples re-tested at an independent laboratory in a third country (instead of the University Hospital of Lausanne (CHUV) in Switzerland), and the independence of the CAS arbitrators appointed to hear her case. The athlete first brought her challenge against the CAS panel before the ICAS, requesting it to replace that panel with a new one, composed exclusively of arbitrators who were not drawn from the CAS list. Later on, she seized the President of the Court of first instance in Lausanne ("Tribunal civil de l'arrondissement de Lausanne") of a request based on Article 179(2) PILA, which enables the court at the seat of the arbitration to act as "juge d'appui", i.e., in support of the arbitral process, inter alia by appointing arbitrators upon request by the parties. Meanwhile, the CAS Court Office had informed the athlete that the ICAS considered her challenge against the panel to have been withdrawn,[112] and, on 10 November 2014, the panel issued the dispositive part of its award (without reasons), in which it ruled that it did not have jurisdiction to hear the athlete's appeal against the IOC decision. On 21 January 2015, the President of the Court of first instance dismissed the athlete's application for the appointment of a panel of arbitrators, mainly on the ground that the appointment, removal and replacement of arbitrators in CAS proceedings are governed exclusively by the CAS Code.

Annulment action and SFT decision
The athlete sought the annulment of the decision issued by the President of the Court of first instance, asking the SFT to remand the case to the lower court, or, alternatively, to rule on her request for the appointment of a new panel directly. The SFT held that the athlete's application was inadmissible pursuant to Article 76(1)(b) SCA, considering that the athlete no longer had an "interest worthy of protection" in the annulment she was seeking, as the CAS panel, in the composition she was

[110]SFT 4A_504/2014, decision of 5 January 2015; SFT 4A_36/2015, decision of 26 January 2015; SFT 4A_609/2014, decision of 20 February 2015; SFT 4A_174/2015, decision of 30 June 2015; SFT 4A_596/2015, decision of 9 December 2015. These cases have been referenced where relevant in the discussion under Sect. 17.2.2 above.

[111]SFT 4A_98/2014, Order of 10 August 2015; SFT 4A_690, Order of 19 May 2015.

[112]The athlete had also unsuccessfully challenged this decision before the SFT (SFT 4A_586/2014, decision of 25 November 2014).

challenging, had already rendered a final and binding award.[113] The SFT added that, once the reasons for the CAS award would be notified to the parties, the athlete could still seek its annulment on the basis of Article 190(2)(a) PILA. At that juncture, if her application was successful, the SFT could annul the award; disqualify the original panel and remand the case to the CAS instructing it to appoint a new panel composed only of arbitrators from outside the CAS list. However, for the purposes of the action then before the SFT, this scenario also confirmed the fact that the athlete no longer had an actual interest in seeking the annulment of the decision issued by the President of the Court of first instance (para 4.2).

17.3.2 Article 190(2)(b) PILA—Incorrect Decision on Jurisdiction[114]

17.3.2.1 SFT 4A_176/2015, Decision of 9 November 2015

Underlying facts, proceedings and decision(s)
This decision concerned a dispute between a football agent and an Ecuadorian club. The club had engaged the agent for representation and counseling services for a sum of $ 140,000, payable in twelve installments over the course of one year. As the club had paid only the first two installments, the agent brought a claim for the outstanding amount before the FIFA PSC. The PSC declared the agent's request inadmissible, finding that he had failed to establish that the activities carried out under the relevant agreement came within the ambit of the 2008 FIFA Regulation Governing the Activities of Agents. The PSC decision expressly indicated that it was subject to appeal before the CAS in accordance with Article 67(1) FIFA Statutes. The agent appealed and the sole arbitrator appointed by the CAS to hear the case upheld his jurisdiction (rejecting the club's argument that the agent's activities in this instance were governed by Ecuadorian law and subject to the exclusive jurisdiction of Ecuadorian courts), and decided in favor of the agent, ordering the club to pay the ten outstanding installments ($ 116,000, plus interest).

Annulment action and SFT decision
The club sought the annulment of the CAS award on the ground that the sole arbitrator had erred in upholding his jurisdiction. The SFT denied the application,

[113]See Sect. 17.2.2.1.c above .

[114]This ground was also (unsuccessfully) relied upon by the applicants in SFT 4A_634/2014, decision of 21 May 2015 (summarized in Sect. 17.3.5.3 below) (para 3), and SFT 4A_374/2014, decision of 26 February 2015 (summarized in Sect. 17.3.5.4 below) (para 5). In case SFT 4A_634/2014, decision of 21 May 2015, the SFT found that the applicant had failed to raise a jurisdictional objection in the arbitration and was thus precluded from doing so at the annulment stage (*Einlassung*). In case SFT 4A_374/2014, decision of 26 February 2015, the applicant had raised the panel's lack of jurisdiction as a subsidiary argument to its complaint of a breach of procedural public policy. Since, as discussed in Sect. 17.3.5.4 below, the public policy ground was upheld, the SFT did not rule on the subsidiary argument.

noting that Articles 66–68 FIFA Statutes provide for the jurisdiction of the CAS to hear appeals against decisions of FIFA's judicial bodies, and that the PSC is such a body. Accordingly, pursuant to Article R47 CAS Code, the CAS had jurisdiction to hear the appeal against the FIFA PSC decision dismissing the agent's claim (as deciding whether the agent's claim was governed by the relevant FIFA Regulations was a matter pertaining to the merits, not jurisdiction). The SFT's decision also confirmed that in CAS appeals proceedings the panel may, pursuant to Article R57 of the Code, issue a new decision replacing the one under challenge instead of remanding the case to the lower instance (para 3.2).

17.3.3 Article 190(2)(c) PILA—Award Ultra, Extra or Infra Petita[115]

17.3.3.1 SFT 4A_684/2014, Decision of 2 July 2015

Underlying facts, proceedings and decision(s)
This decision related to a dispute between an Egyptian football club and a player of British and Ghanaian nationalities. The employment contracts between the parties provided that (i) the player's wages, to be paid in EUR, were tied to the number of games he played over the season, and (ii) the benefits in nature to which he was entitled included compensation for his accommodation costs. The club sanctioned the player on multiple occasions for unjustified absences and misconduct, deducting various amounts from his salaries. Ultimately, the player rescinded the agreements. Thereafter, the club sought damages for breach of contract before the FIFA DRC, while the player requested payment of his outstanding salaries and damages by way of a counterclaim. The FIFA DRC dismissed the club's claim and partially upheld the player's counterclaim. The club appealed before the CAS, where the panel reduced the amount awarded to the player, but (i) set it both in EUR and USD, and (ii) ruled that it included benefits in nature as damages for breach of contract.

Annulment action and SFT decision
The club sought the annulment of the award inter alia on the ground that it was *ultra petita*,[116] arguing in particular that because the player had not appealed the FIFA DRC decision, the CAS panel's award could not rule on the player's claim for benefits in nature, which had been dismissed by the FIFA DRC. The SFT recalled that according to its case law, tribunals are only bound by the total amount claimed in the parties' prayers for relief, but can freely assess and quantify the

[115]In addition to the decision summarized in this section, as mentioned in footnote 121 below, this ground was also (unsuccessfully) relied upon by the applicant in SFT 4A_246/2014, decision of 15 July 2015, para 5.3.

[116]As mentioned in footnote 120 below, the club also invoked Article 190(2)(d) PILA.

individual components of the parties' claims within that amount (para 3.2.1). Thus, the fact that the player did not appeal the FIFA DRC decision was irrelevant for the purposes of Article 190(2)(c) PILA, since the amount awarded by the CAS was less than that claimed in the player's prayers for relief. The SFT also noted in passing that the CAS panel had awarded part of the compensation in a different currency (USD) from that used in the prayers for relief (EUR), but the club had not raised that point as a possible violation of Article 190(2)(c) PILA (para 3.2.2).[117] Accordingly, the application for annulment was denied.

17.3.4 Article 190(2)(d) PILA—Violation of the Parties' Right to Be Heard and Equal Treatment[118]

17.3.4.1 SFT 4A_568/2015, Decision of 10 December 2015

Underlying facts, proceedings and decision(s)

This case related to a dispute between A., an Argentinian football player, and B. and C., two professional agents. The player and the agents had concluded a representation agreement for a fixed period, whereby B. and C. undertook to exclusively represent A., who in turn agreed to pay a EUR 1 million contractual penalty should he decide to unilaterally terminate the agreement. A few months later, A. rescinded the agreement and shortly thereafter he signed a contract with a new club. In response, B. and C. initiated CAS arbitration proceedings claiming € 3 million as a contractual penalty. The CAS panel partially granted B. and C.'s claims, ordering A. to pay them € 1 million.

[117]Commentators have noted that the SFT's obiter statement in this regard may imply that an award in a currency other than that requested may violate Article 190(2)(c) PILA (Voser N and Bell K (2015) Swiss Supreme Court finds CAS award not in breach of *ultra petita* principle. http://www.swlegal.ch/getdoc/a42495ce-4730-450e-a1e5-6dd46ac6fe44/2015_Nathalie-Voser_Katherine-Bell_Swiss-Supreme-C.aspx. Accessed 10 February 2016). In connection with this particular question, see also SFT 4A_654/2011, decision of 23 May 2012, para 5.2, where the Court held that by refusing to convert the amount claimed (and awarded) in a particular currency (as requested by the claimant), the CAS had not breached Article 190(2)(c) because it had concluded—on the basis of its own legal assessment of the relevant contract—that the amount was due in the currency used in the award.

[118]In addition to the decisions summarized below, this ground was also invoked in SFT 4A_634, decision of 21 May 2015 (already mentioned in footnote 89 above), where the applicant argued that the panel had made a "surprising" application of the law by relying exclusively on Swiss law rather than applying the FIFA Regulations. Unsurprisingly, the SFT made short shrift of this argument by reference to the principle of jura novit curia and the fact that the applicant had had ample opportunity to address the applicable law and could not possibly fail to anticipate that Swiss law would apply (para 4 of the decision).

Annulment action and SFT decision

A. sought the annulment of the award on the basis of Articles 190(2)(d) and 190(2)(e) PILA.[119] With regard to the first ground invoked, A. argued, in essence, that the panel had breached his right to be heard by failing to take a number of his evidentiary requests into account in the course of the proceedings, but also by ignoring his explanations to the effect that several allegations made by B. and C. were wrong, and by disregarding the arguments he had developed with regard to his own reasons for terminating the agreement. The SFT underscored that in line with its longstanding case law, the parties' right to be heard does not encompass the right to a substantively correct decision. Accordingly, it is not for the SFT, in annulment proceedings under Article 190(2) PILA, to verify whether the arbitrators have duly considered and correctly understood all the elements in the record.[120] To the extent A. failed to show that the panel had prevented him from presenting and arguing his case, his complaint under Article 190(2)(d) PILA could not be upheld (para 3.2).

17.3.4.2 SFT 4A_246/2014, Decision of 15 July 2015

Underlying facts, proceedings and decision(s)

This decision dealt with a dispute between a football club and nine of its players. The players' employment contracts contained a provision whereby payment of their monthly salaries would be conditional upon their playing in at least 70 % of the matches for the relevant month. In April 2013, the nine players seized the dispute resolution chamber of their federation to obtain an order for payment of outstanding salaries and a declaration that they had validly terminated their contracts with the club for cause.

The chamber granted the players' requests, and the club appealed these decisions before the federation's appeal commission (AC), which found that the appeals against the decisions relating to players 1–7 were inadmissible, reduced the amount awarded to player 8, and upheld the decision concerning player 9. The club appealed the AC's decisions before the CAS, where the cases where consolidated in a single arbitration. After its statement of appeal, the club also submitted two agreements it had concluded with players 6 and 9, whereby the latter waived their claims and withdrew from the proceedings. On 7 March 2014, the sole arbitrator appointed by the CAS to hear the case issued an award declaring that the proceedings had been terminated with respect to players 6 and 9, and dismissing the club's appeal against the decisions regarding the other players.

---

[119]A.'s complaint under Article 190(2)(e) PILA (breach of public policy) is summarized under Sect. 17.3.5.1 below.

[120]The same principle was recalled in SFT 4A_684/2014, decision of 2 July 2015 (summarized in Sect. 17.3.3.1 above), para 4, where the SFT—having nonetheless gone on to thoroughly review the award—also rejected the applicant's complaint that the panel had disregarded or failed to deal properly with several arguments before it.

Annulment action and SFT decision

The club sought the annulment of the CAS award by relying on several grounds, namely violations of the *ne infra petita* rule (Article 190(2)(c) PILA), of its right to be heard (Article 190(2)(d) PILA) and of procedural public policy (Article 190(2)(e) PILA). The SFT denied the petitioner's complaints grounded on *infra petita*[121] and procedural public policy,[122] but partially upheld its challenge under Article 190(2)(d) PILA. Indeed, the SFT found that the sole arbitrator had failed to address in the award certain arguments the club had properly raised and substantiated with respect to the monies due to players 1, 2, and 3. Although some of the arguments at issue were mentioned in the award (in the section summarizing the parties' submissions), the sole arbitrator's decision did not take them into account. Other arguments raised by the applicant with respect to players' 2 and 3's claims had not been mentioned, let alone addressed in the arbitrator's decision, even though they would impact the amounts awarded by him (para 6.3). Recalling and applying by analogy its case law to the effect that the cassatory nature of the annulment action does not exclude that awards may be vacated only partially (when the portions that are challenged are autonomous from the rest), the SFT annulled some of the rulings in the award's dispositive part to the extent they related to players 1, 2 and 3, but confirmed the rest (para 8).

17.3.4.3 SFT 4A_124/2015, Decision of 17 June 2015

Underlying facts, proceedings and decision(s)

This decision related to a transfer dispute between football clubs A. and B., and football player C. Club A. was found by the CAS to be jointly liable with C., pursuant to Article 17 FIFA RSTP, for damages for breach of contract which the player had previously been ordered to pay to club B. by the FIFA DRC.

Annulment action and SFT decision

Club A. sought the annulment of the award, contending that an argument it had raised in its answer to B.'s appeal brief before the CAS had been completely disregarded by the panel, in breach of its right to be heard. According to A., the argument at issue had been set out in two paragraphs in its answer brief, and it went to the question whether the player's registration with the new club was the necessary trigger for holding the latter jointly liable for the player's debt towards the previous club. In a relatively short and blunt decision, the SFT found that the passages A. had referred to in its appeal brief came nowhere close to the proper presentation of a legal argument (they were simply complaints about the player's disloyal

[121] With respect to this ground, the SFT considered that the award had in fact dealt with the allegedly omitted request, as understood by the sole arbitrator (para 5.3).

[122] For a summary of the SFT's decision in relation to this ground, see in Sect. 17.3.5.2 below.

behavior), and thus the panel could not be held to have violated A.'s right to be heard by failing to address them as such (para 4.1). The SFT also noted in passing that while there was no need to consider the merits of A.'s reasoning regarding registration as a condition for the new club's liability, the responsive arguments put forward by the new club were not devoid of interest on this question (which was nonetheless left undecided; para 4.1.2).

17.3.4.4 SFT 4A_426/2014, Decision of 6 May 2015

Underlying facts, proceedings and decision(s)

This decision revolved around a transfer dispute between football clubs A. and B. with regard to player Z. An agreement concluded between A. and B. provided that B. would pay to A. 20 % of any fee it would receive in excess of $ 35 million for the transfer of Z. to a third club. Subsequently, club B. and Z. terminated their employment relationship by mutual consent. Only two days later, Z. entered—as a free agent—into a new employment contract with a third club. Club A. filed a claim against B. before the FIFA PSC, arguing that the termination of the contract between B. and Z. was orchestrated so as to avoid the payment of the transfer fee percentage that would be due to A. as a result of the conclusion of the new contract with the third club. Both the FIFA PSC and the CAS dismissed A.'s claim.

Annulment action and SFT decision

A. sought the annulment of the CAS award on the ground that the panel had violated its right to be heard.[123] Specifically, the club contended that the panel had failed to address an alternative legal argument in its appeal brief. The SFT examined the appeal brief and found that the argument in question was in reality presented as part of the reasoning underpinning A.'s calculation of the amount B. was liable for (in its view), which was set out in the brief's sub-section on quantum, after the sub-section devoted to A.'s legal arguments. Thus, the argument could hardly be understood as a separate legal basis for A.'s claim, and the panel could not be criticized for failing to identify it as such (para 3.2). A. also argued that the CAS had failed to fully review the facts and the law although it was required to do so under Article R57(1) CAS Code.[124] According to A., the panel could not possibly have reached the conclusion that the termination of the employment contract between B. and Z., although unusual, was a 'business decision', for which it was not required to find an explanation, had it accepted to hear the testimony of A.'s

[123]As mentioned in footnote 124 below, the applicant also (unsuccessfully) relied on Article 190(2)(e) PILA, complaining of a violation of substantive public policy.

[124]A. raised this complaint in reliance on both Article 190(2)(d) PILA (right to be heard) and 190(2)(e) PILA (procedural public policy). The SFT noted (para 4.2.1) that procedural public policy is but a subsidiary guarantee, which applies only when other protections are not available. In this case, the complaint fell squarely under the notion of 'formal denial of justice' as developed in the Court's case law under Article 190(2)(d) PILA, and thus it was examined by reference to that provision.

witnesses as to the actual reasons for that termination. In the SFT's opinion, it was apparent from the award that the panel had conducted a full and thorough review of the facts and the law, and the conclusions it reached were based on its legal assessment of the results of that review. Moreover, the SFT noted that A. had not objected after its request for the hearing of the relevant witnesses had been rejected by the panel. Hence, A. had definitively waived its right to complain about the panel's failure to hear those witnesses (para 4).

17.3.4.5 SFT 4A_70/2015, Decision of 29 April 2015

Underlying facts, proceedings and decision(s)

This decision related to a dispute between a football club and one of its players, whose contract was terminated by the club in 2011. The player successfully seized the DRC of various claims including damages for termination without cause. In December 2013, the club, represented by counsel from the Brussels bar, filed an appeal with the CAS. The panel that was appointed to hear the case informed the parties that it had decided to hold a hearing. From then onwards, in spite of several reminders, the club's Belgian counsel no longer replied to the CAS's correspondence. On the day of the hearing, in May 2014, a new (Swiss) counsel appeared before the CAS, purporting to represent the club at the behest of his Belgian colleague. However, the new counsel had no power of attorney and was unable to provide written confirmation of his mandate to represent the club in accordance with Article R30 CAS Code. He was thus not allowed to act as the appellant's representative at the hearing. The hearing was held nonetheless, and the player and his agents were heard by the panel. The day after the hearing, the CAS sent its audio recording to the parties' counsel of record and set a time limit for the club to file any comments it may have. Given that the appellant's counsel had again failed to respond, in June 2014 the CAS wrote directly to the club. In July 2014, yet another counsel wrote to the CAS indicating that he was now representing the club, stating that the latter had been unaware of the hearing held in May until it had received the CAS's direct communication in June, and asking for a new hearing to be held so as to enable the appellant's witnesses to be heard along those of the respondent. The panel rejected the appellant's request for a new hearing, but invited it to file a written submission setting out its arguments and evidence, to which the player was then invited to respond. In December 2014, the CAS issued its award, rejecting the club's appeal and upholding the DRC's decision.

Annulment action and SFT decision

The club sought the annulment of the award inter alia on the ground that its right to be heard in adversarial proceedings had been violated.[125] The SFT recalled the well-established principle that if a party considers its due process rights to have

[125] As mentioned in footnote 126 below, the applicant also (unsuccessfully) relied on Article 190(2)(e) PILA, complaining of a violation of substantive public policy.

been violated, it must raise the objection immediately, in the course of the arbitral proceedings, and clearly maintain the objection if the tribunal does not deal with it in a satisfactory way. Failing that, the aggrieved party is precluded from relying upon the objection before the SFT as a ground for the annulment of the award. In this case, the club's new counsel had not challenged the CAS's decision not to hold a new hearing, and had thus waived the corresponding objection (para 3.2). In addition, the SFT held, by analogy with a principle of Swiss procedural law, that even if the responsibility for the club's failure to participate in the hearing lay with its original counsel, it was for the club to assume the consequences of its counsel's conduct. Hence, given that the appellant's counsel of record had been duly notified of the panel's decision to hold the hearing, the CAS had no duty to hold a second hearing as a result that counsel's failure to attend the original hearing. Be that as it may, the SFT concluded that the appellant's right to be heard had not been violated because it was afforded an opportunity to file a written submission on the matters it would have raised at the hearing (para 3.2.2).

17.3.4.6 SFT 4A_544/2014, Decision of 24 February 2015

Underlying facts, proceedings and decision(s)
This case concerned a disciplinary dispute between FIFA and a player in the Croatian national team. Following a World Cup qualifier between Croatia and Iceland, the player had seized a microphone and shouted political slogans that had been in use at the time of the Croatian fascist movement during World War II. As a sanction, the FIFA DC banned the player for 10 matches and fined him CHF 30,000. The player appealed FIFA's decision before the CAS and then the SFT, arguing that his right to be heard had been breached by the CAS panel when its president had decided to curtail his cross examination of FIFA's expert at the hearing.

Annulment action and SFT decision
The SFT recalled once more that any objections as to the conduct of the arbitral proceedings must be raised immediately, in the course of the arbitration, failing which the aggrieved party will be precluded from relying on them at the annulment stage. In this instance, the player's submissions and the record of the arbitration did not establish that he had objected to the president's decision to cut short his examination of the expert—on the contrary, the applicant's counsel had confirmed, at the end of the hearing, that he was satisfied with the way it had been conducted (para 3.3). The SFT's decision further suggests that in order to demonstrate an actual breach of its right to be heard in relation to the questioning of an expert, the aggrieved party should explain which questions it was prevented from asking and how such questions were relevant to the resolution of the dispute. Be that as it may, in line with its well-established case law on the so-called 'anticipated assessment' of the evidence, the SFT reiterated that the parties' right to be heard does not include an absolute right to question adverse expert witnesses. As

with other forms of evidence, the tribunal can limit or exclude questions which it deems irrelevant or which have already been asked or aim at establishing facts which have already been proven (para 3.4). Accordingly, the application was dismissed.

17.3.5 Article 190(2)(e) PILA—Award Contravening Public Policy[126]

17.3.5.1 SFT 4A_568/2015, Decision of 10 December 2015

Underlying facts, proceedings and decision(s)
The facts in this case have been summarized in Sect. 17.3.4.1 above.

Annulment action and SFT decision
In this decision, also discussed above (Sect. 17.3.4.1), A. argued that the panel's award was incompatible with public policy because it misapplied several provisions of Swiss law. More specifically, according to A., the panel's reasoning and its application of provisions such as Articles 404 CO,[127] 158 et seq. CO[128] and 27 of the Swiss Federal Constitution[129] was wrong, contrary to the principle of legality and simply untenable. The SFT recalled that the understanding and application of the law by the arbitrators is not subject to review in annulment proceedings pursuant to Articles 190–191 PILA. With regard to Article 27 Swiss Federal Constitution, the SFT noted that A. had failed to show how the (reduced) contractual penalty awarded by the arbitrators gave rise to a manifest and excessive impairment of his right to economic freedom such as to violate public policy (para 4). The application for annulment was thus dismissed.

[126]In addition to the decisions summarized below, this ground was also invoked in SFT 4A_426/2014, decision of 6 May 2015 (summarized in Sect. 17.3.4.4 above), para 5, where the SFT dismissed the applicant's argument that the panel had violated the principles of *pacta sunt servanda* and good faith, holding that the complaint was merely a disguised attempt to criticize the panel's application of the law, which is inadmissible in annulment proceedings governed by Article 77 SCA. In similar terms, see also SFT 4A_70, decision of 29 April 2015 (summarized in Sect. 17.3.4.5 above), para 4.

[127]Article 404 CO provides that a mandate or agency agreement can be terminated at any time by either party, but that if the termination occurs at an inopportune time, the terminating party is liable for damages towards the other party.

[128]Arts 158 et seq. CO cover contractual penalties and their reduction by the court or tribunal.

[129]Article 27 SFC guarantees the economic freedom of individuals, including the right to choose one's occupation and to pursue private economic activities.

17.3.5.2 SFT 4A_246/2014, Decision of 15 July 2015

Underlying facts, proceedings and decision(s)
The facts in this case have been summarized in Sect. 17.3.4.2 above.

Annulment action and SFT decision
In this decision the SFT considered the applicant's argument that the parties' right of access to an arbitrator endowed with full power of review forms part of procedural public policy, as encapsulated in the core principles of Article 6(1) ECHR. The Court noted that public policy within the meaning of Article 190(2)(e) PILA does not encompass an absolute obligation for arbitral tribunals to address all the disputes submitted to them with full power of review. In particular, as long as they have validly opted for arbitration and the proceedings comply with Article 182(3) PILA's due process requirements, the parties may, directly or indirectly (by submitting to a set of arbitration rules so providing), agree on the possibility for the tribunal to circumscribe the ambit of its review, as exemplified by Article R57(3) CAS Code, on which the sole arbitrator had relied *in casu* to exclude the evidence (belatedly) tendered by the club (para 7.2.2). The argument relying on this ground was therefore rejected by the SFT (however, as seen in Sect. 17.3.4.2 above, the award was partially annulled for breach of the applicant's right to be heard).

17.3.5.3 SFT 4A_634/2014, Decision of 21 May 2015

Underlying facts, proceedings and decision(s)
This case concerned a dispute arising from two contracts concluded between an Italian football club and an English company to regulate the sale of financial rights deriving from the registration of an argentine player (Paulo Dybala). One of the contracts, which was governed by Swiss law and included a CAS arbitration clause, stipulated that the club was to pay € 6.72 million in two installments. The contract also contained a penalty clause, providing that if the club failed to make one of the agreed payments, all outstanding amounts would be doubled and become due immediately. Given that the club failed to make any of the agreed payments, the company brought its claim before the CAS. By an award dated 26 August 2014, the CAS panel ordered the club to pay € 9,400,000 together with interest. Out of this amount, € 1,680,000 was awarded in application of the contractual penalty, which the panel had reduced to ¼ of the outstanding debt pursuant to Article 163(3) CO.[130]

[130] Article 163(3) CO provides that the court must reduce a contractually agreed penalty if it finds it to be excessive. It is a mandatory provision in the sense that the court must apply it even if the party owing the penalty has not expressly sought a reduction.

Annulment action and SFT decision

The club sought the annulment of the award in reliance on the grounds covered in PILA Articles 190(2)(b) (lack of jurisdiction),[131] 190(2)(d) (violation of the right to be heard),[132] and 190(2)(e) (award contravening public policy). In particular, the club argued that the award violated substantive public policy because the arbitrators had failed to adequately apply Article 163(3) CO, a mandatory provision of Swiss law. The club further contended that the penalty set by the CAS gave rise to an award of compound interest, which is prohibited under Article 105(3) CO. The SFT recalled its jurisprudence whereby mandatory rules such as Article 163(3) CO pertain to *domestic* public policy but are not covered by the annulment ground encapsulated in Article 190(2)(e) PILA, which is only meant to address violations of *international* public policy. Under the latter provision, the scope of review of the SFT with regard to an award enforcing a contractual penalty is limited to the question whether the penalty is excessive to the point of being spoliatory. Such was not the case in this instance, where the CAS panel had significantly reduced the amount awarded on foot of the penalty clause. Moreover, notwithstanding its finding that the club was mistaken in arguing that the panel had awarded compound interest, the SFT also clarified that an order for payment of compound interest is not contrary to public policy within the meaning of Article 190(2)(e) PILA (para 5.2.2).

17.3.5.4 SFT 4A_374/2014, Decision of 26 February 2015

Underlying facts, proceedings and decision(s)

This case concerned a dispute between a Mexican football club and two of its coaches. The coaches' employment contracts contained an arbitration clause providing that disputes should be submitted to specialized labor courts and to the Mexican Football Federation (MFF). In 2009, the coaches brought a monetary claim against the club before the MFF's Conciliation and Dispute Resolution Commission (CDRC). As the club had filed a parallel criminal action in relation to the same dispute, the CDRC issued an order staying the proceedings. Shortly thereafter, the coaches brought their claim before the FIFA PSC. In October 2011, the CDRC, without summoning and hearing the coaches, issued a decision declaring the (hitherto stayed) proceedings before it were terminated. After the FIFA PSC rejected their claims in 2012, the coaches lodged an appeal before the CAS, which overturned the PSC decision and partially upheld the coaches' claims.

Annulment action and SFT decision

The club sought the annulment of the CAS award, arguing that it had been rendered in violation of procedural public policy due to the panel's failure to acknowledge the *res judicata* effect of the CDRC's decision issued in October 2011. To decide on this question, the SFT first had to determine whether the

---

[131] See footnote 114 above.

[132] See footnote 118 above.

CDRC decision was an arbitral award capable of recognition in Switzerland under the NYC. It concluded that such was the case on account of the specific characteristics of the CDRC, which offered sufficient guarantees of impartiality and independence to be considered equivalent to a court (para 4.3.2.1). The SFT also acknowledged that, under Mexican law, the termination of the proceedings in this particular case amounted to a waiver of the coaches' claims, which waiver was vested with *res judicata* effect (para 4.3.2.2). The next question then was whether the FIFA PSC and the CAS had effectively violated procedural public policy by failing to recognize the CDRC decision. The SFT came to the conclusion that there was no such violation as the CDRC decision had been rendered in flagrant breach of the coaches' right to be heard (para 4.3.2.2), and was thus not entitled to recognition under Article V(2)(b) NYC (para 4.4).[133] Accordingly, the FIFA PSC and the CAS had not violated procedural public policy by ruling on the merits of the coaches' claims. The application for annulment was thus dismissed.

***

The table below summarizes the information provided in Sect. 17.2 and provides references to the publications where the decisions just discussed are reproduced and/or commented.[134]

Date	Case no.	Parties	Language	Sources[a] (including commentaries and translations)	Grounds relied upon in annulment action	Outcome
10 December 2015	4A_568/2015	*A. v. B and C.*	D	http://www.swlegal.ch/Publications/Arbitration-Case-Digest.aspx (22 February 2016) www.swissarbitration-decisions.com ASA Bulletin 2016 pp. 178–184	Article 190(2) (d) PILA Article 190(2) (e) PILA	Dismissed
9 December 2015	4A_596/2015	*A. v. B.*	D	http://www.swlegal.ch/Publications/Arbitration-Case-Digest.aspx (26 January 2016)	–	Inadmissible
9 November 2015	4A_176/2015	*Club A. v. B.*	F	http://www.swlegal.ch/Publications/Arbitration-Case-Digest.aspx (3 December 2015)	Article 190(2) (b) PILA	Dismissed
10 August 2015	4A_98/2015	*Club A. v Club B.*	D	–	–	Application withdrawn

(Continued)

[133]Article V(2)(b) NYC provides that "[r]ecognition and enforcement of an arbitral award may be […] refused if the competent authority in the country where recognition and enforcement is sought finds that: […] (b) [t]he recognition or enforcement of the award would be contrary to the public policy of that country".

[134]The data in the table was up-to-date as of 1st March 2016.

Date	Case no.	Parties	Language	Sources[a] (including commentaries and translations)	Grounds relied upon in annulment action	Outcome
15 July 2015	4A_246/2014	*A. SA v. B., C., D., E., F., G., H., I., J., and Federation L*	F	http://www.swlegal.ch/Publications/Arbitration-Case-Digest.aspx (4 August 2015) http://www.internationallawoffice.com (Arbitration & ADR/Switzerland; 3 December 2015) www.swissarbitration-decisions.com ASA Bulletin 34: 190–201 Beffa 2015, pp. 215–216; 247–249; 278–281; 283; 295–296	Article 190(2)(c) PILA Article 190(2)(d) PILA Article 190(2)(e) PILA	Partially upheld (violation of Article 190(2)(d) PILA)
2 July 2015	4A_684/2014	*Club A. v. B.*	D	http://www.swlegal.ch/Publications/Arbitration-Case-Digest.aspx (1 September 2015) ASA Bulletin 33:565–575 Beffa 2015, pp. 213–215	Article 190(2)(c) PILA Article 190(2)(d) PILA	Dismissed
30 June 2015	4A_174/2015	*Association A. v. Association B.*	D	Beffa 2015, p. 176	–	Inadmissible
17 June 2015	4A_124/2015	*Club A v. Club B & C.*	F	Beffa 2015, p. 250	Article 190(2)(d) PILA	Dismissed
21 May 2015	4A_634/2014	*A. SpA v. B. Ltd*	F	www.swissarbitration-decisions.com Beffa 2015, pp. 211; 249; 282–283	Article 190(2)(b) PILA Article 190(2)(d) PILA Article 190(2)(e) PILA	Dismissed
19 May 2015	4A_690/2014	*A. SA v. B.*	F	–	–	Application withdrawn
6 May 2015	4A_426/2014	*Club A v. Club B.*	F	http://www.swlegal.ch/Publications/Arbitration-Case-Digest.aspx (21 July 2015) www.swissarbitration-decisions.com Beffa 2015, pp. 243–245; 267–269; 301	Article 190(2)(d) PILA Article 190(2)(e) PILA	Dismissed

(continued)

Date	Case no.	Parties	Language	Sources[a] (including commentaries and translations)	Grounds relied upon in annulment action	Outcome
29 April 2015	4A_70/2015	*A. Sport Club v. B.*	F	http://www.swlegal.ch/Publications/Arbitration-Case-Digest.aspx (24 June 2015) www.swissarbitration-decisions.com ASA Bulletin 34: 147–157 Beffa 2015, pp. 240–242; 281; 295	Article 190(2) (d) PILA Article 190(2) (e) PILA	Dismissed
14 April 2015	4A_126/2015	*A. v. International Olympic Committee (IOC)*	F	http://www.swlegal.ch/Publications/Arbitration-Case-Digest.aspx (26 May 2015) Beffa 2015, pp. 173–175	–	Inadmissible
26 February 2015	4A_374/2014	*Club A. v. B. and C.*	F	http://www.swlegal.ch/Publications/Arbitration-Case-Digest.aspx (27 May 2015) http://www.internationallawoffice.com (Arbitration & ADR/ Switzerland; 16 July 2015) www.swissarbitration-decisions.com ASA Bulletin 33:576–598 Beffa 2015, pp. 170–172; 259–267	Article 190(2) (b) PILA Article 190(2) (e) PILA	Dismissed
24 February 2015	4A_544/2014	*A. v. Fédération Internationale de Football Association (FIFA)*	D	http://www.swlegal.ch/Publications/Arbitration-Case-Digest.aspx (29 April 2015) www.swissarbitration-decisions.com ASA Bulletin 33: 157–159 Beffa 2015, pp. 228–231	Article 190(2) (d) PILA	Dismissed
20 February 2015	4A_609/2014	*A. SpA v. B.*	I	http://www.swlegal.ch/Publications/Arbitration-Case-Digest.aspx (29 April 2015) www.swissarbitration-decisions.com ASA Bulletin 33:373–377 Beffa 2015, pp. 168–170	–	Inadmissible

(Continued)

Date	Case no.	Parties	Language	Sources[a] (including commentaries and translations)	Grounds relied upon in annulment action	Outcome
26 January 2015	4A_36/2015	*Football Club A. v. B.*	F	Beffa 2015, p. 175	–	Inadmissible
5 January 2015	4A_504/2014	*A. v. B.*	F	–	–	Inadmissible

[a]The sources mentioned in this table are those available in addition to the principal source, being the SFT's website (http://www.bger.ch/fr/index/juridiction/jurisdiction-inherit-template/jurisdiction-recht.htm), where all the decisions summarized in this digest can be accessed

References

Arroyo M (2013a) Article 190 PILA. In: Arroyo M (ed) Arbitration in Switzerland—the practitioner's guide. Kluwer Law International, Alphen aan den Rijn

Arroyo M (2013b) Article 191 PILA. In: Arroyo M (ed) Arbitration in Switzerland—the practitioner's guide. Kluwer Law International, Alphen aan den Rijn

Beffa L (2015) Review of the recent case law of the Swiss Federal supreme court. In: Müller C, Rigozzi A, Besson S (eds) Recent developments in international commercial arbitration. Schulthess, Zurich

Berger B, Kellerhals F (2015) International and domestic arbitration in Switzerland, 3rd edn. Stämpfli, Bern

Bucher A (2011) Article 190 PILA. In: Bucher A (ed) Commentaire romand – Loi sur le droit international privé – Convention de Lugano. Helbing Lichtenhahn, Basel

Corboz B (2014) Article 74 SCA. In: Corboz B, Wurzburger A, Ferrari P, Frésard J-M, Aubry Girardin F (eds) Commentaire de la LTF (Loi sur le Tribunal federal), 2nd edn. Stämpfli, Bern

Dasser F, Roth D (2014) Challenges of Swiss arbitral awards—selected statistical data as of 2013. ASA Bull 32:460–466

Geisinger E, Mazuranic A (2013) Chapter 11—challenge and revision of the award. In: Geisinger E, Voser N (eds) International arbitration in Switzerland—a handbook for practitioners. Kluwer Law International, Alphen aan den Rijn

Göksu T (2014) Schiedsgerichtsbarkeit. Dike, Zurich/St Gallen

Kaufmann-Kohler G, Rigozzi A (2015) International arbitration—law and practice in Switzerland. OUP, Oxford

Schweizer P (2011) Article 393 CCP. In: Bohnet F, Haldy J, Jeandin N, Schweizer P, Tappy D (eds) Code de procédure civile commenté. Helbing Lichtenhahn, Basel

Voser N, Bell K (2015) Swiss supreme court finds CAS award not in breach of *ultra petita* principle, 1 September 2015

List of Jurisprudence—YISA

CAS Awards

CAS 92/63, *Gundel v. Fédération Equestre Internationale*, Award of 10 September 1992
CAS 96/003 & 004, *Korneev and Gouliev v. IOC,* Award of 4 August 1996
CAS 97/169, *Menegotto v. FIC*, Order of 15 May 1997
CAS 97/176, *UCI v. Jogert & NCF*, Award of 15 January 1998
CAS 98/190, *HC Prilly v. LSHG*, Order of 10 March 1998
CAS 98/200, *AEK Athenes & Slavia Prague v. UEFA*, Award of 20 August 1999
CAS 98/202, *Peristeri AC v. FIBA*, Order of 13 July 1998
CAS 98/A/208, *N., J., Y., W. v. FINA*, Award of 22 December 1998
CAS 98/218, *Hall v. FINA*, Award of 27 May 1999
CAS 2000A/274, *Susin v. FINA*, Award of 19 October 2000
CAS 2001/A/324, *Addo & Van Nistelrooij v. UEFA*, Order of 15 March 2001
CAS 2001/A/328, *F. v. ISOD, IPC, DS/USA*, Order of 3 August 2001
CAS ad hoc Division 02/004, *Canadian Olympic Association v. ISU*, Order of 14 February 2002
CAS 2002/O/373, *Canadian Olympic Committee (COC) & Beckie Scott v. International Olympic Committee (IOC),* Award of 18 December 2003
CAS 2002/A/385, *T v. FIG*, Award of 23 January 2003
TAS 2002/O/422, *Besiktas v. FIFA & SC Freiburg*, Award of 10 March 2003
CAS 2003/O/460, *Wüstenrot Salzburg v. Bukran*, Award of 16 June 2003
CAS 2003/O/486, *Fulham v. OL*, Award of 15 September 2003
CAS 2003/O/527, *Hamburger Sport-Verein e.V. v.Odense Boldklub*, Award of 21 April 2004
CAS 2004/A/628, *International Association of Athletics Federations (IAAF) v. USA Track & Field (USATF) & Y.* Award of 28 June 2004
CAS 2004/A/642, *Hertha BSC Berlin v. G. & Club Atlético River Plate & RCD Mallorca*, Award of 1 March 2005
CAS 2004/O/645, *USADA v Montgomery*, Award of 13 December 2005

A. Duval and A. Rigozzi (eds.), *Yearbook of International Sports Arbitration 2015*,
DOI 10.1007/978-94-6265-129-6

CAS 2004/A/676, *Ismailia Sporting Club v. Confédération Africaine de Football (CAF)*, Award of 15 December 2004
CAS 2004/A/691, *FC Barcelona SAD v. Manchester United FC*, Award of 9 February 2005
CAS 2004/A/714 & 718, *Fazeckas v. IOC*, Awards of 31 March 2005
CAS 2004/A/780, *Ch. Maicon Henning v. Prudentopolis SC & FIFA*, Order of 6 January 2005
CAS 2005/A/848, *Sport Club Internacional v. Bayer 04 Leverkusen*, Award of 23 February 2006
CAS 2005/A/871, *FC Rodopa v. Markovitch*, Award of 19 September 2006
CAS 2005/A/876, *Adrian Mutu v. Chelsea Football Club Limited*, Award of 15 December 2005
CAS 2005/A/884, *Hamilton v USADA & UCI*, Award of 10 February 2006
CAS 2005/A/887, *IAAF v SEGAS, Kenteris & Thanou*, (Date unknown)
CAS 2005/A/896, *Fulham FC (1987) Ltd. v. FC Metz*, Award of 16 January 2006CAS 2005/A/990, *Pobyedonostsev v. IIHF*, Order of 19 January 2006
CAS 2005/A/952, *Ashley Cole v. Football Association Premier League*, Award of 24 January 2006
CAS 2005/A/957, *Clube Atlético Mineiro v. Fédération Internationale de Football Association (FIFA)*, Award of 23 March 2006
CAS 2006/A/1008, *Rayo Vallecano de Madrid SAD v. Fédération Internationale de Football Association (FIFA)*, Award of 21 August 2006
CAS 2006/A/1027, *Blackpool F.C. v. Club Topp Oss*, Award of 13 July 2006
CAS 2006/A/1029, *Maccabi Haifa FC v. Real Racing Club Santander*, Award of 2 October 2006
CAS 2006/A/1067, *IRB v. Keyter*, Award of 13 October 2006
CAS 2006/A/1125, *Hertha BSC Berlin v. Stade Lavallois Mayenne FC*, Award of 1 December 2006
CAS 2006/A/1137, *Cruzeiro Esporte Clube v. FIFA & PFC Krilja Sovetov*, Order of 17 August 2006
CAS 2006/A/1141, *M. v. FIFA & FC Krijla Sovetov*, Order of 31 August 2006
CAS 2006/A/1152, *ADO Den Haag v. Newcastle United FC*, Award of 7 February 2007
CAS 2006/A/1180, *Galatasaray SK v. Frank Ribéry & Olympique Marseille*, Award of 24 April 2007
CAS 2007/A/1219, *Club Sekondi Hasaacas FC v. Club Borussia Mönchengladbach*, Award of 9 July 2007
CAS 2007/A/1298, 1299 & 1300, *Wigan Athletic FC & Webster v. Heart of Midlothian*, Award of 30 January 2008
CAS 2007/A/1329, *Chiapas FC v. Cricuma Esporte Clube* and CAS 2007/A/1330, *Chiapas FC v. R.*, Awards of 5 December 2007
CAS 2007/A/1363, *TTF Liebherr Ochsenhausen v. ETTU*, Award of 5 October 2007
CAS 2007/A/1370, *FIFA v. Superior Tribunal de Justiça Desportiva do Futebol (STJD) & Confederação Brasileira de Futebol (CBF) & Mr Ricardo Lucas*

Dodô & CAS 2007/A/1376 *WADA v. Superior Tribunal de Justiça Desportiva do Futebol (STJD) & Confederação Brasileira de Futebol (CBF) & Mr Ricardo Lucas Dodô*, Order of 10 December 2007
CAS 2007/A/1394, *Floyd Landis v. USADA*, Award of 30 June 2008
CAS 2007/O/1440, *P. v. C.*, Award of 21 October 2008
CAS 2008/A/1480, *Pistorius v. IAAF*, Award of 16 May 2008
CAS 2008/A/1517, *Ionikos FC v. C.*, Award of 23 February 2009
CAS 2008/A/1519 & 1520, *FC Shakhtar Donetsk (Ukraine) v. Mr. Matuzalem Francelino da Silva (Brazil) & Real Zaragoza SAD (Spain) & FIFA*, Award of 19 May 2009
CAS 2008/A/1525, *A.FC. v. HFF & O. FC*, Request for Provisional Measures of 21 April 2008
CAS 2008/A/1545, *Andrea Anderson, LaTasha Colander Clark, Jearl Miles-Clark, Torri Edwards, Chryste Gaines, Monique Hennagan, Passion Richardson v. International Olympic Committee (IOC)*, Award of 16 July 2010
CAS 2008/A/1557, *FIGC, Daniele Mannini, Davide Possanzini and CONI v. WADA*, Award of 27 July 2009
CAS 2008/A/1569, *Kurten v. FEI*, Order of 20 June 2008
CAS 2008/A/1574, *D'Arcy v. Australian Olympic Committee*, Award of 7 July 2008
CAS 2008/A/1602, *A. v. Caykur Rizesport Kulübü Dernegi & Turkish Football Federation (TFF)*, Award of 20 February 2009
CAS 2008/A/1617, *Claudio Pizarro v. Federacion Peruana de Futbol*, Award of 15 April 2009
CAS 2008/A/1639, *RCD Mallorca vs. The Football Association (FA) & Newcastle United*, Award of 24 April 2009
CAS 2008/A/1644, *Adrian Mutu v. Chelsea Football Club Limited*, Award of 31 July 2009
CAS 2008/A/ 1656, *PFC Botev 1912—Plovdiv AD v. BFU & Hristov*, Award of 18 November 2008
CAS 2008/A/1677, *A. Enam v. Club Al Attihad Tripoli*, Order of 15 December 2008
CAS 2008/A/1705, *Neue Grasshopper Fussball AG Zurich v. Club Alianza de Lima*, Award of 18 June 2009
CAS 2009/A/1756, *FC Metz SASP v. Galatasaray SK*, Award of 12 October 2009
CAS 2009/A/1757, *MTK Budapest v. Inter Milan*, Award of 30 July 2009
CAS 2009/A/1805 & 1847, *IAAF v. RFEA and Josephine Onyia*, Award of 22 September 2009
CAS 2009/A/1810 & 1811, *SV Wilhelmshaven v. Club Atlético Excursionistas & Club Atlético River Plate*, Award of 5 October 2009
TAS 2009/A/1828 & 1829, *Olympique Lyonnais v. US Soccer Federation*, Award of 18 March 2010
CAS 2009/A/1869, (parties and date unknown)
CAS 2009/A/1870, *WADA v. Hardy*, Award of 21 May 2010

CAS 2009/A/1880 & 1881, *FC Sion & E. v. Fédération Internationale de Football Association (FIFA) & Al-Ahly Sporting Club*, Award of 1 June 2010
CAS 2009/A/1910, *Telecom Egypt Club v. Egyptian Football Association (EFA)*, Award of 9 September 2010
CAS 2009/A/1912, *P. v. International Skating Union (ISU) & CAS*, Award of 25 November 2009
CAS 2009/A/1920 *FK Pobeda and others v. UEFA*, Award of 15 April 2010
CAS 2010/A/1270, *D. Meca Medina & I. Majcen v. FINA*, (date unknown)
CAS 2010/A/2071, *Irish Football Association (IFA) v. Football Association of Ireland (FAI), Daniel Kearns and Fédération Internationale de Football Association (FIFA)*, Award of 27 September 2010
CAS 2010/A/2090, *Aino-Kaisa Saarinen & Finnish Ski Association v. FIS*, Award of 7 February 2011
CAS 2010/A/2091, *Dennis Lachter v. Derek Boateng Owusu*, Award of 21 December 2011
CAS 2010/A/2098, *Sevilla FC v. RC Lens*, Award of 29 November 2010
CAS 2010/A/2170, *Iraklis Thessaloniki FC v. Hellenic Football Federation* and CAS 2010/A/2171, *OF IFC v. Hellenic Football Federation*, Awards of 23 February 2011
CAS 2010/A/2172, *Oriekhov v. UEFA*, Award of 18 January 2011
CAS 2010/A/2229, *WADA v. FIBV & Berrios,* Award of 28 April 2011
CAS 2010/A/2235 *UCI v. Tadej Valjevec & Olympic Committee of Slovenia*, Award of 21 April 2011
CAS 2010/A/2236, *D v. ADoP*, Order of 2 November 2010
CAS 2010/A/2261 & 2263, *Mr. Matuzalem Francelino da Silva (Brazil) & Real Zaragoza SAD (Spain) v. FIFA*, Award of 29 June 2011
CAS 2010/A/2316, *Stoke City FC v. Brescia Calcio* (date unknown)
CAS 2010/A/2500, *Amateur Boxing Association of Thailand v. AIBA*, Order of 15 July 2011
TAS 2011/A/2351, *Calcio Catania v. FIFA*, Order of 16 March 2011
CAS 2011/A/2360 & 2392, *English Chess Federation and Georgian Chess Federation vs. Fédération Internationale des Echecs (FIDE)*, Order of 27 June 2011
CAS 2011/A/2360 & 2392 *English Chess Federation and Georgian Chess Federation vs. Fédération Internationale des Echecs (FIDE)*, Award of 3 July 2012
CAS 2011/A/2410, *A v. IF & G.*, Order of 23 May 2011
CAS 2011/O/2422, *USOC v. IOC*, Award of 4 October 2011
CAS 2011/A/2426, *Amos Adamu v. FIFA*, Award of 24 February 2012
CAS 2011/A/2483, *Iraklis Thessaloniki FC v Hellenic Football Federation & Greek Super League* (date unknown)
CAS 2011/A/2490, *Daniel Köllerer v. Association of Tennis Professionals and others*, Award of 23 March 2012
CAS 2011/A/2551, *Fenerbahce SK v. UEFA & Turkish Football Federation*, Award of 18 June 2012

CAS 2011/A/2561, *FRB v. AIBA*, Award of 20 September 2011
CAS 2011/A/2566, *Andrus Veerpalu v. International Ski Federation*, Award of 25 March 2013
TAS 2011/A/2578, *OGC Nice Côte d'Azur & Yannick Dos Santos Djalo v. FIFA*, Order of 11 October 2011
CAS 2011/A/ 2603, *FC CFR 1907 Cluj SA v. RFF and SC Association FC v. Mateianu*, Award of 4 November 2011
CAS 2011/O/2627, *L. v. K.*, Award of 6 June 2012
CAS 2011/A/2658, *BOA v. WADA*, Award of 30 April 2012
CAS 2011/A/2682, *Udinese Calcio S.p.A. v. Helsingborgs IF*, 23 May 2012
CAS 2012/A/2702, *Göry ETO v. UEFA*, Award of 8 May 2012
CAS 2012/A/2802, *Al-Masry FC v. EFA*, Order of 31 May 2012
CAS 2012/A/2804, *Kutrovsky v. ITF*, Award of 3 October 2012
CAS 2012/A/2821, *Bursaspor Kulübü Dernegi v. UEFA*, Award of 10 July 2012
CAS 2012/A/2824, *Besiktas JK v. UEFA*, Award of 31 October 2012
CAS 2012/A/2857, *Nationale Anti-Doping Agentur Deutschland v. Patrick Sinkewitz*, Award of 24 February 2014
CAS 2012/A/2875, *Helsingborgs IF v. Parma FC S.p.A.*, Award of 28 February 2013
CAS 2012/A/2913, *Mu-yen Chu & Chinese Taipei Olympic Committee v. IOC*, Award of 15 March 2013
CAS 2012/A/2993, *Liberia Football Association v Confederation Africaine de Football (CAF)*, Order of 30 November 2012
CAS 2012/A/3032, *SV Wilhelmshaven v. Club Atlético Excursionistas*, Award of 24 October 2013
CAS 2013/A/3047, *FC Zenit St. Petersburg v. Russian Football Union (RFU)*, Award of 7 October 2013
CAS 2013/A/3139, *Fenerbahçe SK v. UEFA*, Award of 5 December 2013
CAS 2013/A/3140, *A. vs. Club Atlético de Madrid SAD & Real Federación Española de Fútbol (RFEF) & Fédération Internationale de Football Association (FIFA)*, Award of 10 October 2013
CAS 2013/A/3151, *Jonathon Millar v. Fédération Equestre Internationale (FEI)*, Award of 7 October 2013
CAS 2013/A/3194, *SC FC Universitatea Cluj SA v. RFF & RPFL*, Award of 18 November 2013CAS 2013/A/3067, *Málaga CF SAD v. UEFA*, Award of 8 October 2013
CAS 2013/A/3199, *Rayo Vallecano de Madrid SAD v. RFEF*, Award of 22 October 2013
CAS 2013/A/3286-3294, *SC FC Sportul Studentesc SA vs. Romanian Football Federation & several players*, Award of 7 March 2014
CAS 2013/A/3317, *Genoa Cricket and Football Club v. Club Atlético Peñarol*, Award of 26 May 2014
CAS 2013/A/3365 & 3366, *Juventus FC & A.S. Livorno Calcio S.p.A v. Chelsea FC*, Award of 21 January 2015

CAS 2013/A/3437, *International Shooting Sport Federation (ISSF) v. WADA*, Award of 18 December 2014
CAS 2013/A/3453, *FC Petrolul Ploiesti v. UEFA*, Award of 20 February 2014
CAS 2013/A/3647 *Sporting Clube de Portugal SAD v. OGC Nice Côte d'Azur* & CAS 2013/A/3648 *OGC Nice Côte d'Azur v. Sporting Clube de Portugal SAD & FIFA*, Award of 11 May 2015
CAS 2014/A/3471, *FC DNIPRO v. FFU*, Award of 18 February 2014
CAS 2014/A/3474, *Clube de Regatas do Flamengo v. Confederaçao Brasileira de Futebol (CBF) & Superior Tribunal de Justiça Desportiva (STJD)*, Award of 5 October 2015
CAS 2014/A/3486, *MFK Dubnica vs. FC Parma*, Award of 2 February 2015
CAS 2014/A/3488, *WADA v. Juha Lallukka*, Award of 20 November 2014
CAS 2014/A/3508, *FC Lokomotiv v. Football Union of Russia & FC Nika*, Award of 23 March 2015
CAS 2014/A/3518, *Zamalek Sporting Club vs. Accra Hearts of Oak Sporting Club*, Award of 31 October 2014
CAS 2014/A/3629, *Parma FC v. FICG & Torino FC*, Award of 31 October 2014
CAS 2014/A/3701, *Genoa Cricket and Football Club S.p.A. v. AC Sparta Praha*, Award of 11 May 2015
CAS 2014/A/3751, *XX v. WADA*, Award of 10 February 2015
CAS 2014/A/3759, *Chand v. IAAF*, Award of 24 July 2015
CAS 2014/A/3832 & 3833, *Vanessa Vanakorn v. Fédération Internationale de Ski (Vanakorn v. FIS)*, Award of 19 June 2015
CAS 2015/A/3872, *Sheikh Khalid Al Qassimi & Abu Dhabi Racing Team v. FIA, Qatar Motor and Motorcycle Federation & Nasser Al-Attiyah* (date unknown)
CAS 2015/A/3874, *Football Association of Albania v. UEFA & Football Association of Serbia*, Award of 10 July 2015
CAS 2015/A/3875, *Football Association of Serbia v. UEFA*, Award of 10 July 2015
CAS 2015/A/4151, *Panathinaikos FC v. UEFA & Olympiacos FC*, Award of 26 November 2015

Basketball Arbitral Tribunal Awards

FAT 0024/08, *Sakellariou & Dimitropoulos v. Avellino*, Award of 11 May 2009
FAT 0040/09, *Hornbuckle et al. v. Besiktas Jimnastik Kulübü*, Award of 29 October 2009
FAT 0041/09, *Panellinios KAE BC v. Kelley*, Award of 12 November 2009
FAT 0063/09, *Fisher & Entersport Management Inc. v. KK Vojvodina Serbijagas*, Award of 19 February 2010
FAT 0046/09, *Mahoric & Jakse v. BC Kyiv*, Award of 26 February 2010
FAT 0057/09, *Podkovyrov v. Slupskie Towarzystwo Koszykowki Sportowa Spolka Akcyjna*, Award of 15 March 2010

FAT 0062/09, *Harper et al. v. Besiktas Jimnastik Kulübü*, Award of 26 March 2010
FAT 0065/09, *Mikhalevskiy v. Bikov*, Award of 12 April 2010
FAT 0034/09, *Tucker & Pro One Sports Management Inc. v. BC Kyiv*, Award of 3 May 2010
FAT 0069/09, *Ivezic & Draskicevic v. Basketball Club Pecsi Noi Kosariabda Kft*, Award of 27 May 2010
FAT 0075/10, *Tamir & Krayn v. Seastar Apoel Nicosia Basketball Club*, Award of 23 June 2010
FAT 0083/10, *Ilievski v. KK Union Olimpija Ljubljana*, Award of 23 July 2010
FAT 0071/09, *Papadopoulos v. Fortitudo*, Award of 31 August 2010
FAT 0082/10, *Benson & Paris v. Shanxi Zhongyu*, Award of 31 August 2010
FAT 0095/10, *Shabalkin v. "Khimki" Basketball Club*, Award of 24 September 2010
FAT 0092/10, *Ronci & Coelho v. WBC Mizo Pecs*, Award of 15 October 2010
FAT 0104/10, *Pavetic v. GS Trogylos Basket Priolo*, Award of 15 March 2011
FAT 0118/10, *Bracey v. Achilleas Kaimakliou BC*, Award of 23 March 2011
FAT 0143/10, *Tapoutos v. Basketball Club PAOK KAE*, Award of 3 May 2011
BAT 0093/10, *ASD Pallacanestro Femminile Schio v. Braxton*, Award of 11 October 2010
BAT 0107/10, *Kelati & Maravilla v. Olympiacos Piraeus BC*, Award of 13 April 2011
BAT 0130/10, *Thomas et al. v. Baloncesto Fuenlabrada*, Award of 8 June 2011
BAT 0155/11, *Kikowski v. KK Union Olimpija Ljubljana*, Award of 8 August 2011
BAT 0154/11, *Gloger & Bill A. Duffy International, Inc. v. Club C.B. Atapuerca*, Award of 17 August 2011
BAT 0166/11, *Fox v. BC Kalev Cramo*, Award of 17 August 2011
BAT 0172/11, *Jusup & Ivic v. KK Zadar*, Award of 6 October 2011
BAT 0263/12, *Jujka and TP Sports Ltd v. Miejski Miedzyszkolny Klub Sportowy Katarzynki Torun "Energa"*, Award of 11 October 2011
BAT 0139/10, *Sampson & Octagon v. Samahang Basketbol NG Pilipinas Inc.*, Award of 31 October 2011
BAT 0243/11, *Court Side v. Kasnye Krylia Samara*, Award of 2 February 2012
BAT 0224/11, *Bavcic, MEGA Basketball LLC, BeoBasket Ltd. v. KK Union Olimpija Ljublijana*, Award of 9 March 2012
BAT 0225/11, *Djordjevic, MEGA Basketball LLC, BeoBasket Ltd. v. KK Union Olimpija Ljublijana*, Award of 9 March 2012
BAT 0258/12, *Entersport v. Men's Basketball Club Dynamo Moscow*, Award of 25 June 2012
BAT 0230/11, *Zouros v. BC Zalgiris Kaunas,* Award of 9 July 2012
BAT 0231/11, *Kantzouris v. BC Zalgiris Kaunas,* Award of 9 July 2012
BAT 0257/12, *Orlando & DoubleB Management sas v. Besiktas Jimnastik Kulubu Dernegi*, Award of 3 August 2012
BAT 0242/11, *Vrbanc v. KK Cibona Zagreb*, Award of 31 August 2012
BAT 0278/12, *Korstin v. Besiktas Jimnastik Kulübü Dernegi*, Award of 31 August 2012

BAT 0247/11, *Ignerski & Stanley v. Besiktas Jimnastik Kulübü*, Award of 3 September 2012
BAT 0284/12, *Appel & Wasserman Media Group v. Samsun Basketball Kulübü*, Award of 15 October 2012
BAT 0291/12, *Drucker & Beobasket Ltd v. Sutor Basket Montegranaro srl*, Award of 20 November 2012
BAT 0256/12, *Mr Coach and Agency v. Club*, Award of 13 December 2012
BAT 0213/11, *Player v. Club*, Award of 30 January 2013
BAT 0345/12, *FC Bayern München e.V. v. Foster*, Award of 20 March 2013
BAT 0334/12, *Scafati Basket v. Marigney*, Award of 27 March 2013
BAT 0535/12, *Markota & Xl Agency v. Union Olimpija Ljubljana*, Award of 8 May 2013
BAT 0350/12, *Labovic v. BC Krasnye Krylia Samara*, Award of 10 June 2013
BAT 0314/12, *Papaloukas v. Olympiakos*, Award of 15 July 2013
BAT 0318/12, *Hunter & Priority Sports and Entertainment v. Polisportiva Dinamo SRL*, Award of 15 October 2013
BAT 0396/13, *Gaffney & Ayesa v. Club Joventut Badalona SAD*, Award of 16 October 2013
BAT 0429/13, *Coppa v. Basketball Sport Association of Thailand*, Award of 23 December 2013
BAT 0383/13, *Dikeoulakos et al. v. CSM Targoviste*, Award of 22 January 2014
BAT 0385/13, *Liatsos & Antoniou v. BC AEL Limassol*, Award of 22 January 2014
BAT 0421/13 *Berzins & Bill A. Duffy International Inc, db BDA Sports Management v. BC VEF Riga*, Award of 21 February 2014BAT 0439/13, *Burns, Hart Sports Management and Players Group v. SS Sutor Srl*, Award of 19 March 2014
BAT 0449/13, *Steele, Greig and Slay v. SS Sutor Srl*, Award of 20 March 2014
BAT 0463/13, *Johnson v. SS Sutor Srl*, Award of 20 March 2014
BAT 0471/13, *Filipovski v. KK Union Olimpija Ljubljana*, Award of 28 April 2014
BAT 0462/13, *Maresca v. Basket Juvecaserta srl*, Award of 13 June 2014
BAT 0464/13, *Manakian v. FC Bayern München e.V.*, Award of 4 August 2014
BAT 0535/14, *Daniels v. Liaoning Hengye Basketball Club*, Award of 7 August 2014
BAT 0501/14, *De Mondt & Stainier v. Kayseri Kaski Spor Kulübü*, Award of 14 August 2014
BAT 0487/13, *KC Callero & Andrews v. SS Sutor Srl*, Award of 3 September 2014
BAT 0542/14, *Pancotto v. SS Felice Scandone Avellino SpA*, Award of 24 October 2014
BAT 0584/14, *Trinchieri v. Hellenic Basketball Federation*, Award 21 November 2014
BAT 0544/14, *Allred & Greig v. Halcones UV Promotora Deportiva A.C. & Halcones de Xalapa A.C.*, Award of 11 December 2014
BAT 0568/14, *Johnson v. Zhejiang Chouzhou Professional Basketball Club Company Ltd*, Award of 18 December 2014
BAT 0589/14, *Dean v. SS Felice Scandone SpA*, Award of 7 January 2015

BAT 0566/14, *Caracter v. Sichuan Jingqiang Blue Whale Pro Basketball Club*, Award of 27 January 2015
BAT 0593/14, *Tomas v. Fenerbahce Spor Kulübü*, Award of 3 February 2015
BAT 0468/13, *Matic v. Club Sportif Municipal Targoviste*, Award of 4 February 2015
BAT 0477/13, *Denson & Goldansky v. Ramat Hasharon BC*, Award of 3 February 2015
BAT 0562/14, *Zouros v. BC Zalgiris Kaunas*, Award of 3 March 2015
BAT 0502/14, *Banic v. Unics Kazan Basketball Club*, Award of 30 April 2015
BAT 0563/14, *White v. Guaiqueries De Margarita BBC*, Award of 30 April 2015
BAT 0603/14, *Sarkis v. Amchit Club*, Award of 13 May 2015
BAT 0651/15, *Macvan v. Galatasaray Spor Kulübü Dernegi*, Award of 27 May 2015
BAT 0644/15, *Vougioukas v. Galatasaray Spor Kulübü Dernegi*, Award of 13 July 2015
BAT 0640/14, *Smith & Wasserman Media Group v. Galatasaray Spor Külübü Dernegi*, Award of 27 July 2015
BAT 0650/15, *Jawai & Wasserman Media Group v. Galatasaray Spor Kulübü Dernegi*, Award of 30 July 2015
BAT 0668/15, *Familia Basket Schio slr SSD v. Ogwumike*, Award of 26 August 2015
BAT 0630/14, *Kaukenas v. BC Zalgiris Kaunas*, Award of 1 October 2015
BAT 0712/15, *Hamilton v. Saski Baskonia SAD*, Award of 6 October 2015
BAT 0702/15, *Club Sportif Sagesse Beirut v. Kahzzouh*, Award of 7 October 2015
BAT 0539/14, *Dragovic v. BC Spartak St. Petersburg*, Award of 12 October 2015
BAT 0631/14, *Valdeolmillos Moreno v. Comité Olìmpico Mexicano (COM, Asociación Deportiva Mexicana De Baloncesto (ADEMEBA), Liga Nacional de Baloncesto Profesional (LNBP), Instituto Veracruzano Del Deporte (IVD)*, Award of 30 October 2015
BAT 0720/15, *Millage v. Torku Konyaspor Basketbol Kulübü*, Award of 4 December 2015
BAT 0664/15, *Funiciello v. El Jaish Sports Club and Taggard*, Award of 6 December 2015
BAT 0708/15, *Cousin Jr. & Fleisher v. BC Krasny Oktyabr*, Award of 5 January 2016

Swiss national courts

Swiss Federal Tribunal Judgments

SFT decision of 26 November 1980, *Semaine Judiciaire* 1982
SFT 117 II 346
SFT 118 II 199
SFT 119 II 271 *Gundel*

SFT 120 II 155
SFT 123 IV 61
SFT 126 I 207
SFT 127 III 123
SFT 127 III 429
SFT 129 III 445 *Lazutina*
SFT 132 III 389 *Tensacciai*
SFT 133 III 235 *Cañas*
SFT 136 III 345 *Atlético Madrid*
SFT 136 III 597
SFT 136 III 605
SFT 138 III 322
SFT 140 III 477
SFT 140 III 520
SFT 4P.273-283/1999, decision of 20 June 2000
SFT 4P.196/2003, decision of 7 January 2004
SFT 4P.148/2006, decision of 10 January 2007
SFT 4P.240/2006, decision of 5 January 2007
SFT 4A_126/2008, decision of 9 May 2008
SFT 4A_400/2008, decision of 9 February 2009
SFT 4A_600/2008, decision of 20 February 2009
SFT 4A_582/2009, decision of 13 April 2009
SFT 4A_10/2009, decision of 8 July 2009
SFT 4A_548/2009, decision of 20 January 2010
SFT 4A_612/2009, decision of 10 February 2010
SFT 4A_458/2009, decision of 10 June 2010
SFT 4A_144/2010, decision of 28 September 2010
SFT 4A_612/2009, order of 7 December 2010
SFT 4A_392/2010, decision of 12 January 2011
SFT 4A_654/2011, decision of 23 May 2012
SFT 4A_232/2012, decision of 29 May 2012
SFT 4A_636/2011, decision of 18 June 2012
SFT 4A_54/2012, decision of 27 June 2012
SFT 4A_134/2012, decision of 16 July 2012
SFT 4A_314/2012, decision of 16 October 2012
SFT 4A_429/2012, decision of 2 November 2012
SFT 4A_198/2012, decision of 14 December 2012
SFT 4A_576/2012, decision of 28 February 2013
SFT 4A_682/2012, decision of 20 June 2013
SFT 4A_282/2013, decision of 13 November 2013
SFT 4A_112/2014, decision of 28 April 2014
SFT 4A_124/2014, decision of 7 July 2014
SFT 4A_586/2014, decision of 25 November 2014
SFT 4A_504/2014, decision of 5 January 2015
SFT 4A_36/2015, decision of 26 January 2015

SFT 4A_609/2014, decision of 20 February 2015
SFT 4A_544/2014, decision of 24 February 2015
SFT 4A_374/2014, decision of 26 February 2015
SFT 4A_126/2015, decision of 14 April 2015
SFT 4A_70/2015, decision of 29 April 2015
SFT 4A_426/2014, decision of 6 May 2015
SFT 4A_690, Order of 19 May 2015
SFT 4A_634/2014, decision of 21 May 2015
SFT 4A_174/2015, decision of 30 June 2015
SFT 4A_684/2014, decision of 2 July 2015
SFT 4A_246/2014, decision of 15 July 2015
SFT 4A_98/2014, order of 10 August 2015
SFT 4A_596/2015, decision of 9 December 2015
SFT 4A_568/2015, decision of 10 December 2015

Other Judgments by Swiss national courts

Civil Court of the Canton Tribunal Vaud MP 2011/22, *Y. SA v. UEFA*, Order of 27 September 2011
Civil Tribunal Sarine, *X, Y, Z v Fédération Suisse de Basketball, City Fribourg Basketball Club*, Judgement of 20 June 1997

Other national Courts

German courts
LG Bremen, 12 O 129/13, *SV Wilhelmshaven v. Norddeutscher Fußball-Verband e.V*, 25 April 2014
OLG Bremen, 2 U 67/14, *SV Wilhelmshaven v. Norddeutscher Fußball-Verband* e.V. 30 December 2014
OLG München, Az. U 1110/14 Kart, *Claudia Pechstein v. DESG and ISU*, 15 January 2015

French courts
Cass. civ, decision of 4 June 2008
Cass. civ, decision of 30 March 2004
Cass. civ, decision of 11 July 2006

UK courts
Briginshaw v Briginshaw [1938] 60 CLR 336
Miller v Minister of Pensions [1947] 2 All ER 372
Bater v Bater [1951] P 35
Hornal v Neuberger Products Ltd [1957] 1 QB 247
Practice Direction [1966] 3 All ER 77
Arthur Hall v Simons [2000] 3 WLR 543

Miller v Cawley [2002] EWCA Civ 1100
UKHL 47 [2003] 1 AC 153
R (N) v Mental Health Review Tribunal (Northern Region) [2005] EWCA Civ 1605, [2006] QB 468
Re B (Children) (Care Proceedings): Standard of Proof [2008] UKHL 35, [2009] 1 AC 11

US Courts
U.S. Supreme Court, *Baker v. Carr*, 369 U.S. 186 (1962)
United States District Court for the Southern District of Florida, No. 763, *Chelsea Football Club Limited v. Adrian Mutu*, 13 February 2012

CJEU Judgments

C-415/93, *Union Royale Belge des Sociétés de Football Association and others v. Bosman and others*, ECLI:EU:C:1995
C-122/96, *Stephen Austin Saldanha and MTS Securities Corporation v. Hiross Holding AG,* ECLI:EU:C:1997:458
C-176/96, *Jyri Lehtonen and Castors Canada Dry Namur-Braine ASBL v. Fédération royale belge des sociétés de basket-ball ASBL*, ECLI:EU:C:2000:201
C-350/96, *Clean Car Autoservice Gmbh v. Landeshauptmann von Wien*, ECLI:EU:C:1998:205
T-193/02, *Laurent Piau v Commission*, ECLI:EU:T:2005:22
C-519/04, *David Meca-Medina and Igor Majcen v Commission,* ECLI:EU:C:2006:201
C-168/05, *Elisa María Mostaza Claro v Centro Móvil Milenium SL,* ECLI:EU:C:2006:675
C-49/07, *MOTOE v Elliniko Dimosio*, ECLI:EU:C:2008:376
C-325/08, *Olympique Lyonnais SASP v. Olivier Bernard and Newcastle UFC*, ECLI:EU:C:2010:143

ECHR Judgments

ECtHR, n° 1643/06, *Suda v Czech Republic,* decision of 28 October 2010
ECtHR, n° 29369/10, *Morice v/ France*, decision of 11 July 2013

MIX
Papier aus verantwortungsvollen Quellen
Paper from responsible sources
FSC® C105338
FSC
www.fsc.org

If you have any concerns about our products,
you can contact us on
ProductSafety@springernature.com

In case Publisher is established outside the EU,
the EU authorized representative is:
Springer Nature Customer Service Center GmbH
Europaplatz 3, 69115 Heidelberg, Germany

Printed by Libri Plureos GmbH
in Hamburg, Germany